OTHER A TO Z GUIDES FROM THE SCARECROW PRESS, INC.

1. *The A to Z of Buddhism* by Charles S. Prebish, 2001.
2. *The A to Z of Catholicism* by William J. Collinge, 2001.
3. *The A to Z of Hinduism* by Bruce M. Sullivan, 2001.
4. *The A to Z of Islam* by Ludwig W. Adamec, 2002.
5. *The A to Z of Slavery and Abolition* by Martin A. Klein, 2002.
6. *Terrorism: Assassins to Zealots* by Sean Kendall Anderson and Stephen Sloan, 2003.
7. *The A to Z of the Korean War* by Paul M. Edwards, 2005.
8. *The A to Z of the Cold War* by Joseph Smith and Simon Davis, 2005.
9. *The A to Z of the Vietnam War* by Edwin E. Moise, 2005.
10. *The A to Z of Science Fiction Literature* by Brian Stableford, 2005.
11. *The A to Z of the Holocaust* by Jack R. Fischel, 2005.
12. *The A to Z of Washington, D.C.* by Robert Benedetto, Jane Donovan, and Kathleen DuVall, 2005.
13. *The A to Z of Taoism* by Julian F. Pas, 2006.
14. *The A to Z of the Renaissance* by Charles G. Nauert, 2006.
15. *The A to Z of Shinto* by Stuart D. B. Picken, 2006.
16. *The A to Z of Byzantium* by John H. Rosser, 2006.
17. *The A to Z of the Civil War* by Terry L. Jones, 2006.
18. *The A to Z of the Friends (Quakers)* by Margery Post Abbott, Mary Ellen Chijioke, Pink Dandelion, and John William Oliver Jr., 2006.
19. *The A to Z of Feminism* by Janet K. Boles and Diane Long Hoeveler, 2006.
20. *The A to Z of New Religious Movements* by George D. Chryssides, 2006.
21. *The A to Z of Multinational Peacekeeping* by Terry M. Mays, 2006.
22. *The A to Z of Lutheranism* by Günther Gassmann with Duane H. Larson and Mark W. Oldenburg, 2007.
23. *The A to Z of the French Revolution* by Paul R. Hanson, 2007.
24. *The A to Z of the Persian Gulf War 1990–1991* by Clayton R. Newell, 2007.
25. *The A to Z of Revolutionary America* by Terry M. Mays, 2007.
26. *The A to Z of the Olympic Movement* by Bill Mallon with Ian Buchanan, 2007.

27. *The A to Z of the Discovery and Exploration of Australia* by Alan Day, 2009.
28. *The A to Z of the United Nations* by Jacques Fomerand, 2009.
29. *The A to Z of the "Dirty Wars"* by David Kohut, Olga Vilella, and Beatrice Julian, 2009.
30. *The A to Z of the Vikings* by Katherine Holman, 2009.
31. *The A to Z from the Great War to the Great Depression* by Neil A. Wynn, 2009.
32. *The A to Z of the Crusades* by Corliss K. Slack, 2009.
33. *The A to Z of New Age Movements* by Michael York, 2009.
34. *The A to Z of Unitarian Universalism* by Mark W. Harris, 2009.
35. *The A to Z of the Kurds* by Michael M. Gunter, 2009.
36. *The A to Z of Utopianism* by James M. Morris and Andrea L. Kross, 2009.
37. *The A to Z of the Civil War and Reconstruction* by William L. Richter, 2009.
38. *The A to Z of Jainism* by Kristi L. Wiley, 2009.
39. *The A to Z of the Inuit* by Pamela R. Stern, 2009.
40. *The A to Z of Early North America* by Cameron B. Wesson, 2009.
41. *The A to Z of the Enlightenment* by Harvey Chisick, 2009.
42. *The A to Z of Methodism* edited by Charles Yrigoyen Jr. and Susan E. Warrick, 2009.
43. *The A to Z of the Seventh-Day Adventists* by Gary Land, 2009.
44. *The A to Z of Sufism* by John Renard, 2009.
45. *The A to Z of Sikhism* by W. H. McLeod, 2009.
46. *The A to Z of Fantasy Literature* by Brian Stableford, 2009.
47. *The A to Z of the Discovery and Exploration of the Pacific Islands* by Max Quanchi and John Robson, 2009.
48. *The A to Z of Australian and New Zealand Cinema* by Albert Moran and Errol Vieth, 2009.
49. *The A to Z of African-American Television* by Kathleen Fearn-Banks, 2009.
50. *The A to Z of American Radio Soap Operas* by Jim Cox, 2009.
51. *The A to Z of the Old South* by William L. Richter, 2009.
52. *The A to Z of the Discovery and Exploration of the Northwest Passage* by Alan Day, 2009.
53. *The A to Z of the Druzes* by Samy S. Swayd, 2009.
54. *The A to Z of the Welfare State* by Bent Greve, 2009.

55. *The A to Z of the War of 1812* by Robert Malcomson, 2009.
56. *The A to Z of Feminist Philosophy* by Catherine Villanueva Gardner, 2009.
57. *The A to Z of the Early American Republic* by Richard Buel Jr., 2009.
58. *The A to Z of the Russo–Japanese War* by Rotem Kowner, 2009.
59. *The A to Z of Anglicanism* by Colin Buchanan, 2009.
60. *The A to Z of Scandinavian Literature and Theater* by Jan Sjåvik, 2009.
61. *The A to Z of the Peoples of the Southeast Asian Massif* by Jean Michaud, 2009.
62. *The A to Z of Judaism* by Norman Solomon, 2009.
63. *The A to Z of the Berbers (Imazighen)* by Hsain Ilahiane, 2009.
64. *The A to Z of British Radio* by Seán Street, 2009.
65. *The A to Z of The Salvation Army* edited by Major John G. Merritt, 2009.
66. *The A to Z of the Arab–Israeli Conflict* by P R Kumaraswamy, 2009.
67. *The A to Z of the Jacksonian Era and Manifest Destiny* by Terry Corps, 2009.
68. *The A to Z of Socialism* by Peter Lamb and James C. Docherty, 2009.
69. *The A to Z of Marxism* by David Walker and Daniel Gray, 2009.
70. *The A to Z of the Bahá'í Faith* by Hugh C. Adamson, 2009.
71. *The A to Z of Postmodernist Literature and Theater* by Fran Mason, 2009.
72. *The A to Z of Australian Radio and Television* by Albert Moran and Chris Keating, 2009.
73. *The A to Z of the Lesbian Liberation Movement: Still the Rage* by JoAnne Myers, 2009.

The A to Z
of the Old South

William L. Richter

The A to Z Guide Series, No. 51

The Scarecrow Press, Inc.
Lanham • Toronto • Plymouth, UK
2009

Published by Scarecrow Press, Inc.
A wholly owned subsidiary of
The Rowman & Littlefield Publishing Group, Inc.
4501 Forbes Boulevard, Suite 200, Lanham, Maryland 20706
http://www.scarecrowpress.com

Estover Road, Plymouth PL6 7PY, United Kingdom

Copyright © 2006 by William L. Richter

All rights reserved. No part of this publication may be reproduced, stored
in a retrieval system, or transmitted in any form or by any means, electronic,
mechanical, photocopying, recording, or otherwise, without the prior permission
of the publisher.

British Library Cataloguing in Publication Information Available

Library of Congress Cataloging-in-Publication Data

The hardback version of this book was cataloged by the Library of Congress as
follows:

Richter, William L. (William Lee), 1942–
 Historical dictionary of the Old South / William L. Richter.
  p. cm. — (Historical dictionaries of U.S. historical eras ; no. 4)
 Includes bibliographical references.
 1. Southern States—History—1775-1865—Dictionaries. I. Title. II. Series.
F213.R53 2006
975'.03'03—dc22   2005018801

ISBN 978-0-8108-6834-2 (pbk. : alk. paper)
ISBN 978-0-8108-7000-0 (ebook)

∞™ The paper used in this publication meets the minimum requirements of
American National Standard for Information Sciences—Permanence of Paper
for Printed Library Materials, ANSI/NISO Z39.48-1992.

Printed in the United States of America

To the memory of
Miss (that's pronounced *Mee* izz, for you Yankees) Elizabeth Tarver
of Holly Springs, Mississippi,
the quintessential Southern Belle,
and my favorite librarian,
who could effortlessly enunciate the phrase "thank you"
in the five syllables God surely intended for it to have,
and musically drawl the word "Mississippi"
into a luxuriously full sentence.

Contents

Acknowledgments	xi
Editor's Foreword *Jon Woronoff*	xiii
Chronology	xv
Introduction	1
THE DICTIONARY	31
Select Bibliography	383
Appendixes	
A. U.S. Governments during the Antebellum Era, 1790–1861	447
B. U.S. and Confederate Governments during the Civil War, 1861–1865	451
C. The Articles of Confederation and Perpetual Union, 1781	453
D. Constitution of the Confederate States of America, 1861	465
E. Constitution of the United States of America as of 1860	487
About the Author	507

Acknowledgments

A lot of people over the years contributed to this volume. Thirty years ago at Louisiana State University, the magnificent interpretations of Charles B. Dew and T. Harry Williams did much to give a factual basis to my innate love of the South and its historical ironies. John L. Loos and James L. Bolner at LSU, John W. Clark while a visiting professor from Kansas University, and Otis E Young from Arizona State University opened up the constitutional and economic sides of America's past. Several mentors, James E. Sefton from the California State University at Northridge, Burl Noggle, Robert Holtman, and James G. Zeidman from LSU, and Ron Smith from ASU, took an interest in my career early on and have unselfishly helped me countless times. And I am especially grateful to Paul Hubbard, my original advisor at ASU, whose stimulating classes and friendship opened up the world of nineteenth century American history for me. Jon Woronoff at Scarecrow suggested the topic, got me started, and along with Kim Tabor, April Snider, and Niki Averill, kept me on the straight and narrow. Ginger Cullen and the rest of the staff at the main library of the University of Arizona provided critical help in finding needed resources, as did my friend D. Robert Altschul, professor emeritus in geography at the U of A, who suggested several books and articles I might have otherwise missed. My very dear friend, Diana L. Rubino, graciously provided much needed editorial assistance in producing the final draft. As usual, my wife Lynne's constant support and love have been essential. To these people belongs whatever merit this work possesses.

Editor's Foreword

It is rather hard to get a fix on the Old South since one is assailed with so many versions of it. They range from edulcorated visions of high-minded planters and happy slaves to nasty ones of mean-minded whites, whoever they may be, and workers (black and also white) pushed as far as they can go and further. Both visions were probably right, in some cases, and wrong in even more, and the more likely range was somewhere in the middle. Moreover, much of what happened probably had less to do with who they were intrinsically than the rather special situation they were placed in, the "system" if you will. Thus, it is heartening to find a book which covers the whole ground, from the extremes to the middle, and explains how the political, economic, and social structures influenced those living in the Old South. Even more surprising, and welcome, is that this book, although encyclopedic in form, is nonetheless written in such a manner that one can develop a real feeling for the time and place and people.

To understand the Old South, it is necessary to see how it evolved over time—never being exactly the same Old South from one generation or even decade to another. This is best conveyed by the introduction. But there were certain continuities, none stronger than the institution of slavery and the rivalry with the North, both of which can be traced through the chronology. The Old South, perhaps more than many other communities, was strongly influenced and imprinted by people, with the more prominent—if not always quite admirable—appearing in numerous dictionary entries. Others deal with crucial events, political parties and movements, legislation and Supreme Court decisions, and essential economic and social features. There is no end to what can and has been said about the Old South, with a literature that continues expanding from year to year, so the bibliography is a good starting point for those who want to learn more.

The *Historical Dictionary of the Old South* was written by William L. Richter, who also wrote the *Historical Dictionary of the Civil War and Reconstruction*, which could advantageously be consulted on certain aspects of the Old South. Dr. Richter has also written several other books on this region and this period, most of them more scholarly but one a novel. Unlike the vast majority of our authors, while an academically trained historian, he is retired from having operated his own horseshoeing business. This may explain why he is able to combine the basic facts, the same ones we can all find in the history books if we look hard enough, with an insight into the persons and events that goes a bit further than we may be used to and enlivens this latest edition to the series of *Historical Dictionaries of U.S. Historical Eras*.

Jon Woronoff
Series Editor

Chronology

1781 1 March Articles of Confederation ratified.

1783 20 January Treaty of Paris effective, ending American Revolutionary War. **15 April** Congress ratified Treaty of Paris.

1784 23 April Territorial Ordinance proposed 10 states equal to the original 13 be created out of the cis-Mississippi west with slavery prohibited after 1800. Never adopted in Congress, it became the basis of the Northwest Ordinance in 1787. **23 December** New York City made temporary capital of United States.

1785 28 March Mt. Vernon conference between Virginia and Maryland over navigation of the Chesapeake Bay and Potomac River. So successful that Pennsylvania added, then Delaware, then a new conference called for Annapolis. **20 May** Land Ordinance of 1785 created the rectilinear survey system used in all territories from here on out, establishing base lines, townships, and sections. **20 July** Jay–Guardoqui Treaty negotiations began. Considered anti-Southern, its disapproval in Congress within the year led to the requirement that two-thirds of the Senate was to approve all treaties in the new Constitution.

1786 16 January Virginia statute for religious freedom adopted. **7 August** Charles Cotesworth Pinckney proposed that Congress amend the Articles of Confederation. **11–14 September** Annapolis Commercial Convention met but poorly attended so that the delegates agreed to adjourn and meet in Philadelphia the following year with an expanded agenda.

1787 25 May Philadelphia Convention opened. **13 July** Congress passed Northwest Ordinance, creating a territory of up to five future states without slavery, and describing the process whereby territories would become states, on an equal basis with the original 13 states. **17 September** Constitution completed in Philadelphia Convention.

1788 **21 June** Ninth state ratified the new Constitution, putting it into effect.

1789 **7 January** George Washington elected first president of the United States. **9 September–22 December** In response to complaints from several states, Congress proposed 12 amendments to the Constitution limiting the power of the federal government, of which 10 were adopted as the Bill of Rights.

1790 **14 January** Alexander Hamilton's Report on Public Credit, recommending that the debt be funded with new bonds and that all debts from the Revolution be assumed by the federal government. Since South had paid its debts and had none to assume, it would have to pay the nation's debt, in effect, twice. **10 July** Permanent national capital located on the Potomac River between two slave states, Virginia and Maryland. **26 July** Funding passed. **4 August** Assumption passed. **6 December** U.S. capital moved from New York City to Philadelphia until new permanent capital ready for occupation. Combined with Funding and Assumption, this is often called the Compromise of 1790. **16 December** Virginia passed a series of resolves that protested that Funding and Assumption were specific powers granted the federal government in the U.S. Constitution.

1791 **25 February** Congress chartered the first Bank of the United States, under the concept advanced by Alexander Hamilton that there were implied powers in the Constitution. James Madison and Thomas Jefferson protested that implied powers were fraudulent. The result was the formation of two political parties, the Federalists under Hamilton, John Adams, and Washington, and the Democratic Republicans, under Madison, Aaron Burr, and Jefferson. **5 December** Hamilton's Report on Manufactures called for a protective tariff and internal improvements, but Congress failed to act.

1792 **5 December** George Washington reelected to second term as president under the Federalist ticket.

1793 **12 February** Congress passed the Fugitive Slave Law that expedited the return of captured runaways to their owners, no matter in what jurisdiction they were caught. **22 April** Washington declared American neutrality in the Wars of the French Revolution. **31 December** Jefferson resigned as Secretary of State to gain a free hand to oppose the Federalists.

1794 **5 March** Eleventh Amendment to the Constitution prevented the U.S. Supreme Court from taking jurisdiction in cases where citizens from one state sued another state. This was to prevent Tories (British loyalists) from collecting for property seized during the American Revolution. **14 March** Eli Whitney patented the cotton gin after a year's invention and modification. **5 June** Congress passed Neutrality Act which reinforced Washington's earlier Neutrality Proclamation. **19 November** Jay's Treaty with Great Britain opposed by the South, which denied funding in the House.

1795 **27 October** Pinckney's Treaty signed at Madrid, set Florida boundary at 31° and gave U.S. right to navigate the Mississippi River and access to port of New Orleans. The treaty was passed in conjunction with funding of Jay's Treaty.

1796 **23 February** In *Hylton v. U.S.*, the U.S. Supreme Court ruled that a law passed by Congress was constitutional. **17 September** Washington's Farewell Address warns against permanent foreign entanglements. **7 December** Federalist John Adams elected president. Democratic Republican Thomas Jefferson elected vice president, the only time in U.S. history the executive was split between two parties.

1797 **31 May** Undeclared Quasi-War against France for stopping American ships on the high seas. **18 October** X-Y-Z Affair in which France tried to bribe American delegates.

1798 **18 June–14 July** Alien and Sedition Acts prevented criticism of the government and discriminated against non-citizens. **16 November** Kentucky state legislature passed the Kentucky Resolves. **24 December** Virginia state legislature passed the Virginia Resolves. Both resolutions maintained that when the Constitution did not specifically grant a power to the federal government, it was the right and duty of a state or states to intervene and negate the effects of that action.

1799 **30 January** Logan Act passed in Congress prevented private citizens from negotiating behind the back of the government. Still good law.

1800 **30 August** Gen. Gabriel Prosser's Henrico Slave Revolt plot. **30 September** Convention of 1800 or Treaty of Morte Fontaine ended Quasi-War and Franco-American Alliance of 1777 from the American Revolutionary War. **3 December** Democratic Republicans Thomas Jefferson and Aaron Burr tied for the presidential electoral vote.

1801 **13 February** Congress created an expanded judiciary to preserve Federalist power. The appointments came so late in Adams's term that they were called Midnight Judges. **17 February** Thomas Jefferson elected president in the House of Representatives.

1803 **24 February** In the case of *Marbury v. Madison*, Supreme Court declared an act of Congress invalid and unconstitutional for the first time. **30 April** Louisiana Purchase agreed to.

1804 **5 December** Democratic Republican Jefferson reelected as president over Federalist Charles Cotesworth Pinckney. **25 December** Twelfth Amendment ratified that recognized the political party system in the electoral college.

1807 **2 March** Congress outlawed African slave trade after 1 January 1808, as a part of Compromise of 1808 from the Constitutional Convention of 1787. **22 December** Congress passed an embargo act against Britain for transgressions against American ships and seamen on the high seas.

1808 **1 January** African slave trade outlawed. **7 December** Democratic Republican James Madison elected president over Federalist Charles Cotesworth Pinckney.

1810 **1 May** In Macon's Bill No. 2, Congress allowed the president to declare a trade embargo against either Britain or France, whichever nation refused to admit to the American position of free ships equaled free trade. **27 October** Lone Star Rebellion in West Florida (Gulf coast from Baton Rouge to Mobile) led to its annexation.

1811 **20 February** Congress failed to renew charter of First Bank of the United States. **4 November** War Hawks emerged in Congress. **7 November** Gen. William Henry Harrison defeated Northwest Indians leagued with Tecumseh at the Battle of Tippecanoe.

1812 **18 June** Congress declared War of 1812. America lost every land battle in this year. **2 December** Democratic Republican James

Madison reelected president over anti-war Democratic Republican and Federalist DeWitt Clinton.

1813 **27 April** Americans burned Canadian capital at York (Toronto). **10 September** Americans under Capt. O. H. Perry won Battle of Lake Erie at Put-in-Bay. **5 October** Americans under Harrison defeated British–Indian forces decisively at Battle of the Thames in Ontario near Detroit. Tecumseh killed by Richard Johnson's Kentucky Mounted Rifles.

1814 **9 August** Gen. Andrew Jackson defeated the Creek Nation, ending the Creek War. **24 August** British defeated American force at Battle of Bladensburg and burned public buildings in Washington, D.C. **11 September** Capt. Thomas MacDomough defeated British fleet at Battle of Lake Champlain. **14 September** Americans defeated British attack on Baltimore at Ft. McHenry. **15 December** At the Hartford Convention, New England states under Federalist auspices threatened to secede from the Union over the war. **24 December** Treaty of Ghent ended the War of 1812 in status quo antebellum.

1815 **8 January** Americans under Jackson defeated British invasion at the First Battle of New Orleans.

1816 **10 April** Congress chartered a Second Bank of the United States. **4 December** Democratic Republican James Monroe elected president over Federalist Rufus King, the last time the Federalists fielded a presidential candidate.

1817 **3 March** Congress voted to apply all bonuses paid by the Second Bank of the United States to internal improvements, but Monroe issued the Bonus Bill Veto, calling it all beyond the Constitution. **28 April** In the Rush–Bagot agreement, the U.S. and Britain began to demilitarize the Great Lakes. **8 July** By the Treaty of Rattlesnake Springs, the Cherokees agreed to exchange lands east of the Mississippi for lands west of the river. Those who moved were called the Old Settlers.

1818 **7 April** First Seminole War began as an attempt to return escaped slaves to their owners. **20 October** Anglo-American Convention of 1818 settled the Canadian–American border west of the Great Lakes to the Rocky Mountains at 49°.

1819 Panic of 1819. **22 February** Adams–Onís Treaty created the southern boundary of the Louisiana Purchase and ceded East Florida to the U.S.

1820 3 March Missouri Compromise admitted Maine as a free state and Missouri as a slave state, with no slavery allowed in the Louisiana Purchase north of the southern boundary of Missouri, 36°30'. **15 May** Congress declared participation in the international slave trade to be piracy. **18 October** By the Treaty of Doak's Stand, the Choctaw Nation agreed to exchange a third of their land east of the Mississippi for land west of the river. **6 December** Democratic Republican James Monroe reelected president without opposition.

1822 4 May President Monroe vetoed the extension of the National (Cumberland) Road, calling for a constitutional amendment to build internal improvements. **14 June** Charleston Plot involving Denmark Vesey's alleged slave revolt betrayed.

1823 10 March In *Johnson v. McIntosh*, U.S. Supreme Court ruled that Indian Nations occupy their homelands at the pleasure of the Federal government. **17 April** Treaty with Russia set the southern boundary of Alaska and the northern boundary of Oregon at 54°40'. **18 September** By the Treaty of Camp Moultrie, a part of the Seminole nation agreed to remove to land west of Arkansas. **2 December** Monroe Doctrine, actually the work of Secretary of State John Adams, declared the Western Hemisphere to be off limits to further European colonization.

1824 30 March Henry Clay introduced the American System in Congress. **1 December** No one won a majority of the electoral vote and presidential election was thrown into House of Representatives. John C. Calhoun elected vice president, eventually splitting with Adams and joining the Jacksonians.

1825 9 February Second place popular-vote winner, National Republican John Quincy Adams elected president in the House of Representatives amid charges of a "corrupt bargain" as speaker of the House Henry Clay, who also ran for president and came in third in popular votes, was appointed secretary of state, and by implication, the next presidential candidate. Popular-vote winner Andrew Jackson was cut out of the results and announced his immediate campaign for the presidency for 1828. **12 February** Treaty of Indian Springs called for Creek removal to land reserved for the Indian Nations to the west of Arkansas.

1826 January 24: Treaty of Washington voided Treaty of Indian Springs, 1825.

1827 26 July Cherokee Constitution drawn up.

1828 19 May Congress passed the high protective Tariff of 1828, known in the South as the Tariff of Abominations. **3 December** Andrew Jackson elected president and John C. Calhoun elected vice president, this time on Jackson's ticket. **19 December** South Carolina legislature passed a series of resolves to nullify the tariff, and printed the *South Carolina Exposition and Protest*, authored in secret by Vice President John C. Calhoun, which told how Nullification would work.

1830 19–27 January In Webster–Hayne Debate, Senator Robert Y. Hayne of South Carolina defending the compact theory of the Union through states rights and Nullification, with Senator Daniel Webster of Massachusetts advocating an insoluble Union with fewer state prerogatives. **13 April** Jefferson Day Dinner, where President Jackson toasted the permanency of the Union and Vice President Calhoun saluted liberty over Union. **27 May** In the Maysville Road Veto, the first pocket veto in U.S. history, Jackson refused to allow a branch to the National Road to be built past Henry Clay's home. **28 May** Congress passed Indian Removal Act, which called for eviction of all tribes living east of the Mississippi. **1 June** Georgia legislature declared Cherokee law inoperative in the state. **31 August** By the Treaty of Franklin, the Chickasaw Nation agreed to remove to lands west of Arkansas. **28 September** By the Treaty of Dancing Rabbit Creek, Choctaw Nation agreed to remove to lands west of Arkansas by 1833.

1831 18 March *Cherokee Nation v. Georgia*, U.S. Supreme Court ruled that Indians were wards of the federal government and beyond state law. **7 April–8 August** Jackson reorganized his cabinet, getting rid of Calhoun supporters. **13 August** Nat Turner led Southampton Slave Rebellion on Virginia's Southside. **26 July** Calhoun confirmed his authorship of Nullification in Ft. Hill Letter. **26 September** Organization of the Anti-Masonic Party and the nomination of William Wirt for president. **12 December** National Republicans nominated Henry Clay for president at Baltimore convention.

1832 3 March *Worcester v. Georgia*. U.S. Supreme Court ruled that Georgia had no power to interfere with Indian lands. Indian Removal began, nonetheless, as Jackson ignored the court. **6 April–2 August** Black Hawk War in Illinois and Wisconsin. **9 May** By the Treaty of

Payne's Landing, the Seminole nation agreed to remove to lands west of Arkansas. **22 May** Democrats nominated Jackson for president and dumped Vice President Calhoun in favor of Martin Van Buren. To show Van Buren's supposed popularity in the party, Democrats adopted the two-thirds rule for all nominations, a rule that lasted to 1936. **10 July** Jackson vetoed the rechartering of the Second Bank of the United States. **14 July** Tariff of 1832 passed Congress with Jackson's blessing. Nullification crisis began. **20 October** By the Treaty of Pontotoc, the Chickasaw Nation agreed to sell its lands east of the Mississippi to the federal government. **24 November** South Carolina state convention nullified tariffs of 1828 and 1832. **5 December** Democrat Andrew Jackson reelected president over National Republican Henry Clay and Anti-Mason William Wirt. **10 December** Jackson's Proclamation to the People of South Carolina denounced Nullification as treason.

1833 14 January Georgia released white missionaries Samuel Worcester and Elizur Butler from jail to expedite negotiations for Cherokee removal. **2 March** Congress declared federal deposits in Second Bank of the U.S. to be safe. **1 February** Date Nullifiers were to begin resistance to enforcement of U.S. laws passed without incident. **1 March** By the Force Act, Congress granted Jackson full military powers to suppress Nullification. **2 March** Compromise Tariff of 1833 ended the Nullification Crisis. **18 March** South Carolina nullified the Force Act as a last shot at Jackson. **28 March** Seminole Nation representatives signed Treaty of Ft. Gibson, agreeing on which lands west of Arkansas to occupy. Seminole left in Florida refused to leave, killing one of the signers, an Indian agent, and massacring Maj. Francis Dade's army command. **3 April** Attorney General Roger B. Taney declared federal deposits at risk and liable to removal at the president's desire. **20 May** Secretary of the Treasury Louis McLane refused to remove deposits when Jackson asked and resigned. **23 September** New Secretary of the Treasury William Duane refused to remove deposits as Congress had declared them safe. Jackson fired him. **26 September** Secretary of the Treasury *ad interim* Roger B. Taney removed federal deposits from Second Bank of the U.S, while Congress was out of session.

1834 28 March Senate censured Jackson for his actions against Second Bank of the U.S. **14 April** Jackson's opponents adopted the name Whig Party, comparing King Andrew I of Veto Memory to George III during the American Revolution. **28 June** Congress refused to confirm Taney as secretary of the treasury.

1835 **14 March** Draft of the Schermerhorn Treaty to remove Cherokee from Georgia. Tribe asked for a renegotiation. **28 December** Treaty of New Echota expelled the Cherokee from Georgia under nearly the same terms as Schermerhorn Treaty.

1836 **2 March** Texas declared its independence from Mexico in a Lone Star Rebellion. **6 March** Alamo fell. **11 March** Gag Rule began in Senate. **15 May** The Creek War resulted in the Creek Nation being forcefully escorted in chains to lands west of Arkansas one year later. **26 May** Gag Rule fight in House for next eight years. **27 March** Massacre of Texas troops after surrender at Goliad. **21 April** Texas army defeats Mexicans at San Jacinto, near present-day Houston. **14 May** Treaty of Velasco granted Texas its independence. **23 June** The Federal Deposit Act created state banks to receive the deposits removed from the Second Bank of the U.S. **11 July** Jackson issued the Specie Circular, requiring the payment of cash for all land sales to slow rampant inflation. **7 December** Democrat Martin Van Buren elected president over Whig candidates Hugh Lawson White, William Henry Harrison, and Daniel Webster. Democrat vice presidential candidate, Richard M. Johnson, selected in the Senate because his racial proclivity of living with a black woman and admitting to fathering her children denied him a majority in the Electoral College. **18 December** Second Seminole War began with ambush at Kanapaha, Florida.

1837 **17 January** By the Treaty of Doaksville, the Chickasaw Nation finally left for the West, to live in a district obtained from the Choctaws. **1 March** Jackson pocket vetoed congressional attempt to eradicate Specie Circular, resulting in the Panic of 1837, the deepest economic depression before the Civil War. **3 March** Jackson recognized the Republic of Texas. **4 August** Texas asked for annexation to U.S. **25 August** Texas annexation refused as Jackson feared it would bring up the slavery issue. **18 October** The Army violated flag of truce and arrested Seminole Chief Oseola, sending him to Charleston to die in jail. The war continued.

1838 **21 May** Congress repealed the Specie Circular. **1 October** Cherokee forcibly removed to lands west of Arkansas in a march called the Trail of Tears. **25 December** Battle of Lake Okechobee drove the Seminoles deeper into the Everglades. **29 December** Anglo-American tensions over the *Caroline* Affair, where Canadians attacked an American ship on the U.S. side of the border that had been ferrying Canadian separatists over to raid British installations.

1839 **12 February** Aroostook War in Maine over the boundary with Nova Scotia. **15 July** Seminoles agreed to a truce in Florida and retired south of the Pease River into the Everglades. **13 November** Organization of the Liberty Party, first moderate anti-slavery political party in American history.

1840 **4 July** Independent Treasury established to hold U.S. funds independent of the Jacksonian pet banks. **2 December** Whig William Henry Harrison elected president over Democrat Martin Van Buren.

1841 **9 March** Amistad Case. **4 April** Death of Harrison, succeeded by John Tyler. First time a vice president became president by "accident." **13 August** Repeal of independent treasury and federal deposits returned to select state banks after rejection of another U.S. Bank. **11 September** Whig cabinet left over from Harrison resigned en masse because Tyler was acting more like a Democrat.

1842 **1 March** *Prigg v. Pennsylvania*, decided in U.S. Supreme Court, ruled that the fugitive slave issue was a federal matter beyond the states' interference. **21 March** *Creole* Case. **18 May** Dorr Rebellion against antiquated Rhode Island constitution. **9 August** Webster Ashburton Treaty settled all outstanding border issues except the line west of the Rocky Mountains to the Pacific. Henry Clay resigned from the Senate to concentrate on becoming president in 1844. John J. Crittenden was his successor. **14 August** Most of the rest of the Seminoles agreed to leave for lands west of Arkansas to avoid continued Florida militia campaigns.

1844 **27 April** Clay and Van Buren agreed to keep Texas annexation out of the presidential race. **1 May** Whigs met in convention at Baltimore and nominated Clay. **27 May** Democrats met in convention at Baltimore and nominated James K. Polk. He stood for re-annexation of Texas and reoccupation of Oregon. **4 December** Democrat James K. Polk elected president over Whig Henry Clay.

1845 **1 March** Tyler annexed Texas before Polk could take office. **28 March** Mexico broke off relations with United States over Texas annexation. **28 May** U.S. army ordered to Corpus Christi, Texas. **27 December** Use of term *Manifest Destiny* to justify American expansion to the Pacific for the first time.

1846 **13 January** Polk ordered Maj. Gen. Zachary Tayor and his army to cross the Nueces River and advance to Río Grande. **12 March** Mexico refused to negotiate Texas problem. **23 April** Mexico declared a defensive war against the U.S. **25 April** War with Mexico began near present-day Brownsville. **13 May** Declaration of war upon Mexico. **15 June** Settlement of U.S.–Canadian boundary at 49° to the Pacific. **6 August** Independent Treasury reestablished. **8 August** Introduction of Wilmot Proviso, declaring that no slavery be allowed in any territory gained from Mexico.

1847 War with Mexico, conquest of Santa Fé, the Great Southwest, and California. **29 December** Lewis Cass announced that he was for Squatter Sovereignty on the question of slavery in the territories.

1848 **24 January** Gold discovered at Sutter's Mill (today's Sacremento) on the American River in California. **2 February** Treaty of Guadalupe Hidalgo ended War with Mexico. **22 May** Democratic Convention at Baltimore nominated Lewis Cass of Michigan for president. **7 June** Whig Party Convention at Philadelphia nominated war hero Maj. Gen. Zachary Taylor for president. **22 June** Antislavery Democrats, meeting at Utica, New York, nominated Martin Van Buren for president. **9 August** Liberty Party supporters, Antislavery Democrats, and Conscience Whigs met at Buffalo, New York, and formed the Free-Soil Party and jointly nominated Van Buren for president. **8 November** Whig candidate Zachary Taylor won the election of 1848.

1849 **3 January** In *Luther v. Borden*, a case growing out of the Dorr Rebellion in 1842, the U.S. Supreme Court ruled that Congress determines the constitutionality and legality of all state governments and elections by seating its representatives. This case would determine the acceptance of Southern states back into the Union after the Civil War.

1850 **29 January** Senator Henry Clay of Kentucky introduced a series of resolutions calling for compromising of a multitude of issues concerning slavery. **5–6 February** Senator Henry Clay of Kentucky spoke in favor of compromise, North and South. **4 March** Senator John C. Calhoun of South Carolina spoke in favor of the Non-Exclusion Doctrine and equal Southern rights to the territories. **7 March** Senator Daniel Webster of Massachusetts spoke for no action on slavery in the territories because climate determined it would not last there. **11 March** Senator William H. Seward of New York spoke for a higher law that justified excluding slavery from the West. **8 May** Clay's committee in the Senate introduced the Omnibus Bill covering slavery in the territories and a second bill prohibiting the slave trade in the District of Columbia, but they failed to be passed. **10 June** Nashville Convention. **9 September** Anti-compromise President Taylor died, allowing pro-compromise Vice President Millard Fillmore to become president. **13 August–7 September** Led by Senator Stephen A. Douglas of Illinois, the Compromise of 1850 was passed as a series of individual acts, the first of which was the admission of California as a free state, upsetting the 50-50 balance in the Senate. **15 August–6 September** Texas and New Mexico Territory Act, Texas Republic debt assumed by United States, and Texas surrendered all claim to Santa Fé with no mention of slavery. **15 August–6 September** Utah Territory Act created a new territory with no mention of slavery. **23 August–12 September** Fugitive Slave Act provided for the return of all fugitives as an exclusive federal prerogative. **16–17 September** Abolition of the domestic slave trade in District of Columbia act passed. **13–14 December** Georgia platform called for adherence to Union until the North ignored any part of the Compromise of 1850.

1851 **1 September** Narciso López publicly garroted in Havana for filibustering expeditions against Cuba.

1852 Young American Movement became a national passion. **20 March** Harriet Beecher Stowe's *Uncle Tom's Cabin* published and became a best-seller. **1 June** Democratic Convention at Baltimore nominated Franklin Pierce of New Hampshire for president standing for the Compromise of 1850 and Popular Sovereignty deciding slavery in the territories. **16 June** Whig Convention at Baltimore nominated Lt. Gen. Winfield Scott for president standing for the Compromise of 1850 and an end to further anti-slavery agitation. **11 September** Free-Soil Party met at Pittsburgh and nominated U.S. Senator John P. Hale of New

Hampshire for president and condemned the Compromise of 1850 and stood for free soil and free men. **2 November** Franklin Pierce selected with the abandonment of the Whig Party for the Democrats in the South.

1853 4 March Pierce was inaugurated calling for support of the Compromise of 1850 and acquisition of more territory by peaceful means. **30 December** Gadsden Purchase completed U.S. acquisitions from Mexico.

1854 23 January-30 May Congress passed the Kansas–Nebraska Act. **28 February–13 July** Organization of the Republican Party in several states. **26 April** Eli Thayer organized the Massachusetts Emigrant Aid Society which was reorganized as the New England Emigrant Aid Society on 21 February 1855. **18 October** Ostend Manifesto called for U.S. annexation of Cuba by purchase or force.

1855 Kansas–Missouri Border Wars. **June–October** William Walker exploited a local civil war to subjugate Nicaragua. **20 December** Third Seminole War began when U.S. survey team sacked plantations of Seminoles in the Everglades.

1856 Kansas–Missouri Border Wars. **22 February** The American (Know Nothing) Party met at Philadelphia and nominated Millard Fillmore for president on a Nativist platform. **14 May** After repudiating William Walker's takeover of Nicaragua, President Pierce received his emissary, a virtual recognition. **19–20 May** Senator Charles Sumner of Massachusetts delivered his "Crime against Kansas" Speech. **22 May** Representative Preston Brooks (S.C.) assaulted Senator Charles Sumner (Mass.) in the senate chamber for insulting his uncle and home state. **2 June** Democratic Party convention met at Cincinnati and nominated James Buchanan for president on a platform of Popular Sovereignty and support for the Kansas–Nebraska Act. **17 June** Republican Party met at Philadelphia and nominated John Charles Frémont for president on a platform opposing the twin evils of slavery and polygamy in the territories and supporting a Free State Kansas. **17 September** Whig Party met at Baltimore and nominated Millard Fillmore of the American Party for president. **4 November** James Buchanan elected president.

1857 Kansas–Missouri Border Wars. **4 March** President Buchanan inaugurated, pledged federal non-interference and Popular Sovereignty in the territories. **6 March** *Dred Scott v. Sanford* decided by U.S.

Supreme Court, ruling that African Americans were not citizens, that slavery had an extraterritorial quality, and that the South was correct in its doctrine of federal non-interference with slavery in the territories. **1 May** Filibusterer William Walker surrendered to U.S. Navy after being run out of Nicaragua by Cornelius Vanderbilt, his original sponsor. **24 August** Panic of 1857 began. **25 November** Walker landed at Greytown, Nicaragua, only to be expelled by the U.S. Navy.

1858 Kansas–Missouri Border Wars. **8 May** Third Serminole War ended, about one-third of the Seminoles in southern Florida moved to lands west of Arkansas. Rest of tribe stayed behind, where they remain today. **27 August** Abraham Lincoln asked Stephen A. Douglas the Freeport Question and Douglas stated the Freeport Doctrine that slavery can be stopped in a territory before the vote on a state constitution, winning Illinois (the only Democrat to win in the North, except for some in Indiana) but losing the South in 1860, because he had repudiated Popular Sovereignty.

1859 **9 May** Southern Commercial Convention at Vicksburg, Mississippi, urged reopening the international slave trade from Africa. **16 October** John Brown's raid on Harper's Ferry, Virginia. **2 December** Brown hanged.

1860 **23 April–3 May** Democratic Party met in Charleston and adopted the Cincinnati Platform of 1856, but could not come to an agreement on a presidential candidate, with the Deep South States walking out. **9 May** The former Whig American Party met at Baltimore as the Constitutional Union Party and nominated John Bell of Tennessee as its presidential candidate, condemning sectionalism and standing for Constitution and Union. **16 May** Republican Party met in Chicago and nominated Abraham Lincoln of Illinois as its presidential candidate on a platform of economic improvement and the Wilmot Proviso. **18 June** Democrats met again in Baltimore and, after another Southern walkout, nominated Stephen A. Douglas of Illinois for president. **28 June** Meeting at Richmond since June 11, Southern Democrats nominated Vice President John C. Breckinridge of Kentucky as their presidential candidate for 1860, standing for non-exclusion of slavery from the territories and the acquisition of Cuba. **12 September** William Walker executed in Honduras after landing in August to subjugate the country. **6 November** Abraham Lincoln elected president with 39 percent of the popular vote. **10 November** South Carolina state legislature called a convention to meet on December 17 to consider secession from the Union. **13 December** Seven Senators and 23 Representatives from the South urged secession and creation of a Southern Confederacy. **14 December** Georgia state legislature asked South Carolina, Mississippi, Alabama, and Florida to appoint delegates to a convention to establish a Southern Confederacy. **20 December** South Carolina seceded from the Union.

1861 **9 January** Mississippi seceded. **10 January** Florida seceded. **11 January** Georgia seceded. **19 January** Louisiana seceded. **29 January** Kansas admitted as a free state. **1 February** Texas seceded. **4 February** Drafting of the Confederate Constitution began in Montgomery, Ala. **4 February** Washington Peace Conference began. **8 February**: Confederate Constitution adopted. **9 February** Provisional Government of the Confederacy established. **19 February** Jefferson Davis inaugurated as president of the Confederacy. **12 April** Confederates fired upon Ft. Sumter; Ft. Pickens at Pensacola reinforced without incident. **14 April** Ft. Sumter surrendered. **15 April** President Lincoln called up 75,000 volunteers to suppress the Confederates. **17 April** Virginia seceded. **6 May** Arkansas seceded. **7 May** Tennessee seceded and established a military alliance with the Confederacy. **20 May** North Carolina seceded. **20 May** Confederate government moved to Richmond. **11 June** Western Virginia refused to secede. **31 July** Loyal convention established Union government in Missouri, its elected government having fled to the Confederacy. **19 August** Confederate Congress agreed to a military alliance with Rebel Missouri. **20 August** Western Virginia Convention at Wheeling established Free State of Kanawha. **31 October** Missouri formally seceded from the Union. **6 November** Confederate election of 1861 selected a permanent government and Congress. **7 November** Confederate commissioners to Britain and France, James M. Mason and John Slidell taken from the British mail ship *Trent* by Capt. Charles Wilkes of U.S.S. *San Jacinto*. **26 November** The convention at Wheeling adopted a new constitution for the proposed state of West Virginia. **4 December** U.S. Senate expelled Senator John C. Breckinridge of Kentucky from its body as an avowed Rebel. **10 December** Kentucky formally seceded from the Union. **26 December** Lincoln ordered the release of Confederate diplomats James M. Mason and John Slidell.

1862 **9 April** Confederate Congress passed the first conscription act. **27 September** Confederate Congress passed the Second Conscription Act. **4 October** Confederate Governor Richard Hawes inaugurated at Frankfort, Kentucky. **1 December** Lincoln asked Congress to consider gradual emancipation of the slaves by 1 January 1900, compensation for the owners, and deportation of freed slaves out of the nation.

1863 **29 January** Confederate Congress authorized the Erlanger Loan for $15 million.

1864 **7 February** Confederate Congress authorized the enrollment of blacks, slave or free, as military laborers. **28 February** Union Kilpatrick-Dahlgren Raid to free prisoners held in Richmond and kidnap or execute members of the Confederate government began. **1 March** Kilpatrick-Dahlgren failed and its controversial orders fell into hands of the Confederates. **10 June** Confederate Congress passed the Third Conscription Act. **18 July** New York newspaper editor Horace Greeley went to Niagara Falls to discuss peace with Confederate emissaries but that came to nothing. **9 August** Two Confederate secret agents blew up Lt. Gen. Ulysses S. Grant's main supply base at City Point, Virginia. **12 October** U.S. Supreme Court Chief Justice Roger B. Taney of Dred Scott and Non-Exclusion Doctrine fame died.

1865 **12 January** Frank Blair, Sr., a Northern Democratic politician with sons in the Republican Party, conferred with Confederate President Jefferson Davis on a possible peace conference. **16 January** Frank Blair, Sr., reported to President Lincoln on his discussions for peace with Confederate President Davis, but Lincoln refused to act as if there were two nations. **18 January** President Lincoln told Blair that he would talk informally of peace with any representative from the South. **23 January** Confederate Congress created the position of general-in-chief and President Davis appointed Robert E. Lee on 31 January. **30 January** President Lincoln issued a pass to permit three Confederate peace commissioners to come to Union-held Fortress Monroe, Virginia. **2 February** President Lincoln and Secretary of State William H. Seward met with Confederate Senator R. M. T. Hunter, Assistant Secretary of War John Campbell, and Vice President Alexander H. Stephens aboard the *River Queen* in Hampton Roads to discuss peace to no avail. Lincoln allegedly told them that his policy toward freed blacks was they were now on their own: "root, hog, or die." **13 March** Confederate

Congress approved the use of black combat troops. **2 April** Confederate army and civilian government abandoned the Richmond and Petersburg lines. **14 April** President Lincoln assassinated by Confederate agent John Wilkes Booth at Ford's Theater. **10 May** Confederate President Davis and party captured by Union cavalry at Irwinsville, Georgia, ending the Confederate government and the Old South.

Introduction

The American Civil War was fought to promote Union, Freedom, and Equality. At least that is what one learns in public schools and even colleges and universities. But that is only partially true. What the war really was all about was raw political power—about which white people would rule the United States. It was the successful attempt to take the political imperium from the Southern agrarian, slaveholding aristocracy that governed this nation until the most terrible of all American wars, and transfer it to the industrial, shipping magnates of the North, who have run it since, which is one reason the war produced a reborn Union, but only a technical freedom, and little equality, legacies that haunt the United States even today.

The chronicle of the Old South is the story of how the supporters of slavery had others use that institution to destroy them and set a different course for the nation's future, under new leadership, with a new Constitution, and an interventionist governmental philosophy. The man who would lead that change, in his own words, "scorn[ed] to tread in the footsteps of any predecessor, however illustrious," and predicted that he or some other "[t]owering genius" would do it "at the expense of emancipating slaves, or enslaving freemen" in a public speech given at a local Young Men's Lyceum in 1838. That meeting took place in Springfield, Illinois. The speaker's name was Abraham Lincoln.

As an earlier president, Thomas Jefferson, once warned, "The natural progress of things is for liberty to yield and government to gain ground." The irony in the early history of the United States was that those who favored the most liberty for white Americans denied it to black slaves. The history of the Old South is their story. It is also the saga of the governance of the United States before the war that changed everything, the war that, paraphrasing Lincoln's words, emancipated the slaves and enslaved the free.

WHAT WAS THE OLD SOUTH?
THE CENTRAL THEME OF SOUTHERN HISTORY

If one is to read a book about the Old South, it might be useful to know what the author thinks the Old South is, or was. One way to define the Old South is to give it arbitrary historical dates: to assert, along with many historians, that the Old South was a part of the present United States that existed before the beginning of the American Civil War. That is, the Old South was an antebellum South; it was extant before 1861. But that makes the Old South include something that might better be called the Colonial South. If the colonial era is dropped out of the picture, the Old South now becomes something that existed between the American Revolution and the Civil War. It is antebellum only in relation to the Civil War.

But is the Revolution an ending to the colonial period or a beginning of a new nation? Perhaps it is both. So for clarity, let us consider that the United States was something that began in 1781, with the adoption by the 13 rebelling British colonies along the Atlantic coast of their first constitution, the Articles of Confederation. This new nation was confirmed with the Americans' defeat of the British at Yorktown that led to the Treaty of Paris in 1783 and that established boundaries for the United States, of which the Old South was a part. So now the Old South is a component of the United States that existed between two of America's greatest wars. In that sense, by 1861, it was hardly "old" at all.

What then separated the Old South from the rest of the nation, the North and the West? One answer was climate. The Old South had less snow, more rain, and a greater number of balmier days per year than other sections of the United States. This allowed it to grow certain staple crops. Of all of these crops, none dominated the Old South like the cultivation of upland cotton. The natural climate for upland cotton existed in few places in the world, and none was as ideal as the 19th century American South.

But to define the Old South by the natural climate for cotton is to lose many border regions that were part of it. Southern agriculture was actually quite diverse and included more than cotton. There was upland cotton's lowland cousin, Sea Island cotton, and rice, indigo, hemp, and tobacco. But then there was also corn, wheat, livestock, and naval stores (pitch, turpentine, and such). These "crops" help extend the Old South northward to the Ohio River and the Mason–Dixon Line, the northern border of Maryland, and Delaware.

The North and West, however, grew many of the same crops, particularly foodstuffs, as the Old South. They were as rural as the Old South. Northern and Western states supported states rights, another supposedly exclusive Southern trait. The North and West had the same evangelical religions as the South and participated fully in the religious fervor of the Second Great Awakening. Even the preference of some historians for defining the Old South by its peoples, Anglo-Saxon and Celtic, overlooks the fact these existed in large numbers elsewhere in the United States, too.

Other commentators prefer to emphasize that the Old South was dominated by a country gentry that was learned, landed, chivalric, paternal, responsible, and interested in government. This has often been enshrined in the concept that Southerners were cavaliers, gentlemen like the monarchical-supporting class in 17th century Britain. The Yankees to the north have been stereotyped as Puritans, Roundheads, modern-day Oliver Cromwells, common people who knew God's will and were not shy in telling others about it and how to live it. But there were Northern counterparts to the rustic gentlemen of the Old South, surely as noble and paternal and landed as those in the Old South. And there were Southerners fully as Calvinistic and plebian and sanctimonious as the Cromwellian North.

What, then, distinguished the Old South from the rest of the nation and made it unique? According to the dean of Southern historians, Ulrich B. Phillips, it was the Southern whites' dedication to a cultural principle, embodied in an institution, slavery. Phillips called that principle the "Central Theme of Southern History." It was the belief that the Old South (and the New Souths that followed) had been, was, and shall "remain a white man's country." Slavery was the distinguishing feature that marked the Old South. But slavery was more than a labor system; it was a social system guaranteed to keep the African American more African than American. The black people were to be ensconced in a well-defined secondary position in the Old South for life.

Sure, the North and West had their reserved second-class place for the African Americans they freed after the American Revolution. It came to be called segregation. But they faced a small demographic problem when compared to the defeated Civil War South, which had its plantation belts with 90 percent black populations. It would take a New South to make segregation into the pervasive Jim Crow system that aped peonage for a hundred years after the war that promised Union, Freedom, and Equality.

THE OLD SOUTH AND THE PECULIAR INSTITUTION: THE CENTRAL THEME IN ACTION

The institution of slavery, the peculiar institution, as it came to be called, was neither peculiar nor Southern in 1619, when the first slaves arrived at Jamestown to be sold off a "Dutch man of warre" to local tobacco farmers. It was simply a medieval answer to a labor shortage that was more pronounced in the lush, semi-tropical, Southern, British mainland colonies than in the rocky, non-productive soils of the North. But slavery soon spread to all 13 British colonies in North America, plantations being as common in the old Dutch areas of the Hudson Valley and the truck gardens of New Jersey as the tobacco farms of Virginia and Maryland, and the later rice, cotton, and indigo plantations of South Carolina and Georgia.

The first black slaves were probably not chattels at all, but indentures. Just like the white immigrants from England and northern Europe, they "owed" a sponsor a sum for their transportation to the New World, that amount to be worked off in a term of years. Indeed, until a decade or two before 1700, there were no slave laws on the books anywhere in British North America. But gradually the terms of indenture were lessened for whites and lengthened for blacks until, for the latter, it came to 99 years. By 1714, the year the last Stuart monarch, Queen Anne, died in Britain, black codes in every colony defined slavery as a racial matter handed down from mother to child. Thus the off-spring from miscegenation, generally between white males and black women, expanded the labor force and could be disposed of as deemed convenient.

By the time of the American Revolution, slavery north of Maryland was a stagnant institution, while that south of Pennsylvania was entrenched and growing. Thomas Jefferson hoped to stigmatize King George III in the Declaration of Independence for imprinting slavery on America as part of the British Navigation Acts that forced colonies to purchase certain enumerated items and sell their produce to the mother country. But the hypocrisy of it all—the colonies never sent a slave ship out of port with its cargo unloaded or unsold, as they had with tea, for example—caused this clause to be stricken. However, a reference to the king's ministers, like the colonial governor of Virginia, John Murray, the Earl of Dunmore (Lord Dunmore to his American subjects), encouraging slave rebellion against their patriot masters ("domestic insurrections," Jefferson called them) was kept.

During and after the Revolution, the Northern states began to free their slaves, influenced by the natural rights philosophy of freedom and independence. But the black codes remained on the books as early statements of racial discrimination. Indeed, special laws had to be passed to prevent Yankee slaveholders from selling their slaves out of state to the Old South instead of freeing them. Many Southerners, motivated by the same philosophy of revolution, freed their slaves by individual action (George Washington, James Madison, James Monroe), but Thomas Jefferson, like most Southerners, did not. The social separation of racial slavery was too much of an impediment, with slaves outnumbering whites in many districts, as they did.

Actually, the Old South needed more and more slaves to raise the labor-intensive staple crops of Sea Island cotton, hemp, indigo, and rice. Since the British had liberated thousands of American slaves during the war, these needed to be replaced, too. When the Constitutional Convention met, the Old South insisted that the international slave trade remain legal until 1 January 1808. On that date the trade was outlawed. The slave states of Virginia and Maryland were among the leaders of the ban, realizing that their numerous chattels now had a heightened value, as the Old South began to expand westward in the Great Migration.

The westward movement of the plantation system was made possible by the domestic slave trade, centered in Washington, D.C., in the Upper South and New Orleans in the Lower South. The active domestic market in slaves revealed one of the oddities of slavery in the Old South, when compared to all the slave systems active in the Western Hemisphere over the centuries. In the 19th century, the Old South thrived on its own reproduction without resort to the international slave trade so necessary in Latin America. Some historians posit that the reason for this was that the Old South had the kindest form of slavery—if there is such a thing—one that allowed a semblance of normal family life.

Shortly after the Constitutional Convention, an invention that made the Old South and slavery part of a viable economic entity, the cotton gin, was perfected. Now there was a product that thrived in the climate and soils of the upland South, from the rolling hills of the Piedmont to the plains of Texas, and could be raised with gangs of slave labor, and readied for market with a simple machine that for the first time easily separated seeds from fiber. It was upland cotton on its way to becoming King Cotton.

It was no accident that, until the opening of the Erie Canal in the mid-1820s, the westward expansion of the United States relied primarily on the advance of the cotton culture and the slave labor that grew it. Cotton spurred the War of 1812 in the Old South, crushing the British and their Spanish and Native American allies for the fertile soils of Florida, Alabama, Mississippi, Louisiana, and, ultimately, Texas. This land grab continued throughout the first half of the 19th century, thinly disguised as an alleged social reform called Indian Removal.

THE POLITICS OF THE OLD SOUTH INSIDE THE UNION: THE COOPERATORS

Even with federal domestic and foreign policy support to abet the expansion of slavery and the cotton culture westward into new lands below the Mason–Dixon line, as the North abandoned slavery after the American Revolution, the Old South became more and more a conscious white minority within the nation. From the very beginning, there was an argument between those Southerners who believed that their right to slaves was best protected within the Union under the Constitution of 1787 and those who thought that the Old South ought to opt to become a nation in its own right with its own pro-slave fundamental law. The first theory was called state sovereignty, and its success was condemned by the North as the Slave Power Conspiracy. The second was called secession and was always a thorn in the side of Southern cooperators and their Yankee political allies, Northern men of Southern principles when it came to slavery and race.

Contrary to popularly held notions of modern Americans, a clear majority of the white South was very much against limiting the power of the federal government before the Civil War—when it came to slavery.

This was the difference between those who advocated cooperation and those who wanted secession. The cooperators realized that the Constitution offered the South many advantages in preserving their "peculiar institution." This has been concealed because historians have usually interpreted the Constitutional Convention as a quarrel between big states and small states. In reality there was a more important division—between those who opposed slavery and those who wished to protect it, under the Constitution of 1787.

The process was simple. The delegates from South Carolina and Georgia, led by such luminaries as Charles Cotesworth Pinckney of South Carolina, refused to endorse the new document without certain pro-slavery concessions. Sufficient Northerners from New England wanted the new document for its free trade, common market advantages badly enough to yield to Southern blackmail and worry about the consequences later. It was a deal that the Northerners' grandchildren would refuse to live under, and the Southerners' progeny would refuse to modify in 1861.

The South had many reasons to laud the new fundamental document that replaced the Articles of Confederation. All treaties had to be approved by a two-thirds vote in the upper house of Congress where all states had equal representation, regardless of physical or demographic size, giving the Old South a virtual veto. In the lower house, where membership was based on free, white population, the South managed to get three-fifths of all "other persons" (read: enslaved black men and women) counted for purposes of direct taxation and representation. As direct taxes were levied only briefly four times before the Civil War to finance the commercial wars of the early Union (such as the Quasi-War and the War of 1812), the Old South got a real bargain.

In addition, when it came to apportioning the original representation among the states at 30,000 for each congressional district in 1790, Secretary of State Thomas Jefferson, with the concurrence of President George Washington, rounded the numbers off in such a manner as to give the Old South a couple of extra congressmen more than the North. Then, in the Compromise of 1808, the importation of slaves from Africa and the Caribbean was allowed without limit until 1 January of that year. To his credit, then-President Jefferson saw to it that it was stopped on that date.

But these were all icing on the surface of the cake. It was the filling deep inside the pastry that made the real difference. Unlike the Articles of Confederation, the new Constitution had a stated and an unstated concept of extraterritoriality when it came to slavery. The overt statement came through the fugitive clause, which guaranteed the return of anyone held to "service or labor" to his or her state of origin (art. IV, sect. 2). What this phrase did was give slavery an extraterritorial nature. That meant the peculiar institution could be enforced outside the boundaries of the slave states in the so-called free states of the North. This was a compulsory thing—quite separate from criminal extradition, a voluntary legal process between states.

But it was the covert concept of extraterritoriality that brought the final break between North and South. This concerned the advance of slavery into the Western territories. Not only was this attempt subtle, but very involved. Both sides, pro-slave and anti-slave, realized that the territories were the key to breaking the Old South's hold on the constitutional argument for an extraterritorial application of slave law in the West.

The question in the West revolved around a problem in the Constitution. The document recognized two legitimate governing authorities existing in the United States: federal and state. But in reality, there were three: federal, state and territorial. The administration of territories was reserved to the federal government (art. IV, sect. 3, clause 2), but the Constitution defined federal territories as only the District of Columbia, federal forts, and federal dockyards (art. I, sect. 8, clause 17). The territories in the West were not mentioned.

The key was who would administer the police powers (health, safety, morals, well-being) in the unorganized West. The Old South maintained that powers not specifically defined in the Constitution (art. I, sect. 8) were reserved to the states and the people through the Bill of Rights, especially the Ninth and Tenth Amendments to the Constitution. The Old South admitted that the many states and divers peoples could not enforce the wide variety of state and local laws in the territories. So that right had to be granted to the federal government, not as a sovereign, but as a trustee (agent) of all the states and peoples.

Hence, the Old South argued that the federal government had no right to make policy (as it lacked sovereignty) but only to enforce any extraterritorial powers of the sovereign states as recognized in the Constitution. The only such power was the extraterritoriality of slavery, recognized through the fugitive clause.

This meant that of all the theories that Congress entertained over the years that referred to slavery in the West, only one obtained, the Non-Exclusion Theory. This held that all territories had to be opened to slavery until the territory achieved popular sovereignty. That happened only when Congress accepted the territory as a state, after the occupants wrote their state constitution. Only states had the sovereignty the territories lacked and could abolish or keep slavery.

The North argued that the nation ought to accept congressional laws on excluding slavery from the West, and that the precedent had been set even before the Constitution was written. In 1787, under the Articles' last gasp, Congress had passed the Northwest Ordinance creating the Old Northwest Territory (current Ohio, Indiana, Illinois, Michigan, Wisconsin, and parts of Minnesota) with slavery excluded from the whole area at its inception. Again, in 1820, under the Constitution, Congress had legislated the Missouri Compromise, which admitted Maine (free state) and Missouri (slave state) into the Union but excluded slavery in the West, synonymous then with the Louisiana Purchase, north of the southern boundary (36°30' line of latitude) of Missouri.

Because Congress had passed the Gag Rule, designed to keep the slavery debate off the floor from 1835 to 1845, and there were no new territories annexed after the acquisition of Florida in 1819 and the enactment of the Missouri Compromise of 1820, the question of slavery in the territories became moot. This lasted until Texas joined the Union in 1845 and Mexico was defeated and dismembered in 1848. With the Mexican Cession (the desert Southwest of today), the problem of slavery in the territories became the single most important issue in the Old South's relation with the Free States. Much of this new land lay south of the Missouri Compromise line and was open to slavery.

To preserve the West for free, white, non-slaveholding men only, Free-Soil congressmen coalesced around the Wilmot Proviso, a Northern proposal that no slavery be allowed in the territory won from Mexico (already a sovereign state, Texas was excluded from the measure). In the election of 1848, Democrats proposed that slavery be decided by those living in the territories as soon as a territorial legislature was created. This came to be called Squatter Sovereignty.

But the Old South would have none of that. Non-exclusion of slavery in the territories meant non-exclusion. Southern Democrats countered with the Alabama Platform that urged Popular Sovereignty—a popular vote on slavery's permanence in a territory, only after the populace ratified a proposed state constitution and achieved sovereignty or self-rule. Squatter Sovereignty cost the Democrats the election of 1848 because the Old South went for the Whig candidate, Louisiana planter and military hero Maj. Gen. Zachary Taylor, who was allegedly safe on the slavery question. In the ensuing Compromise of 1850, Congress sought to bury the problem of slavery in the territories by avoiding mention of it altogether. The implication was popular sovereignty, but it was only an unmentioned hint.

The issue sprang up again in the election of 1852. This time, the Democrats adopted popular sovereignty openly and carried the South. Then, Southern senators moved to hold the organization of the Great Plains west of the Missouri River hostage. They had four critical votes and forced the creation of two territories, Kansas and Nebraska, implying Kansas to the south was for slaveholders and the other for Free-Staters. The Old South got its way in Congress because men like Democrat Senator Stephen A. Douglas of Illinois were more interested in developing railroads in the West, come what may on slavery. But as Kansas was above the Missouri Compromise line (36°30' north latitude), Congress overrode that limitation in the Kansas–Nebraska Act.

Douglas and the Old South had underestimated the impact of the slavery issue. Both North and South headed for Kansas and ignored Nebraska. The resulting Kansas–Missouri Border Wars presaged the coming Civil War, as outnumbered Southern settlers struggled in vain against overwhelming numbers of Free-State settlers to write the first state constitution. Meanwhile, back east, the new Republican Party arose, dedicated to stopping the advance of slavery westward.

Then the thunderclap of the decade struck. The U.S. Supreme Court ruled on the question of slavery in the territories. The 1857 court case was *Dred Scott v. Sanford*. In it the court ruled 7 to 2 in favor of the Southern position, the Non-Exclusion Doctrine, on slavery in the West. But the justices could not agree on why. Chief Justice Roger B. Taney of Maryland, a slaveholder who had already manumitted his own chattels, wrote the definitive opinion.

What Taney did was to confirm the Southern position on slavery and its extraterritorial rights, direct and implied, in the Constitution. When added to the unanimous pro-Southern decision in *Ableman v. Booth* two years later, legitimizing the 1850 Fugitive Slave Act, the Old South's concept of slavery and the United States government's obligation to support its extraterritoriality was complete.

The Cooperators believed that each state was sovereign within it own borders, immune to outside control on all domestic matters. But beyond state borders, the Old South held that, because of the extraterritoriality guaranteed to slave institutions through the Constitution, it was the duty of the federal government to enforce state laws on slavery everywhere in the United States—in the free states and in the territories. This is what Abraham Lincoln referred to in his 1858 "House Divided" speech—that the nation could not exist half slave and half free but would soon become all one or the other.

There are historians who theorize that most of this was accidental and not intended by the Founding Fathers. But there would seem to be more to the mix than sharp Southern politicians twisting the Constitution to their own liking. It was that the pro-Southern tilt was endemic in the original document, merely waiting to be utilized.

THE SLAVE POWER CONSPIRACY: HOW THE OLD SOUTH DOMINATED NATIONAL POLITICS BEFORE THE CIVIL WAR

The success of the program advocated by Southern Cooperators can be seen in the Northern notion of the existence of a Slave Power Conspiracy. Between 1789 and 1861, in a nation where free, white males (potential voters) in the Northern states outnumbered Southern whites at least two to one, the South secured fully half of all major cabinet and diplomatic appointments and had 22 extra representatives in the lower house of Congress from counting three-fifths of its slaves. The Old South, more or less, according to this theory, unfairly and disproportionately ran the whole nation.

Not counting numerous clerkships, secretaries, sergeants at arms, and pages in every executive and congressional department of the federal government, which in that age of difficult and expensive travel frequently went to local Washingtonians, Marylanders, and Virginians (who backed the institution of slavery if they were not slaveholders themselves), individual presidential administrations were even more lop-sided in their appointment policies. Fifty-one percent of John

Adams's appointments were Southern slaveowners; and Adams was never an apologist for the Old South's peculiar institution. But Thomas Jefferson made 56 percent of his appointments from the Old South, while Andrew Jackson found 57 percent of his appointments among slaveholders.

In the 62 years between 1789 and 1850, slaveholders controlled the presidency for 50 years, and five slaveholders (George Washington, Thomas Jefferson, James Madison, James Monroe, and Andrew Jackson) served two consecutive terms. No Northerner was reelected, regardless of his stance on slavery (Adams and his son, John Quincy, against; Van Buren for; and William Henry Harrison, born in Virginia but elected from Ohio and dead one month after taking office, probably against). The Northern-born, pro-slave presidents of the 1850s (Millard Fillmore of New York, Franklin Pierce of New Hampshire, and James Buchanan of Pennsylvania) continued this trend to the Civil War.

Additionally, the Speaker of the House was a slaveholder for 51 of the 62 years, and the longest serving were all Southerners: Henry Clay (Kentucky), Andrew Stevenson (Virginia), and Nathaniel Macon (North Carolina). The chairman of the powerful House Ways and Means Committee (which determined what legislation reached the floor) was a slaveholder for 41 of those 62 years. Eighteen of 31 Supreme Court justices from the same period were from the Old South, as were the two more important chief justices, John Marshall (Virginia) and Roger B. Taney (Maryland).

There is more involved in this political ascendancy than the three-fifths compromise in the Constitution, which guaranteed the Old South 22 extra congressmen in the 1850s, based on the enumeration of slaves in the U.S. census. This Southern dominance was made possible by the support that non-slaveholding, Northern congressmen, Democrats after the rise of Jackson, rendered to Southern positions on slavery. These men actually came to the fore during the debates on the Missouri Compromise. It was their votes that made the adjustment of sectional argument over the admission of Missouri as a slave state possible. They were condemned as "unblushing advocates of domestic slavery" by their opponents in the North.

But it took the invective of a Southerner, who distrusted them as much as their Northern critics, to give them the sobriquet by which they would be forever known all the way to the Civil War. John Randolph of

Roanoke, Virginia, called them "dough faces," Northerners of Southern principle, and he despised them for being bought off by political patronage and deemed them unreliable for the future. Martin Van Buren organized these dough faces, and others of like philosophy, into a paramount part of his New York political machine, the Albany Regency. Known as Bucktails, from their identifying hat adornments, and buttressed by New Englanders, Pennsylvanians, and Northwesterners of similar political leanings, they became an important segment of Van Buren's new national Democratic Party that made Andrew Jackson and his successors president.

Randolph was correct in his prediction of their final fecklessness, but it would take the bitter anti-slavery quarrels of the 1850s and the rise of the Republican party to cause the dough faces to break their bond with the Old South. Those who had stayed loyal to the Southern wing of the Democratic party, the old Jacksonians from New York and elsewhere, men who had traditionally delivered 15–25 votes in Congress to protect Southern rights in slaves and territorial expansion, ultimately either became strong anti-slavery men or lost election to Republicans or Free-Soil independents.

To blunt the Slave Power Conspiracy argument, John C. Calhoun of South Carolina kept track of all those from Connecticut—anti-slavery Yankees in the government was the notion—and maintained that half of Congress came from or had been educated there (which included, oddly enough, himself). But no one cared. The Slave Power Conspiracy was hard to parry and impossible to beat.

Almost everyone who was anyone, North or South, believed in it. U.S. Senator William H. Seward (New York, Republican presidential candidate and later Lincoln's secretary of state), one-time U.S. Representative Abraham Lincoln (Illinois, eventual president of the United States), U.S. Representative Henry Wilson (Massachusetts, who wrote a multivolume history on the slave power and became a Republican vice president), and U.S. Senator Thomas Morris (Ohio, who coined and popularized the term "Slave Power Conspiracy" during the Jackson administration) backed the notion of a Slave Power Conspiracy.

So did Southerners like U.S. Senator James H. Hammond (South Carolina secessionist, who gloried in it, "You dare not make war against cotton, cotton is king!"), U.S. Representative Edward Stanly (North Carolina, later Civil War military governor of the state for Lincoln),

Benjamin Perry (South Carolina, moderate and Unionist, a rarity in that hotbed of *avant-garde* secession), and U.S. Representative Alexander H. Stephens (Georgia, close congressional friend of Lincoln, later vice president of the Confederacy, who called slavery the "cornerstone" of Southern civilization).

But it went further. The belief in the Slave Power Conspiracy became so all-encompassing as to cause it to be accused of sponsoring presidential assassinations. As the story went, whenever a president free from Old South control emerged, he was cut down in his prime, allegedly poisoned by unknown Southerners bent on guaranteeing the primacy of the Slave Power Conspiracy. William Henry Harrison (who, history says, actually died of the flu), Zachary Taylor (who died from gastroenteritis), and James Buchanan (who suffered from constant dysentery or the National Hotel disease, as it was popularly known) were all allegedly poisoned by anonymous members of the slave power cabal.

Only Buchanan survived, to remain infirm and positively intimidated by the Southerners who made up the 6–3 majority of his cabinet throughout most of his administration. Although a disinterment of Taylor recently found no DNA poisoning evidence in his case, the fact that he was dug up at all vividly demonstrates the continued vigor of the idea of a Slave Power Conspiracy a century and a half after its historical demise.

The ability of the Old South to control much of antebellum national politics, through the use of the clause in the Constitution that based representation in Congress on a count of the white population plus three-fifths of the Old South's slaves, led to the notion that there was a conspiracy to deny the more populous North its fair share of national power, which came to be seen as the Slave Power Conspiracy. But the real key to the Old South's ability to control the government came from its Northern allies, the dough faces, men who had disappeared by the time of the congressional by-election of 1858 and presidential election of 1860 in favor of Republicans. With them went an important political influence that led to Republican victory and boosted the Old South's interest in secession. By 1860, the Old South could still block much legislation, but it could no longer advance its program defending slavery because of the loss of its Northern allies.

Ironically, with the end of slavery at the termination of the Civil War, and the counting of the African Americans as full persons, the Northern victory actually increased the native-born political power of the South in Congress during Reconstruction and after. This meant that the expanded black vote became necessary to the North as a loyal, anti–white Democrat, pro-Republican counterforce on the Southern scene. To the New South, black enfranchisement was something to be curtailed, but the increased representation counted just as it had under the Three-Fifths Clause before the war. It took to the 1890s before that goal was fully accomplished, and the North gave up on trying to reconstruct the South until 60 years into the 20th century.

THE POLITICS OF THE OLD SOUTH OUTSIDE THE UNION: THE CHIVALRY

The Cooperators and their political opponents in the Old South, the chivalry or the Secessionists, essentially agreed on each state's existence as a sovereign entity. Within its borders, a state had full control of its domestic institutions, in this case, slavery. Where they disagreed was what to do if the North challenged the extraterritorial rights of slavery outside state boundaries, in the rest of the United States and its territories.

Unlike the Cooperators, the chivalry were quick to threaten to sunder the Union if the North did not play by Southern rules. Secessionists believed that eventually the faster growth of the free, white, nonslaveholding population in the North and West would cause them to outvote the Old South in the nation as a whole. The chivalry doubted the North's dedication to the Constitution as a slaveholders' document, that is, as it was written. Yankees would use the "necessary and proper" clause of the Constitution (art. I, sect. 8, clause 18) to get around all prohibitions. Why wait for the inevitable?

Even before the Constitution was ratified, the Old South threatened to play the disunion card. No matter what the *Federalist Papers* promised, it was obvious that the Constitution of 1787 was going to allow the central government much more power than had the Articles of Confederation of 1781. The preambles said it all. The Constitution began, "We the People of the United States." The Articles had opened, "We the undersigned delegates of the state." The Old South wanted certain constitutional and legislative guarantees as regarded its peculiar institution that would exempt slavery from possible adverse effects of the power change.

Among these guarantees were a two-thirds vote confirming treaties to protect the agricultural South from the trading and industrializing North; the counting of three-fifths of all "other persons" for representation and, at the North's insistence, direct taxation; the extraterritoriality of slavery through the fugitive clause, later extended to the territories by way of the Ninth and Tenth Amendments in the Bill of Rights; the guarantee of the international slave trade until 1 January 1808; equality of representation of the states in the new upper house of Congress, the Senate (the Articles had had a unicameral congress with each state having one vote); and later, the move of the national capital to a slave state in exchange for the Funding and Assumption of Revolutionary War debts on behalf of Yankee bankers and investors.

The terms were simple and openly stated by delegates from Georgia and South Carolina. Either the North agreed to the slaveholders' Constitution or it would not get the trade benefits inherent in the creation of a new common market between the states and national regulation of trade and tariffs. The new Union and its promised economic advantages were more important to the Northern Framers than quibbling over Southern slavery. Constitution ratified first, slavery reformed later.

Two things changed the picture for the next quarter century and kept secession before the American people as a paean for those dissatisfied with the course of government. The Old South did not reckon on the first anti-slavery Quaker petitions concerning the international slave trade which, though tabled because the Compromise of 1808 pledged the import of slaves from outside the United States until that year, led to the pro-slave argument justifying slavery and maintaining Southern interest in secession.

On the other hand, the North did not reckon on the retention of slavery in the Old South and an aggressive southern and westward movement into what was primarily Spanish territory, spurred on by the cotton gin and mercenary armies, called filibusters, often financed in secret by pro-Southern American presidential administrations. New England's increasing political isolation, in particular, even led to a Northern interest in secession by 1814 at the Hartford (Connecticut) Convention.

But events broke both secession movements before they could be effective. The outward question at hand was the rights of Americans on the high seas during the wars of the French Revolution and Napoleon in Europe. The seizure of American sailors and ships, and the quarantining of contraband and the ineffectual blockades of Britain and Continental Europe, put the trading North and agricultural South at loggerheads and stimulated the growth of American political parties. Again, the general rule (there were notable exceptions, mostly in New York and coastal South Carolina) was a North-South orientation in the division of the nation.

Powerful in the commercial North, the Federalist Party's Quasi-War against France dominated John Adams's administration. More reliant on British trade agreements, the Federalists blamed the entirety of America's navigation problems on Britain's enemy in Europe, France. The Federalists' domestic political opponents, the Democratic-Republicans, led by Thomas Jefferson and James Madison, were threatened by the Alien and Sedition Acts, which tried to limit public criticism of Federalist governmental policy.

In protest, Jefferson and Madison responded with the Kentucky and Virginia Resolves, written in 1798, and passed by their respective state legislatures, before the U.S. Supreme Court reserved for itself the examination of all federal laws for constitutionality in Marbury v. Madison (1803). In the Kentucky Resolves, Madison asserted that the individual states in combination ought to look at unconstitutionality of federal laws. Jefferson, author of the Virginia Resolves, went further. He hinted at secession by several states as a group as an ultimate check on federal excesses.

As Virginia (along with Rhode Island and New York) had a reserve clause in its ratification of the Constitution that allowed it to resume all its rights and leave the Union if the Constitution were perverted into a tyranny, Jefferson's position was not as radical as it might seem. But chivalry were blocked when the "Revolution of 1800," the election of Jefferson as president, put their advocate in charge of the very government they hoped to destroy. Nothing succeeds like success.

With Jefferson's accession to power, the Quasi-War ended even before he assumed office. But the problem of America's rights as a neutral on the high seas persisted as before. As a pro-French Revolution, Southern agrarian, Jefferson now blamed the same set of international circumstances on Britain. France, as anti-British, was the Democratic Republican's natural ally in Europe, and many Americans still hated Britain from the American

Revolution. So began a chain of events epitomized by the Embargo Act, which curtailed New England shipping in a vain attempt to protect American neutrality by eschewing use of the high seas, that led to the Second War of American Independence, the War of 1812.

The Old South's War of 1812 against Britain led to another brush with secession. Although ostensibly to gain American neutral rights on the high seas, the war was really a fight to conquer British Canada (an unachieved goal of the original Revolutionary War, liberating the so-called "Fourteenth Colony") and Spanish Florida (both also havens for runaway slaves), and expand American hegemony in the West by destroying the Native Americans in the way of the westward movement. Many of the states that would come of these territories would be slaveholding provinces and have their representation in Congress buttressed by the three-fifths clause of the Constitution.

This was all too much for New England and its Federalist Party. Once a dominant influence in American politics under Washington and Adams, the rise of the Jeffersonians to power and the expansion of the peculiar institution westward had seen New England become the first legitimate political minority in the nation. Led by a group of ultra-secessionists called the Essex Junto (once in cahoots with Jefferson's one-time vice president, the slightly disreputable Aaron Burr, until he totally ruined his reputation by killing Alexander Hamilton in a duel), delegates met in the Hartford Convention and threatened secession if the national government did not agree to terms.

The irony was that the convention's demands, which centered around repealing the three-fifths clause of the Constitution to limit Old South political power extending into the Southwest (as suggested by Federalist leader and stylist of the Constitution of 1787, Gouverneur Morris), became public at the same time as the Treaty of Ghent, which ended the War of 1812 in a draw. Seen in the rest of the nation as a traitorous wartime activity, these demands pretty much killed off the opposition Federalist Party. Although secession would later be picked up in the North again by the abolitionists, who spoke of a purifying disunion from the slaveholding Constitution, "a covenant with death and an agreement with hell," serious secession schemes would hereafter be reserved to the Old South.

With the secessionists North and South defeated, the nation embarked on a New Nationalism and Era of Good Feelings. The only viable political party remaining was the pro-South Democratic-Republicans. Southerners like John C. Calhoun and Andrew Jackson initially led the drive for a more powerful application of federal power. As with all one-party situations, personalities dominated, and the Election of 1824 saw four candidates run for president under the same party label. The fall-out from the deals that produced a president, John Quincy Adams, and the entrance of Martin Van Buren on the national political scene, caused the destruction of American unity through the creation of new political parties and the tariff used to rebuild them.

The Tariff of 1827, often called the Tariff of Abominations, was the highest tax on imported goods until the American Civil War. It was designed to get New York and Pennsylvania to vote with Van Buren and join the new party coalition that became the Democrats. Van Buren figured that the Old South would have to eat it. They had no other place to go, as the incumbent administration of John Quincy Adams was the most grasping for federal power until the Civil War government of Abraham Lincoln, or maybe even that of Franklin D. Roosevelt in the 20th century.

The lack of real choice between Adams and Van Buren (who confused the issue in the Old South by forming his party around the popular Southern military hero, Andrew Jackson) opened the opportunity for the chivalry once again in American history. This time the divisionists would come out of the Old South and be a continuing force to be reckoned with until they succeeded in 1861 in breaking the nation in twain, only to be crushed once and for all in the Confederate surrenders of 1865.

The Tariff of Abominations demonstrated to Southern planters what their forefathers and economic historians of mercantilism had discovered long ago. The control of natural resources (the naval stores of North Carolina, sugar cane of Louisiana, tobacco of Virginia and Kentucky, hemp of Kentucky and Missouri, and cotton of the rest of the American South) enabled distant colonial powers to oppress the locals—be those powers foreign, as Britain before the Revolutionary War, or home-grown, as the Yankee North after the War of 1812.

Whether true in this case or not, many in the Old South subscribed to this theory after the Tariff of Abominations passed Congress. The industrial and shipping North reaped an economic advantage from the tariff, while the agrarian and importing South paid for it. The heart of secession was in South Carolina, where the once divided plantation oligarchy (Federalists versus Democratic Republicans) that controlled the state's government organized to act in unison to defeat the tariff. The chivalry used as a basis for their program the *South Carolina Exposition and Protest*, a work written by then-Vice President John C. Calhoun, that detailed the process by which a federal law might be declared unconstitutional by a state action he called Nullification.

Nullification seemed to be a seceder's dream. In it, Calhoun offered a step-by-step primer that ultimately led to secession. According to Calhoun, any state offended by a federal enactment could call a state constitutional convention through a special election. As the body closest to the people in democratic theory, the convention would debate the law in question and vote as to its propriety. If the convention approved of the law, the whole process stopped. But if the convention rejected the law, it was nullified or invalidated within that state's boundaries.

Then Calhoun postulated that other states would follow suit with their own conventions. If three-fourths of the rest of the states approved of the law, it would become an amendment to the U.S. Constitution. If not, the law would be nullified for the whole nation. If the law passed muster at state and national levels and the original state still could not abide its effect, that state could reconvene its convention and secede from the Union. Secession was now available as an individual state action.

But there was a subtle trick in the process that initially escaped the would-be seceders. Calhoun was a nationalist, in his own states'-rights sort of way. He hoped that the continued debate would move the law's original congressional supporters to debate their measure some more and modify it to overcome the objections of the Nullifiers. Thus the Union would be made stronger by Nullification, not weaker.

This may have been true, but it is questionable that a theory of the Concurrent Voice, as Nullification was formally called, which historians assert Calhoun based on the rights of Polish nobles to check their central government in the 18th century, would strengthen much of anything, even in Calhoun's idealized presentation. After all, the Concurrent Voice had resulted in a weak, indecisive government that cost Poland its very existence, as Prussia, Austria, and Russia gobbled it up in the 1790s.

Calhoun's political ideas also got bound up in the quarrel between himself and Martin Van Buren as to who would succeed Andrew Jackson as president. Through several converging events, Calhoun lost that fight. Moreover, Jackson was not consistent in his attack upon nullification. While he did not allow it to happen in South Carolina over the tariff (which Jackson, Henry Clay, and Calhoun did compromise), he fully permitted Georgia to nullify the adverse decisions of the U.S. Supreme Court over its eviction of the Cherokees from traditional lands held within the state's boundaries. This skillfully undercut secession support for South Carolina's opposition to the tariff from the rest of the Old South, eager like Georgia to dispossess the Native Americans from ancestral lands in their states, too. Once more, the chivalry had been checked.

The Southern secessionists had a rough time for the next couple of decades. Each time they seemed on the verge of gaining new adherents in the Old South, they faltered. The chivalry were blocked by differences over economic issues like the tariff, the Second Bank of the United States, the Panic of 1837, government assistance for internal improvements (roads, canals, railroads, harbor advancements), various land laws, and, finally, James K. Polk's campaign for the "Re-annexation of Texas and Re-occupation of Oregon."

But when Polk went to war with Mexico, the North responded with the Wilmot Proviso designed to curb the expansion of slavery into any territory obtained from Mexico. The Old South objected vehemently. As a compromise, the Democratic presidential candidate in 1848, Northerner Lewis Cass, suggested a theory he called Squatter Sovereignty, which would allow the rejection or acceptance of slavery as soon as a territorial legislature assembled.

Southerners held out for the Non-Exclusion Theory that allowed slavery in the territories initially until a territory submitted a constitution for statehood, whereupon a popular vote would be held on slavery's existence in the new sovereign state. This quarrel over slavery in the Mexican Cession led to a revival of the secession movement in the Old South.

President Zachary Taylor sought to avoid the question of slavery in the territories altogether by making all territories states. But since most early settlers were non-slaveholding Hispanics and Yankees, this would have made all the new states free, which was one problem with Squatter Sovereignty all along. It took more time to move a plantation and its slaves westward than a single family farm. The Old South would not abide any hurrying of the settlement process or a vote before a territory achieved the necessary sovereignty as a state. It was especially offended that a slaveholding president from Louisiana would turn his back on the Constitution, his section, and its peculiar institution.

Forced to act after an agonizing debate, Congress passed the Compromise of 1850. The Old South got a new, strong fugitive slave act and an implied recognition of the Non-Exclusion Theory, now called popular sovereignty, in the territories of New Mexico and Utah, organized from the Mexican Cession. Finally, Texas gave her Republic of Texas debt to the United States for the cession of all land it claimed north of El Paso between the Rio Grande and the 103rd meridian to New Mexico Territory.

The North received the end of the slave trade in the District of Columbia and the admission of California as a free state. On its face, California's admission upset the balance between slave and free states in the U.S. Senate, but one of California's senators throughout the 1850s was originally from Mississippi, and there remained a half dozen dough face Northern allies in the Senate. The Slave Power Conspiracy was still intact. Nonetheless, Taylor vowed to veto the whole deal. But he died before he could make good on his threat and Vice President Millard Fillmore signed the Compromise into law.

The chivalry claimed that the South had yielded too much in the Compromise of 1850. Meeting at the Nashville Convention, however, they were blocked by the cooperators, who claimed that the U.S. Constitution still protected the South better than independent nationhood, and the refusal of another state to lead secession in the place of South Carolina. The state of Georgia, dominated by Cooperators, reached a compromise with its Georgia Platform. The Old South would stay in the Union provided that the North followed the Compromise of 1850 in its entirety. Cooperators narrowly swept the Southern state elections that followed, destroying any chance the chivalry had to act independently.

The fight between the Old South and the North nationally, and inside the Old South between its Cooperators and Secessionists, continued unabated during the decade of the 1850s. The cooperators seemed to be advancing their cause ably through the passage of the Kansas–Nebraska Act at home and so-called Spread Eagle Diplomacy overseas. But both efforts failed as Northern congressmen and citizen groups rallied to block pro-slave settlement in the Kansas–Missouri Wars and the forceful expansion of slave territory into the Caribbean basin by filibuster expeditions. But the cooperators did achieve a complete victory in the U.S. Supreme Court with favorable decisions on all aspects of extraterritoriality, from slavery in the territories in *Dred Scott v. Sanford* (1857) to the fugitive issue in *Ableman v. Booth* (1859).

Then Kansas asked to become a state in the Union. It was obvious that the Northern Free-Staters had won the race to populate the state. But the Old South cried foul. The race had been contrived through organized Yankee emigration and had not been a natural process. President James Buchanan agreed and demanded that Kansas be made a slave state. He also supported the Dred Scott decision that confirmed the Southern view of the extraterritoriality of slavery in the nation as a whole.

Unlike Buchanan, Democrat U.S. Senator Stephen A. Douglas of Illinois, the major advocate of Popular Sovereignty, refused to force slavery upon Kansas. He was likely to be the next Democrat candidate for the presidency, with strong Southern support. But first he had to win reelection to the U.S. Senate in 1858 by beating his opponent, an anti-slavery extension Republican, Abraham Lincoln. Lincoln lost the contest, but destroyed Douglas' Southern support in the Lincoln–Douglas Debates by forcing Douglas to admit that Popular Sovereignty could be had ahead of time if a territorial legislature simply refused to pass, as a part of its police powers, a black code supporting slavery. This was known as the Freeport Doctrine, from the debate site where it was announced.

In effect, Douglas was saying that there was little practical difference between Popular Sovereignty and Squatter Sovereignty. But the Old South still maintained that there was a difference, and it was crucial and constitutional—the Dred Scott decision had said so. Then came John Brown's Raid on Harper's Ferry. The Old South saw this as the Republican's ultimate goal revealed—to destroy slavery and the white South by encouraging, or even assisting, servile rebellion—the same thing Jefferson had accused the British of in the Declaration of Independence.

This caused the Democrats to split their support in the presidential election of 1860 between the Northern Freeport Doctrine wing represented by Douglas, and the Southern state sovereignty group led by Buchanan's vice president, John C. Breckinridge of Kentucky. This division guaranteed that the Republicans, running Abraham Lincoln, who pledged to ignore the Dred Scott decision, would win the election with a majority of electoral college votes and a minority (39 percent) of the popular vote, next to none of it coming from the Old South. But had all of Lincoln's opponents joined in a fusion ticket, they would have still lost the electoral college majority, even with 61 percent of the popular vote. Lincoln narrowly won the correct states. However, a unified opposition might have stood a better chance to deny him at least one of the closely contested states and the electoral college majority.

Lincoln's victory gave the chivalry their chance to strike, at last. There would be no time-wasting nullification. This time, the radical chivalry, called the fire-eaters, learning from the earlier nullification crisis, would go straight to secession. Emissaries traveled from state to state, lining up support and receiving pledges that, if South Carolina were to lead the way, at least Mississippi and Florida would follow, with Alabama probably close behind.

The Compromise of 1850 had been violated and was dead. The North had sold out the Old South completely—even the dough faces were voting Republican. Lincoln was pledged to end any slavery in the territories and to overturn the Dred Scott case, the central statement of Southern extraterritorial rights in slavery. In 1860, the election of Lincoln meant that secession would finally be successful, at last, after 70 years of defeat.

SECESSION TRIUMPHANT:
THE CONFEDERATE STATES OF AMERICA

Southerners were united more than usual in 1861. Secession was to be a conservative turn back to the Founding Fathers and the real Constitution, unpolluted by political parties and Yankee notions of modernity, which had been covered up over the years since by the term "progress."

By seceding from the Union, the radical secessionists expected to purify the South, much as the North hoped to do the same through the Republican Party's eradication of slavery and introducing governmental financial and legal assistance to business and agriculture. This was seen in the Republican platform of 1860, which was basically a restatement of Whig policies, introduced by Henry Clay in the presidential election of 1824 and rejected by the nation's voters before the war so many times. These included a high tariff, a centralized banking system, free land in the West without slaves or free blacks, government-assisted agricultural and mechanical colleges, and internal improvements (roads, canals, railroads), all financed by the nation at large. The Old South had been pivotal to blocking these federal programs since Alexander Hamilton had first tried to start them in the 1790s. Such proposals had been a major reason why James Madison and Alexander Hamilton had created political parties to hinder or support them. Parties had led to the spoils system, where presidents appointed their lackeys to government jobs. It had gotten so bad that succeeding Democrat administrations, like Franklin Pierce and James Buchanan's, had kicked out supposedly loyal party members who backed the other man in the pre-election conventions.

This corruption, epitomized in Alexander Hamilton's 1790 Economic Program, Henry Clay's 1824 American System, and the Republican Party's 1860 Platform, and condemned as early as 1820 by John Randolph of Roanoke in the Missouri Compromise debates, was what the Confederacy sought to end. It was not for nothing that the Great Seal of the Confederate States of America was a picture of an equestrian-mounted George Washington, the portrayal of American integrity.

Secession was not a true revolution in 1861, but a reaction to all that had passed since 1789 that the Old South saw, correctly or not, as a corruption of the American political process as envisioned by the Founding Fathers. It was with this attitude that the Confederacy approached the War for Southern Independence and it may help explain why the Old South would lose the struggle for its very existence as a separate nation.

It is commonplace to attribute the Southern loss of the Civil War to the overwhelming numbers and resources of the North. This seems to imply that the Confederacy had no chance to win the war—that Southern defeat was inevitable. Yet history is full of examples where the weaker side prevailed in a war. And although the Civil War was seemingly fought as a conventional 19th-century war, it was different from the many European wars that had preceded it.

This has led many modern writers, most recently Ethan S. Rafuse of the U.S. Army Command and General Staff College at Ft. Leavenworth, to assert that the Confederacy was not really fighting a traditional war, but an insurgency. Military scholars define an insurgency as "an organized movement aimed at the overthrow of a constituted government through the use of subversion and armed conflict." As Confederate President Jefferson Davis recognized upon assuming office, the War for Southern Independence was much the same in character as the American War of Revolution had been 90 years earlier.

The two armed forces, Union and Confederate, were contending less with each other and more for the support and control of the civilian population. The application of force was shaped by the social, political, and cultural factors that had caused the conflict. The attempt to create the new Southern nation was not an end in itself. It was instead a means the Confederate government believed was necessary to defend its way of life and its institutions, like slavery, from outside interference by Yankees. If the Confederacy convinced the white population of the Old South of the necessity to keep the Northerners out and demonstrated its ability to do that, its leaders would maintain the consent of the people. If they failed, the Confederate government would lose the hearts and minds of its citizens and fall before the Yankee juggernaut.

With this in mind, military historians see four factors as critical to the success of an insurgency—the possession of a conventional army, the backing of irregular forces, some kind of external assistance, and a safe sanctuary. The degree to which an insurgency possesses these elements determines its chance to succeed in its desire for independence.

The Confederacy certainly had a conventional army of some power. This undermined the standing of the United States government in the South and questioned the authority of the United States over the seceded states among nations abroad. The ability of the Confederacy to exist no matter what its loses were forced the Union to divert much of its armed forces to occupation duties.

But the second component of successful insurgencies, an irregular force, eluded the South. It was not that the South lacked irregular forces as much as it worked actively to discourage their formation and acceptance as a legal means to fight the Yankee occupation. Irregulars are the closest expression of popular support. They operate in a military and political fashion. Here the hierarchical nature of Old South society and politics worked to limit those who fought outside the boundaries of established authority.

The Old South had a proud guerrilla tradition. Men like Francis Marion and Thomas Sumpter were invaluable to the American effort in the Revolution against Great Britain. But irregular operations were disorderly and involved the leveling of Southern society. It also meant that conventional forces could concentrate in key areas of the Confederacy to confront the Yankee invasion, abandoning large parts of the South to occupation by the Northern armies. The South just could not do this. The government deemed it politically suicidal not to maintain its territorial legitimacy in the eyes of its public and economically unwise to cede its most populous and best industrial areas to the enemy.

Unlike insurgency, both the North and the South were aware that foreign intervention could prove critical to winning the Civil War. The key to foreign interference was the stance of Britain and the Royal Navy, from which all continental European powers took their cue. This was especially true as France was tied up with its ongoing intervention in Mexico. The British government, with some backsliding like allowing the Confederacy to buy occasional sea raiders, approached the American Civil War with cold self-interest. The British population was patently anti-slavery in attitude. The North threatened to make anyone who interfered on behalf of the South pay dearly (as Britain did ultimately in the *Alabama* claims). There were limits to British power and what it could achieve in the American Civil War. The South's embargo on cotton, while severe in its effects on British industry early in the war, soon was overcome by substitutes from Egypt and India. In the final analysis, foreign interference never proved as great as Northern leaders feared and Southern statesmen hoped.

Finally, as the balance of power between an existing government and an insurgency is usually on the side of the former, insurgents need a place of sanctuary to maintain their existence and build up their strength until they can attack their opponents at more favorable odds. The great American interior had provided such a place of safety for the American revolutionaries in the 1770s. Ninety years later, the Confederacy had the same sanctuary advantage, but failed to use it.

The Confederacy proved its unwillingness to employ a "Fabian strategy" of strategic retreat by placing its capital at Richmond, Virginia, within 100 miles of the federal center of Washington, D.C. It was a typically Southern move, daring, gutsy, and manly—"Come and take it," was the challenge. The Confederacy, particularly in the person of President Davis, eschewed the strategic retreat policy of Gen. Joseph E. Johnston for the more aggressive strategy of Gen. Robert E. Lee. While Lee won spectacular victories, he cost the Confederacy casualties that it could ill afford in the long run. But it was hard to argue against Lee's successes on the field until it was too late.

The South lost the Civil War according to the insurgency theory because it was unwilling to adopt revolutionary methods to achieve its independence. The fate of the Confederacy was sealed long before secession became a reality. Southern society, its culture, and its political structure were too ingrained with the mores of conventional warfare to take advantage of the requirements necessary to achieve victory by unconventional means.

This allowed the stronger conventional forces of the North methodically to destroy Southern resources and revealed the inability of the Confederate government to protect slavery, repel the Yankee occupation, and defeat the advancing Union armies. The leaders and people of the Old South imposed severe limits upon themselves on what they were willing to sacrifice to secure victory—an achievable triumph as their grandfathers had demonstrated in the years leading up to Yorktown, but only available to a society dedicated to innovation for the future, not to preservation of the past.

Safeguarding the past hurt the Confederacy in another way, too. Had the Old South but taken time to listen, it might have realized that Abraham Lincoln's preferred plan to end slavery, as presented to Congress in December 1862, was through a gradual apprenticeship program that would have extended black servitude, in one form or another, well into the 20th century. Even the Emancipation Proclamation actually freed few slaves except in areas the North did not control. As a wartime measure, Lincoln had doubts as to its constitutionality.

The Union president was a mighty conservative emancipationist, and even slower on guaranteeing black civil rights. It was Confederate intransigence on the battlefield that allowed those against slavery to have the time necessary to force the peculiar institution's end just after the war in the Thirteenth Amendment. Agreeing to this amendment was one of the prime conditions for the defeated Southern states' re-admission to the Union after Appomattox.

Perhaps it was the Civil War, the shared experience by all Southerners, that made the South truly a unified region. In many ways, there was no Old South until its time had passed and Southerners coalesced once again around U. B. Phillips' central theme—no longer slavery, but the dominance of white control under other guises, nonetheless. If Confederate nationalism actually created a Confederate mind, the demise of the Old South made it truly "old," at last.

As for the nation as a whole, the United States "are," the correctly used grammar before the Civil War, had become the United States "is." Lincoln's new, revitalized national government, as envisioned in his 1838 speech at the Young Men's Lyceum at Springfield, had become reality—something he now cleverly called a New Birth of Freedom. But, to achieve this, as he had foreseen, the slaves had to be freed and the freemen enslaved.

The Dictionary

– A –

***ABLEMAN v. BOOTH* (1859).** Two years after the U.S. **Supreme Court** decided the issue of **slavery** in the territories in favor of the Southern **Non-Exclusion Doctrine** embodied in **Popular Sovereignty** in *Dred Scott v. Sanford*, the Court struck again, deciding the fugitive slave issue in favor of the South, too. The Dred Scott case was a bit of a stretch, the Court having to interpret a complicated rendition of the Ninth and Tenth amendments to the U.S. Constitution. The fugitive issue was easy, by comparison, the fugitive clause (art. IV, sect. 2) being openly stated.

Since the fugitive clause was there for all to see, the South held it to be a fundamental constitutional right. Even **Abraham Lincoln** and the mainstream of the Republican Party agreed to enforce it in 1861, before the war changed things. The Court had ruled on fugitive slaves being returned to their owners upon claim in the 1842 case, *Prigg v. Pennsylvania*. In the **Compromise of 1850**, the South demanded and received a strong **fugitive slave act**.

In response, states under strong abolitionist influence had passed personal liberty laws, preventing any state official from interfering to assist a federal officer returning a fugitive. These went so far as to deny sheriffs allowing their jails to be used to house a federal fugitive slave even momentarily. In addition, states required better procedural guarantees, like requiring the presence of all witnesses and denying the use of depositions, which required planters to come North in person and confront a hostile community to reclaim a slave. After Dred Scott declared no African American was a citizen, several Northern states gave blacks citizenship to nullify that. They also provided public defenders to represent indigent fugitives.

The Booth case came up through Wisconsin. A fugitive had been apprehended by his master in Wisconsin. Newspaper editor Sherman M. Booth led a mob to the jail and freed the slave from the custody of U.S. Marshall Stephen V. R. Ableman; then Booth spirited the slave over the border to British Canada, free country. When federal courts tried to prosecute Booth for violating the Fugitive Slave Law of 1850, Wisconsin state courts intervened with a writ of *habeas corpus*, freeing Booth. On appeal, the Wisconsin supreme court declared the fugitive act to be unconstitutional.

In 1859, Chief Justice **Roger B. Taney** again wrote the decision in this Wisconsin case, now called *Ableman v. Booth*. Unlike the divided bench in Dred Scott, he spoke for a unanimous Court. He said that the fugitive clause in the U.S. Constitution was a guarantee that no state could violate. He maintained that when Wisconsin joined the Union it lost its absolute sovereignty and could not interpose to prevent the enforcement of federal laws. It is still good case law today.

The significance of Booth and Scott as court cases is that they illustrate that the South actually wished to enhance federal power before 1860, as regards protection of slavery in the territories and the return of fugitive slaves, while the North wished to limit federal power in these instances. This is the opposite of what many historians and students believe today.

ABOLITION OF SLAVERY IN THE NORTH. At the time of the drawing up of the Constitution of 1787, **slavery** was becoming an anachronism in the states north of the Mason–Dixon Line, the southern border of Pennsylvania. There were several important influences at play in the Northern states. One was the influence of Quakers, especially in Pennsylvania. Another was the willingness of African Americans to enlist in the revolutionary cause. Somewhere around 5,000 blacks fought for American independence, which caused whites to change their support of slavery as an institution. Finally, the idealism and natural rights philosophy of the Revolution itself, caused many whites to reevaluate the notion that any man could be enslaved. As whites rejected the notion of British tyranny, so they questioned the compatibility of slavery in the new nation.

The result was that by 1804 chattel slavery had been rejected in the Northern states. This took the form of outright manumission or gradual freedom, depending upon the state. In some cases, gradualism took so long that slavery was not completely ended in the North until the advent of the Thirteenth Amendment in 1865.

ABOLITIONISTS. Abolitionists made up a small faction of the **antislavery** movement in the United States in the 19th century, with 1,300 groups comprising 150,000 to 200,000 individuals. Early abolitionists from the prior century were mostly Quakers, but the founding of William Lloyd Garrison's newspaper, the *Liberator*, created a new crop of believers who formed groups throughout the 1830s. Abolitionists differed from anti-slavery people in that they saw **slavery** as an evil they could not easily eradicate due to the difficulty of amending the U.S. Constitution. Rather than fight the system, abolitionists preferred to withdraw. They favored **secession** more than the South before the Civil War, seeing the Constitution as a "covenant with death and an agreement with hell."

Traditionally, Americans saw abolitionists as ignorant of the institution of slavery. But modern scholars believe that abolitionists tolerated slavery because they were politically, socially, and morally detached from the issue—to them, slaveholders were not sinners and evil men, but good, moral Christians. But when the abolitionists circulated tracts and pamphlets detailing the evils of slavery or dispatched petitions to Congress, the South prevented their delivery through the mail. Southern congressional leaders also tabled their petitions without allowing them to be heard, leading to the **Gag Rule** fight.

Abolitionists maintained that the real enemies of free men were those, North and South, who condoned slavery. Treatment of the slave was irrelevant, as blacks were still slaves. To prove their point, the abolitionists publicized and distributed atrocity stories that came north with **runaway slaves** on the **underground railroad**. Rather than convince the public that cruelty existed in slavery, its purpose was to show evidence of the tyranny that crushed independence, resourcefulness, and fostered adaptation to the system, deceit of the slaveowner, and the slaves' vacillation for personal survival.

ADAMS, JOHN (1735–1826). Massachusetts born and bred, John Adams went to Harvard and became a lawyer in Boston. He attacked

British colonial taxes, but defended the soldiers accused of the Boston Massacre in 1773. He served in both houses of the colonial General Court and was a delegate to the First and Second Continental Congresses. Adams was instrumental in having **George Washington** appointed commanding general. Adams saw him as rich (which meant respectable in those days), with as much military experience as anyone else, but most important, as a Southerner.

Adams did not want the American Revolution limited to Massachusetts or New England. He wanted all 13 colonies fighting against Britain and saw Washington as the man to bring them all in. Adams went as an American delegate to France and came home to write the new Massachusetts state constitution. He was one of three negotiators, along with Silas Deane and Benjamin Franklin, of the Peace of Paris (1783), which ended the Revolutionary War.

During the 1780s, Adams served as American minister to Great Britain. He came home to be George Washington's first vice president, a job he saw as the most foolish creation of the Constitutional Convention. But in the position of president of the Senate, he broke 20 tie votes on some of the key issues of the day. He succeeded Washington as chief executive, fighting the **Quasi-War** with France and enforcing the **Alien and Sedition Acts**, with which he disagreed.

While vice president, he began his feuds with **Thomas Jefferson** and **Alexander Hamilton** that would estrange them all. Jefferson and Hamilton saw the power of the government differently; Adams wanted a strong central government, Jefferson did not. His quarrel with Hamilton was over who should control the **Federalist Party**. As the president following Washington, Adams thought he should be party leader as well. Hamilton, as the originator of the party, was unwilling to allow that. Hamilton and Adams never reconciled. He and Jefferson would over the years, writing copiously until they died, oddly enough, on the very same day, just hours apart.

Adams was not a well-liked personality. He was blunt to a fault. He could not hold his tongue. He was insufferably right. But his brilliant mind did much to forge the United States from the Declaration of Independence to the constitutional issues facing the first three administrations of the new government. Above all, he was one of only two Northern presidents (the other was his son, John Quincy) before the Civil War who was not dominated by Southern political interests, characterized as the **Slave Power Conspiracy**.

ADAMS, JOHN QUINCY (1767–1848). Son of **John Adams**, John Quincy traveled with his father to Europe and received one of the best educations available for a boy at that time in France and the Netherlands. He became secretary to his father and traveled to Russia and Scandinavia. He returned home to finish his education at Harvard and was admitted to the bar.

A defender of **Federalist** foreign policy in the 1790s, Adams returned to the Netherlands as American minister. He also traveled to Sweden and Prussia, until the **election of 1800** brought **Thomas Jefferson** to power. Massachusetts sent him to the U.S. Senate where he stayed until he backed Jefferson's **Embargo Act** as a realistic way for America to stay out of the Napoleonic Wars. He then had to resign as a Federalist.

Adams became a **Democratic Republican** diplomat serving in Russia and a negotiator of the Treaty of Ghent after the **War of 1812**. In 1817, Adams was rewarded with the position of secretary of state under **James Monroe**. This implication was that he would be the party's next nominee for the presidency. As secretary he negotiated the **Adams–Onís Treaty** with Spain that gained East Florida for the United States and wrote the misnamed **Monroe Doctrine** that became the centerpiece of American diplomacy.

In the **election of 1824**, his hope to become president was threatened when the Democratic Republican Party broke into factions around personalities. The second of four candidates, Adams won when the election had to be decided in the House of Representatives. Speaker **Henry Clay**, who backed the same nationalistic economic policies, shifted his support to Adams. In exchange, Adams made Clay secretary of state, with the usual implication that he would be the next president. The top candidate of the voters, **Andrew Jackson**, accused the two men of a corrupt bargain and vowed to destroy them in the **election of 1828**.

With Jackson sniping at his every move and being blunt like his father, Adams was soon the most hated man in Western and Southern America. He called himself a **National Republican** and was for Henry Clay's **American System**—an expansion of **Alexander**

Hamilton's notion of government intervention in business. Jackson beat Adams decisively in the election of 1828.

After his defeat, Adams was returned to Congress where he remained the rest of his life. He fought against the expansion of **slavery** in the territories, for the freedom of the Africans accused in the *Amistad* **Case**, and for the right to petition in the **Gag Rule** debates, in which he earned the nickname of "Old Man Eloquent." He and his father were the only two of six Northern presidents before the Civil War who were not dominated by the **Slave Power Conspiracy**. Appropriately, Adams died of a stroke on the floor of the House, attending to interests of his constituency.

ADAMS–ONÍS TREATY. After the conclusion of the **War of 1812**, during which Maj. Gen. **Andrew Jackson** had defeated the Creek Nation, East Florida (roughly the present-day state) remained under the control of the Spanish. As such, it provided a convenient sanctuary for **runaway slaves** from nearby American plantations. The Seminole Nation, an offshoot of the Creeks, accepted the fugitives into their tribe, often intermarrying with them. The Spanish really had minimal control over the region, and the blacks tended to gather at the old, abandoned British Ft. Apalachicola, on the river of that name, just below the boundary of the 31st parallel.

The disgruntled American slaveholders to the north soon gave it the name "the Negro Fort." Under fire from the state of Georgia, the United States Army was sent down to capture and destroy the fort in July 1816. This touched off the First Seminole War, a series of cross-border raids of red and black warriors on American plantations, which resulted in more runaway slaves and much property destruction. It seemed natural to send down a more aggressive officer who knew the territory to stop the raids. So the American government sent Andrew Jackson.

Jackson believed that Florida ought to have been kept from the War of 1812, when he had taken and burned Pensacola to the ground. Now he believed that British agents were encouraging the raids by providing guns, ammunition, and supplies to the Seminoles and their black allies. Jackson swept across the boundary in 1817 and captured St. Marks and Pensacola. He also captured two British citizens, whom he court-martialed and executed for helping the Indians attack Americans.

Great Britain protested Jackson's action, but did nothing else. When Jackson invaded Florida, Secretary of State **John Quincy Adams** had been trying to negotiate outstanding matters with Spain. Encouraged by Jackson's aggression, Adams pointed out to the Spanish minister, Luís de Onís, that the United States could and would take Florida if Spain could not control its inhabitants. Better to sell out now, Adams suggested. Onís took the hint. Hoping to safeguard the more valuable Spanish province of Texas, he yielded Florida.

The resulting Adams–Onís Treaty of 1819 sold East Florida to the United States for $5 million. It also established the southern boundary of the Louisiana Purchase between the Spanish (soon to be Mexican) province of Texas and the United States. This transcontinental line followed the Sabine River from the Gulf of Mexico to the 32nd parallel, north by compass to the Red River, west along the Red to the 98th meridian, north by compass to the Arkansas River, west to the Rocky Mountains, north along the continental divide to the 42nd parallel, and west along that line to the Pacific. This extinguished the existing Spanish claim to Oregon.

Although Adams got a pretty good line, the South was dissatisfied. In the **election of 1844**, the Democratic presidential candidate, Tennessean **James K. Polk**, campaigned on the slogan "the re-annexation of Texas," implying that the United States, particularly the South, had somehow been robbed of what the Louisiana Purchase really ought to have been.

ALABAMA PLATFORM. *See* ELECTION OF 1860; YANCEY, WILLIAM L.

ALAMO, THE. *See* LONE STAR REBELLIONS.

ALBANY REGENCY. *See* VAN BUREN, MARTIN.

ALIEN AND SEDITION ACTS. As a part of the war hysteria that accompanied the **Quasi-War**, the **Federalist**-dominated Congress passed a series of four measures designed to suppress activities of French agitators and spies in the United States called the Alien and Sedition Acts. But in reality, the acts were designed to stifle **Democratic Republican** newspaper criticism of the undeclared war.

Federalists (especially **George Washington**) deplored opposition and could not understand it. They believed everyone ought to support the national government because it was a virtuous institution. **Thomas Jefferson** was more open to criticism, especially when his political friends were the critics.

To unify Americans against the perceived French threat, the Alien and Sedition Acts had four parts. The first was the Naturalization Act that changed the residency requirements for citizenship from 5 to 14 years. The idea was that recent immigrants were all Jeffersonians. The next measure was the Alien Friends Act that allowed the president in peacetime to deport or jail aliens suspected of being foreign agents. Then came the Alien Enemies Act, which allowed the president to do the same in time of war. These two measures got around the fact that the **Quasi-War** had been undeclared by Congress. Finally, there was the Sedition Act which placed restrictions on press, assembly, and criticism of the government, supposedly to provide for good order and decorum in the political debate. This was used to jail Democratic Republican newspaper editors who attacked the Federalist war. It was also a blatant violation of the First Amendment of the Bill of Rights, but it was hoped it would put an end to opposition criticism of Federalists' refusal to declare war, even after they obtained a majority in Congress. In fact, the debate got so hot that regular fistfights broke out in Congress over the matter.

The Alien and Sedition Acts were a great mistake. They allowed the Democratic Republicans to attack the Quasi-War without appearing to be disloyal to the men in uniform. The Jeffersonians maintained that they were merely defending the Constitution. To prove their point, the Democratic Republicans attacked them in two Southern-inspired documents, the **Kentucky and Virginia Resolves** of 1798.

ALMONTE, JUAN N. *See* WAR WITH MEXICO.

AMERICAN COLONIZATION SOCIETY. After the **War of 1812,** Americans considered the merits of emancipating and returning slaves to Africa because the profitability of **slavery** was eroding along with the soils in the Southeastern Atlantic states, due to intensive agriculture and the accompanying erosion. Pressured by their constituents who supported ending slavery, influential Americans tried to convince slaveowners to eradicate the "**peculiar institution**." In 1816, President **James Monroe**, former President **James Madison**, and Speaker of the House **Henry Clay** formed the American Colonization Society to free Negroes from slavery and send emancipated Negroes to an area on the African coast that would become the nation of **Liberia**. The new **tariff** on imports would fund their transportation as well as various **internal improvements** and also act to protect the nation's fledgling industries from the import of cheap foreign goods.

AMERICAN PARTY. A short-lived faction of the old Whig Party, the American Party was the fastest growing political party in the country in the 1850s, initially gaining more popularity than the **Republicans**. After taking 25 percent of the popular vote in the **election of 1856**, with most Northern Whigs having supported the Republicans, it dissolved by the **election of 1860** amidst the slavery controversy that led to the South's **secession** in 1860–1861. The quarrel over slavery in the territories didn't entirely cause its demise, however. The Whigs had successfully run as pro-slavery in the South and anti-slavery in the North. Other issues manipulated the American Party, resulting in the appropriate nickname "Know Nothings."

The American Party was a response to two factors that dominated the 1850s: the **slavery** issue and the problem of increased immigration, much of it Roman Catholic. Anti-Catholicism was a constant undercurrent, occasionally surfacing with violence as in the Philadelphia Riots of 1844. It took the election of John F. Kennedy in 1960 to finally undermine the issue. Another persistent theme in American history was disdain of foreigners. The **Alien and Sedition Acts** at the end of the 18th century were an attempt by Whig Party forerunners to limit the power of foreigners in domestic political life, a theme taken up by the **Anti-Masonic Party** in the 1830s. But the failure of the revolutions of 1848 in Europe and the Irish potato famine about the same time brought masses of immigrants to the United States, many of them Catholic. Also disturbing to old Protestant America was Rome's control over the Catholic clergy and hierarchy, an attitude fostered by the refusal of John Cardinal Hughes in New York City to mute his allegiance abroad. When **Franklin Pierce** appointed a Catholic to his cabinet as postmaster general in charge of patronage, Protestants and "Old Americans" protested vehemently. The result was the Know Nothing movement.

Officially known as The "Order of the Star Spangled Banner," the Know Nothings began in New York in 1849 as a semi-secret organization of patriotic Americans. Their purpose was to support long-accepted values and traditions of conservative politicians. Their secret rituals, degrees of membership, and local, state, and national councils likened the organization to the Freemasons. When asked by outsiders about their rituals, a member responded, "I know nothing," hence their popular name. As Northern anti-slavery Whigs became Republicans, those who still wanted to oppose the **Democrats'** economic policies in favor of the American System joined the Know Nothings, calling themselves Whig-Americans, or, by 1856, the American Party.

The American Party swept state and local elections in 1854, taking Delaware and Pennsylvania. In 1855, they won Rhode Island, New Hampshire, Connecticut, Maryland, and Kentucky. That same year they also captured Virginia, Georgia, Alabama, Mississippi, and Louisiana, barely losing out to the Democrats in Tennessee, their total Southern vote only 16,000 less than the regular Whigs and the Democrats. American Party supporters believed that the regular Whigs, Democrats, and Republicans failed to offer a solution to the social problems brought on by immigration, such as Catholicism, Mormonism, Sunday imbibing, selling corrupted immigrant votes, and a declining economy which predominantly affected the North.

By virtue of its platform vagueness, the American Party attracted followers with divergent political beliefs. Once in power, the American Party did even less than its opponents, who denounced them as "Owe Nothings," "Do Nothings," and "Say Nothings." Then the **Kansas–Missouri Border Wars** eclipsed the issue of slavery in the territories, bringing about the **Kansas Settlement**, a crisis that lasted to the advent of the Civil War. The Americans and the regular Whigs endured to 1860 as a party of compromise over the slavery issue, making their last stand as the **Constitutional Union Party** in the **election of 1860** and contributing most of the members to the failed **Washington Peace Conference of 1861**.

AMERICAN SYSTEM. Even before he became leader of the **Whig Party** in the 1830s, **Henry Clay** developed the American System in 1824 so that the federal government could guide the development of the United States through regulated economic growth. Clay's theory evolved from the principles of **Alexander Hamilton**, President **George Washington**'s first secretary of the treasury, and economists Friedrich List and Matthew Carey, who opposed free economy based on supply and demand, a theory that Adam Smith devised in the mid-1700s. Clay disagreed with Smith's belief in natural economic laws, maintaining that it was the government's duty to secure its nation's economic well-being by providing new jobs, protecting old jobs, diversifying production, and preventing foreign competition.

Clay's economic development was called the American System to place the onus on opponents who backed what he believed were un-American programs. Its four basic components comprised a high protective **tariff** to guard American industry against foreign competition; a central banking system to regulate the overall economy and national currency (at that time, banks issued their own paper money, which eventually became worthless); a vigorous program of governmentally financed **internal improvements**; and the distribution of the proceeds from the sales of public lands (for $1.25 an acre) back to the states for internal improvements or the liberation and **colonization** of American slaves in Africa.

The American System was the platform of the Whig Party throughout its existence. The **Democrats** were among its many opponents and detractors, who believed that an unregulated economy was more beneficial to the common man, and Southerners, who believed that the high **tariff** unfairly penalized the South and its export/import economy based on **staple crops**. The American System survived Henry Clay's death in 1852 and became the **Republican Platform of 1860**.

AMERICOS. *See* LIBERIA.

AMISTAD **CASE (1841).** In 1839, a schooner was reported sailing erratically off the Atlantic Coast of the United States. Whenever other ships approached, armed black men would warn them off. Finally, a U.S. Navy ship approached the mystery ship off the eastern tip of

Long Island and, under cover of its guns, a boarding party found 53 slaves, including four children, and two Spanish-speaking white men on the ship. None of the blacks could speak English. But the whites spoke some English, and the American sailors some Spanish. The whites said that they were all that remained of a slave mutiny that had killed their captain and three crew members of the Spanish coastal trading ship *La Amistad* (Friendship) out of Cuba.

The navy took the ship to New London, Connecticut, and laid claim to the ship and its slave and non-slave cargo. The two Spaniards also laid claim on behalf of the Spanish consul at Boston to the ship and cargo. A hearing before the local federal magistrate resulted in the blacks being arrested and jailed for murder and mutiny.

Meanwhile the Spanish government asked that the *Amistad* be turned over under the **Pinckney Treaty** (1795) and the **Adams–Onís Treaty** (1819), and that the blacks be transported back to Havana, since the ship's papers listed the chattels as legally enslaved, and that no United States court intervene. But the Spanish were too late. The federal courts had already taken jurisdiction.

Asked by the local federal judge for an opinion, U.S. Attorney General Felix Grundy, a Tennessee slaveholder, referred to the earlier **Antelope Case**, and said that the ship's papers were enough to dispose of the *Amistad* affair in short order. Send the Africans back to Havana on the *Amistad*, Grundy said. Instead, in the surprise of the whole incident, Judge Andrew T. Judson, a noted Connecticut racist, ruled on behalf of the Africans.

The case was quickly appealed up the federal court system to the U.S. **Supreme Court**. Taking no chances, the **abolitionists** asked former president **John Quincy Adams** to handle the defense. Adams spoke for more than eight hours over two days. He denied that any existing treaty between the United States and Spain, one of which (Adams–Onís) he had negotiated himself, covered the case. Human beings were not in the treaty clauses for returned cargo.

Again, the *Amistad* blacks beat the odds since a pro-slave majority dominated the high court. Yet the Supreme Court agreed entirely with the lower courts. The Africans were free men because they had asserted their freedom. They did not come to the United States as slaves or to be slaves and violated no laws. But freeing the *Amistad's* black cargo now meant that the United States was free of all responsibility for their care. The abolitionists again appealed for funds and eventually transported them back to their native Africa.

ANGLO-AMERICAN RAPPROCHEMENT (1816–1823). Following the **War of 1812**, Britain took the initiative in securing the Canadian border and American friendship that would pay off so mightily in the 20th century. They were met in their objectives by **John Quincy Adams**, the **Federalist** turned **Democratic Republican**, who always wanted to negotiate rather than fight with Britain. Imbued with the **New Nationalism** of the **Era of Good Feelings**, the Old South backed these agreements that basically benefited the North.

In 1817, the Rush–Bagot Agreement demilitarized the Great Lakes, making the U.S.–Canadian border the longest undefended border in the world. Each side was restricted to one war vessel on Lake Champlain, one on Lake Ontario, and two vessels each above Niagara Falls. It would take until after the U.S. Civil War before the agreement was fully in force, but it was a critical first step.

The Rush–Bagot Agreement was followed by the Anglo-American Convention of 1818, which guaranteed American fishing rights at the Grand Banks in the Atlantic and extended the U.S.–Canadian border at the 49th parallel from Lake of the Woods at the tip of Lake Superior to the Rocky Mountains. The country from the Rockies to the Pacific, then called Oregon, was to be jointly occupied until further notice.

The final Anglo-American agreement (actually more of an unofficial understanding) to follow the War of 1812 is usually seen as a bit of American chicanery that became the central tenant of American foreign policy for nearly a century. This was the **Monroe Doctrine**.

***ANTELOPE* CASE (1825).** In the spring of 1820, an American ship, operating as a privateer, stood out to sea from Baltimore. The goal of the trip was to capture a Spanish slaver or two and sell the cargo at an appropriate place. The expedition proved lucrative. The privateer took 25 slaves off a Rhode Island slaver, 156 from a ship flying Portuguese colors, and the Spanish slaver *Antelope* and its cargo of 200 slaves fresh from Africa.

Taking the *Antelope* in tow, the two ships sailed into a vicious storm off Brazil. The American ship sank, but most of its men and cargo were transferred to the *Antelope*. But fate determined that the

Antelope would be seized by a U.S. Coast Guard ship and hauled into Savannah, Georgia.

The Spanish and Portuguese governments filed claims for their parts of the *Antelope's* slave cargo. The coast guard captain who seized the *Antelope* also filed a salvage claim. The federal circuit court ruled that the coast guard officer would receive 25 percent of the value of the ship and cargo. The slaves from the Rhode Island ship were to go free. The Spanish and Portuguese would receive the slaves taken from their ships and the Spanish also receive the *Antelope*.

Everything was appealed to the U.S. **Supreme Court** as a case between two nations. Chief Justice **John Marshall** ruled that a ship's papers were to be considered valid on their face without going behind the papers to ascertain any other facts. To receive its claim beyond the ship itself, the Spanish had to offer absolute proof of ownership of any and all slaves. No matter how unjust or unnatural the **slave trade** might be, it was not illegal in international law. But each nation could rule as to its illegality as regarded its own citizens and enforce that law. This did not permit any nation to adjudicate any case involving the slave trade when its own citizens were not involved, even if the violators were from a nation that had declared the trade illegal. Marshall's ruling would influence the ***Amistad* Case** that was to follow.

ANTI-FEDERALISTS. Those politicians and people opposed to the new Constitution that had been put forward in place of the **Articles of Confederation** were labeled by the Constitution's supporters (called **Federalists**) as Anti-Federalists. The implication was that somehow these people wished to weaken the nation from within because they opposed the Federalists' coup. Instead of modifying the Articles of Confederation, the Philadelphia Convention had illegally brought forth an entirely new governmental framework and then justified it in the *Federalist Papers*.

This led some historians to call this process a conservative counter-revolution. The notion was that the Articles of Confederation represented a government closer to the people with little or no centralized executive power. The Federalists, conservative businessmen in the North and coastal slaveholding planters in South Carolina, wanted to remove government from the voters by installing a government protected from direct control of the states and the people. To achieve this, the Federalists installed a layer of indirect election, like the U.S. Senate (elected by the state legislatures in those days) and the Electoral College.

In reality, the old establishment of strong state politicians supported the Articles of Confederation because it was subordinate to their desires. The men who fought in the Revolutionary armies, finding this establishment hard to break into and remembering its reluctance to finance the war adequately, contrived to create a new establishment with a stronger central government, permitting them to bypass the old, entrenched state politicians and install themselves at the top. The ploy worked.

ANTI-MASONIC PARTY. *See* ELECTION OF 1832.

ANTI-SLAVERY. Before the Civil War, the majority of Northerners was anti-slavery, believing that **slavery** should end gradually throughout the entire United States, precluding expansion of slavery into the Western territories.

Anti-slaveryites and **abolitionists** differed in nature and philosophy. While many abolitionists favored withdrawing from political participation with a government corrupted by pro-slavery attitudes, anti-slaveryites sought to achieve their goals through political action, backing parties that represented their beliefs, such as the **Liberty Party** in 1840 and 1844 and the **Free-Soil Party** in 1848 and 1852. Their program of **Free Men, Free Soil, Free Speech** became part of the **Republican platform** in 1856 and 1860.

The anti-slaveryites saw the federal government as essentially good but corrupted by the **Slave Power Conspiracy**, which unfairly empowered the South politically by allowing three-fifths of all slaves to be counted for representation. The South also held unfair political sway in that 9 of the first 15 U.S. presidents had been Southerners, and 5 of the Southerners had held two terms. They believed these circumstances corrupted the federal government's basic integrity.

APPEAL, THE. *See* SOUTHAMPTON REVOLT; WALKER, DAVID.

AROOSTOOK WAR. *See* CANADIAN BOUNDARY DISPUTE; SCOTT, WINFIELD.

ARTICLES OF CONFEDERATION. In order to turn the Second Continental Congress that broke the colonies away from England through the Declaration of Independence into a permanent national government, Congress submitted a plan called the Articles of Confederation to the states. Written mostly by John Dickinson of Delaware, the Articles created a weak central government subordinate to the power of the states.

According to the Articles, there would be a unicameral Congress, with each state having one vote. All legislation required nine votes to pass. The national government had the power to engage in foreign policy, borrow money, coin money, set standard weights and measures, handle Indian affairs, and ask the states for taxes.

Certain powers were denied to the central government. It could not force tax contributions from the states, regulate commerce, settle disputes between the states, or compel a citizen of one state to do anything without the state's approval. There would be no executive or national court system. This smacked too much of tyrannous kings and appointed colonial courts. Congressional committees would handle these matters. It was a perfect response to the strong central British government that the colonies believed had led to the Revolution in the first place. The Articles were submitted to the states in 1777, but arguments over the **Western Lands Cession** held up final approval until 1781.

ASHBURTON'S CAPITUALTION. *See* CANADIAN BOUNDARY DISPUTE.

ATCHISON, DAVID. *See* ELECTION OF 1852; KANSAS–MISSOURI BORDER WARS; KANSAS–NEBRASKA ACT (1854).

AUSTIN, STEPHEN F. *See* LONE STAR REBELLIONS.

– B –

BAILEY, FREDERICK AUGUSTUS WASHINGTON. *See* DOUGLASS, FREDERICK.

BALTIMORE PLOT (1861). On his way to be inaugurated in 1861, President-elect **Abraham Lincoln** took an extended trip through the North, a "Swing around the Circle," to introduce himself to the Northern electorate, publicize his upcoming administration, and demonstrate his calm demeanor to the tense population. In Philadelphia, Lincoln met railroad detective Alan Pinkerton, who tipped Lincoln off about a plot to assassinate him in Baltimore, recommending that Lincoln alter his schedule to foil the attempt.

At that time, the railroads did not pass directly through Baltimore. Upon arriving at its own station, the railcars were drawn by horses between the lines, or passengers were transferred to horse-drawn carriages. Removing his stovepipe hat and donning a cape and slouch hat to impersonate a sick passenger, Lincoln boarded a locked car hitched to the rear of a regularly scheduled train. It was hauled through the streets of Baltimore at 3:30 a.m., then attached to the overnight Baltimore & Ohio train to Washington, arriving at 6 a.m.

Outwitted, the plotters, led by John Merryman, proceeded to burn rail bridges and tear up track to cut Washington off from the rest of the North. They were among the first to be arrested when Lincoln, as president, suspended the writ of habeas corpus by executive proclamation. Merryman achieved fame with his successful appeal to U.S. **Supreme Court** Chief Justice **Roger B. Taney** to annul his incarceration at old Ft. McHenry in the case *ex parte* **Merryman**. But Lincoln, in a precedent set by **Andrew Jackson** on the question of **Indian Removal,** ignored the court order.

BANK OF THE UNITED STATES. Along with **Funding and Assumption, George Washington**'s Secretary of the Treasury **Alexander Hamilton** proposed that a federal bank be established to regularize the national money and banking system. Called the Bank of the United States, the government would purchase 20 percent of the stock. The purpose of the bank was to store U.S. monies, issue federal paper currency, and regulate state and private banks through a discounting of their paper notes.

This would create more debt, the very thing Hamilton said he wished to pay off through his measures. Worse than that, according to **James Madison**, the Southern leader in the House of Representatives, the purchase of bank stock was not a governmental power enumerated in the Constitution, which ought to be construed strictly. A Constitution not followed was no document at all, Madison maintained. Hamilton saw this as too restrictive. He said the Constitution was a living, breathing document that ought to be viewed and used expansively. The bank was allowable under the open "necessary and proper" clause. Madison retorted that necessary and proper referred to the actual listed powers of Congress in the Constitution, about 20 in number.

Nonetheless, the bank bill passed the Congress and arrived on Washington's desk. He asked Hamilton and Secretary of State **Thomas Jefferson** what he ought to do, sign or veto it. Hamilton said sign it. Jefferson recommended a veto but also argued that the veto was a presidential prerogative that ought to be used wisely and rarely. Washington took Hamilton's expansive argument of the Constitution and Jefferson's idea that the veto ought not to be exercised often and signed the bill, chartering the bank for 20 years, over Madison's complaints. It was one more breach between Southern agricultural interests and Northern commercial interests that led to the formation of the first political parties, the **Federalists** (mostly, but not exclusively, in the North) and the **Democratic Republicans** (mostly, but not exclusively, in the South).

In 1811, as the impending **War of 1812** approached, Congress failed to renew the charter of the bank by one vote. The lack of finances to fight the war and the economic havoc it wrought on American business and agriculture led to its recharter in 1816 as a part of the **New Nationalism**. Now called the Second Bank of the United States, it was to be headquartered in Philadelphia. There would be branches in key cities, the bank would sell 20 percent of its stock to the U.S. Government, it would be a depository for U.S. Treasury funds, and it would discount paper notes to create a common currency—just like the First Bank of the United States.

Interestingly, the Federalists, who had sponsored the original Bank of the United States, opposed the Second Bank. New England banks were already the best in the nation. But the Federalist Party had for all practical purposes been killed by the **Hartford Convention,** so the measure passed. America was now to enter the **Era of Good Feelings** with a Democratic Republican Party that was Jeffersonian in name but Federalist in constitutional philosophy. But within 20 years the **Andrew Jackson** administration would make the **Bank War** a centerpiece of its domestic policy.

BANK VETO. Chartered in 1817, the **Second Bank of the United States** got off to a rough start. Poor management made it very susceptible to the ravages of the **Panic of 1819**. President **James Monroe** turned to a strict Southern conservative, Langdon Cheves. He called every loan he could, stabilized the situation, and saved the bank but ruined the people. Once the institution was on a solid footing, Cheves resigned. He had not wanted the job in the first place.

Cheves' replacement was Nicholas Biddle. A Philadelphian of prominent social status, and a graduate of the University of Pennsylvania at age 13, Biddle had been refused a degree because of his youth. But he was brilliant—perhaps the last of a dying breed, a man of letters and a man of public affairs in one person, a holdover from the 18th century Age of Reason. He had no prior banking experience but ran the bank well until 1830. Biddle was actually quite popular because he increased the bank's note circulation, creating a mild inflation. He also kept strict control over its branches by placing Philadelphians he knew and trusted as cashiers. Then he ran afoul of **Andrew Jackson**.

Biddle has a strange historical reputation. He is thought of as a man of stratagems, full of intrigue and devious. Even his contemporaries thought this. But one man knew better. He was **Martin Van Buren**. The little redhead knew that the exact opposite was true. Biddle was too honest, too frank, and too unable to defend himself or the bank against criticism at the critical time. He was a sitting duck for the artful in the Jackson administration, led by Van Buren.

All of this leads one to wonder why to the end of his days Jackson thought of his destruction of the banks as his proudest moment as president. What happened was that a half dozen elements united in 1830 to crush the nation's finest monetary institution for 100 years. In general America was a debtor nation of farmers who hated banks, no matter how well run. Banks kept them from overextending their investments in land and slaves. In addition, politicians of the times were predominantly state oriented. The Second Bank of the United States was beyond their control. In 1819, Chief Justice of the U.S. **Supreme Court**, **John Marshall**, said so in *McCulloch v. Maryland*.

There was also a feeling that the federal charter of the banks made it seem an entrenched monopoly. This was an age of raw economic power. People were aggressive, individualistic, intolerant, and even lawless. Businessmen especially believed that the bank kept them on a tight rein. They wanted expansion, factories, shipping, and inordinate wealth, free of any outside controls.

But the most important was the emergence of two new factors that came to galvanize public opinion against the bank. Jackson believed that to the victor belonged the spoils of office. The bank was a part of the lucre of being in charge. Finally, Wall Street (New York City) was jealous of Chesnut Street (Philadelphia). It was the new wealth from the Erie Canal and the biggest port in the land against the old wealth from colonial and revolutionary days. And Van Buren represented this new wealth.

Biddle and everyone else knew that the bank's charter was up for renewal in 1836. He was confident that Congress would vote for the bank but feared Jackson might veto the recharter bill. Biddle went to Louis McLane, the Secretary of the Treasury, and asked his advice. McLane said to wait until after the **election of 1832**. But Jackson's potential opponents for the presidency, **Daniel Webster** and **Henry Clay**, needed an issue to skewer Old Hickory with. They told Biddle that, if he waited, Jackson would be off the hook. Pressure him now, came their advice.

Biddle foolishly caved in to their recommendation. No one openly challenged Andrew Jackson and got away with it. On 6 January 1832, the recharter bill was introduced in Congress. Jackson's cronies launched a senatorial investigation and proved that the bank was unconstitutional, unwise, and antagonistic to free enterprise.

The whole purpose of this investigation was to arouse the public against the bank, and it worked. Webster and Clay quickly modified their bill to include some of the committee's criticisms. They reduced the charter from 20 to 15 years, limited the bank's ability to create new branches, prohibited the bank's investment in real estate, added a presidential appointment to each branch board, and gave Congress he right to stop the issue of federal bank notes.

The modified bill passed both houses of Congress with one-third of the votes for it coming from Democrats. On 10 July 1832, Jackson vetoed the measure. He said that the federal government should not be prostituted before the power of money. The bank had too many privileges, Jackson said. It was an institution that had too many rich investors, many of them foreign, and their policies harmed the poor and simple American citizen. Southern and Western supporters called Jackson's veto a Second American Declaration of Independence, which severed the ties between government and capitalistic wealth. Jackson made this the theme of the election of 1832, not the concurrent **Nullification Crisis and Compromise of 1833** in South Carolina. *See also* ECONOMY.

BANK WAR. The Second **Bank of the United States** was chartered to last until 1836, but with the ringing endorsement of his policies in the **election of 1832**, President **Andrew Jackson** moved immediately to crush the institution. He would withdraw the federal deposits that were the basis of the bank's power. According to law, this could be done if the secretary of the treasury would determine and declare the deposits to be "unsafe."

Seeking to move with the outward appearance of legality, Jackson asked Congress to investigate the security of the federal deposits. There was no reason to suspect otherwise, so Congress voted the deposits to be safe by a large majority and adjourned and went home. Foiled here, Jackson decided to move before Congress reassembled in December 1833. He asked his Secretary of the Treasury to ignore Congress' report and pull the deposits out. Louis McLane, the secretary, was an old **Federalist**. He was not about to play this game. But as a friend of the president, he offered to resign and permit Jackson to appoint another man to effect the transfer.

Jackson decided that he would kick McLane upstairs, rather than let him leave. He turned to Edward Livingston of Louisiana, his Secretary of State, and asked him to step down to become the American minister to France. A loyal party man, Livingston did so at once. McLane then became the new Secretary of State. For the treasury position, Jackson turned to William Duane. Known as unfavorable to the bank, Duane took the job without promising to withdraw the federal deposits. Jackson assumed he was smart enough to know. Duane said that since Congress had voted the deposits safe, they were. Besides, to pull them out would shake public confidence in all banks and cause economic panic.

Events would prove Duane's objections valid, but Jackson was not interested in economics, but in politics. He also had a deadline—to change the deposits before Congress got back in session. Jackson had already sent his advisor Amos Kendall around to soundly run private banks in New York City, Boston, Philadelphia, and Baltimore, asking them if they would accept the federal deposits. Of course they would. Jackson told Duane he had two days to change his mind. Duane refused, and Jackson fired him. He was the first cabinet official in American history dismissed for refusing to carry out a presidential directive.

Jackson was not about to allow for any more slip-ups. He promoted his attorney general, **Roger B. Taney**, to the treasury job. Taney immediately announced that the federal deposits at the Second Bank of the United States were found to be unsafe. He had the deposits withdrawn in a week. The deposits were placed in banks certified sound, both in management and political leanings. They became known as the "Pet Banks" (there would soon be 92).

When Congress returned, Jackson's opponents went wild. They refused to receive Jackson and Taney's reports. Then they rejected Taney's appointment as *ad interim* secretary. Finally, the Senate censured Jackson himself, another first in American history (later expunged when the Democrats got their Senate majority back in 1836). But Jackson's critics were destroyed when Nicholas Biddle began to call in the loans he had outstanding, to pressure Congress to save the bank and recharter it. This merely proved Jackson to be correct in his assessment that the bank had too much power.

There matters stood. Without its federal deposits, the Second Bank of the United States was a shell of its former self. In 1836, it applied for and received a Pennsylvania state charter. It was just another state bank, and not even a pet bank, either. Biddle unwisely invested heavily in cotton shares and he and his bank went broke in the **Panic of 1837**.

The pet banks' investment of their federal deposits as loans to their customers, combined with another congressional act, which sent surplus federal income to the states, resulted in runaway inflation. People bought outrageous amounts of land, cotton, slaves, and expanded their businesses—all on credit—as the economy boomed. The government had to do something. As usual, Jackson acted in his all-or-nothing manner. On 11 July 1836, he issued the Specie Circular. All land sales were to be paid for in full with gold or silver coin (specie). Land sales collapsed overnight. The government was overextended and had to call in its deposits in the pet banks to meet costs. The banks had to foreclose on their loans to pay the government. The result was the Panic of 1837, the worst before the Civil War. Duane had been right—the deposits should not have been messed with.

BARBOUR–CLAY COMPROMISE. *See* MISSOURI COMPROMISE.

BARRACOON. *See* SLAVE TRADE, INTERNATIONAL.

BATES, EDWARD. *See* DRED SCOTT v. SANFORD.

BATTLE OF BAD AXE. *See* INDIAN REMOVAL.

BEAR FLAG REVOLT. *See* WAR WITH MEXICO.

BELL, JOHN (1797–1869). A Tennessee native, John Bell studied in local academies and graduated from Cumberland College (now the University of Nashville) in 1814. He read law and was admitted to the bar two years later. He practiced in Franklin. He served in the state senate and then removed to Nashville. Bell was elected to the U.S. Congress and served from 1827 to 1841. He was initially a **Democrat**, but broke with President **Andrew Jackson** over the **Bank War** and became a **Whig**.

With the election of **William Henry Harrison** to the presidency, Bell was made Secretary of War. He resigned when **John Tyler** replaced Harrison. He served in the state legislature before being elected U.S. Senator, serving from 1847 to 1859. He supported the **Compromise of 1850**, opposed the **Kansas–Nebraska Act** and the pro-Southern Lecompton Constitution as part of the **Kansas Settlement**.

In the **election of 1860**, Bell ran for the presidency on the Constitutional Union ticket and lost. He opposed **secession**, but ran an iron works during the Civil War that supported the Confederate war effort. He died after Tennessee was readmitted to the Union without reentering politics again.

BENJAMIN, JUDAH P. (1811–1884). Judah Philip Benjamin was born on the island of St. Croix to Sephardic Jewish parents. During his childhood, his family moved to Charleston, South Carolina, where he was educated. Having become a compulsive gambler, he later was expelled from Yale College, probably a result of his addiction. Benjamin relocated to New Orleans to study law and was admitted to the bar. After marrying into a prominent Creole family, he and his wife had one daughter. His wife's unconventional libertine lifestyle led to their separation without divorce. His wife and daughter eventually moved to France.

A gifted intellectual, Benjamin devoted himself to his profession, representing the insurance company seeking to reclaim the cargo in the *Creole* **Case**. In addition, he authored a prominent law book and became a prosperous planter. He served in the state legislature in the 1840s and attended two state conventions representing the **Whig Party**. From 1853 to1859, he served in the U.S. Senate as a Whig, switching to the Democratic Party from 1859 to 1861. He became a devout secessionist after **Abraham Lincoln**'s victory in the **election of 1860** threatened his expulsion from the party. **Jefferson Davis** then appointed Benjamin as attorney general in the provisional government of the Confederacy.

Benjamin grew close to Davis and his wife and became Davis's most trusted civilian advisor. Benjamin was secretary of war from late 1861 to early 1862 but performed poorly. Davis then made him secretary of state, a position he served with distinction to the end of the war. He negotiated several important foreign loans for the Confederacy and figured prominently in the development of the Confederate secret service. His alleged involvement with the attempted kidnappings and later assassination of Lincoln is unknown as Benjamin diligently destroyed all incriminating personal and state department records.

After the war, Benjamin left the fleeing Confederate government and relocated in London, where he launched a second successful law career and published another key legal treatise. On a brief visit to Paris to rejoin his family, he died and was buried in Pere Lachaise Cemetery.

BENTON, THOMAS HART (1782–1858). The first man to serve 30 consecutive years as U.S. Senator in American history, Thomas Hart

Benton was born in North Carolina. He studied at the Chapel Hill College and William and Mary College. He moved to Tennessee and was admitted to the bar at Nashville. He served in the state legislature, fought in the **War of 1812**, and engaged in a street gunfight with **Andrew Jackson**. Believing he had killed Jackson only to find him still alive, Benton wisely moved on to Missouri. There he fought other duels and entered local politics before the **Missouri Compromise** allowed the state legislature to send him to Washington as the state's first U.S. Senator.

In Washington, Benton made amends with Andrew Jackson. He held Jackson's arm as the old bullet he shot into it was finally removed to prevent further infection. Then Benton stood by Jackson through **Jackson's first administration** and **Jackson's second administration**, warning **John C. Calhoun** that when Jackson talked hanging, "smart men get rope." Benton was instrumental in fighting the **Bank War** and opposed to all paper money. This earned him the nickname "Old Bullion." He was also responsible for suggesting the old 16 to 1 ratio between silver and gold, which became standard in the late 19th century.

Benton opposed the extension of **slavery** into the West, although he favored the **War with Mexico**. His **anti-slavery** extension stand led to his defeat for the senate in 1851, but he returned to the House to oppose the **Kansas–Nebraska Act** in 1854. Again, his anti-slavery extension stand cost him his seat and the upcoming gubernatorial campaign. He was the father of a ravishing, intellectual daughter, Jessie, who married **John C. Frémont** and wrote up his journals of exploration as popular bestsellers. But Benton refused to support Frémont for president in 1856 on the first national **Republican** ticket. He died before the nation split to fight the Civil War.

BICKLEY, GEORGE W. L. *See* FILIBUSTERING.

BIDDLE, NICHOLAS. *See* BANK VETO; BANK WAR.

BILLY BOWLEGS. *See* INDIAN REMOVAL COMPLETED.

BIRNEY, JAMES G. *See* ELECTION OF 1844, FREE-SOIL PARTY.

BLACK CODES. The laws that defined the role of people of African descent in the United States were called the Black Codes. Because Black Codes treated the legal position of both slaves and free persons of color, they existed in one form or another in all states, North and South. Indeed, the Black Code of Illinois was deemed one of the cruelest in denying blacks the right to live and earn a living in the state.

In the slave states, the Black Codes were extremely tough in the colonial period, but became more humane after the **abolitionists** used them to criticize the system as a whole. Most important, every master or mistress was a law unto himself or herself. They alone determined what part of the Black Code they and their "people" would obey. Exception was the rule.

But the law was there, always ready to be applied to the fullest. The Black Code established a master's property right in the slave. The state was charged through the law to protect the right of the master through the courts, police, and militia. No slave was allowed to be off the plantation without a pass. If the slave passed a certain distance (8 miles in Mississippi or 20 miles in Missouri), he or she became a **runaway** by law. Slaves were not allowed to raise their own crops, own their own livestock, learn to read or write, be employed in a print shop, hire their own time, preach the Gospel, or gather in groups of three or more without white supervision. Slaves were not allowed to beat drums, blow horns, or possess a firearm. Slaves could not buy or sell goods of any kind. Slaves were not allowed to possess or use alcoholic beverages. Masters and the local authorities were to search slave quarters regularly for contraband.

The master had both rights and obligations in owning a slave—but legally, as well as actually, the slave was more property than a person. The exception was if a slave committed a crime. Then the chattel could be punished in a special court for any misdemeanor or felony.

Slaves were "chattels personal" under the law. This gave the owner a property right in the person of the slave. As property, a slave was different from a horse or a cow, but not much. There were laws requiring certain basic levels of food, clothing, shelter, and care. These laws got more demanding after the abolitionists used actual neglect to attack the **peculiar institution** as a whole. By 1850, any cruelty to a slave was a crime punishable by a stiff fine and social ostracism. But the exceptions to the law were telling. The law did not apply if a slave "accidentally" died from "moderate" correction.

The Black Code also stated who was a slave. It was important that **slavery** was racial in its make-up. Skin color carried the presumption of non-free. The actual legal term was *partus sequitur ventrem*—the child inherited the condition of its mother. This was contrary to old British common law, which assumed that the child inherited the father's social position. But there were too many mixed-race children born out of wedlock in what became the United States to limit slavery in this manner.

Because of **miscegenation**, not all slaves were black nor were all slaveowners white. Only in Delaware were all blacks considered legally slaves without proof to the contrary. Most Southerners assumed that one drop of black blood (the Black Codes were written without the assistance of modern sociology and its sensitivity for multiculturalism and racism) meant one was all black. In general, all mixed bloods were called mulattos (from the Spanish for mule—it was once assumed they could not reproduce). Only in Louisiana, where miscegenation developed into a fine art, did the varying gradations of color confer extra privileges to the whiter.

By the 1830s, some 3,600 blacks in the South owned slaves. For the most part, these slaves were family members, kept enslaved because chattels often had more legal protection than free blacks. In certain places, like southern Louisiana with its French heritage, blacks held as many as a hundred slaves and owned and managed large plantations. Only in Arkansas and Delaware were free blacks prevented from holding slaves.

The Black Codes in the South applied to free persons of color as well as slaves. Denominated as free man or woman of color, blacks who were not slaves were a real anomaly in the slave states. They were looked upon as an alien force, necessitating much regulation. Any blacks visiting from outside the state, like Negro seamen, for example, were jailed until their ship left.

The Black Codes showed that slavery was a solution to a white-perceived racial problem of living with blacks. It defined a less than equal place for African Americans in white society. As slavery disappeared in the North, and traditional slave controls lessened in

Southern cities, the Black Codes developed a new national racial separation concept, segregation. Here laws kept free African Americans in a subordinate legal, political, and social position much as the slave codes had in the past.

BLACK WARRIOR INCIDENT. *See* SPREAD EAGLE DIPLOMACY.

BLAIR, FRANK, JR. *See DRED SCOTT v. SANFORD.*

"BLEEDING KANSAS." *See* KANSAS–MISSOURI BORDER WARS.

BONUS BILL. *See* ERA OF GOOD FEELINGS.

BOOTH, SHERMAN M. *See ABLEMAN v. BOOTH.*

BORDER STATES. *See* SECESSION AND THE BORDER STATES.

BORÉ, ETIENNE. *See* SUGAR.

BRECKINRIDGE, JOHN C. (1821–1875). John C. Breckinridge was born into a politically powerful family in Lexington, Kentucky, his grandfather having served as **Thomas Jefferson**'s attorney general. Completing an academy education and law school at Kentucky's Transylvania College and Yale, he settled in his home state, where he married in 1843 and taught and practiced law. After serving with a Kentucky regiment in the **War with Mexico**, he served in the Kentucky legislature as a **Democrat** for a short time before being elected to Congress from 1850 to 1856. His nomination as Buchanan's vice president in 1857 made him the youngest vice president the United States has ever had. He lost his bid for president on the Southern Democratic ticket in the **election of 1860**. Kentucky sent him to the U.S. Senate where he worked to compromise the coming war and was expelled for treason in the fall of 1861 for his unsuccessful efforts in helping Kentucky secede from the Union.

As brigadier general in the Confederate army, he fought in the Shiloh Campaign at Pittsburg Landing and Baton Rouge. He also led a division during the Perryville Campaign at Stone's River, and at Chickamauga and Missionary Ridge in the Chattanooga Campaign. In 1864, he fought in Virginia at New Market, the Richmond Campaign, and the Raid on Washington. In 1865, he became the Confederacy's last secretary of war. Fleeing Richmond with the **Jefferson Davis** cabinet, Breckinridge reached Cuba. He traveled on to Canada where he lived in exile until he received permission from the federal government to return to Kentucky in 1868. He lived out the rest of his life practicing law as a private citizen.

BREDA, TOUSSAINT. *See* HAITI.

BROOKS, PRESTON S. (1819–1857). On 19 May 1856, Republican Senator Charles Sumner of Massachusetts took the floor in the capitol building at Washington, D.C., and for two days spoke out against what he characterized as "the Crime against Kansas." An ardent **abolitionist**, Sumner referred to **Stephen A. Douglas**'s doctrine of "**Popular Sovereignty**" as a cover for "Popular Slavery." He called the **Kansas–Nebraska Act** a "swindle." He suggested that Kansas be made a free state immediately, a solution he labeled a "Remedy of Justice and Peace."

As he spoke, Sumner castigated Senator Andrew Pickens Butler of South Carolina as a Southern "Don Quixote," who "has chosen a mistress, . . . the harlot, Slavery." Senator Douglas and others were shocked at Sumner's venomous attacks. Already characterized by Sumner as "the squire of slavery, its very Sancho Panza, ready to do all its humiliating offices," Douglas muttered prophetically to anyone who would hear, "That damn fool will get himself killed by some other damn fool."

That "damn fool" turned out to be Congressman Preston S. Brooks of South Carolina, Butler's cousin, who heard Sumner's invective from the Senate gallery. A native South Carolinian, veteran of the **War with Mexico**, Brooks was believed to be very pro-Northern by Southern standards, too ready to compromise. But he was also a believer in a strict code of chivalry. And since Senator Butler happened to be absent, Brooks took it upon himself to defend his family's insulted honor. No true gentleman would go to court over such a personal matter, and to challenge Sumner to a duel would elevate the Massachusetts senator to

Brooks's high social level. Besides, Sumner would refuse to fight. So he decided to "chastise" Sumner as a social inferior.

Brooks took a gutta percha walking stick, an inch in diameter at its big end, hollow core, weighing eleven and a half ounces, and confronted Sumner sitting at his desk on 21 May. There were ladies present, so Brooks waited several minutes until they left. Then he came up and spoke. "Mr. Sumner, I have read your speech twice over carefully. It is a libel on South Carolina, and Mr. Butler, who is a relative of mine." Sumner sought to rise, but Brooks caned him over the head. He gave Sumner at least 30 "stripes," as he called them, breaking his cane on the third one but continuing until he was exhausted, and Sumner lay in a pool of blood on the floor, his fixed desk ripped off the floor in his struggle.

No one intervened, but several observers shouted encouragement; "Hit him again." Brooks was arrested, posted bond, and ultimately paid a $300 fine for assault, but beat off an attempt to kick him out of the House of Representatives. He resigned his seat instead. In the furor that followed, canes like the one Brooks used sold out all over the South, some carved with "Hit him again," or "Use Knock Down Arguments." Brooks was the hero of the hour. Everyone wanted a splinter of the true cane. His constituents bought him a new cane with a gold head, and re-elected him overwhelmingly.

Meanwhile, Sumner spent three years recovering from a posttraumatic stress syndrome, a condition that manifested itself only when he tried to return to his public duties. But his constituents cared little for fancy analyses. They re-elected "Bleeding Sumner" to his Senate seat. Throughout the North, he too became a symbol. And better yet was "the Vacant Chair of Sumner" which was eulogized in rhyme as a tribute to Southern **violence and white militancy**.

Sumner finally beat his psychic problems and returned to the Senate on 4 June 1860, where, at precisely noon, he began a four-hour speech on the "Barbarism of Slavery." This time, he had nothing to fear from "Bully" Brooks. The South Carolinian had died two years earlier from an agonizing disease. As Sumner said to a friend, "The Almighty has settled this better than you or I could have done."

BROWN, ALBERT GALLATIN (1813–1880). Born in South Carolina, Albert Gallatin Brown (named after **Thomas Jefferson**'s Secretary of the Treasury) went as a boy with his parents to Mississippi. His father entered planting and did quite well. The younger Brown was educated at several local colleges and took such an interest in military affairs that he was elected brigadier general in the state militia at age 19. He was admitted to the bar in 1834 and served in the state legislature and the U.S. Congress as a **Martin Van Buren Democrat** and opposing the **Second Bank of the United States**. He was judge of the circuit superior court and governor throughout the 1840s. He was an opponent to **Jefferson Davis** and Thomas Quitman.

Brown returned to Congress for the **Compromise of 1850**, called for the non-exclusion of **slavery** from the territories, and served as U.S. Senator until Mississippi seceded from the Union. Brown was against single state **secession** but in favor of several states acting together. He contributed money to the war effort and raised a company of infantry and fought the early Civil War with the 18th Mississippi Volunteer Infantry.

In 1862, Brown was elected to the Confederate senate and served in Richmond for the rest of the war. He supported the Jefferson Davis administration until 1864, when he joined the opposition. He advocated white conscription, arming slaves to fight for the South and their freedom, and spoke out against the promotion of incompetent generals. After the Confederate defeat, Brown advocated cooperation with the Reconstruction programs of the North. His stance was so unpopular that he never again stood for election. He died in 1880 having lived the quiet life of a farmer.

BROWN, JOHN. *See* HARPER'S FERRY RAID.

BROWN, JOSEPH E. *See* SECESSION OF THE SOUTHERN STATES, FIRST.

BUCHANAN, JAMES (1791–1868). Born to a Scots-Irish family near Mercersburg, Pennsylvania, James Buchanan was educated in Franklin County and studied law at Dickinson College. He served two terms in the state legislature and was admitted to the bar in 1821. That same year, he was elected to Congress (1821–1831) and became a loyal **Jacksonian Democrat**. He served as minister to Russia (1832–1833), U.S. Senator from Pennsylvania (1834–1844), Secretary of State (1845–1849), minister to Great Britain (1853–1856), and the last **Democrat** to be president (1857–1861) for the next 24 years. He was a party hack in many respects and bowed to his constituents' wishes, putting up no resistance. An expansionist, he supported the **War with Mexico** and the **Spread Eagle foreign policy** of the 1850s. He was dedicated to the law and revered the U.S. **Supreme Court**. A self-starter, he rarely delegated details, preferring to micro-manage in solitude.

Buchanan entered the presidency overconfident that his 42 years in politics had taught him everything. But he did not understand city politics, speculative interests, the intensity of Southern Nationalism, or the moral aspects of the **anti-slavery** issue. In 1856, Buchanan's policies and beliefs were outdated and passé, his ideology mired in the past. A lifelong bachelor, his true love died when her parents prevented their marriage. But he enjoyed feminine company and cut a striking figure on the ballroom floor. His First Lady was his niece, Harriet Lane.

Although ruddy, tall, and hearty in appearance, Buchanan was weak in body and spirit. He suffered from the "National Hotel disease," a form of dysentery. He was myopic and always held his head cocked to the left. An operation left him with unsightly scars on his neck which he concealed with high, stiff collars. At age 65, he was a crotchety old man whose faith still had failed to grace him with a saving religious experience, which deeply troubled him.

President Buchanan faced enormous opposition as a party regular. He questioned the personal loyalty of all prior appointments, even if they were Democrats. When faced with insoluble problems in the territories that led to the **Mormon War** and the **Kansas settlement,** he waffled on minor party issues. He enforced the U.S. **Supreme Court**'s pro-slavery decisions in ***Dred Scott v. Sanford*** and ***Ableman v. Booth***, which his critics say he manipulated. He watched the nation suffer through the **Panic of 1857**, a depression that hit the North harder than the South. This allowed the panic to seem to confirm the South's belief of superiority of the slave economy and gave impetus to the drive for secession to be rid of the Yankee albatross of free labor at the mercy of the rise and fall of the industrial business cycle.

He supported the **John C. Breckinridge** Southern Democrats in the **election of 1860**, believing that the South had many just complaints about slavery and the nature of the Union. He was against **secession**, but his belief in governmental non-interference led him to do little during the secession crisis. He retired to his Pennsylvania home, Wheatland, in 1861, announcing his support of the **Abraham Lincoln** administration's prosecution of the war for Union (as opposed to the ending of slavery) and quietly living out his days until his death in 1868.

BUCKTAILS. *See* SLAVE POWER CONSPIRACY; VAN BUREN, MARTIN.

BURR, AARON (1756–1836). Born in New Jersey, but a New Yorker most of his life, Aaron Burr applied for admission to Princeton at age 11. When he was turned down, he read on his own, pestered the faculty, was admitted two years later, and ultimately delivered the commencement address at graduation at age 16.

Burr served in the Continental Army. He began as a private on the failed expedition to Quebec. He was promoted to major for bravery and was on the staff of Gen. Israel Putnam. Burr endured the winter at Valley Forge, where he became disillusioned with the leadership of Gen. **George Washington**. He plotted with the Conway Cabal and backed Gen. Charles Lee, whom Washington ordered off the field at Monmouth.

Burr was in the New York legislature, became a notoriously successful lawyer, organized the northern half of the **Democratic Republican** Party, ran for president three times (through his mentor George Clinton in 1792, for himself in 1796 and 1800) and became **Thomas Jefferson**'s vice president after the **election of 1800**. But first Burr tried to claim the presidency as both he and Jefferson had the same electoral vote. This episode resulted in the **Twelfth Amendment** to the U.S. Constitution and ruined Jefferson's faith in Burr forever.

His suggestions for political appointment ignored by Jefferson, Burr ran for governor of New York in 1804, but his campaign failed when **Alexander Hamilton** exposed Burr's dabbling in a possible plot with the Essex Junto, an extremist Federalist group, to dismember the United States. This same group would later back the **Hartford Convention of 1814**.

His honor slurred by Alexander Hamilton's constant political meddling and a public reference to possible and "despicable" relations between Burr and his own daughter, Burr challenged the prominent figure to a duel. Usually Hamilton is seen as a noble figure, firing in the air to avoid a murder. Burr then killed him with a single shot.

After fleeing possible prosecution and extradition, Burr reportedly sought to detach the West from the Union and form his own personal "mini-empire" in the Burr Conspiracy. It is usually believed that Burr was cooperating with Gen. James Wilkinson to detach Louisiana or Texas (the trans-Mississippi West) from the U.S. and Spain. But in reality Burr was interested in the Old Southwest (Alabama and Mississippi) and possibly Tennessee and Kentucky (the trans-Appalachian West).

Burr figured that these areas had been ignored by the federal government and that they would follow anyone who could promise them the use of the Port of New Orleans, where Wilkinson, a shady figure in his own right, was in command. This angered Jefferson, who saw such national dismemberment as a threat to the South's power in Congress through the **Three-Fifths Compromise**. He had Burr tried for treason. But Chief Justice **John Marshall**, sitting in Richmond on circuit, ruled that the government (Jefferson and Congress) had failed to supply adequate evidence (which was readily available) to make a case of overt treason. Burr, with further charges pending, skipped bail for refuge in France. Burr returned to New York in 1812, practiced law to an old age characterized by vitality—at 80 he was divorced on grounds of adultery. All of which lends much credence to the observation of an old New Yorker that Aaron Burr's sole claim to virtue lay in the fact that he never claimed it for himself.

BURR CONSPIRACY. *See* BURR, AARON.

BUTLER, ANDREW PICKENS. *See* BROOKS, PRESTON S.

– C –

CABELL, JOHN L. *See* SLAVERY AS A POSITIVE GOOD, THEORY OF.

CALHOUN, JOHN C. (1782–1850). Known as the "Cast Iron Man," from his tough, humorless expression, John C. Calhoun had two forbidding, steely eyes that bore into acquaintances from beneath a prominent forehead. He was Scots-Irish in ethnicity, Calvinistic in religion. Born to a fairly wealthy family in South Carolina, he was tall and handsome, a wiry fellow with coal-black hair. His education was the best America had to offer. He attended Moses Waddell's academy in his home state, Yale College, and the Litchfield Law School in Connecticut. Like all rich Southerners from the South Atlantic, the Calhouns kept a summer home on Connecticut's shore of Long Island Sound. His home in South Carolina was Ft. Hill. His wife was Floride Bonneau, from a family far tonier that his.

Calhoun tended to be brilliant, but humorless and legalistic. He spent his life in public service. He was a state legislator before going to Washington as an original **War Hawk** in 1811. He was instrumental in promoting the war and the **New Nationalism** that followed. Calhoun was **James Monroe**'s secretary of war, considered one of the best (along with **Jefferson Davis** in the 1850s) before the Civil War.

In the **election of 1824**, Calhoun ran for vice president, a clever move that was designed to put him in line for the presidency. He served one term under **John Quincy Adams** and another under **Andrew Jackson** before **Jackson's break with Calhoun** over the scope of the federal government. Calhoun spent his political career trying to hold back hotheads in his home state from seceding from the Union. He developed a lengthy process of how this could be done, which he called the **Concurrent Voice and Nullification**, but resigned the vice presidency to prevent his state from carrying the process out in 1833. He continued to serve as senator, secretary of state, and senator again. He developed the **Non-Exclusion Doctrine** over **slavery** in the territories, and was in favor of the **annexation of Texas**. But he opposed the **War with Mexico**, the annexation of all of Mexico after the war, the **Wilmot Proviso**, and the admission of California as a free state in the **Compromise of 1850**, as it would upset the 50-50 balance of North and South in the senate. He died before the Compromise was passed.

CALLENDER, JAMES. *See* HEMINGS, SALLY.

CANADA. *See* CANADIAN BOUNDARY DISPUTE; WAR OF 1812.

CANADIAN BOUNDARY DISPUTE. By 1841, it began to look as if the **Anglo-American Rapprochement** from the end of the **War of 1812** was about to collapse. The British decided to give negotiation one more try, sending over Alexander Baring, Lord Ashburton, to iron things out. He was a jovial man with an American wife, a close friend of Secretary of State **Daniel Webster**, and with an abiding hatred for Washington's weather. The result was the Webster–Ashburton Treaty of 1842, better known in British history as "Ashburton's Capitulation."

Capitulation is a good description for what followed, because Webster took Ashburton for all he was worth. It began with the boundary between Maine and Canada, which had spawned a local border conflict, the Aroostook War. It seems that an American historian had been looking through old records in Paris, France, and found an original of the Treaty of Paris of 1783. The line for the northern boundary of Maine was clearly drawn, giving Britain all of the area but a small swatch along the coast. Webster showed it to Maine's congressional delegation and told them he would try and save the state. Then Webster and Ashburton divided everything along the St. Johns River. This was less than Maine wanted—even less than an earlier Dutch arbitration had offered, but more than the old treaty line gave.

The other big deception Webster pulled off was the boundary between Lake Superior and Lake of the Woods in Minnesota. Webster knew of the Messabi iron range—Ashburton did not. Webster suggested that everything be divided along the Pigeon River, half to the U.S. and half to Britain. The iron was in the American half. Ashburton also gave up little pieces of land in New York and New Hampshire, the latter containing the headwaters of the Connecticut River.

Finally, Webster promised to reserve enough ships to provide 80 guns a year to enforce the ban on the slave trade. He would also seek to prevent the U.S. flag from being used by slavers in the international **slave trade**. This was accomplished by the American and British navies patrolling in pairs of ships. The Webster–Ashburton Treaty had settled the Canadian boundary to America's advantage. The North was pleased, but the South looked askance at the slaving patrols in the Atlantic. But the Oregon boundary was another matter.

Oregon became a crisis after the **election of 1844**, when **James K. Polk** had been elected pledging "54°40' or Fight." This meant that the Americans wanted all of Oregon, which comprised all of present-day Oregon, Washington, and British Columbia. Common sense dictated that the 49th parallel be extended from the Rockies, although the British wanted the Columbia River to be the boundary. The disputed area between the 49th parallel and the Columbia River was called the Columbia Quadrilateral.

The American rush to Oregon in the 1840s gave the United States a big population just south of the Columbia River. If Polk wanted to fight, the Americans could take the Columbia Quadrilateral any time they wanted. The 1846 Oregon Treaty extended the 49th parallel line, gave the United States access to Puget Sound, and avoided a war.

Everyone was happy but Northerners. It was they who had settled Oregon. Now that Southerner, Polk, had given away half of Oregon needed for their future free states, but annexed all of Texas to the Río Grande and took the Desert Southwest in the **War with Mexico** for the expansion of the slave South and its **Three-Fifths Compromise** representation in Congress. The **Slave Power Conspiracy** lived on. But Northerners hoped that the **Wilmot Proviso** would set that issue straight.

CANE RIDGE REVIVAL. *See* SECOND GREAT AWAKENING.

CAREY, MATTHEW. *See* AMERICAN SYSTEM.

CAROLINA GAP. *See* PANIC OF 1837.

CARSON, CHRISTOPHER "KIT." *See* FRÉMONT, JOHN CHARLES.

CARTWRIGHT, SAMUEL A. *See* SLAVERY AS A POSITIVE GOOD, THEORY OF.

CASS, LEWIS (1782–1866). Born in New Hampshire, Lewis Cass was educated at Exeter Academy. At 19, he set out on foot for the Northwest Territory, read law in the new state of Ohio, was admitted to the bar, served in the state legislature and as U.S. Marshal. During the **War of 1812**, he enlisted in the army and rose to brigadier general, instrumental in fighting in the battles against the British and Native Americans led by Shawnee chieftain Tecumseh. From 1813 to 1831, he was the governor of Michigan Territory and President **Andrew Jackson**'s secretary of war, directing the Black Hawk War and southeastern **Indian Removal**. He was President **Martin Van Buren**'s Minister to Britain, but resigned over his disagreement with the Webster–Ashburton Treaty.

In 1844, Cass sought the **Democratic** Party's presidential nomination by supporting the annexation of Texas. After losing to **James K. Polk**, Cass served as Michigan's U.S. Senator from 1845 to 1848, where he backed the annexation of Oregon and the War with Mexico, and opposed the **Wilmot Proviso**. Cass's solution to the question of slavery was **Squatter Sovereignty**, the notion that the people in the territories ought to decide the future of slavery by a vote. But he would allow this vote at any time during the territorial process, which the South would not abide, preferring the **Non-Exclusion Doctrine** and a decision in the first state convention, a process later called **Popular Sovereignty**. This cost Cass the presidency in 1848 as the South voted for the **Whig** candidate, **Zachary Taylor**.

Upon returning to the U.S. Senate from 1849 to 1857, Cass favored the **Compromise of 1850**. He was secretary of state under President **James Buchanan**, resigning when Buchanan refused to take a strong stand against **secession**.

CHALMETTE, BATTLE OF. *See* WAR OF 1812.

CHARLESTON PLOT (1822). In the early 1820s, the **Era of Good Feelings** was coming to an end as the **Missouri Compromise** debates and the high protective **tariff** caused a rift between North and South in Congress. Among many slaveholders, the specter of the St. Domingue slave revolt and the creation of the independent black nation of **Haiti** still rankled. The coming schism in the United States was particularly felt in slave-heavy South Carolina and other Gulf states where many of the French slaveholders had fled with their bondspeople to escape the Caribbean holocaust that had ravaged the island of Hispañola.

One of the blacks who followed the **Missouri Compromise** debates and believed that the North would help blacks in the South gain their freedom and create their own version of Haiti was Denmark Vesey. Ominously, Vesey was from St. Domingue. He had been sold in 1780 as "sound," but his purchaser had returned him to the slave trader, one Vesey, as "defective," because he was subject to epileptic fits. Vesey took Denmark with him around the Caribbean for the next 20 years. Denmark worked on numerous ships in varying capacities, learned to read and write, picked up several languages, and in 1800 won a lottery with which he bought his freedom.

The 40-year-old freeman moved to Charleston and took up carpentry. In 1821, Vesey gave up his carpentry to devote himself full time to revolution. He enlisted many local slaves and free men of color in his plot. Most were mixed bloods and two were the house slaves of the current governor of South Carolina. Using local blacks as recruiters, Vesey's influence spread among slaves as far as 80 miles into the countryside. Slowly he organized seven companies of special assault troops who were to attack arsenals and gun shops to arm the others. Then a general massacre was to ensue, a la Haiti.

Vesey picked a Sunday to revolt, as white Charlestonians allowed their slaves to go into the city unsupervised. But, on 25 May 1822, just before the attack was to be sprung, a slave told his master about it. A half dozen slaves and free men were arrested, but no one admitted anything and all were let go for lack of evidence. Vesey moved the day of reckoning up.

Two days before the revolt was to begin, another slave informed on Nat Bennett, one of the governor's slaves. This time 18 were arrested, including Vesey. All were hanged. One of his henchmen, Gullah Jack, took over but he too was ratted on. This time the authorities were more than thorough. They arrested Gullah Jack and 130 others, of whom 37 were executed, 43 sent out of the country, and the rest received severe whippings.

There was just one problem. Except for the informers, no one ever admitted to anything. Not one. Some modern historians claim that there was no real plot, just a lot of brag from Vesey and Gullah Jack. But they went silently to the gallows allegedly with knowing smiles on their faces. *See also* SLAVE RESISTANCE AND REBELLION.

CHEROKEE NATION *v.* GEORGIA (1830). *See* INDIAN REMOVAL.

CHEVES, LANGDON. *See* BANK VETO; PANIC OF 1819; WAR HAWKS.

CHICAGO, TREATY OF (1833). *See* INDIAN REMOVAL.

CHINN, JULIA. *See* JOHNSON, RICHARD MENTOR.

CHURCH AND RELIGION. One of the ironies of American history is that as the old line Puritan churches in the North became more Unitarian, that is, more rational, in their approach to salvation, religion in the Old South became more evangelical, in the sense that people are drawn into a relationship with God through faith in Christ. There were a half dozen church sects that dominated the Old South before the Civil War. Catholicism was dominant in Maryland, along the Gulf Coast in the former French and Spanish colonies, and up the Mississippi River in the **Louisiana Purchase**. There were also isolated Catholic areas in almost every Southern state, but they were dwarfed by the Protestant majority. These included the Episcopal or old Anglican church in the older, established areas of the Southeast, and the Presbyterian, Methodist, Baptist, Cumberland Presbyterians, Campbellite Baptists, and Disciples of Christ. Often each valley seemed to have its own sect, with a different one available just over the next mountain. All were distinctly evangelical in their approach to salvation, even the Episcopal in it own staid way.

In spite of the Southern reputation for religious belief, not one in 10 belonged to an establish church in the 1820s. But there was a distinct movement away from the deism that marked the Age of Enlightenment the century before. These 19th-century Christians saw God as a forceful, demanding, and intimate reality in their everyday lives. The Episcopalians, Presbyterians, and Catholics all required an educated priesthood, which did much to forward Southern higher **education**. But many, on the frontier in particular, relied on preachers who received the call through a personal encounter with the Holy Spirit. These men usually had other jobs during the week and devoted Sundays to church work, often preaching out of a building on their own property.

The standard weapon that the preachers wielded against all evil was the sermon. Each divine had his own style of preaching, be it florid, reasoned, intense, or restrained—or all of above in varying combinations as circumstances required. The devil, after all, was a slippery demon to defeat. The Southern Protestants were masters of the jeremiad, an indictment of the local, regional, or national culture, followed by a call to reform one's own inner being. The congregation was treated as "sinners in the hands of an angry God," as an earlier Yankee divine, Jonathan Edwards, once put it.

In expanding the frontier to the Southwest during the **Great Migration**, settlers often moved out of the realm of organized religion. The void was made up by circuit riders, a concept developed by Methodist Francis Asbury from John Wesley's notion that preachers ought to be rotated among congregations. Asbury assigned preachers to cover a circuit, showing up on a more or less regular schedule. Itinerant circuit riders, usually not affiliated with any particular denomination, also made their irregular rounds in the far reaches of the settlements.

The **Second Great Awakening** pulled all of these styles together in massive camp meetings that lasted days on end. Dozens of preachers might be emoting at one time, each in his own corner of the gathering. Sinners abounded, souls had to be saved, and the gullible fleeced, as Mark Twain described it in *The Adventures of Huckleberry Finn*. But after the Second Great Awakening, it was no longer sufficient for a man or a woman to be well-born and well-educated. Now one had to be a Christian gentleman or lady to reach the apogee of the **social hierarchy** in the Old South. The slaves were also caught up in the evangelical frenzy that would characterize their own churches before and after emancipation.

Along with the Whig and Democratic parties, various business organizations, and the Masonic Lodge before its condemnation as an undemocratic secret organization in 1832, the churches were instrumental in reinforcing the concept of the American Union before the Civil War. Various doctrinal schisms, in which the Protestants specialized, amounted to little when compared to the one great division that occurred among American churches over the issue of **slavery**. It was quite apparent that many Northern **abolitionists** were prominent church members. They believed that the peculiar institution was sinful. Southerners, on the other hand, were quite convinced that slavery was condoned in the Bible, as many **pro-slave theorists** maintained.

The parting between the Northern and Southern branches of American churches in the 1840s was one of sorrow as much as of bitterness. In the case of the Presbyterians, it also had to do with Southern church members' opposition to the Plan of Union with the Congregationalists, a devoted **anti-slavery** group if there ever was one. But it presaged the splitting of the political parties in the 1850s and the nation in 1861, and gave each side the moral consensus necessary to accomplish its role in the **secession** crisis.

CHURCH OF JESUS CHRIST OF LATTER-DAY SAINTS. *See* MORMON WAR; SECOND GREAT AWAKENING.

CINCINNATI PLATFORM. *See* CHARLESTON CONVENTION (1860), ELECTION OF 1856, POPULAR SOVEREIGNTY.

CLARK, ADAM. *See* SLAVERY AS A POSITIVE GOOD, THEORY OF.

CLAY, CASSIUS M. (1810–1903). Originally from Madison County, Kentucky, Cassius Marcellus Clay was a distant cousin to **Henry Clay**. He received a Jesuit education at Bardstown and attended Transylvania College and graduated from Yale. He then studied law again at Transylvania and entered politics as a **Whig**.

In the Kentucky state legislature, Clay sponsored the common public school system and the jury system of law. He supported a law to prevent the introduction of more slaves into the state. With **Texas annexation**, Clay became an opponent of the **War with Mexico** as the aggression of the **Slave Power Conspiracy** (although he served in the army and was held as a prisoner of war) and then became an **anti-slavery** agitator, calling for the gradual emancipation of all slaves. He freed his own slaves in the meantime.

Clay established an anti-slavery newspaper, the *True American*, in Lexington in 1845. Outraged locals assaulted the building and sent the press to Cincinnati. Clay printed the paper there and distributed it in Kentucky. Finally he moved the operation back to Lexington and set up two four-pounder cannons loaded with nails and scrap iron and covering the door to discourage opponents from attack. He carried a spring-loaded knife (a long, double-edged dagger known as an

"Arkansas Toothpick") hidden up his sleeve for self-defense and later wrote a book on the finer points of knife fighting.

Although Clay stood for public office several times, his antislavery sentiments doomed him to defeat. He became a **Republican**, was appointed brigadier general by **Abraham Lincoln**, but, having no military talent, opted to serve as U.S. Minister to Russia. He had an affair with a ballerina, sired an illegitimate son by her, and was divorced by his wife when he returned home. He later married a 14-year-old and single-handedly drove off a sheriff's posse sent to arrest him for debauching an underaged girl, whom he then sent back home to her parents.

Clay opposed Radical Republican Reconstruction after the war and switched between the Republican and **Democratic** parties as issues changed. He was ostracized at social functions and died an isolated, lonely man.

CLAY, HENRY (1777–1852). Born in Virginia, Henry Clay read law and moved to Lexington, Kentucky, where he practiced law, served in the state legislature, and was a congressman and U.S. Senator off and on for the rest of his life. In the midst of everything else, he ran for president numerous times and never won, and earned the title "the Great Compromiser" or "the Great Pacificator" for his efforts to adjust quarrels over **slavery** between North and South in the **Missouri Compromise** of 1820, the **Nullification Crisis and the Compromise of 1833**, and the **Compromise of 1850**. He also served as delegate to the peace treaty ending the **War of 1812**, and Secretary of State under **John Quincy Adams**. Clay was an originator of the **National Republican** Party and the **Whig** Party and developed a federal program of economic development known as the **American System**.

Clay had an intuitive grasp of politics and how to manage people. He could speak so movingly as to bring tears to the hardest soul. On occasion he would break down in tears himself, for effect. While he was trained in law, Clay was no intellectual. He had a certain Southern lazy charm about him. He showed elaborate courtesies to anyone who could cast a vote or who wore a skirt. He had a plantation home outside of Lexington called Ashland, owned 600 acres, 18 slaves, and, as befitted a Kentuckian, 64 horses. Of all the men in Washington during his era, Clay had true vision. Show him a barren plot of land and he envisioned farms, factories, mines, houses, and prosperous people, all prompted by federal policies.

CLINTON, DEWITT. *See* ELECTION OF 1812.

CLINTON, GEORGE. *See* ELECTION OF 1792, ELECTION OF 1804, ELECTION OF 1808.

COBB, HOWELL (1815–1868). Born at Cherry Hill, Georgia, Howell Cobb graduated from Franklin College (now the University of Georgia) and became a lawyer and soon entered Congress as a **Democrat,** interested in free trade and compromise over **slavery**. He became Speaker of the House, before returning to Georgia to serve as governor. He was a strong Union man and opposed all opposition to the **Compromise of 1850.**

Cobb returned to Congress in 1855 and was appointed Secretary of the Treasury by his good friend, President **James Buchanan**. As **secession** approached in 1860, Cobb recognized Buchanan's latent Unionism. Cobb was Buchanan's closest friend in the cabinet and his resignation over Buchanan's address to Congress in 1860, calling for Union, was a blow. Egged on by the **Harper's Ferry Raid** and the **Republican** majority in the lower house of Congress, Cobb was becoming as staunch a Secessionist as he had earlier been a Union man.

Cobb supported the walkout of Southern representatives in the Charleston Convention in the **election of 1860**. He became chairman of the convention that drew up the **Confederate Constitution** and was president of the provisional Congress. With the advent of the Civil War, Cobb became colonel of the 16th Georgia Volunteer Infantry and was promoted to general shortly after. He served in Virginia from Seven Pines to Antietam before taking over the Confederate command of Georgia.

In Georgia, Cobb did much to mediate between Governor Joseph Brown and various general officers opposed to the **Jefferson Davis** regime's conduct of the war. He also helped defeat a cavalry raid at Macon. After the war, Cobb practiced law in Macon. He opposed the

Republican plans for Reconstruction and was not allowed to run for office. Cobb died in New York City in 1868 on a business trip, a Confederate to the end.

COFFLE. *See* DOMESTIC SLAVE TRADE.

COIRON, JEAN JACQUES. *See* SUGAR.

COLONIZATION. Many early American statesmen, like **Thomas Jefferson** and **James Monroe,** believed that **slavery** might best be ended if the freed slaves were transported out of the United States back to their homelands in Africa. **Henry Clay** expressed their feelings well when he stated that there was "moral fitness in the idea of returning to Africa her children, whose ancestors have been torn from her by the ruthless hand of fraud and violence." To accomplish this goal, Monroe and Congress set up the colony of **Liberia** to receive American blacks released from slavery.

After his inauguration, **Abraham Lincoln**, long an advocate of Clay's political and economic policies, looked into colonization as a way to handle the large numbers of blacks who had fled to Union lines for protection from their masters. Congress endorsed the president's suggestions on 16 April 1862, when it passed a law to end **slavery** in the District of Columbia. Part of the measure called for $100,000 to be appropriated to remove such manumitted slaves to Liberia or **Haiti**, or anywhere they wished to go and would be well received. Each immigrant was to receive not more than $100. Later, on 16 July, an additional $500,000 was appropriated to extend the project further. Both equal rights advocates, Senator Charles Sumner of Massachusetts and **Frederick Douglass**, and most blacks themselves, protested the plan as unfair. Blacks had fought in the Civil War for their own freedom, so it became morally and politically impossible to propose that they leave the country of their birth.

COLUMBIA QUADRILATERAL. *See* CANADIAN BOUNDARY DISPUTE.

COMET. *See CREOLE* CASE.

COMMITTEE OF THIRTEEN. *See* **CRITTENDEN COMMITTEE OF THIRTEEN.**

COMMITTEE OF THIRTY-THREE. *See* **CORWIN COMMITTEE OF THIRTY-THREE.**

COMPENSATED EMANCIPATION. Since shortly after the American Revolution, many Americans publicly favored abolishing the institution of **slavery** by paying slaveowners to emancipate their slaves. By the end of the War of 1812, these compensation schemes became linked with the notion of colonizing liberated slaves in **Liberia** or the Caribbean.

In 1816, **Henry Clay** and former Presidents **Thomas Jefferson**, **James Madison**, **James Monroe** and other noted politicians formed the **American Colonization Society** . Not only did they fear the difficulties of absorbing freed blacks into white society and government, but saw transportation overseas as a logical, albeit racist, solution.

In 1824, Henry Clay introduced compensated emancipation as a part of his **American System** of financing economic growth through the proceeds from public land sales. To overcome Southern opposition, he emphasized that his was not an abolition program but a government effort to allow individual slaveowners a choice of emancipation.

In his annual message to Congress in December 1862, President **Abraham Lincoln** proposed that Congress compensate, in U.S. bonds, those who freed their slaves by 1 January 1900. Lincoln's true plan of eradicating slavery failed when Congress narrowly defeated a vote to pay Missouri $15 million for freeing its slaves through state action.

It was not until the passage of the Thirteenth Amendment in 1865 that Southerners were willing to consider compensation for their slave property. Many held their slaves until 1866, hoping that Congress might vote some form of compensation. But their hopes were in vain.

COMPROMISE OF 1808. Upon the recommendation of President **Thomas Jefferson** in 1806, and through a law passed by Congress in 1807, on 1 January 1808, the **international slave trade** was abolished through agreement reached in the **Constitution of 1787** (art. I, sect. 9). Anyone caught violating the law would be liable to loss of ship and cargo, with the seized slaves being disposed of by the state law in which the ship was condemned. In 1820, informers were granted a $50 bounty on each illegally imported slave, and violators were declared pirates, liable to hanging if American citizens and convicted.

It was important that the enabling acts be passed because the Compromise of 1808 was open ended—a simple law, as was tried in 1858, could have reopened the international slave trade. The South was happy to back the Compromise of 1808. The slave states of the Atlantic coast (Maryland and Virginia) and upper South (Kentucky and Tennessee) wanted to force up the value of their excess slaves, which now gave them a monopoly market through the **domestic slave trade** to the lower South (Georgia to Texas).

COMPROMISE OF 1833. *See* NULLIFICATION CRISIS AND COMPROMISE OF 1833.

COMPROMISE OF 1850. The introduction of the anti-slavery **Wilmot Proviso**, countered by the pro-slavery **Non-Exclusion Doctrine**, intensified the potency of the slavery issue in the Western territories, bringing the United States to the brink of Civil War by 1849. **Democratic** presidential candidate **Lewis Cass** had tried to compromise these two extremes by proposing **Squatter Sovereignty** (letting the residents of the territory decide), which Southern voters rejected by voting against him in the **election of 1848**.

The newly elected President **Zachary Taylor** was a slaveholding member of the **Whig Party** and hero of the **War with Mexico**. Never having voted, Taylor was not an active party member, so his views on the slavery issue in the territories were unknown. But Taylor needed to take a stand. The discovery of gold in California in 1849 brought 100,000 prospectors swarming to the territory. But California wanted to be more than a territory; it had sufficient population to qualify it for statehood.

This became Taylor's solution to the problem of slavery in the territories: grant statehood to the territories taken from Mexico, eliminate the territorial stage of government, and end the slavery problem in the territories. Everyone agreed that the question of slavery could be decided at a state constitutional convention prior to California's admission to the union. But to admit California as a state would upset the 50-50 balance between North and South in the U.S. Senate. Politicos questioned the president's power to dictate to Congress the solution to the most important issue facing the country.

Taylor's solution was way too simplistic. Many problems faced the nation by 1850: California's impending statehood; slavery in the rest of the Mexican Cession; the unpaid Republic of Texas' debt after its admission to the Union, which helped to cause the War with Mexico, and Texas' claim to Santa Fé and the Río Grande; slavery and the slave trade in the District of Columbia, especially odious to all Northern congressmen; Southern desires for a strongly worded and strictly enforced fugitive slave law, which would return escaped slaves to their rightful owners and negate personal liberty laws in Northern states that interfered with **slave catchers**.

As a result of prompting by New York's anti-slave, Whig U.S. Senator William H. Seward, Taylor said that California must be admitted as a free state before addressing any other issues and that he would veto all other measures. **John C. Calhoun** spoke for Southern hardliners, pledging no compromise. Slavery must be allowed in all territories until statehood. As a possible solution, **Henry Clay**, the Great Compromiser of the 1820s and 1830s, introduced the Omnibus Bill, combining all five problems into one single legislative proposal.

Clay's measure would admit California as a free state; set up territorial governments in Utah and New Mexico under the no-slavery laws of Mexico; have the United States assume the Texas Republic debt for which Texas would give up all land claims along the Río Grand north of El Paso; eliminate the despised slave trade from the District of Columbia; and pass a strict fugitive act, negating personal liberty laws and paying federal commissioners, who ruled on an African-American's status, twice the amount if he ruled for slavery. But an insufficient number of votes caused its defeat. Enough congressmen and senators stood against each section to prevent a legislative majority. Clay gave up any hope of success.

Then Calhoun died of old age on 31 March of that year, and President Taylor died five days after participating in ceremonies at the Washington Monument on a sweltering 4 July. Taking control of

Clay's Omnibus Bill, Senator **Stephen A. Douglas** of Illinois realized that each section had a congressional majority so long as it was not combined with the others. He split the Omnibus Bill into its original five parts, omitting mention of New Mexico and Utah slavery issues during their initial organization. The new president, **Millard Fillmore**, indicated that he would abide by anything Congress agreed to, and signed it all into law.

In response, the Southern states called a unified convention at Nashville and created the Georgia Platform, which supported the Union if the North obeyed every article in the Compromise of 1850, including the fugitive act. Combined with the failure of the pro-secession Southern movement, the Compromise of 1850 delayed the inevitable Civil War for another 10 years.

CONCURRENT VOICE AND NULLIFICATION. John C. Calhoun had been first elected to the U.S. House of Representatives just before the **War of 1812** as a **War Hawk**, that group of nationalistic Westerners and Southerners who wanted America to project its power into British Canada, Spanish Florida, and onto the high seas. But Calhoun and other Southern nationalists were different from the Western War Hawks. They based their nationalism in great part on America's needs for defense.

After the War of 1812, Calhoun and other Southern politicians joined the **New Nationalism** that preceded the **Era of Good Feelings**. They supported the **Second Bank of the United States** mostly to finance future wars and **internal improvements** like roads and canals to make for military mobility (one of the first railroads in the nation was a Calhoun project from Charleston into the interior). Even the later-to-be-hated **tariff** was to provide for domestic industry to produce goods for the army. And that army was to be an "expansible army," incorporating militia and professional cadres, brilliantly developed by Calhoun as Secretary of War during the **James Monroe** presidency.

But when the New Nationalism seemed only to benefit New England over the South, and there was no external threat to the United States, Calhoun and his supporters quickly retrenched and returned to a weak central government with restricted powers. Calhoun was always under fire for his nationalism from within his state.

The big states' rights advocate at home was William Smith. When Smith defeated Calhoun's right-hand man for the U.S. Senate in 1822, it was time to regroup. The **Denmark Vesey Plot**, the increased Tariff of 1824, and the growing interest of the North in abolition caused Calhoun to treat Smith and his exaggerated states' rights views with previously unheard-of consideration. But when the Tariff of 1828 was passed, which Smith and his radicals labeled the Tariff of Abominations, Calhoun knew he had to do something to slow down Smith and his backers, who wanted to forcibly prevent tariff collection at Charleston.

Calhoun began to feel alienated from his own state. He needed a device to regain leadership of his state and win back his supporters. The result was his publication of the *South Carolina Exposition and Protest*. Essentially what Calhoun said was that the tariff was unfair to the South, it was indeed unconstitutional, and that the people of any single state were sovereign and could interpose between the federal government and its enforcing of such unconstitutional laws.

In effect, Calhoun was saying the same thing that Jefferson and **James Madison** had asserted in the **Kentucky and Virginia Resolves** against the **Alien and Sedition Acts**. But unlike Jefferson and Madison, Calhoun maintained that one state, not several, could act alone to declare laws unconstitutional. This competed with **John Marshall**'s assertions in *Marbury v. Madison* that it was the U.S. **Supreme Court**'s responsibility to protect the people from unconstitutional actions of Congress. But things were still up for grabs then, and, theoretically, Calhoun's ideas were as good as Marshall's.

What Calhoun was saying was that any majority could ride roughshod over the rights of a deserving minority. So somehow the rights of the minority had to be protected. Calhoun's proposal was the Concurrent Voice. What it said was that no majority could act unless a majority of the minority concurred in that action. The process by which this theory was to be asserted was nullification.

One state, if it acted correctly, could nullify or invalidate a federal law if its governor would ask the state legislature to call for the election of a state convention. In republican theory, a convention is the body closest to the people. The convention would meet and debate the federal law in question. If a majority of the convention agreed, the law would be nullified and have no further effect in the state. Then the law would automatically be admitted to the other states as a constitutional amendment.

If three-fourths of the other states agreed to the law in question, it would become an amendment to the **U.S. Constitution**. If not, the law would be invalidated as unconstitutional. If three-fourths of the other states agreed to the law and made it a constitutional amendment, the original nullifying state could drop its opposition, and the law would go into effect nationwide. But if the original nullifying state still opposed the law, it could reconvene its convention and secede from the Union.

This is a highly legalistic approach, typically Calhoun, typically Southern. But the key here is not **secession**. The point is the prolonged debate. Calhoun figured that if any state were willing to go through all this, Congress would reconsider the law and modify it before secession ever became necessary. But Calhoun was logical. Secession was there because it was a logical final step.

The South Carolina state legislature published the *South Carolina Exposition and Protest* anonymously in 1828, but most suspected Calhoun was behind it. South Carolina radicals eagerly embraced Calhoun's ideas and decided to use them on the **tariff**, leading to the **Nullification Crisis and the Compromise of 1833.**

CONFEDERATE CONSTITUTION. *See* CONSTITUTION, CONFEDERATE.

CONFEDERATE GOVERNMENT. The South in the Confederacy was not the Old South or the postwar New South, but unique—*sui generis*—an independent South entire unto itself. The Confederate Constitution was designed to encourage unity in government, merging the executive with the legislative by granting cabinet members non-voting seats of the floor of Congress and extending a single term of the presidency to six years.

The men selected to be the provisional executives of the new Confederacy were **Jefferson Davis** of Mississippi as president, and **Alexander Stephens** of Georgia as vice president. Both were regular party men (Davis a **Democrat**, Stephens an old-line **Whig** and friend of **Abraham Lincoln**). The **fire-eaters**, or radical secessionists, were generally excluded from the Confederate government right from the start. This was to be a conservative enterprise, based on tried and true principles inherited from the Founding Fathers of 1776 and 1787, not some wild-eyed experimental nonsense. That was left up to Yankees and **abolitionists** who, in Southern eyes, had destroyed what the Founders wrought and caused the Confederacy to be necessary.

There were no competitors for election to the national government, named Confederate to show its obeisance to the states and localities. There were few contested races for the Congress, as pre-war conservative Southern cooperators moved to reassert their leadership and to exclude the fire-eaters from nomination as too radical. The South was supposed to display unity in the face of Yankee aggression. But the ideal never was truly achieved. Soon congressmen were opposing the government and its military and foreign policies.

One historian, in a burst of present-mindedness, called those in favor of the Confederate government Nationalists, while those opposed, interested in individualism, liberty, and states' rights even at the cost of losing the war were named Libertarians. The Confederate government, headed by Jefferson Davis, an ardent Libertarian advocate, at least in theory, sacrificed the conservative cause of states' rights in all of its manifestations (governance, aristocracy, **slavery**, racism) for the radical causes of nationalism and centralization to try and win the war. Although stymied by the inertia of an inefficient bureaucracy and opposition from many Libertarian governors (especially in Georgia and North Carolina), the Confederate administration at Richmond acted with revolutionary zeal, often beating the Lincoln government's response to the same issues in the North.

The Rebel authorities conscripted troops and labor and materiel, created a viable national army and a secret service (which many credit as the best organized covert American administration until the advent of the Central Intelligence Agency), suspended the writ of habeas corpus, and issued rules for manufacturing, railroad operation, and allocation of vital raw materials. It impressed goods, fixed consumer prices, brought white women and blacks of both genders into the wartime workplace, and brought about an astounding industrialization and urbanization. It also tried to create a **cotton** shortage to influence European governments to support its bid for continued independence.

Finally, the Confederacy destroyed the very reason the Old South left the Union, the cornerstone of its uniqueness, the institution of slavery. Under prodding from **Judah P. Benjamin**, Jefferson Davis, Gen. **Robert E. Lee**, and others, over vociferous Libertarian opposition, the Confederate government began to enroll slaves as soldiers in 1865. The Davis administration had fought on in every imaginable way for Southern self-determination despite continued military losses, winning many battles but losing the campaigns and, ultimately, the war. It is possible, however, that the Confederate government did a more credible job than many modern critics have been willing to admit.

CONSCIENCE WHIGS. *See* WHIG PARTY.

CONSTITUTION, CONFEDERATE. As each Southern state seceded separately, they tacitly agreed to unify and form a central government. South Carolina, the first state to leave the Union, conferred with other Southern states about to follow suit and seceded with support from Mississippi and Florida. In February 1861, delegates from seceded states Alabama, Georgia, Mississippi, Louisiana, Florida, and Texas met in Montgomery, Alabama, and established a new nation, the Confederate States of America. Texas, having seceded later than the others, sent their delegation in March. It agreed with that which had preceded its arrival.

The delegates chose Montgomery as the first capital of the independent South, "the Cradle of the Confederacy," due to its central location and distance from the coast, unlike the port cities Charleston, Mobile, Savannah, and New Orleans, which were vulnerable to Union naval expeditions. When Virginia seceded as a part of the **second secession movement**, Richmond became the new capital of the Confederacy. Larger, more cosmopolitan, Richmond represented the dedication to the Border South. It also typified Southern defiance with its proximity to the North.

With less than a month before **Abraham Lincoln**'s inauguration, the delegates at Montgomery hastened to form a solid government. The convention did some unconventional things: acted as a constitutional convention and elected a provisional president and vice president. It acted as a provisional unicameral Congress for five sessions from 18 February 1861, to 22 February 1862, acts which, in republican theory, are not traditionally carried out by the body that authors the Constitution. But the Montgomery delegates knew they were part of a unique moment in American history.

The Southerners' commitment to a written constitution demonstrated their dedication to the American way of government. A written fundamental document is America's great contribution to world political history. They called themselves the Confederate States of America. Confederation implied a looser bond than United States, as stated in the preamble: "We, the People of the Confederate States, each State acting in its sovereign and independent character...." The delegates built on the premise that the U.S. Constitution was the most just and equitable document ever created until it was compromised by what they saw as pernicious Yankee influences. So the delegates made only minor changes in their Constitution, retaining and honoring the essence of the original Founding Fathers' principles.

But the Confederate Constitution was far from inconsequential. The framers distinguished it from the U.S. Constitution with several unique points. First, they made the executive and the legislative bodies closer than in the U.S. Constitution. Cabinet members were permitted to take a seat in either house of Congress and debate but not vote. The Confederate presidency held more power than under the U.S. Constitution. Allowed a six-year term, the president could not succeed himself, but he could remove cabinet members and diplomats at his pleasure (all other civil officials could be removed only for cause, not political leanings) and had the right to introduce all appropriations bills. Congress could act to introduce appropriations only with a two-thirds vote. In effect, the Confederate Constitution foresaw the U.S. Constitution's Twenty-Second Amendment on presidential term limits, a budgetary system of appropriation, precluded impeachment of executive officials prior to removing them from office, and created a protected civil service.

Second, the Confederate Constitution changed the relationship between the states and the central government. Only the states, acting individually or in cooperation with each other, could pass a **tariff**. The amendment process was simplified: any three states could call for a convention to amend, with only a two-thirds majority to approve it (the figures in the U.S. Constitution are two-thirds to call the convention and three-fourths to approve the amendment). Any Confederate official could be impeached by the state in which he served, to be tried before the Confederate Senate. **Secession** was omitted, not because the Confederacy denied this right to its member states, but because it was so essential it needed no mention.

Finally, Negro **slavery** or slaves were mentioned openly three times in the Confederate Constitution. Slavery was guaranteed by the central government, although theoretically any state could abolish it. A slaveowner was guaranteed the right to transport his or her slaves throughout the Confederacy, and slavery was guaranteed in any Confederate territory, such as the seceded territory of Arizona.

Other changes included the addressing of "the favor and guidance of Almighty God" and omitting any mention of "general welfare," the clause that led to much dispute in interpreting the U.S. Constitution. The first 12 amendments to the U.S. Constitution were placed in the main body of the Confederate text. Each law was to concern only one topic, which was to be stated clearly in its title. The Post Office Department was to be self-sustaining by 1863. States could be admitted by a two-thirds vote of both houses of Congress. The Confederates anticipated many Middle Atlantic and Old Northwestern states eventually joining this purified form of government to solidify a Southern Reconstruction of the Union under the Confederacy.

The men selected to be the provisional executives of the new Confederacy were **Jefferson Davis** of Mississippi as president, and **Alexander Stephens** of Georgia as vice president. Both were regular party men (Davis a Democrat, Stephens an old-line Whig and friend of **Abraham Lincoln**). The radical secessionists, or **fire-eaters**, were generally excluded from the Confederate government right from the start. This was to be a conservative enterprise, based on tried and true principles inherited from the Founding Fathers of 1776 and 1787. Provisional experimentation and insurgency was for Yankees and **abolitionists** who, according to the Old South, had forced the Confederacy's creation as a result of destroying what the Founders had wrought.

CONSTITUTION, U.S., AND SLAVERY. When delegates met in Philadelphia in 1787, professing only to amend the Articles of Confederation, representatives of the Southern colonies made sure their special interest, the **peculiar institution,** was well protected. As it became obvious that the Constitutional Convention's backers were intent on replacing the articles, the South needed to step in and safeguard their agenda.

Four special areas concerned the South: commerce, representation, treaties, and **extraterritoriality**. After securing complete control of trade, the federal government would oversee the exports of **staple crops** and the international **slave trade**. To protect their interests, the South requested all commerce laws be passed by a two-thirds vote in Congress. The convention refused, but offered a compromise: simple majorities would pass trade laws, but no taxes would be allowed on exports, like **staple crops**. Commerce also affected the slave trade. By importing slaves from Africa, South Carolina and Georgia hoped to replace laborers lost during the Revolution, but the North would allow this only until January 1, 1808. Then this **Compromise of 1808** would be up for a second vote.

The most important commerce agreement was the creation of a free-trade area encompassing several states to prevent discriminating against other states' produce. The federal government would regulate all currency, money-lending, **tariffs**, weights and measures, and interstate commerce. In guaranteeing payment of all business debts by honoring contracts in federal courts, creditors could now collect debt across state lines.

Because slaves were not allowed to vote and therefore were not counted, the South felt it would be underrepresented in Congress. The South wanted its slaves counted for representation but not taxed. The **Three-Fifths Compromise** solved the problem by partially counting the slaves for both. With few direct taxes until the Civil War, the South benefited greatly from this compromise.

A common fear below the **Mason–Dixon Line** was that New England would try to reduce the South's vast agricultural interests by forcing the south to accept a tariff on imports. New England would be raising prices on goods the South traded her cotton for and also invite trade retaliations by European nations by limiting the market for cotton imports abroad for trade advantages for Northern shipping and manufacturing, as in the failed **Jay–Guardoqui Treaty** of 1786. The South insisted on a two-thirds vote in the Senate, where each state would have equal representation for all treaties. Fearful that the eventual admission of Western states might isolate New England, Massachusetts voted with the South on this measure.

Finally, the South demanded and received the **extraterritoriality of slavery**. In effect, slaves remained in service anywhere in the United States, regardless of local law. This was pledged through the fugitive clause that guaranteed return of slaves to their state of origin. *See also* RUNAWAY SLAVES.

CONSTITUTIONAL UNION PARTY (1860). Acting on fear that extremists in the other major political parties would choose war if the **election of 1860** did not go their way, members of the **Whigs**, Know Nothings, and **American Party**, primarily in the border states of Missouri, Kentucky, Maryland, and Delaware, formed the Constitutional Union Party on December 29, 1859. Knowing this war between North and South would be fought on their home ground, they dreaded the inevitable destruction and devastation.

The Constitutional Unionists held their first convention on 1 May 1860 in Baltimore. Their goal was to force the election into the House of Representatives where each state would have but one vote, with a view to a compromise between North and South to preserve the Union. Believing that written promises restricted their planned stratagem and repulsed potential voters, the party stood on no platform, only for the enforcement of all public laws and on what their name implied—Constitution and Union. The object of their opponents' ridicule, they became known as the "Soothing Syrup" Party. In fact, the John Brown **Harper's Ferry Raid** had pretty much killed reasonableness on all sides already. There was little to no more room for compromise; everyone was stuck in their ways.

Their presidential candidate was **John Bell** of Tennessee, an old-time moderate Whig who had served as Speaker of the House, Secretary of War, and U.S. Senator. His running mate was Edward Everett of Massachusetts, who was considered the greatest orator of his time. He was best renowned for his three-hour main speech at the dedication of the Gettysburg National Cemetery before President **Abraham Lincoln** spoke for two minutes in November 1863. Although they failed to affect the election, the Constitutional Unionists emerged again at the **Washington Peace Conference**.

CORN. Although the Old South was best known as an area that produced **staple crops**, it also was a region that produced much corn and consumed even more than it grew. Corn was a peculiarly American crop, obtained from the Native American tribes by the earliest settlers. Even though it was considered the first crop frontiersmen planted, corn never lessened in its overall importance to agriculture nationwide. The hogs and cattle were often turned loose in corn fields to fatten and fed corn fodder (as opposed to hay) in the bare winter months. Many places in the Old South were described by early travelers as "beyond bread," that is, wheat bread, dependent upon corn bread fried in some sort of "oleaginous matter," combined with various species of game.

Even in the most civilized parts of the Old South, corn was combined with pork or catfish and often was the more important food. Corn was used in many ways. In early summer it was boiled green on the cob, cut from the cob, and creamed. It was also roasted in the shuck. After the ears were ripe in the fall, it was ground into meal from which an endless array of breads was cooked. The most common was meal, salt, and water which baked into cakelike corn pone. Added to this basic recipe were milk, buttermilk, eggs, shortening, or cracklings (renderings left over from making lard).

No matter how wealthy Southern farmers became, they never seemed to lose their taste for corn bread. The slaves ate it all the time, presumably because it was cheap. Besides corn breads, the crop could be turned into mush (porridge), griddle cakes, and waffles. Often the broth poured off vegetables, which Southerners boiled for hours on end, was served as pot-likker, and crumbled corn bread added to the mix to thicken it. Hominy, boiled whole grain corn, was common, as was grits, dried coarsely ground corn cooked into a thick porridge. Moreover, both of these could be fried in grease for variety.

Corn grew well in the South with very little extra work beyond a couple of hoeings for weed control. In the hillier areas, it usually surpassed **cotton** production and was seen as a cash crop rather than subsistence farming. Often beans or peas were planted among the cornstalks. The Southern corn belt generally was north of the cotton belt. This meant that Virginia, Tennessee, Kentucky, Arkansas, and Missouri raised the most corn. In the rest of the South, corn was confined to the hills and less fertile lands in which cotton grew poorly. While the corn belt of the old Northwest out-produced the Old South, the lands south of the **Mason–Dixon Line** ran the Old Northwest a close second over the badly trailing Northeast. The only other grain grown in the Old South in quantity was wheat, which had the same growing area as corn and **rice**, which tended to grow in the Sea Islands of Georgia and South Carolina before the Civil War. *See also* ECONOMY.

CORNERSTONE SPEECH. *See* STEPHENS, ALEXANDER H.

CORRUPT BARGAIN. *See* ADAMS, JOHN QUINCY; DEMOCRATS; ELECTION OF 1828; JACKSON, ANDREW.

CORWIN COMMITTEE OF THIRTY-THREE. Upon the **first secession** of the Southern states, the press, the clergy, local governments, and the general public pressed Congress to act upon the situation by preventing more states from leaving the Union. The daunting task before Congress was to rectify the errors of a generation, and in the beginning it looked little better than hopeless.

The factionalism that splintered Congress, especially in the House of Representatives, was a huge obstacle hindering its progress, but the House felt obliged to try and overcome. When South Carolina seceded, Congress formed the Committee of Thirty-Three chaired by Thomas Corwin of Ohio. The committee put forth several proposals: The first was to open the territories, until achieving statehood, to all slave owners with **slavery** protected, essentially the Southern **Non-Exclusion Doctrine,** rejected by all **Republicans** and Douglas **Democrats**. Also proposed was for states to pay for the fugitive slaves they shielded, and no African Americans would be granted citizenship or the right to vote. Because several Northern states allowed both, this proposal was unacceptable to Republicans.

Finally, the committee passed the so-called Corwin Amendment, disallowing future amendments to the **U.S. Constitution** regarding slavery. This was to guarantee the continuance of slavery in the Southern states, but raised the question, could Congress act to prohibit future Constitutional amendments? The Committee of Thirty-Three eventually earned its macabre moniker "the coffin" because everything seemed to die there, leaving the responsibility to the **Crittenden Committee of Thirteen** in the Senate.

CÓS, MARTÍN PERFECTO DE. *See* **LONE STAR REBELLIONS.**

COTTON, SEA ISLAND. Distinctive yet related to **upland cotton** was its long-staple cousin, Sea Island cotton. It was grown in a narrow band within 40 miles of the sea, among the Atlantic coastal islands affected by tidal flow, in South Carolina, Georgia, and Florida. It was never driven out of the market by its upland competition because of its quality—silky, soft, and strong. Sea Island cotton was called long staple because its fiber was double the length of upland or short-staple cotton.

The Sea Island cotton fields were full of elaborate ditching. Unlike **rice**, the object was to drain moisture from the plants, not to irrigate them. Most fields were subdivided into quarter-acre plots or tasks. The seeds were planted every two feet in high ridges set up in rows four feet apart. In South Carolina and Georgia, the hoe was the only tool used. In Florida, however, planters relied less on tradition and used horse- and mule-powered tilling equipment. Either way, the crop was hoed eight times a year.

Harvest time was very arduous because the crop had to be picked quickly to prevent damage from wind or moisture. Most fieldhands picked 25 pounds a day, less trash. Although the seeds were easy to remove by hand, an adaptation of the **cotton gin** called the McCarthy gin came into use in the 1840s. This had the usual two rollers working in opposition with a chopping bar mounted before the front roller to flatten the fibers.

Sea Island cotton was pressed by hand and bagged and roped into a round bale that weighed 300–400 pounds. It took 40–50 man-hours of labor to produce one bale. Bales brought almost $30 each on the market—compared to 50 cents for a short-staple bale of similar weight. There was actually little profit in the Sea Island variety because it was so labor intensive and the prices fluctuated. It was good from the American Revolution to the **Panic of 1819**, bad to 1834, good until the **Panic of 1837**, bad to 1850, and good to the Civil War. Growing Sea Island cotton was more a way of life than a business. It was truly a "gentlemanly" pursuit. *See also* ECONOMY.

COTTON, UPLAND. Of all the crops raised in the Old South, short-staple upland cotton was a real obsession. It was discussed incessantly everywhere. Yankee travelers and women, Northern and Southern, opined that the topic was mentioned at least 1,000 times a day and seen moving by every conveyance possible. One Northern drummer mentioned that he finally got a good night's sleep on a steamboat packed with cotton right up to the pilot house, although he admitted he dreamed of cotton as he slept.

Upland cotton culture expanded after the **War of 1812** because of three things: vast virgin lands available at a low price, rapid expansion of demand from British cotton mills, and cheap labor in the form of black slaves. If there was one factor that could not keep up with the expansion of upland cotton culture, it was the availability of labor. Slave prices constantly rose until a slave worth $600 in Virginia was valued at $1,200 or more in Louisiana and Texas.

Prices for cotton fluctuated from 1815 onward. It was generally downward to 1844 (three to six cents a pound) and then upward to 1860 (11 cents a pound). Cotton proved very susceptible to the economic depression of the antebellum period. Both the **Panic of 1817** and the **Panic of 1837** decimated cotton planters. But the **Panic of 1857** was hardly noticed in the South, and Southerners smugly assumed that the cotton boom of the 1850s proved Southern economic and cultural superiority and the immunity of cotton to Yankee industrial economic cycles. The Civil War and Reconstruction would soon disabuse the South of those quaint notions as cotton prices bottomed out for decades because of war damages, excessive postwar production, and drought.

In growing cotton, the fields were plowed into parallel ridges about four feet apart. The ridges were creased on top with a thin slit and the seed sown. Some fertilizers were used before the Civil War—a regular guano mania swept the Southeast—but not extensively, as when growing **tobacco**. Much of the work in upland cotton was done by machines like planters and plows at the general ratio of two field-hands per mule. Then the sprouting crop was thinned or chopped out by hand, leaving plants 12 inches apart.

The crop was hoed on a regular basis until mid-July when lay-by season occurred. Everyone went off to other work and left the cotton to grow. In the fall, picking season occurred. Everyone, regardless of gender, from adult to children, house servants or fieldhands, helped with the picking. The cotton was picked over three times, bottom, middle, and top of the plant. The middle picking was generally considered the best. In 1860, it was not unusual to expect a male to pick upwards of 200 pounds a day, quadruple the rate in 1800.

The picked cotton was taken to racks and spread out to dry, turned with a rake, and had the dirt and trash removed. Then it was ginned. A newer variety of **cotton gin** removed not only the seeds, but dirt and trash, too. Three men generally ran the cotton gin. The output was up to six bales per day, depending on the model of the gin. Then the cotton was baled. Upland cotton bales weighed around 400 pounds in 1860, up from a mere 225 pounds in 1800. The difference was the press that packed the hemp-covered bales. A good cotton press was expensive, so a planter generally opened it up to his less fortunate small farmer neighbors. It was generally a large screw worked by a team of mules or a steam engine.

The soils of the Southwest (Louisiana, Mississippi, Arkansas, Texas) were noted for their fertility. It was not unusual for plantations located on bottomland to produce two 500-pound bales per acre on average, double what was raised on weaker soils in the Atlantic Coast South. Numerous rusts and worms affected cotton no matter where it was raised. These were combated by letting chickens and turkeys run wild in the fields. The one innovation in upland cotton was a new seed found south of the border during the War with Mexico. It was crossed with native Southern varieties at Rodney, Mississippi, and named Petit Gulf after this region. The finest seed was that developed by Henry W. Vick, whose family lent its name to the river city, Vicksburg. *See also* ECONOMY.

COTTON FACTORS. *See* FACTORS, COTTON.

COTTON GIN. Developed in the 1790s in response to a need to strip the tightly ensconced seeds from the fibers of short-staple **upland cotton**, the cotton gin made it possible to gin the cotton in quick time with little effort compared to heretofore meticulous handwork. A transplanted Connecticut teacher, **Eli Whitney**, developed the gin in Georgia on the plantation of Mrs. Nathaniel Greene, widow of the Revolutionary War general. Whether Whitney did the work himself or stole and altered the work done by unknown slave artisans has been hotly disputed. Nevertheless, financed by Phineas Miller, executor of the Greene estate and soon-to-be new husband of Mrs. Greene, Whitney got credit for the invention from the U.S. Patent Office in 1794 and several Southern state legislatures paid him for its use, so important was the invention. But Whitney took much less than he wanted, as patent infringements ate up his profits. Before Whitney could collect on patent infringements, the document had expired, and the cotton gin became public property at the insistence of several Southern state legislatures. Various versions of the cotton gin soon appeared throughout the South as upland cotton cultivation spread westward during the **Great Migration**. A different version designed for long-staple **Sea Island cotton** was called the McCarthy gin. *See also* ECONOMY.

COTTON WHIGS. *See* WHIG PARTY.

CRAWFORD, WILLIAM H. *See* ELECTION OF 1816; ELECTION OF 1824; ERA OF GOOD FEELINGS; JACKSON'S BREAK WITH CALHOUN; VAN BUREN, MARTIN.

CREEK WAR. *See* INDIAN REMOVAL COMPLETED; WAR OF 1812.

***CREOLE* CASE (1842).** Dealing in transporting American slaves from the upper South to the marketplace in New Orleans, the *Creole* left Chesapeake Bay in 1841 and began its journey south with 135 slaves and a cargo of tobacco. Eleven days later the ship sailed into a harbor in the British Bahamas. There the crew soon was overpowered by loose, armed slaves on the ship and the survivors chased up the mainmast, from which perch they surrendered shortly. One white and one black died in the rebellion, with several whites being wounded and one black rebel being hurt.

The *Creole* incident was one of an estimated 55 slave insurrections at sea from 1699 to 1840. The freed slaves directed one of the white survivors to take the ship to nearby Nassau. There, despite protests of the American consul, the slaves were all freed, including those who had led the mutiny. The *Creole* was then allowed to continue its journey to

New Orleans, the rest of its cargo intact. Immediately several Southern state legislatures protested British interference with the **domestic slave trade** and demanded that Britain pay restitution for the slaves lost. Americans pointed to the recently settled *Amistad* **Case**, in which illegal participants in the **international slave trade** had received no restitution, and said since this case was legal trade, restitution ought to be immediate.

The British were not so sure. They pointed out that there had been other similar cases, the *Comet*, the *Encomium*, and the *Enterprise*, in which ships blown into the Bahamas by bad weather had had their slave cargoes liberated. Another slave ship, the *Formosa*, had been wrecked off the Bahamas, with the same result.

But the real threat the *Creole* incident presented was the scuttling of the pending Webster–Ashburton Treaty over numerous issues affecting the **Canadian Boundary Dispute**. Although the British government refused to placate American hostilities over the *Creole*, Lord Ashburton gave private assurances in a letter to U.S. Secretary of State **Daniel Webster** that Britain had no policy of consistently interfering with the American domestic slave trade. On the other hand, Britain would not return **runaway slaves** to their owners, even if they stole items to expedite their journey, which made them susceptible to extradition.

This unofficial Ashburton letter seemed to appease South and North, and the Webster–Ashburton Treaty passed through the U.S. Senate unimpeded. The *Creole* Case was finally settled in 1855, when Britain agreed to pay damages of $110,330 to the owners of the liberated slaves. Britain also stated that **slavery**, while reprehensible and illegal in the British Empire, was not illegal under international law or in the United States, a statement taken from the U.S. **Supreme Court** decision in the *Antelope* **Case** in 1825.

"CRIME AGAINST KANSAS." *See* BROOKS, PRESTON S.

CRITTENDEN, JOHN J. (1887–1863). Born and raised in Kentucky, John Jordan Crittenden attended local academies, studied at Washington College (now Washington and Lee), and graduated from William and Mary College in 1806. He read law and was admitted to the bar a year later.

Crittenden soon entered public service, first as secretary to the governor of Illinois Territory, and then as aide to the governor of the State of Kentucky. Resuming his law practice, Crittenden served in the state legislature where he was speaker and was elected to the U.S. Senate in 1817, where he was chairman of the Judiciary Committee.

Crittenden resigned his Senate seat and returned home to serve in the state legislature. He was a **National Republican**, which led President **John Quincy Adams** to nominate him to the U.S. **Supreme Court**. The **election of 1828** intervened, and with the election of **Andrew Jackson** and the **Democrats**, Crittenden was never confirmed. He also lost his position of U.S. District Attorney for Kentucky.

Switching to the **Whig** Party, Crittenden again served Kentucky as U.S. Senator during the **Martin Van Buren** administration, With the election of **William Henry Harrison** to the presidency, Crittenden became attorney general of the United States. He was reelected to the U.S. Senate and served on the committee on military affairs during the **War with Mexico**. He resigned in 1848 to become governor of Kentucky.

With the rise of **Millard Fillmore** to the presidency, Crittenden was again made U.S. Attorney General. He returned to the U.S. Senate and served until 1861. He opposed reopening the issue of **slavery** in the territories through the passage of the **Kansas–Nebraska Act**, preferring to stick with the old **Missouri Compromise**.

He was a leader in the compromise movement preceding the Civil War and chaired the **Crittenden Committee of Thirteen.** His family typified the agony of Kentucky during the war, one son serving the Union and the other and a nephew fighting for the Confederacy. Returning to Congress as a Union man, Crittenden was running for reelection for his old house seat when he died in 1863.

CRITTENDEN COMMITTEE OF THIRTEEN. When it formed its compromise Committee of Thirteen chaired by Senator **John J. Crittenden** of Kentucky in 1861, the U.S. Senate was not as splintered as the House of Representatives' **Committee of Thirty-Three.** However, the result was equally devoid of any sound resolutions. Only one-quarter of the Senate was willing to compromise in any way. The root of the problem was that Northerners, especially President-elect **Abraham Lincoln**, did not take **secession** seriously and believed the

South would reconsider and crawl back to the Union. But the slave states believed secession was the most effective answer to what they saw as a generation of unfair and unconstitutional attacks on their guaranteed institution of slavery.

Crittenden's family situation echoed the consequences of Civil War for the nation, and he feared its splitting up to join opposite sides. The Crittenden Committee of Thirteen proposed that Congress prevent ending **slavery** in any territory surrounded by slave states, not interfere with the domestic **slave trade**, pay slaveholders who could not recover fugitive slaves, prohibit any constitutional amendment abolishing slavery in slave states, and extend the **Missouri Compromise** line to the eastern border of California to solve the slavery problem in the territories.

Most Southerners favored the Missouri Compromise extension. But Abraham Lincoln could not. It violated his most sacred tenet, the **Wilmot Proviso,** as the solution to the extension of slavery into the West. He also believed the South would take advantage of the extension by spreading slave territory into the Caribbean, especially Cuba. Lincoln pledged to protect slavery in the states where it existed by enforcing the **Fugitive Slave Act of 1850** from the **Compromise of 1850.** But he did not allow Crittenden's proposals to be voted on in a national referendum, asserting that avoiding the problem through compromise was not to the nation's advantage. The failure of Crittenden's proposals and Corwin's Committee of Thirty-Three necessitated a body other than Congress to forestall the threat of war, putting the onus on the **Washington Peace Conference**, then in session.

CUFFEE, PAUL. *See* LIBERIA.

CUMBERLAND ROAD. *See* NATIONAL ROAD.

– D –

DALLAS, GEORGE M. *See* ELECTION OF 1848.

DALONEGA GOLD RUSH. The first major gold rush in United States history was not in California in 1849, but in northern Georgia in 1829. The Dalonega gold rush exacerbated the whole problem of **Indian Removal** because the gold was located in lands traditionally held and recognized by treaty as belonging to the Cherokees. But as other **Native Americans** would find out in later years, the surest way for their treaty rights to be ignored and eradicated was the discovery of gold.

Sought unsuccessfully by the Spanish in the 1500s, Georgia's gold was mined for centuries by the Cherokees in small amounts for decorative purposes. But in the late 1820s, white men began to come north into Cherokee country, at first driven by land hunger and then, a ravenous desire for gold riches. Governor George Gilmer was no friend of Indian treaty rights, but he hoped to regulate the trade through state law. The governor soon found out that the Twenty-Niners were not about to wait for Gilmer and Georgia law any more than they were to respect Cherokee treaty rights. They invaded the area as illegal trespassers. Their mining activities became known as "swindling" in the parlance of the times.

The Georgia state legislature soon passed the Act of 30 July 1830, which declared all Indian lands in the state under its jurisdiction and ordered all miners out of the area pending proper licensing and regulation. The Georgia State Guard was to enforce the law. The Cherokees appealed everything to the U.S. **Supreme Court** but won what turned out to be a Phyrric victory.

Governor Gilmer refused to obey the court's edict to back off. He was backed up by President **Andrew Jackson** and the U.S. Congress, which passed a law that called for total Indian Removal. Gilmer declared the Cherokee to be hostile to the interests of the people of the state, an aggravation that had to be ended.

At this moment, Gilmer was in the midst of a gubernatorial election. His opponent, Wilson Lumpkin, called for the immediate opening of all Cherokee lands to white exploitation. He called Gilmer's plans undemocratic as they would create a state-run monopoly. Georgia voters agreed and installed Lumpkin in office. The legislature established 10 new counties from Cherokee land and set up a land lottery to distribute the area to white participants.

The gold miners did not wait for any lottery. They flooded the area and began placer operations to secure the gold. It was estimated that 40,000 miners and settlers swarmed into the gold-rich area, centered on the town of Dalonega. Lawlessness was rife. The miners would pan for gold and quickly spend it in the nearest saloon or house of ill repute if they were not robbed or killed for their poke beforehand.

Many planters took part in the gold rush, bringing in their slaves to do the mining, one of the early uses of **industrial slavery** in the Old South. One of the more important of these slaveowners was none other than the Vice President of the United States, **John C. Calhoun**, who used 20 slaves as miners on his claims. But even though Georgians sympathized with Calhoun's affinity for **Nullification and the Concurrent Voice** and possible **secession** over the **tariff** question, President Jackson's removal of the Cherokees kept them loyal to the Union and Georgia's gold.

The gold industry in Georgia lasted until the Civil War, with about $50 million in ore produced. Modern estimates are that only one-third of the gold deposits were mined, and from these only half of the ore available was taken. *See also* INDIAN REMOVAL COMPLETED.

DANCING RABBIT CREEK, TREATY OF (1830). *See* INDIAN REMOVAL.

DAVIS, HENRY WINTER (1817–1865). Henry Winter Davis was born at Annapolis, Maryland, to an Episcopal rector who was president of St. Johns College. Raised in an upper-class setting, he graduated from Kenyon College in 1837 with an education in the classics and an interest and skill in forensics. He went on to study law at the University of Virginia and practiced his profession at Alexandria, later relocating to Baltimore, where he lived the rest of his life. A polished orator, Davis was a Baltimore politician of the old **Whig** Party. He was elected to Congress in 1855 and served three terms. After a two-year retirement, he returned for one more term that ended just before his premature death. He gleaned much of his political power from a gang of dockworkers known as the "plug-uglies" whose riots in select places on election day intimidated and scared off Davis's opposition voters.

In Congress Davis was known for his outspokenness and hatred of the **Democrats**. He spoke out against the crooked, pro-slave Lecompton Constitution in Kansas and criticized every aspect of **James Buchanan**'s administration. In 1859, he cast his vote for the **Repub-**

licans to organize the U.S. House of Representatives, giving them the majority in the House for the first time. Davis's unpopular vote earned him the castigation of "Black Republican," the censure of the Maryland State Assembly, and cost him his reelection in 1861.

During his term beginning in 1863, Davis appealed to white middle-class town dwellers, small farmers, and artisans to purge Maryland of what he, as a Radical Republican, saw as the anachronism of **slavery**. He shrewdly pointed out that black soldiers allowed the poorer whites to avoid serving in the war, while the richer slaveholders could buy an exemption. With the aid of federal soldiers to shield his crooked election-day antics, Davis and his Republicans elected an emancipationist majority to the state legislature. In the election of November 1864, he was instrumental in freeing the slaves of Maryland by act of the state legislature approved by the people. Davis went on to champion black suffrage, seeing in the black vote a way for his political machine to move into previously Democratic bastions.

Along with his U.S. Senate ally Benjamin Wade of Ohio, Davis introduced the Wade–Davis Bill into Congress. When President **Abraham Lincoln** pocket vetoed the bill, the two men issued their Wade–Davis Manifesto. A civil libertarian, Davis believed that President Lincoln had abused his presidential powers when he denied the writ of habeas corpus and relied on military courts to try wartime dissenters. He also stood forthrightly against the prevalent notions of transporting the freed slaves to the Caribbean or back to Africa, maintaining that their labor and service in the Union armies had earned them the right to be Americans. At the height of his state power, Davis died of pneumonia in December 1865.

DAVIS, JEFFERSON (1808–1889). Jefferson Davis was born in Kentucky, but his family soon removed to Mississippi where he was educated in private schools before returning to Kentucky to attend Transylvania College. Receiving an appointment to the United States Military Academy, where he was a contemporary of **Robert E. Lee**, Joseph E. Johnston, and Albert Sidney Johnston, Davis graduated in 1828. He served as an officer for seven years along the Western frontier. In 1835, he married the daughter of his regimental colonel, **Zachary Taylor**, but soon resigned his commission and took his new wife to a plantation in the Felicianas north of Baton Rouge,

Louisiana, where she died of a fever. Heartbroken, Davis returned home to Mississippi and lived the life of a recluse for several years at his brother Joseph's landholdings.

Through the influence of his brother, Davis read widely and ran for Congress in 1843. He lost the election but did serve as a presidential elector in 1844 for **James K. Polk**. He ran for Congress again in 1845 and won, but resigned his seat to serve in the **War with Mexico**. Davis fancied himself a military strategist, and his influence and education gained him the rank of colonel in the First Mississippi Rifle Regiment, the Red Shirts. He and his regiment took a conspicuous part in several battles, notably Buena Vista.

Davis parlayed his military reputation into a national political career in the 1850s. He was elected to the U.S. Senate, served as chairman of the Military Affairs Committee, and spoke out for the retention of all of Mexico conquered by the United States during the war on behalf of Southern rights in the debates over the **Compromise of 1850**. He even suggested that the South secede rather than submit to what he saw as Yankee perfidy, stealing the fruits of war by preventing the westward movement of **slavery**. Davis resigned his Senate seat, returned home to run for governor on the Secessionist ticket, but lost the race to a Union man by less than 1,000 votes.

The loss greatly discredited Davis, but he recovered when his old friend President **Franklin Pierce** invited him to serve as Secretary of War. As one of the most innovative secretaries the department ever had, he experimented with camels as beasts of burden, established numerous forts to protect Western travelers, and reorganized the variety of mounted regiments (dragoons, mounted rifles, and cavalry) in the army into five units of modern light cavalry. He also supported the building of a transcontinental railroad and was instrumental in completing the Gadsden Purchase for a Southern route out of New Orleans or Memphis.

At the end of Pierce's term, Mississippi returned Davis to the Senate. There he stood for the repeal of the **Missouri Compromise** and the extension of slavery to all of the Western territories. In 1860, Davis and other Southerners bolted the **Democratic Party** and set up Vice President **John C. Breckinridge** as their candidate. With a split Democratic Party, the rival **Republicans** easily nominated and elected **Abraham Lincoln** as president. Davis was mortified, but he urged the nation to stay whole. Unfortunately the crisis had passed beyond the politicians' control, resulting in the **first secession** of the lower South.

To his complete surprise, Davis was elected president of the provisional government of the Confederate States of America at Montgomery, Alabama, despite his procrastination. Once in office, he organized a cabinet of conservative Southerners like himself and set about to unify the South. The refusal of the Lincoln government to give up Forts Sumter in Charleston and Pickens in Pensacola forced the Confederates to fire the first shot to save face. The result was to unify the South—and the North—and cause a **second secession** of the upper South, followed by Davis's popular election as president of the Confederacy, headquartered in Richmond, Virginia.

Much has been written about Davis's inability to work with people of all beliefs, his favoritism to old West Point cronies, his preference for field command over political leadership (he had a neuralgia of the eye that intensified while he was in Richmond and mysteriously disappeared when he went out into the countryside to campaign or inspect the troops), and his willingness to argue an issue to its fine points. But he did manage to take a nation built from scratch and in four years nearly break up the United States.

With the defeat of the Confederate armies in the East, Davis fled South, hoping to get to the western part of the Confederacy but was captured by Union cavalry in Georgia. Davis spent the next two years under government arrest in Fortress Monroe, Virginia. He was released on May 13, 1867, upon a bail bond signed by Yankee publicist Horace Greeley and other long-time Davis opponents. The Virginia federal circuit court moved a *nolle prosequi* (no further prosecution) motion be entered in the Davis case and the appeal to the **Supreme Court** was dismissed. Davis was freed on February 26, 1869, not liable to prosecution in any jurisdiction of the United States.

Davis spent his retirement traveling and finally settled down in Beauvoir, a home near Biloxi, Mississippi, a gift from a friend. There he lived out his days, writing a defense of his actions as Confederate president (*The Rise and Fall of the Confederate Government*, in two long volumes). Relishing the role of elder statesman, while stripped of his rights as a citizen, he'd never surrendered, unreconstructed to the end. He died in New Orleans on a business trip. His body was later disinterred and shipped to Richmond in a procession across a half dozen Southern railroads that rivaled Abraham Lincoln's journey to Springfield 23 years earlier.

DE BOW'S COMMERCIAL REVIEW. Although its circulation was only 5,000 copies a month at its height in the 1850s, *De Bow's Review* or the *Commercial Review*, as many called it, was the premier Southern magazine of business, economics, and politics. Its founder and editor was James Dunwoody Brownson De Bow, a Charlestonian by birth. He had been educated as a lawyer and admitted to the South Carolina bar, but soon was contributing articles to the *Southern Quarterly*, a local magazine, of which he was soon editor. His most noted article was a lengthy justification of United States expansion into Oregon, then jointly occupied by the U.S. and Britain.

In 1845, De Bow moved to the biggest commercial center of the Old South, New Orleans. Here he established the *Commercial Review*, usually known simply as *De Bow's*. Copied after *Hunt's Merchant's Magazine* of New York City, De Bow discussed the growth of staple crops (like **tobacco, sugar**, and **cotton**), soil depletion and how to avoid it, plantation management, the expansion of the Cotton Kingdom into the Desert Southwest and the Caribbean, **slavery as a positive good, industrial slavery**, and Southern rights under the Constitution, including **secession**.

In 1853, De Bow became superintendent of the 1850 U.S. census and prepared the bound volumes of that counting of the American population, a statistical analysis, and an independent volume of "Industrial Resources of the Southwest." Such income was necessary because De Bow never made enough cash off his magazine to keep it going. He was especially miffed that no Southern printer could do a proper job publishing it and he had to farm out the task to Yankees, a fact he kept quiet from his subscribers. He also let out advertising in the late 1850s and found that Northern businesses bought most of it.

Although the subscription rate was low, the magazine had more influence in the South than the rate showed. He advocated Southern commercial, business, and industrial independence from the North. De Bow kept on publishing the magazine after the start of the Civil

War until the Union Army occupied New Orleans. De Bow resumed publication after the war, but his death in 1867 caused the *Commercial Review* to disappear forever.

DE LEON, EDWIN. *See* YOUNG AMERICA.

DEMOCRATIC REPUBLICANS. Because of the disenchantment that many felt, not with President **George Washington** so much as with the men behind him, opponents to these measures formed around **James Madison** in the House of Representatives. But Madison worked hard and successfully to bring **Thomas Jefferson** over as the front man for his political group, the Democratic Republicans, often called the Old Republicans (to differentiate them from the modern Republican Party chartered in 1854) or the Jeffersonians.

Madison and Jefferson came to believe that **Alexander Hamilton** and his **Federalists** were willing to play fast and loose with the Constitution as written. To expand their party northward, they allied themselves with an ambitious New York politician who had run for president in 1792, **Aaron Burr**. Conveniently, Burr was a political enemy of Hamilton in their home state and disliked Washington from his generalship during the war, which he found lacking in ability and aggressiveness.

Because Jefferson erroneously saw the French Revolution as a mirror of the American Independence movement, the Democratic Republicans tended to back the French side in the European wars. They favored **Pinckney's Treaty** with Spain, opposed Hamilton's economic program (**Funding and Assumption**, and the **Bank of the United States**), **John Adams**'s **Quasi-War** against France, the **Alien and Sedition Acts**, and the appointment of the **Midnight Judges**.

The Democratic Republicans would see Britain as America's natural enemy, an attitude that would lead to the **Embargo Act** and the **War of 1812**, as a second War for Independence. The good fortune that led to losing no territory in that war plus the Federalists' mistaken supplying of the British navy and support of the **Hartford Convention** led to the Democratic Republicans' domination and destruction of their political opponents. The result was the **Era of Good Feelings**, a one-party era that would dissolve in the **election of 1824**.

The Democratic Republicans tended to be strongest in the agrarian areas of the nation, North and especially South. Whatever their faults in relying on the **Slave Power Conspiracy**, the **Three-Fifths Compromise**, they looked West, because that was where potentially more three-fifths slave states lay. This often had little to do with **slavery** itself, but everything to do with Southern national political power in relation to the North, as typified by the **Virginia Dynasty** of American presidents.

DEMOCRATS. Those politicians called Jacksonians, who coalesced behind the figure of **Andrew Jackson** in 1828, went on to declare themselves Democrats by 1832. The party owed its existence to a loose North-South coalition between Virginia and New York as in the days of **Thomas Jefferson** and the **Virginia Dynasty**. Only this time, New York was in command.

The driving spirit in the formation of the Democratic Party was **Martin Van Buren**, a forgotten president nowadays, but a feared and respected politician in his own time. Andrew Jackson really had no stated political philosophy. He did everything by gut instinct, devil take the hindmost. But Van Buren did have something very specific in mind. He created a philosophy that the Democrats adhered to until the inauguration of Franklin D. Roosevelt in 1933.

Van Buren believed in restricted central power. Part of this was in his soul, part of it was to safeguard New York state's interests in the Erie Canal, the Port of New York, and Wall Street. New York had done everything on its own in the 1820s and surged ahead of other states and localities. Van Buren was damned if the federal government was going to help the others catch up. He remembered **Alexander Hamilton** and **Funding and Assumption** and how the South had to pay twice.

As the **Democratic Republican** Party became more and more **Federalist** in its outlook after the **War of 1812** and the formulation of the **New Nationalism** in the **Era of Good Feelings**, Van Buren wanted to end this Monroe Heresy, as he called it, and return to first principles of a weak federal government. He knew he was not alone. There were others who felt the same: William Crawford, Monroe's secretary of the treasury, and Thomas Ritchie of the Richmond Junto, a Virginia political machine, for example. Van Buren believed that if these Southerners would combine with the Albany Regency, his own New York political machine, they could make for a strong national political presence.

So Van Buren traveled south in the 1820s visiting politicos opposed to strong central government such as the Sage of Monticello, Jefferson, and receiving the benediction of the author of limited government. What he needed was a leader who would inspire the American people to vote his way, even if they did not understand why. That man was the hero, Andrew Jackson. Old Hickory was still boiling over the corrupt bargain in the **election of 1824**. His national popularity from the War of 1812 and the First Seminole War appealed to the new average-man-as-voter. He was more than happy to win the presidency for the new coalition, now labeled the Jacksonians, and, after he left the presidency, the Democrats.

Jackson's whole administration was subtly steered into a program of reduced patronage and economy by driving **John Quincy Adams**'s supporters into the **National Republicans**, steering a middle course on the **tariff**, keeping it strong enough to entice New York and Pennsylvania support, limiting public works to protect the Erie Canal, getting rid of Calhoun as a competitor for the presidency, placing businessmen in government to destroy the **Second Bank of the United States** and allow expansion of the economy, and removing the **Native American**s from the Old Northwest and Old Southwest to let the little man in on the economic expansion. And Van Buren controlled the whole thing. His reward was the presidency in the **election of 1836** and a party coalition that would last a hundred years.

DENMARK VESEY'S PLOT. *See* THE CHARLESTON REVOLT (1822).

DESERET, STATE OF. *See* MORMON WAR.

DEW, THOMAS R. (1802–1846). Born and raised in the Virginia tidewater, Thomas R. Dew was educated at William and Mary College where he became a professor of history, metaphysics, natural law, and political economy. Asked to review the Great Debates over **slavery** in Virginia in 1832, Dew used the opportunity to review the history of **slavery as a positive good**.

Dew pointed out that slavery was one of man's oldest institutions. Greece and Rome both had it and democracy, as did the American South. Indeed, slavery was seen as a merciful way to treat prisoners of war. There were also instances in which people sold themselves into slavery for self-protection as during the feudal age. The Old Testament showed the general nature of slavery as an institution sanctioned by God. Slavery, properly maintained, promoted paternalism and happiness in slave and master.

Dew then turned to Negro slavery in particular. Dew said that blacks had to be held in bondage because no other practical alternative was available. The property rights of the slaveowner had to be protected under the federal and state constitutions. To free the slaves would prove too costly. He pointed to the massive black rebellion in **Haiti** when French slaves were freed as a part of the Revolution of 1789. Slavery offered the only practicable manner in which to control the unbridled lusts of the African.

Dew's analysis was the first of many justifications for slavery. He used nearly every argument that others would employ in years to come. He would be rewarded by constant reprinting of his opinion and promoted to president of William and Mary College in 1836.

DISTRIBUTION. *See* JACKSON AND THE PUBLIC LANDS.

DOAKSVILLE, TREATY OF (1837). *See* INDIAN REMOVAL COMPLETED.

DONATION. *See* JACKSON AND THE PUBLIC LANDS.

DOUGH FACES. Invented by **John Randolph of Roanoke** in the 1820s, the term referred to Northern politicians who sided with Southerners on the *slavery* issue. Randolph disparaged such men as unreliable in the long run, easily bought out, issue by issue.

Although it would take until the 1850s for Randolph's prediction to come true, the dough faces were a key element to what Northerners saw as the Southern grip on the machinery of the federal government, which was known as the **Slave Power Conspiracy**. The **Jeffersonians** and the **Jacksonians** were both dependant on three facts of political life in the days of the Old South. One was the **Three-**

Fifths Compromise, another was the equal numbers of senators from the free and slave states, and the final factor was the presence of many Northern politicians in the federal government's executive, legislative, judicial branches, and national party caucuses who voted with Southerners on matters concerning slavery.

Indeed, four of the six Northerners (**Martin Van Buren, Millard Fillmore, Franklin Pierce, James Buchanan**) who served as president of the United States before the Civil War were transparently "dough faces." Only **John Adams** and his son, **John Quincy Adams**, were truly and consistently **anti-slavery** and pro-Northern. But dough face or not, all of the Northerners served single-term presidencies. Only real Southern slaveholders (**George Washington, Thomas Jefferson, James Madison, James Monroe,** and **Andrew Jackson**) received two-term tenures.

DOUGLAS, STEPHEN A. (1813–1861). Originally from Vermont, Stephen A. Douglas attended Canandaigua Academy in New York before relocating to Illinois. He studied law and taught school at Jacksonville and was admitted to the bar in 1834. Between 1835 and 1843, he served the **Democratic Party** and Illinois as state attorney, state legislator, secretary of state, and judge of the state supreme court. He was usually addressed as "Judge," but his nickname was the "Little Giant" because of his diminutive size.

In 1843, Douglas was elected to the U.S. House for two terms and served in the U.S. Senate from 1847 until his death 14 years later. Douglas was an expansionist on both Oregon and Texas, a supporter of the **War with Mexico,** and an opponent of the **Wilmot Proviso**. By proposing a separate vote for each measure in Henry Clay's Omnibus Bill, he got the **Compromise of 1850** passed in the Senate. Through his first wife, a Mississippi plantation owner with over 100 slaves, he had a personal connection to **slavery** in the South.

Douglas was leader of the **Young America Expansionist Movement** in the 1850s and a practitioner of "**Spread Eagle foreign policy**." He sponsored the **Kansas–Nebraska Act**, but opposed the pro-Southern Lecompton Constitution, drawn up in Lecompton, Kansas, which legalized slavery. To him this was a violation of **Popular Sovereignty**. Senior Southern Democrats coerced Douglas, then chairman of the committee on territories, to back Popular Sovereignty.

This caused him to break with President **James Buchanan,** who demanded that Congress admit Kansas as a slave state. Douglas used his influence to persuade western Democrats in the House to vote against the bill, and it was killed.

In 1858, Douglas agreed to debate his opponent for the Illinois Senate seat, **Abraham Lincoln.** Even though the election was by the state legislature, the two men gave seven speeches throughout the state to influence the vote. In the Freeport Debate, Douglas admitted that a territory could keep slavery from its borders prior to statehood by voting against laws in its favor. This **"Freeport Doctrine"** was a violation of his Popular Sovereignty concept, which won him the senatorial election in 1858 but cost him the presidential **election of 1860,** when the South deserted the party. Douglas's many attempts to compromise the coming of the Civil War met with failure. Weakened from exhaustion, he died from typhoid in 1861.

DOUGLASS, FREDERICK (ca. 1817–1895). Born into **slavery** in Talbot County, Maryland, of a black mother, Harriet Bailey, and an unknown white father, and originally named Frederick Augustus Washington Bailey, Frederick suffered the usual torment of slavery: neglect, cruelty, and hard labor, with an occasional respite from the drudgery and strife. But the tyranny of slavery thwarted Frederick's ambition and talent. In 1838, he escaped to New York City and assumed the name under which he became famous, Frederick Douglass.

In New York Douglass married a free woman of color whom he had met in Baltimore and they moved to New Bedford, Massachusetts where he worked as a common laborer. There he made his initial contact with **abolitionists** and became a lecturer for the Massachusetts Anti-Slavery Society. In addressing a meeting of the society in 1842, he displayed his famous oratorical style: "I appear before the immense assembly this evening as a thief and a robber. I stole this head, these limbs, this body from my master, and ran off with them." Thus began his lifelong commitment to free blacks from slavery and the noxious consequences of the second-class citizenship they suffered in the aftermath. In the process he was mobbed, beaten, mocked, and humiliated by being refused access to public accommodations, but those indignities never discouraged him.

Douglass carried himself with the comportment of a leader. Over six feet in height, he did not lower his eyes, mumble apologies, smile, or shyly retreat to the background as did so many blacks of his time, slave or free. His imposing appearance belied the fact that he had ever been in bondage. Douglass also founded an abolitionist journal, the *North Star*, and authored his memoirs, *Narrative of the Life of Frederick Douglass* in 1845, a best seller in the U.S. and Europe, where he vacationed until the controversy over his book died down.

The respect with which he was treated in Britain made him realize, for the first time in his life, that he was truly a free man. His concern with emancipation of his people made him the premier spokesman for their social equality and African-American economic and spiritual freedom. Besides abolition, Douglass supported advancing the rights of **women** and counseled John Brown in his **Harper's Ferry Raid**.

The Civil War brought Douglass to the forefront of black liberation activities. He devoted the rest of his days to the hope that future generations would see the conflict from an African-American and abolition perspective rather than a war where all were brave soldiers for their own brand of right. Douglass's view became the historical standard in the world of academia by the dawn of the new millennium.

When he died in 1895, five states adopted resolutions of regret, and two U.S. senators and a Supreme Court justice were among the honorary pallbearers. By the end of his life in the late 19th century, the cause of freedom had suffered a setback. Never giving up hope, he went to his death believing the African American could rise to the standard of American democracy by which all else must be measured.

DRED SCOTT v. SANDFORD (1857). In 1857, the only truly viable national political party belonged to the **Democrats.** They fought the **Republicans** in the North and the **Whig-Americans** in the South. While the other parties espoused extreme views on various issues, especially **slavery**, the Democrats moderated their principles to attract the widest variety of voters from all regions. In one of the most controversial and momentous decisions of the antebellum era, Democrats naïvely hoped that the Dred Scott case would solve the slavery issue in the territories and allow the nation to move forward to more pressing political issues such as settlement of the West, the building of the transcontinental railroad, and party building, graft, and the corruption rampant in the East.

One reason the Democrats were naïve in their expectations was that five of the seven Democratic justices on the **Supreme Court** were Southern slaveholders, with only one Whig and one Republican. President **James Buchanan** violated good protocol when he used his influence to persuade the Court to render a decision on slavery on the territories. He actively intervened with Justice Robert C. Grier from Pennsylvania to vote with the Southerners to give the decision a non-sectional appearance. Buchanan publicly denied in his inaugural address that he knew the Court's decision in advance, but he asked all good citizens to submit to the Court's decision as he promised he would.

Dred Scott had been a slave in Missouri all his life. While employed at Jefferson Barracks near St. Louis, army surgeon Dr. John Emerson legally bought Scott. Emerson's career necessitated frequent relocation to different posts. His next duty station was Ft. Armstrong at Rock Island, Illinois, where he brought Scott, even though Illinois was free territory under the **Northwest Ordinance** (1787) and by its own state constitution (1818). Later, Emerson was ordered to Ft. Snelling in Minnesota territory, free soil under the **Missouri Compromise** (1820). Scott accompanied him there and married another slave, Harriet, whom Emerson bought at Dred Scott's request. Their child, Eliza, was born on a Mississippi River steamboat between the free territory of Iowa and the free state of Illinois.

After returning to St. Louis, the doctor died in 1843, passing his slave property along to his wife and daughter. Mrs. Emerson's brother and executor to the estate was John F. A. Sanford of New York. He moved to St. Louis and regularly hired Dred Scott out, a common practice in the South. As an officer's aid during the war, Scott went to Mexico, where slavery had been illegal since 1821. He returned to St. Louis after the war and asked Mrs. Emerson for permission to buy himself and his family out of slavery. Mrs. Emerson, through Sanford, refused. Dred Scott then sued in state court for his freedom, on the grounds he had been illegally enslaved in a free territory and a free state. The Missouri district ruled him to be free but the state supreme court overturned the decision.

By now Scott had become a cause célèbre. Prominent lawyers Frank Blair, Jr. and Edward Bates appealed his case to the U.S. Federal Courts on the legal pretense that Scott was a citizen of Missouri and Sanford was still a resident of New York. Meanwhile, Mrs. Emerson married Massachusetts **abolitionist** Dr. Calvin Chaffee and they moved to his home state. He convinced her to free Scott, regardless of the court's decision, the U.S. District Court having ruled Scott still a slave. Just before the **election of 1856**, the case went to the nine-member U.S. Supreme Court. Chief Justice **Roger B. Taney**, prominent one-time Maryland slaveholder and **Jacksonian Democrat**, presided.

The Court ruled 7 to 2 that Dred Scott was still a slave but could not agree as to why. Each judge wrote a separate opinion. The chief justice's opinion became the prevailing explanation. Taney gave three reasons why Scott was still a slave:

First, Scott had no right to bring suit. He claimed to be a citizen of Missouri, but most free or slave states did not grant citizenship to blacks. This reason was adequate for Taney to dismiss the case, but he further pursued his agenda on behalf of the South by ruling that Scott's residency in a free territory or state was not reason enough to liberate him. This was because the **U.S. Constitution** gave slaveowners a legal **extraterritorial** protection to hold their slaves anywhere in the United States. Moreover, slavery was legal in territories until statehood, whereupon the new state could vote to become free or remain slaveholding. Just as Congress could not legislate against slavery without a constitutional amendment, neither could a creature of Congress, such as a territory. This meant that **Squatter Sovereignty** (the Democratic Party platform of 1848) was wrong, as was the **Missouri Compromise** in 1820; and **Popular Sovereignty** (the Democratic Party platform of 1852 and 1856) was correct, as was the **Kansas–Nebraska Act** in 1854. The **Republican Party** platform of 1856 disallowing slavery in the territories was unconstitutional.

Rather than deciding the slavery issue, Taney stirred up a tempest that energized all **anti-slavery** proponents throughout the North. It caused **Abraham Lincoln** to campaign against the Dred Scott case in the Illinois U.S. Senate race in 1858, when he challenged incumbent **Stephen A. Douglas** to a series of debates known as the **Lincoln–Douglas Debates**.

DRIVERS, SLAVE. A driver was a slave who set the pace of work of labor in the fields for the job that had to be accomplished on a day-by-day basis. He was in effect a black foreman for the gang system of labor. But drivers usually had the respect of the entire slave community on the plantation. They set a pace that most of the slaves could adapt to without being unduly fatigued and would still please the **overseer** or the slaveowner.

The drivers also administered the punishment of other slaves, including whippings. They were known for their leadership and ability to make the system function as fairly as possible. Overseers were usually not allowed to punish drivers without the intercession of the slaveowner or his **plantation steward**. Often the planter dispensed with white overseers and entrusted the running of the plantation to slave drivers. The big problem here was not the capabilities of the black foremen, but the fact that their abilities upset preconceived white notions of black inferiority. Free men of color were used as foremen, overseers, and stewards only in southern Louisiana, where preconceived notions of racial inferiority often yielded to practicality.

DUANE, WILLIAM. *See* BANK WAR.

DUELS. *See* VIOLENCE AND WHITE MILITANCY.

– E –

EATON, JOHN. *See* JACKSON'S BREAK WITH CALHOUN.

ECONOMY. While there is no key to a nation's economic growth, particular factors loom greater at specific times. For example, there are geographic sections, economic sectors, industries, and business firms. Thus it is possible to isolate one item and study it. In the Old South, this invariably leads to **cotton** and how it became King Cotton.

Cotton is a good example of how a negligible crop in the 18th century evolved into the single most important part of the American economy before the Civil War. It was assisted in its development by the **cotton gin**, fired by the demand of British textile growth, encouraged by a vast tract of virgin land that inspired the **Great Migration**, and cultivated by dint of a cheap labor source, **slavery**.

Along with the growth of cotton came the growth of New England's industry and the Old Northwest's agriculture. Also expanding was the American transportation system of roads, canals, riverboat traffic, trans-Atlantic shipping, and railroads. This was accomplished with a minimum of federal assistance because of Congress' rejection of **Henry Clay**'s so-called **American System** during the **Bank War**. Clay's proposal had relied on the limited credit provided by the **Bank of the United States**. The Andrew Jackson administration preferred the looser regulations and easy credit of the poorly regulated state and often totally unregulated private banks to finance Northern and Southern economic growth before the Civil War.

Overseas, Britain was advancing in its ability to turn out cotton products. A series of inventions pushed cotton milling forward. There was Arkwright's water frame (1769) that made thread and wound it on a spindle. Hargreaves' spinning jenny (1770) made finer, more malleable thread. Kay's flying shuttle (1773) doubled the production of each handworker. Crompton's mule (1779) combined the features of the water frame and spinning jenny into one machine. Cartwright's power loom (1785) mechanized the whole operation. And Watt's steam engine (1764, but not practicable until 1785) transformed cotton cloth production from a cottage industry into a centralized mill, the first real factories in the world, powered independently of waterfalls and streams.

The demand of Britain's mill industry for quality cotton was insatiable by 1800. Supply came from the Levant, Bermuda, the West Indies, Brazil, India, and Egypt. The American South contributed the long, silky **sea island** variety. But none of this was enough. It was into this market that **upland** short-staple **cotton** arrived. The United States could outproduce the rest of the world in cotton. It had the technology, the soil, the climate, the entrepreneurs, and the labor. And it was closer to Britain than other sources, making costs of shipping reasonable.

In 1784, a British customs official had seized eight bags of American upland cotton on the plausible grounds that the United States could not possibly grow that much. In 1791, America produced two million pounds of cotton—by 1860, it harvested one billion pounds, a 500-fold increase. Cotton was indeed King Cotton. Although much of the literature is aimless and wandering, slavery is often blamed for holding back the economic growth of the Old South before the Civil

War and condemning the large mass of whites to poverty. The critique falls in three general areas: slavery's effect on industrial labor; slavery's effect on the industrial market; and slavery's effect on hindering alternate forms of investment.

The first assertion revolves around the notion that **industrial slavery** was a contradiction in terms. Over 90 percent of slaves worked in simple agricultural pursuits because slaves were unable or unwilling to adapt to skilled trades. Yet this assertion is patently false. Most historians simply have failed to realize that slavery offered great possibilities of application to the industrial revolution that had been untapped before the Civil War. The future expansion of slavery into the mountain West through its employment in mining also loomed large.

A corollary to the inability to transfer slaves over to industrial labor is the assertion that the presence of slavery denied white **non-slaveholders** the opportunities of gaining skilled trades, too. Many of them fled the South to the Old Northwest, like Abraham Lincoln's parents, to be rid of slavery's economic influence and its demeaning of all labor. Yet it was these very Southern migrants who tried to get slavery introduced in the Old Northwest and nearly succeeded in the case of Illinois in the 1820s. Those left behind in the South eschewed industrial employment because of the innate independent streak that caused whites to prefer subsistence farming.

The second assertion, that slavery limited the industrial market in the South, relies on the notion that all southern farmers, non-slaveholders and planters alike, were self-sufficient or in the process of becoming so. This stifled the growth of industries and cities. Yet this ignores the fact that the Southern market for industrial goods averaged $200 million a year for Northern and European industries. The self-sufficiency argument is based on river trade, which did indeed decline. But the critics ignore the expanding railroad trade that took its place.

The third assertion, that slavery limited other forms of investment, has two parts. One is that Southern money was tied up in long-term investments in slaves. But this overlooks the profits the Atlantic Coast South and Kentucky made in the **domestic slave trade** when combined with the profits made in **staple crops**, like upland cotton's lowland cousin, Sea Island cotton, and **rice**, **indigo**, **hemp**, and **tobacco**. There was also **corn**, wheat, **livestock**, and **naval stores** (pitch, turpentine, and such), but cotton was over half of the total value of America's exports from the end of the **War of 1812 to secession**. Wheat and flour combined ran second at 16 percent and unmanufactured tobacco was third at 15 percent, but both declined after 1820. Foodstuffs from the Old Northwest then went to feeding the Old South's slave population. This made the South the most profitable economic force in the development of the nation at that time.

Others believe that planters wasted their earnings by living beyond their means. Although figures are hard to come by because of faulty accounting methods employed in plantation account books, throughout American history the wealthy have not only spent much on personal lifestyles, but invested much in various commercial ventures, too. There is no reason to suspect that rich Southerners did not do the same, speculating in Western lands, railroads, bonds, cotton mills, and other industries. Whatever industry the South did have by 1860 was built with the slaveowners' money from the **profitability of slavery**.

If the North's record in industrial development is better, it is because it did not have the profitable agriculture present in the South and no other place to invest but in industry, guarded by a protective **tariff** paid in large part by the South. It was not until after losing the Civil War that the South began its long and quite un-American experience with poverty as an economic colony of the North, providing raw materials for Northern industrial interests. Maybe it was slavery's fault after all.

EDUCATION. Because of the rural nature of the South, which led to a sparsely settled population and a weak tax base, public education was poorly attended to. Although some of the bigger towns had academies, the so-called "three R's" were all the average student was likely to receive, and often at scattered intervals, as teachers were poorly paid and unavailable. The upper classes, the children of planters, employed tutors. Boys were instructed in such topics as classical languages and history, mathematics, geography, and rhetoric. Girls were taught "polite" subjects like music, drawing, fancy needlework, dancing, French, geography, ciphering, letter writing, and elocution.

Most academies relied on some form of tuition to survive. Often they were taught and administered by people of much talent. But all in all, about one-third of the white population, especially in the states further to the Southwest, were illiterate. As it was against the law in most states to educate blacks, the figures for the slaves and free people of color were even more dismal.

During the 1830s, and once again during the 1850s, much effort was made to better the public education of white boys and girls through state-run schools backed by public taxation. South Carolina led the way, followed by Virginia and Georgia. But competition between education and **internal improvements** for the same limited tax base usually turned out to the detriment of education as a whole. This meant that a lot of educational improvement was theory on paper as opposed to practical reality.

Early in the 19th century, it was common for richer parents to send their boys to Northern colleges and universities, particularly Princeton, Harvard, and Yale. By 1820 there were as many as a dozen institutions of higher learning in the Old South, but they struggled to stay open. William and Mary College at Williamsburg, Virginia, had only 11 students in 1824. Others were lucky to graduate four or five students a year. The best college was Transylvania in Kentucky, which had an enrollment of 140 students in 1819. Military schools on all levels were available for boys. The colleges of the Citadel in South Carolina and Virginia Military Institute were among the best.

But college graduates had a great impact on the leadership of the Old South in politics, **church and religion**, law, and education. For example, 40 percent of the 111 Representatives and Senators of the Sixteenth Congress in 1819–1821 were college educated, half from Northern and half from Southern colleges and universities. Most institutions of higher learning in the Old South were allied with churches, Episcopal and Presbyterian predominating, with the Catholics running the College of Georgetown in the District of Columbia. The competition between religious sects meant that the education impetus was divided among too many institutions for the available money, public or private.

All colleges emphasized a classical education, based on Latin and Greek. Besides the subjects that students were expected to know from their academy educations, the colleges offered astronomy, philosophy, science, history, English grammar, surveying, navigation, and agriculture. The moral conduct of the student was often deemed more important than any scholarly subject, but then as now, most students were known as well for their extra-curricular activities as their scholarship.

One of the major problems facing Southern education was the predominance of Yankee-oriented textbooks, often with an **anti-slavery** tinge. In the 1850s there was a drive to produce Southern-oriented texts that grew with the advent of the Civil War. Proper questions might posit, as did one algebra textbook, "A Yankee drummer was selling jars with 10 real nutmegs and 5 wooden nutmegs. What percentage of the nutmegs were wooden?"

ELECTION OF 1788. The first U.S. presidential election was held in January 1789. Depending on the state, the legislature or the people chose the electors. It did not matter much. Everyone knew that **George Washington** would be the unanimous choice in a non-partisan, non-sectional election. The second place went to **John Adams**. The votes were opened and counted and Washington inaugurated by 30 April.

ELECTION OF 1792. Once again, **George Washington** was the choice of all the electors, three votes abstaining. As the abstentions showed, the notion of political parties was beginning to take root. This was seen particularly in the vote for vice president, where **Aaron Burr**'s mentor, George Clinton, calling himself an **Anti-Federalist**, received 50 votes to **John Adams**'s 77. Parties were not wholly sectional, North and South being represented in each party on a more or less equal basis.

ELECTION OF 1796. The first real presidential election in American history was the election of 1796, the first one in which the hallowed **George Washington** did not participate. His absence put everyone before the American people on a more or less party basis, but not by North or South. The **Federalists** ran Washington's vice president, **John Adams**, and Thomas Pinckney of **Pinckney's Treaty** fame. The **Democratic Republicans** put up **Thomas Jefferson** and his New York ally, **Aaron Burr**.

One might have expected **Alexander Hamilton** to have entered the lists, but he had so many enemies that he could not. Besides, in the middle of the contest, his affair with a married woman came to light, damaging him politically forever. But Hamilton was the true head of the Federalist Party and operated behind the scenes. This galled Adams because, throughout his term, the party reacted to Hamilton's desires more than to his as president. No Adams was ever satisfied to be number two.

Because of their enmity, the Federalists stupidly allowed Hamilton to manipulate the electoral vote to try and make Pinckney the winner and force Adams to stay as vice president. Pennsylvania and South Carolina were to vote for Pinckney and Jefferson. When the New England states heard of this, they voted Adams and Jefferson. The upshot was that Adams was elected president in the Electoral College, but Jefferson wound up as vice president. Worse for the future of the Democratic Republicans, Jefferson foolishly allowed Virginia delegates to vote for Pinckney rather than Burr. Four years later, in the **election of 1800**, Burr would remember this slight.

ELECTION OF 1800. Having turned up short in 1796, the **Democratic Republicans** were not about to lose in 1800. This time there would be no mistakes. Every elector in the Electoral College would vote for **Thomas Jefferson** and **Aaron Burr**. The key to getting the correct electors would be the 12 votes from the slave South guaranteed by the **Three-Fifths Compromise** and the dozen votes from New York City produced by Burr.

Jefferson did not like Burr. There was something shady and untrustworthy about the man. Still, to win, the Democratic Republicans had to have Burr's New York and Jefferson's Virginia. But the errors came fast and hard. Exactly what Jefferson and his Virginia electors feared happened—the two men, Jefferson and Burr, tied. Now the election would have to go the House of Representatives, with each state having one vote. It would be decided by the lame-duck House— the one left over from the by-election of 1798. It had a **Federalist** majority. But each state delegation was free to choose, as it desired, the election results be damned. And a tie vote among a state's delegation meant no vote in the presidential contest. But first, knowing that they had lost the executive and legislative branches of the federal government, the Federalists' lame-duck Congress passed the Judiciary Act of 1801, which packed the federal court system with loyal party men known as **Midnight Judges**.

It was obvious that Burr was slick enough to appeal to the Federalists. Jefferson was an ideologue. He tried to get Burr to commit to being vice president. Burr hedged. The Federalists meanwhile got James Bayard of Delaware to present their views. They wanted a guarantee that neither Jefferson nor Burr would dismantle their programs, like Alexander Hamilton's **Funding and Assumption** Program and the new navy, wholesale. Jefferson was vague, but promising. Burr refused to deal. So Bayard arranged to have enough Federalists abstain from voting to let Jefferson beat Burr. But no Federalist had to vote for Jefferson. This peaceful transition of political power from one party to another came to be called the "Revolution of 1800."

ELECTION OF 1804. Thomas Jefferson and the **Democratic Republicans** had pretty well destroyed the **Federalists** outside of New England by the end of his first term as president, creating a political party based in the South and dependent on **Three-Fifths Compromise** votes to win. All Jefferson had to do was find a replacement for the discredited **Aaron Burr**. He did this by turning to Burr's greatest Democratic-Republican political competitor in New York, his former mentor, George Clinton. The Federalists put up Charles Cotesworth Pinckney of South Carolina (to conceal their Northern emphasis) and Rufus King of New York. The only real opposition Jefferson faced was from within his own party. Led by **John Randolph** of Roanoke, a dissident element, the Tertium Quids, broke from supporting Jefferson over the **Yazoo Land Frauds**. But Jefferson and Clinton carried a majority in the electoral college.

ELECTION OF 1808. By the end of his second term as president, **Thomas Jefferson** willingly stepped down to honor the two-term tradition set by **George Washington** in 1796. His successor as presidential nominee was Secretary of State **James Madison**, the originator of American political parties with his creation of the **Democratic Republicans** to oppose Alexander Hamilton's **Federalists** in the early 1790s. To solve the perennial problem of **Aaron Burr**, Madison kept George Clinton as vice president, head of the anti-Burr Democratic-Republican faction in New York.

The Federalists ran Charles Cotesworth Pinckney of South Carolina and Rufus King of New York. The election was pretty one-sided, with

Madison winning easily, despite opposition of **John Randolph** and the Tertium Quids from his own party. The Quids supported **James Monroe**. Some backers of the Clinton family in New York wanted their man to succeed Jefferson, but Clinton was really too old and would die in office soon after the election. The election of 1808 confirmed the primacy of the **Virginia Dynasty** and the succession of the secretary of state as next president, making the vice presidency more irrelevant than ever.

ELECTION OF 1812. Because of the disastrous first year of the **War of 1812**, there was much opposition to **James Madison** being re-elected to the presidency. Of course the New England **Federalists** were against what they saw as the capstone to a ruinous campaign of destroying American trade to Europe through the **Embargo Act** and now war. But many members of the **Democratic Republican Party** disliked the war, too. Southerners could see no reason to fight for Canadian soil, and many northern Democratic Republicans sided with the Federalists. They tended to see Madison as a willing tool in the hands of the **War Hawks** and **Henry Clay**.

Madison managed to assuage southern members to gain unanimous renomination. As Vice President George Clinton had died in office, the party picked New England Democratic Republican and Federalist defector (over the X, Y, Z, Affair) Elbridge Gerry as vice president. The Clinton faction was outraged. They put up DeWitt Clinton of New York (nephew of George Clinton) as their presidential nominee. The Federalists also turned to Clinton, who vowed he was an American Federalist (whatever that meant) against the war, with Federalist Charles J. Ingersoll of Pennsylvania as vice president.

Madison managed to carry the presidency—just barely. Had Pennsylvania gone Federalist (which is why Ingersoll was on the ticket), the Federalists would have won. Madison's political coattails were not long either. The Federalists took every state north of the Potomac except Pennsylvania and Vermont, and managed to double their representatives in Congress.

ELECTION OF 1816. Immediately after the **War of 1812** came a new presidential election. President **James Madison** chose to follow the two-term tradition—he probably would not have won had he run. The

Democratic Republican nominee was Madison's Secretary of State **James Monroe**. As Vice President Elbridge Gerry had died in office, the second spot on the ticket went to Daniel D. Tompkins, a jovial, drunken party hack from New York.

Younger party members and the **War Hawks** of 1812 wanted some one more exciting than staid old James Monroe. They settled on William H. Crawford of Georgia. In the party caucus that did the nominating, Monroe won by only six votes.

The **Federalists**, isolated by the recent **Hartford Convention** to support in New England, advanced no candidate. They hoped to give the Democratic Republicans a lot of room to splinter, hoping to pick up the pieces. But Federalist electors all voted for their old standby, Rufus King of New York. There was no vice presidential candidate. It was the last time the Federalists ran a national ticket. They ran locally in the states and sent some members to Congress, but nothing else. Monroe won the presidential election easily.

ELECTION OF 1820. In his try for a second term, **James Monroe** ran unopposed with Vice President Daniel Tompkins of New York in the second slot. He was expected to win all of the electoral votes, but one elector voted for **John Quincy Adams**. Supposedly this was to keep **George Washington** as the only unanimously elected president. But the elector admitted that he thought Monroe lacked foresight and neglected his duty. He was not alone. There were plenty of younger party members who wanted the presidency, but they all knew that a bid during the **Era of Good Feelings** against a popular president would bode ill for their future public appeal. They would all wait for 1824.

ELECTION OF 1824. As frequently happens in a one-party situation, one gets a multitude of candidates, each one running on personality or similar issues. The election of 1824 was such a case. A half dozen men entered the race, all **Democratic Republicans**, a situation made possible because President **James Monroe** refused to endorse a successor. All of his predecessors had done so, and it was one of the things that had kept the **Virginia Dynasty** strong. But no Virginian entered the 1824 contest and Monroe remained noncommittal.

The first man to enter the race was William H. Crawford of Georgia, a noted duelist and the current secretary of the treasury. Crawford was an original Jeffersonian, a man who believed in strong state government rather than power emanating out of Washington. He had been in favor of the **New Nationalism**, but the **Missouri Compromise** had changed his viewpoint. He was nominated by the Democratic Republican Party caucus composed of senators and representatives. But the caucus was on the way out and few of its members even bothered to attend. Crawford's chances were hurt when he suffered a stroke in mid-campaign.

The next man to announce was expected. This was the current secretary of state, **John Quincy Adams**. The secretary of state's job had been the traditional entry position for Democratic Republicans desiring to become president. But Adams had a weakness. He was a former **Federalist** and believed in a stronger central government than most of his opponents. He was nominated by officeholders from Massachusetts, his home state.

Like Adams, **Henry Clay** was a strong government man. He had been a **War Hawk** in 1812, and now he had a well-developed program designed to build America's economy, much as **Alexander Hamilton** had acted 35 years before. It was called the **American System**. But its emphasis on **tariffs** and industrial power discriminated against the slave South, although Clay really did not intend it.

A fourth candidate was William Lowndes, a War Hawk like Clay. A South Carolina aristocrat and slaveholder (as were all of the candidates except Adams, showing the Southern prejudices of the party), he hated Crawford for not being a proper gentleman. He had been nominated by his state's legislature, but had died before his campaign could get under way. But South Carolina would not be found wanting. Lowndes was replaced by **John C. Calhoun**, Monroe's secretary of war. Calhoun had a cold, legalistic mind that was shifting from the New Nationalism to states' rights. Indeed he was exactly like Adams in personality but the complete opposite in political philosophy.

Suddenly, Calhoun did something strange. He announced that he would seek the vice presidency, an office for which no one else was running. The reason was soon apparent. A new entry in the presidential field came out of Tennessee. He was the great hero of the **War of 1812**—none other than **Andrew Jackson.**

When the electoral votes were counted, Calhoun won the vice presidency handily—he had been on everyone else's ticket, after all.

But no one had a majority of the electoral votes for president. There were too many candidates for that. Jackson came in first in popular votes and electoral votes, Adams came in second in both votes, Crawford had the third place in electoral votes but fourth in popular votes. And Clay had fourth in electoral votes and third in popular votes. The House of Representatives would make the decision from among the top three in electoral votes, each state having one vote. As it happened, the Speaker of the House was none other than Clay, the odd man out. He would count the votes.

It was obvious that Clay and Adams had the most similar programs, so Clay threw his support to Adams, and Jackson, even though he had won the most popular and electoral votes, lost. Adams was inaugurated in March 1825, with Clay appointed as his secretary of state and presumptive heir.

ELECTION OF 1828. Among the four presidential candidates in the 1824 election, **Andrew Jackson** had received the larger number of popular and electoral votes, but not enough for victory. By constitutional prescription, the House of Representatives had to decide the outcome. Ultimately, second place **John Quincy Adams** received the support of fourth place (and conveniently also Speaker of the House) **Henry Clay** which guaranteed Adams the prize, and he obligingly appointed Henry Clay secretary of state in the new administration, the traditional position at that time for the next president. The Jacksonians immediately proclaimed the deal to be a "Corrupt Bargain," a charge that was never proved, but one that tainted Quincy Adams' administration forever and led to a four-year election campaign against him.

As early as October 1825, the Tennessee legislature named Andrew Jackson as their choice for 1828. Then Jackson's supporters in Congress began to oppose anything and everything Adams proposed. This was not hard, as Adams was about a century ahead of his generation in his concept of what the federal government ought to do. Adams supported a Pan-American Conference his opponents said would give away U.S. sovereignty. He refused to remove the **Native Americans** supposedly impeding the spread of cotton culture and the exploitation of gold discoveries in the South.

But there was more. Adams wanted to found a national university, finance national scientific expeditions, establish standard weights and measures, build a national observatory, create a Department of the Interior, reform patent laws, and finance roads and canals all over the country. He also asked that it all be passed on one act. Congress rejected it all. In 1826, Adams became the first president in U.S. history to lose both houses of Congress to his opposition. By the end of his term, the only piece of legislation to his credit was the **Tariff of 1828**, so high it became known as the Tariff of Abominations in the South.

Jackson supporters presented him as the "Hero of New Orleans," "the People's Candidate," "the Farmer from Tennessee," anything to enhance his image as an average man made good. Because of his toughness, he came to be known affectionately as "Old Hickory" (the first American president to have an endearing nickname). At rallies and barbecues his "Hurra Boys" (campaign workers) handed out hickory sticks, canes, and hickory-handled brooms designed to sweep the corrupt Adams men from office and purify American politics once again.

The corrupt bargain was a constant theme, fortified by Adams use of gambling furniture in the White House (he had bought a billiards table with his own funds, but such things get twisted around in the heat of an election). The Adams family was characterized as the American House of Stuart, a reference to the high-handed British royal family thrown out in the Glorious Revolution of 1688.

Adams supporters compiled a list of Old Hickory's sins, which included everything just short of sodomy. Among Jackson's misdeeds were adultery, gambling, cock fighting, slave trading (which revealed Adams to be a Yankee with no sympathy for the South and its peculiar institution), bigamy, drunkenness, theft, lying, and murder.

The Adams men even distributed a single-sheet "Coffin Handbill" bordered in black which pictured six coffins and names of six militiamen whom, they charged, Jackson had murdered in cold blood (Jackson had executed them for mutiny) during the **War of 1812**. It was further charged that Jackson was but one of several offspring of a "common prostitute" brought to the U.S. by British troops and who eventually married a "mulatto man." Pro-Adams crowds paraded before a Nashville hotel where Jackson was staying, waving banners that said, "The A B C of Democracy: Adulterer, Bully, Cuckold."

Jackson swept the whole nation but New England, Delaware, Maryland, and New Jersey. This was the first election in which property rights were not a prerequisite for voting. After Jackson won, the people, the common man, decided to come to Washington for the inaugural. Drunk and rowdy, they tore up the city and the White House. Jackson, old and frail from his numerous bullet wounds, was very nearly crushed to death as the crowd surged to meet him. He was only rescued when a quick-thinking aide pulled the whiskey barrels outside. First things first. The White House lost a few full-length French doors with windows, but the action saved the president.

ELECTION OF 1832. Three parties put forward presidential candidates in 1832. The first was the Anti-Masonic Party. It had been created in western New York state on a platform of opposing secret societies. The Masons were supposedly an anti-papist, Protestant and Jewish group descended from medieval stonemasons that now devoted their time to studying the Bible and engaging in secret quasi-religious ceremonies.

Many important politicians were members. One William Morgan had revealed some of their rituals in a book and he had later been arrested on a trumped-up charge, kidnapped from jail, and dumped over Niagara Falls. When the public demanded an accounting, supposedly office-holders who were also Masons had prevented justice from being done. The result was a political movement against privilege that fielded many candidates in New York, Ohio, Massachusetts, and Pennsylvania. These Anti-Masons were largely **anti-slavery** reformers who later became prominent in the **Whig** and **Republican** parties.

The Anti-Masonic Party held the first national convention in American history at Baltimore in 1831. All other political parties down to the present day would copy it. The party nominated James Monroe's attorney general, William Wirt of Maryland. His vice presidential running mate was Amos Elmaker from Pennsylvania. It adopted the first party platform (against privilege and elites) and was the first third party in American history, too.

The second party to field candidates was the Old **National Republicans**. Now they called themselves **Whigs**. The notion was that they opposed King Andrew I of veto memory, much as the American and British Whigs had opposed the evil King George III during the

American Revolution. The party's presidential nominee was **Henry Clay** of Kentucky. Running with Clay was John Sergeant of Pennsylvania. They offered the nation a choice. Clay stood for civilian politicians as opposed to "General" Jackson, opposed the spoils system, **Indian removal**, and Jackson's all-too-frequent veto. But their main issue was that Jackson was ruining the American economy by vetoing the Bank bill. They too held a convention at Baltimore.

Finally, the **Democrats** nominated **Andrew Jackson** for president and **Martin Van Buren** for vice president, also in a Baltimore convention (it was the most centrally located city in a nation with few roads). As the nation entered the election of 1832, it was not obvious that Jackson would win. Indeed Jackson had promised to serve but one term before stepping down for **John C. Calhoun** or Van Buren.

But now his blood was up, and Jackson would run to get his job completed. **Jackson's break with Calhoun** and denial of the **Concurrent Voice and Nullification** had alienated the Southeast. Indian Removal had angered religious groups in the Northeast. The **Maysville Road Veto** had hurt him in the West. The **bank veto** had hurt him with business groups, North and South. And his selection of Martin Van Buren as his vice presidential nominee alienated the whole South, including Jackson's home state of Tennessee.

To make Van Buren look popular, Jackson insisted that the party nominate him with a two-thirds vote. This rule would linger on for 100 years because it gave the South an absolute veto over the party's national candidates. The Democrats had no real platform. They just put Jackson forth as the hero who had vetoed the renewal of the **Second Bank of the United States** and stood against all privilege.

The Democrats easily won the electoral vote. The election of 1832 stabilized the Democratic coalition around Jackson and Van Buren and gave what Jackson saw as a mandate from the people to destroy the Second Bank of the United States in his **Bank War**.

ELECTION OF 1836. Henry Clay was pretty much used goods but refused to admit it, so **Daniel Webster** accepted the nomination from his home state of Massachusetts. Most party men believed that he was the best candidate, particularly in his home area of New England. He was the most regular in support of the Whig economic philosophy, Clay's **American System**.

But Webster had competition for the presidential nomination. **Hugh Lawson White** of Tennessee had much support in the Old Southwest. White and his political ally, **John Bell**, resented that Jackson had cut them out of all political patronage, giving it instead to **James K. Polk**. Moreover, like many Southerners, neither man could stomach **Martin Van Buren** as head of the **Democrats** and now forced on the party by Jackson. So they bolted and put up White as a better candidate than Webster. The Tennessee and Alabama legislatures nominated White.

Clay may not have been the nominee, but he hoped to be the kingmaker. He supported **William Henry Harrison** of Ohio. Give Clay credit for a good choice. A hero of the **War of 1812**, negotiator of numerous Indian treaties that opened the Old Northwest to white settlement, "Old Tippecanoe" was as close to Andrew Jackson in popularity with the average voter as either party came.

But no one but Nicholas Biddle, the loser of the **Bank War**, saw this. Biddle wanted to give Harrison his head and make him another Jackson with a "hurrah" campaign like the one that elected Old Hickory in 1828. But party elders demurred. Instead they loaded the party with a platform of negatives. They accused Jackson of not reforming the government as he had promised. They accused him of arbitrary use of the veto. They charged him with corrupting the government through appointments to office and postmasterships. And they accused him of disrespecting Congress and the Supreme Court.

The party could not agree as to who should represent them as the nominee. So they ran all three men, hoping to throw the election into the House of Representatives as in the **election of 1824**. Webster would appeal to New England, White to the Southeast and Southwest, and Harrison to the Northwest and mid-Atlantic states.

The Democrats nominated Van Buren, who had to garner two-thirds of the convention votes. For their vice presidential nominee, the Democrats went with **Richard Mentor Johnson** of Kentucky. Johnson was a hero from the War of 1812 and the reputed slayer of the famed Shawnee chief, Tecumseh, at the Battle of the Thames. But Johnson had a problem. He had a black wife, or mistress, depending upon one's point of view. Johnson did not try and hide her or her mulatto children by Johnson. The result was that while Van Buren won the electoral vote, Johnson did not take sufficient electoral votes to win in his own right. So the vice presidential race was decided in the U.S. Senate, with the party whip cracking loud and clear.

The election of 1836 showed that Biddle had been right about Harrison. If the party had dropped all of the anti-Jackson statements and the American System and run Harrison as their hero, he might have swept the day. The same mistake would not happen in the **election of 1840**.

ELECTION OF 1840. The **Democrats** were stuck in 1840 in a bad situation. They would have liked to ditch both President **Martin Van Buren** and his running mate, Vice President **Richard Johnson**. But to do so would be to admit to **Whig** charges of incompetence and blame for the **Panic of 1837**. So the party renominated both men and awaited the inevitable onslaught.

The Whigs met at Harrisburg, Pennsylvania. As usual, **Henry Clay** was available and wanted the nomination. He was not too shy about it, either, referring to his being "forced" into the presidential arena. But the party had other ideas. Of special importance was the old **Anti-Masonic** element, led by Thurlow Weed of New York and his political front man, William H. Seward. They rejected Clay as a slaveholder, a man reprehensible to other former Anti-Masons, and too much in favor of the old **Second Bank of the United States**, the issue that had cost the party the **election of 1832**.

What Weed and Seward wanted was a military hero. They wanted a Whig **Andrew Jackson**. Their choice was Maj. Gen. **Winfield Scott**, hero of the **War of 1812** and the recent **Canadian Boundary Dispute**. Clay quickly took a "vacation" to western New York. But Weed and Seward refused to budge. Clay bitterly withdrew his name and took another vacation to Europe. The electoral field was open to victory—with the appropriate candidate. At the convention, **Daniel Webster** agreed with the New Yorkers that a military hero was needed as the party's nominee. But he proposed it be **William Henry Harrison**, a proven vote getter from the **election of 1836**.

To appease Clay's disappointed supporters, the convention chose **John Tyler** of Virginia as the vice presidential nominee. He was a friend of Clay, a strict interpreter of the Constitution (but Clay and the convention were not aware of how deeply these views were held).

The party was now united on national and local levels because there was no platform to disagree on.

The Democrats took heart at seeing Harrison at the head of the Whig ticket. He was dismissed as a "granny" or "old lady." They said that Harrison would look better getting his $2,000 military pension, sitting in front of a log cabin, drinking cider from a jug. The Whig publicists read this and thought why not? The result was the "Hurrah" campaign of "Tippecanoe and Tyler, too, against "Martin Van Ruin."

Slogans, songs, rhymes, bands, and barbecues were the order of the day. "With Tip and Tyler we'll bust Van's biler," the Whigs boasted. But the crowning achievement was to call Harrison the "Log Cabin" candidate. Then a Cincinnati distiller names E. C. Booz put up little shots of hard cider in tin log cabins. Crowds everywhere shouted, "Bring on the Booze," and a new word entered the American language.

It was all over before it started. The popular vote was 50,000 apart but the electoral vote gave four times the numbers to Harrison. The Democrats screamed, "We have taught them to conquer us!" and dismissed the Whigs as "bastard Federalists."

But there was a discord that went unnoticed by the major parties. A third party, calling itself the **Liberty Party**, ran an anti-slavery ticket. Stimulated by the lynching of **abolitionist** newspaper editor E. P. Lovejoy in Alton, Illinois, they accused both Whigs and Democrats of kowtowing to slave interests and being unwilling to support free speech, necessitating a new party. This problem of **slavery** and the **Slave Power Conspiracy** would take on new meaning as the 1840s ground on toward a **War with Mexico**.

ELECTION OF 1844. The election of 1844 is a perfect example of how politicians can misread the minds of the people. It all began when the Texas issue popped up again. An election in the Republic of Texas had given it a new president, or rather, an old one back again. Mirabeau B. Lamar, an expansionist and republic advocate, had lost out to Sam Houston. Houston was against Texas invasions of Mexican Territory that had marked the Lamar administration. He believed that Texas' true destiny lay with annexation to the United States.

But until now, no one had been able to pull it off. U.S. domestic politics worked against it. But there was a new movement loose in

America, one that emphasized American expansion to the Pacific coast as God's **manifest destiny** for the nation. It would extend the area of freedom and democracy—never mind that this extension would be accompanied by its antitheses, black **slavery** and the **Three-Fifths Compromise,** which kept the **Slave Power Conspiracy** in power.

It was the quarrel between President **John Tyler** and **Whig** Party leader **Henry Clay** that made it all possible. Clay had resigned as secretary of state to get ready to capture the presidency from the hated Tyler. In his place, Tyler appointed his secretary of the navy, a fellow Virginian with his political sensibilities, Abel Upshur. Devoted to the spread of slavery and the Three-Fifths Compromise, Upshur went right to work.

Suddenly, Upshur (the former secretary of the navy) was killed in a naval gun explosion during a demonstration on board ship. Tyler turned to **John C. Calhoun** as his new secretary of state. Calhoun had avoided the Tyler administration up to now, but the possible annexation of Texas was too much to pass by. Calhoun completed the negotiations. Texas was to be admitted as a territory. This way the maximum number of slave states with **Three-Fifths Compromise** congressmen could be created in the future. Texas would cede its public lands to the U.S. and America would assume the debt of the republic up to $10 million.

The whole North rose up in protest. The Senate killed the Texas Treaty. Calhoun saw in this incident something he held dear to his heart—a chance to get even with **Martin Van Buren** over the Eaton Affair during Andrew **Jackson's first administration**. Everyone assumed that Van Buren would be the Democrat nominee for the presidency in 1844. So Calhoun had a friend write Andrew Jackson and ask his opinion of the annexation. Annex Texas now, came the reply.

But Van Buren and Henry Clay, everyone's favorite to be the Whig presidential nominee, had already made a deal to keep **Texas annexation** out of the election. There would be no annexation of Texas at this time, they said. Clay received the Whig nomination without a hitch. But on his way to the nomination, Van Buren ran up against his previously loyal Southern Democrats. They were not amused. Stop the expansion of America, especially Southern slave America! No way, said the Southerners at the convention.

The Democratic convention still had the two-thirds rule for nomination—the one Jackson passed in 1836 to show Van Buren's popularity as his successor. But here was Jackson and the whole slave South calling for annexation. Van Buren could not get the votes. For the first time in American history, an issue, manifest destiny as represented by the annexation of Texas, caused the Democrat convention to nominate a dark horse, a candidate not in the running before the convention met. Introduced by expansionist Robert J. Walker of Mississippi, he was **James K. Polk**, Jackson's neighbor from Tennessee. His vice presidential nominee, George M. Dallas, was actually better known than he at the time.

Unlike Clay and Van Buren, Polk was in favor of what a clever Ohio Democrat newspaper called the "Re-annexation of Texas and the Re-occupation of Oregon." It was so compelling that John Tyler, who sought the presidential renomination as an Independent Whig, switched sides to Polk, Walker easing the way. Tyler was a Democrat again, and the first American president not to be renominated for a second term. He would later be elected to the Confederate Congress, just before his death in 1862.

The **abolitionists** were so worked up at the idea of Texas extending the domain of domestic slavery that they ran James G. Birney, a transplanted Alabama planter who was against slavery, in the Liberty Party. Birney pledged to divorce the federal government from promoting slavery in the West. The Liberty Party wanted non-extension and no-annexation.

Polk cleverly dodged the hot **tariff** issue, the only one that could trip him up. He said he wanted a revenue tariff that would protect industry, more or less a contradiction in terms. "Polk, Dallas, and the Tariff of '42," went the slogan. To keep the Northern Democrats happy, it was "54°40' or Fight!" That is, Polk wanted all of Oregon, including today's Washington, Oregon, and British Columbia. Clay tried to hedge on his no-annexation promise, but all that did was cost him key votes in western New York that went to Birney.

The result was that Polk won by capturing the electoral vote of New York. Had Clay taken it, as he should have, he would have been president. He won not a single electoral vote south of Tennessee. The election of 1844 showed that whenever Southern issues were involved, Southern Whigs and Democrats would stand together to guard slavery and its expansion, party be damned.

ELECTION OF 1848. Although both major political parties, the **Democrats** and the **Whigs**, were bi-sectional and, as such, affected by the **slavery** issue as proposed in the **Wilmot Proviso,** which called for excluding slavery in the territories, the Democrats were hit the hardest during the election of 1848. Party regulars were determined to work out some sort of compromise on slavery in the territories. Developed by Vice President George M. Dallas of Pennsylvania and publicized by their 1848 presidential nominee **Lewis M. Cass** of Michigan, the party regulars' solution was to let the people in the territories vote on the slavery issue, a measure they termed **Squatter Sovereignty.**

Obstacles stood in their way, however. **John C. Calhoun**, slowly dying after 40 years of public service, saw the trick in Squatter Sovereignty—only Mexicans and Yankees occupied the territories. The South and its slaves would be excluded before they could think of moving west. Southern **fire-eaters**, led by **William L. Yancey** of Alabama, objected by backing the **Non-Exclusion Doctrine,** allowing slavery in the territories until a proposed state constitution was drawn up and the territory admitted to the Union as a state.

Yancey's northern counterparts in New York state, called Barnburners (their opponents accused them of being so extreme as to burn down the barn [the nation] to get rid of the rats [slavery]), stood for the Wilmot Proviso—no slavery in any territory. Cass refused to support either extreme. In a letter to Democrat stalwart A. O. P. Nicholson, he stated his neutrality, support of Squatter Sovereignty, and the rule of the majority. Extremists on both sides refused to back him as a nominee, especially after President **James K. Polk** created Oregon Territory north of the **Missouri Compromise** line and therefore without slavery. Feeling betrayed by Polk, a slaveholder, the South could not trust the centrist, non-slaveholding Cass.

The slavery issue also divided the Whigs, who craftily nominated military hero Gen. **Zachary Taylor**, the victor of Buena Vista, despite his drawbacks. His being a slaveholder pleased the South, but never having voted in his entire life, he declared himself a Whig but not an ultra-Whig. He backed certain **tariffs** and **internal improvements**, but not to the extent of lifetime Whig candidate **Henry Clay**. Taylor won the nomination, but Northerners known as Conscience Whigs deserted the party.

The Conscience Whigs joined the Northern Democrats in backing the remnants of the anti-slavery Liberty Party. Salmon P. Chase brought them together at Buffalo, New York, where they declared themselves the **Free Soil Party**. They nominated **Martin Van Buren**, who had created the **Democratic Party** in 1828 with slaveholding **Andrew Jackson** as their candidate. Now old Van had seen the **anti-slavery** light—or at least, another route to the presidency.

With the support of Southern Democrats and most Whigs, Taylor won the election with 163 electoral votes to Cass's 127. Van Buren received no electoral votes, but garnered 10 percent of the popular vote. Taylor's first task in office was to solve the problem of slavery in the territories, which became the **Compromise of 1850**.

ELECTION OF 1852. Even though **Whig** President **Millard Fillmore** had signed the **Compromise of 1850**, the measure was essentially a creation of the **Democrats** with support from Southern Whigs. The Northern Whigs were lukewarm on the Compromise of 1850, as was U.S. Senator **William H. Seward** of New York, who spoke of a "higher law" than the **U.S. Constitution** that justified opposition to slavery.

The Whigs agreed on three possible candidates for president: Millard Fillmore of New York, who had signed and promoted the Compromise of 1850; **Daniel Webster** of Massachusetts, by whom many Northerners felt double-crossed because of his vote and public support for the **Compromise of 1850**; and Bvt. Lt. Gen. **Winfield Scott** of Virginia, who had not been personally involved in political controversies such as the Compromise of 1850, but represented the victory in the **War with Mexico** that had brought about the need for compromise.

Both Fillmore and Webster were unacceptable to Seward and his allies. However, Scott could potentially repeat the 1848 triumph, being the military hero of the age. Although not a pro-slave advocate, he was a Virginian. But Southern Whigs wanted Scott's assurance that Seward's influence would not compromise his Southern loyalties, as had been the case with Taylor. Vaguely maintaining his beliefs, Scott refused to give any specific guarantees.

Meanwhile, the Democrats moved to secure the Compromise of 1850 coalition of Northern and Southern Democrats and Southern Whigs. Their candidate, **Franklin Pierce** of New Hampshire, was also a war hero, one of the few New Englanders who had supported the war as a brigade leader. Like many junior volunteer officers, he despised the arrogant Scott. Marketed to the public as the Northern version of "Old Hickory" **Andrew Jackson**, the "Young Hickory of the Granite Hills" appealed to New England and **Martin Van Buren**'s New York supporters, strengthening the party. He also publicly favored the Compromise of 1850.

The election was a foregone conclusion. Pierce won by over 200,000 popular votes. His vice presidential candidate, William R. King of Alabama, brought Southern Whigs back into the Democratic fold, as had the passage of the Compromise of 1850. Upon King's death in April 1853, David Atchison of Missouri, the Senate's president *pro tempore* and one of the nation's staunchest pro-slavery proponents, assumed King's functions of office, such as presiding over the Senate. The Pierce administration would fulfill the South's fondest expectations, instituting the **"Spread Eagle" foreign policy** and the **Kansas–Nebraska Act** domestic policy.

ELECTION OF 1856. The presidential candidates in the election of 1856 represented three parties. What remained of the old **Whig Party** was now called the **American** or Know Nothing Party. The **slavery** issue had virtually destroyed the Whigs. The Conscience Whigs believed compromise over slavery was wrong and impolitic and joined the new **Republican** anti-slavery party. The pro-slavery Cotton Whigs believed limiting slavery in the states or territories interfered with domestic institutions and hoped to oppose the **Democrats** on the traditional economic issues of **Andrew Jackson**'s term: a national banking system, government assistance to farmers and education, a high protective **tariff**, the colonization of freed slaves overseas, and federally funded internal improvements. The Cotton Whigs defected to the American Party, which found support among the native-born Americans of the Atlantic states, now becoming densely populated with refugees of the Revolution of 1848 in Germany and the Irish potato famine. These mostly Roman Catholics drank heavily even on Sundays and corrupted the big-city Democratic machines which provided jobs and welfare in exchange for the correct vote, making many Americans nostalgic for old-time Protestant values.

The American Party nominated **Millard Fillmore,** who the Whigs had passed over in favor of Gen. **Winfield Scott** in 1852. Appealing on the surface due to his basic integrity and support of the **Compromise of 1850**, he was against the **Kansas–Nebraska Act** which had repealed the **Missouri Compromise**, causing many Southern Whigs to distrust the Buffalo, New York, native. Southern Whigs feared that if the South split its vote in 1856, the **Republicans** might win and reopen the slavery issue.

The Democratic convention was held on June 2, 1856, in Cincinnati, the "Queen City of the West." This marked the first time a national convention was convened west of the Appalachians. The city had been chosen four years earlier to entice Western Democrats to support New Englander **Franklin Pierce** back in 1852. By 1856, years of victory had made the Democratic Party sluggish, out of touch with the moment, and faction ridden.

Its potential nominees for the election of 1856 illustrated that point well. Franklin Pierce's support of the Kansas–Nebraska Act and the **Kansas–Missouri Border Wars** precluded his chances of a successful campaign in the future. He had won an easy victory in 1852 over the old, outdated **Lewis Cass**, who had lost in 1848. The young, brassy, outspoken **Stephen A. Douglas,** disliked by old-time party regulars, represented the new blood in the Democratic Party. He was also burdened with originating the Kansas–Nebraska Act, whose central tenet was the failed **Popular Sovereignty** doctrine, which was nonetheless incorporated into the convention's Cincinnati Platform. This left the 42-year party veteran, **James Buchanan**. The crafty, plodding Old Buck was uninspired but reliable and safe on the slavery issue.

The party's Southern wing, hoping that his party loyalty would give them the unity they had not enjoyed since the Jackson era, secured Buchanan's nomination. Buchanan's backers proposed to Douglas, the strongest opponent, that he yield to Buchanan until 1860, when Buchanan would be entering his seventh decade, too old to serve again. In deference to die-hard Southern Pierce supporters, Charleston was the chosen venue for the 1860 convention.

The two-year-old **Republican** Party needed someone moderately **anti-slavery** and nativistic to take votes from Fillmore and the Americans. Old Frank Blair, Sr., once an advisor to Andrew Jackson but now in the opposition, suggested California U.S. Senator **John Charles Frémont**. An attractive war hero, the conqueror of California, Western explorer of note, and advocate of a transcontinental railroad, Frémont, in the words of one observer, possessed all of the qualities of genius except ability. To assure his nomination, Frémont denounced the Kansas–Nebraska Act for the first time.

The Republican platform included a congressional ban on the twin evils of slavery and polygamy in the territories. It omitted traditional Republican positions on nativism, the Missouri Compromise, the Kansas–Nebraska Act, and banning slavery in the District of Columbia. The party slogan was "**Free Men, Free Soil, Free Labor,** and Frémont." As extreme **abolitionists** ran a candidate under the Free Soil Party label, Frémont looked moderate by comparison, a boon to the party.

The close election results made the Democrats uneasy. Fillmore took eight electoral votes (Maryland) and 25 percent of the popular vote; Frémont took 114 electoral votes (all Northern) and only 30 percent of the popular vote; Buchanan took 174 electoral votes (North and South) and 45 percent of the popular vote. While Buchanan won by a comfortable margin, the Republicans looked ahead to 1860. Holding the same states and taking Pennsylvania (27 electoral votes) and either Indiana (11) or Illinois (13) would win them the White House with a majority of the electoral vote and a minority, approximately 40 percent, of the popular vote. All they needed was a viable candidate in place of Fremont.

ELECTION OF 1860. For the first and last time in American history, four equally powerful parties contested for the presidency in 1860. The **Democratic Party**, splintered into two factions based on sectional lines, held three conventions. Charleston, chosen four years earlier, hosted the first, although it was the center of Southern Nationalism, to the detriment of party unity. The Southern delegates, in backing the so-called Alabama Platform, insisted that the party adopt their doctrine of **non-exclusion** of **slavery** in the territories. Unable to gain compliance, the Gulf South delegates abandoned the convention, forcing party regulars to adjourn and reconvene at the Baltimore Convention six weeks later.

The **Constitutional Union Party**, comprising the remnants of the old **Whig**, Know-Knothing, and **American Parties,** nominated **John Bell** of Tennessee for president and Edward Everett of Massachusetts for vice president. Mostly representing the border states, the Constitutional Union Party abandoned any attempt to fool the public with a complex set of political ideas as a party platform. It stood for the vague ideals of Constitution and unity. The goal of the Constitutional Unionists was to take enough electoral votes to force the election into the House of Representatives, in hopes that an acceptable compromise could save the slowly crumbling Union.

The **Republicans** held their convention in Chicago. Only their second try at the presidency, the Republicans had recently managed to obtain a majority in the House when Representative **Henry Winter Davis** of Maryland shifted his vote from Whig-American to Republican. In 1856, the Republicans realized that by keeping the states they had won and adding Pennsylvania and either Indiana or Illinois to their column, they could now win with a minority of popular votes, but a majority in the Electoral College. They nominated **Abraham Lincoln** of Illinois, a moderate on most issues who favored the Whig economic program and no slavery in the territories.

The Democrats reconvened their convention in Baltimore. Before leaving Charleston, their leading candidate, **Stephen A. Douglas**, had agreed to accept the nomination only with a two-thirds majority of the original convention's delegates. But now, Douglas agreed to run as their candidate with two-thirds of those attending in Baltimore. Many Southern delegates met in Richmond, awaiting an invitation from Douglas and his cronies in Baltimore to return to the party. Upon Douglas's nomination, those few Southerners who had gone to Baltimore walked out again and, joining with the Richmond delegates over the telegraph, nominated then-current vice president, **John C. Breckinridge** of Kentucky, as their candidate for president.

As each state voted on its own timetable, finishing by November, the Democrats showed early signs of increasing their number of congressmen. But only Douglas, and perhaps Bell, seemed to realize that the South's Seceders were increasingly absorbing the regular Southern Democrats. If Lincoln were elected, the South saw itself opened to domestic violence brought on by Lincoln's own party's abolition wing. Breaking with precedent, Douglas, as the only compromise candidate of national stature, toured New England and the South, hoping to appease extremists on both sides.

The possible loss of a majority in federal power devastated the Southern politicians. In a sense they believed the Republicans' **Slave Power Conspiracy,** which had supposedly controlled American federal government from the days of George Washington and the following **Virginia Dynasty** of presidents. The only way to maintain the South in power was to secede and form its own nation. They substituted their own men for the radical secessionists, the **fire-eaters** or the chivalry, in state after state. The regular Democrats would lead the way to Southern independence as they had led the whole United States from the 1830s. **James L. Orr** took over from **Robert Barnwell Rhett** in South Carolina, **Jefferson Davis** from **Albert Gallatin Brown** (Mississippi), **John Slidell** and **Judah P. Benjamin** from **Pierre Soulé** (Louisiana), **Howell Cobb** from Alfred Iverson, Sr. (Georgia). This is what Douglas saw, and it scared him.

Douglas and Breckinridge combined took 47 percent of the popular vote, up 2 percent from 1856. The Constitutional Unionists captured 14 percent of the popular vote, down 9 percent from the Whig-Americans in 1856. The Republicans took the remaining 39 percent, a 7 percent increase from 1856. Most importantly, the Republicans won the electoral vote in every state as in 1856, and added Pennsylvania and Illinois. Indeed, every free state except half of New Jersey gave Lincoln their electoral votes. Lincoln would have won even if all his opponents had created a fusion ticket. While the race was close for the Republicans, they won every state they needed. To the South's disadvantage, Lincoln and Douglas together took 70 percent of the popular vote, a forewarning of a ban on slavery in the territories, rendering the slave South a greater minority within the nation than ever before.

In November, Governor William H. Gist, no fire-eater by any means, requested a meeting of South Carolina's legislature, elected in October 1860. They called for a constitutional convention to consider the concept of secession and began to buy weapons to arm an increased state militia, marking the advent of the **First Secession movement**.

ELECTION OF 1861, CONFEDERATE. The Provisional Congress of the Confederacy, functioning as a unicameral national legislature until February 1862, elected **Jefferson Davis** and **Alexander H. Stephens** president and vice president. However, their **Confederate Constitution** called for national elections in 1861 to select permanent executives and a regular bicameral Congress. Jefferson Davis ran unopposed and won reelection by a landslide in both the popular and electoral vote, despite Confederate military setbacks on the South Atlantic coast, western Virginia, Kentucky, and Missouri. However, Vice President Stephens was perceived as apathetic towards a Confederate victory or a viable Confederate state. His opposition to secession caused others to see him as a spoilsman, enforcing the corruption policies of the antebellum Union. The protests against Stephens were too weak, however, to produce an opposition candidate or prevent his reelection.

In the congressional elections, each state was allotted its normal number of U.S. Representatives elected popularly, plus two senators elected by state legislatures. The parties did not label themselves, and although pockets of **Whig** and **Democratic** areas remained, the parties utilized former political machines whenever possible. But the Democrats and the Whigs had long ceased to battle over traditional economic issues and were now united in their quest for national independence. States in which Whigs and Democrats had been balanced before the war generally selected one senator from each party.

Many voters and commentators groused that the war had taken away the ablest men, leaving election campaigns suffering from moral turpitude. The contenders who remained behind offered themselves as individuals, often with an explanation attached to their names advertising their patriotic support of the troops and independence. Any other issues were purely local. The governors of Missouri and Kentucky, amidst their governments' exile, selected their two senators and encouraged soldiers and refugees to vote whenever possible. Despite the low voter turnout in these two states, which reflected the entire Confederacy, the First Confederate Congress was elected to meet in Richmond for four sessions, 18 February–21 April 1862; 18 August–13 October 1862; 12 January–1 May 1863; and 18 November 1863–21 February 1864

EMBARGO ACT. Caught between France and Britain fighting the Napoleonic wars, each side wanting American trade and hoping to deny it to the other, President **Thomas Jefferson** had the exact opposite response from the **John Adams** administration. As a **Federalist**, Adams sought to blame America's woes at sea, the seizure of American ships by foreign powers, on France alone. As a **Democratic Republican**, Jefferson now turned his ire to Britain.

There was good reason for Jefferson to direct his response toward Britain. In 1807, the British ship, H.M.S. *Leopard*, fired on the U.S.S. *Chesapeake* in Hampton Roads, when the Americans refused to allow the British to search the ship for deserters from the Royal Navy. Three Americans were killed and 28 wounded. The boarding party from the *Leopard* removed three alleged deserters from the American ship. The nation demanded that Jefferson do something. The United States lacked men, money, and munitions for a war. The president's answer was the Embargo Act.

Passed in 1807 and strengthened the following year, the Embargo Act called for a suspension of all American trade with any foreign nation or its colonies. American ships engaged in coastal trade between American ports had to post a bond worth twice the value of the ship and cargo to sail. Foreign vessels could enter an American port and deposit a cargo from overseas, but they could not take any cargo out of that port.

The result was an economic slump that adversely affected New England, New York, and Pennsylvania for a decade or more. It was Massachusetts **Federalist John Quincy Adams**'s support of the Embargo Act that made him anathema to his party and caused him to become the Democratic Republicans' point man on all foreign policy questions. He would serve as diplomat and secretary of state until his election by the House of Representatives as president in 1824.

The Embargo Act raised smuggling and evasion of the law to high art forms. Each new measure to enforce the embargo caused more hostility the farther North one went along the Atlantic coast. New Englanders saw this as Democratic Republican retribution for voting

Federalist. Southern congressmen, all pro-Jefferson, supported the measure. Jefferson was noted for his predilections for agriculture over all forms of business and trade. He saw the violations of the embargo as treason.

What Jefferson failed to realize was that his measure was not protecting New England shippers from having their vessels seized and their seamen impressed into the British Navy. Even though half of the American seamen were British deserters, and numerous ships had been seized, the New England shippers were willing to run the risk. The profits were high and not every ship was challenged. Southerners began to change their minds in support of the measure, when the finished goods they needed to run their plantations were not forthcoming. Actually, the only nation hurt by the embargo was the United States.

In the end, Jefferson agreed to suspend the embargo in favor of the Non-Intercourse Act. This reopened trade with all nations except Britain and France. It pledged the United States to reopen trade with either of them if they suspended their attacks on American ships on the high seas. This measure was modified by Macon's Bill No. 2, which permitted open trade with France and Britain, but allowed the president to reestablish non-intercourse against the enemy whichever country suspended its attacks on American shipping. France responded positively first. This did what the Democratic Republicans really wanted—it isolated the British and led to the **War of 1812**—the Second War of American Independence against Britain.

EMERSON, JOHN. *See DRED SCOTT v. SANFORD.*

EMPRESARIOS. *See* LONE STAR REBELLIONS.

ENABLING ACT. *See* NORTHWEST ORDINANCE.

ENCOMIUM. *See* CREOLE CASE.

ENGLISH BILL. *See* KANSAS SETTLEMENT.

ENTERPRISE. *See* CREOLE CASE.

ERA OF GOOD FEELINGS. James Monroe's two terms as president have been labeled the Era of Good Feelings. This was based on the **New Nationalism** that marked the last months of his predecessor, **James Madison**. The New Nationalism saw the passage of the **Tariff of 1816** and the **Second Bank of the United States**. To the discerning eye, these were all a part of **Alexander Hamilton**'s original economic program, the one so vigorously opposed by Madison and **Thomas Jefferson** as to be the basis of the two original political parties (**Federalist** and **Democratic Republican**) under the Constitution.

The Era of Good Feelings was marked by the settlement of the Old Northwest with its subsistence and commercial agriculture, and the Old Southwest with its **cotton** culture. Four new states came into the Union, Indiana and Illinois north of the Ohio River and Alabama and Mississippi along the Gulf Coast. Congress passed the Land Law of 1820 that created the $100 farm. Under its terms, the minimum amount of land one had to buy in the West was 80 acres at $1.25 an acre. It would last unchanged until the Civil War. The catch was that one had to pay the whole amount in cold cash—no credit. This was a response to the **Panic of 1819**, an economic depression supposedly begun by undue land speculation with credit purchases.

Monroe's able Secretary of State **John Quincy Adams** engineered an **Anglo-American Rapprochement** that regularized and demilitarized the Canadian border and created the misnamed Monroe Doctrine. After Maj. Gen. Andrew Jackson had invaded Florida in the First Seminole War, Adams also obtained Florida and set the southern border of the Louisiana Purchase from Louisiana to the Pacific from the Spanish in the **Adams–Onís Treaty**.

But in the Era of Good Feelings there were some ominous rumblings for the nation's future. As a part of the New Nationalism, Congress had funded extension and repair of the **National Road,** begun under Jefferson's tutelage. But Monroe, in a burst of strict construction of the Constitution, had vetoed this Bonus Bill, named because it would have placed profits (bonuses) from the Second Bank of the United States into the road. But the issue of **internal improvements** would not go away. The nation needed roads and canals to bring finished goods to the hinterland and ship food and staples to the cities.

But the worst was yet to come. In 1820, **slavery** became a topic of congressional debate when the first state fully west of the Mississippi River, Missouri, asked to be admitted to the Union, upsetting the free state-slave state balance in the U.S. Senate. The ensuing **Missouri Compromise** was achieved when Massachusetts allowed its disconnected county of Maine to become a free state. But its ease of settlement was deceptive for the future of the South's place in the nation.

Then there was the more immediate "Monroe Heresy." Within the Democratic Republican Party was a remnant of Federalist support, represented by three men, although there were others. **John C. Calhoun**, **Henry Clay** and his **American System**, and John Quincy Adams had backed the New Nationalism so much so that they could best be classified as **National Republican**s. A senator from New York, new to the national political scene, **Martin Van Buren**, saw these men and their nationalistic programs from Washington as threatening to the Jeffersonian view of restrictive central government.

Van Buren would rally like-minded politicians, mostly Southerners, into a new **Democratic** Party, first under the leadership of William H. Crawford of Georgia in the **election of 1824**, then behind **Andrew Jackson** of Tennessee in the **election of 1828**. Van Buren's goal was to stop the Monroe Heresy, the mindless political appointments of men tainted in the past with Federalist principles of strong central government. In effect, Van Buren would be the new **Aaron Burr**, seeking his Thomas Jefferson in the person of Andrew Jackson. His biggest disappointment was Monroe's refusal to appoint a successor, allowing the party to splinter behind personalities, rather than adhering to original Jeffersonian principles in the election of 1824.

ESSEX JUNTO. *See* BURR, AARON; HARTFORD CONVENTION.

EX PARTE MERRYMAN. *See* MERRYMAN, EX PARTE.

EXPANSIBLE ARMY. *See* CONCURRENT VOICE AND NULLIFICATION.

EXTRATERRITORIALITY OF SLAVERY. The Framers of the Constitution wrote that the institution of **slavery** had a legal aspect that adhered to the slave and legalized **slavery** wherever an owner might take a slave within the boundaries of the U.S. It was key to understanding the difference between **Squatter Sovereignty** and **Popular Sovereignty** and determined the outcome of the U.S. Supreme Court case ***Dred Scott v. Sandford***.

– F –

FACTORS, COTTON. All **staple crops** in the South were sold through commission merchants called factors. The factorage system began in the Middle Ages. A factor was a broker who acted in his own name. Thus he was different from a broker or agent who acted in the name of his employer. The crop remained the property of the planter until the factor sold it, but the factor was free to deal as he saw fit, provided he did not exceed conditions for sale set by the planter or act in a fraudulent or negligent manner. The planter had no right of redress otherwise. Because a factor had expenses associated with the sale, he acquired a lien on the planter's crop, which gave him a right to use or sell it in his own interest first.

Originally, in the colonial era, many planters acted as their own factors and dealt directly with the London merchants or their ship captains. But as Americans moved west, they wound up too far from the coast to make this possible. The advantage to using a middleman, the factor, was that the factor could store the crop until the best price was available. Planters believed that factors knew the ups and downs of the market better because they specialized in its fluctuations. The **upland cotton** market could fluctuate as much as 18 cents a pound at various times during the year. The factor also could sell to any place in the world.

Some planters restricted their factors with very specific orders as to how, when, and where to sell. The problem was that the planter was removed from the port cities and had poor information upon which he acted days or weeks too late. Factors knew more accurately what was happening and had to move quickly to secure a good price. A factor always advertised for new clients and kept old clients informed through letters and brochures. A factor could sell at any time the price exceeded the planter's desired minimum or whenever he had to satisfy a debt of his own. These terms were spelled out in the

U.S. **Supreme Court** case, *William & James Brown & Company v. Thomas McGran* **(1840)**.

Factors acted as buyers as well as sellers. They provided such items as bagging, rope, food, tools, cloth, and whatnot. Most planters operated on account, with payment due or deducted at the end of a given year or planting season. The books kept by factors are often the only records extant today on any plantation's operations. The standard factor's fee was 2.5 percent on the gross price for buying goods or selling a crop, 8 percent interest on unpaid loans, and deductions for all costs of shipping, storage, and services provided.

Most modern writers have condemned the factorage system as costly and a means of keeping the planters in perpetual debt. It encouraged the growth of a single cash crop, rural backwardness, and a colonial **economy** that exchanged finished goods for raw materials, delaying the growth of native Southern industries. In short, the factors were representatives of Yankee money power.

It is a bit exaggerated and certainly unfair to blame Southern economic woes on factors. The real culprits here were the planters, who created their own debt by inordinate borrowing triggered by social pressures to buy more slaves and land than they could use profitably. The planters sold themselves to the Northern financiers, who had the money to lend. Much of the inordinate debt came due in the **Panic of 1837**, which led to much criticism and finger pointing by Southern Nationalists at Northern financial interests, the **Second Bank of the United States**, and the protective **tariff**.

The solution was very simple, in theory. All the South had to do was break the one-crop cycle and expand into food crops and industry. In actuality, however, the solution ran up against the whole concept of what it meant to be a planter, a Southern gentleman. It would have meant changing a whole lifestyle. It also might have meant giving the **abolitionists** fodder for their criticism of **slavery** as an institution. So planters dug their heels in and kept on with things as they were.

The factors really could do little to change the system. They had to borrow from Northern financiers because the South had too little liquid capital to run the system. The factors were "King Cotton's Retainers," providing services, not setting policy. So long as Southern planters refused to change their socially rewarding lifestyle, it was necessary to grow more and more cotton for the factors to sell.

FALL LINE. The imaginary line drawn along the first waterfalls in any navigable river in the South is called the fall line. Most early, larger Southern cities (Washington, D.C., Richmond, Raleigh, Columbia, Augusta) sprang up here as shipments from oceangoing vessels had to be off loaded for further shipment. It is also a dividing line between the Old South's geographic regions known as the **Tidewater** and the **Piedmont**.

FANNIN MASSACRE. *See* LONE STAR REBELLIONS.

FEDERAL RATIO. *See* THREE-FIFTHS COMPROMISE.

FEDERALISTS. When the Constitutional Convention completed its work in Philadelphia, it sent the new fundamental law to the states for ratification. Remembering how the **Articles of Confederation** had been delayed by the need to get all 13 states to approve before it went into effect, the Convention said the Constitution would go into effect for all states after nine endorsed it.

The people in favor of ratifying the new document cleverly called themselves Federalists. Federalism implied that they supported a loose Union with the states and central government having specific and divided powers. That was exactly what the Articles of Confederation had had. In reality, the Federalists simply did not want people to realize how big a power the central government would become under the Constitution.

The Federalist view was presented to the people in a series of essays written by **James Madison**, **Alexander Hamilton**, and **John Jay**, collectively entitled the *Federalist Papers*. These treatises sought to reassure the states that numerous checks and balances would limit the central government from becoming all-powerful, as had the British government before the Revolution. The ploy worked and the Constitution achieved ratification in fairly short order.

The new government was installed with **George Washington** elected as the new president and **John Adams** as vice president. Washington's cabinet read like the duty roster of his army staff, with Hamilton as secretary of the treasury and Henry Knox as secretary of war. At first things were pretty much all-inclusive, with **Thomas Jefferson** back from France as Secretary of State and Virginian Edmund

Randolph installed as attorney general, men who had not been in Washington's wartime retinue.

Soon it was obvious that two major factions existed in Congress and the cabinet. Those in favor of a strong central government, primarily from the Carolina Tidewater and commercial centers of the North, coalesced around Hamilton. In foreign policy, they supported the British side in the wars of the French Revolution in Europe, and a mercantile policy at home. The result was **Jay's Treaty**, **Funding and Assumption**, and the creation of the **Bank of the United States**. Hamilton's men, still called Federalists, held hostage measures that the South desired—**Pinckney's Treaty**, the permanent location of the federal seat of government below the **Mason–Dixon Line**, protecting **slavery in Washington, D.C.**—passing them only when an economic program favoring Northern commercial interests was approved, too.

Hamilton's ascendancy in the cabinet drove Jefferson to resign. Because of a personal scandal, Hamilton soon followed. But because Washington basically favored Hamilton's policies as good for the nation, the Federalists became strong. It was only under the John Adams administration, following the **election of 1796**, that the Federalists began to overplay their hand. The **Quasi-War**, the **Alien and Sedition Acts**, and the packing of the federal judiciary system with the so-called **Midnight Judges** after the **election of 1800** cost them much, especially in the South.

The real problem was that the Federalists in the North were essentially the descendants of New England Puritans. They were interested in purifying themselves at home, creating the old Puritan perfection, city on the hill, and did not want nor see the need to expand into the American West. The South realized that the West held the key to the future. The more slave states admitted with extra "Negro congressmen" those whites elected under the **Three-Fifths Compromise**, the more powerful what the North called the **Slave Power Conspiracy** would become through the **Virginia Dynasty**.

When this became evident, the Federalists opposed the **War of 1812** and became treasonous in the eyes of the American people. The **Hartford Convention**'s proposals to amend the federal government to lessen Southern and Western power effectively killed off the party and resulted in the **Era of Good Feelings**, where all politicians became **Democrat Republicans**.

FILIBUSTERING. In the 1850s, the United States followed the same **Spread Eagle foreign policy** of Manifest Destiny in the Americas as it did in Europe and Asia. In the early 19th century, private armies led by filibusterers (from the Spanish *filibusteros*, an old corruption of the Dutch *vribueter*, similar to the English freebooter) began attempting expansion expeditions to the Gulf of Mexico and into Texas. These **Lone Star Rebellions** had conquered West Florida in 1810 and Texas in 1836. In 1819, because of the First Seminole War, **Andrew Jackson** and the U.S. Army had intimidated Spain into signing away East Florida in the **Adams–Onís Treaty**.

One of the great mysteries of the mid-19th century is why the United States never annexed Cuba and Puerto Rico, the Spanish colonies left over from the Latin American revolutions for independence before the Civil War. With Puerto Rico's meager economic value and less strategic location, American antebellum interest centered on Cuba, the "Pearl of the Antilles," the fertile island "sugar bowl" which guarded the mouth of the Mississippi River. Every American president from **Thomas Jefferson** to William McKinley, with the exception of **Abraham Lincoln,** offered to buy Cuba from Spain, **James K. Polk** offering a staggering $100 million. This was far more generous than the mere $40 million he offered Mexico for New Mexico and California, before taking them by force, giving Mexico an even more insulting $15 million in return.

The **War with Mexico** spurred American interest in expansion to the south. Although they considered the Mexican Cession a barren desert wasteland, Cuba, with its solid slave economy and lucrative staple crop of sugar, was worth pursuing. But Spain, preferring to see Cuba "sink into the ocean" rather than relinquish it, would not sell. Knowing the impossibility of getting a declaration of war through Congress, the supporters of Cuban annexation devised other means.

When the War with Mexico ended, many unemployed soldiers were willing to embark on reckless missions for the right price. Most Americans believed that, with support from American freedom-loving slaveholders, Cubans would rebel against the Spanish monarchy. One of several aborted revolutions had involved Narciso López, a native of Venezuela. He was now in the United States promising recruits all the glory of conquering Cuba.

Detained upon leaving New York harbor with a force of volunteers in 1849, the resilient López transferred his operations to the more amenable New Orleans. But he and his followers reached a Cuban shore devoid of rebel followers. A Spanish fleet chased the López party to Key West, where the United States arrested him for violation of the neutrality laws. After a trial by jury, he emerged a hero upon his acquittal. Faithful followers soon flocked to his cause. In 1851, the Spanish massacred his new army of 500 filibusters on the Cuban beaches. Survivors surrendered to the Spanish, who executed López and 50 of his leaders. They became known as the "Gallant Fifty-one." A contrite President **Millard Fillmore** paid Spain $25,000 in damages, whereupon Spain released the 100 surviving prisoners.

Franklin Pierce's victory over Winfield Scott in the **election of 1852** was a sign of expansionist support. He demonstrated this by making fellow expansionist **Pierre Soulé** of Louisiana American minister to Spain. So emphatic was Soulé's insistence on America's right to own Cuba that Spain took his appointment as an insult. The European diplomatic corps thought no better of him. In Spain, the French ambassador's disparaging remark about Mrs. Soulé's décolletage galvanized Soulé to challenge him to a duel. A bullet wound to the hip maimed his opponent for life. While Europe was outraged, America basked in the glow of its upheld honor.

Soulé soon was immersed in Cuban affairs. Because of the Lopez debacle, Spain now enforced strict shipping laws against American seamen. After a series of minor incidents, Spain seized the American registered ship *Black Warrior* for lacking a proper cargo manifest. Soulé took the liberty of delivering a contemptible demand of $300,000 in damages to the Spanish, who replied directly to Washington. The *Black Warrior*'s owners agreed to accept $53,000. But Soulé had scored another point for the expansionist crowd of **Young America**.

During the Crimean War, Pierce offered Spain $130 million for Cuba, which Spain again refused. Secretary of State William Marcy ordered Soulé to detach Cuba from Spain, if possible, and Soulé obligingly invited John Y. Mason, the U.S. minister to France, and James Buchanan, minister to Great Britain, to a clandestine meeting at Ostend, Belgium, where they issued the inaccurately titled "Ostend Manifesto." It was not a manifesto; it was merely a set of reasons the

U.S. should purchase Cuba from Spain for $120 million: to suppress the African slave trade, to promote Cuban-American trade, to prevent further slights to American pride like the *Black Warrior* incident, and for its favorable location in the name of national security. In the wake of Spain's likely refusal, the Spanish monarchy would be seen as threatening United States interests in the Gulf, and the U.S. would be justified in taking Cuba by force.

Marcy first glimpsed the manifesto in the press, leaked by overanxious reporters. Europe and the American North's **anti-slavery** advocates deemed it a Southern attempt to extend American **slavery** into new territory. Marcy firmly rejected the manifesto's conditions and omitted his order to Soulé from the documents sent to Congress. Soulé took this gesture as an insult and promptly resigned. Buchanan and Mason disclaimed all blame and involvement. The incident lost the **Democrats** many seats in the 1854 congressional by-elections, and the new **Republican Party** eagerly anticipated presenting its first presidential candidate in the **election of 1856**.

But Cuba was not America's only filibustering interest in Latin America. Newspaper editor William Walker set his sights on expanding American control into Nicaragua and Honduras. A compact 5'6" and 100 pounds, Walker was known as the "Grey-Eyed Man of Destiny." Having rushed for gold in California, his adventurous nature provoked his ambition to capture Central America and exploit it as potential U.S. slave territory. He also saw the potential for an isthmian canal. After a failed 1853 expedition into Baja California, Walker led three campaigns into Nicaragua, in which he fronted for William Vanderbilt's railroad and shipping interests. Although the distance across the isthmus was longer overland than the route to Panama, Nicaragua offered fewer jungle hazards.

Walker's plans bore fruit until he revoked the Vanderbilt company's charter. A formidable opponent, Vanderbilt financed a nationalist revolution against Walker's dictatorship. Walker was deposed but foolishly returned only to suffer another defeat. A third try in Honduras in 1860 brought British opposition. They captured him and turned him over to the government of Honduras, where he was executed.

Walker's quests to Central America were echoed by expeditions into northern Mexican states such as Sonora. A wide belief still prevailed in the United States that Mexico should have been annexed after the 1848 treaty. This issue was brought to the forefront once again when Cincinnati doctor George W. L. Bickley became president-general of the Knights of the Golden Circle. The Knights were an organization named after a mythical crusading force of a current popular novel, the *Knights of the Golden Horseshoe*. Hoping to be a modern-day William the Conqueror, Bickley raised castles throughout the United States, with a concentration in the West and South. Under the sponsorship of U.S. Senator William Gwinn of California (by way of Mississippi), Bickley plotted a military expedition of "energetic Anglo-Saxons" to conquer and "Texas-ize" Mexico, hoping to divide it into as many as 25 slave states.

Northern pro-slavery advocates became his loyal supporters. But many thought the pro-Southern Copperheads' campaign against the Union war effort was Bickley's grand brainstorm. Bickley was arrested during the war with a Southern army and jailed for two years without trial. Upon his release, he emerged defeated and subdued. Filibustering, although still glamorized by modern Hollywood, dissipated as the real war began in 1861.

FILLMORE, MILLARD (1800–1874). Born in a log cabin in the Finger Lakes country of New York, Fillmore spent his youth fraught with the hardships of frontier life. While attending one-room schools, he worked his father's farm and was apprenticed to a cloth dresser. In 1823, he was admitted to the bar and seven years later moved his law practice to Buffalo.

Like fellow up-stater and **Whig** lawyer, William H. Seward, Fillmore was an associate of Whig politician Thurlow Weed. Fillmore served in the state assembly and, during two terms in the U.S. Congress, he was chairman of the Ways and Means Committee and an advocate of **Henry Clay**'s **American System**. For eight years he was a member of the House of Representatives. In 1848, while comptroller of New York, he was elected vice president to balance the Whig ticket under slaveholding Southerner and war hero **Zachary Taylor**.

Unlike Taylor, Fillmore supported the **Compromise of 1850**. When Taylor died suddenly in July of that year, Fillmore's accession to the presidency created a momentary calm between pro- and antislavery advocates. He quickly signed the Compromise and strongly enforced the **Fugitive Slave law**. This caused him much unpopularity with the Northern branch of the Seward-led Whig Party, the Conscience Whigs, which lost him the renomination for the presidency in 1852. He ran as the **American Party** or Know Nothing candidate in 1856, but the **slavery** issue, having irrevocably divided the old Whigs, rendered his chances of victory extremely slim. He retired to Buffalo where he died in 1874.

FINNEY, CHARLES GRANDISON. *See* SECOND GREAT AWAKENING.

FIRE-EATERS. Those antebellum Southern politicians who championed the break-up of the **Democratic Party** and the Union were called fire-eaters or chivalry. They were generally led by **William Yancey** of Alabama, but included **James L. Orr** (South Carolina), **Albert Gallatin Brown** (Mississippi), **Pierre Soulé** (Louisiana), **Alfred Iverson, Sr.** (Georgia), and **Louis T. Wigfall** (Texas), among others.

FITZHUGH, GEORGE (1806–1881). From Port Royal, Virginia, born into a planter family that had fallen on hard times, George Fitzhugh was a self-educated man who practiced criminal law. As such, he alone of the writers who presented **slavery as a positive good** rejected racism, John Locke and the social contract, the **Concurrent Voice and Nullification**, free trade, and **secession**. Instead, Fitzhugh turned to Sir Robert Filmer, a British anthropologist and sociologist who emphasized the importance of the patriarchal family.

Fitzhugh also used many of the same sources employed by Karl Marx to argue that society was not progressing toward freedom, but retrograding from it. Fitzhugh saw all labor, not merely black chattels, as enslaved by necessity. He argued that **slavery** could survive only if the capitalistic world market were destroyed. His work was a call for a war against the modern world. Only when the servile nature of all labor was recognized could class war be avoided and the anarchy of capitalism avoided, because capital and labor were united in the black slave. Thus he contrasted the social disorder in the North and its free labor with what he saw as the ordered, peaceful South with slavery.

It was Fitzhugh's books, S*ociology for the South, or the Failure of Free Society* (1854) and *Cannibals All, or Slaves without Masters* (1856), that made his national reputation. They were read by **Abraham Lincoln** and used in his assertion in the "House Divided" speech that the nation could not perpetually exist half slave and half free, but must become either all one or the other.

With the advent of the Civil War, which Fitzhugh supported, even though he was initially against secession, he lapsed into obscurity. He eventually became a racist and moved to Texas where he died in 1881. As one historian put it, Fitzhugh actually died at Appomattox — the rest of his life was denouement.

FIVE CIVILIZED TRIBES. *See* INDIAN REMOVAL COMPLETED.

FLETCHER, JOHN. *See* SLAVERY AS A POSITIVE GOOD, THEORY OF.

FORCE ACT. *See* NULLIFICATION AND THE COMPROMISE OF 1833.

FORT GIBSON, TREATY OF. *See* INDIAN REMOVAL COMPLETED.

FORT MIMMS MASSACRE. *See* WAR OF 1812.

FORT SUMTER. *See* SECESSION OF THE SOUTHERN STATES, SECOND.

FRANKLIN, TREATY OF (1830). *See* INDIAN REMOVAL COMPLETED.

FREE MEN, FREE SOIL, FREE LABOR. This slogan of the **Republican Party** in the **election of 1856** was borrowed from the defunct **Free-Soil Party** of 1848 and 1852, and became the embodiment of Republican ideology before, during, and after the Civil War. "Free Speech" was sometimes included, which opposed Southerners' attempt to prevent Congress from receiving abolition petitions through the **Gag Rule.**

FREE-SOIL PARTY. By the early 1840s, two distinct factions divided the **anti-slavery** issue. One group wanted the political system to reform the government and the Constitution to eliminate **slavery** and formed the Liberty Party. The opposition, feeling that slavery had corrupted the system too badly for it to be saved, did not participate. The Liberty Party contested for local, state, and national political offices and opposed the annexation of Texas as a slave state. It held little sway in the election of 1840, but in 1844, it ran a national ticket for president and vice president under James G. Birney and Thomas Morris, originator of the term "**Slave Power Conspiracy.**" Although they numbered a mere 63,000 nationally, their votes in New York and Michigan shifted them from the **Whigs** to the **Democrats**, giving **James K. Polk** the presidency.

By 1848, it was clear few voters would support a party favoring **abolition**. The **Wilmot Proviso** prohibited slavery from any territory acquired in the **War with Mexico**. The Liberty Party, led by Salmon P. Chase and John P. Hale, combined with Conscience Whigs led by Charles Sumner and Charles Francis Adams and free-soil Democrats led by ex-President **Martin Van Buren** and **David Wilmot**, into the Free-Soil Party. In Buffalo, New York, the party nominated Van Buren and Adams, declaring " **Free Men, Free Soil, and Free Labor**."

Lacking in ideology, the pragmatist Van Buren saw his political career destroyed when the Free-Soil Party lost to the **Whigs** (**Zachary Taylor** and **Millard Fillmore**) and Democrats (**Lewis Cass**) in the **election of 1848.** They did, however, elect Chase and Hale to the U.S. Senate and 14 men to Congress, including George W. Julian of Indiana, later a **Republican** congressman of note.

Hale and Julian led the Free-Soil Party to another defeat in the **election of 1852** on their platform of opposition to the **Compromise of 1850** and the **Fugitive Slave Law**, which to them exemplified the sin and crime of slavery. Once again, the Democrats (**Franklin Pierce**) and Whigs (**Winfield Scott**) dominated national politics, forcing a merger of the Free-Soil Party with the new Republican Party in 1854, whom they supported in the **election of 1856**.

FREEPORT DOCTRINE. Republican **Abraham Lincoln**, in the 1858 **Lincoln–Douglas Debates** in the U.S. senatorial race, asked **Democrat** Stephen Douglas whether **slavery** could be prohibited in a territory despite the **Dred Scott** decision. This became the **Freeport Question**. Douglas's reply is known as the Freeport Doctrine, in which he maintained that slavery could be excluded from Western territories if no positive law were enacted in any territory endorsing the institution of slavery. Slavery could not exist in any locality without such a law. This duplicitous position alienated the South by contradicting his theory of **Popular Sovereignty** and the Southern **Non-Exclusion Doctrine**, and lessened his chances for the Democrat nomination in the **election of 1860**.

FREEPORT QUESTION. In the race for the U.S. senatorial seat from Illinois in 1858, **Republican** candidate **Abraham Lincoln** debated **Democrat** opponent **Stephen A. Douglas** in what became the famed **Lincoln–Douglas Debates.** At one point, Lincoln asked Douglas a question that would put him in a difficult position whether he answered yes or no: Could **slavery** be prohibited in a territory despite *Dred Scott v. Sanford*, the recent U.S. **Supreme Court** case ruling it could not? In answering "yes," Douglas would likely gain enough support to ensure his reelection to the U.S. Senate but alienate the South to the point of preventing his Democratic Party presidential nomination for **election in 1860**. Saying "no" would maintain his Southern support for the presidential election at the cost of losing the senate seat in Illinois to Lincoln. Douglas's answer, in the affirmative, became known as the **Freeport Doctrine**.

FRÉMONT, JOHN CHARLES (1813–1890). John Charles Frémont was born in Savanannah, Georgia, and educated at Charleston College. He taught mathematics before joining the Army Topographical Engineers Corps as second lieutenant. He joined a party led by Joseph N. Nicollet that surveyed and mapped the region between the upper Mississippi and Missouri rivers. Frémont surveyed the Des Moines River in 1841, and the same year he married Jessie Benton, the daughter of the influential U.S. Senator from Missouri, **Thomas Hart Benton**, who was instrumental in furthering Frémont's career the rest of his life.

A successful publicist and writer, Frémont's wife edited his three 1840s diaries detailing his Western expeditions that made him a household name in the United States as the "Pathfinder." In 1843, with Kit Carson and Tom Fitzpatrick as his guides, Frémont and his party ventured into the Laramie Mountains. He then crossed the Rocky Mountains via the South Pass and Green River, following the Bear River until it reached the Great Salt Lake.

Frémont made his third expedition in 1845 to the Great Basin and the Pacific Coast. While this was taking place, the **War with Mexico** began. As a major in the United States Army, he helped annex California. Commodore Robert Stockton appointed Frémont as military governor of California. However, in 1847 Frémont clashed with Brig. Gen. Stephen W. Kearney, President James K. Polk's appointment as military governor. Frémont was court-martialed, although his father-in-law persuaded President Polk to reverse a guilty sentence for mutiny and disobedience of orders.

Needing to regain his reputation, Frémont undertook an expedition into the southern Colorado mountains without Carson, but a blizzard stranded his team, forcing them to resort to cannibalism. In 1849, gold was discovered on his California estate, making him a multimillionaire. In 1850, Frémont was elected as senator for California, and in the **election of 1856,** the **Republican Party** chose him as its first presidential candidate, but he was defeated by **Democrat James Buchanan.**

The North would ensure his victory in 1860 by keeping the states Frémont won and adding Pennsylvania and Illinois or Indiana. But this was to be the destiny of **Abraham Lincoln.** After a less than sterling Civil War career in 1861 and 1862, Frémont spent the rest of the war in New York City awaiting orders that never came.

In 1864, he represented certain radical Republicans in opposing Lincoln's re-nomination for president, only to withdraw his candidacy under pressure. After the war he served as governor of Arizona Territory (he spent most of his time in the East lobbying for his mining interests) and bilked French investors in the transcontinental railroad (for which he was tried and found guilty in a French court *in absentia*). He died from food poisoning in New York state in 1890, after being placed on the army's retired list as major general.

FUGITIVE SLAVE ACT OF 1793. *See PRIGG v. PENNSYLVANIA.*

FUGITIVE SLAVE ACT OF 1850. The Fugitive Slave Act was the part of the **Compromise of 1850** that favored the South in declaring the **extraterritoriality of slavery**. This maintained that under the **U.S. Constitution** (art. IV, sect. 2) slaveholders were secure in their rights of holding their slaves beyond their home state in either slave or free states. Fugitives were to be denied jury trials and their cases heard before a special federal commissioner, who was doubly compensated if the defendant was determined to be a slave. The commissioner's decision was to be an answer to any state application for a writ of *habeas corpus* from any other court, state or federal. The commissioner could also call upon any citizen as part of a *posse comitatus* to assist him in the arrest and detention of any fugitive.

Northern states moved immediately to make it a crime for any state official to assist a federal commissioner. These laws were called personal liberty laws. The U.S. **Supreme Court** ruled in 1859 in *Ableman v. Booth* that the Fugitive Slave Law aptly demonstrated federal power over states rights, and that the personal liberty laws were unconstitutional as the states had given up such rights to join the Union. In many Northern states, outraged citizens, black and white, resisted enforcement of the law and several attempts were made to rescue captured fugitives. The Fugitive Slave Acts of 1850 and 1793 were still valid laws until 1864, when a Republican-dominated Congress managed to repeal them after years of wrangling.

FULTON, ROBERT. *See* SHREVE, HENRY MILLER.

FUNDING AND ASSUMPTION. As the first Secretary of the Treasury, **Alexander Hamilton** proposed to restore the public credit of the United States through decisive governmental action. He wanted the government to interfere with the free market system and regulate the economy to promote the Industrial Revolution.

Hamilton's first goal was to restore the creditworthiness of the United States by paying off the public debt left over from fighting the Revolutionary War. He saw three kinds of debt. There was the foreign debt, the money owed by the United States to foreign creditors and governments; the domestic debt that the state and federal governments owed to individual Americans, and various private debts, owed by individual Americans to British merchants from before the Revolution.

To pay off these debts, Hamilton proposed two measures. The first was Funding. This proposed to call in all old outstanding debts and issue bonds for the face amount plus interest owed. The new bonds would be paid off in time with 6 percent interest in gold. The problem was that the South was an agricultural area that needed to balance its books at the end of each year. So Southerners had sold their then-worthless debts heavily discounted for ready cash to plant future crops. Northern bondholders stood to make as much as 900 percent on this deal. Worse yet, many of these profiteers were Hamilton's close friends. It left a bad taste in one's mouth.

The second measure was Assumption. Under this proposal, Hamilton proposed to take all state debts and have them assumed by the federal government. The problem here was that the Southern states had paid most their state debts already. The Northern states had been remiss. Now they were to be rewarded and the South would in effect have to pay twice. Worse yet, both of these measures would also add to the overall federal debt owed.

The old story is that Hamilton and **James Madison**, the Southern leader in Congress, met at **Thomas Jefferson**'s house in Philadelphia and cut a deal. The South would vote for Funding and Assumption and the new national capital would be located below the **Mason–Dixon Line**. In reality, it seems the dinner was more about determining that Virginia's cost for these measures would equal the amount assumed. Prior to the dinner, Virginia's tax burden was nearly double the amount assumed. But Funding and Assumption for a capital in the South was a good public cover for all. This deal is often called the Compromise of 1790. It also gave the South control over **slavery in Washington, D.C.** for years to come.

– G –

GABRIEL'S PLOT. *See* "GENERAL" GABRIEL'S PLOT.

GADSDEN, JAMES. *See* WAR WITH MEXICO.

GADSDEN PURCHASE. *See* KANSAS–NEBRASKA ACT; WAR WITH MEXICO.

GAG RULE. With the rise of the **abolitionists** during the 1830s, Congress began receiving numerous petitions critical of all aspects of **slavery** and the federal government's role in preserving the **peculiar institution**. Abolitionists who dared go below the **Mason–Dixon Line** to voice their opposition to slavery were lynched. There were 300 such hangings of white questioners of slavery before the Civil War.

In the Senate, **John C. Calhoun**, reflecting earlier Southern complaints from similar tactics in the First Congress in 1790, demanded that the petitions not be received. Led by Senator **James Buchanan** of Pennsylvania, a front man for **Martin Van Buren**'s presidential ambitions, the Senate received the petitions and rejected them. This gave both sides a chance to voice their feelings, both for and against slavery.

But in the House of Representatives the fight was long and bitter. The leader for receiving the petitions was **John Quincy Adams**. The former president was now a congressman, and this became his last great stand. Adams never believed that Congress ought to interfere with slavery in the states where it existed, but he was against its extension and in favor of an absolute right of petition. He worked mightily to get slavery mentioned in every measure he introduced. He was a laughing stock at first. Then he became admired. Then he was cheered, and the Gag Rule became the joke. Angry Southerners refused to sit with him on committee assignments.

Buttressed by the so-called three-fifths representatives, those who represented the South's advantage from the **Three-Fifths Compromise** in the Constitution, the House passed the Gag Rule in 1836. It stated that Congress would lay all petitions regarding slavery or its abolition on the table without comment. The House also adopted resolutions stating the Congress had no power over slavery in the states where it existed, and no desire to interfere with **slavery in Washington, D.C.**

But as House and Senate rules had to be renewed each session in those days, the quarrel came up every session. The House repassed the Gag Rule, Adams objecting and refusing to vote, as usual. In the Senate, Calhoun offered six resolutions affirming slavery as a unique institution and that no section of the nation had the right to use the federal government to attack another part of the nation. Five of the six were passed, with some minor alterations in wording.

The Gag Rule was passed again and again in the House, but each time the majority in favor lessened until in 1844 it was abolished altogether. In the Senate, **Henry Clay** spoke on the question in 1839 at length, with an eye to the **Whig** Party's nomination for president in the **election of 1840**. He maintained that the abolitionists preferred civil war to allowing slavery to prevail in the Southern states. He also asserted that Congress had no authority to interfere with slavery where it already existed.

After the speech, one Southern senator suggested that Clay's stand might harm his support among Northern Conscience Whigs. Clay replied, "I trust the sentiments and opinions are correct; I had rather be right than be president." Later events proved that he would be neither.

"GALLANT FIFTY-ONE." *See* FILIBUSTERING.

GALLATIN, ALBERT. *See* NATIONAL ROAD.

GASPAR RIVER CHURCH. *See* SECOND GREAT AWAKENING.

"GENERAL" GABRIEL'S PLOT (1800). At the turn of the 19th century, with the success of the St. Domingue revolt, the new nation of **Haiti** became second only to the 13 British colonies to gain its independence in the New World. The idea of a black republic, terrifying as it was to American slaveholders, electrified their bondspeople. This soon became evident on 30 April 1800, when Mosby Sheppard's two slaves, Tom and Pharoah, reported that a slave army was to march from Henrico County north of Richmond upon the Virginia capital.

The informants fingered Gabriel Prosser, a favorite slave of his owner Thomas Prosser, as the rebels' leader. Gabriel, or "General" Gabriel," as he liked to be called now, was a tall black man in his mid-twenties, trained as a blacksmith. In addition, Prosser illegally taught him to read and write. Gabriel soon became a great Bible reader. He especially liked the story of Samson from the Old Testament, and grew his hair long to emulate his biblical hero.

With the informants' frightening story, Virginia Governor **James Monroe** ordered up the all-white militia and rounded up suspected blacks for the next two weeks. But Gabriel and the other leaders were not to be found.

Finally, slaves at Norfolk pointed out the ship on which they were hidden. The insurrectionists were arrested just before they were to set sail for freedom. Gabriel and the leadership refused to confess or to inform on whom else was involved. In the end 41 were hanged. White Virginians believed that slaves from all over the state had been aware of the plot, which left an uneasy feeling among slaveholders for years to come. *See also* SLAVE RESISTENCE AND REBELLION.

GEORGIA PLATFORM. *See* COMPROMISE OF 1850.

GERRY, ELBRIDGE. *See* ELECTION OF 1812, X, Y, Z AFFAIR.

GHENT, TREATY OF. *See* ADAMS, JOHN QUINCY; WAR OF 1812.

GIST, WILLIAM H. *See* SECESSION OF THE SOUTHERN STATES, FIRST.

GLIDDEN, GEORGE. *See* SLAVERY AS A POSITIVE GOOD, THEORY OF.

GOLDEN CIRCLE, KNIGHTS OF THE. *See* FILIBUSTERING.

GOODE, WILLIAM O. *See* VIRGINIA SLAVERY DEBATES.

GREAT COMPROMISER. *See* CLAY, HENRY.

GREAT DEBATE. *See* VIRGINIA SLAVERY DEBATES.

GREAT MIGRATION. Between 1815 and 1850, the United States experienced a huge westward movement called the Great Migration. Uncounted thousands of Americans crossed the Appalachians and settled the vast area from the mountains to a line that paralleled the western edge of the state of Missouri, before jumping the plains and Rocky Mountains to California and Oregon. This migration was made possible by several pivotal events. The end of the **War of 1812**

meant that the defeated **Native American** tribes in the Old Northwest were finished as an obstacle to the advance of white farmers. In the Old Southwest, the same vacating of the land by former inhabitants was achieved by **Andrew Jackson**'s aggressive policy of **Indian Removal**. The infiltration into the Mexican Empire's outposts west of the Sabine River and the **Texas Revolution** pushed the cotton culture on toward the 97th Meridian. This process was accelerated by Capt. **Henry Miller Shreve**'s clearing of the massive Red River Raft, a tangle of uprooted tree stumps that had blocked exploitation of northwest Louisiana, northeast Texas, and southwest Arkansas for eons.

The main problem in developing the West was to turn the place from an area of subsistence farming into one of commercial agriculture. Most of the products (wheat, flour, **corn**, butter, pork, **tobacco**, **hemp**, lead) produced in the West, particularly the Old Northwest, had a high weight to value and were bulky and expensive to ship by road. It was cheaper to ship all such produce by river to New Orleans and then transship them to the Atlantic Coast ports of New England.

But the items produced in New England (textiles, hardware, hats, tea, and machine tools) had a greater value to weight, and could cross the mountain roads by wagon at a profit. The result was that travel of goods tended to be one way and limited the growth of more than subsistence agriculture in the West.

But **cotton** changed all that. In 1815, the area of cotton culture was pretty much limited to the Piedmont of South Carolina and Georgia. But with the end of the war with the British and the opening of new trade opportunities there and in Europe as a whole, the production of cotton became a passion that knew no boundaries. Pushed by the **soil depletion** of the Atlantic Coast South, and pulled by the demand of cotton profits, adventure, and restlessness, Americans moved west in a continuous stream. Profits in cotton often topped 35 percent a year in the 1830s. One Alabamian bought his plantation for $16,000 and valued the place at $65,000 in just two years. By 1850, there were 388,000 Virginians and 128,000 Marylanders alone transplanted to the Southwest.

As more and more farmers in the Old Southwest turned to growing cotton, there came a demand for food that hastened the development of commercial agriculture in the Old Northwest. Hence, many historians credit the entire westward movement to cotton and its side effects. Everyone grew rich off the crop grown by slave labor.

This whole process was made more attractive by the development of the steamboat. This is not Robert Fulton's invention, but its modification by Capt. Shreve and others into the flat-bottomed cargo and passenger carrier that made the Western rivers famous. Now cargoes of whatever weight could be moved easily in both directions on the waters of the West. This meant more profit for both the farmer and the cotton planter through lower shipping rates and more flexible schedules and markets.

When combined with the development of the Erie Canal, the Pennsylvania Main Line Canal, and various branch canals in Ohio and the rest of the Old Northwest and then the railroads in the 1850s, the transportation of goods and services from all sections of the United States relied on Southern cotton more than might be expected from a casual glance. *See also* ECONOMY.

GREAT PACIFICATOR. *See* CLAY, HENRY.

GREEN SEED COTTON. *See* COTTON, UPLAND.

GRUNDY, FELIX. *See AMISTAD* CASE; WAR HAWKS.

GUADALUPE HIDALGO, TREATY OF. *See* WAR WITH MEXICO.

– H –

HAITI. Now the western third of what Christopher Columbus called the island of Hispañola (Place of the Spanish), Haiti is a local Indian word meaning "Place of Mountains." The French took over the whole island during one of the incessant colonial wars in the Caribbean and called it St. Domingue, from the Spanish phrase, Santo Domingo (Holy Sunday), the day it was first seen. Tragically, its history has been anything but holy. In the 1790s, it was the richest **sugar** and coffee producer in the world. Over a half million slaves worked the island, about the size of Maryland, at a time when the American South had 700,000 slaves overall.

St. Domingue has the distinction of being the second European colony, after British North America, to declare its independence. But Haiti had a problem with the United States from the beginning. The independence fighters were black slaves in rebellion against their masters. This made the whole Haitian Revolution anathema to the Old South.

But when the invasion never materialized, rebel leader Toussaint Breda, now called by his revolutionary name, "L'Ouverture" (The Beginning), asked for trade agreements. U.S. President **John Adams** agreed, if Haiti would deny French ships access to their former colony. The result was not only a trade agreement but also the assistance of a U.S. warship or two during L'Ouverture's battles with his pro-French opponents.

But when **Thomas Jefferson** became president in 1801, things changed. He tilted toward the French retaking the island and putting down the slave revolution. Jefferson, indeed the whole American South, saw nothing but bad from the notion that slaves could kill their masters and take over a whole country. Jefferson also wanted to deal with the new French ruler Napoleon I for Louisiana.

L'Ouverture's opponents conspired with Napoleon's general of the invading French army, Charles Leclerc. L'Ouverture was captured and spirited away to Europe and eventual death. Yellow fever began to decimate LeClerc's army, which pleased Jefferson, because he feared that it might next secure Louisiana. Finally L'Ouverture's successor, Jean-Jacques Dessalines, declared Haiti's total independence from France. Jefferson refused to recognize the new nation.

It would take until 1862 before **Abraham Lincoln**'s administration would extend U.S. diplomatic relations to Haiti. But the French military disaster at the hands of the black revolutionaries and the ravages of yellow fever guaranteed that Louisiana would be cut off from Europe and ripe for America to make the **Louisiana Purchase**, denying that part of the old French Empire to Britain or anyone else.

HAMILTON, ALEXANDER (1757–1804). Born on the island of Nevis in the West Indies, possibly a light-skinned mulatto by race, Alexander Hamilton was abandoned by his parents and raised by

James Hamilton, whose last name he took. At age 12, Hamilton had to go to work as his guardian had gone broke. The young man proved to be a genius at business and was running the counting house that employed him within two tears. Friends provided him with enough money to come to British North America for his education. He attended several institutions, finally graduating from King's College (now Columbia University).

By the 1770s, Hamilton had become converted to the cause of American Independence. When the war began, he enrolled as a captain of artillery. His unit being a model of efficiency and organization, Hamilton earned a promotion to lieutenant colonel and a position on the staff of Gen. **George Washington** as his confidential secretary. A reprimand from the general in 1781 led Hamilton to resign his position. He became the commander of an infantry regiment and led the assault on Yorktown. He was elected to Congress but regarded the institution as such a disappointment that he resigned a year later.

Returning to the practice of law, Hamilton became one of numerous officers from the Continental Army who saw the need for a stronger central government in the 1780s. He attended the Constitutional Convention and spoke on behalf of an American monarchy. He wrote in defense of the final document in the *Federalist Papers* and worked successfully to get New York to ratify the document.

With the election of Washington as president, Hamilton received an appointment as the first secretary of the treasury. He issued several reports on public credit and the state of manufactures that led to his proposing **Funding and Assumption** and the **Bank of the United States**. His advocacy of what many assumed at best to be unconstitutional actions led to his organization of the **Federalist** Party, which was opposed by **James Madison** and **Thomas Jefferson** and their **Democratic Republican** Party. Hamilton's support of trade with the British in **Jay's Treaty** and opposition to America's old Revolutionary ally, France, helped cement domestic political differences.

About this time it was revealed that Hamilton had fallen victim to the old badger con game and had had an affair with Maria, the wife of one James Reynolds. While under arrest for another crime, and hoping to beat the charges by revealing a bigger scandal, Reynolds claimed that Hamilton had paid him off with government funds to keep silent. This was never proven, but the damage was fatal to Hamilton's office-holding career.

Hamilton resigned his cabinet position, declined the position of chief justice of the U.S. Supreme Court, and went back to practicing law. Breaking with **John Adams**, who as Washington's successor thought he should lead the party, too, Hamilton continued to be the head of the Federalists in Congress. The undeclared **Quasi-War** with France and the **Alien and Sedition Acts** were more Hamilton- than Adams-inspired policies.

In the **election of 1800**, Hamilton was instrumental in getting the Federalists to support Jefferson over **Aaron Burr** for president. In 1804, he revealed Burr's flirting with the Federalist Essex Junto to set up a seceded New England, costing Burr the governorship of New York. Words were exchanged resulting in the Hamilton-Burr duel in Weehawken Heights, New Jersey. Hamilton was mortally wounded and died the next day at home in New York City.

HAMMOND, JAMES H. (1807–1864). Admitted to the bar in 1828, James Hammond became the editor of a political journal in Columbia, South Carolina, that was dedicated to the states rights view and supported negating the **Tariff of Abominations** during the **nullification Crisis** of 1832–1833. He was active in organizing state military forces to defend the state and later elected to Congress, but had to decline assuming his seat because of ill health that dogged him most of his life.

Hammond actively defended the **"Slavery as a Positive Good"** argument and published a book of collected essays on the subject in 1853. He propounded the Mud Sill Theory, that all decent society was based on a lower class that acted as the mud sill for its betters, freeing the latter to pursue more gentile, intellectual, and political endeavors. He also popularized the phrase "Cotton Is King" and warned that the North dared to make war on cotton.

He is also known for his instructions to his overseer expounded in his "Plantation Manual." Typical entries warn that the overseer needs to plan for everything and keep everything in its place. Inventory was to be taken each New Years' Day and 1 July. The overseer was to supervise the stock tenders, count the animals, check the water supply, inspect fences and gates, look after wagons and carts and the storage of all equipment. The overseer was allowed to give as many as 20 lashes on his own volition—more required Hammond's permission. The hierarchy of crime was running away, drunkenness, theft, absent from the job without permission, neglect of tools or animals. The overseer was to feed and clothe the slaves, select washer women each week to wash, mend, and iron all clothes. No work was to be done Sundays, but all slaves were to wash their persons, change their clothes, and comb their hair during that day. No work was to be done in the rain and none after dark, unless harvest time required it. The overseer was also to inspect the slave quarters regularly. Each morning he was to see that mothers took their children to the nursery. After the slaves left for work, all cabins were to be securely locked to prevent loitering. The sick were to be examined daily and cared for, calling a doctor when necessary.

A record of all births and deaths was to be kept. In addition, the overseer was to keep a record of all crops raised and amounts of harvest. The sale prices of all items taken to market and sold were to be noted. If an overseer did not make the cash crop expected or put up too little corn or meat, he was to be terminated. Failure to follow the instruction would mean that the overseer would not be rehired.

In 1850, Hammond was considered as Calhoun's replacement in the U.S. Senate, but he was passed over in favor of **Robert Barnwell Rhett**. Wade Hampton said that he would have to present evidence of Hammond's sexual liaison with Hampton's teenage daughters. The same problem kept him from assuming the senate seat when Rhett resigned over South Carolina's acceptance of the **Compromise of 1850**. This time, Andrew Butler won. But Hammond was elected to the U.S. Senate in 1857 and served until his state seceded in December 1860. He died during the war from lifelong physical disabilities. *See also* PLANTATION MANAGEMENT.

HAMPTON ROADS PEACE CONFERENCE. *See* STEPHENS, ALEXANDER H.

HARPER'S FERRY RAID (1859). In almost every state election in 1859, **Democrats** were voted out of office. As the Northern states overwhelmingly voted **Republican,** only **Stephen A. Douglas** retained his Senate seat. Virginia was the only Southern state to retain

Democrats, as **Whigs** or independents captured the rest of the South. Radical Southern Democrats, known as the chivalry or **fire-eaters**, led by **William L. Yancey**, overtook Georgia, Mississippi, and Louisiana. In their victory rallies, Yancey and his followers emphasized that even moderate Republicans, not just **anti-slavery** radicals, spoke about not having a nation half slave and half free (**Abraham Lincoln**'s "House Divided Speech"), and the inevitability of war over **slavery** between North and South (William H. Seward's "Irrepressible Conflict Speech"). In winning reelection to the U.S. Senate from Illinois, Douglas had to admit in his **Freeport Doctrine** that his support of **Popular Sovereignty** was a ruse. Further upsetting the balance between North and South in the U.S. Senate, Oregon and Minnesota had been admitted as free states.

However, the raid on the federal arsenal at Harper's Ferry, Virginia, in October 1859 gave Yancey's rhetoric sudden credibility in the South. John Brown, already infamous for executing Southern settlers in Kansas even though they were not slaveholders, organized a group of **abolitionists** to capture federal arsenals in the South and liberate slaves by force. Those unwilling to join would be sent to Canada, but participants would be supplied with arms and urged to spread the revolution throughout the South.

Unfortunately for Brown, the local African Americans did not flock to his cause. But President **James Buchanan** rushed a force of United States Marines commanded by **War with Mexico** hero Col. **Robert E. Lee** to Harper's Ferry. His chief aide was another Virginian whose star would rise during the coming Civil War, cavalryman Lt. J. E. B. Stuart. They surrounded Brown and his followers in a firehouse and, after a brief siege, they arrested Brown and a half dozen of his men. Ten of Brown's followers, including several of his sons, were killed in the gunfight. Among Brown's effects were maps of the South marking concentrated slave areas. Tried in a Virginia state court, Brown was found guilty of treason. Rumors spread that fellow abolitionists would try to free Brown, prompting the state militia to guard the execution proceedings, but no uprising occurred. A group of wealthy abolition businessmen and philanthropists called the "Secret Six" suspected of financing the raid denied any involvement.

The point was moot, as the South saw the Republicans as backing a slave rebellion through hiring surrogates, which this event proved.

The election of a Republican such as Lincoln would negate the South's hard-won victories in the U.S. **Supreme Court**, *Dred Scott v. Sanford* and *Ableman v. Booth*. **Secession** now seemed inevitable.

The Southern Whig-**American Party** centrist revival of 1859 dissolved after the Harper's Ferry Raid, leaving Republicans in the North and secessionist Democrats in the South as the only choices in the **election of 1860**. The splintering of the Democrats in 1860 led to war, during which Yankee troops marched south singing the ditty "John Brown's Body Lies A-Moldering in the Grave, But His Soul Goes Marching On" which evolved into the "Battle Hymn of the Republic."

HARRIS, ISHAM. *See* SECESSION OF THE SOUTHERN STATES, SECOND.

HARRIS, TOWNSEND. *See* SPREAD EAGLE FOREIGN POLICY.

HARRIS TREATY OF 1858. *See* SPREAD EAGLE FOREIGN POLICY.

HARRISON, WILLIAM HENRY (1773–1841). Born on the Virginia Peninsula east of Richmond, William Henry Harrison studied medicine before entering the army in the 1790s. He attained the rank of captain before he resigned his commission to accept the secretaryship to the governor of the Northwest Territory. He was elected territorial delegate to Congress and was made governor of Indiana Territory in 1801. Harrison was also a special Indian agent as he negotiated several big land concessions before the Shawnee chief, Tecumseh, put an end to such treaties.

Harrison led American forces against Tecumseh's Indian alliance at the Battle of Tippecanoe, winning a victory, mostly because he managed to hold his ground and the Indians retreated. He was made major general during the **War of 1812** and defeated a British–Indian alliance at the Battle of the Thames in 1813, destroying **Native American** power forever in the Old Northwest. He received the nickname "Old Tippecanoe" or "Old Tip" for his wartime experiences.

After the war, he served as state senator, congressman and U.S. Senator before being appointed as American minister to Colombia.

He retired to his Ohio estate, but was drafted as one of several **Whig** Party candidates for the presidency in the **election of 1836**, losing to **Martin Van Buren**. He became the party's sole candidate in the **election of 1840** and won a brilliant campaign ("Tippecanoe and Tyler, too") against the incumbent, Van Buren. Harrison died within a month of assuming the presidency, leaving the party in a shambles over his successor, **John Tyler**.

HARTFORD CONVENTION OF 1814. Ever since the election of **Thomas Jefferson** as president, the **Federalists** had questioned his policies, domestic and foreign. What the Federalists saw was that Jefferson hoped to extend **slavery** into the West through the creation of a never-ending series of **Three-Fifth Compromise** territories that were destined to become slave states. The more the Federalists objected to Jefferson and **James Madison**, who followed him into the presidency, the more Southern members of the Federalist Party dropped out to become **Democratic Republicans**. This limited the Federalists to the New England states and some of New York.

The measures leading up to the **War of 1812** were the last straw for the Federalists. They hated the **Embargo Act** and opined that it was a deliberate step to impoverish New England manufacturing and shipping while protecting Jefferson's beloved agrarian South. New England dragged its feet in supporting the war, becoming "Blue Light Federalists," those who signaled British warships ashore at night for reprovisioning and dispensing American military intelligence.

As the War of 1812 turned against the Americans and British forces prepared to invade coastal cities like New Orleans, Baltimore, and Washington, D.C., the Federalists, led by an ultra group called the Essex Junto, met at Hartford, Connecticut, to petition the government over perceived grievances. The delegates asked that military conscription be stopped within their boundaries, federal revenues collected in their states be spent in their states alone, no embargo be passed that lasted over 60 days, a two-thirds vote in Congress be necessary for declaring war and admitting new states, there be prohibitions against naturalized citizens holding federal office, there be laws limiting the president to one term of office and unable to be succeeded by anyone from his own state, there be a repeal of the **Twelfth Amendment** and repeal of the Three-Fifths Compromise. Should these things not be done, the delegates would opt for secession from the Union.

The real thing was to protest the government and reform it—the original goal of the Essex Junto—rather than secede, but the latter was always an option. But its sessions had been held in secret and its delegation arrived in Washington just as news came in that Gen. **Andrew Jackson** had won a great victory in the First Battle of New Orleans. Then came the announcement that the war had been concluded at Ghent, the Netherlands (today's Belgium), on the formula of status quo ante bellum—no loss of territory. The Federalists were accused of treason, sedition, and conspiracy. It killed their party forever. Jefferson's Revolution of 1800 speech ("We are all Federalists, we are all [Democratic] Republicans") had been proven half correct—Americans were now all Democratic Republicans. The **Era of Good Feelings** was on.

HAYNE, ROBERT Y. *See* JACKSON'S BREAK WITH CALHOUN; NULLIFICATION AND THE COMPROMISE OF 1833; RHETT, ROBERT BARNWELL; WEBSTER, DANIEL.

HELPER, HINTON ROWAN (1829–1909). From Davie County, North Carolina, born to a non-slaveholding family, Hinton Rowan Helper was educated in a local academy and worked as a store clerk. Accused of embezzling $300 from the till, Helper admitted to the charge and left the state for New York City. There he caught a boat to the California gold fields, but came home some years later, broke.

Helper decided to publish a book on his experiences out West and when his publisher objected to certain passages that made unfavorable comparisons between slave and free labor, Helper had to change the sections to suit the company. Helper angrily decided that freedom of expression and the press were denied in the slave South and worked to expose this in a new book, *The Impending Crisis of the South and How to Meet It* (1857).

Published in New York under the condition that he would pay ahead of time for the volume, Helper's book attacked **slavery** from an economic point of view. He claimed that slavery caused the South to stay backward from areas that used free labor. To prove his point, Helper used statistics, which he salted in favor of his argument. He claimed that the hay crop in the North was more valuable to the nation than cotton, which was patently untrue. He also said that the South lagged behind the North in imports and exports, manufactures, railroad mileage, bank capital, and overall wealth. The South was dependent on the North for manufactured articles, and Southern culture overall was inferior in terms of literacy, schools, colleges, libraries, newspapers, post offices, and publishers of books and magazines.

The true salvation of the South would be to abolish slavery by taxing it out of existence and make slaveholders unable to vote. To secure that end, Helper said he would vote **Republican**. Helper's book did not make much of an impact until Horace Greeley of the *New York Tribune* published an abridged version of it in 1859 as a Republican campaign piece.

Helper realized little profit from his writings. He could not return to the South and lived in New York City. **Abraham Lincoln** made him the minister to Argentina, where he married a local woman. Returning to New York, Helper spent the rest of his years calling for the expulsion of the now freed slaves from the United States to help the poor whites economically in the South. This also showed a racial prejudice that kept almost all Southern whites, regardless of social or economic station, supporting the **peculiar institution** and the Confederacy. They had no sympathy for black people living among them, slave or free. Neither did Helper.

HEMINGS, SALLY (1766–1835). Sally Hemings was **Thomas Jefferson**'s female house slave, a beautiful light-skinned quadroon (one-fourth black). Jefferson's father-in-law John Wayles had originally owned and fathered Sally, which made her the half sister of Jefferson's wife. When Jefferson married Martha Wayles Skelton, Sally went along as a wedding present. Tragically, Martha Jefferson died at a young age. According to the stories, the bereaved Jefferson did not need to find a new wife; he had a spare at home, Sally, whom he made his concubine and by whom he fathered five children.

The story of Jefferson and his ebony paramour was compelling enough that historian Fawn Brodie built a large section of her biography of her *Sage of Monticello* around the alleged love story (she elevated it above an affair) between Jefferson and his servant. Up to this point, Jefferson's **miscegenation** was but a local rumor. But it would not be for long.

Sally Hemings' public story begins with Jefferson's political relationship with an English publicist named James Callender, who was drawn to Jefferson's attention by his tract *The Political Progress of Britain*, which excoriated King George III as one of the "ruffian race of British kings." Callender did some good work for Jefferson. He was the man who revealed Alexander Hamilton's shenanigans—in the treasury illegally speculating in government securities and outside the administration romancing Mrs. James Reynolds—in his *History of the United States for 1796*, which got Callender arrested under the Alien and Sedition acts. Jefferson made his first mistake pardoning Callender and getting him out of jail. But the marshal refused to remit Callender's fine. Jefferson raised the money but Callender wanted more. He wanted a political appointment. Jefferson refused. Callender threatened to do him in as he had done Hamilton. Still Jefferson was adamant.

Callender then got a job with a Federalist newspaper, the *Richmond Recorder*, and made it into a widely read scandal sheet. The trouble was that Callender never investigated anything; he merely published innuendoes, the sexier the better. He found a gold mine in Jefferson. Under the principle that the people must know, Callender asserted that Jefferson had fathered children not only by Sally Hemings, but also by a veritable "Congo Harem," the progeny of which he sold on the slave market to hush it all up.

If the Jefferson–Hemings love story is true, wrote one biographer, who like most disbelieves it, then Jefferson stands condemned as one of the "most profligate liars and consummate hypocrites ever to occupy the presidency." Unfortunately for Jefferson's advocates, modern DNA research on African Americans claiming to be heirs of Jefferson indicates that the story is at least partially true. That is, someone with the Jefferson family's DNA was intimately involved with Sally Hemings and produced some progeny.

Whether he loved Sally or took advantage of her, of all the Founding Fathers who spoke out against slavery and of the freedom of man, Jefferson was the only president from the **Virginia Dynasty** not to free all of his slaves upon his death. He was in too much debt to throw away that much capital. His heirs did free Sally Hemings's progeny over the years, but not her. According to state law, she would have had to leave Virginia had they done so, an old woman without support. But his daughter did emancipate her after Jefferson's death, ridding Monticello of the physical traces of Sally's story, if not the prurient rumors, at last.

HEMP. Closely related to **cotton** economically was hemp culture, which produced the bagging and rope that made up the exterior of a cotton bale. Originally grown in the back country during the colonial era, hemp culture there was wiped out by the expansion of upland cotton. But the product was a necessity, so it shifted westward to Kentucky, Tennessee, and Missouri. By the Civil War, 75 percent of the crop was grown in the Missouri River bottomlands from St. Louis to Kansas City. Kentucky and Tennessee found **tobacco** and the **domestic slave trade** with Louisiana and Texas to be more profitable business endeavors.

Hemp did well in the river valleys and on the blue grass prairies of the upper South interior. It wore out the land just as much as did tobacco. Originally pulled up by hand, by the 1840s a special curved cutting knife was used to speed harvest. The fibers were then broken out of the stalks by hand at a rate of 40–50 pounds a day. It required the strongest slaves to do this. One acre of hemp produced about 600 pounds of fibers and 10 acres was considered the right amount of work for one fieldhand. From the Great Migration to the Civil War, the price of American hemp doubled because of the rapid increase in the growth of upland cotton. *See also* ECONOMY.

HENRICO PLOT (1800). *See* "GENERAL" GABRIEL'S PLOT.

HIDALGO Y COSTILLA, MIGUEL. *See* LONE STAR REBELLIONS.

HONOR. *See* VIOLENCE AND WHITE MILITANCY.

HOUSTON, SAMUEL. *See* LONE STAR REBELLIONS; SECESSION OF THE SOUTHERN STATES, FIRST.

HUGHES, JOHN CARDINAL. *See* AMERICAN PARTY.

– I –

IMPENDING CRISIS. See HELPER, HINTON ROWAN.

INDIAN REMOVAL. Another issue in which **Andrew Jackson** proved himself a Westerner and a Southerner was Indian Removal. Unlike **John Quincy Adams**, who would not evict **Native Americans** from their ancestral lands, Jackson would. The traditional view has been that Jackson was an Indian-hater, but more recent historians have suggested that Jackson knew only too well that it was either removal or extinction by land-hungry and gold-crazed settlers.

Jackson was aware that in both the Northwest (Wisconsin, Illinois, Indiana) and Southwest (Georgia, Alabama, Mississippi, Florida), Native Americans still held onto at least 40 million acres of land. Indian Removal was not new. **Thomas Jefferson** first proposed a constitutional amendment to allow Indians to swap lands east of the Mississippi for lands in the **Louisiana Purchase** beyond the western border of Arkansas. But Jefferson was against force being used, so few Native Americans left.

Unlike the tribes of the Old Southwest, the Indians of the Old Northwest had been crushed in the **War of 1812**. Reduced to 20 or so small tribal units, their removal west of the Mississippi had been an ongoing process ever since, largely directed by **Lewis Cass** of Michigan. In 1832, the U.S. government engaged in the brutally quick Black Hawk War in Illinois and Wisconsin against the stubborn Sauk-Fox tribe, which resulted in the Battle of Bad Axe and their removal in the Trail of Death. The following year saw the Treaty of Chicago negotiated between the Ottawa, Pottawatomie, and Chippewa, the last tribes to hold major tribal lands in the Old Northwest. Many of these tribes wound up in Kansas only to be moved once again, south into Indian Territory after Kansas was made a territory in the **Kansas–Nebraska Act** in 1854.

The tribes of the Old Southwest presented a bigger problem for removal. For one thing, they were larger and better organized. They had also adopted white ways. They owned plantations, farmed, raised **cotton**, used slave labor, and had white names and governmental organization. They were referred to as the Civilized Tribes.

With the influx of whites after the War of 1812 in the **Great Migration**, some Cherokees (the Old Settlers) agreed to leave the South for western Arkansas in 1817. Three years later, after signing the Treaty of Doak's Stand, a few Choctaws left to join them. In 1823, the Georgia legislature passed a resolution demanding that the United States remove Indians from the state under a prior agreement, the 1802 cession of its western lands. The problem was complicated by a gold discovery in the heart of Cherokee country at Dalonega, leading to the first gold rush in American history.

When a portion of the Creeks agreed to their own removal in the Treaty of Indian Springs, President John Quincy Adams refused to enforce it and the Creeks assassinated their chief, William McIntosh, who had negotiated it. Adams' position cost him what few votes he might have received from the South in the **election of 1828**.

But when all was said and done, Jackson knew that everything depended on what the Cherokees would do. If they accepted removal, everyone else would have to go, too. The Cherokees were so important because they had accepted white civilization, including the plantation economy and **slavery**, more than any other tribe. The Cherokees put up a spirited resistance based on Anglo-American legal tradition.

The first thing the tribe did was to declare its independence from Georgia, the state in which most of them lived. Georgia immediately protested to the federal government. The U.S. Constitution said no new state could be created from another state without the original state's approval. Georgia then declared the Cherokee to be mere tenants and extended Georgia law into the area, nullifying all Indian laws and creating counties and all-white governments.

Jackson backed up Georgia by having Congress pass the Indian Removal Act of 1830. The law was based on the U.S. **Supreme Court** case, *Johnson v. McIntosh* (1823), which stated that Native Americans were mere residents (tenants, not owners) on any land they claimed by right of conquest. The Indian Removal Act created an Indian Territory (eastern part of present-day Oklahoma) and proposed to trade land east of the Mississippi for land in the new territory. It also promised to buy the territory from the existing Native Americans who already claimed it, and ordered the president to provide for tribal government for the removed Indians when they arrived in the West. The new lands were guaranteed to the removed peoples forever—as usual. The federal government would pay for all improvements to Indian lands in the East and throw in an extra half million dollars to pay for removal, new homes in the West, tools, and other amenities. By the end of **Jackson's second administration**, 46,000 Native Americans had been removed from east of the Mississippi under the 1830 law, freeing up 25 million acres of land to white settlement.

The Cherokees took it all to the U.S. Supreme Court, Chief Justice **John Marshall** presiding. The court examined the case as the *Cherokee Nation v. Georgia* (1830). Georgia refused to appear, alleging its sovereignty was being impugned by both the court and the tribe. Marshall ruled that the Cherokees were a domestic, dependent nation in a state of pupilage; that is, the Cherokees were wards of the federal government. They were not independent because they had no right to deal with foreign nations. Georgia was rebuked for not guaranteeing them their rights as landowners as granted by federal treaty.

Borrowing a page from South Carolina and its theory of the **Concurrent Voice and Nullification**, Georgia nullified the Court's decision. It also passed a law preventing whites from entering land claimed by the Cherokees without taking an oath to the state and purchasing a license. The belief was that the white missionaries were providing legal advice to the Indians. A state guard was created to enforce the law.

Meanwhile, in Mississippi, the Choctaw Nation took note and signed the Treaty of Dancing Rabbit Creek (1830). It called for the removal of all Choctaws to Indian Territory by 1833. Those Indians not desiring to leave could accept a parcel of land in Mississippi and become citizens of the state and hence the United States. By 1842, most who stayed behind had been cheated out of their land. The federal government agreed to make up their losses only if they followed their brethren to Indian Territory.

The year after the Choctaw agreed to move west, the Seminole Nation agreed to the Treaty of Payne's Landing. This exchanged all of their land in Florida for a tract in Indian Territory. Unlike the earlier Treaty of Moultrie Creek (1823) that had been signed by a fraction of the tribe and rendered unenforceable, every Seminole faction was present. All of the chiefs signed but Osceola, who drove his knife through the treaty pages in a rage and walked out.

Meanwhile, Georgia arrested two unlicensed missionaries for violating state laws. One of them, Samuel Worcester, took his case to the U.S. Supreme Court. Georgia refused to appear. In *Worcester v. Georgia* (1832), Marshall repeated what he had said earlier, accompanied by an extensive history lesson of treaties and other relations between whites and reds. Georgia had no jurisdiction over Cherokee lands, Marshall concluded. Worcester should be set free. Georgia nullified the decision. Andrew Jackson did, too. "John Marshall has made his decision; let him enforce it," the president is alleged to have said. Worcester served most of a four-year jail sentence before following the Cherokees to the West.

Jackson condoned Georgia doing what he would nearly go to war to prevent in South Carolina. He was very inconsistent but politically astute in this. He wanted to be sure that nullification in South Carolina did not spread to another state. If he had to remove the Native Americans to prevent the spread of nullification, he would do so. Georgia became the key to his being able to isolate the South Carolinians from other Southern states and blocking their nullification action against the **Tariff** of 1828 and the **Tariff** of 1832.

INDIAN REMOVAL ACT (1830). *See* INDIAN REMOVAL.

INDIAN REMOVAL COMPLETED. In his second term, **Andrew Jackson** was determined to wrap up as much of the resettlement of the Five Civilized Tribes (Cherokee, Creek, Chickasaw, Choctaw, and Seminole) as possible. The going got difficult right away. The Creeks in Alabama were old nemeses of Jackson from the **War of 1812** and after. In fact, Jackson had signed nearly a dozen treaties with the Creek (sometimes called the Muscogee) Nation, each taking more land for white settlement. In this he rivaled **William Henry Harrison** in the Northwest for numbers of treaties and acreage yielded.

By 1836, the Creeks still left in Alabama were worn out. Whites had cheated them out of land that those who refused to leave had received. Houses and barns were shot up and burned by white raiders. The Creeks retaliated in what came to known as the Creek War of 1836. This only allowed the whites to bring in the soldiers. Creeks were rounded up, put in chains, and shipped to Indian Territory in small groups all thorough 1837. Some traveled by steamboat on the Tennessee River, and others went by ship to New Orleans and by steamboat up the Arkansas. Others fled to neighboring tribes, only to be sent to the West with them.

Having won their legal appeals in the Supreme Court only to see it all nullified by the state of Georgia, the Creeks' eastern neighbors, the Cherokees (at least, part of the tribe), signed the Treaty of New Echota in 1835. In it, the whole tribe agreed to removal to Indian Territory within two years, but few left. In 1837, Maj. Gen. **Winfield Scott** and 9,000 soldiers rounded up the whole tribe and lodged them in holding stockades. Some remnants fled into the mountains in western North Carolina where they still live today. The great majority was divided into traveling groups and escorted to Indian Territory. The march, known as the Trail of Tears, took a northern route down the Tennessee River to the Ohio and west across Missouri and saw 4,000 Indians die. After their arrival in the West, tribal factions fought against each other, joined opposite sides in the white man's Civil War, and finally came together late in the century.

Other tribes, North and South, followed. The last of the Civilized Tribes, the Chickasaws from northern Mississippi, finally agreed to leave for Indian Territory in 1837. As early as 1828, the government invited tribal representatives to look over possible settlement sites out West. Mississippi had destroyed the legality of tribal government and the authority of the chiefs, and it was obvious something had to be done.

The Chickasaw Nation had agreed to the Treaty of Franklin in 1830. It provided for the usual annuities and funded the removal as soon as the tribe picked out a parcel of land in Indian Territory. But every time a piece of land was designated, the tribal delegations demurred. Then the tribe agreed to the supplemental Treaty of Ponotoc in 1832. This allowed their land in Mississippi to be surveyed and sold immediately, which put great pressure on completing the move west.

In 1837, at the Treaty of Doaksville, the Chickasaws agreed to pay the Choctaws for the western half of their Indian Territory grant and the tribe made the arduous journey westward. Although the trip was not without its difficulties, the Chickasaws seem to have suffered less than those who preceded them.

With the pending departure of the Chickasaws, all that was left was the Seminole Nation in Florida. There were two problems with the Seminole's Payne's Landing Agreement. The Seminoles had long been a refuge for **runaway** slaves. The treaty said that fugitive blacks had to be given up to their "rightful owners." The blacks were fully integrated into tribal affairs and most Seminoles disliked this turning on a loyal portion of the tribe. As a matter of fact, this had been the main bone of contention leading to the First Seminole War in 1818.

Then the treaty called for the removal to begin three years after the treaty was ratified. This did not take place until an exploratory party returned from Indian Territory in 1834. The Seminoles said they now had until 1837 to move. But white authorities counted from 1832, meaning the tribe had but one year to leave.

When the exploratory party that agreed to accept the lands set aside in Indian Territory at Ft. Gibson in 1833 returned home to begin the removal process, hostilities began. A dissenting chief, Osceola, executed one of their number, Charlie Emathla, for confirming the removal treaty. War parties killed U.S. Indian Agent Wiley Thompson near Ft. King, and another ambushed Maj. Francis Dade's two companies of soldiers on the road from Tampa. The Second Seminole War was on.

Attacking from the Florida swamps, the Seminoles bled the U.S. Army until 1842. The war compromised the careers of nearly every general officer associated with it and decimated the ranks of subalterns and the regulars and militia that fought it. And always the Negro-Indians were a point of contention and a center of resistance.

To separate the former slaves from the Indians, the army offered them their freedom from being returned to **slavery** if they would but surrender. Then Maj. Gen. Thomas Jesup committed the dirtiest and most effective move of the war in 1837, when he seized Osceola, Wildcat (who later escaped), and a half dozen other chiefs who had come in under a flag of truce. Jesup was condemned then and now, but he believed he did what had to be done. Every other captured Indian was put in irons and shipped out to Indian Territory. Jesup sent the Negro-Indians with them.

Finally, Maj. Gen. Alexander McComb figured out that the war was dying out. Military columns were not being attacked, not even unescorted wagons. Only the Florida Crackers (settlers) and the

Seminole hotheads were fighting. The general decided to try out a plan. He would ask the Indians to withdraw south of the Pease River into the Everglades and stop the war. It worked. President **Martin Van Buren** declared the area to be a full-fledged reservation, no whites allowed.

Floridians were very unhappy with the army's plan. The Indians still could raid out of the Everglades and some did. Then in 1842, Wildcat came in to talk to Col. William Worth, the new army commander. The Seminoles had been burned out, their crops destroyed, and their warriors, women, and children were starving.

Worth told Wildcat that he was to convince as many of the Seminoles as he could to go with him to Indian Territory or be hanged. Wildcat sent out numerous messengers and the Seminoles began to come in to be transported west. The black Indians went with them, no longer a point of contention. Osceola sickened and died shortly after at Ft. Moultrie in Charleston.

The war was over. All but 300 Seminoles removed to Indian Territory. The others stayed in the Everglades area and farmed in peace until 1857. Then, after their defeat in a brief Third Seminole War, instigated when a military column destroyed an Indian encampment in a drunken spree, about a third of these, under Billy Bowlegs, joined the rest of the tribe in the West.

INDIAN SPRINGS, TREATY OF. *See* INDIAN REMOVAL.

INDIGO. A plant native to the Atlantic Coast of South Carolina, Georgia, and Florida, indigo was not cultivated until the 1740s. At that time, Eliza Lucas, the wife of Charles Pinckney and mother of Charles Cotesworth and Thomas Pinckney of **Federalist Party** fame, brought a variety from the West Indies, which was developed into a seed crop. The reason that indigo arrived late in the North American colonies was that its production was not feasible until the West Indies converted solely to **sugar** production. Only then were the poorer soils of South Carolina able to compete with the richer Caribbean islands' soils.

By the end of the decade, 138,334 pounds of indigo (used as a dyestuff for the burgeoning British textile industry) was being shipped to Britain from Charleston annually. A bounty of one shilling per pound made indigo an extra special crop. Indeed, one could easily double one's initial investment in three years. In combination with **rice**, indigo made South Carolina the richest planting area in North American before the introduction of **upland cotton**.

Indigo was grown inland in South Carolina, especially after the Sea Islands emphasized the production of rice and long-staple cotton. One slave could cultivate up to four acres. It was planted in holes a foot apart, five seeds per hole. It was cut with a sickle before the stalk got woody, but the plant had a bluish or purple tinge. Then the cuttings were taken to a shed that had three large vats in it, each draining into the next through a spigot. In the first vat the cuttings were soaked until the dye was given up by the leaves. In the second vat, the blue water was beaten vigorously and allowed to settle. Then the clear liquid was slowly drawn off to the third vat. The indigo solids left in the second vat were lifted out in bags and spread to dry. Then the solids were cut into squares and packed into barrels for shipment. *See also* ECONOMY.

INDUSTRIAL SLAVERY. One of the greatest weaknesses in the notion that there were **natural limits of slavery expansion** was industrial slavery. The natural limits theory assumed that slaves could only work at the simplest tasks. Yet the very existence of slave artisans on the plantations themselves gave lie to this racist notion inherent in pro-slave thought. The South in its industrial output during the Civil War produced enough goods to keep the war going for four long years. By 1860, the South had 20 percent of the invested industrial capital and 15 percent of the total industry of the nation as a whole (North and South). Five percent of the slaves in the South were owned by factories or employed in industrial applications. Most of these slaves were male and many hired their own time and lived pretty much unsupervised after hours in towns or cities. It was possible for slave and free blacks to work side by side in the same plant, alongside of free white workers.

Industrial slaves worked at numerous skilled and unskilled jobs in **cotton** mills, iron furnaces, **tobacco** warehouses, **hemp** walks, light machine fabrication shops, the processing of all agricultural crops, mines (precious metals, coal, salt), lumberyards, fishing, all forms of transport (firemen on Southern railroads were by and large African Americans), and in public works for local, county, state, and federal governments. As industrial workers, slaves received better treatment than workers, white or black, for hire. Slaves had an intrinsic value in the health of their own bodies. Accidents were common in all industrial jobs before the Civil War, and if a slave were hurt or killed, his owner (not necessarily the factory owner) received whatever compensation was adjudicated.

In industry, discipline was a matter of the production schedule. No slackers were abided. Rewards like free time, holidays, or cash bonuses were allotted for good and extra work or denied for sloppy or inferior production. **Abolitionists** likened this to a breakdown in the usual white control, but factory owners recognized it for what it really was—a clever way to enforce discipline short of the lash. Above all, while free workers had the habit of striking at crucial moments in the work schedule, no slave had such a chance. Physical compulsion as regards the slave was always a last resort. It was not uncommon for a white worker to teach his slave apprentice the job only to be fired in turn, and the slave introduced permanently into his old job.

Industry was a relatively new field for **slavery** in 1860 that had not been fully exploited. This made the climate and rainfall necessary to produce **upland cotton** irrelevant to slavery's expansion into the West. For 400 years, the Spanish in Latin America had shown the future for American slavery to expand without natural limits into the mining areas of the new Rocky Mountain West. The **Wilmot Proviso**, artificially limiting the expansion of slavery, was the North's only chance to stop a vibrant, growing institution before the Civil War.

INTERNAL IMPROVEMENTS. These are transportation projects financed by state or federal appropriations, The big question was whether they were within the scope of the **Constitution** as written. The answer was affirmative for years as illustrated by the **National Road**. But **Andrew Jackson** was not so sure and restricted federal participation in the **Maysville Road Veto**. His arch political enemy, **Henry Clay**, however, made federal financing of internal improvements a central part of his **American System**.

ITURBIDE, AUGUSTÍN. *See* LONE STAR REBELLIONS.

IVERSON, ALFRED, SR. (1783–1873). Georgia-born and educated, Alfred Iverson, Sr., attended Princeton University as a young man. He returned home to read law and opened a very successful practice at Columbus, Georgia. In the 1840s, he served three terms in the state legislature before rising to the state senate. He helped finance a Georgia volunteer regiment for the **War with Mexico**. He then served for seven years as judge of the superior court for the Columbus circuit. Iverson was a presidential elector in 1844 and in 1846 was elected to Congress as a Democrat. As the sectional conflict heated up between the North and the Old South, Iverson was elected to the United States Senate in 1855.

While in the senate Iverson backed the concept of the **extraterritoriality** of slavery and the Old South's absolute right to have slavery in the territories as expressed through the U.S. **Supreme Court** case, ***Dred Scott v. Sanford*** (1857). He was an open advocate of the disunion movement. Upon the success of **secession**, Iverson withdrew from the Senate and practiced law back in Columbus until 1868. He then bought a plantation and farmed until his death five years later.

– J –

"JACKAL DIPLOMACY." *See* SPREAD EAGLE FOREIGN POLICY.

JACKSON, ANDREW (1767–1845). A South Carolinian by birth, Andrew Jackson grew up during the most violent days of guerrilla warfare that plagued the state during the American Revolution. His family was Scots-Irish and Presbyterian, two qualities that built the South and made it great before the Civil War. Like his people, Jackson was stubborn, righteous, knew the Lord's will, and did it. When Jackson was beaten by a British officer during the Revolution, the incident revealed another Jackson quality—he never forgot a slur and he was a very good hater. His admirers did not call him "Old Hickory" for nothing.

As a young man, Jackson went to Tennessee, where he made his fortune and built his home, the Hermitage. He settled at Nashville and became an attorney, state legislator, judge, and head of the state militia. Unlike most militias that stood around and got drunk on drill days, Jackson saw to it his men were well-trained and disciplined. Jackson was of above average intelligence, but he liked to overawe his opponents with an aggressive personality.

In Nashville, he met Rachel Donelson. Mistakenly, he and Rachel thought her former husband, living in Kentucky, had obtained a divorce. He got one all right, but it was dated two years after Andrew and Rachel had married. So the Jacksons married a second time. This caused all sorts of unwise people to accuse Andrew Jackson and his wife of committing adultery.

In a brawling section of the country like Tennessee, this was tantamount to challenging Jackson to a **duel**. He never backed down. His life was filled with violence. He was noted for duels, gunfights, street battles, canings, and fistfights and had the reputation of killing or maiming a large number of men in his lifetime. Jackson wound up with two bullets in his body, one in his arm that was extracted years later in the White House without anesthetic. The other was so close to his heart it was never removed. It just bled and suppurated on an irregular basis until the day he died.

Jackson led the Southern army in the **War of 1812**, fighting the Creeks and the British. They won victory after victory culminating in the First Battle of New Orleans, which made him a national hero. After the war, he fought the Indians again, captured Pensacola, Florida, and hanged two British citizens he accused of inciting the war. Elected to the U.S. Senate, Jackson stood for the presidency in the **election of 1824**. He lacked a majority of electoral votes and lost to **John Quincy Adams**.

When Adams appointed **Henry Clay**, another candidate and the man who counted the electoral votes as speaker of the house, to his cabinet as secretary of state and, by implication, the man to succeed him in the White House, Jackson accused them of a "Corrupt Bargain." The result was a four-year-long campaign that put Jackson in as president in the **election of 1828**. The campaign was very dirty, and at the end of it Rachael sickened and died.

Jackson's first administration saw him unite his backers into the **Democrat Party** and challenge South Carolina's nullification of the **Tariff of 1828** and the rechartering of the **Second Bank of the United States**. In **Jackson's second administration** he finished off these problems and engaged in **Indian Removal** from the cis-Mississippi west, opening the lands to white settlement.

Jackson retired, leaving the presidency in the hands of his political crony, **Martin Van Buren**. When he died some years later, there was much debate over whether he went to Heaven or Hell. The general agreement was that if Jackson wanted to go to Heaven, he would manage it. He always did.

JACKSON, THOMAS J. "STONEWALL" (1824–1863). Born on 21 January 1824 in what would become West Virginia, Thomas J. Jackson became an orphan at an early age. Raised by his uncle, Jackson was a very lonely child, so much so that he refused to discuss it in later years with anyone. Still, he developed a great sense of integrity, personal responsibility, and honesty.

But what Jackson pined for most was **education**. He sought a military education at West Point, a common approach for poorer boys of ambition in those days. At the Military Academy, Jackson withdrew into himself even more as he worked hard to make up for his shortcomings as a scholar. He eschewed all frivolity, although some cadets remembered him engaging in a few drunken parties. But Jackson made few close friends and felt awkward in the company of others. He became a disciplined young man who hated surprises and did not tolerate mistakes in himself or others. He was quite successful, all things considered, as he graduated 17th in his class of 59 at West Point in 1846.

He won three brevets for bravery during the **War with Mexico**, but resigned his commission in 1851 to teach tactics at the Virginia Military Academy (VMI). At Lexington, Jackson became a devout Presbyterian, tended to be humorless (he laughed by throwing his head back but making no sound), rarely spoke, believed in predestination, was a fatalist, gave out Sunday school tracts to his military students, and lived a simple life of hard work and few outwardly perceived enjoyments besides constant prayer. His whole life was one of the perfect schedule. Each day was the same as the day before and the day to come. The only exception was Sunday, which he devoted to **church and religion**.

Like many Southern men, Jackson married twice. His first wife died during the birth of their still-born baby. His second would bury

Jackson during the Civil War. He owned six slaves in the 1850s, making Jackson an average slaveholder as far as numbers of chattels was concerned. He received most as gifts and treated them all with kindness, although life in the Jackson home was one of regulation and discipline that might challenge any being of any color, slave or free. He rented one of his bondsmen to the Virginia Military Academy; the others worked at home and in the garden.

Jackson found **secession** to be a religious necessity. He firmly believed that the Yankees were violating the commandments of God and Constitution by meddling to create a new society with little adherence to both. Not to fight the North would lead to subservience to the forces of evil. Like **Robert E. Lee**, Jackson was loath to draw his sword against his native state or his Lexington neighbors. But Jackson went a step further when he hoped to create an "army of the living God" as he led the VMI cadets to war.

When Jackson joined in the defense of Virginia at Harper's Ferry, in 1861, he presented a not-too-inspiring sight. He wore a broken brimmed kepi, a threadbare jacket from his War with Mexico days, and a pair of floppy boots of a very large size. He was tall at six feet, and powerfully built. He liked to ride about holding one arm up in the air (allegedly to improve his circulation), and often sucked on lemons or other fruit (it quelled his dyspepsia) while in thought. He was deaf in one ear and could not hear distant sounds. He never shared his battle plans with anyone, which drove subordinates crazy with anxiety. He was fearless in battle, trusting his life and commands to the Lord. His eccentricities caused the soldiers to give him a multitude of nicknames from the endearing "Old Jack," to the less loveable "Fool Tom," to "Old Blue Light" for the haunting gaze in his pale eyes. Jackson disliked fighting on Sundays, although he never delayed engaging in battle on the Lord's Day, especially when victory presented itself, as it often did.

As a brigade commander at the battle of First Manassas, he and his men held Henry House Hill "like a stone wall," permitting the Rebel counterattack that swept the Yankees from the field. For this both he and his brigade received the nickname, "Stonewall." In the spring of 1862, Jackson fought the famous First Shenandoah Valley Campaign in which he defeated three Union Armies sent against him. Called to Richmond, Jackson took a lackluster part in Robert E. Lee's defense of the Confederate capital of Richmond. That summer, Jackson was his old self as he led half of Lee's army at the Second Manassas Campaign and at Antietam Creek. Jackson circled the Union Army at the Battle of Chancellorsville and made a crushing flank attack, during which he was mistakenly shot down by his own men. Losing his left arm, Jackson seemed to be mending well when he suddenly took ill from pneumonia and died at Guiney Station on 10 May 1863.

JACKSON AND THE PUBLIC LANDS. Andrew Jackson believed in the Land Law of 1820 ($1.25 an acre, 80 acres, or the $100 farm) from the **Era of Good Feelings**. But often the settlers got ahead of the survey teams. Then when the land was surveyed, it was bought out from the farmers by speculators. Jackson's solution was the Preemption Act of 1830. This meant that the resident on the public lands who got there ahead of everyone else had an uncontested first right to buy the land he had improved at $1.25 an acre, up to 160 acres.

But Jackson had much competition on what was right in land policy. **Thomas Hart Benton** of Missouri championed two other theories. The first was donation. Benton wished to donate unsold public lands to the states in which they were located. The states could sell such land at whatever price they could get, the proceeds to be used for internal improvements. The Swamp Lands Acts of 1848 and 1854 instituted this policy. Benton also favored graduation of federal land prices. If land did not sell after so long, Benton wanted the price reduced or graduated until it did sell. This would fill up empty spaces and assure some income from vacant areas. It took until 1854 before Congress made this federal policy in the Graduation Land Act.

Henry Clay of Kentucky, like Benton, had his own favorite solution to land sales profits. He favored distribution and made it a part of his **American System**. This was a policy whereby the proceeds of all land sales would be given out to the states for their own use, preferably on internal improvements or **colonization** of freed slaves back to Africa. The state or territory in which the land was located would be given a guaranteed percentage of all sales within its boundaries for the same uses.

Jackson reserved the pocket veto for the Distribution Bill (the president can let the bill expire without comment if Congress is not in session), a first in American history, a special slap at his **National Republican** opponent, Clay. Jackson knew that Clay wanted to reduce federal income from land sales to force a higher **tariff** to please the national Republicans' New England manufacturing constituency. Later in 1842, the **Whigs** under **John Tyler** would place preemption, donation, and graduation in the tariff of that year, providing that the tariff never rose above a rate of 20 percent.

JACKSONIANS. *See* DEMOCRATS.

JACKSON'S BREAK WITH CALHOUN. The man who suffered most from **Andrew Jackson**'s initial political appointments was Vice President **John C. Calhoun**. Jackson early on realized that Calhoun was out for himself. Secretary of State **Martin Van Buren** saw to that, reporting any event that might cast aspersions on Calhoun's loyalty. Jackson had the habit of taking a fast horseback ride every morning. Van Buren was a lousy rider, but he went with the president regularly. Along the way, artful political discussions placed Van Buren firmly in Jackson's camp. Or was it the other way around?

Three things did in Calhoun's political alliance with Jackson. First was the marital problem of Secretary of War John Eaton. Eaton had married a flashy young woman, Peggy O'Neal, with a shady past, at least according to the better people in Washington society, that is, the wives of the rest of Jackson's political retinue. Those ladies refused to admit Peggy into their affairs.

This angered Jackson, who had seen the same done to his wife, Rachel, after their marriage had been interrupted by the discovery that her first union had not been ended by the divorce her ex-husband had promised. The Jacksons had had to remarry after the divorce came through, resulting in charges of adultery. Jackson fought **duels** over such things. He saw Peggy Eaton suffering from the same kind of unfounded accusations. Jackson ordered his political allies to tell their wives to stop their whispers and for everyone to treat her respectfully. Only Secretary of State Van Buren, a widower, complied. Once again, Calhoun, whose wife led the campaign against Peggy, turned up on the wrong side.

Then Van Buren arranged for Jackson to discover that Calhoun had wanted him recalled as general for his brash actions in the First

Seminole War. Jackson had always assumed that **John Quincy Adams** had made the protests in **James Monroe**'s cabinet. Calhoun had let the matter ride, but now was caught, revealed in documents that Jackson saw for the first time. William Crawford, Monroe's old secretary of war and Calhoun's sworn enemy, had provided them to Van Buren through Virginia newspaper editor Thomas Ritchie, an important Jackson supporter.

Finally, Jackson began to suspect that Calhoun was behind South Carolina efforts to nullify the **Tariff of 1828**. Calhoun was, but his motives were to try and stop possible **secession** of the state by suggesting how one state might declare an act of Congress unconstitutional. Hopefully the prolonged process would lead to discussion and compromise.

When **Daniel Webster** of Massachusetts and Robert Y. Hayne of South Carolina debated the issue in the U.S. Senate, Hayne, a true radical secessionist, wanted to get Jackson to take a stand. At the Thomas Jefferson birthday celebration, Hayne arranged for written toasts to all forms of states rights and nullification. Many Northern delegates walked out in disgust.

When impromptu toasts began, Jackson gave the first. "Our Union, it must be preserved," Jackson said. This was a shock to the Southerners, who assumed that Jackson was a states rights man. Later Jackson allowed Hayne to publish the toast as, "Our Federal Union," to indicate the importance of the states under the Constitution. Quickly Van Buren, short in stature, leaped upon his chair to see over the crowd. The second toast, from Calhoun was "Our Union, next to our liberties, most dear." Van Buren saw Calhoun's hand shake ever so imperceptibly and some of the liquor dripped to the floor. Jackson, and everyone else present, took this correctly to indicate that Calhoun was the author of the nullification process.

Unlike the South Carolinians, many of whom believed in states rights and secession, Jackson believed that the interests of the South could best be protected within the Union under the Constitution, with its **extraterritoriality** guarantees for **slavery** and the **Three-Fifths Compromise**. The result was that Jackson, at Van Buren's suggestion, asked his original cabinet, including Eaton, to resign and appointed a new batch completely loyal to him. The loyal Mr. Van Buren wound up as minister to Britain, but Calhoun blocked the appointment. Once again, Jackson and Calhoun had split over a party loyalty issue.

JACKSON'S FIRST ADMINISTRATION. Arguably the most important administration between **George Washington** and Civil War, **Andrew Jackson** was instrumental in creating a new political party system, comprising the **Democrats** or Jacksonians and **National Republicans** or anti-Jacksonians, later called the **Whigs**. He was the last president to serve two full terms until Ulysses S. Grant. Jackson was a blend of the two most dynamic, expansionist sections of the nation, the West and the South. His policies fluctuated between them.

Important to understanding his actions in the White House was Jackson's concept of the presidency. He had a more activist attitude than anyone since **Thomas Jefferson**, envisioning himself as party leader, using outside advisors instead of his cabinet, and seeing public office as open to all through his policies of rotation and the spoils system.

Right away, Jackson had trouble with his Vice President **John C. Calhoun**. Much of it was over trivial matters, but half of his cabinet was more loyal to Calhoun than Jackson. **Jackson's break with Calhoun** was in part a successful attempt by Martin Van Buren to create a new political coalition imbued with the philosophy of limited federal government with Jackson as a figurehead. One way in which this was assured was Jackson's **Maysville Road Veto** and his attitude toward sale of the public lands. The solution to **Jackson and the Public Lands** issue was embodied in preemption—that the first squatter there had unchallenged right of first purchase.

When it came to other issues of interest to the West, like **Indian Removal,** Jackson was willing to challenge all comers, especially the U.S. **Supreme Court**, when it tried to protect the **Native Americans** from forcible eviction from their traditional areas in the Old Northwest and Old Southwest. Here Jackson was willing to allow the state of Georgia to nullify federal court decisions to get his way.

But when it came to South Carolina and the **Tariff** of 1832, Jackson refused to permit Calhoun's home state to use Calhoun's theory of the **Concurrent Voice and Nullification**. This led to the **Nullification Crisis and the Compromise of 1833** over the tariff. Jackson labeled nullification a form of treason.

Finally, Jackson's first term ended with the **Bank Veto** when **Henry Clay** and his **National Republicans** decided to try and get the Second **Bank of the United States** charter renewed early while Jackson was busy with the nullifiers in South Carolina. Jackson proved up to the task when he used this issue to spearhead his reelection campaign in the **election of 1832**.

JACKSON'S SECOND ADMINISTRATION. After his successful return to office in the **election of 1832**, **Andrew Jackson** would be the last president to win reelection until **Abraham Lincoln** in 1864, and the last to serve two terms until U. S. Grant. He faced two big issues left over from his first term. He handled the **Nullification Crisis and the Compromise of 1833** first. Here Jackson proved to be an artful statesman, cajoling, threatening, compromising until U.S. Senators **John C. Calhoun** and **Henry Clay** drew up the **Tariff** of 1833 that allowed a solution to the crisis without violence.

Having solved the tariff problem, Jackson turned to the rechartering of the Second **Bank of the United States**, the so-called **Bank War**. Jackson decided that he had a mandate to destroy the bank through his reelection. He determined to accomplish this by withdrawing the federal deposits that made the bank unique. It took him three secretaries of the treasury before he got the job done through **Roger B. Taney**, whom Jackson rewarded with appointment to chief justice of the **Supreme Court** upon the death of **John Marshall**.

Next the president turned to what might best be called Jacksonian foreign policy. His biggest problem was the **Lone Star Rebellion** in Texas. Although Jackson wished to annex Texas immediately to extend slavery westward and bring in more **Three-Fifths Compromise** states, he knew that the North was so heated up over the **Slave Power Conspiracy** that it could not be done without seriously disrupting the nation he had just brought together. Texas would have to exist as an independent republic for the near future. Instead he turned to European countries and, through his usual approach of persuasion and threats, managed to collect various claims owed the United States in Europe and pay off the national debt.

As he solved other problems, Jackson aggressively wanted **Indian Removal completed**. Defeated in the Black Hawk War, the tribes in the Northwest, the Sauk-Fox, Peoria, Shawnee, Kickapoo, Delaware, and Miami accepted the inevitable and headed for Kansas. While he managed to get the army to escort the Cherokee, Creek, Choctaw, and Chickasaw from the Southeast and Southwest to Indian Territory (modern Oklahoma), the Seminole in Florida refused to go without a fight. This Second Seminole War became a bloodbath that decimated West Point classes for years to come, until American skullduggery as much as military victory won out in the end.

At the end of his second term, Jackson saw to it that his vice president, **Martin Van Buren**, was nominated to succeed him. To make Van Buren look more popular than he was, Jackson installed the two-thirds rule in the **Democratic** Party for nomination, subtly giving the South one more way to veto who might run the country, which lasted until the New Deal of the 1930s. As Jackson left office, legend has it that he was asked by one reporter if he had any regrets. Wistfully, Old Hickory admitted to having but two—he had not hanged John C. Calhoun nor shot Henry Clay.

JAY–GUARDOQUI TREATY (1786). In an effort to draw a definitive boundary between Spanish Florida and the United States, John Jay went to Spain. Representing New York–New England shipping interests more than anything else, Jay obtained a treaty proposal to permit American trade throughout the Spanish colonial empire if the United States would relinquish trade rights on the Mississippi River for 25 years. This would have delayed slave interests from exploiting the Southwest and obtaining more **Three-Fifths Compromise** states to bolster the Slave Power Conspiracy in Congress. The South used the two-thirds requirement for all matters passed under the Articles of Confederation to block this treaty. The South would remember this episode and insist that a two-thirds vote of the Senate, where all states were represented equally, be required to approve of any treaty as a part of the **Constitution** of 1787. The problems with the Spanish on the Southern frontier would be solved in **Pinckney's Treaty** (1796), and the **Adams–Onís Treaty** (1819).

JAY'S TREATY (1795). One of the most explosive episodes in world history was the French Revolution. Americans responded to the overthrow of the French monarchy with enthusiasm, seeing it much as its overthrow of the British colonial system. The United States recognized the French Revolutionary Government and was thrown into the vortex of the wars that followed.

In general, Secretary of the Treasury **Alexander Hamilton** and the **Federalist** Party supported Britain as the leader of the opposition to the violence of the French Revolution. Secretary of State **Thomas Jefferson** and the **Democratic Republicans** sided with the French, as did most average Americans. Both sides in Europe wanted to restrict American shipping and carrying trade exclusively to their cause. So, all things being equal, when the Federalists were in power, they blamed solely the French for interfering with American neutral rights on the high seas. When the Democratic Republicans were in power, they blamed the same transgressions only on the British. But in truth both sides in Europe seized American ships and impressed American sailors into their navies.

Since **George Washington**'s administration was Federalist and 75 percent of American trade was still with Britain, it moved to settle difficulties with the British. John Jay was sent over to get a treaty. Jay was to threaten to renew the old Franco-American alliance from 1778 to get favorable terms. Hamilton went behind his back and informed the British that Jay was bluffing. President Washington wanted nothing to do with the French.

The result was Jay's Treaty. It required the United States to declare trade with France off-limits, to force the states to pay for the seizure of Tory property during the American Revolution, and to force individual Americans to pay off the claims of British banks and merchants from before the American Revolution. Most of the Tory claims and business claims were held by Southerners, once again alienating them from the Federalist Party.

In exchange, Britain agreed to open all of its colonies to American trade, pleasing Hamilton's commercial supporters in the North, and to evacuate various forts they still held in America in the territory northwest of the Ohio Rivers. But no mention was made of the prime issue of disagreement, impressment of American sailors on the high seas or American sovereignty over Native Americans in the Ohio country.

The South used the two-thirds Senate vote to approve of treaties to block passage of Jay's Treaty, but failed. It passed by one vote. President Washington signed it. The Democratic Republicans said it violated America's traditional friendship with France and refused to appropriate the money to enforce it in the House of Representatives. Instead the nation passed the Eleventh Amendment to the Constitution, denying the federal courts any jurisdiction over the problem of Tory indemnification. Jay himself was hanged in effigy all over the country as a traitor. Then a new proposal came to the Senate, **Pinckney's Treaty** with Spain, which changed everything. Presenting the two treaties as a package resulted in the passage of both.

JEFFERSON, THOMAS (1743–1826). A philosopher-statesman of the Enlightenment, Thomas Jefferson was born and raised and lived near Charlottesville all his life. He was educated by private tutors and attended William and Mary College from 1760 to 1762. He studied law for five years and was a practicing attorney for two years before being elected to the House of Burgesses. He served from 1769 to 1774 and published *A Summary View of the Rights of British America*, which made him an open revolutionist.

At this time, Jefferson married a rich widow, Martha Wayles Skelton, by whom he had two daughters who survived to adulthood. He then was a member of the Virginia conventions on the coming of the Revolution in 1774 and 1775 and a member of the First and Second Continental Congresses. He was co-author of the *Declaration of Independence*.

Jefferson next served in the Virginia state legislature to 1779, during which time he helped create a republican state government, authored measures calling for abolition of primogeniture and entail, of separation of church and state, and creation of a public school system, all of which passed mostly through the efforts of his political ally, **James Madison**. Jefferson also supported proposals to discontinue the international slave trade and impose gradual state emancipation of slaves (he owned about 150), both of which failed. Becoming governor of Virginia in 1779, Jefferson succeeded Patrick Henry. When the British army raided the state, he was accused of cowardice in fleeing Richmond without putting up a fight.

At this time Jefferson's wife died and he began a life-long affair with **Sally Hemings**, a mulatto slave who was his wife's half-sister. Jefferson was elected congressman in 1783 and authored measures leading to the land ordinance of 1784 and proposals to convert weights and measures and money to the decimal system. Appointed minister to France, Jefferson served from 1784 to 1789, succeeding Benjamin Franklin. Jefferson worked for open trade with France, wrote his *Notes on the State of Virginia*, and witnessed the beginnings of the French Revolution.

Serving in France, he missed the Constitutional Convention, but he acted as an **anti-Federalist** in opposing its assumption of more federal power *vis à vis* the states. With the election of **George Washington** as president, Jefferson joined the cabinet as secretary of state, serving three years, He was opposed to **Alexander Hamilton**'s **Funding and Assumption** programs, the creation of a national **Bank of the United States**, and Hamilton's creation of the **Federalist** Party. Jefferson also worked to locate the national capital in Washington, D.C., in the South, and cooperated with Madison to found the Democratic Republican Party based on a decentralized federal government and a society of freeholding farmers.

Elected vice president under **John Adams,** the only time the president and vice president were of different political parties, Jefferson opposed the Adams administration's policies of the **Quasi-War,** the **Alien and Sedition Acts**, and was co-author with Madison of the **Kentucky and Virginia Resolves** as an alternative method of checking unconstitutional acts of Congress through state action. Neither Jefferson nor Adams, once good friends, spoke to each other for years afterward because of their political enmity.

Jefferson won the presidency in 1800 after defeating his ally **Aaron Burr** when the House of Representatives broke the electoral college tie. As president, Jefferson continued Hamilton's economic policies with some modification, fought the Barbary Pirates, backed the **Louisiana Purchase** as an early statement of the later **Monroe Doctrine**'s denial of further European colonization in the Americas, sponsored the Meriwether Lewis–William Clark Expedition, instituted the **Embargo Act,** and split his political party by using as loose a construction as had Hamilton, the bolters being the Tertium Quids, led by **John Randolph** of Roanoke.

Retiring in 1809, honoring Washington's two-term tradition, Jefferson returned to his home, Monticello, leaving the presidency to Madison, creating the so-called **Virginia Dynasty**. Continuing his public service, he founded the University of Virginia, becoming known as the

"Sage of Monticello." Jefferson was a poor businessman. He went broke with his version of Southern hospitality (often putting as many as 50 guests up for a prolonged period) and the outward life of a prosperous planter. He healed his quarrel with John Adams after leaving the presidency and died on 4 July 1826. With some exceptions, he personified the Southern gentleman of the Enlightenment in many ways: character, grace, vision, scholarship, and leadership.

JEFFERSON, THOMAS, AND SLAVERY IN VIRGINIA. One of the greatest myths in American history after the Revolutionary War was that the South was ready to duplicate the **abolition of slavery in the North**, but the invention of the **cotton gin** prevented it from happening. The problem was that the South never changed its mind on slavery—the North did that. A look at Virginia and **Thomas Jefferson** during the period from the creation of the **cotton gin** to the **Nullification Crisis** confirms this fact.

One of the features of this period, before the assertion of **slavery as a positive good**, was that statesmen from the South, like Jefferson, thought it proper to denounce the existence of slavery but few did much else about it. Only St. George Tucker put forward an actual plan to end the **peculiar institution**. He proposed that all females born after a certain date be freed at age 28. Their progeny would be freed at the same age. After the first generation of males died, slavery would be ended gradually in two or three generations. He coupled this plan with a stricter black code that would force all freed blacks to leave the state, presumably for the West.

But, unlike Jefferson, Tucker was not a politician. Had Jefferson, or any political figure, proposed or voted for such a plan, he would have been defeated in the next election. This is because Virginians held certain "truths" about slavery and black people in general. Most Virginians felt no fault in the creation of slavery. Instead they blamed the British colonial system, as did Jefferson in the Declaration of Independence, which forced them to allow the international slave trade. This overlooked the fact that no British king ever forced a colonial to buy a slave, or forced slavery to be introduced where it was not wanted, but consistency was not always part of political arguments, then or now.

Another supposed verity Virginians, like Jefferson, held about slavery was that they believed that blacks were innately inferior to whites. Freedom would thus be a disaster for society in America, resulting in race war, race mixture, and a general lowering of the morals, intellect, and industry of the white race. One only had to look at the history of **Haiti** to see this was true.

While certain key statesmen never felt guilty about slavery, the average Virginian hesitated to discuss the problem publicly or privately lest slaves learn that whites were divided in their stances on slavery. The result was that politicians described a problem but rarely if ever put forth a solution as had Tucker. Virginia's premier statesman of the period, **Thomas Jefferson**, fit this mold.

Jefferson's opinion was so important because so many looked up to him for leadership. His central dilemma was that he, like virtually all Virginians, hated slavery, but thought blacks to be inferior to whites. Jefferson believed in the natural rights philosophy of all men created equal, but he believed in another facet of natural rights philosophy more—the passion for order, solitude, and an awe for nature. He was more like Latin American revolutionaries of the era. He wanted freedom, but as a controlled force. He was an enlightened despot or a benevolent dictator when it came to slaves.

Jefferson was especially concerned with slavery's effect upon whites, not blacks. He never felt it was anything but wrong in the abstract and he felt personal guilt as a slaveowner. But he also feared turning the United States into a larger version of Haiti. Blacks had an inherent inability to handle themselves responsibly in a free society, according to Jefferson. He could not compliment any black without adding a racial qualification. He believed African Americans needed less sleep, were less serious in thought, brave, adventuresome, sexually ardent, had a short span of attention, and were light-hearted.

More than any one man, Jefferson formed and influenced white prejudices that are still commonplace today. He suffered from these prejudices in his own relationship with his alleged slave mistress, **Sally Hemings**. The significance of his affair with Sally was the scandal, not the fact that it occurred or not. Behind it all was a universal assumption that blacks were inferior in mind and different in appearance.

Jefferson, like most Americans, was accustomed to seeing things in pairs of good and bad, white and black, America against King

George III, and so on. He did the same thing in his anthropology. But there was a problem in that. There were three races in America—white, black, and red. Jefferson turned the three into two by absorbing the Indians into the white race. Here he was aided by the Enlightenment view of the noble red savage and his belief in the innate inferiority of black people.

Like all Founding Fathers, Jefferson was confronted with two sacred entities, liberty and property, and could not choose between them when they conflicted, one with the other. This is the key to the tragedy of Southern history, the paradox of the slaveholders' devotion to liberty, which moved the caustic 18th-century British literary and social critic Samuel Johnson to query, "How is it that we hear the loudest *yelps* for liberty among the drivers of negroes?" This plus their fervent adherence to the Union through state sovereignty theory, as represented in the U.S. **Supreme Court** decision *Dred Scott v. Sanford* **(1857)**, made the Southern slaveholders the most loyal of Americans until the **secession** crisis of 1861.

JEFFERSONIANS. *See* DEMOCRATIC REPUBLICANS.

JESUP, MAJ. GEN. THOMAS. *See* INDIAN REMOVAL COMPLETED.

JOHNSON, RICHARD MENTOR (1780–1850). Born and raised in Kentucky, Richard Mentor Johnson was educated at Transylvania University and practiced law at Lexington. He served in the state legislature and entered Congress in 1807, where he sided with a pro-war, anti-British faction called the **War Hawks**. Johnson took command of the Kentucky Mounted Rifles in the **War of 1812** and led them to victory under Maj. Gen. **William Henry Harrison** at the Battle of the Thames.

Johnson's men broke through the British lines and isolated the Indian forces under Tecumseh. There he received credit for personally killing the Indian chief, although many others had as good a claim. He used the fame he received in politics afterward, under the little ditty, "Rumsey Dumsey, Colonel Johnson killed Tecumsey." It took him from the U.S. House of Representatives to the Senate and to the vice presidency under **Martin Van Buren** in the **election of 1836**.

Although Johnson was a very popular politician, he had one quirk for the times that kept him from presidential nomination. He lived openly with one of his ex-slaves, Julia Chinn, and sired two daughters by her. While he might be looked on as eccentric walking the streets of Lexington, the idea of him parading his brood around the White House was too much for 1840s America. Johnson retired after Van Buren lost the presidency in 1840. His legislative triumphs included securing soldier pensions for the Revolution and the War of 1812, continuing Sunday mail service, and abolishing debt imprisonment in Kentucky.

JOHNSON v. MCINTOSH. *See* INDIAN REMOVAL.

JUDICIARY ACT OF 1789. *See MARBURY v. MADISON*; MIDNIGHT JUDGES.

JUDICIARY ACT OF 1801. *See* MIDNIGHT JUDGES.

– K –

KANE, THOMAS LEIPER. *See* MORMON WAR.

"KANSAS, CRIME AGAINST." *See* SUMNER, CHARLES.

KANSAS–MISSOURI BORDER WARS. In 1853, President **Franklin Pierce** believed the issue of **slavery** in the territories was finally settled, and with **Popular Sovereignty** the issue was now out of Congress and in the hands of the territories. But Northern feelings were unequivocal in 1854 when passage of the **Kansas–Nebraska Act** reopened the issue of slavery expansion into the territories. Introduced by Senator **Stephen A. Douglas**, the act exacerbated the issue in the territories rather than calmed it. Pierce had not considered Northern public opinion when signing this act. Not Nebraska, opposite the free state of Iowa, but Kansas, opposite the slave state of Missouri, was the focal point where the Northerners hoped to defeat what they believed was a plot for a sweeping expansion of slavery westward.

The Kansas issue involved more than the pro-slave vs. Free-Soil conflict. The new territorial government's leaders would have the power to assign land grants to railroads, issue business licenses, and ensure high profits for speculators. No one would have legal title until all land ownership was registered. This had yet to be accomplished, so physical violence often ensued for other than pro-slave or Free-Soil reasons. But the people back East heard only the bottom line—slavery or freedom.

Trying to defuse the issue, President Pierce appointed Andrew Reeder of Ohio as the first territorial governor, a man noted for his centrist attitude on the issues. But when he discovered that Yankees paid more for smaller lots than Southerners, Reeder declared himself a Free-Soiler and began to spread rumors about Southern unrest and violence. Missouri Senator and acting U.S. Vice President David Atchison demanded Reeder be replaced. Reeder charged that fraud had been committed in the elections of the new territorial legislature because Atchison had led pro-slavery advocates from Missouri into Kansas to cast pro-slavery votes. When Reeder explained the situation to the president, Pierce refused to challenge the results. Instead, at the suggestion of Secretary of War **Jefferson Davis** of Mississippi, he removed Reeder from office.

Northerner Wilson Shannon, also a Free-Soil moderate, replaced Reeder. But acting alone, the Free-Soilers elected their own legislature in Topeka with Charles Robinson as governor. Reeder, now in Congress as the territorial delegate from the Topeka government, petitioned for statehood under a Free-Soil constitution. In response, Southerners dispatched a militia from Missouri, the so-called Border Ruffians, in November 1855. The Topeka government then formed a militia under James H. Lane. The resulting skirmish was exaggerated as the Wakarusa War. This demonstrated to Pierce that civilians were no match for the professional army in bringing peace to Kansas.

By April 1856, slavery advocates needed to stop the infiltration of Yankees. Backed by Jefferson Buford, who had recruited 600 Alabama volunteers, Judge Samuel D. Lecompte asked for a grand jury indictment of Free-Soil government members for high treason. Sheriff S. J. Jones was ambushed near Lawrence, the center of Free-Soil sentiment, when he arrested a group of Free-Soilers charged in Lecompte's warrants. Along with Buford, Missouri and Alabama volunteers, Jones invaded Lawrence, destroying several businesses, "Governor" Robinson's house, and the Free State Hotel. Unable to fight back against so large a force, Free-Soil leaders retreated into the hills. The North called this incident the "Rape of Lawrence." After U.S. Senator from Massachusetts Charles Sumner made a speech he titled "The Crime Against Kansas," South Carolina Congressman **Preston Brooks** attacked him on the floor of the Senate with his walking stick, breaking it over Sumner's bleeding head. As the South cheered Brooks's action, eight Free-Soilers in Kansas led by a staunch **abolitionist, John Brown,** hacked seven alleged Southerners to death in the "Pottawattomie Massacre."

These events confirmed the failure of Popular Sovereignty. The irony lay in the necessity of army intervention to uphold a policy that stood for no federal intervention. The Free-Soilers had skillfully exaggerated the myths and rumors of a shooting war, portraying a grim, revolting image of "Bleeding Kansas" in the minds of the nation for their own purposes. Citizens blamed tragedies such as the "Rape of Lawrence" and the "Wakarusa War" on the Missouri Border Ruffians and Pierce, ensuring his defeat for re-nomination in the next presidential election.

KANSAS–NEBRASKA ACT. The Kansas–Nebraska Act was focused on the idea of a transcontinental railroad and North–Old South politics. The 1849 California Gold Rush, followed by California statehood as part of the **Compromise of 1850**, and the four-month-plus coast-to-coast journey proved that connecting the Far West with the center of American population east of the Mississippi was becoming a necessity. The railroad was the apex of technology at the time, but its prohibitive expense necessitated huge public demand to justify its construction.

Unfortunately, railroad customers were few beyond the 95th meridian, where the Missouri River turns north at Kansas City. The Great American Desert stretched between there and the California gold fields. This meant that the railroad needed to be taxpayer funded, but the price tag limited the federal government to financing only one route, a formula not designed to promote sectional harmony.

The most practical starting points for the rails heading west were Chicago, St. Louis, Memphis, and New Orleans. After surveying all four routes, the Army Corps of Engineers determined that the only all-weather routes would have to originate as far south as possible. Steamboat-oriented St. Louis was content with the status quo and Memphis could not handle a major depot, leaving Chicago and New Orleans as the remaining contenders. This immediately provoked the sectional politics of the North against the Old South.

The **Whigs** had lost their political sway in 1853, the **slavery** issue having thwarted their growth, dividing North from South within the party. In the **election of 1852**, the **Democrats** had elevated **Franklin Pierce** to the presidency with the support of Southern Whigs. But the Democrats were also fragmented, especially in New York and New England. Moreover, three **Free-Soil Party** men, Salmon P. Chase, John P. Hale, and Charles Sumner, elected in 1848, were up for re-election in 1854 and needed a hot issue to run on.

In the early 1850s, confused as to their political roles by the slavery issue, politicians needed a piece of legislation that would create solidarity, and the railroad west was just the timely issue. **Jefferson Davis** of Mississippi, Pierce's secretary of war and chief advisor, backed New Orleans for the railroad's starting point. The South's great advantage over the North was the Texas population, which spread farther west than that of any other state. Davis made sure the Southern route prevailed when James Gadsden of Alabama included the best land for railroad construction south of the Gila River in the Gadsden Purchase from Mexico in 1854.

In response to Davis' pro-Southern policy, U.S. Senator **Stephen A. Douglas** of Illinois wanted Chicago to win the railroad contest. In 1854, he believed a new territorial government west of Iowa or Missouri would negate the Texas population advantage by encouraging settlers to migrate onto the Great Plains beyond Kansas City. He called his new territory Nebraska (present-day Kansas and Nebraska). Southern opposition in 1853 prevented the passage of the measure.

Southerners in the Senate would agree to rails originating in Chicago if Douglas offered something in return: the **Non-Exclusion Doctrine** on slavery in the territories, updated as **Popular Sovereignty**. This meant that until a territory applied for statehood, it was to be open to slaveholder and non-slaveholder alike. Only in the constitutional convention for the new proposed state would the slavery issue be decided. According to the "voice of the people," Congress would admit the new state according to its convention's vote.

In 1854, Douglas and Pierce needed four Southern votes to pass a Nebraska Act and get the Gadsden Purchase treaty through the Senate. One of the four Southern votes was Senator David Atchison, president *pro tempore* of the Senate and acting vice president of the United States. Atchison promised that no legislation would pass until a slave territory was established on Missouri's western border.

Douglas, as chairman of the committee on territories, gave in by rewriting his Nebraska Bill to provide for two territories: Kansas directly west of Missouri, and Nebraska west of Iowa and Minnesota. Atchison had finally achieved the open repeal of the **Missouri Compromise** (the 36°30' line dividing slave territory from free territory), and the substitution of Popular Sovereignty.

The Kansas–Nebraska Act passed both houses of Congress, with Pierce cracking the patronage whip. Atchison got the Democratic support he wanted for the Non-Exclusion Doctrine without **Martin Van Buren**'s New England and New York supporters. Southern Whigs started defecting to the Democratic Party again, which began the one-party South that would emerge after the end of the Civil War and Reconstruction. The Gadsden Purchase confirmation soon followed.

In response, Northern Whigs, New England Democrats, and Free-Soilers formed the **Republican Party.** They saw that Atchison's voters had come from **Three-Fifths Compromise** supporters, white Southern slaveowners representing their slaves. This reinforced the viability of the **Slave Power Conspiracy** in Congress.

Presidential hopeful Douglas, who thought that he had paved the way for Western expansion and the construction of a transcontinental railroad, believed the Kansas–Nebraska Bill would strengthen his position in the North and make him an adequate candidate in the South. Popular Sovereignty recognized the theoretical rights of slaveholders in these territories.

But Douglas knew that Popular Sovereignty still had a lie deep within it. No matter when the popular vote was taken, in territorial stages or as the territory became a state, **anti-slavery** Northerners and immigrants, unburdened by slaves, outran their Southern counterparts in the trek out west. Topography now dictated the **natural**

limits of slavery expansion, as the arid land towards the west was not conducive to cultivating cotton crops. Douglas showed characteristic duplicity by backing slavery while in Washington, but pandered to his anti-slavery constituents in Illinois. **Abraham Lincoln** would expose this blatant guile in the **Lincoln–Douglas Debates** of 1858.

KANSAS SETTLEMENT (1856–1861). In 1856, after a lengthy struggle, **Democrats** chose **James Buchanan** of Pennsylvania as their presidential candidate. His platform, which called for overseas expansion, free trade and **Popular Sovereignty,** won him the election. The federal government now needed to avoid the political turmoil that **slavery** in the territories had provoked and leave the issue to the people.

But the **Republicans** wanted Buchanan to violate Popular Sovereignty. In the 1856 campaign, their candidate John Frémont denounced "those twin relics of barbarism, polygamy and slavery" in the territories. Republicans wanted Buchanan to suppress the Mormon uprising in Utah Territory and leave his pro-slave Southern allies in Kansas to their own devices. Buchanan's zealous complicity resulted in the **Mormon War** in Utah and the final Kansas Settlement.

President Buchanan tried to resolve the difficulties created by the explosive situation in Kansas peacefully. Unlike his predecessor, **Franklin Pierce,** Buchanan understood the importance of a first-rate administration to govern Kansas. For territorial governor, he appointed Robert Walker, an old-time Democrat and Popular Sovereignty advocate who had served as **James K. Polk**'s treasury secretary. A native New Yorker, Walker was a lifelong Mississippi planter. Buchanan assigned Brig. Gen. William S. Harney to support Walker, but the demands of the **Mormon War** soon decimated his command of 1,500 soldiers. Buchanan also appeased the South with the appointment of pro-slave Judge Samuel Lecompte.

Walker, in a swift flurry of diplomacy, asked the Free-Soilers to delay their Topeka Constitution and to submit any clause on slavery separately. When the newly elected constitutional convention met at Lecompton, Walker's strategy backfired. The Kansas Free-Soilers boycotted the elections, unable to trust a Mississippian, and pro-slavery forces dominated the convention. The convention drew up the Lecompton Constitution, which legalized slavery, and sent the document to Washington without submitting it to a vote of Kansas residents, as Popular Sovereignty called for.

The Congressional Committee on Territories, insisting the residents vote, sent the Lecompton Constitution back to Kansas. Again, the Free-Soilers boycotted the vote. Walker journeyed to Washington to dispute Congress' accepting Kansas as a slave state. Admiring his insistence on a full vote on any constitution, Northerners made the slaveholding Walker the **anti-slavery** hero of the hour. Buchanan, determined to have Kansas admitted to the Union as quickly as possible, was not impressed. He told Congress that the Free-Soilers' refusal to vote should not preclude admission of Kansas as a slave state and that party loyalty demanded a vote for Lecompton.

Senator **Stephen A. Douglas** joined with Walker against Buchanan over the legality of the Lecompton Constitution. In an attempt to push the bill through Congress, Buchanan tried to force Douglas to support his position, threatening him with political reprisals. Nonetheless, Douglas used his influence to persuade Western Democrats to vote against the bill. He refused to support Buchanan; he believed the events in Kansas were a travesty of Popular Sovereignty. He based his position on political considerations as well as principle. Opinion in Illinois opposed the admission of Kansas under Lecompton, and Douglas was up for re-election in 1858.

The Republican-dominated Kansas legislature called for another referendum on the Lecompton Constitution, which the Free-Soilers participated in. This time Lecompton was overwhelmingly defeated because Democrats refused to vote. It was killed by a coalition of Western Democrats, Republicans, and anti-Nebraska Know Nothings. The two elections added together produced 11,000 votes against the Lecompton Constitution and 6,000 in favor. Obviously, at the end of the day, Kansas should be admitted as a free state.

Buchanan refused to relent, and by stubbornly refusing to accept political realities in Kansas, he intensified sectional hostilities, further dividing the Democratic Party. With the aid of moderate Congressman **Alexander Stephens** of Georgia, who was popular in the North, Buchanan had Representative William English of Indiana draw up the English Bill, allowing Kansas immediate admission under Lecompton, under the condition of accepting a much reduced land grant. Kansas's refusal to accept these terms would result in delayed statehood until the population reached 93,000, the number each congressman represented at the time.

The English Bill passed both houses of Congress, although Douglas voted against it. The anti-Lecompton Democrats who favored it were defeated in 1858. Douglas credited his re-election to the Senate in the face of a capable opponent, **Abraham Lincoln**, to his (Douglas') vote against the English Bill. This resulted in the rejection of Kansas for statehood, but a new free state constitution was drawn up during a subsequent state convention, and, after the South seceded in 1861, Kansas finally achieved statehood.

KEARNY, STEPHEN WATTS. *See* WAR WITH MEXICO.

KENTUCKY AND VIRGINIA RESOLVES (1798). Written by the two leaders of the **Democratic Republican** Party, **Thomas Jefferson** (Virginia Resolves) and **James Madison** (Kentucky Resolves), in response to the Federalist passage of the **Alien and Sedition Acts**, the Resolves asserted that the Constitution was a compact between the sovereign states. It had been voluntarily adhered to for mutual advantage. The states could resume their sovereignty at any time and interpose that sovereignty between the federal government and their own citizens to protect them from the operation of such obviously unconstitutional laws as the Alien and Sedition Acts. Better yet, since states had joined the United States under their own free will, they could withdraw from it and resume their sovereign powers in the same manner. Indeed, Virginia's approval of the Constitution had been done with such a reservation explicitly stated, just as other states (New York and Rhode Island) had. This idea of states declaring federal law unconstitutional was developed before the U.S. Supreme Court claimed that right for itself in *Marbury v. Madison*. It would be a continual thorn in the side of the federal government from then through the **Nullification Crisis,** all the way up to **secession** of the South in 1860.

KING, RUFUS. *See* ELECTION OF 1804, ELECTION OF 1808, ELECTION OF 1816.

KNIGHTS OF THE GOLDEN CIRCLE. *See* FILIBUSTERING; VIOLENCE AND WHITE MILITANCY.

"KNOW NOTHINGS." *See* AMERICAN PARTY.

KOSSUTH, LAJOS. *See* YOUNG AMERICA.

KOSZTA, MARTIN. *See* YOUNG AMERICA.

– L –

LAKE OCHEKOBEE, BATTLE OF (1838). *See* INDIAN REMOVAL COMPLETED.

LAMAR, MIRABEAU. *See* ELECTION OF 1844.

LAND LAW OF 1820. *See* ERA OF GOOD FEELINGS; JACKSON AND THE PUBLIC LANDS; LONE STAR REBELLIONS.

LAND ORDINANCE OF 1784. *See* NORTHWEST ORDINANCE.

LAND ORDINANCE OF 1785. Providing for the rectilinear survey of the **Western Lands Cession**, the Land Ordinance of 1785 created townships six miles square that were measured from a series of baselines and prime meridians and subdivided into 36 sections of 640 acres each. Sale would be at $1 per acre, with a minimum purchase of 640 acres necessary. (Later laws would raise the price to $1.25 an acre and reduce the amount to be purchased to 80 acres, known as the $100 farm.) Proceeds from section 16 would be used to finance public schools. This cost tended to open the public lands to speculative companies that resold smaller amounts at higher prices. This law replaced the old colonial surveys based on compass readings from prominent landmarks, and was used in all areas west of the Appalachian Mountains except Texas, California, Kentucky, and Tennessee. According to Congress, all land was to be bought from the Native Americans before white settlement, an ideal rarely achieved.

LAND ORDINANCE OF 1787. *See* NORTHWEST ORDINANCE.

LAW OF SLAVERY. *See* BLACK CODES.

LAWRENCE, RAPE OF. *See* KANSAS–MISSOURI BORDER WARS.

LECOMPTE, SAMUEL. *See* KANSAS–MISSOURI BORDER WARS.

LECOMPTON CONSTITUTION. *See* KANSAS SETTLEMENT.

LEE, ROBERT E. (1807–1870). Son of a famous Virginian, Richard Henry "Light Horse Harry" Lee, an inveterate gambler who died early in his son's life, Robert E. Lee was raised by his mother, Anne Hill Carter Lee, in what one commentator called "genteel poverty."

Lee spent his formative years in Alexandria. Educated at local academies, the youth had a gift for mathematics. This, plus the lure of a free **education**, led him to gain an appointment to the U.S. Military Academy. In 1829, he graduated second in his class at West Point with a perfect conduct record. After graduation, Lee married Mary Custis, a distant relative to himself and through marriage to **George Washington**. In this manner Lee came to live in the Custis mansion, Arlington, across the Potomac River from Washington, D.C.

He went into the Army Corps of Engineers and spent much of his military career working on rivers and fortifications. He did especially good work at Fortress Monroe at the tip of the Virginia Peninsula and in designing the port of St. Louis on the Mississippi River. During the **War with Mexico**, Lee was on the staff of Maj. Gen. John E. Wool in northern Mexico as a staff engineer. He transferred to Brevet Lt. Gen. **Winfield Scott**'s command for the decisive campaign on Mexico City out of Vera Cruz. It is not known if Lee angled for the transfer or if Scott asked for him. With Scott, Lee served as chief scout, winning many of Scott's battles before they started with timely information on enemy positions and roads to the Mexican rear. In one famous incident, Lee spent the night hidden behind a fallen log as Mexican soldiers encamped on the other side.

After the war, Secretary of War **Jefferson Davis** recommended Lee as superintendent of West Point, where he was one of the best and most respected leaders the institution ever had. He later received an appointment as lieutenant colonel of the crack Second Cavalry, but he remained in Virginia caring for his wife and her father who were seriously ill.

Thus Lee was available to lead the federal troops who recaptured **Harper's Ferry** from John Brown, after which he finally went to Texas briefly. In March 1861, he was appointed colonel of the First Cavalry but, because of the onset of war, never took command. He resigned his commission after the firing on Ft. Sumter, refusing the command of all federal forces to put down the rebellion. There is some dispute as to whether Lee actually accepted a position with Virginia state troops before he resigned.

Although Lee is usually seen as an apolitical soldier before and during the Civil War, a man devoted to "duty," which word he described as the most perfect in the English language, he was a supporter of **slavery** and the **extraterritoriality** of slavery in the territories. Where Lee differed from most of the planter class and **pro-slave theorists in the Old South** was his unwillingness to define the peculiar institution as a moral one. But he never countermanded orders that had his army return actual or suspected runaway slaves or free blacks to the South when he invaded Pennsylvania.

Lee saw slavery as an unfortunate but necessary reality, as he revealed in an 1856 letter to his wife and an 1865 letter to Andrew Hunter of the Virginia state senate. He thought it the best relationship between the races and worried about the effects of emancipation on the two races. But he consigned abolition to God, "who sees the end; who chooses to work by slow influences." While Lee condemned those of the North who would interfere with the Old South's institutions, he was more than willing to free any black who would enlist in the Confederate Army, something that the March 1865 law calling on the creation of slave regiments refused to endorse. He also oversaw the voluntary manumission of his father-in-law's slaves in 1862, although surrounded by national separation and war.

Lee received appointment to be the chief military advisor to President Jefferson Davis. On 1 June 1862, with the wounding of the general commanding the forces defending Richmond from Yankee attack, Davis turned to Lee to save the Confederacy. Re-naming his troops the Army of Northern Virginia, Lee proceeded to beat the Union forces arrayed against him for a solid year before advancing into Pennsylvania to be defeated himself at Gettysburg.

The next spring, Lee fought the reorganized federal armies at the Wilderness, Spotsylvania, the North Anna River and Totopotomy Creek, before enduring the nine-month siege of Petersburg and Richmond. Attempting to break away from Richmond to join other Confederate forces in the Carolinas, Lee was brought to bay at Appomattox Courthouse.

Forced to surrender, Lee received a parole to Richmond, and then spent the rest of his life as president of Washington University at Lexington, Virginia. Upon his death in 1870 (Lee had suffered from continual heart attacks of varying import during the war), the institution was renamed Washington and Lee University and Lee was buried there.

LEON, EDWIN DE. *See* YOUNG AMERICA.

LETCHER, JOHN. *See* SECESSION OF THE SOUTHERN STATES, SECOND.

LIBERIA. In the aftermath of **"General" Gabriel's Plot**, several people approached President **Thomas Jefferson** with an idea. They proposed that the United States sponsor a "colony" in Africa to which might be sent black persons deemed dangerous to the peace and good order of society. Jefferson thought well of the idea, but the trade embargoes leading to the **War of 1812** prevented any immediate action.

Following the War of 1812, after a black sea captain, Paul Cuffee, successfully transplanted a shipload of freed American slaves to Sierra Leone, several prominent white Americans took a new look at transporting freed American slaves back to Africa as a philanthropic policy. **Henry Clay** explained the group's policy as a pragmatic one of avoiding the seemingly insurmountable barrier of racial prejudice against the presence of free blacks in the United States. Along with Francis Scott Key of "Star Spangled Banner" fame; Bushrod Washington, **George Washington**'s nephew and a noted jurist; President **James Monroe**, whose support for an American colony of freed American slaves caused its capital to be named Monrovia; and **Andrew Jackson**, Clay organized the **American Colonization Society**. Although Monroe referred to the African colony as "Little America," it soon came to be called Liberia, from the Latin for liberty or freedom.

Most of the early supporters of Liberia were Southern American slaveholders, who freed some or all of their slaves on condition they emigrate to Liberia. Branches of the Society opened in Louisiana, Mississippi, Maryland, Ohio, Pennsylvania, and New York. Under Monroe's prodding, the federal government provided a grant of $100,000 in 1819 to get things started. Between 1820 and 1867, approximately 13,000 African Americans, freed slaves and free men and women, returned to Liberia in West Africa near where it was believed they were enslaved.

Using Society funds, the settlers bought land from the natives or took it by force, if necessary. Eventually, they set up a miniature American-style government, including a Congress and court system and elected their first president, Joseph Jenkins Roberts, in 1847. The new nation, which remained unrecognized by its parent country until 1862, also adopted a flag with red and white stripes and a blue field adorned by a single star. The colony also had a noble motto: "The love of liberty brought us here."

Local Africans were not amused, as warfare between the "Americos," as the settlers came to be called, and the numerous indigenous people became common. Backed up by the U.S. Navy, the Americos always came out on top. The Americos also built plantations, much like those they had left behind in the United States, and exploited local labor in a manner Southern white Americans would have recognized. The clash between the Americos, represented eventually by a political party called the True Whigs, and the various tribal groups rages on today in varying intensity, ranging from open warfare to political contests.

LIBERTY PARTY. *See* FREE-SOIL PARTY.

LINCOLN, ABRAHAM (1809–1865). Abraham Lincoln was born on February 9, 1809, in a log cabin near Hodgensville, Kentucky, the second child of carpenter/farmer Thomas Lincoln and his wife, Nancy Hanks Lincoln. Abe was named after his paternal grandfather who was killed by Indians in 1786. In 1817, the family moved to southern Indiana, near Gentryville, and Lincoln's mother soon succumbed to milk sickness (undulant fever). After searching the countryside for a bride and stepmother for his children, Thomas Lincoln married Sarah Bush Johnston, a widow with three children. She was a robust, hearty homemaker who rejuvenated the Lincoln homestead and instilled the value of an education in Abe over his father's objections.

Well-read and mostly self-educated, young Lincoln worked hard at physical labor and clerked at Gentry's store. At age 19 he accompanied the Gentrys down river on a raft to New Orleans, where he encountered **slavery** for the first time. Seeing how slaves were treated created in him what became a lifelong hatred for the institution. The Lincolns moved to Illinois, but Abe soon set out on his own. A delayed flatboat journey down river from New Salem necessitated his taking a job as a store clerk. Lincoln held down a series of jobs and became a popular resident in New Salem. During the Black Hawk War, he enlisted as a private and was elected captain of the local militia. By now he had reached his full height of 6'4".

Lincoln returned home after serving a quiet, inconsequential hitch. He made an entrepreneurial attempt at storekeeping, which plunged him into debt which he was unable to repay until he became a congressman 10 years later. In 1846 he was elected to the state legislature as a **Whig,** the party opposed to the policies of **Andrew Jackson,** and actively participated in having the state capitol moved from Vandalia to Springfield. As Springfield was in his own district, he relocated there. Choosing the legal profession, he read law and was admitted to the bar. Lincoln and many other young local men, including his good friend **Stephen A. Douglas**, courted a visiting Kentucky belle, Mary Todd, whom Lincoln married in 1842 after he had backed out of their first engagement and left her standing at the altar some months earlier.

The Lincolns settled in Springfield, where he cultivated a steady client base as a top-drawer lawyer. Mary was known as a sharp-tongued hot-tempered shrew who dominated her husband at home. Lincoln served one term in Congress in the mid-1840s, during which he opposed the **War with Mexico**. Lincoln retired after the one term, supposedly by prior agreement, but his anti-war attitude would probably have cost him the seat in pro-war Illinois, anyway.

Lincoln dabbled in local politics and practiced law until the opening of Kansas to slavery above the old **Missouri Compromise** line prompted him to pursue a full-time political career. Lincoln helped organize the **Republican Party** in Illinois, which urged him to challenge the architect of slavery in the territories, his boyhood friend and political opponent **Stephen A. Douglas**, known as the Little Giant.

Now a powerful **Democrat** and U.S. Senator from Illinois, Douglas hoped to make his 1858 re-election the springboard for the presidency in 1860. Lincoln agreed to run against Douglas during his famous "House Divided Speech," in which he said that the United States could not remain half free and half slave. He feared that the U.S. **Supreme Court** case, ***Dred Scott v. Sanford***, showed that the whole nation would become like the Old South and support slavery. Because of the expense of the campaign, the Lincolns and Douglases traveled together on a special campaign train and engaged in a series of **Lincoln–Douglas Debates** (seven, one in each of Illinois' congressional districts) on the issues of the day.

Lincoln lost the race by a closer margin than expected by bedeviling Douglas with the so-called **Freeport Question**. He asked Douglas if slavery could be legally excluded from the territories, violating his **Popular Sovereignty** doctrine, which allowed slavery until a territory voted on statehood. This posed a serious dilemma for Douglas, who had to answer "yes" to win the Illinois Senate seat, but "no" to win the South in his 1860 presidential bid. Douglas crossed his political bridges as he came to them and answered "yes." His answer became the **Freeport Doctrine**. He won the Senate seat with the Illinois legislature's support, but lost the Old South forever, as Lincoln's question had exposed his unabashed duplicity.

Lincoln's skill in discrediting Douglas brought him invitations to speaking engagements throughout the North. He was now able to carry three key states (Illinois, Indiana, Pennsylvania) the Republicans had failed to win in the **election of 1856**. If the party could maintain its 1856 results, these three states could win Lincoln and the Republicans the presidency without a single electoral vote below the Ohio River. Although not yet a household name, Lincoln surpassed several potential candidates in his ability to take the three states. Even if Douglas had obtained a solid majority of the popular vote, Lincoln still would have taken the presidency. The vote in the Electoral College resulted in a simple majority to the Northern states that supported Lincoln in close popular races. Lincoln's potential presidential appointments to executive offices and the U.S. **Supreme Court** caused the rabid Southern secessionists to leave the Union. Lincoln's moderate inaugural speech was an attempt to bolster their confidence, but he refused to submit to two issues: the advancement of slavery into the territories and the yielding of federal properties still held in the seceded states. When the Old South forcibly asserted its rights to federal property within its boundaries, the war began, bringing further **secessions** as Lincoln assigned a quota of militia to every state to quell the growing rebellion.

LINCOLN–DOUGLAS DEBATES (1858). In 1858, **Democratic** U.S. Senator **Stephen A. Douglas** sought reelection. The Illinois **Republican Party** nominated **Abraham Lincoln**, who had stolen the party from its organizers in 1856. Because U.S. Senators were not directly elected until the 20th century, the vote was made in the Illinois state legislature in 1860. Lincoln boldly challenged Douglas to debate the current issues before the state legislature met. Although not obligated, Douglas accepted, his stand on **slavery** in the West being the most crucial item before the South as well as Illinois. Douglas' reputation in Washington and his likely Democratic presidential nomination, along with the publicity of the articulate debates, made Lincoln an immediate household name and a likely Republican presidential nominee in 1860.

Lincoln and Douglas engaged in seven debates between August and October 1858 in counties that had supported **American Party** candidate **Millard Fillmore** in 1856, now likely to vote either way. In each three-hour debate, one candidate spoke for the first hour and his opponent spoke for the next 90 minutes, followed by a half-hour rebuttal from the first speaker. Douglas and Lincoln took turns speaking first.

Upon accepting his party's nomination in Chicago on June 16, 1858, Lincoln, in his famous "House Divided Speech," insisted that the United States could not survive with both slave and free states; one or the other must prevail. The U.S. **Supreme Court** had decided the ***Dred Scott v. Sanford*** case in favor of the Old South and slavery. Douglas cunningly spun the implications of Lincoln's speech to his advantage, convincing Illinois voters that Lincoln was an ardent **abolitionist** intent on achieving his ends at the expense of the Union. In subsequent debates, Lincoln needed to show Illinois citizens and legislators that he agreed with their objection to full citizenship and equality of African Americans. In his defense, he resorted to several compromising statements to refute Douglas' allegations, pledging not to tamper with slavery or spread it westward. He also promised not to force Illinois to admit free blacks as voting citizens.

In what became known as the **Freeport Question,** Lincoln found his opportunity to retaliate by asking Douglas if slavery could lawfully be excluded from a territory before a proposed state constitution were drawn up. This forced Douglas to admit to supporting Squatter Sovereignty rather than his favored **Popular Sovereignty**—the pro-Southern **Non-Exclusion Doctrine.**

This posed a serious dilemma for Douglas, who had to answer "yes" to win the Illinois Senate seat, but "no" to win the South in his presidential bid. In Washington, Douglas supported the South in slave expansion, but at home he took the opposite position. His reasoning was that whether popular votes were cast while still a territory or as a new state, **anti-slavery** Northerners and immigrants, unburdened by slaves, outran their Southern counterparts in the journey west. He was now forced to admit this publicly at the risk of losing his U.S. Senate seat. But he could not win his Senate seat and expect clear sailing for his Southern-dominated party's nomination for the presidency in 1860.

In Douglas's solution, known as the **Freeport Doctrine,** a territory's not passing a positive law to establish slavery would deny the peculiar institution the laws necessary to sanction and protect it. Douglas, the only Democrat who voted against the Lecompton Constitution in the **Kansas Settlement** question to survive politically in the North, won his U.S. Senate seat by a vote of 54-46 in the state legislature.

Douglas won in the Illinois legislature, but Abraham Lincoln immediately achieved national fame for the Republican Party. Not only had he had bested Douglas in the debates as a shrewd orator, but the former railsplitter's homespun quality endeared him to his fellow Illinois frontiersmen. Republicans needed Illinois to win the presidency in the **election of 1860,** and the people, not the state legislature, voted in 1860.

LIST, FRIEDRICH. *See* AMERICAN SYSTEM.

"LITTLE GIANT." *See* DOUGLAS, STEPHEN A.

LIVESTOCK. Although it not well-known today, cotton had a big competitor in livestock for economic importance to the Old South. In the area east of the Mississippi River, drovers were a big part of an economic activity that is usually associated only with stock raising in Texas as inherited from the Spanish. These Southeastern drovers often walked behind their herds as they took them to market.

Cattle and hogs were common on the public lands in the South, essentially running wild to the outsider, but gathered in round-ups annually and driven to market. The tradition of stock herding grew up in the Carolinas and spread westward in the **Great Migration**. Hogs, particularly, fattened on the acorns and roots of the original hardwood forests.

Using old Celtic methods, Southern whites began to collect animals for profit. When the local Native Americans saw how it was done, they joined in the effort—one of the things that made them "the Civilized Tribes." In more open areas, like Florida, the herders actually rode horses, developing a cowboy tradition separate from that of Spanish Texas. Many of their slaves, whose ancestors from West Africa had herding traditions of their own, quickly adapted to Southern herding styles and proved invaluable. This would feed into the trail drives of the post–Civil War days out of Texas, up to a third of the cowboys being black. In the cis-Mississippi region before the Civil War, the whip replaced the lariat, hence the origin of the common term "cracker" for non-slaveholding whites, who dominated this industry.

In the autumn geese were killed and plucked, while December was set aside for hog killing on the plantations, pork being preferred among both whites and blacks over beef. Many planters came from the ranks of drovers and continued their interest in cattle and hogs by controlled breeding to produce better, meatier, and more disease-resistant animals. By 1860, it has been estimated that 8 million cattle and 10 million hogs lived in the Old South, a vibrant industry that was almost totally destroyed by the Civil War and the passing of the armies of both sides. Its absence after the war and the fencing of the open range forced many former herders out of the woods and into the cotton mills, lowering their lifestyle immeasurably. *See also* ECONOMY.

LOGAN ACT (1798). *See* QUASI-WAR.

LONE STAR REBELLIONS. In the 19th century, the all-blue flag with a single white star was the banner of democratic revolution, well before the red flag used and abused later in the century. Better known from its use by pro-secessionists during the American Civil War, the Bonnie Blue Flag was the symbol for pro-American democratic revolutions until its association with the Confederacy ended its use. These revolutions were also known as Lone Star Rebellions, a form of **filibustering**, of which there were two important cases to the Old South, West Florida and Texas.

Although the **Louisiana Purchase** made no mention whether the Spanish Floridas were a part of the deal, President **James Madison** chose to think that they were. At this time Florida was divided into two parts. East Florida included the present-day state. West Florida comprised the areas of the Gulf Coast below the 31st parallel from the Perdido River just west of Pensacola to Mobile and on to Baton Rouge on the Mississippi. New Orleans was a separate part of West Florida and, although it lay east of the Mississippi River, had been included in the Louisiana Purchase.

Because the rivers in the American South ran through West Florida into the Gulf of Mexico at Mobile, it was important to future American commerce that this area be taken over. Madison sent William Wycoff with sufficient funds to encourage the predominantly Spanish inhabitants to revolt against Spain by raising the blue flag and asking for American protection. Madison annexed all of West Florida immediately by executive proclamation. Congress later endorsed his action.

The **Federalists** and the **Tertium Quids** of Madison's own **Democratic Republican** Party protested, to no avail. Gen. James Wilkinson occupied Mobile in 1813. More **Three-Fifths Compromise** territory soon to become parts of slave states (Louisiana, Mississippi,

Alabama) had joined the Union. This was the only territory taken during the era of the **War of 1812** that America managed to keep.

Madison secretly tried to obtain $100,000 from Congress to cause a Lone Star Rebellion in East Florida, but the revolt failed to come off. Gen. **Andrew Jackson** took the area around Pensacola in 1814, on his way to the First Battle of New Orleans, but the territory was returned to Spain after the War of 1812. It would later be annexed to the United States in the **Adams–Onís Treaty** of 1819, which confirmed the cession of West Florida and defined the southern boundary of the Louisiana Purchase.

But Florida would not be enough to sate the South's drive for more and more slave territory, so marked by the **Great Migration**. No sooner had Spain defined the southern boundary of the Louisiana Purchase as the Sabine and Red rivers than the Americans sent filibustering expeditions into Texas to initiate internal revolt on behalf of the United States. The process was made more attractive as the newly freed colony of Mexico was in constant turmoil, creating a situation much like the one that had led to the annexation of the Floridas.

But Texas was a little more complicated than the Floridas had been. In 1810, Mexico had revolted against Spanish rule. What began as a peasant revolt under Father Miguel Hidalgo y Costilla soon turned into what the American Revolution had been—a revolt of colonists for home rule. Led by Vincente Guerrero, the revolutionists called themselves the Federalists. They wanted an independent Mexico ruled by common people like themselves under a constitutional government. Friendly Americans crossed the border to lend support, but most were captured and executed.

By 1821, after the Adams–Onís Treaty, a new revolution sprang up. This one was led by the upper classes. They feared the democracy of the French and American revolutions. They wanted a strong government, favored monarchy, the church, the army, the wealthy, and were anti-American. They were called the Centralists. Their leader was Augustín Itrubide, who took over the government as dictator (unlike **George Washington**).

Certain army officers revolted against this empire of Augustín I, as he styled himself, and led by Gen. Antonio López de Santa Anna, created a Federalist constitutional government in 1824. This United States of Mexico had 19 states, four territories, a bicameral congress, and a federal court system. The people elected their local state governments which, in turn, elected federal officials.

It was about this time that settlers from the American South began to cross the Sabine River, looking for new land. And someone in the Mexican Federalist government got the bright idea to seal off the American border much as the Romans had—invite the barbarian interlopers in, make them Mexican citizens, and let them defend the frontiers against others of their kind. After all, the Americans sided with the Federalists in political principle. They would surely learn Spanish, convert to Catholicism, give up or leave their slaves behind, and become Mexican citizens for cheap land.

So Mexico contracted with American land agents, called *empresarios*, to bring in settlers to land grants in select areas of Texas. At a time when Americans could buy an 80-acre farm for $100 in the United States, land in Texas was available by the league (4,000 acres) at $30, no money down. An equivalent homestead in the United States would have cost $5000. By 1830, Americans, mostly from the slaveholding South, outnumbered Mexicans in Texas by 10 to 1.

Although everything looked good on paper, the scheme did not work out well. The lead empresario, Stephen F. Austin, did his best to live up to the terms of the deal and encouraged his settlers to do likewise. But most American settlers simply lied. They took their oaths of loyalty to Mexico and ignored them. They spoke English, stayed with their Protestant evangelical faiths, kept their slaves, and got nasty when Mexican authorities pointed out their falsehoods. In the best traditions of the earlier American Revolution against Britain, they even attacked and threw out customs collectors at Anahuac, and threatened to establish an independent republic.

American Presidents **John Quincy Adams** and **Andrew Jackson** offered to buy Texas, causing much consternation in Mexico over the open immigration policy. In April 1830, the Mexican Congress passed a new immigration law, restricting American access to Texas. But Americans ignored the law and kept coming to settle. Meanwhile, back in Mexico City, the political situation was pure chaos. Between 1824 and 1865, Mexico had 36 different governments and 73 presidents. The Federalists would win election after election, and the Centralists would lead military revolt after revolt. Then someone would call for elections and the process would repeat itself. Finally, in 1833, Santa Anna switched sides to the Centralists and took over and suspended the constitution of 1824 for personal rule. The ousted Federalists fled to the provinces and started a rebellion to restore the constitutional republic. Santa Anna moved his army out to suppress these combinations without mercy. By 1835, he was ready to put down the last rebel stronghold—Texas. The native-born Mexicans (Tejanos) and Americans (Texians or Texicans) in Texas proved a hard nut to crack. They threw out a Mexican army led by Gen. Martín Perfecto de Cós, Santa Anna's militarily inept brother-in-law. At first they claimed to be fighting for the Mexican Constitution, and raised the Mexican tri-color with 1824 in its center. But the Texians went further. With the connivance of many Tejanos, they formed an army and called a constitutional convention, established a slaveholding government, and invited other Americans to cross the Sabine line and join the fight.

Santa Anna had had it. He condemned all Americans as *filibusteros*, whom he characterized as pirates and adventurers deserving of death. His forces moved into Texas in mid-winter, taking the rebels by surprise, and destroying their advance guards at San Antonio (the Battle of the Alamo) and Goliad (the Fannin Massacre). Then Santa Anna spread his troops out and headed for Liberty, where rebel refugees were fleeing across the river, high-tailing it for Louisiana. But at San Jacinto, the rebels under Texian Gen. Sam Houston turned and, in a surprise attack, crushed Santa Anna's main force and captured him. The result was the treaty of Velasco, where Santa Anna (in exchange for his life) granted Texas its independence, with the border being the Rio Grande, miles south of the traditional Spanish-Mexican border of Texas, the Nueces River.

The Mexican Congress repudiated the treaty in short order. Texas asked for admission to the Union. Jackson wanted **Texas annexation**, as did most Southerners. But the rise of the **abolitionists**, the **Gag Rule** fight, the upcoming **election of 1836**, and the **Panic 1837** caused him to hold back. He would not destroy the **Democratic** Party for Texas, even if it promised more Three-Fifths Compromise states. Texas annexation was inevitable, but it would have to await a more propitious moment. So it became the Lone Star Republic until **Manifest Destiny** swept Texas and America along to their fate, a national war against slavery.

LOOSE PACKERS. *See* SLAVE TRADE, INTERNATIONAL.

LÓPEZ, NARCISO. *See* FILIBUSTERING.

LOUISIANA PURCHASE. As Napoleon Buonaparte emerged to lead the French revolutionary armies sweeping through Europe, he decided to restore the old French colonial empire in the New World. This involved suppressing the slave revolt on **Haiti** and regaining Louisiana from the Spanish, who had obtained it for siding with the British at the Peace of Paris in 1763. So Napoleon threatened Spain with a French invasion unless the Spanish agreed to the Treaty of San Ildefonso (1801). According to this document, Louisiana was transferred back to the French. If the French decided to divest themselves of Louisiana in the future, Spain was to get first refusal at buying it back.

Although the terms of San Ildefonso were supposedly secret, the American spy network, the best in the world at the time, soon found out that Napoleon not only had Louisiana but, because of his failure to suppress Haiti, he might be willing to sell to the Americans the section that included New Orleans, the treaty with Spain notwithstanding. The Crescent City was the only way for Americans living west of the Appalachian Mountains to move cargoes to market. There were few roads available, everything moved by water, and all rivers wound up flowing to the Mississippi and then to the Gulf of Mexico past New Orleans.

President **Thomas Jefferson** wasted no time in sending **James Monroe** as a special negotiator to buy New Orleans. Monroe arrived at exactly the right moment. Napoleon was reordering his priorities in the never-ending wars of the French Revolution. His plan to reconstitute the French Caribbean empire was failing. Although his supporters had captured and sent Haitian patriot Toussaint L'Ouverture to his exile and death, yellow fever had destroyed the French Army in Haiti as a viable fighting force.

It was time for Napoleon to cut his losses and find some nation rich and eager enough to buy what was left under French control, Louisiana, but not strong enough to affect the wars in Europe or resell it to the British. Spain had too often been a British ally against France to be trusted. With Monroe's arrival, the United States became the perfect choice. Monroe had $2 million from Congress to deal with. He made the American offer for New Orleans and was surprised when the French countered by offering to sell all of Louisiana for $15 million. No one knew what exactly Louisiana was, but it comprised all of the territory west of the Mississippi River as far as America could assert its power—to the Rocky Mountains or even the Pacific. Make the most of it, the French said, it is all yours. Monroe agreed to the deal immediately.

The incoming Jefferson administration saw Monroe's Louisiana Purchase as a fine way to extend the **Slave Power Conspiracy**, as his opponents called the drive of the South to create new slave states that could enter the Union under the **Three-Fifths Compromise**. As Jefferson saw it, the lands below the 31st parallel would be new slave states, while the land above it could be reserved for displaced Native Americans subject to **Indian Removal**. This would allow slaveholding Southerners to move into the rich territories that would become Alabama and Mississippi.

But there was a problem about acquiring Louisiana. The purchase of new territory was not mentioned in the Constitution, and Jefferson prided himself in following the fundamental law to the letter—or more so than his **Federalist** opposition. But this was an emergency. So Jefferson decided to approve Monroe's $2 million down payment and finance the rest in three installments with 6 percent bonds due in 15 years. He would amend the Constitution afterward, when he would ask Congress to provide a government for the new territory that would make the existing residents American citizens.

Until the time that Congress would act, Jefferson envisioned ruling the new addition by executive fiat. This meant that the French and Spanish whites living there would be an occupied people, more of a military concept than a republican one. Northerners immediately moved to restrict slavery in Louisiana, even though it already existed under prior colonial regimes. Jefferson wanted to restrict the international slave trade, but not the domestic institution.

The Northern congressmen responded by proposing that the Three-Fifths Compromise be amended out of the Constitution. They claimed that the clause had been envisioned only so long as the original 13 states comprised the nation. New slave states and now new slave territories meant that the South could no longer maintain that it needed the Three-Fifths Compromise to equalize congressional representation. After all, few direct taxes had ever been levied, which left the South with all the advantages of the compromise and none of the disadvantages seen when it was written a decade earlier.

None of the Northern proposals would pass, and Jefferson got his way when he cracked the patronage whip. After he got Congress to approve of the Louisiana Purchase, there was no need to amend the Constitution anymore. It was a done deal. The Louisiana Territory would enter the Union equal to all other territories and Louisiana would be admitted as a slave state in 1813. It was this fear that the position of the North, especially New England, would become increasingly marginalized as a national political power that would lead to the **Hartford Convention of 1814**.

But Jefferson would also face opposition to reading powers into the Constitution from with in his own party in the **Tertium Quids**, who had just begun to challenge what they saw as the increasing Federalist proclivities of the once ideologically pure Democratic Republican president. Jefferson stopped following the strict interpretation of the Constitution whenever it interfered with extending the slave power westward.

L'OVERTURE, TOUSSAINT. *See* HAITI.

LOWNDES, WILLIAM. *See* ELECTION OF 1824; WAR HAWKS.

LUCAS, ELIZA. *See* INDIGO.

– M –

MACON'S BILL NO. 2. *See* EMBARGO ACT.

MADISON, JAMES (1751–1836). Born in his grandfather's home at Port Conway, Virginia, James Madison grew up in a privileged atmosphere. He was privately educated as a boy and graduated from Princeton. As a student, he was strong in religion and philosophy and read the law. A short man, "Little Jimmy" served as a politician from the Revolution to his retirement from the presidency.

Madison was on the local Committee of Public Safety, helped write the constitution of Virginia, won a seat in the House of Burgesses, and served on the Governor's Council until he was elected to the Second Continental Congress in 1780. There he realized that the central government under the Articles of Confederation was too weak to be effective. Madison was instrumental in summoning the Constitutional Convention in 1787 and became the "Father of the Constitution" for his work there. He wrote in favor of its ratification in the *Federalist Papers*, with **Alexander Hamilton** and John Jay.

Madison served in the Virginia Convention that ratified the Constitution. He wished to be elected to the U.S. Senate, but had antagonized the influential Governor Patrick Henry and had to settle for a seat in the House of Representatives. There Madison opposed the expansive interpretation given the Constitution by Secretary of the Treasury Alexander Hamilton in his economic program of **Funding and Assumption** and the **Bank of the United States**.

Madison's opposition to what he thought was Hamilton's butchering of the true meaning of the Constitution led him to form one of America's first political parties, the **Democratic Republicans**. Uniting with **Thomas Jefferson**, Madison opposed the opposition party, Hamilton's **Federalists**, and their attempts to ruin the Franco-American Alliance of 1778. He also criticized the **Alien and Sedition Acts** by writing, along with Jefferson, the Kentucky part of the **Kentucky and Virginia Resolves**.

When Jefferson became president in 1801, Madison was appointed secretary of state. He supported the **Louisiana Purchase** and the **Embargo Act**. Acceding to the presidency as a part of the **Virginia Dynasty**, Madison tried diplomacy but finally agreed to Congress declaring the **War of 1812**. Madison supervised an incompetent prosecution of that conflict, going forth in 1814 to command American troops at the Battle of Baldensburg outside Washington, D.C., the only American president to command an army in the field while in office. The British victory allowed the enemy to enter the capital city and burn its public buildings. Heroic work by his wife, Dolley, saved many of the nation's more precious artifacts and paintings.

After the war ended, Madison became a part of the **New Nationalism**. He signed several measures, like the **Tariff** of 1816 and the rechartering of the Second **Bank of the United States**, which he had argued against as unconstitutional when originally proposed by Hamilton in the 1790s. After the **election of 1816**, Madison retired to his home, Montpelier, and lived in peace the 20 years until his death.

MANIFEST DESTINY. By 1844, the **Panic of 1837** was coming to an end. America was ready to move forward politically and economically to new horizons. At first this was expressed in a renewed interest in the West, territory claimed by Mexico or Britain. Later it would spill over into American **"Spread Eagle" foreign policy** abroad in Europe and the Pacific Rim.

The ideological force that spurred this interest was called *Manifest Destiny*. It was a doctrine that maintained that America had a preeminent social worth, a lofty mission, and a unique right in the application of moral principles. This was a nation God had selected to spread its society, government, traditions, and culture over an unidentified area to the west in North America, the entire Western Hemisphere, and eventually to the world overseas.

John L. O'Sullivan, a Democrat newspaper editor, had coined the phrase Manifest Destiny. He was a college graduate (present-day Columbia University), had sponsored **filibuster** expeditions, served as U.S. Minister to Portugal, and later sympathized with the Confederacy from a self-imposed exile in Britain. In the 1840s, Manifest Destiny called for free, white self-government on a continental scale in a loose confederation of states, and had a decided Southern tinge to it.

Supporters wanted a single-term president, white male suffrage, frequent elections of all officials (later incorporated in the **Confederate Constitution**), and homesteading free land in the West (later part of the **Republican Platform of 1860**). They believed that the West belonged to those who occupied it, namely white America, because it was the refuge for the world's oppressed. It also saw red, black, and brown people in need of regeneration, which boded ill for the future of Native Americans, slaves, and Mexicans. It called for the United States to expand to the full limits of its natural geographic boundaries, all the way to the Pacific, into the Caribbean, north to Alaska.

Many forces influenced Manifest Destiny. There was the end of the debilitating economic depression, the Panic of 1837. There was a sense that land was growing more and more limited in availability, with the Great Plains seen as the Great American Desert. Business needed more homegrown markets to expand. Manifest Destiny was part of all sorts of reforms which permeated the American psyche at the time—government by the common man, temperance, prison reform, abolition, socialism, dietary reform (Graham Crackers), and clothing changes (Bloomers).

Manifest Destiny would lead to the **Canadian Boundary Dispute**, the **War with Mexico**, the **Spread Eagle foreign policy** of the 1850s, and the **Young America** Movement. It would also lead to the exacerbation of the problem of slavery in the territories by way of the **Wilmot Proviso**, the **Compromise of 1850**, the **Kansas–Missouri Border Wars**, the **Dred Scott** decision, **secession**, and the Civil War.

MANN, A. DUDLEY. *See* YOUNG AMERICA.

MARBURY v. MADISON **(1803).** The first of numerous **Supreme Court** decisions that Chief Justice **John Marshall** wrote designed to enhance the power and prestige of the judiciary branch of the federal government, *Marbury v. Madison* concerned the commission of William Marbury, one of the many **Midnight Judges**, who had failed to receive his commission. Under the Judiciary Act of 1789, men like Marbury could ask the Supreme Court for a writ of mandamus to force the government to hand over their commissions.

Marshall very cleverly gave the president, **Thomas Jefferson**, what he wanted. Marshall said that Marbury had no right to an undelivered commission. By implication the other Midnight Judges who had not received their commissions did not have a right to them, either. But the reason why Marbury was out of luck was revolutionary, making this the most important judicial decision in American history. Marshall said the Judiciary Act of 1789 had given the Supreme Court original jurisdiction over writs of mandamus. Since the original jurisdiction of the Court had been strictly defined in Article III of the Constitution of 1787, this part of the congressional law was unconstitutional and void. Congress could not add to or subtract from the Constitution without proposing a constitutional amendment.

This decision is what gives the Supreme Court its power today to rule on the constitutionality of laws of Congress. Jefferson knew that the Constitution did not really grant the Court this power. But he wanted Marbury and his fellow Federalist appointees even less. So he let the decision pass, satisfying himself with a verbal condemnation of the Court's ruling. Jefferson spoke out against what he saw as an independent judiciary that can decide what laws are constitutional or not, not only for themselves within their own sphere of jurisdiction, but for the federal legislative, executive, and the states as well. He saw the courts ultimately becoming a despotic branch of government, wholly independent of the nation and embodying in themselves the germ of dissolution of the federal government. It was a process, Jefferson said, that would advance little by little until the courts would usurp and subvert the Constitution in its entirety.

Marshall's opinion of court review of laws passed by Congress would be reinforced by his successor, **Roger B. Taney**, in the case *Dred Scott v. Sanford* (1857), which ruled the **Missouri Compromise** of 1820 unconstitutional.

"MAROON" COLONIES. See RESISTANCE AND REBELLION, SLAVE.

MARSHALL, JOHN (1756–1835). John Marshall was born in Fauquier County, Virginia, in 1756. He was privately tutored, served in the Revolutionary War, and studied law at William and Mary College. He practiced in Richmond. He was in favor of the adoption of the Constitution of 1787 and served in the state legislature as a **Federalist**, where he argued for a strong central government. He accompanied the American delegation to Paris during the **Quasi-War** as secretary. He served in the U.S. Congress, then as **John Adams**'s secretary of state, and was appointed to be Chief Justice as a **Midnight Judge** in 1801, after his predecessor John Jay, had quit the post because he thought the Court had outlived its usefulness.

John Marshall spent the next 34 years on the federal bench, making the Supreme Court a powerful third branch of government through the skill of his decisions. Marshall operated on three cardinal principles. First, he established the prestige of the federal judiciary in *Marbury v. Madison* (**1803**), gaining the Court the right to overrule acts of Congress; *Fletcher v. Peck* (1810), guaranteeing the sanctity of contracts and the right to overrule acts of state legislatures; and

Martin v. Hunter's Lessee (1816), and *Cohens v. Virginia* (1821), gaining the right to overrule decisions of state courts.

Second, Marshall enhanced the implied powers of the Constitution, so hated by Jeffersonians, in *McCulloch v. Maryland* (1819), sustaining the superiority of federal institutions over state law; and *Gibbons v. Ogden* (1824), guaranteeing federal regulations over interstate commerce.

Third, Marshall protected private property from acts of state legislatures in *Dartmouth College v. Woodward* (1819), guaranteeing the sanctity of contracts; and *Craig v. Missouri* (1830), guaranteeing federal control of the money supply.

Finally, he protected the rights of **Native Americans**. In *Johnson v. McIntosh* (1823), he admitted that no tribe had an innate title to its land, but in the *Cherokee Nation v. Georgia* (1830), he asserted that the United States could grant such title by treaty, and in *Worcester v. Georgia* (1832), that no state had a right to interfere in any way with granted Indian territory, as it was exclusively a federal question.

Marshall fell in 1831 and went through a dangerous operation, but his health was never the same. Upon the death of his wife, he sickened and died at Philadelphia in 1835.

MASON–DIXON LINE. The traditional border between the free and slave states after 1800 was the southern border of Pennsylvania and the northern border of Maryland and Virginia commonly known as the Mason–Dixon Line. Charles Mason and Jeremiah Dixon surveyed the line between 1763 and 1767 to solve a dispute between the Penn and Baltimore families. The line runs along 39°43' 26.3" north latitude.

As Americans moved west as part of the **Great Migration**, the Mason–Dixon Line as a division between **slavery** and freedom was, in effect, extended. From the western line of Pennsylvania, the line between slave and free states to the Mississippi became the Ohio River as determined by the **Northwest Ordinance**. Then, with the exception of Missouri, the slave-free line ran south along the Mississippi River to the border between Arkansas and Missouri at 36°30' north latitude. After that the line ran west as determined by the **Missouri Compromise** until it was modified by the **Kansas–Nebraska Act** to include all the West in slave territory until admitted to statehood.

MAYSVILLE ROAD VETO. As president, **Andrew Jackson** believed that roads, canals, and later railroads, so-called **internal improvements**, ought to be sponsored by the states in which they were located. Unless a project were multi-state and truly benefited the nation, he would not allow it. He was probably encouraged in this by New Yorker **Martin Van Buren**, who wanted to protect New York's state-financed Erie Canal from improvements being built elsewhere with federal money.

To make his point, Jackson vetoed the Maysville Road Bill, introduced by **Henry Clay** to run a road from his hometown, Lexington, Kentucky, to Maysville on the Ohio, where it could connect to the **National Road** across the river. This was too limited in approach to Jackson. Besides, the veto only hurt Clay's constituency and none other.

Jackson's Maysville Road Veto forced the other states to construct their own transportation projects to compete with New York's Erie Canal, with varying degrees of success. Virginia built the Chesapeake and Ohio Canal, the James and Kanawha Canal, and the Dismal Swamp Canal. Ohio interlaced its numerous rivers to Lake Erie with canals. Illinois connected the various tributaries of the Mississippi River to Lake Michigan at Chicago. Pennsylvania tried to cross the Appalachians, but the task had to await the coming of railroads to succeed. And Indiana went broke in the **Panic of 1837**, leaving its numerous canals lying unfinished.

McCARTHY GIN. *See* COTTON, SEA ISLAND.

McCOMB, MAJ. GEN. ALEXANDER. *See* INDIAN REMOVAL COMPLETED.

McINTOSH, WILLIAM. *See* INDIAN REMOVAL.

McLANE, LOUIS. *See* BANK VETO, BANK WAR.

MERRYMAN, *EX PARTE* **(1861).** During the Civil War, the U.S. **Supreme Court** backed the Yankees' cause in many respects. One exception was *ex parte* Merryman, in which Chief Justice Roger B. Taney censured military arrest outside the civilian court system of ordinary citizens showing seditious tendencies. In early 1861, John Merryman led a mob accused of burning railroad bridges between Baltimore and Philadelphia to prevent Union reinforcement of Washington. These Yankee Southern sympathizers were later called Copperheads. Merryman was arrested, imprisoned in Ft. McHenry, where Francis Scott Key had penned the *Star Spangled Banner,* and denied the writ of *habeas corpus.*

While on circuit later that year, Marylander Chief Justice Roger B. Taney issued *ex parte* Merryman, an opinion stating that military arrest of civilians and their trial before military commissions were prohibited while civil courts were operating freely. Both the Army and President **Abraham Lincoln** rejected his proposal. In 1866, it was restated by the whole U.S. Supreme Court in *ex parte* Mulligan, but Taney had died two years earlier, and the war had ended, rendering it academic.

MERRYMAN, JOHN. *See* BALTIMORE PLOT; MERRYMAN, *EX PARTE.*

MEXICAN CESSION. *See* WAR WITH MEXICO.

MIDDLE PASSAGE. *See* SLAVE TRADE, INTERNATIONAL.

MIDNIGHT JUDGES. After **Thomas Jefferson** won the election of 1800, his **Democratic Republican** Party taking the executive and legislative branches of the national government, the **Federalist** Party in the outgoing, already defeated Lame Duck session of Congress moved to secure the third branch of government, the federal court system, for itself. The process was simple. They would pack the courts with new Federalist judges, appointed for life. The measure that achieved this was the Judiciary Act of 1801.

The Judiciary Act expanded the federal court system and provided for the appointment of Senate-approved judges to fill those posts. The new judges were needed in the growing country, but the timing of the act, and the fact that it decreased the number of **Supreme Court** judges from six to five (Jefferson would have to await the death of two sitting judges before he could appoint one), caused the **Democratic Republicans** to cry foul.

Because the Judiciary Act was passed so late in outgoing President John Adams' term, and he allegedly stayed up until midnight on his last day in office to appoint the new judges, the new appointees became facetiously known as the "Midnight Judges." Communications being what they were in 1801, not all of the commissions were mailed before the incoming Jefferson administration arrived in March. Secretary of State **James Madison** saw all the undelivered commissions on his desk and put them in the fire. The new Democratic Republican Congress confirmed his action by abolishing all of the vacant new posts when it met in December.

One of the Federalist appointees who failed to receive his commission was William Marbury. He knew he had been appointed, so he sued Secretary of State Madison for it by asking the still-Federalist dominated U.S. **Supreme Court** for a writ of mandamus (a court order to a public official to do something). The decision, *Marbury v. Madison*, was written by **John Marshall**, a Midnight Judge who had received his commission.

Marshall wrote the majority opinion of the court. Marbury's request was invalid, Marshall said, because the Judiciary Act of 1789 that had granted the Supreme Court original jurisdiction for writs of mandamus in cases such as this was unconstitutional. It was wrong because the original jurisdiction of the U.S. Supreme Court had been set by the Constitutional Convention in Article III of the Constitution, and Congress could not change it except through a constitutional amendment.

What Marshall had done was to very cleverly agree with Jefferson that Marbury ought not to be a judge. But he had also assumed the right of the Supreme Court to declare laws of Congress unconstitutional. This competed with the compact theory advanced by Jefferson and Madison in the **Kentucky and Virginia Resolves**. But Jefferson decided to accept what little he had won and save the battle with the court for later. Of course, neither theory is in the Constitution, but Marshall's won out over time.

MILLER, PHINEAS. *See* COTTON GIN.

MISCEGENATION. The union of the black and white races, generally black women with white males, is something that many authors present as rape—the dominance of the weak by the strong, a typical result from something so exploitative as **slavery**. In reality it was something that ranged from an act of love to sadistic violence. Most miscegenation fell somewhere in between. Allegedly today about three-fourths of African Americans have some white ancestry. But in 1860, the number was more like 13 percent if the U.S. census is accurate, which it usually was not. Hence scholars believe it was closer to 20 percent. According to the census, the occurrence was twice as likely in the upper South than the Gulf States—with the exception of Louisiana.

The problem with antebellum statistics is that whatever involved white ancestry was estimated by observation and personal opinion. If a slave were not coal-black, he or she might be determined to be "yellow," or a mulatto, of mixed blood. This overlooks the fact that many enslaved Africans came from lighter colored peoples in their homeland. Many novels about the slaveholding South depict it as a society full of plantations that were, at best, a lustful harem. Yet most race mixing occurred in towns and cities where single, white men and single, black women lived in close quarters and looser morality.

Of all the incidents of miscegenation under the slave regime, two stand out. The most looked at and controversial to this day is the relationship between **Thomas Jefferson** and his slave, the half-sister of his deceased wife, **Sally Hemings**. But Jefferson never admitted to anything.

Only one early public figure admitted to an open affair with a black woman: **Richard Johnson** of Kentucky, vice president under the **Martin Van Buren** administration and reputed killer of Tecumseh at the Battle of the Thames in the **War of 1812**. Johnson even paraded down the main street in his hometown of Lexington, Kentucky, with her, their mulatto children in tow. He never made it to the presidency, allegedly because of it. Upon his death his white relatives successfully contested his will, which left most of his property to his black progeny.

Not all miscegenation was between white males and black females. There were recorded instances where white women engaged in sexual relations with black men, slave or free. It was remarkable that such incidents did not lead to the lynching of the black man as it did after slavery ended. Miscegenation in the Old South remains as the great black historian, W. E. B. Du Bois, characterized it, "stark, ugly, painful, beautiful."

MISSOURI COMPROMISE. The conquest of the West surged across the Mississippi River during the **Era of Good Feelings**. As in the past, the South led this **Great Migration**. Southerners poured from Kentucky and Tennessee into Arkansas and Missouri. By 1819, Missouri had enough population in the Missouri River valley and the key city of St. Louis to ask to be admitted to the Union as a state—a slave state.

It so happened that between 1800 and 1819, the new states of the West had come into the Union in pairs, North and South. As the first state west of the Mississippi, Missouri would upset the 11 to 11 balance. The South would not only have two more senators, it would also have a whole new set of "Negro congressmen," white representatives based on some of its slave population, under the old **Three-Fifths Compromise**. The North was not about to allow that.

So when Missouri applied for statehood, Congressman James Tallmadge of New York added the Tallmadge Amendment to the measure. He proposed that no more slaves, beyond the 10,000 already there, be allowed into the proposed state. Further, Tallmadge wanted all slave children born in Missouri after it became a state to be freed at age 25. Tallmadge believed that slavery was immoral and the South got too much from the Three-Fifths Compromise. The House of Representatives agreed. The Senate refused to consider the measure and adjourned.

By 1820, the situation had changed. Massachusetts had agreed to grant its detached county of Maine the right to become a state—a free state. **Henry Clay** attached the two enabling acts together. Then Jesse B. Thomas of Illinois proposed the Thomas Amendment, which became the First Missouri Compromise of 1820. It had several provisions. First, Maine was to be admitted into the Union as a free state. Second, there would be no more slavery allowed in the Louisiana Purchase above the line of 36°30', the southern boundary of Missouri. Third, Missouri would be allowed to draw up a slave state constitution. But Missouri was yet to be admitted into the Union

Missouri, however, maintained that it ought to have already been admitted as a slave state and cast its electoral vote for **James Mon-**

roe in the **election of 1820**. This necessitated a Second Missouri Compromise of 1820, often called the (Philip P.) Barbour–(Henry) Clay Compromise. This proposed that all of the electoral votes submitted in 1820 be counted. If Missouri's votes were challenged (they were), then the electoral votes would be counted again. In either case, Monroe and Daniel D. Tompkins would be re-elected.

Finally, in 1821, the Third Missouri Compromise was reached. The Missouri slave state constitution prohibited the entry of free persons of color into the state. Years before, New York and Massachusetts had granted free blacks citizenship and protested that not all of their citizens would be granted the privileges and immunities of citizenship under the Missouri prohibition. So Missouri agreed not to enforce this provision, but refused to remove it from its constitution. The result was the admission of Missouri to the Union as a slave state in 1821.

The Third Missouri Compromise did not end the state's problem with Northern **anti-slavery** forces. In 1837, Congress allowed Missouri to annex the Platte Region, a rich hemp and tobacco-growing area along the eastern bank of the Missouri River in the northwestern part of the state, north of present-day Kansas City and west of the 94°40' line of longitude that marked the state's original boundary. This was accomplished only after treaties evicted ten Eastern **Native American** tribes, who had already been given the land as a part of Indian Removal from the Old Northwest. This annexation was a technical violation of the original Missouri Compromise, but anti-slavery forces could not get any interest aroused in Congress because it did not affect the equality of North and Old South in the Senate. Within little more than a decade, the **War with Mexico**, the **Wilmot Proviso**, and the **Kansas–Nebraska Act** would change all that.

MISSOURI COMPROMISE, REPEAL OF. See *DRED SCOTT v. SANFORD*; KANSAS–NEBRASKA ACT.

MONROE, JAMES (1758–1831). The last president of the **Virginia Dynasty**, James Monroe was born in Westmoreland County, Virginia. He left William and Mary College to enlist in the Continental Army and fought from Harlem Heights to Monmouth. Then his commission expired, and he returned to Virginia to study law under

Governor **Thomas Jefferson**. He served in the Virginia state legislature and the Congress under the **Articles of Confederation**. He was an Anti-Federalist and opposed ratification of the new U.S. Constitution. But he was elected U.S. Senator after it was ratified.

As a senator, Monroe joined with fellow Virginians Jefferson and **James Madison** in the **Democratic Republican** Party. He was U.S. Minister to France but returned to serve as governor of Virginia during the slave rebellion known as **"General" Gabriel's Plot**, which he suppressed with vigor. After the election of Jefferson in 1800, Monroe returned to France to negotiate the **Louisiana Purchase**. He served in other European diplomatic positions for the next several years. He returned to Virginia to become governor once again. But James Madison asked him to serve as secretary of state, with its implication of succession to the presidency in the **election of 1816**.

As president, Monroe served two terms, known as the **Era of Good Feelings**. His presidency was especially active in foreign affairs, thanks to the abilities of his secretary of state, **John Quincy Adams**. The **Anglo-American Rapprochement** settled the Canadian boundary issues, and the **Adams–Onís Treaty** bought East Florida and established the southern boundary of the Louisiana Purchase. The **Monore Doctrine** became a cardinal principle in American foreign policy. Domestically, Monroe signed the **Missouri Compromise** and the Land Law of 1820, weathered the **Panic of 1819**, and vetoed the Bonus Bill that would have financed repairs to the **National Road** from profits earned by the Second **Bank of the United States**.

Monroe retired to his home in 1825. He served in the Virginia Constitutional Convention in 1829 and, because of economic troubles, sold his papers to the U.S. government. He died suddenly while in New York City in 1831. His body was returned to Virginia in 1858, the centennial year of his birth, amid solemn ceremonies.

MONROE DOCTRINE. In the 1820s, after the end of the Napoleonic Wars, Spain wished to restore her Latin American Empire, which had declared its independence. Only Britain refused to go along, for trade reasons. Britain suggested that the United States might wish to go in on a joint resolution to restrict the reestablishment of the Spanish Empire in the New World.

President **James Monroe**'s Secretary of State **John Quincy Adams** saw that the United States might assert its own power independently of Britain by acting unilaterally behind the shield of the Royal Navy. After all, Britain and the United States had the same objectives, trade with independent countries freed from Spain. So Adams wrote the speech that Monroe planned to give in Congress in 1823. It came to be called the Monroe Doctrine.

The Monroe Doctrine has three principles: non-colonization, which states that the U.S. would allow no more European colonies to be created beyond those already in the New World; non-intervention, which asserts that the U.S. would stay clear of European problems if Europe would do the same in the New World; and no-transfer, which is the idea that no European power could transfer an existing colony in the New World to another European power. They must free them or hold them, or, by the Old South's interpretation, give them to the United States for future slave states.

The European nations laughed at America's haughtiness. But Britain did not. If the Americans could not enforce the Monroe Doctrine, Britain's fleet could. And that was the way it stood until America entered onto the world stage in the Spanish–American War of 1898.

MONROE HERESY. *See* DEMOCRATS; ERA OF GOOD FEELINGS.

MOORE, THOMAS. *See* SECESSION OF THE SOUTHERN STATES, FIRST.

MORGAN, WILLIAM. *See* ELECTION OF 1832.

MORMON WAR (1857). John C. Frémont, the **Republican Party** nominee in the **election of 1856,** declared that "the twin relics of barbarism—polygamy and **slavery**" ought to be prohibited in the territories. Polygamy was a reference to the Mormons—the Church of Jesus Christ of Latter-day Saints. Fleeing violent religious persecution in the East in 1846, they settled in Utah's Great Salt Lake valley, then Mexican territory. But two years later, as a part of the territorial adjustments in the **War with Mexico,** the Mormons found themselves back in the United States on the direct overland trail to California's gold fields and in need of a territorial government.

The Mormon State of Deseret included what the United States called Utah Territory, and spread north to Idaho's Salmon River and south to San Diego, California. The Compromise of 1850 created the Utah Territory including present-day Colorado west of the Continental Divide and what is now Utah and Nevada. President **Millard Fillmore,** concerned with more urgent items, like the **Compromise of 1850**, appointed Mormon church leaders as his territorial officials.

Fillmore's governor was Brigham Young, the prophet and first president of the Council of Twelve. For this piece of perspicacity, the Mormons named one of their counties Millard and its county seat Fillmore. Under Governor Young's administration, the Church took precedence over national interests. Unfortunately, Fillmore's successor as president, **James Buchanan.** would not be smart enough to leave well enough alone in Utah.

The Republican Party's common denominator in 1856 was its opposition to the twin evils of **slavery** expansion and polygamy in the West. This duality was designed to ensnare Buchanan into intervening in Utah to show the Democrats' inconsistency in supporting **Popular Sovereignty**, or non-interference, in Kansas. Buchanan succumbed to this ruse by appointing a secular territorial government of the usual **Democratic Party** political hacks, which Young rejected and threw out of the territory.

About the same time, a wagon train of rowdy Gentiles from areas that had persecuted Mormons in the East headed to San Diego via Utah. Mormon militia and local Native Americans confronted and massacred most of the group at Mountain Meadows near St. George. Young and the Church's involvement is unknown, but this was all that Buchanan needed to justify sending in the U.S. Army to "stabilize" the situation.

Buchanan appointed a top army officer, Col. Albert Sidney Johnston, to lead an expeditionary force of troops onto the Great Plains out to Ft. Bridger in Wyoming to intimidate Mormon officials. Supplies were freighted out from Kansas City by wagon train. Upon his arrival, Johnston's column found Ft. Bridger in ruins; raiding Mormon militia had burned it down. Next, the militia attacked and destroyed Johnston's supply train, forcing the army to spend a long, cold, hungry winter in what was left of Ft. Bridger.

Meanwhile, Thomas Leiper Kane of Pennsylvania, an important Gentile friend of the Mormons, voyaged across the Isthmus of Panama and traveled the trail from San Diego to Great Salt Lake City to effect a compromise. He persuaded Young to punish the Mountain Meadows Massacre leaders and allow the army to encamp south of Great Salt Lake City. Young would also have to accept a new secular government. The real significance of the Mormon War, besides showing the vulnerability of long federal army supply lines, which Confederate commanders would demonstrate time and time again during the coming Civil War, was that the army was too busy in Utah to do much in the **Kansas Settlement,** which is exactly what antislavery forces desired.

MORRIS, THOMAS. See FREE-SOIL PARTY; SLAVE POWER CONSPIRACY.

MORTE FONTAINE, TREATY OF (1800). See QUASI-WAR.

MORTON, SAMUEL G. See SLAVERY AS A POSITIVE GOOD, THEORY OF.

MOULTRIE CREEK, TREATY OF (1823). See INDIAN REMOVAL.

MOUNTAIN MEADOWS MASSACRE. See MORMON WAR.

– N –

NASHVILLE CONVENTION. See COMPROMISE OF 1850.

NAT TURNER'S REBELLION. See SOUTHAMPTON REVOLT.

NATIONAL REPUBLICANS. The most nationalistic of the **old Democratic Republicans**, those who supported the **New Nationalism**, the Monroe Heresy, the **John Quincy Adams** administration, and **Henry Clay**'s program, the **American System**, against the decentralizing tendencies of **Martin Van Buren** of the Albany Regency and Thomas Ritchie of the Richmond Junto and William Crawford of

Georgia, declared themselves to be National Republicans. There is some truth that these men represent the old **Federalists** in their approach to government, as typified by **Alexander Hamilton's** program of **Funding and Assumption** and the chartering of the **Bank of the United States**. These men would eventually be a critical element in founding the **Whig** Party.

NATIONAL ROAD. When **George Washington** left office, the old road from Baltimore to Pittsburgh was so rough that it actually improved when covered with snow and ice. The problem was how to justify financing the building of a national road to the west in a manner so as not to compromise states' rights guaranteed in the Constitution. This means little to a modern American; the Constitution has been so stretched to justify anything nowadays, it is rarely read anymore.

But to the Americans in 1800, as **Thomas Jefferson** came to power under the guise of states' rights and weak central government, it was a key issue. Secretary of the Treasury Albert Gallatin solved the problem to Jefferson's satisfaction. Gallatin urged that 2 percent of the income from the sale of public lands be held aside to build a National Road. Later the sum was raised to 5 percent (to keep the state from selling the lands for taxes), and ultimately $20 million was spent.

In 1806, Congress passed an act authorizing the construction of a National Highway between Cumberland, Maryland, and Wheeling, Virginia (West Virginia not being a separate state until 1863). It was popularly called the Cumberland Road. The route meant life or death for the towns included or bypassed by the highway. Pennsylvania withheld its approval until the survey was changed to include Uniontown and Washington (the process was for the federal government to get permission to build from the state and then advance the money needed against the future sales of land). It was deemed politically smart to include the capitals of the states and territories through which it passed (Columbus, Ohio; Indianapolis, Indiana; and Vandalia, Illinois).

Because of political delays and the **War of 1812**, it took until 1818 to complete the section to Wheeling. Even though the land sales rarely kept up with the demands of construction and repair, the government kept on building from Wheeling (1818), to Columbus

(1833), to Vandalia (1839). At least that is what was planned — the actual road never got beyond Terra Haute.

Repairs were halted with **James Monroe**'s veto in 1817 of the Bonus Bill, which would have allowed proceeds from the **Second Bank of the United States** to be applied to the road. With the **Maysville Road Veto** in 1830, President **Andrew Jackson** began a project of divesting the road and turning it back to the states. Under no constitutional restraint, the states made their sections into toll roads. But it had taken so long to build the National Road that it began to suffer from fierce competition, particularly from the Erie Canal and the later railroads. The highway's heyday was pretty much over by the 1840s.

An odd effect of the National Road was that civilization changed north and south of it, irrespective of state boundaries. North of the highway, Yankee mores ruled. South of the highway, society had a distinct Southern feel, so much so that Illinois tried to institute slavery upon statehood in violation of the intent of the **Northwest Ordinance** of 1787, which prohibited it north and west of the Ohio River. During the Civil War, southern parts of Ohio, Indiana, and Illinois were decidedly lukewarm to federal policies like the military draft and emancipation.

NATIVE AMERICANS. At the time of the creation of the United States, at least half of all the territory south of the Ohio River was occupied by some 50,000 members of various Native American tribes. They held sway over nearly all of what would become Mississippi and Alabama, four-fifths of Georgia and Tennessee, all of Kentucky west and south of the Cumberland River, and most of the mountain regions of North and South Carolina. Each tribal group was independent and militarily powerful and posed a barrier to the expansion of white settlement into the Old Southwest. Three of the tribes, the Cherokees, the Creeks, and the Choctaws, were or had been hostile to American interests throughout the 18th century. Only the Chickasaw, the weakest of the tribes, could be considered friendly to white settlement west of the Appalachian Mountains.

The earliest Native American arrivals into what became the Old South were believed to be the Creeks. They ultimately divided into Upper and Lower Confederations. The Upper Creeks settled in what is now Tennessee, Alabama, and Georgia. The Lower Creeks lived along the Gulf Coast and were ultimately enticed by the Spanish to move into northern Florida to act as a barrier to English expansion southward from South Carolina.

Soon the Creeks were pressured from all sides by newer native peoples like the Cherokees from the East, the Chickasaws and their brethren the Choctaw from the West, and the Shawnee from the North. Constant warfare existed between tribes, which allied with each other and then divided to join others at will. In this manner the Creeks were driven south, while the Shawnee eventually wound up north of the Ohio. The ground in between, the Dark and Bloody Ground known as Ken-tuck-ee, was fought over and hunted in by each. This battling generally was fairly low-grade, consisting of small war parties that ambushed their enemies and took prisoners to be held as slaves or ransomed or traded.

The first contact of any of these peoples with whites occurred in the mid-1500s when Hernando de Soto's Spanish army showed up looking for food, gold and other valuables, and women and men for slaves. The Spanish were very brutal in their practice of war, destroying entire villages. But, worst of all, they left behind European diseases like smallpox which decimated the whole region, leaving many areas without population at all.

Soon the various tribes found themselves caught between European powers competing for colonial advantage, the Spanish on the south, the French to the west, and the British to the north. The Native Americans played the Europeans off against each other, angling for trade and military advantages. The Cherokee, for example, used an alliance with the English to drive the Tuscarora all the way to their Iroquois relatives in New York.

With the Tuscarora buffer gone, the Cherokee found that they had made a deal with the devil. South Carolinians began to raid isolated towns for prisoners to sell as slaves to the West Indies. The resulting Cherokee Wars were stopped only after the South Carolina militia won a few victories and bribed the Native Americans with a large gun and ammunition gift. But, by 1721, the Cherokees gave up their first land cession to the encroaching British.

Similar wars and treaties followed throughout the century, with the whites managing to buy, bribe for, or conquer small sections of land.

Generally the tribes sided with the French or Spanish against the British until England won most of the cis-Mississippi west except Florida in the French and Indian Wars. Then the tribes sided with the British, who created the Proclamation Line of 1763 down the spine of the Appalachian Mountains, beyond which there was to be no American westward movement. But United States victory in the Revolutionary War left the Native Americans to stand alone against America's rapacious hunger for Western land.

Indian policy in the new United States went through three different stages between the War for American Independence and the **War with Mexico**. The first has been called the **Federalist** policy, named after the political party that dominated America at the end of the 18th century. It was a continuation of older concepts of Native American management inherited from the Confederation period and the British colonial era. Essentially this boiled down to extending the influence of the U.S. government among the tribes to keep them at peace with each other and the United States, and to "civilize" them in place in their traditional homelands, which were given more exact boundaries. The main concessions expected were some land cessions and the right to build roadways.

In the Old South, all Native Americans, regardless of tribe, were supervised by one federal agent who usually delegated his powers among sub-agents responsible for relations with one tribe. These sub-agents were of a differing character as to honesty, ability, and concern for their human charges. Several feared to go among their charges, much less live among them as the government desired.

As the Southwest Territory became populated with more whites and states were formed, the federal Indian agent found that, not only did he have to engage in arguments over policy with his subordinates, he had to mediate between territorial and state governors, whose concept of Indian rights were vastly different from his. The governors often bypassed the federal Indian agent and his subordinates and took their quarrels straight to influential politicians in Washington, D.C.

In addition, the U.S. government moved to create both private and federal trading posts to provide the tribes with the necessities of life and to make wide-ranging hunting and war unnecessary. The private licensed traders had a big advantage over a government that was often strapped for cash and could not stock its shelves with sufficient goods for the job. But while the private traders could provide more to the Indians, they did so at a bigger cost to the tribes in the form of business profits the government did not charge.

Finally, the federal government exerted a small but influential military presence along tribal boundaries with white settlements. This was deemed especially important among the Creeks, who were restless from the start about American willingness and ability to regulate settlements to lawfully ceded land areas.

With the accession of the **Jeffersonians** to power in 1801, a new wrinkle in American Indian management developed. The trading posts and military garrisons were as before, but the concept of the civilizing process was expanded to include voluntary removal to "Indian Territory," a vaguely defined land that would change its boundaries over the years, in the new **Louisiana Purchase**. Seeing the handwriting on the wall, individual Cherokees, those in the most direct contact with advancing white settlement in Tennessee, began to move voluntarily to what would become western Arkansas. They were known as the Old Settlers.

The Jeffersonians made considerable progress in talking the various tribes into land cessions, but the Native Americans resisted any overall **Indian Removal**. When the **War of 1812** occurred, skillful work by the various Indian agents managed to keep the Cherokees, Choctaws, and Chickasaws allied to the United States. But the Creek Nation fell under the influence of the Shawnee from the north, Tecumseh (his mother was Creek), and it went to war. The ensuing massacre of white settlers at Ft. Mimms was one of the worst in American history. The whites reacted with great vengeance and, in defeating the Creek uprising, made the end of the fighting dependent upon massive land cessions in Alabama.

The end of the War of 1812 brought a new turn to American Indian policy. The Native Americans were placed under the tutelage of the Department of War. The secretary was none other than **John C. Calhoun**, one of the foremost advocates of westward expansion in Washington. Calhoun knew that the Native Americans, especially in the Old South, were disorganized, dependent on the government for subsistence, and too feeble to oppose government desires.

It was obvious that with the advent of the **Great Migration** the Indian tribes were in the way. This was so despite the success of civilizing the tribes to the degree that the Southern nations (Cherokee, Creek, Chickasaw, Choctaw, and Seminole) became commonly referred to as the Five Civilized Tribes. Many, especially among the Cherokees, had farms and plantations and even owned slave property just like prosperous whites. So Calhoun made Indian Removal compulsory, by any means, fair or foul. He appointed as sub-agents among the tribes men who believed in despoiling the tribes without mercy. The Southern state and territorial governors cooperated as if their political lives depended on it, which they did. The rush of the "Twenty-Niners" for gold found on Cherokee land at **Dalonega** only increased the imperative.

Calhoun's main negotiator in securing treaties through the application of fraud, chicanery, and force was **Andrew Jackson**. Soon to be president of the United States, Jackson, who had already defrauded several tribes of large sections of their homelands, signed the Indian Removal Act of 1830, which made eviction legal federal policy. It remained but for his successors, principally Martin Van Buren, to see **Indian Removal completed**, often with dreadful results for the native peoples as the army forcefully escorted them west to Indian Territory (present-day Oklahoma), opening the rich soils of the Old South to **slavery** and the **upland cotton** cultivation.

NATURAL LIMITS OF SLAVERY EXPANSION. The natural climate for **upland cotton** existed in few places in the world, and none was as ideal as the 19th-century American South. Generally, a planter desired a mean summer temperature of 77°, a year-round mean temperature of 70°, and 23 inches of annual rainfall. In the United States, before the advent of irrigation, this was marked by a line beginning at the northeastern border of North Carolina at the sea and curving with the Appalachian Mountains until it reached the Georgia–Alabama border at 31° north latitude. The line then curved gently north to take in southeastern Missouri and dropped back south around the Ozark Mountains into Arkansas and northeastern Texas. Next the line went up into central Oklahoma (then called Indian Territory), and dropped south to the Gulf of Mexico along the 97th meridian. Depending on the price and demand for cotton, the line shrank or expanded into Maryland, Virginia, the Nashville basin, and parts of Kentucky, Illinois, and Missouri.

Before cotton became important and **Indian Removal** took place, migration into the Southwest was through the mountain gaps in Kentucky and Tennessee, across the Mississippi into Missouri, and the main crop was **tobacco** and various subsistence crops, like **corn**. But after the **Panic of 1819**, cotton lured the **Great Migration** forward into the interior of Alabama and Mississippi, displacing the Indian tribes. A Florida boom came with the Seminole Wars, before the **Panic of 1837** and the clearing of the Red River Raft necessitated another pause. With the solution of these problems, cotton planters stormed into the rich lands of Arkansas, northwestern Louisiana and northeastern Texas. Then, with the end of the **War with Mexico** came the so-called Texas Fever, opening an area as big as Alabama and Mississippi combined. The Lone Star State tripled its white population, increased its slave population three and a half times, and raised its cotton culture eight-fold in the 1850s.

Just how aware politicians were of the natural limits of slavery expansion is debatable. It seems that **Stephen A. Douglas** was willing to repeal the 1820 **Missouri Compromise** in the 1854 **Kansas–Nebraska Act** because he knew that cotton, and thus slavery, were at their natural limits. But to others there was a principle involved in not limiting or denying the expansion of slavery that transcended geography and entered the realm of morality. This would be called the **Non-Exclusion Doctrine** in the South, and the **Wilmot Proviso** in the North, and lead directly to **secession** and the Civil War.

NAVAL STORES. The 100-mile-wide coastal plain from Virginia was home to the long-leaf pine, a highly resinous tree that can be tapped for tar, pitch, and turpentine much like the maple is for syrup in the hardwood forests of the North. The products were highly prized in the age of sailing ships and utilized in waterproofing hulls and sails. The lack of shipbuilding harbors meant that most of the product was exported to areas where shipyards abounded, up North and in Britain.

Of all the colonies and later states, North Carolina specialized in these products, from which the nickname "Tar Heel" emerged for its native sons. The tar was baked from pine lumber in a kiln. The longer the wood was heated, the more pitchy the sap became. After the **War of 1812**, the production of tar declined and production shifted to turpentine and its various derivatives, used in paint and the preservation of wood. One product of great importance was camphene, a turpentine derivative mixed with alcohol and used to light lamps between the decline of whale oil and the introduction of kerosene. Because of the poor soils in the **Tidewater** plain, North Carolina stayed with turpentine products and never shifted to **cotton** as did much of the rest of the South.

The turpentine business was an area in which industrial slavery could be practiced with much success. The slaves worked at tasks, assigned duties of a day's work, generally covering 50 to 100 acres of trees. Quick workers could secure much free time if their allotted tasks were completed with alacrity. The slaves went through the woods in shifts. Boxers would cut holes in the tree base to collect the juices. Chippers would open the gashes regularly to ensure better flow. Dippers removed the saps from the boxes. Distillers refined the juices into products needed. Coopers made the barrels in which the final product was shipped.

The average life of a pine was about ten years in production. Then the producers would have to move their operations to new trees. By the time of the Civil War, North Carolina and other turpentine areas earned $12 million annually. *See also* ECONOMY.

NEGRO FORT, THE. *See* ADAMS–ONÍS TREATY.

NEW ECHOTA, TREATY OF (1835). *See* INDIAN REMOVAL COMPLETED.

NEW ENGLAND EMIGRANT AID SOCIETY. The North, seeing the **Kansas–Nebraska Act** as a Mephistophelean plot to render the West a haven for slavery, organized a movement to rescue Kansas from this atrocious fate. Eli Thayer, a Massachusetts educator and businessman, founded the New England Emigrant Aid Society to help Free-Soilers settle Kansas and vote to make it free.

An initial 30 settlers in July 1854 named the town of Lawrence in honor of the financier, businessman, and philanthropist Amos Lawrence, who had built many cotton mills in Lowell, Massachusetts. The Kansas settlers constructed the residences and the centrally located Free State Hotel from brick and stone. These fortified edifices were defensive **anti-slavery** strongholds during the **Kansas–Missouri Border Wars**.

NEW NATIONALISM, THE. The period immediately following the **War of 1812** was one of euphoric nationalism in the United States. There was a feeling that the nation had shamed Britain once again. This was, of course, public denial that the nation had escaped defeat only because of war weariness in Europe, but Americans did not care. All they remembered was the First Battle of New Orleans. It was time to get on with building the nation.

James Madison shared in this happiness, something he had not experienced since the adoption of the **Constitution** 30 years before. The nation was expanding westward in the **Great Migration**. Within the next four years, the United States admitted six new states since the beginning of **Thomas Jefferson**'s administration. Gone were the old constitutional arguments involving **Alexander Hamilton**'s economic program. Jefferson himself had continued **Funding and Assumption** and the **Bank of the United States**. Madison had become a convert and now moved to revive the Hamiltonian program as his own.

The first Hamiltonian institution that Madison put forth was the Bank of the United States. The original charter had expired in 1811, just as war fever had gripped the nation. The bank had failed by one vote in Congress. Since then hundreds of wildcat banks had sprung up. With the absence of a discount rate, they had printed thousands of dollars in worthless paper money. Expanding business needed a supervisory agent to guarantee a viable monetary policy.

Led by **Henry Clay** and **John C. Calhoun**, the Congress established the Second Bank of the United States. It was to be headquartered in Philadelphia, have branches in key cities, sell 20 percent of its stock to the U.S. government, be a depository for U.S. Treasury funds, and discount paper notes to create a common currency. Interestingly, the Federalists, who had sponsored the original Bank of the United States, opposed the Second Bank. New England banks were already the best in the nation.

Another Madison-sponsored project was the first tax to protect infant American industries, the **Tariff** of 1816. Even Hamilton had been unable to pass this. The early tariffs before 1816 were solely for revenue purposes—very slight. Jefferson had said in 1800, "We are all Federalists, we are all Republicans." Madison proved this true in 1816 with his New Nationalism. It would not stay that way for long.

NEW ORLEANS, FIRST BATTLE OF. *See* WAR OF 1812.

NICHOLSON, A. O. P. *See* ELECTION OF 1848.

NON-EXCLUSION DOCTRINE. This Southern political theory held that the **U.S. Constitution** guaranteed the **extraterritoriality** of **slavery** as an institution in the Western territories of the United States. When the territory applied for statehood, slavery could be confirmed or abolished within the boundaries of the proposed new state. This would be determined by the state constitutional convention or a later popular vote. More widely known as **Popular Sovereignty,** it was a crucial component of the 1857 U.S. **Supreme Court** case *Dred Scott v. Sanford.*

NON-INTERCOURSE ACT. *See* EMBARGO ACT.

NON-SLAVEHOLDERS. The usual myth about white society in the Old South was that there were only two visible white classes: the wealthy planters and the poor whites. The general pattern was for the poor non-slaveholding whites to open up Western lands and then to be supplanted by the planters and their slave labor force in time. This process did not exist before the rapid influx of slaves from Africa in the early 1700s. But as the planters began to dominate the coastal settlements, the poor whites moved westward into the Great Valley, the Shenandoah and it adjuncts along the Appalachian front range. When the **cotton gin** was introduced, the process intensified and the poor whites led the way over the mountains into the valley of the Mississippi and its tributaries.

The result was geographic specialization. The poor whites remained poor because they farmed the barren sand hills, the piney woods, and the mountain valleys. The planters dominated the rich soil of the deltas and the prairies. If the farmers were not shoved out because of not being able to compete with cheaper slave labor, the planters' willingness to pay high prices for the best land proved irresistible. As for white artisans and other skilled laborers, they merely filled in the interstices in the small towns between the big plantations. Industry was minimal in such a society.

Not all historians agree with the classic description of antebellum Southern white society. Because the critics mostly came from Vanderbilt University in Tennessee, their viewpoint is called the Vanderbilt School. These writers posit that there was actually a prosperous and large Southern white middle class. The reason prior researchers failed to see it was that they relied on descriptions written by Yankee and European travelers. These accounts depict the ornate plantation homes served by numerous slaves, and the six to seven million poor whites, all of whom were infested with hookworm, lived in squalid huts, ate little better than the slaves (meal, fatback, and molasses), drank to excess, fought anyone and everyone, and epitomized what the slaves called them: "white trash."

The Vanderbilt scholars decided to see if the stereotype was true. Using the U.S. census, they discovered a thriving middle class that was constantly expanding in wealth, many of whom in time became planters themselves. Land ownership, slave ownership, and fluidity of wealth marked the pre–Civil War white South, not poverty. While slave labor was cheap, it also was rigid. Slaves had much of their work fixed by custom. Agriculture was so simple at this time that large scale meant little. Indeed, non-slaveholding whites grew half of all pre–Civil War **tobacco** and **cotton**.

Planters also had higher overhead. There were slaves to be cared for, overseers to pay, and a poor utilization of the excessive slaves most owned. The fieldhands were inadequately supervised and the house servants too many in number. Indeed, the only real advantage the planter had over the average white farmer was that the planter had much leisure time to devote to politics and government.

The old stereotype also failed to realize that most of the movement of non-slaveholding whites was voluntary and involved much profitable land speculation. Those not involved in raising staples ran a self-sufficient unit that needed less tending than farms in the North or Europe. Crops and livestock literally grew wild in the South. The only real work was the harvest or round-up.

So small farmers allowed nature to do the work and appeared lazy to outside observers. Most important, small farmers and non-slaveholders never felt competition from slavery because it kept the numerous blacks in a fixed position in the white-only Southern society. Indeed, most planters were but a small step above the middle class, holding less than 20 slaves as a rule. The plantation society was easy to buy into at this level. There were few really big plantations in most areas.

But it is possible that the Vanderbilt School drew too bright a picture of the Southern white middle class. Modern critics grant that there was a large middle class and that too many historians had ignored its contributions to Southern history. But size was not the problem. The problem was the proportion of wealth the white middle class held in the Old South.

In the 1850 Alabama Black Belt (named for the soil, not the presence of the large number of slaves), two-thirds of the land was held by 17 percent of the population. In the Mississippi Delta (a triangle of fertile river bottomland stretching from Vicksburg to Memphis and bordered by the Mississippi and the Yazoo) for the same time period, the census showed that 3 percent of all farmers held one-third of all land. The poorer 50 percent of farmers held only 12 percent of the land. The critics of the Vanderbilt critics also questioned the ability of the white middle class to advance into the slaveholding ranks.

In conclusion, the picture was closer to the stereotype drawn by the 19th-century visitors. There was a large middle class, but it was farming less fertile lands and being crowded out of the best land locations in the South. Examinations of individual counties all over the South failed to draw a definitive picture of how well the middle class lived. It all seemed to depend on which county, in which state, and in which time period the historian looked.

NORTHWEST ORDINANCE. With the completion of the **Western lands cession, Thomas Jefferson** wrote a measure that came to be called the Land Ordinance of 1784. It proposed that the West be divided into 10 districts that would be admitted into the Union as they were settled, as states on an equal basis with the original 13, whenever nine of the original states approved. After the year 1800, slavery would be prohibited in all of these Western territories. Jefferson went so far as to name the 10 territories with fanciful Greek and Roman names (what became Illinois was to be Vandalia, for example). But Congress passed Jefferson's proposed Land Ordinance of 1784 without a ban on slavery in the West. A year later, Rufus King of Massachusetts tried to get slavery banned in the West immediately, but Congress took no action.

Two years later, Congress acted without Jefferson, who had meanwhile gone to Paris as America's minister to France. Considered the greatest achievement of the national government under the **Articles of Confederation**, the Land Ordinance of 1787, more popularly known as the Northwest Ordinance, established a territorial government and steps for admission to statehood for the territory northwest of the Ohio River to the Canadian border. This was essentially Virginia's old, original, colonial grant minus Kentucky. (A later **Southwest Ordinance** would cover the rest of the West below Kentucky).

From three to five states were to be created (five were Ohio, Indiana, Illinois, Michigan, and Wisconsin). The territory was to be free of **slavery** initially, although after admission, the new state gained complete sovereignty and theoretically could establish slavery within its boundaries. Illinois tried to introduce slavery several times in the 1820s but failed. Many historians think that the reason all of the South Atlantic Southern states voted for the exclusion was that they knew it had little purchase north of the Ohio, as the failed Illinois attempts proved.

To achieve statehood and sovereignty, the territory had to go through a series of steps. At first all sovereignty rested with the federal government. Congress would appoint a governor, a secretary, and three judges to administer the territory on behalf of all the states. When the select area reached a population of 5,000 free white males, the territory would advance into a condition of shared federal and local sovereignty by electing a bicameral territorial legislature to help govern. When the select area reached a population of 60,000 free white males, it would ask Congress to pass an enabling act. This allowed the territory to call a constitutional convention, write a proposed state constitution, and ask Congress to admit it into the Union. If Congress agreed, the new state would enter the Union on an equal basis with all existing states.

This method, reconfirmed by Congress under the new **Constitution,** was used for all territories becoming states, except that slavery was not prohibited outright from the beginning, as with the Northwest Ordinance, because the Old South asserted that it had qualities of **extraterritoriality**. This was the biggest change from Jefferson's original Land Ordinance of 1784, which abolished slavery everywhere in the West. This meant that the big question before the Civil War became if and when the population of a territory could abolish slavery. If it was to be done by the territorial legislature in the second stage of territorial government, as the North preferred, when sovereignty was shared federally and locally, it was called **Squatter Sovereignty**. If it was to be done in the third stage by the Constitutional Convention, which had total sovereignty, as the South preferred, it was called **Popular Sovereignty**. The South maintained that only a sovereign state could abolish slavery. During the territorial stages, Congress had to administer the territories as a trustee of all Americans, and slavery had to be admitted. This was also called the **Non-Exclusion Doctrine**.

NOTT, JOSIAH. *See* SLAVERY AS A POSITIVE GOOD, THEORY OF.

NULLIFICATION CRISIS AND THE COMPROMISE OF 1833. The first time **John C. Calhoun**'s idea of the **Concurrent Voice and Nullification** came up before the whole nation was in the Webster–Hayne Debates in 1829 and 1830. Calhoun sat as presiding officer of the U.S. Senate and did not speak. A New England senator started things off by suggesting limiting the sales of Western land. Robert Y. Hayne immediately suspected the real reason was to limit federal income so that the **tariff**, the only other source, would have to be raised. Western senators blasted the notion of limiting the move west propelled by cheap land.

Daniel Webster rose and challenged Hayne to debate the nature of the Union. By changing the subject, Webster hoped to get Hayne to alienate Western senators at the concept of destroying the Union. Hayne could not refuse—Southerners do not step down in face of challenges of any kind. Hayne was not as clever as Webster and was verbally crushed in the debate, with Webster maintaining that the states gave up their absolute sovereignty permanently upon joining the Union, embodied in the phrase, "Liberty and Union, now and forever, one and inseparable."

In spite of all this, Calhoun still believed that he could win the presidency in 1832. He expected **Andrew Jackson, Martin Van Buren, Thomas Hart Benton**, and **Henry Clay** to split apart and Calhoun, with his limited nationalism, would step forward to pick up the pieces. If only he could hold back the radical secessionists in South Carolina.

But the Nullifiers were not going to allow Calhoun to delay them. Jackson prodded them on by sending a public letter that equated Nullification with treason. Most Nullifiers could not believe that Jackson would permit Georgia to nullify U.S. Supreme Court decisions in **Indian Removal** only to deny South Carolina the same right in the tariff question. Realizing that he could not stop the Nullifiers in any way, Calhoun came out openly for Nullification in his Ft. Hill Letter on 4 July 1831.

Then Jackson signed the Tariff of 1832 that reduced tariff rates and schedules on raw materials (the Abomination of 1828) and raised them on cotton and woolen products and iron manufactures. Although still fairly high, it was seen as so much better than the Tariff of 1828 that South Carolina's congressional representatives and senators all voted for it. It was hailed as the compromise that Calhoun had sought. But the Nullifiers saw this as their only chance to test the efficacy of Nullification. On 31 November 1832, they defiantly nullified the tariffs of 1828 and 1832. After 1 February 1833, no tariffs would be collected in the Port of Charleston.

Immediately Hayne resigned as senator and was elected governor. With his man in control of the state government, Calhoun resigned the vice presidency and was elected as the new U.S. Senator. He had stepped down from the dais to the senate floor to lead the fight against the tariffs.

Jackson moved to solve the Nullification Crisis by 1 February. He pulled the army out of the Citadel and Castle Pinckney in Charleston to outlying Ft. Moultrie where an incident was less likely to occur. He then issued his Nullification Proclamation of 10 December 1832. In it he said that once a state joined the Union, it was there to stay. The states had no right to nullify a law or to secede and leave the Union. To attempt either was treason, Jackson said. He asked South Carolina to repeal its nullification of the **tariff**s and yield to federal law. Then Jackson formed a civilian posse comitatus under **Joel R. Poinsett**, a

South Carolina Union man. Poinsett's posse would put down any armed attempt to enforce Nullification. It would be South Carolinian against South Carolinian—the U.S. Army would stand aside.

Next Congress gave Jackson a free hand when it passed the Force Act of 1833. It was actually misnamed—it was to avoid force. Jackson was authorized to use the navy to collect all tariffs at sea before a ship entered the harbor. Any goods seized would be stored in Ft. Moultrie. Special jails in the fort were set up to hold violators of the tariff laws. He also received a blank check to employ federal forces without having to declare insurrection or appeal to Congress again.

From the moment that the Nullification Act was passed in South Carolina, many worked to moderate the state's position. This is why Calhoun got Hayne elected governor. Hayne pledged that Jackson would have to fire the first shot, if it came to that. But he did call up the state militia. When the "Fatal First" came and passed with nothing happening, it began to look like cooler heads would prevail. Calhoun and Hayne had held off the hotheads who wanted secession.

In Congress, Henry Clay stepped forward and, with Calhoun's backing, took control of the compromise efforts to block Jackson from getting all the glory. He introduced a new tariff bill that would lower tariff rates gradually to 20 percent by 1842. Congress passed it and Jackson signed the Force Act and the Tariff of 1833 on the same day. Calhoun raced to South Carolina to get the state to take the Compromise of 1833, as the new tariff was called. The state convention accepted the Compromise of 1833, repealed its nullification of the tariffs of 1828 and 1832, and, as a final act of defiance, nullified the Force Act and adjourned.

The crisis was over. The failure of Nullification in 1833 caused Calhoun to suggest other methods whereby the United States could be kept whole by using the Concurrent Voice. These ideas were developed in the 1840s and published three years after Calhoun's 1850 death in two treatises, his *Disquisition on Government,* and his *Discourses on the Constitution and Government of the United States.* Calhoun suggested, as one approach, a dual presidency, one Northern and one Southern, both necessary to sign all laws. Another method would be to amend the Constitution so that all laws would need a two-thirds vote to pass Congress. Or, alternately, the United States could spilt the control of Congress, with the North controlling one house and the South the other. Of course, the problem with any of this is that a minority exploits the majority.

None of Calhoun's suggestions for maintaining a Concurrent Voice were seriously considered. From there on out, the South assumed Jackson's more traditional position, that the South's position within the Union could be maintained by the state sovereignty positions of **extraterritoriality of slavery** and the **Three-Fifths Compromise**. This would hold, with an underlying threat of disunion, until 1861. Then, in a flurry, the secessionists would skip all of the Nullification process and go straight to states rights and **secession**.

– O –

"OLD BULLION." See BENTON, THOMAS HART.

OLD REPUBLICANS. See DEMOCRATIC REPUBLICANS.

OLMSTEAD, FREDERICK LAW (1822–1903). A landscape architect based in New York City, where he built Central Park, Frederick Law Olmstead was noted for his books about his trips through the slave South before the Civil War. Olmstead's trips originated when the *New York Times* commissioned him to travel through the slave states and write of the **peculiar institution** and conditions in the South. His letters to the editor were collected and published as *A Journey in the Seaboard Slave States* (1856).

Olmstead continued his travels in the South and Southwest, publishing two other volumes, *A Journey through Texas* (1857) and a *Journey through the Back Country* (1860). The books proved quite popular and were collected and edited in London in 1861 and issued as *The Cotton Kingdom*. His observations are considered to be without parallel and very accurate, although some modern historians point out that he was patently against slavery, a friend to abolitionists, and often turned away from some of the more important plantations in his travels. His viewpoints were widely quoted by British politicians anxious to keep Britain from intervening on the Confederate side in the American Civil War.

OMNIBUS BILL. *See* COMPROMISE OF 1850.

ONE HUNDRED DOLLAR FARM. *See* JACKSON AND THE PUBLIC LANDS; LONE STAR REBELLIONS.

O'NEAL, PEGGY. *See* JACKSON'S BREAK WITH CALHOUN.

ONÍS, LUÍS DE. *See* ADAMS–ONÍS TREATY.

ORDER OF THE STAR SPANGLED BANNER. *See* AMERICAN PARTY.

OREGON TREATY (1846). *See* CANADIAN BOUNDARY DISPUTE.

ORR, JAMES L. (1822–1873). Although he was born in South Carolina, James L. Orr was educated at the University of Virginia. He returned to his home state and became a lawyer and newspaper editor. Entering politics as a **Democrat**, Orr served two terms in the state legislature before going to Congress. There he served throughout the 1850s, becoming speaker of the house, until the Democrats lost their thin majority when **Henry Winter Davis** of Maryland switched sides from the **American Party** to **Republican**.

A **Stephen A. Douglas** Democrat until South Carolina seceded from the Union, Orr quickly switched viewpoints to block **fire-eaters** like **Robert Barnwell Rhett** from dominating the state. He was among the negotiators who tried to get the North to surrender the forts in Charleston harbor to prevent a war. Once the shooting started, Orr was one of the first to raise a regiment, Orr's First South Carolina Rifles, to defend the Confederacy. He led the regiment until 1862, when he was elected to the Confederate Senate. There, he was an opponent of the policies of President **Jefferson Davis**.

After the war, Orr supported President Andrew Johnson and was elected governor of South Carolina until replaced by the army during Military Reconstruction. He changed to the Republicans in 1868, opposed the Ku Klux Klan, and was appointed minister to Russia under the Ulysses S. Grant administration. While on duty in St. Petersburg, Orr died of pneumonia in 1873.

OSCEOLA. *See* INDIAN REMOVAL COMPLETED.

OSTEND MANIFESTO (1854). *See* FILIBUSTERING; SPREAD EAGLE FOREIGN POLICY.

O'SULLIVAN JOHN. *See* MANIFEST DESTINY.

OVERSEERS. On larger plantations, the planter's direct representative in day-to-day management of the crops, care of the land, livestock, farm implements, and slaves was the white overseer. It was his goal to work the labor force to produce a profitable crop. He was an indispensable cog in the plantation machinery.

The overseer has usually been portrayed as an uncouth, uneducated character of low class whose main purpose was to harass the slaves and get in the way of the planter's progressive goals of production. More than that, the overseer had a position between master and slave in which it was hard to win. Directing slave labor was looked down upon by a large number of people, North and South. He was faced with planter demands that were at times unreasonable. He was forbidden to fraternize with the slaves. He received inadequate pay in relation to his responsibilities. He had no chance for advancement unless he left the profession. He was bombarded with incessant complaints from masters, who did not appreciate the task he faced, and slaves, who sought to play off master and overseer against each other to avoid work and gain privileges.

The very nature of the job was difficult, The overseer had to care for the slaves and gain the largest crop possible. These were very often contradictory goals. There were three factors in determining an overseer's success: the size of the plantation—the larger the better; the state and county in which it was located—critical as to soil fertility; and the actual residence of the owner—on the land or absentee, the latter guaranteeing the most freedom of operation.

Because of the difficulty of the operations, overseers from the **rice** and **sugar** areas were the most skilled. The worst were in the **upland cotton** regions. But it was the planter himself, and the degree to which he meddled in the overseer's job of **plantation management,** that caused the most problems. The adding of new rules, expectations, and constant changes could sabotage any operation. The same applied if the owner was an absentee who had several plantations supervised by a **steward**, who then regulated several overseers. *See also* SOCIAL HIERARCHY.

– P –

PANIC OF 1819. One of the more important events that helped destroy the **New Nationalism** after the **War of 1812** was the first major economic depression America had faced in the industrial era. It struck the nation in four ways.

First there was a collapse of the market for industrial goods. The War of 1812 was part of the Napoleonic wars in Europe that ended at the same time. British warehouses were loaded with tons of goods stored until shipping could move them freely to other markets. These industrial goods were often better made and lower priced than their American counterparts. They flooded the American market and the **Tariff of 1816** was too low to stop them. Very often the British would sell an expensive version of a product to an American wholesaler and then sell a cheaper version themselves without the middleman. The result was a double profit.

Things were not better in agriculture. Although European nations experienced several crop failures that boded well for American farmers, the Americans made an erroneous assumption that good markets would last forever. They began to overproduce and exceed the demand. The Americans also began to speculate in Western lands, most bought on credit. Then the markets collapsed. One of the worst price reductions was a 26-cent drop per pound in **cotton** at New Orleans in one day.

Finally there was a shortage of specie worldwide. The source of the world's gold was Mexico and Peru, and both nations were in the throes of revolution from Spain. There was a great demand for specie in France as it tried to pay the indemnity exacted on it at the Congress of Vienna for the Napoleonic wars.

By 1819, there was a shift away from American goods and crops. Added to the land speculation, farmers went broke by the hundreds. This was worsened when the **Second Bank of the United States** insisted that all debts be paid in specie rather than discounted paper.

There was simply not enough specie to meet the demand, resulting in numerous bankruptcies. Many people in the South and West would remember the Panic of 1819, especially one broke planter named **Andrew Jackson**. That memory would prove fatal to the aspirations of the bank in the **election of 1832**.

PANIC OF 1837. The worst single economic depression before the Civil War, the Panic of 1837 destroyed the **Martin Van Buren** administration before it could get running. The cause was the independent treasury system that replaced the **Second Bank of the United States**, which allowed local banking institutions to overextend their production of notes. With such easy credit, the American economy was soon overheated and inflation ran wild. Excessive speculation on land, livestock, industrial plants, and slaves was commonplace. With **Andrew Jackson**'s issuance of the Specie Circular before he left office, specie was drawn from the West to the East. No one could cash in their paper because there was no gold or silver available.

All of this was blamed on the **Democrats**. The Democrats cried foul and blamed it all on the **Whig** financiers. The Democrats said the shortage of specie was intentional to force the Democrats to recharter the Bank of the United States. The voters were not convinced of the Democrats' innocence. The wily Van Buren had been ensnared in his own duplicitous actions at last. There was nothing that could be done. Under the economic theories of the day, the nation would just have to ride it out.

But Van Buren made it worse by refusing to repeal the Specie Circular and allow discounted paper notes to be used to pay debts. Banks began to suspend all specie payments, even on their own notes. Van Buren and the Democrats passed a measure that declared any bank bankrupt that refused to honor its own notes. He also refused to transfer government specie to the independent treasury banks for deposit.

Finally, Van Buren accepted a **John C. Calhoun** plan to ease up on the Specie Circular immediately (1837) and gradually restore it by 1843. This allowed Calhoun to rejoin the Democratic Party through the "Carolina Gap," as his plan was called. In effect, the result of this plan was to withdraw the government from any banking regulation until the National Banking Act during the Civil War.

PANIC OF 1857. The indecisive Crimean War on Russia's Black Sea had upset the world's economy in 1857 by excluding Russia's wheat from the world markets for several years. The shortfall had been made up by increased American production, but in 1857, this was no longer needed, causing a market glut and a corresponding fall in prices. At the same time, British banking interests decided to cash in their American bonds, draining gold from American banks, most located in the North. The whole crisis came to a head when the expected gold shipment from California was lost aboard the SS *Central America* off Cape Hatteras. The loss of that cargo, involving millions in gold minted in California since 1849, which totaled 20 percent of the gold reserves then held on Wall Street, proved catastrophic. Many institutions could not meet the call for cash and folded, sending the New York Stock Market into a tailspin and collapse. But while the North suffered, cotton was booming. This led the Old South to see its slave **economy** and staple crop system as stronger than that of the industrial North. The solid Southern economy was of great help to the seceders in 1861 who pointed to 1857 and how the South was actually stronger economically than the North and no longer needed it as an albatross pulling the South down.

PARTUS SEQUITUR VENTRUM. See BLACK CODE.

"PATHFINDER." *See* FRÉMONT, JOHN CHARLES.

PATROL. Instrumental to controlling the chance of running away was the **patrol**, an outfit that enrolled all male whites in the effort to check out slave cabins for stolen goods and the roads for runaways. The paderollers, as the slaves called them, could enter anyone's property, search any building, and terrorize slaves at will. Planters did not like such violations of their rights and often refused to cooperate with patrols, enough to compromise their effectiveness at all times except when there was a fear of inordinate slave **resistance and rebellion**. *See also* RUNAWAY SLAVES.

PAYNE'S LANDING, TREATY OF (1832). *See* INDIAN REMOVAL.

PEARL INCIDENT. No single event more demonstrated the connection between the federal government and **slavery in Washington, D.C.** than the voyage of the schooner *Pearl*. Arriving in the national capital with a load of wood, the *Pearl* left on the following Saturday night with 76 slaves, all hoping to achieve freedom on the *Pearl's* trip out of the slave states. **Runaway slaves** frequently left the capital. Pennsylvania was only 70 to 80 miles away, and, for a slave serving a congressman and his family from the Deep South, freedom would never be closer.

Saturday was picked because it was a traditional night of relaxation in a slave's routine, a time to go enjoy the various diversions that Washington provided to all visitors and residents, regardless of race. Most slaveowners would not be aware that their chattels had disappeared until Monday morning.

It was a good plan, but its plotters, Daniel Drayton and ship's captain Edward Sayres had not reckoned that the wind would unexpectedly change its direction at the mouth of the Potomac and cause the ship to anchor in the bay to await a new weather front. By Monday morning the tale was out. A free black drayman, who had not been paid for hauling some of the slaves from Georgetown to the wharf, revealed the slave-stealing, abolition plot.

The Washingtonians promptly swore in an armed posse of 30 and, boarding a steamboat, soon overhauled the schooner still at rest. The slaves and the two white instigators were placed under arrest. Back in Washington, the whites were placed in the city jail and the slaves returned to their owners. The whites were allowed bail at the rate of $100 per slave taken. The re-enslaved blacks were, amid the wails of family and friends, shipped to New Orleans to be disposed of on the cotton and sugar plantations of the Southwest.

Drayton and Sayres stood trial four months later and received fines that totaled over $20,000 per defendant. Unable to pay, they rotted in the city jail for four years until President Millard Fillmore pardoned them in 1852. Their treatment revealed just how Southern the national capital was and the completeness of federal involvement in slavery, as Congress administered it under the **Constitution** as a federal territory. It also did much to heighten the angry debate between North and South over the terms of the **Compromise of 1850**.

PECULIAR INSTITUTION. Another more diplomatic name for American Negro **slavery** that denoted its uniqueness as a social-labor system was the title "Peculiar Institution."

PERRY, MATTHEW C. *See* SPREAD EAGLE FOREIGN POLICY.

PERSONAL LIBERTY LAWS. *See ABLEMAN v. BOOTH* (1859).

PET BANKS. *See* BANK WAR.

PHILADELPHIA RIOTS. *See* AMERICAN PARTY.

PICKENS, FRANCIS. *See* SECESSION OF THE SOUTHERN STATES, FIRST.

PIEDMONT. The land that lay between the first waterfall (the **fall line**) on navigable rivers to the foothills of the Appalachian Mountains is known as the Piedmont. It was a fertile region that became the first home to **upland cotton.**

PIERCE, FRANKLIN (1804–1869). Franklin Pierce, the "Young Hickory from the Granite Hills," became the youngest antebellum president at 49. Born in Hillsboro, New Hampshire, of a political family, he attended the prestigious institutions of Hancock, Francestown, and Phillips Exeter. He graduated third in Bowdoin College's class of 1820 with fellow schoolmates Henry Wadsworth Longfellow and Nathaniel Hawthorne. He studied law in Portsmouth under prominent Jacksonian **Democrat** Levi Woodbury. Pierce served in the New Hampshire state legislature at 24 and two years later became its speaker. During the 1830s he went to Washington, first as a representative, then as a senator. He had boyish good looks and a pleasant personality. Although a loyal Democrat, he was non-committal on political issues. His rare speeches were characteristically lacking in substance.

He enlisted as a private during the **War with Mexico** and used his political connections to rise in rank to colonel and later brigadier general. At that time, President **James K. Polk** sought loyal Democratic officers to offset the many **Whig** hero-generals. After bringing in reinforcements from Vera Cruz to Puebla and fighting off six guerrilla attacks along the way, Pierce reaped little reward. One shortfall was his penchant for pre-battle injuries and not commanding attack units. He later defeated his opponent, Whig Party candidate Bvt. Lt. Gen. **Winfield Scott**, his former commander, believing this vindicated him and his war record in the public's eye.

Two months before he took office, he and his wife saw their 11-year-old son Bennie killed when their train derailed and rolled off an embankment. Mrs. Pierce spent the rest of her life in deep mourning, believing that God had taken the boy to leave Pierce's presidency unencumbered by family problems. As first lady, her unhappiness and resentment divested him of his prior optimism and the self-assurance he needed to effectively carry out his duties.

Pierce made the stock promises in his inaugural address: a more economical government, to uphold the Constitution and support the **Compromise of 1850** as the solution to the **slavery** conflict in the territories. He also denounced **anti-slavery** agitators. To demonstrate the accord he sought in his administration, he appointed a Catholic as postmaster general, his cabinet being a cross-section of influential Democrats representing various party factions.

Despite his best efforts, Pierce's administration proved far from harmonious. An expansionist wing of the party, **Young America**, tainted his foreign policy by using **filibusters** to advance American interests in the Caribbean. To Northerners, this was merely a substitution for slavery expansion into the American West. Domestically, he backed **Popular Sovereignty** in the Western territories through the **Kansas–Nebraska Act**, which repealed the **Missouri Compromise**. The Kansas–Nebraska Act led to an armed conflict in Kansas and the organization of **anti-slavery** forces nationwide into the new **Republican Party**. His appointment of incompetent Northern hacks to govern Kansas alienated Southerners. By 1856, Pierce's waning popularity hindered any chance of renomination, as the party turned to the less controversial **James Buchanan**. Pierce completed his single term, discredited as a "**dough face**," a Northern man with Southern principles. He retired to New Hampshire, where he died in 1869.

PINCKNEY, CHARLES COTESWORTH. *See* ELECTION OF 1804; ELECTION OF 1808.

PINCKNEY, THOMAS. *See* PINCKNEY'S TREATY.

PINCKNEY'S TREATY. At the same time John Jay went to Britain to negotiate what became **Jay's Treaty**, Thomas Pinckney was sent to Spain to negotiate the boundary between the American South and Spanish Florida. Pinckney was to use the same bluff that Jay was to use against Britain: If Spain did not sign what the United States wanted, American would renew the Franco-American Alliance of 1778. Since Secretary of the Treasury **Alexander Hamilton** had no interest in Spanish–United States relations, he did not tip Spain off as to America's bluff.

Without Hamilton's interference, everything went like clockwork. A treaty with Spain was needed since the **Jay–Guardoqui Treaty** had been rejected some years earlier. Spain had wanted the northern border of Florida to go up the Chattahoochie River, over to the Tennessee River, up to the Ohio, over to the Mississippi, then down to the Gulf of Mexico. It would have cost the United States most of the Old Southwest gained in the Treaty of Paris (1783).

Under the fear that the United States might back France in its European war, Spain gave the United States all it wanted. The northern boundary of Florida was set at the 31st parallel. Spain agreed to stop supplying hostile Native Americans in their war against American settlers. Americans in the West received the right to use the length of the Mississippi River and the Port of New Orleans.

When the treaty reached the U.S. Senate, the Federalists threatened to turn it down unless the House of Representatives would appropriate the monies needed to enforce Jay's Treaty. The South gave in, but Hamilton's **Federalists** lost much of what little support they had in the area as voters went over to Jefferson's **Democratic Republicans** *en masse*.

PINKERTON, ALAN. *See* BALTIMORE PLOT (1861).

PLAIN FOLK. *See* NON-SLAVEHOLDERS.

PLANTATION MANAGEMENT. Slavery was first and foremost a labor system in which the planter valued the slaves for the work they could do. On smaller farms of fewer than a half dozen slaves, management was no real problem. The farmer worked in the fields right along with his slaves and supervised everything directly. Most slaves, however, never saw their masters in the fields. On those farms with more than six chattels, the farmer became a manager and left day-to-day supervision to others. On a plantation of 30 or more slaves, management and supervision became a real problem.

It was generally held that maximum efficiency was obtained on plantations with somewhere between 30 and 100 slaves. Over half of all African Americans lived on such plantations, and there were 25,000 such plantation units in the slave South. If a planter owned more than 100 slaves, he usually placed them on separate plantations (sometimes in different states), each with its own **overseer**, and operated as an absentee landlord. Most of the planters of such units delegated actual field supervision to a white **overseer** and numerous black **drivers**. The slaveowner limited his supervision to casual inspection of the fields, the market prices for the **staple crops** he grew, general administration, and issuing instructions to his overseer. Perhaps the most famous of these instructions to the overseer was **James Hammond**'s book of "Plantation Management."

In general, slaves were worked in one of two forms of field management, the gang system or the task system. Under the gang system, the fieldhands were divided into groups handling one assignment, supervised by the overseer, or drivers who were also slaves. Gang work caused the weaker hands to suffer at the pace set by the stronger. But it had one advantage. Nearly every hand touched a piece of the work, so no one of them could be blamed for a mistake. This was particularly common on **upland cotton** plantations.

The task system was different. Here each hand was assigned a task or a total job for the day, after the completion of which he or she could go home. Often the slave was tempted to hurry up the work to go home early. But responsibility for mistakes or sloppy work was easy to establish and punishment exacting. This was especially preferred on **rice** plantations, where the fields were divided into manageable lots for work.

Southern whites were universal in condemning the slaves as lazy. Modern historians feel that the plantation owner got a full day's work out of each slave, by one means or another. The custom was to work from "day clean to first dark," or from "kin to cain't." A horn was blown an hour before daylight to roust the slaves. A second blast told them to form up into gangs and be assigned the day's work. After all morning in the fields, the gang usually rested and ate lunch from 1 p.m. to 3 p.m., during the heat of the day. Then they worked until dark, arriving back in their quarters for a 9 p.m. curfew.

PLANTATION MASTER. Nowhere was the integration of black and white society more thoroughly personified than in the plantation owner. In every word, gesture, emotion, idea, and attitude, in every conception and misconception of what **slavery** was all about, the white master embodied his boyhood upbringing by black women, playing with black children, and relishing black folktales and folklore. His boyhood mentors were black men and the most stalwart of these were his flesh and blood boyhood heroes, often surpassing the white heroes he knew only from books.

As a plantation owner, the planter was master of all he surveyed. His attitudes towards his chattels could make slavery pure hell or merely a compulsory work experience. But regardless of how he treated and respected his slaves as individuals, the master's first objective was to make them submissive to his every command and deferential to the presence of himself, his family, and all other whites. Many planters enrolled the more diligent bondsmen and women in their corps of command. These were **slave drivers** and house servants, like the black mammy who dominated the domestic staff.

The key to black-white relations was the manner in which the master preserved order. The master was every slave's policeman. He had to control his anger and rely upon the exact right measure of force to keep everyone on the plantation, black or white, in line. Many were cruel beyond belief. Others were considered just and benevolent. But masters were people, too, and a bad day could lead a planter to take out his anger on the slave force.

The planter determined what medical care the slaves received, how much they ate and what they were fed, what clothes they wore, what kind of shacks they lived in, and how many lived in each building. The master also punished the slaves for lying, fighting, theft, breaking tools, and all sorts of offenses that might better be seen as forms of familial survival strategies or resistance to and rebellion against the peculiar institution.

While some planters merely whipped those deemed at fault, the cleverer masters restricted some privilege, like passes to town, or assigned some degrading form of work, or demoted a slave leader to the ranks, as it were. Public disapproval of violent punishment became more potent as the **anti-slavery** movement gained momentum in the North. The master and his help rarely saw eye to eye on labor demands, but the clever slave managers usually turned a blind eye to work slowdowns that allowed the weaker to keep up with the more physically fit. **Religion** and duty and law compelled masters to care for the aged, although many planters sold off older slaves before age became an obvious problem.

In the end, planters managed to sell slavery to the non-slaveholding Old South as a system of opportunity that offered them possible wealth and social advancement as future planters in their own right and kept blacks in a well-defined place in a white society worth fighting for. When this was challenged by the North, the result was **secession** and a Civil War that cost the Old South the whole system. *See also* SOCIAL HIERARCHY.

PLANTATION MISTRESS. She carried the keys, literally and figuratively, to every building and locked closet and room on the plantation. The plantation mistress was the one who kept the whole operation functioning smoothly because she saw to it that the slaves were fed and cared for, tended to medically if ill (June through September were the "sick" months), and that the food and supplies were kept secure and available to all members of the plantation family and work force.

The plantation mistress' domain was the so-called Big House—although it was often not as grand as modern Americans envision it as portrayed in the movies and novels about the Old South. But there was more than the planter's residence involved in the Big House. It included the stables, barns, workshops, warehouses and storerooms, and the slave quarters. Housekeeping included gardening, dairy activities, salting meat (usually pork), preserving fruits and vegetables, mixing home remedies, making candles, wax, soap, rag rugs, pillows, linens, bedding, and clothes. And of course their were children to birth, raise, and educate, both slave and free. The small fry were kept together until the young blacks could help out in some job, somewhere. Then the reality of slave and free reared its head.

On bigger plantations this work might be divided up, but on smaller farms, the plantation mistress had to do much of it herself with little help. For really big jobs, often kinfolk would come in from miles around and help out each plantation on a circular basis. On top of the physical labor, the plantation mistress also kept track of money matters, expenses, and purchases. At least the smart women did this. Those who failed to take a close interest found that upon their husband's death, that assumption of total control could be a daunting task. Since marriages were often arranged among older planters and younger women (childbirth taking its inevitable toll), the plantation mistress being left alone to run the plantation, no matter its size, was a real possibility. But rarely did men **duel** over women—duels were for really important matters like gambling, debts, or a personal slight.

All in all, the job of plantation mistress was a lonely thing. **Women of the Old South were not allowed to travel without a proper escort or chaperone.** Plantations and farms were very isolated, towns few and far between. If the plantation was built on the frontier, isolation was even greater. The result was the famed Southern hospitality and an occasional grand ball or barbeque that would do *Gone with the Wind* proud. But, in general, at best life on the plantation proved to be tedious even for the privileged class of white owners and especially for their wives. *See also* SOCAL HIERARCHY; SOCIALIZATION.

PLANTATION STEWARDS. A plantation steward was a white man who supervised several plantations in an area, the owner of which was an absentee. This meant that the steward occupied a socially advantageous position between the planter and the **overseer** of a single plantation's operations. As the planter's direct representative, the steward often interfered too much in the day-to-day **plantation management**, which led to much quarreling with the overseers under his supervision.

The steward was really a financial administrator, a man of much management talent, highly educated, and of the same social class as the planter. As such, he could pass on any malfunctions he was responsible for to the backs of the overseers under him. Stewards tended to last on the job much longer than overseers did and found their relations with the planter to be quite cooperative. *See also* SOCIAL HIERARCHY.

PLANTER. *See* **PLANTATION MASTER.**

POINSETT, JOEL R. (1779–1851). Charleston-born Joel Poinsett studied medicine and military science in Britain. After he studied law back in the United States, Poinsett became a special agent of the State Department and traveled for 10 years in Europe and Asia, before becoming American Minister to Río de la Plata and Chile, studying Latin American revolutions against Spain. He returned to America and served in the South Carolina legislature and in Congress until he was appointed the first American Minister to Mexico in 1825.

The Mexicans did not like or trust Poinsett. He was regarded as an intriguer with imperialist designs on Mexico's province of Texas. Sent home in 1830, bringing with him the flower named after him (poinsettia), Poinsett served as **Andrew Jackson**'s representative in South Carolina during the **Nullification Crisis and the Compromise of 1833**. For his loyalty as leader of the posse comitatus that was to back up the federal collection of the **Tariff of 1832**, Poinsett was made secretary of war in the **Martin Van Buren** administration. He reorganized the army, saw **Indian Removal completed**, and fought the Second Seminole War. He retired to sponsor several museums until his death.

POLK, JAMES K. (1795–1849). If **Andrew Jackson** was "Old Hickory," James K. Polk was "Young Hickory," Jackson's protégé in Tennessee politics. Born in North Carolina, Polk was well educated, holding a degree from Chapel Hill College. He read law and was admitted to the bar, running his practice out of Columbia, Tennessee. He was a **Democrat** state legislator, congressman (during which time he was Andrew Jackson's hatchet man and driver of all legislation), and state governor.

But after years of success, Polk lost out to Tennessee **Whigs** in the early 1840s. He lost two elections for governor and seemed to be doomed to inactivity. Then came the Democrat convention preceding the **election of 1844**. Both **Henry Clay** of the Whigs and **Martin Van Buren** of the Democrats had agreed to leave the **annexation of Texas** out of the election. But when Van Buren had fallen prey to the two-thirds rule for being nominated, Polk emerged on the ninth ballot as the first "Dark Horse" nominee in American history. Polk ran on an expansionist platform calling for the "Re-annexation of Texas and the Re-occupation of Oregon."

Polk swept the country at a time when American westward movement was deemed the nation's **Manifest Destiny**. Texas having been brought into the Union by outgoing President **John Tyler**, Polk skillfully negotiated a compromise with Britain over the Oregon question. But angered by the annexation of Texas, the Mexican government and Polk began sparing over Texas boundaries and the annexation.

The inevitable first shot being fired, Polk aggressively pursued the **War with Mexico**. He changed his commanding generals on a regular basis, not because of lack of victory but because of their successes. As Polk feared, they all turned out to be Whig politicians and potential presidential candidates.

Polk refused to back the "all of Mexico" demands of certain congressmen after the war and took only certain sections of Mexico. But as he feared, **Zachary Taylor** became the Whig candidate and swept the **election of 1848**. Polk went home to Tennessee by way of the Atlantic and Gulf, taking a steamboat up the Mississippi and Ohio and coming down the Tennessee. He was exhausted by his personal involvement in every aspect of the war, in which he set a precedent for every wartime president that followed. He died in 1849, at just over 55 years of age.

PONOTOC, TREATY OF. *See* INDIAN REMOVAL COMPLETED.

POPULAR SOVEREIGNTY. This was the political concept that incorporated the **Non-Exclusion Doctrine** favoring the South in allowing **slavery** in the Western territories until achieving statehood. While drawing up the new state constitution, the convention could then approve or abolish it by a simple vote. U.S. Senator **Stephen A. Douglas**, a Popular Sovereignty advocate, made it law in the **Kansas–Nebraska Act** of 1854, which led to the **Kansas–Nebraska Border Wars**, a harbinger of the Civil War. The U.S. **Supreme Court** in the case *Dred Scott v. Sandford* gave it constitutional viability in 1857. But **Abraham Lincoln** showed the impracticality of Popular Sovereignty during the **Lincoln–Douglas Debates** in 1858 when he asked his so-called **Freeport Question**. In reply, Douglas was forced to admit that slavery would fail everywhere without a positive law enforcing it. Douglas's duplicity on the issue split the **Democratic** Party into Northern and Southern wings. This secured Lincoln's nomination for president on the rival **Republican** ticket and his presidential victory in the **election of 1860**.

PORTER, PETER B. *See* WAR HAWKS.

PREEMPTION ACT OF 1830. *See* JACKSON AND THE PUBLIC LANDS.

PRIGG v. PENNSYLVANIA **(1842).** In most of the cases under his supervision, Chief Justice **Roger B. Taney** of the U.S. **Supreme Court** took the position of granting the states maximum freedom from the centralized control of the federal government. The exception was state interference with the **extraterritorial** rights of slavery.

The fugitive clause of the Constitution guaranteed any slaveholder or his agents the right to pursue **runaway** slaves into any other state or territory and forcibly return them to their master. In response to **slave catchers** kidnapping free Negroes and selling them into slavery, Congress passed a **Fugitive Slave Act in 1793** to enforce this constitutional provision. All the claimant had to do was to get any of a wide number of magistrates, state or federal, to rule that the slave was a **runaway**. The law was so vague as to permit slave catchers to in effect legally kidnap at will blacks living in the North. Several Northern states found this practice reprehensible and passed state personal liberty laws banning the forcible removal of fugitive slaves from within their borders.

In the Prigg case, an escaped female slave had been living in Pennsylvania for five years before she was brought before a state judge. But unexpectedly the judge refused to declare her a runaway to be returned to her master. So the slave catchers merely kidnapped her. Pennsylvania then arrested and tried the kidnappers and found them guilty. The slave catcher, Edward Prigg, appealed his case as a violation of the fugitive law of 1893.

Justice Joseph Storey of Massachusetts wrote the decision on which Taney concurred. Storey said that personal liberty laws were unconstitutional because the fugitive clause made this problem a federal concern to the exclusion of the state. No state was obliged to enforce the fugitive law in any way. As a result, Northern states rewrote their laws to prohibit state officials from aiding federal slave catchers in any manner. The Prigg decision would be expanded and clarified after the new, tougher **Fugitive Slave Law of 1850** in the court case *Ableman v. Booth*.

PROPHET, THE. *See* WAR OF 1812.

PRO-SLAVE THEORISTS IN THE OLD SOUTH. Pro-slave thought, although it has never approached historians' interest in abolition, is very instrumental in understanding the issues that instigated the Civil War. Historians have successfully perpetuated the myth that the South, like the North, had nearly abolished **slavery** by the end of the American Revolution. They maintain that the invention of the **cotton gin** in 1793, which literally created an industry, was responsible for slavery nationwide, not just in the North where the cold climate rendered a cotton-based economy unprofitable or difficult.

Many saw Virginia, the largest slave state at the time, as the reason the institution thrived. Wealthy planters such as **Thomas Jefferson**, whose words in the Declaration of Independence professed the equality of all men, which implied his objection to slavery, had somewhat contradictory beliefs about the institution. Virginians doubted that Africans were able to function in society as free persons as they would inevitably interbreed with whites, diminishing the level of intelligence and industry necessary to preserve democracy.

Few Virginians outside the aristocratic classes expressed any guilt over keeping slaves. Nonetheless, St. George Tucker, a Virginian, proposed a plan of gradual abolition based on freeing all black women at age 28 because slavery passed through the mother, partly because of white male-initiated **miscegenation**. But the fear of the black and white races being contaminated by their own human inability to stay clear of each other sexually was the basis of most freedom plans including some form of **colonization** of blacks overseas, somewhere. *See also* SLAVERY AS A POSITIVE GOOD, THE THEORY OF.

– Q –

QUASI-WAR. Federalist John Adams faced a rough time as president in 1797. His vice president, who also presided over the Senate, was **Thomas Jefferson**, leader of the opposition **Democratic Republicans**. The rest of the party in the Senate and the House of Representatives was more loyal to **Alexander Hamilton** than to Adams. As if this were not enough, foreign relations between the United States, France, and Britain were falling apart as a result of the Wars of the French Revolution.

Naturally, as a Federalist, Adams believed that the problem overseas was caused by France. He had **Jay's Treaty** with Britain, but none with France. But the French were still laboring under the notion that the Franco-American Alliance of 1778 should apply. Adams sought to straighten out the French situation, once and for all. He sent to France a commission comprised of **John Marshall**, Charles Cotesworth Pinckney, and Elbridge Gerry to negotiate with three French diplomats, named X, Y, and Z.

The reason for their anonymity became obvious when the French demanded that the United States pay France $64 million damages and a quarter of a million to the three diplomats as an outright bribe, and that the Americans pledge to reactivate the Franco-American Alliance of 1778. This X, Y, Z Affair outraged Marshall and Pinckney and they came home in a huff. But not before Pinckney said defiantly, "No, no, not a sixpence!" A more publicity-wise congressional investigation later altered this bit of whimpery into one of the greatest statements of American principle on file, "Millions for defense, not one cent for tribute."

But Elbridge Gerry stayed on in France to see if the price could be made more reasonable. Fellow Federalists called him a traitor, and when Adams tried to send over an unofficial delegation to help Gerry, Congress passed the Logan Act. This prevented a private citizen from treating with the enemy in the name of the United States without prior formal government authorization. When Adams threatened to resign as president in favor of Jefferson, Congress relented and approved of a new treaty attempt.

The result was an undeclared conflict (the United States specializes in such things) called the Quasi-War. American privateers and the French navy shot up each other's merchant fleets. Adams responded by creating the Department of the Navy and Congress by passing the **Alien and Sedition Acts**. But the war suddenly ended when Napoleon I came to power. He was more interested in land warfare in Europe and signed the Treaty of Morte Fontaine (1800). The French recognized the American principle of free (neutral) ships means free goods, and both sides declared the Franco-American Alliance of 1778 to be ended for good.

When Gerry came home, he joined the Democratic Republicans and ultimately became vice president under James Madison in 1813. Meanwhile he developed the grand old American tradition of gerrymandering—unfairly dividing up a state's congressional districts in such a manner that one's own party wins.

QUIDS, TERTIUM. *See* DEMOCRATIC REPUBLICANS; RANDOLPH, JOHN, OF ROANOKE.

– R –

RANDOLPH, JOHN, OF ROANOKE (1773–1833). In the Early National Era, no one epitomized firm adherence to the cause of a weak central government based on a literal reading of the Constitution better than John Randolph of Roanoke. Randolph was falsely ennobled by the addition of the place of his birth to his surname to differ him from the many John Randolphs Virginia produced in those times.

Randolph was a Jeffersonian who guided the **Louisiana Purchase** appropriation (his one break with strict construction) and much of **Thomas Jefferson**'s first-term legislation through the House of Representatives. But soon Randolph was dismayed to find that Jefferson and his advisors were becoming more and more like the hated **Alexander Hamilton** in their reliance on the "general welfare" clause of the Constitution to justify actions that were plainly not intended by the framers' hallowed written document.

When Jefferson asked Congress to bail out the investors in the **Yazoo Land Frauds**, Randolph and others of his persuasion broke with the administration. They formed an independent political group, the "Tertium Quids," to preserve the written Constitution from questionable interpretation. The group took its name from the Latin for a substance that shares the qualities of two other objects (in this case, **Federalists** and **Democratic Republicans**) yet is apart from them. His opposition to the **War of 1812** cost him his seat in the House, although he was returned in 1815 and later served briefly in the Senate.

As a national figure, Randolph had a speaking style that made him unique. Tall and thin (so much so that one wag characterized him as "the advance agent for a famine"), he suffered from a hormonal deficiency that caused him to speak in a distinctive soprano and be unable to have or desire sexual relations with women. His face was boyish at a distance, but closer inspection revealed that it was covered with fine wrinkles that gave him the appearance of an unwrapped mummy. His often cynical comments were very quotable, such as calling Northerners, who supported the South before the Civil War, "**dough faces**."

Throughout his public service, Randolph held to the notions of Old Republicanism, those things that Jefferson believed when he originally challenged Hamilton's theory of expanding government—that political power tended to grow at the expense of human liberty, that human liberty in the United States depended upon resistance to the supreme central power of national sovereignty, and that this resistance was served by supporting the individual states in their exercise of their reserved rights under the Ninth and Tenth Amendments. It but remained for others to take these ideas and fashion a political defense of **slavery** and **secession** that **fire-eaters** would employ to break up the nation in 1861.

RANDOLPH, THOMAS JEFFERSON. *See* VIRGINIA SLAVERY DEBATES.

RECTILINEAR SURVEY. *See* LAND ORDINANCE OF 1785.

REEDER, ANDREW H. *See* KANSAS–MISSOURI BORDER WARS.

RELIGION. *See* CHURCH AND RELIGION.

REPUBLICAN PARTY, BEGINNING OF. Many third parties have come and gone in the framework of American politics. The **Anti-Masonic Party** (1827–1832), the **Liberty Party** (1840–1848), the **Free-Soil Party** (1848–1856), and the **American Party** (1854–1856) briefly survived before the Civil War. Eventually, a major party would incorporate the manifesto of a third party and destroy its reason for existence. The one antebellum exception was the Republican Party. Since its organization at Ripon, Wisconsin, in 1854, it has been the **Democrats'** major contender to this day.

Anti-slavery crusaders formed the Republican Party after Senator Stephen A. Douglas introduced the **Kansas–Nebraska Act** during the **Franklin Pierce** administration. This brought about the question of the extension of slavery into the territories, which Douglas and Pierce sought to solve by **Popular Sovereignty** and the **Non-Exclusion Doctrine**. With the opening of the West to slavery, Northern anti-slavery advocates held "Anti-Kansas" meetings. The Ripon Convention adopted the name "Republican" so as not to be classified extremist, as had happened to the earlier Free-Soil Party. The party presented several candidates in the 1854 Wisconsin elections that immediately followed and carried the state.

It was quite possible that the Republicans would never have survived their first electoral victory had not the **Kansas–Missouri Border Wars** kept slavery in the territories an issue before the American people. To promote their moderate anti-slavery platform, as opposed to that of the radical **abolitionists,** the Republicans called an "Opposition to Kansas" convention at Pittsburgh on Washington's Birthday in 1856. But by then the Kansas issue was old news and the convention failed to attract any converts.

In May 1856, Kansas once again rose to the forefront with the Sacking of Lawrence, the Brooks-Sumner Affair, the Pottawattomie Massacre led by John Brown, and the imprisonment of the Free-Soil Topeka government. Scores of new adherents joined the party, including a hack **Whig** politician from Illinois named **Abraham Lincoln**. Lincoln persuaded **Senator Stephen A. Douglas**'s opponents to support him, stole the Illinois party from its original 1854 organizers, ousted its anti-slavery agitators, and made it into an anti-Kansas, anti-Douglas organization that carried him to the presidency in 1860.

REPUBLICAN PLATFORM OF 1860. The **Republican Party** Platform of 1860 barely touched on the **slavery** issue, although the party owed its existence to the opposition to the extension of slavery in the territories. The discussion centered mostly on **Henry Clay**'s old **American System** proposals from the 1820s. The platform's planks were designed to bring diverse groups together under the Republican label. For the idealists and white, small farmers there was the pledge of no slavery in the West. To win industrial Pennsylvania, one of the key states the party had to have to carry the presidency, was the promise of a high protective **tariff**. For old-time **Whigs** and New England financiers the party's enticement was the vow of a national banking act. To develop the West and provide free land to immigrants and white, family farmers, the Republicans promised a homestead act. To hold the Old Northwest, especially **Abraham Lincoln**'s state of Illinois, critical to his winning the presidency, there were to be internal improvements on a large scale, especially a transcontinental railroad emanating out of Chicago. Finally, to carry the Old Northwest and the immigrant and farm vote, the party pledged to create land grant colleges to teach agricultural and military sciences to help their progeny advance intellectually, professionally, and economically. Unlike many political platforms, which are enunciated and forgotten, the Republicans had delivered on every platform issue by 1865.

REPUBLICANS, OLD. *See* DEMOCRATIC REPUBLICANS.

"REVOLUTION OF 1800." *See* ELECTION OF 1800.

RHETT, ROBERT BARNWELL (1800–1876). Originally born Robert Barnwell Smith, Rhett changed his surname to that of a prominent ancestor in 1837. He read law and served in the state legislature from 1826 to 1832. He was a strong Nullifier and took more radical positions for states' rights and secession than most. Rhett was the kind of man that **John C. Calhoun** and Robert Y. Hayne tried to rein in to keep the protest against the **tariff** from getting out of hand and forcing President Andrew Jackson to use force to subdue the application of Nullification and the **Concurrent Voice**.

After serving as state attorney general, Rhett was elected to Congress in 1837 and served until 1849. He created the Bluffton Movement, a group dedicated to the eventual secession of the South from the Union. Upon Calhoun's death he was picked to be the new U.S. Senator from South Carolina. Rhett opposed the **Compromise of 1850**, was a delegate to the Nashville Commercial Convention and the Southern Rights Convention, resigned his senate seat in 1852, and became editor of the *Charleston Mercury*, a newspaper advocating immediate secession from the Union.

He drafted South Carolina's secession ordinance in 1860 and represented his state at the Montgomery Convention that drew up the **Confederate Constitution**. He was considered a possible candidate for president of the new nation, but his radicalism caused the delegates to turn to the more conservative **Jefferson Davis** of Mississippi. Although he lost his first bid to serve in the Confederate House, he used his newspaper to criticize the Davis administration throughout the war.

After Confederate defeat, Rhett was a delegate to the 1868 Democrat Convention. Disappointed in the Republican victory in 1868, Rhett removed to Louisiana near New Orleans where he died in 1876, just after the end of Reconstruction and the state's redemption through the return of white rule.

RICE. Experimented with in Virginia with little success, rice became a major product of South Carolina when Thomas Smith imported a variety from the Island of Madagascar in 1694 that grew well in the American climate. By 1715, rice had become a mainstay of the colony and was accepted in lieu of cash payments for debt.

Initially, rice was grown in swamps above tidewater and irrigated by stream water stored in dammed-up ponds behind the fields. It was planted in rows 18 inches apart in the spring and harvested in the fall. It received two flowings, as irrigation was called then, one in the spring and another in the summer. Then the fields were allowed to dry and the weeds hoed by hand, one slave working every three acres.

When the grains were harvested, they were flailed by hand, the wind removing the chaff. Then the outer husk and inner cuticle were removed by rolling the grains through wooden rollers. Next the rice was then sifted twice to remove dirt and broken grains. The latter were used to feed slaves while the whole grain was exported to

Britain. By the time of the split with Britain, South Carolina and Georgia exported 165,000 barrels of rice annually.

After the American Revolution, rice returned to and stayed steadily at pre-war production levels. There was much competition for slave labor as **upland cotton** began its expansion. Production was also harmed by a flat price, compounded by the economic depressions that accompanied the **Panic of 1819** and the **Panic of 1837**. The main change in rice cultivation was that the growing area shifted to the Sea Islands along the coast. In 1783, Gideon DuPont discovered that keeping the crop underwater throughout the growing season killed the weeds. This required more water than streams and dams could provide.

The best conditions for tidal irrigation occurred between Cape Fear, North Carolina, and Fernandina Island off northern Florida, where the tides were about seven feet. Anything else was too insignificant a tidal flow to work. The rivers had to have water free from salt, but close enough to the coast to be affected by the tides. The fields were divided into plots of 12 to 22 acres by large irrigation ditches, often 15 feet deep, with high embankments and a complicated network of gates that allowed water to flow in or out, based on the cycle of the tides and the setting of the gate.

Then the fields were subdivided into plots of about a quarter acre each, called tasks. A task was the amount of crop a slave could cultivate in a day. By the time of the Civil War, one slave was responsible for a half dozen acres, double the work rate in colonial times.

The fields were kept inundated until planting time. Then they were drained, cultivated into rows 14 inches apart, and the crop planted by hand. It took much skill to keep the rows straight and the fields level so that the water flow was evenly distributed. The first flow was the sprout flow. Every hand was called out to keep birds from devouring the young plants. Horns, whistles, clanging pans, and motion were used to frighten off the birds.

After the crop was established, the point flow was applied for a week to kill grass and weeds. Then the crop, once drained, was hoed carefully several times. Then came the long flow, lasting up to 20 days and covering two-thirds of the plant stems. The crop was drained once again and time allotted for the roots to grow and the plants to mature. Then came the lay-by flow, which was continued until the plants fully developed. Once again the main problem was to keep the birds away. Any plant that showed rust was destroyed at this time. Then the fields were drained and the crop harvested, flailed, and rolled as usual for sale and local consumption.

RITCHIE, THOMAS. *See* DEMOCRATS; JACKSON'S BREAK WITH CALHOUN.

ROBERTS, JOSEPH JENKINS. *See* LIBERIA.

ROBINSON, CHARLES. *See* KANSAS–MISSOURI BORDER WARS.

ROUGH AND TUMBLE. *See* VIOLENCE AND WHITE MILITANCY.

RUFFIN, EDMUND (1794–1865). Born and educated in Virginia, Edmund Ruffin was a graduate of William and Mary College, a volunteer in the **War of 1812** (he saw no action), and a state senator in the 1820s. He was an early convert to the concept of **Nullification and the Concurrent Voice** and believed the **tariff** to be unconstitutional and unfair to the South.

Seeing Virginia being depopulated in favor of the **Great Migration** to the fertile Southwest, Ruffin was a primary advocate of agricultural improvements through fertilization of the worn soils of the **Tidewater** and **Piedmont**. Building on earlier recorded experiments of John Taylor of Caroline, which Ruffin dismissed as virtually useless, he used his own chemical analyses of the local soils to produce a thesis on how to improve fertility. He found that sterility in earth was due to a lack of calcareous earth and too many acids from crops like **tobacco**.

Ruffin believed that calcareous earth reduced plant acids, returning the soils to a natural fertility. When this condition had been achieved, then one could add manures to act as fertilizers, the preferred product being Peruvian guano. Ruffin believed that almost any soil could be made productive again using his methods. The growth of diversified farming, replacing **staple-crop** agriculture in Virginia, Maryland, and North Carolina in the 1850s, seemed to prove him correct.

He was president of the state agricultural society and editor of its newsletter for some years, making his ideas commonplace.

With the death of his wife in 1846 and the **War with Mexico** and the **Wilmot Proviso**, Ruffin returned to politics as a Southern nationalist in favor of secession. Influenced by the writings of Virginians **Thomas R. Dew** and **George Fitzhugh**, and a close friend of South Carolinian **James Hammond**, Ruffin saw slavery as the only answer to keep the South from becoming a North American version of **Haiti**.

Well ahead of his home state in his political sentiment, Ruffin rejected the **Compromise of 1850**. Terrified by what the results of the **election of 1856** showed, namely that the North could take the presidency with a minority of the popular and a majority off the electoral vote, Ruffin turned to warning his fellow Southerners of their precarious spot in the Union with articles in publications like *DeBow's Review* and the *Charleston Mercury*. He also traveled widely and spoke all over the Old South.

Ruffin was cheered in South Carolina and even granted a seat at its secession convention. He joined the Palmetto Guard and fired the first shot on Ft. Sumter, beginning the Civil War. He also fought with an artillery battery at the Battle of First Mannassas and participated in the blasting of the stone bridge over Cub Run that precipitated the Yankee rout. He visited the troops defending Richmond and Charleston. But as black soldiers in blue entered Richmond, Ruffin refused to surrender to Northern dominance. He wrote a defiant letter to the conquerors and blew his own brains out—symbolically firing the last shot of the greatest of American wars.

RUNAWAY SLAVES. Running away was a common tactic used by slaves in their **resistance and rebellion** to the travails of **slavery**. By 1850, some 20,000 slaves had run away to their freedom, often through the **underground railroad**, up North or to Canada, where they were outside all attempts of **slave catchers** to retrieve them for their owners.

Most runaways (80 percent) were young males in their late teens or twenties. The rest were from differing age groups and gender. But **women** had great difficulty escaping slavery because by the time they wanted to they already had children, who would make the attempt too chancy. Young men by the age of 20 realized that they had to make a choice: try for freedom now or be a slave for life. The older a slave got, the harder it would be, physically and mentally, to make the break with his past.

Initially, most runaways were black, although by the mid-19th century, more and more mulattos joined the throng. Mulattos were often house slaves or slave artisans. They had a better chance to affect the demeanor of free blacks, and generally more education and experience with handling white people. They also had the knowledge to forge their own passes and freedom papers.

Regardless of color, scars and disfigurements marked many runaways. There was a direct correlation between the marks and prior punishment, like whippings, beatings, brandings, and the cropping of ears and such. These were males who were harder to control as slaves. The numerous advertisements mentioning these scars became fodder for the **abolitionists**, who used them to good effect in their criticisms of slavery as an institution.

Because the average slave gang dressed like modern-day homeless in a variety of cast-off and crudely made clothing, one of the first things the runaway tried to do was dress for the occasion. A different set of clothes was made for a disguise, especially if they ran to a city, where blacks, slave and free, dressed better than a plantation slave gang. Another thing that whites took notice of was straight hair; also, long hair was practically non-existent.

Most successful runaways were bright, cheery people to all they met. They were amicable, cordial, well-mannered, and congenial. Many, particularly from Louisiana or border regions, could speak two or more languages. Only rarely did an advertisement speak of a slave being bold or surly, probably because such a description might indicate the owner feared his slave.

Runaways usually left at night and on a weekend, when they would be least missed. This might give them a day's lead on the inevitable pursuit. The actual act might be precipitated by some form of punishment, the sale of a child or spouse, decision of a master to move or sell the runaway, the sighting of a known slave dealer in the area, or the death of the master. When the master died, it was not uncommon for him to leave behind numerous debts that would necessitate the sale of some or all of his slaves to settle.

Running away was one of the more persistent ways of resistance and rebellion against the enslaved condition African Americans found themselves in before the Civil War. It showed that blacks were not necessarily docile or submissive and showed that the idea of **slavery as a positive good** was a white myth.

– S –

ST. DOMINGUE. *See* HAITI.

ST. JOHN THE BAPTIST PARISH REVOLT (1811). The biggest slave revolt in American history in terms of numbers, yet the one with the least impact on the nation and the Old South as a whole, occurred in 1811 in Louisiana's St. John the Baptist Parish (a political subdivision that corresponds to a county elsewhere) just north of New Orleans on the eastern bank of the Mississippi. As with **"General" Gabriel's Plot (1800),** the **Charleston Plot (1822),** and the **Southampton Revolt (1831),** the St. John the Baptist Parish Revolt drew from the 1790s St. Domingue Revolution that created the free black nation of **Haiti.**

The Haitian revolutionary experience had a greater effect on Louisiana than the rest of the United States. Haiti, like Louisiana, had been a French colony. It had linguistic and cultural similarities that drew fleeing white slaveholders from the island to the refuge of the Louisiana mainland. With the white refugees came many of their slaves, also affected by the violence their masters had fled.

There had been an alleged conspiracy upriver in Pointe Coupee Parish as early as 1795 that ended in many arrests and executions of black suspects. The 1811 revolt in St. John the Baptist Parish was led by a free man of color, Charles Deslondes, a mulatto immigrant from Haiti. In January 1811, he organized local slaves into several combat groups totaling over 500 men armed with cane knives, hoes, axes, and pikes who razed numerous plantations, but killed only two whites. The rest of the white population fled toward New Orleans, followed by Delondes' drum-beating rebels. Before the insurgents reached the Crescent City, U.S. troops, backed by local militia, attacked, killing 66 out-gunned slave rebels in pitched battle.

Part of the militia units were composed of free blacks from the city, who backed the white authorities as they would again four years later in Gen. **Andrew Jackson**'s victory over the British at the Battle of New Orleans. Dividing up the prisoners to isolate the leaders, authorities tried and executed 16 men, whose heads were cut off and placed on poles along the river in St. John the Baptist Parish to discourage future slave rebellion. *See also* SLAVE RESISTANCE AND REBELLION.

SANDERS, GEORGE N. *See* YOUNG AMERICA.

SANFORD, JOHN F. A. *See DRED SCOTT v. SANFORD*.

SANTA ANNA, ANTONIO LÓPEZ DE. *See* LONE STAR REBELLIONS; WAR WITH MEXICO.

SCHERMERHORN TREATY. *See* INDIAN REMOVAL COMPLETED.

SCOTT, SIR WALTER. *See* VIOLENCE AND WHITE MILITANCY.

SCOTT, WINFIELD (1786–1866). Winfield Scott remained near his Virginia birthplace in Dinwiddie County near Petersburg to graduate from the College of William and Mary in 1805. His law practice took him throughout the circuit around Petersburg. He began his army career in 1807, receiving a captain's commission. During the **War of 1812** on the Niagara frontier, he was captured at Queenstown and exchanged. His attacks at Chippawa and Lundy's Lane made him a hero as he advanced to major general by war's end.

Scott served on various commissions and military boards, coordinated the army response in the Black Hawk War, and commanded at Charleston during the **Nullification Crisis**. He fought briefly in the Seminole War and supervised Cherokee **Indian Removal**. He became a prominent **Whig Party** politician in 1839, losing the presidential nomination to **William Henry Harrison**. By 1841, he was general in chief of the army. He participated in the so-called Aroostook War in Maine, part of the ongoing **Canadian Boundary Dispute,** and unsuccessfully mediated in a Canadian boundary disagreement over the Puget Sound islands in 1859.

As a **Whig** and potential presidential candidate, Scott withstood the rebuffs of his personal and political archenemy President **James K. Polk** during the **War with Mexico**. Polk would not give him, as senior American general, a field command. But when Gen. Santa Anna repudiated his bargain to a settlement along the lines the Americans demanded, President Polk permitted Scott to plan a campaign to capture Mexico City.

With Maj. Gen. **Zachary Taylor** also a potential Whig presidential possibility, Polk sent Scott southward to the coastal city of Vera Cruz, hoping the two men would counteract each other in a future election. Scott captured the city after a three-week siege and prepared for the march inland to Mexico City. After eliminating Taylor, Santa Anna planned to meet the new threat posed by Scott. But although he attacked Taylor's army at Buena Vista and inflicted heavy casualties, the Mexican general did not achieve a victory and he withdrew. But Santa Anna proved no match for Scott at Mexico City. After a campaign still deemed to be a military classic, Scott returned to Washington, D.C., a hero. But instead of allowing the two heroes to knock each other off, the Whigs nominated Taylor for president in 1848 and Scott in 1852. Scott lost to one of his former military subordinates, **Franklin Pierce**.

In 1855, Scott was the first man since George Washington to hold the rank of brevet lieutenant general. His legendary brawls with subordinates gave him the nickname "Old Fuss and Feathers." Scott moved army headquarters to New York to avoid Washington politics. Now a corpulent 300 pounds, for reviews he needed to be hoisted onto his equally stout horse with an A-frame crane.

Scott returned to Washington to supervise the Inauguration of President **Abraham Lincoln** and act as chief military advisor at the outbreak of the Civil War. But Lincoln retired Scott in November 1861. More renowned as an army general than a politician, his Mexican Campaign was his claim to fame. A prolific writer in retirement, he authored a wide range of material, from military manuals to a self-congratulatory autobiography. When he died in 1866, he was given a fitting burial at West Point.

SECESSION, ATTEMPTS TO COMPROMISE. As the likelihood of Civil War increased, concerned politicians made several attempts to avoid it. The U.S. House of Representatives formed the **Committee of Thirty-Three,** and the U.S. Senate organized the **Crittenden Committee of Thirteen.** The border states and the **Constitutional Union Party**, predominantly comprising Virginians, assembled at the **Washington Peace Conference**. The compromisers' proposals centered around extending the old **Missouri Compromise** line west to California's border, leaving half of the West free and half slave. These ideas were contrary to the **Republican Platform of 1860** and never came to fruition because President-elect **Abraham Lincoln** had his own notions of limiting the extension of **slavery** into new areas.

SECESSION, BUCHANAN'S CABINET AND. After President **James Buchanan** and the 1858 Congress were defeated in the **election of 1860**, they served out their "Lame Duck" term until **Abraham Lincoln** was inaugurated on 4 March. But the Republican-dominated Congress would not meet until December. Not wishing to call what he believed to be the Old South's bluff, Buchanan paid little heed to **secession** until South Carolina actually left the Union. In his address to Congress in December 1860, Buchanan gave a lengthy uninspiring diatribe on the legal aspects of secession. In his usual indecisive way, he decided against a proclamation against secession, as **Andrew Jackson** had done in 1833 during the **Nullification Crisis** in South Carolina.

Buchanan laid most of the blame on Northern agitation against **slavery**. An election defeat was no excuse for the Old South's impulsiveness. But he pledged to uphold all federal laws, collect customs revenue, and maintain federal property. Congress, now handling the issue, formed the **Corwin Committee of Thirty-Three** in the House and the **Crittenden Committee of Thirteen** in the Senate in attempts to compromise secession.

Although Buchanan is known to history as an inconsequential figure, many Southerners, especially his seven cabinet members, took umbrage at his speech to Congress. His cabinet had been divided 6–3 in favor of Southern Democrats in 1857. But in December 1860, this coalition dissolved into a ratio of 5–4 in favor of the Old South. By January 1861, Buchanan's cabinet was 3–6, favoring the North. This inversion further confused the already inconsistent and faltering Buchanan. He neither wished to surrender federal installations in the

Old South nor provoke a fight. The decision to declare war would be Lincoln's. In the end, Buchanan endured the secession crisis as a Northerner, but with no true allegiance to either side.

SECESSION, THEORY OF. Despite the Republican Party's belief that it was illegal, secession was based on a theory of states' rights. The people's sovereignty was the theoretical idealized conviction on which the government was based. The supremacy clause of the United States **Constitution,** written by the people's sovereign representatives, by definition did not make the federal government supreme over the people. Under the Ninth and Tenth Amendments, all rights and powers not listed in the Constitution are retained by the people, yet the federal government requires compliance as long as they uphold those amendments. But at the time the Constitution was a compact that the people could repeal through state conventions if the federal government overstepped its written bounds.

Far from a revolution, secession was the assertion of immutable rights. Several steps were required to ensure its legality. A state legislature would authorize the state governor to call a special election to select delegates, who most closely represented the people, to a convention with the sole intention of discussing secession. After debate, the convention would vote to either secede or not. A state's vote to secede dissolved the Union between it and the other states. The people's election of delegates made a referendum unnecessary. Secession was a taking back of a state's sovereign rights which had been conditionally granted to the federal government upon achieving statehood.

The Old South believed that the events that had transpired by 1860 entitled it to leave the Union. The timing was as crucial as the issue itself, producing two groups at each state convention, the Seceders and the Cooperationists. The Cooperationists favored waiting for a forthcoming overt act by the Republican **Abraham Lincoln** administration before seceding, while the Seceders preferred taking immediate action. These circumstances differed from 1850, when the Old South considered leaving the Union over the Mexican Cession issue, and the Cooperators, mostly **Whigs**, denied the right of secession. They had proposed instead that the Old South industrialize and compete with the North in the domestic markets.

But the eventual collapse of the Whigs left secession as the only alternative. The Seceders' advantage in 1860 was their belief in immediate action. By contrast, the Cooperators offered more indecision and delay to solve a problem, Yankee economic and social dominance, that had been ongoing for the past 30 years. The Seceders also maintained that the North's disdain for the Old South was so great that it would happily facilitate secession.

SECESSION AND LOYALTY IN THE BORDER SOUTH. The refusal of the border slave states of Delaware, Maryland, Kentucky, and Missouri to secede brought numerous strategic, psychological, and economic consequences upon the Confederacy. The ideal of **secession** carried less credibility, especially abroad, because the **Confederate States of America** did not represent all the slave states. The border states' joining the Confederacy would have doubled their white population. The South needed the 50,000 troops Kentucky alone could have provided the Confederate Army. Finally, the border states would have extended the South's boundary along the Ohio River in the Western Theater and placed the Union capital behind the lines in Maryland. The Union would have been greatly disheartened in either instance.

Both the Union and Confederate presidents, **Abraham Lincoln** and **Jefferson Davis**, being Kentuckians illustrates the political problem of the border states. Lincoln went North, Davis went South, and Kentucky was split family against family and within families, North and South. Kentucky had supported the Constitutional Union Party's **John Bell** over the Northern Democrats' **Stephen A. Douglas** and the Southern Democrats' **John C. Breckinridge** in the **election of 1860**. In the spring of 1861, Kentucky's **John J. Crittenden** was the leader of compromise in the U.S. Senate. Governor Beriah Magoffin refused to contribute to Lincoln's call for troops after Ft. Sumter, but the state legislature had not asked for a state convention, and Kentucky tried to remain neutral.

Kentucky's refusal to secede was to the Union's advantage as was a state and local election in June. This pro-Union neutrality endured until September 1861, when Confederate Maj. Gen. Leonidas Polk moved into Columbus to facilitate blockading the Mississippi River. Both sides had recruited soldiers from Kentucky, but Union troops retaliated by taking strategic towns along the Ohio River. The remaining Confederate Army occupied Bowling Green but secession never happened. However, pro-Southern elements in Kentucky sent representatives to the Confederate Congress and soon had a star on the Confederate battle flag. The Rebels tried to install a Kentucky governor, Richard Hawes, in Frankfort during the Perryville Campaign in 1862, but were driven out by a Union counterattack.

Missouri, another important border state, was across the Mississippi from Kentucky. Missouri's secession would outflank Illinois with Confederate soldiers halfway to Chicago. Governor Claiborne Jackson and Lieutenant Governor Thomas Reynolds, staunch secessionists, had the state legislature call a convention, which being pro-Union, took no action. Federal officers and politicians based in St. Louis during the Missouri Campaign (1861–1862) forced secession-minded men to head South with Maj. Gen. Sterling Price or become guerilla raiders. Missouri held for the Union although it also sent representatives to Richmond, had a government in exile in Shreveport, and merited a star on the Confederate battle flag.

Kentucky and Missouri were important buffer zones, but pro-Union Maryland was the key to the Border South. If Maryland were lost, Lincoln would have had to move the capital to Philadelphia or New York City. Maryland's western reaches were especially loyal to the Union. The eastern shore was too far from the South to be considered a military factor. But ardently pro-Confederate Baltimore and the peninsulas southeast of Washington recruited soldiers and spies to the Rebel cause.

To Lincoln's advantage, Governor Thomas Hicks was pro-Union. Postponing the state legislature until April 1861, Governor Hicks called the legislature to meet in Unionist Frederick rather than Secessionist Annapolis. Then Lincoln, with little margin for error, ensured a Union majority by ordering the army to arrest 19 members and occupy Baltimore. When the state elected a new legislature that fall, Union soldiers occupied the polls, and Maryland's Union soldiers were furloughed home to vote. Maryland stayed in the Union, but fortunately, Confederate Gen. **Robert E. Lee** fought his Maryland Campaign in the Unionist areas to a dearth of popular support.

Delaware, the final border slave state, had little choice other than to remain in the Union due to its location, sheltered between Maryland and Pennsylvania's southern border. With few slaves and its people divided in outlook, Delaware was the last border state to remain in the Union, but was pro-South until late in the war, maintaining its belief that the South should have been allowed to secede peacefully.

SECESSION OF THE SOUTHERN STATES, FIRST. The **Republican** victory of **Abraham Lincoln** coincided with November's meeting of the South Carolina state legislature immediately following **Abraham Lincoln**'s victory in the **election of 1860**. Consequently, the emotions and fears engendered by the national election were still riding high when the state's politicians convened to decide the **secession** issue. Governor William H. Gist, a moderate, did not wish to take immediate action, but the legislature called for the December meeting of a state convention to consider South Carolina's relationship to the Union. At the convention, Gist approved the purchase of $100,000 in arms and ammunition for the state's defense.

The state legislature needed to elect a new governor, according to state law, and chose Francis Pickens, a regular Democrat turned fire-eating Secessionist. Meanwhile, Mississippi and Florida pledged their cooperation in seceding with South Carolina. This differed from earlier efforts to split the Union during the **Nullification Crisis and Compromise of 1833** and the **Compromise of 1850**. On 20 December 1860, South Carolina unanimously dissolved the bonds of Union and declared itself a free and independent state—a nation co-equal to all others. The Secessionists faced little opposition, although Union man James L. Petigru quipped that South Carolina was too small to be an independent republic and too large to be an insane asylum.

As promised, Mississippi held its scheduled convention and seceded with an 84–15 vote on 9 January 1861. The few opponents objected to timing rather than the act itself, in anticipation of other states. Florida voted 62–7 the following day, the last state to secede easily. An active group of Cooperationists, wishing to wait until after Lincoln and his Republicans took office, confronted the **fire-eaters** or chivalry, as the Seceders were called, in the remaining Southern states.

Alabama seceded quickly on 11 January, despite the opposition, especially in the northern counties along the Tennessee River, whose citizens were economically dependent on Tennessee's support. The Cooperationists suggested postponing action until the meeting of a Southern States Convention. But the Seceders rejected the delaying tactic, voting 54–45 against it. Secession passed 61–39, as some Cooperationists, wishing to show solidarity, accepted their fate. Georgia followed Alabama a week later, delayed by powerful Cooperationist influence. As the core of the Deep South, Georgia's remaining in the Union would geographically divide the Southern nation—and the Seceders always planned on a Confederacy.

Georgia's decision would affect the Cooperationist movement in other states. To assist the Seceders in furthering their agenda, Governor Joseph E. Brown had state militia capture the federal installation at Ft. Pulaski. Although the state legislature had already appropriated a $1 million defense budget, the Cooperationists proposed a motion to delay until after Lincoln took office. After heated debate, as in Alabama, the motion lost 164–133. But the convention overwhelmingly voted to secede by 208–89. The South was finally united geographically, with Georgia as its crux.

Of the states west of the Mississippi River, Louisiana was the first to consider secession. Both Governor Thomas Moore and a key politician, U.S. Senator John Slidell, rescinded their Unionist allegiance and initiated secession proceedings. As in all other Deep South states, the regular **Democrats** took over the secession movement and emerged victorious, beating the chivalry at its own game. The chivalry was trying to cut the regular Democrats and **Whigs** out of the political process, but the regular politicians took over the secession movement and made it their own so that the populace would support the normal politicians and also achieve secession.

As was typical in Louisiana politics, the convention members were elected by corrupt means. The returns, not published until after the state left the Union, showed the closeness of the race, 20,000 to 17,000, giving rise to suspicion that the Cooperationist candidates actually had won. When the close election held up the secession movement, the governor ordered the militia to seize the Baton Rouge arsenal and the New Orleans mint, technically acts of treason, as had happened in Georgia.

With New Orleans as the only large city in the South, Louisiana had a sophisticated citizenry who carefully considered the consequences of a swift secession. But the Seceders argued that Louisiana's critical location at the mouth of the Mississippi was an advantage. As part of the Confederacy, Louisiana could strike a better deal with the North, especially the Northwest—by controlling the mouth of the Mississippi, Louisiana could make better trade and political arrangements with the Old Northwest (Illinois, Indiana, Ohio, Iowa, Wisconsin, and Minnesota) as Louisiana controlled their access to the outside world through New Orleans. On 26 January at the convention, these arguments resulted in a vote of 113–17 in favor of seceding, although 10 of the 17 delegates refused to sign the final document. Louisiana also passed a special "Resolution to the Northwestern States," pledging the continuation of river trade. But Mississippi intervened by stopping all river movement to now-fortified Vicksburg.

Texas seceded six days after Louisiana on 1 February. The convention vote was a landslide of 166–8. But it was widely misrepresentative of a large portion of the state. Governor Sam Houston, an old Jacksonian Democrat, called secession treason and unwise. He believed issuing the call for the secession convention would lead to war. But the state legislature suggested that county judges issue the call. Unable to delay the inevitable, Houston finally agreed to call the convention election. Irregular pro-secession militia units were already seizing federal installations in San Antonio. Texas was the only Gulf Southern state to have a public referendum on the convention's actions, which showed that the frontier dwellers, on a band stretching along the Red River and south to San Antonio, accounting for about a quarter of the population, opposed secession.

The first six states to secede sent delegates to Montgomery, Alabama, in February 1861 to form the **Confederate States of America**. The Texas delegation appeared in March, delayed by the referendum results and the lengthy journey, becoming the seventh Confederate state. But Governor Houston, who stayed behind, refused to take the oath to the Confederacy. As a result, he was deposed in favor of his more deferential lieutenant governor, pro-secessionist Edward Clark.

SECESSION OF THE SOUTHERN STATES, SECOND. The effect of the Battle of Ft. Sumter forced both North and South doubters and

Cooperators to choose sides and they generally went with their section. President **Abraham Lincoln** called up 75,000 state militia for three months to put down "combinations" of seven states, "too powerful to be suppressed by the ordinary course of judicial proceedings," that is, to suppress **secession** by armed force. Every state received a quota, including Southern states that had not seceded. U.S. Senator **Stephen A. Douglas** of Illinois, Lincoln's political opponent, immediately became his staunchest advocate and traveled extensively to muster federal support, dying from exhaustion on 3 June 1861.

The seceded South rallied to their own Confederate cause, fearing that the federal government would overpower them and force them to forfeit their rights. Having previously considered and rejected the idea a few months earlier, Virginia led the second wave of secession, although the western area was strongly pro-Union, and Douglas and **Constitutional Union Party** candidate **John Bell** had won the statewide popular vote in 1860.

The convention that Governor John Letcher called in January 1861 voted 85–45 not to secede on 4 April, but asked the federal government for concessions on the question of the **extraterritoriality of slavery** and not to coerce the seceded states. Virginia spearheaded the **Washington Peace Conference of 1861**. Three days after the firing on Ft. Sumter, Virginia voted 88–55 to secede, when more members had joined from the West. Virginia had a popular referendum on 23 May that approved the convention's platform, as Texas had.

Although Arkansas had refused to attend the Washington Peace Conference and the northern part of the state was mostly pro-Union, it followed Virginia when Lincoln sent it a troop quota to put down secession in other Southern states. On 4 March, the convention reached a compromise to let the public vote on secession on 5 August. But the convention voted 65–5 to secede on 6 May, after militia units seized local federal installations.

Tennessee was much like its fellow upper South states, initially. Governor Isham Harris strongly advocated secession, although eastern Tennessee strongly objected. The state legislature called for a convention on 19 January, but voted against it, even though delegates had been elected. The state elected a majority of Union men, a double defeat for the secessionists.

Even after Ft. Sumter, prevailing Union sentiment prevented Harris from calling another convention. He asked the pro-secessionist state legislature to pass a secession law, which he signed on 7 May. After Harris signed a military alliance with the Confederacy, the state legislature enrolled 55,000 soldiers in the state's Army of Tennessee to occupy polling places and the state's voters ratified secession, as a fait accompli, on 8 June—105,000 for secession, 47,000 against.

North Carolina, with its strong pro-Union element, was the upper South's last state to secede. The state, like Tennessee, had a strong pro-Union element, and the state convention called for by the governor and the state legislature for the secession convention narrowly lost by 1,000 votes. But the combination of Lincoln's troop call-up and its location between now-Confederate Virginia and South Carolina destroyed North Carolina Unionism. In a special session, the governor and state legislature called for a convention on 20 May, which voted unanimously to secede. North Carolina, like the rest of the upper South, believed that if Lincoln had shown more forbearance, the firing on Ft. Sumter would not have happened. In the end, they could not endure the call for troops to put down their Southern brethren.

SECOND GREAT AWAKENING. Like the Great Awakening in the 18th century, before the American Revolution, the Second Great Awakening swept the nation in the first half of the 19th century. In many respects it was a response to the deism that marked much of what the Founding Fathers had professed. One can see the difference in reading the preamble to the Constitution of 1789 and comparing it to the preamble of the Confederate Constitution. God is present in both, but with much greater force and definite Christianity in the latter.

The Second Great Awakening gave birth to many new forms of belief, although much of this came from the Northern branch with its Church of Jesus Christ of Latter-day Saints (Mormons) and the Seventh-day Adventists. In the South, the Second Great Awakening was much more an expansion and modification of traditional Methodism and Baptism. Both North and South, the evangelical nature of the movement was made clear in its emphasis on the camp meeting or revival, which was honed to a fine art form, particularly through the work of Charles Grandison Finney.

The first real camp meeting took place in southwestern Kentucky at Gaspar River Church. The following summer, a larger meeting took place at Cane Ridge, in Logan County, Kentucky, led by James McGready and William and John McGee. Upwards of 25,000 people attended and primarily Methodist and Baptist preachers exhorted. People would stay in an area under massive tents and sheds, hear preaching that went on 24 hours a day, and move on in about a week, after food supplies were exhausted.

These revivals were religious democracies in which various denominations joined under the vast umbrella of Protestantism. The essential religious doctrine was a reformed Calvinism, which the early Puritans would have condemned as heresy, stressing one's inner faith as central to salvation on an equal basis for all. The Second Great Awakening spread rapidly into the sparsely settled areas of the West and South, where it provided a form of social stability to those of all ethnic backgrounds through a common religion. The important factor was emotion in the face of an Almighty God.

Many of these Methodist, Baptist, and Campbellite denominations not only believed in religion for all white people, but threw in blacks and Indians as well. But most Southern forms of this equality were tempered with a fear of where these equal black and red people would fit into white society. This was answered simply by stressing the view of **Slavery as a Positive Good** and **Indian Removal**. But there was a realization that evangelical religion was not just for whites alone. Many African denominations of Protestant churches traced their origin to the Second Great Awakening.

Since the evangelicals were from the outset interested in expanding church membership, they defined religious experience in a very practical manner. They set forth the promise of the individual being reconnected to a higher form of community in the emotional experience of a revival church. They closed the gap between the individual and the Divine. They also sought to close the gap between the possessed and dispossessed, be they male or female, black or white, within the strictures of racial separateness by way of **slavery** or segregation of freed Negroes through the **Black Codes**.

SECRET SIX. *See* HARPER'S FERRY RAID.

SEGREGATION. See SLAVERY IN THE CITIES.

SEMINOLE WAR, FIRST. *See* ADAMS–ONÍS TREATY; ERA OF GOOD FEELINGS.

SEMINOLE WAR, SECOND. *See* INDIAN REMOVAL COMPLETED.

SEMINOLE WAR, THIRD. *See* INDIAN REMOVAL COMPLETED.

SEVENTH-DAY ADVENTISTS. *See* SECOND GREAT AWAKENING.

SHANNON, WILSON. *See* KANSAS–MISSOURI BORDER WARS.

SHORT STAPLE COTTON. *See* COTTON, UPLAND.

SHREVE, HENRY MILLER (1785–1854). Born in New Jersey, Henry Shreve went west as a young man to engage in river navigation on the Mississippi and Ohio. It gradually dawned on him that steam might offer a solution to the difficult journey against the river's powerful current. He was aware of Robert Fulton's success in the Hudson, but he knew that such a deep-draft boat would not make it up the shallower Western rivers. Nonetheless, during the **War of 1812**, he bought the first Fulton boat he saw, loaded it with powder and shot, and set out for the Gulf. Conscripted by Gen. **Andrew Jackson**, his boat helped supply the American forces at the Battle of New Orleans (1814). In 1815, he ascended the Mississippi and Ohio Rivers by steam, the first time it was done. But because of the draft of his craft, Shreve knew that the trip was possible only because of the spring flood.

In 1816, he built a flat-bottomed shallow-draft sternwheeler. It rode on the water rather than in it. Space came in the multiple decks reaching into the sky. Power came from a rebuilt high-pressure steam engine, which Shreve installed horizontally to save space. Although he ran aground and suffered a boiler explosion and two dozen casualties horribly scalded by escaping steam (another river first of dubious honor), Shreve repaired his boat, which continued on its trip to New Orleans. Then he turned around and made the upstream trip in just over three weeks, a feat that took any other craft four to six months to accomplish.

All of this was in violation of the Fulton Company's patents and monopolies. When the Fulton interests tried to have him arrested, a New Orleans mob went crazy. No one in the West cared about monopoly, least of all Captain Henry Miller Shreve. Sixty more boats were built by various concerns in the next two years. Soon Shreve rebuilt his sternwheeler into a sidewheeler, with each wheel operated by a separate engine. His design became a riverboat standard for power and control.

Shreve also invented a boat to remove snags from rivers and a steam ram, for harbor defense. In 1826, he was made federal superintendent of improvements on Western rivers. He was best known for removing the Red River Raft, a historic jam of floating timber (so solid that one could ride a horse across parts of it) that prevented navigation of the Red River above Alexandria, Louisiana. He left something else at the head of the logjam, a camp that became the town named for him, Shreveport. He retired in 1841 and died at St. Louis on March 6, 1851.

SIERRA LEONE. *See* LIBERIA.

SLADE, ELI AND ELISHA. *See* TOBACCO.

SLAVE CATCHERS. Because of the constant problem of **runaway slaves**, slave catchers, professionals who hunted slaves for the reward, were employed by planters, who lacked the time and resources to devote to the problem. Catching runaways was important in making slavery an inescapable condition for blacks. Each slave who escaped to freedom made that concept a lie. In addition to slave catchers, sheriffs, constables, jailers, justices of the peace, and other local, state, and federal officials made the idea of escaping slavery a difficult proposition to enact.

Indeed, according to Southern state laws, any white person could apprehend any slave at large without a proper pass, have the prisoner jailed or hold the slave himself, and be paid for mileage and incidental expenses, plus a reward for his efforts. There were often legal disputes as to ownership and monetary claims, but generally the planter had to pay or see his slave sold at auction for expenses.

In the end, the slave catchers were the universal answer to keeping slavery intact as an institution. They had tracking knowledge, were aware of likely hideouts, and had the dogs (bloodhounds to track and mastiff crossbreeds to hold and maul the captive), horses, nets, chains, and manacles to do the job up right. They also had the time and inclination to track runaways anywhere in the South and even into the North, especially after congressional passage of the **Fugitive Slave Act of 1850**. The tracking of fugitives was so profitable that local white farmers and artisans did it on the side for extra cash.

SLAVE DRIVERS. See DRIVERS, SLAVE.

SLAVE POWER CONSPIRACY. Coined by Ohio Free-Soil Democrat and **Liberty Party** vice presidential candidate, Thomas Morris, the ability of the South to control much of antebellum national politics through the benefits of the **Three-Fifths Compromise** in the U.S. **Constitution,** determining the make-up of the House of Representatives, equal representation of each state in the Senate, and the manipulation of national party caucuses led to the notion that there was a Slave Power Conspiracy to deny the more populous North its fair share of national power.

Instrumental in the Old South's control of national politics before the Civil War was a group of Northern politicians, Jeffersonian **Democratic Republicans** before the **Era of Good Feelings** and Jacksonian **Democrats** afterward. Called **dough faces** from their willingness to be molded like a loaf of bread into voting against the desires of many of their anti-slavery constituents, it seemed that the Old South could rely on at least four or five such votes in the Senate and as many as 60 in the House of Representatives.

These Northern men came from two main areas of the free states, New York and New England, and Pennsylvania and the Old Northwest. Prior to the **Missouri Compromise** of 1820, the Slave Power Conspiracy was just under the surface, there but not publicly noticed. Northern votes, principally from western New York, helped confirm the **Louisiana Purchase**, pass the **Embargo Act** (**John Quincy Adams** being the most notable here), make up the congressional **War Hawks** who declared the **War of 1812**, and legislate the **New Nationalism**.

But it was the political effort of the South to protect and expand slavery into the West and protect slavery's **extraterritoriality** in the North, as opposed to slavery in existing Southern states, that publicized the Slave Power Conspiracy for the first time and gave its Northern adherents a nickname, **dough faces**. In the passage of the Missouri Compromise, 17 northern congressmen (14 by voting, three by being absent at crucial moments) were critical to getting the measure passed. Five Northern senators stood by the Old South in the Senate to obtain Missouri's admission into the Union as a slave state.

The reorganization of American political parties into the **Democrats** and **National Republicans** or **Whigs** followed. Key to dough face availability was **Martin Van Buren**'s creation of the Democrats. Building his Northern branch on his own New York state political machine, the Albany Regency, Van Buren's allies (known as Bucktails, from their public symbol of identification) based their membership on following the party line. Van Buren extended his party organization and discipline into New England, where it was centered on New Hampshire, which would provide a successful dough face presidential candidate in **Franklin Pierce**. Since the rest of the party was comprised of Southerners, Van Buren made support of slavery on the national level imperative.

Later, when **anti-slavery** groups began to multiply in the Northeast, Bucktails began to lose their congressional seats. So the dough face support shifted to Pennsylvania (**James Buchanan**) and the Old Northwest (**Stephen A. Douglas**). But still the support was there for the Slave Power Conspiracy to remain potent until just before the Civil War.

On fundamental Old South-supported issues, dough face votes were critical to Southern success. Although the dough faces were chary in their support of **Indian Removal** in the House of Representatives, where the measure barely passed, nine northern dough face senators guaranteed its ultimate passage. On the **Gag Rule**, as many as 60 Northern congressmen voted with the South. On the **Wilmot**

Proviso, 27 dough face votes bolstered a losing Southern position in the House but five Northerners blocked the proviso in the Senate. On the draconian **fugitive slave law** in the **Compromise of 1850**, 35 Northerners voted for passage in the House, while three voted for it in the Senate and 15 missed the vote altogether. And when it came to repealing the Missouri Compromise in the **Kansas–Nebraska Act**, 58 dough faces guaranteed a Southern victory in the House with the support of 14 in the senate.

Moreover, the Slave Power Conspiracy extended into the 900 appointive offices at the disposal of the American president. In a nation where the Northern free white male population outnumbered that of the Old South by two to one, half of all appointments went to Southern men. And while no **abolitionist** was appointed to a position of importance before the Civil War, radical Southern secessionists regularly achieved senate approval in numerous positions.

The Slave Power Conspiracy extended into the U.S. **Supreme Court**. Both chief justices, slaveowners **John Marshall** and **Roger B. Taney**, were respectful of slaveholding rights in court. Presidents Andrew Jackson and Van Buren filled the court with eight pro-slave justices from the South and two other who were reliable on the issue. The trend continued until Southern **secession**.

Northerners believed that the **Louisiana Purchase**, American expansion into West Florida and Texas through **Lone Star Rebellions**, the purchase of East Florida in the **Adams–Onís Treaty**, the cession of land in the **War with Mexico**, and the Ostend Manifesto designed to obtain Cuba from Spain in the **Spread Eagle foreign policy** of the 1850s, demonstrated this Slave Power Conspiracy in action even beyond America's borders, and made it a centerpiece of **Republican** anti-South ideology in the 1850s.

The event that broke the dough face representatives was the **Kansas Settlement**. When crooked voting produced the pro-slave Lecompton Constitution, President Buchanan insisted that the Northern Democrats get in line and vote for it. The congressmen from the North refused to go along. Everyone that did was defeated in the upcoming by-elections of that year. But the Senate still produced four dough face votes for Lecompton, despite Stephen A. Douglas's harsh attacks and vote against it. It saved him in the senatorial election that year against **Abraham Lincoln**.

It was the loss of Northern dough face support in the Congress, with Democrats being replaced by Republicans in district after district, that led to Republican control of Congress in 1859 when Henry Winter Davis changed from Whig-American to Republican. This, combined with Lincoln's electoral victory with a minority of popular votes, all from the North, led the Old South to secession and the creation of the Confederate States of America.

SLAVE RESISTANCE AND REBELLION. Even if black persons could not totally escape the demands of **slavery**, there were ways in which they could mitigate the system through passive and more active forms of resistance—a common enough occurrence to cause Southern whites to label their chattels "a troublesome property." Whites classified all misdeeds as "slave crime" and took it as a matter of course that their black charges would at least skirt work and responsibility.

The real problem was intent. Slaveowners never could agree whether the smart slaves or the stupid ones were the most exasperating—nor could they agree if the alleged stupidity was real or feigned. The only solution seemed to be closer white supervision of their chattels. More recent observers, however, point out that a suppressed people achieves self-respect by attacking its oppressors, whether this resistance is planned and obvious or subconscious and more subtle. In this light, much of the alleged black inability to work as their white owners desired makes considerable sense.

In one of his famous tours of the South, New York landscape architect **Frederick Law Olmstead** (the originator of Central Park) commented on how a long line of slaves hoeing a cotton field would stop work each time the **overseer** turned away, only to chop weeds with renewed vigor each time he faced their direction. Other blacks seemed too dumb to catch on to the task at hand, chopping up cotton as well as weeds. This inability to learn extended to all tasks—a form of resistance that led whites to disparage all black work, and ignored the obvious contribution of African Americans to the building of America's economic wealth.

Still others faked illness—the most noted example being a Mississippi slave who convinced his master that he was blind, only to emerge as the best farmer in the county with perfect vision after Emancipation.

Women used "female complaints" to beg off work, something no man, regardless of his medical abilities, seemed able to predict or cure. A good whipping was not the solution that first glance gave it. A fieldhand or house servant whipped for no good reason led to the whole gang slowing up its work and "forgetting" how the tasks were done. Worse yet, for the planter, the whole gang might take to the woods and swamps, stopping all work indefinitely. After two or three weeks of "labor negotiation," the recalcitrants would come back, the disliked condition would change, and usually some form of punishment was agreed upon to help the harried slaveowner save a little face.

These mysterious slave work habits the slaveowners condemned as "rascality," and they were marked by broken tools, lame livestock, the shuffle-walk, thieving, lying, sullenness, feigned sickness, and stupidity. But in reality these so-called faults or crimes among slaves masked a different code of behavior acceptable to African Americans, but not condoned by white authorities. To steal from the master and get away with it showed much cleverness, especially if the theft helped raise the living standard of the whole black plantation community, as in the case of purloined food and drink.

Arson was another crime to whites that was a form of revenge acceptable among slaves who were wronged. Fires of mysterious origin cropped up on a regular basis all over the South, especially in times of racial tension. Murder of a cruel master or overseer was not unusual. Usually no one from the quarters knew who did it. In extreme cases, slaves were known to mutilate themselves "accidentally," or even commit suicide, the ultimate form of individual protest.

But there were less severe means to defeat the travail of slavery. **Runaway slaves** were a constant plague in the plantation South (newspapers were full of such ads), and blamed on abolitionist propaganda or the activities of the **underground railroad** and "conductors" like **Harriet Tubman**. Most took to the free states, particularly slaves from the upper South along the Mason–Dixon Line and the Ohio River, hoping that the professional bounty men, the slave catchers, would not find them. But federal law guaranteed a slave's return if captured, making it a risky proposition not to go to any foreign jurisdiction, like Canada or Mexico. Estimates of the number of permanent runaways hover around the 60,000 figure for the period of 1790–1860.

Farther south, many slaves just took off for a few weeks' "vacation" and returned home to accept what punishment was in store for them. But running away in the Deep South could be permanent, too. Entire runaway or "maroon" colonies in the woods and swamps of every Southern state lived beyond the pale of slavery and all white authority. Slaves from nearby plantations often succored them with food, clothing, medical aid, and information.

But sometimes the frustrations of bondage became too much and broke forth in the violence of armed rebellion. One of the most disturbing events that inspired the hope of freedom among African Americans and fear of violent slave revolution among white Americans was the 1790s revolution in St. Domingue. **Haiti** was the outgrowth of the philosophy of liberty and equality of the French Revolution and the American Revolution before it. Many refugees came to the American South from Haiti and brought their slaves with them. Southern whites saw this influx as akin to some sort of silent epidemic.

The American slaves also felt other forces that inspired revolt. Important was the ratio of blacks to whites in an area's population. The blacker areas tended to be more susceptible to rebellion. As America grew, so did its cities. The bigger the city, the more the controls so essential to slavery's functioning lessened in influence, leading to unsupervised activities among urban blacks. Finally, economic depression increased the likelihood of a disturbance. As their masters went broke, food and clothing amounts and quality declined, and the chance increased that whole plantation communities would be sold into the Deep South to pay for planters' debts. This meant the division of friendship, marriages, and family, a very disrupting possibility. Examples of outright armed rebellion in the Old South include **"General" Gabriel's Plot, St. John the Baptist Parish Revolt,** the **Charleston Plot,** and the **Southampton Revolt.**

SLAVE TRADE, DOMESTIC. At the Constitutional Convention, anticipating the 1790 census, the South divided over the efficacy of reintroducing the international slave trade in America. Virginia and Maryland were opposed, seeing their great numbers of domestically grown blacks as a physical danger, then a great economic boon, as the nation spread the **peculiar institution** westward. But Georgia and

South Carolina wanted to replenish the slaves they had lost to the British during the Revolutionary War through reopening the international slave trade. All parties finally agreed to the **Compromise of 1808**. The international trade would be legal until 1808, when it would be ended forever.

By 1808, the economic effects of the **cotton gin** and the beginnings of the **Great Migration** were evident. The excess slaves in Maryland and Virginia were worth a fortune in the cotton lands of the Southwest. At the same time, the problems of soil depletion from **tobacco** raising and excessive debt drove many planters to sell their one cash commodity in high demand, their black slaves. The domestic slave trade instantly became a big business.

The center of the domestic slave trade, to the utter shame of **antislavery** people and **abolitionists**, was the national capital, Washington, D.C. Strategically located between Maryland and Virginia on the Potomac River, Washington was a gathering point. Itinerant traders would bring in small groups of slaves and sell them to the big companies, which had the facilities for holding them until a large coffle, as gangs of slaves on the road were called, could be assembled for the trip south and west.

The slaves came from three sources. The first was bills of sale. These were individual sales to the **slave trader** for ready cash. Upon a planter's death there would have to be a settlement of the estate, the second and most likely way the traders obtained their slave coffles. Finally, slave criminals were shipped out of state if the crime committed was not punished by execution.

Many times there have been accusations that individual planters actually ran slave-breeding farms. If forced cohabitation is meant, this was very rare. But no planter was averse to allowing nature to take its course by condoning young black males and females to consort freely at all levels of social conduct.

The trip to the Deep South was by ship, train, steamboat, or on foot. The latter allowed the slave trader to sell and buy at each small town along the way. The male slaves were handcuffed and then chained by the neck to each other. Women were joined by tying ropes between their necks. The long walk allowed the slaves to be acclimated thoroughly by the time they arrived at their destination. Usually the other forms of transportation were reserved for slave coffles destined for sale in places like Natchez (at Forks of the Road one mile east of the city), Vicksburg, New Orleans, or Shreveport. These forms of transport had the advantage of being easy on the slave in health and short in duration. But if the ship had trouble, it was likely that whatever aid it received would be from the Bahamas, and the British freed all slaves without question.

The prime slave market in the Deep South was New Orleans. By 1842, its city directory listed 185 full-time dealers in slaves. The dealers operated on a simple principle—fast sale, large profits, and all risk to the buyer. During the 1850s, the South experienced what was called "negro fever." There were never enough slaves to buy and prices shot sky high. The demand grew to such an extent that serious men suggested that the international trade be opened through a constitutional amendment. Prices in Virginia for a prime fieldhand rose from $300 in 1790 to $1,000 in 1860. The same slave in 1860 New Orleans would fetch as much as $2,500. *See also* SLAVERY.

SLAVE TRADE, INTERNATIONAL. All immigrants to the New World took what was essentially a three-part journey. First they had to reach a port and board a ship, then they had to sail across the Atlantic Ocean, and finally they had to disembark and move to their new home. The crossing of the Atlantic was thus the middle part of their journey and became known as the Middle Passage. Frequently locked below decks for the duration, it was a terrifying, painful, and daunting part of their journey.

While for white Europeans it was more or less a voluntary trip, for black Africans it was a forced voyage into lifelong bondage, in conditions that made the admittedly appalling conditions on white immigrant ships look solicitous by comparison. The movement of slaves from the barracoons (slave-holding pens in Africa) to the seagoing slave ships was a critical part of the journey. The blacks were well aware that this was their last chance to stay in Africa. Many had never seen the sea before. None had ever taken a sea journey. Once at sea, they knew they were lost.

The slavers knew that rebellion was a real possibility at this stage of the transaction. The surf was crashing, the coast was very shallow, and the slaves had to be taken out in lighters to the slave ships standing off the shore a half mile or more. Professional men, Captains of the Sand, specialized in taking slaves from the barracoon to the ship. They were generally Kru tribesmen who used long canoes capable of holding up to 80 slaves per trip. Slip-ups were fatal. Sharks patrolled the bays, hungrily awaiting anyone overboard.

Once aboard ship, the slaves were placed like spoons on rough planks. On a rough trip with high seas, it was not unheard of for slaves to be rubbed raw to the bone. There were two schools of thought on loading slave cargoes. Loose packers realized that the more room, food, and fresh air on deck the slaves were allowed, the more of them would survive the trip. Tight packers, and most slavers were of this notion, believed that numbers would make up losses in life. For safety, all slaves were chained below on the shelves. One could fatten slaves up on arrival, if it were necessary at all.

Room depended on the ship's construction and the captain's concept of profit. Generally there were 20 to 30 inches between shelves. Each man was allotted a space six feet by 16 inches, females, five feet 10 inches by 16 inches; each boy, five feet by 14 inches; and each girl, four feet six inches by 12 inches. These were "lawful" clearances. One can imagine what a real tight packer might deem satisfactory.

Given the unsanitary conditions, the decks of slave ships often ran red with blood from dysentery. If smallpox or some other epidemic were detected, the sick would be chained to each other and a cannon ball and heaved over the side. The same treatment awaited whole shiploads of slaves if a British man-o'-war came up after the trade was outlawed. The rule was that no evidence in the form of captive live Africans meant no charge could be brought.

Total mortality in the slave trade was hard to figure. But if one figures 4.5 percent in Africa before sale, 12.5 percent for the trip, and 33 percent for seasoning in the New World, it comes to around 50 percent overall. The rate for free, white immigrants was almost as bad. They had less value than the slaves and were rarely allowed up out of the holds. The sailors suffered the worst because they made a triangular route from Britain to Africa, Africa to the New World, and the New World back to Britain. Parliament estimated the sailors' rate of death at 21 percent, the same rate as suffered by British forces in World War I. Abolitionists claimed that the sailors' death rate was more like 40 percent.

SLAVE TRADER. Before the Civil War, the buying and selling of African Americans was as legitimate a business, in the legal sense, as any other exchange. Yet slave traders were despised by the "better classes," North and South. The hatred of Northerners, many of whom were ardent **anti-slavery** people and **abolitionists**, is understandable. The dealer in slaves represented all of the evils of the **peculiar institution** in one person. Blacks had reason to fear and hate the dealers, too. They could tear slaves away from home and loved ones in an instant, if the price were right. But why Southerners?

The slave trader allowed many in the South to feel superior. The traders took the blame for all that was distasteful about **slavery**, while the planters kept a clear conscience and their hands clean. But this was really unfair. The planters knew that the dealers would separate families, sell to unscrupulous buyers, and emphasize profit above all other considerations. The slave trader made the system function by providing a mobile labor force, and the planters ought to share in that condemnation.

While admittedly many slave traders were pillars of the community and ran a good, clean operation, the ostracism emphasized their methods. They took advantage of someone down on his luck and made a substantial profit off of it. They were the 19th-century version of used car dealers: brutal, keen, ruthless, and an exploiter of weakness in their fellow man. Somehow, the dealer always seemed to know when the planter needed a sale to get out of debt.

So planters assuaged their consciences by portraying the slave trader as a superficially artful and compliant combination of unscrupulous horse dealer, tavern keeper, hard drinker, low politician, and fast-talking sharpie. They sold a bill of goods to the unwary in the form of another human being. Buyers had to be wary. They examined a potential purchase's teeth for soundness and age; watched for those with dyed hair or shaved heads as older than they appeared; ran them up and down the aisle to check for wind, disease, blemishes, and whip marks, all of which could be concealed; and looked out for fake buyers who ran up the auction prices.

But in reality, the slave traders always moved up in society as they profited, not down. They associated with the best men in the county, they assisted them by getting rid of surly or unwanted slaves, and they sold them the replacements they needed. Actually, as a type the slave traders were as varied a people as any other members of the business world.

SLAVERY. One of the more difficult things for modern Americans to understand is that slavery has been the norm in the world from time in memoriam, not freedom. The reason for this misunderstanding is that England, unlike continental Europe, has had a long tradition of assuming all humans are free and equal before the law. Americans are the heirs to this tradition, which made slavery an aberration instead of normal.

To grasp how slavery came to British colonies in the New World, one needs to comprehend what colonies meant to the mother country in the 16th century. The main economic theory of the time was mercantilism. Under mercantilism, colonies existed to provide raw materials for sustaining the infant industries back home. But there were two types of British colonies. The first were those in North America from Pennsylvania to New England comprised of diversified economies of self-sufficient small farms and an adequate labor force that needed to import little from the mother country. The second were those colonies south of the **Mason–Dixon Line** to and including the West Indies. These colonies were constantly short of labor and provided staple crops and raw materials that fed the industries back home. These colonies could not exist without importing all types of finished goods from Britain itself.

Under the mercantile system, labor was simply another commodity. There was no overt discrimination by race or religion. It could be white, red, brown, black, yellow, Protestant, Catholic, or Pagan. As Britain had an idle, surplus population, mercantilists decided to ship it to the colonies where it would do the most good.

Actually, there were three sources of impressed labor before the U.S. Civil War. One was the Native American. But unlike the Spanish and Portuguese, the British had an ethnic cleansing policy from the beginning. Besides, Indians refused to work, died like flies from white man's diseases, and were too individualistic to labor as a team.

The British then sent over its surplus, unemployed white population to labor in the colonies. These were indentured servants who signed a contract to labor for their upkeep and travel; redemptioners, who went on credit to the ship's captain with a promise to pay for the trip in a certain amount of time or be indentured later; and convicts, who went over as a part of their punishment for crime, usually unpaid debts or political opposition (although there were 300 capital crimes on the books in Britain). So the Catholic Stuart kings sent the Protestant levelers, the Protestant Roundheads sent the Catholics, and the Hanoverian kings sent the Scottish Jacobites, and everyone sent the unemployed poor.

The indentures and the rest went over just like the Africans in the **international slave trade**, less the chains. They were locked in ships' holds, maltreated and malnourished, many dragooned by kidnappers, called "Spirits," working for planters and businesses in the New World. Running out of British subjects, the Spirits turned to the German Palatinate, where they were called "Neuländer."

But then the Industrial Revolution hit Britain hard in the late 1600s. The useless, unemployed laboring class now had jobs at home. But the colonies still needed labor. The colonies were also tired of new white settlers with limited terms of service. If they ran away, they were hard to distinguish from other free whites. When freed, they became competitors. Besides, most were English, too. So the British turned to a new source of labor, one that the Spanish and Portuguese had been using for over a century—black Africans.

There were few Africans in the British North American mainland before 1675. Those who arrived involuntarily from Africa via the West Indies were at first indentures, just like the whites before them. But gradually a change took place. When the British colonies decided to make their laws of voluntary servitude more exact and limited, blacks were left out. There was no need, reasoned the colonial assemblies. Blacks came involuntarily anyway.

In late 1600 Virginia and Maryland, the indentures for non-Christians were extended to life. Obviously the current laws for bastardy, extension of involuntary servitude for nine more years, now had no meaning. So the children of such indentured women were granted to the owner of the indenture as payment for work lost during pregnancy. The condition of the child now followed the virtual enslavement of its mother. It was not until after 1700 that the colonies felt compelled to write the **Black Codes** that defined the position of the black as different from all whites. The blacks had become slaves.

See also CARE AND MAINTENANCE OF SLAVES; INDUSTRIAL SLAVERY; PLANTATION MANAGEMENT; PROFITABLY OF SLAVERY, SLAVERY IN THE CITIES.

SLAVERY, INDUSTRIAL. *See* INDUSTRIAL SLAVERY.

SLAVERY, LAW OF. *See* BLACK CODES.

SLAVERY, PROFITABILITY OF. The traditional view is that slavery was an undue economic burden on the South before the Civil War. Maintaining that slavery was primarily a race accommodation device, the traditionalists believe that the South kept slavery around to keep the black slaves in a predetermined, subordinate place in a predominately white American society. Stuck with an institution that once was very profitable in the colonial and early national eras, slavery by the 1850s was economically no longer viable. It had reached the **natural limits of slavery expansion** in the deserts of the Southwest and Great Plains. Soil exhaustion made **staple crops** no longer profitable in the Southeast.

In more recent times, revisionist historians have reexamined the profitability question and challenged the traditional view. Under existing circumstances, the raising of large staple crops like **tobacco, indigo, rice, cotton, sugar,** and **hemp** by slave labor was actually quite efficient. As for all those plantation books that showed the planter losing money, they were nonsense. Using modern accounting methods, these new historians-turned-accountants found that planters had placed assets in the debit columns and not even counted other related profits like natural slave increase. If Southern white slaveholders were poor, it was because they overspent on a luxurious lifestyle. It was not slavery itself that broke them.

Depending upon where a planter lived, he could expect a return on economic investment as high as 14 percent, twice what Northerners were gaining from the most profitable sectional investment they had—railroads. Why should Southerners change from slavery-generated, sky-high profits to mediocre returns? Add to this the social division that protected the white-dominated United States, and one has an unbeatable institution that is not as "peculiar" as modern Americans think. Politics, not profit, challenged the slave system.

SLAVERY AS A POSITIVE GOOD, THEORY OF. The Civil War South believed that **slavery** benefited the entire nation. But **antislavery** and **abolitionist** Northerners of the **Republican** Party did not share their views, especially after the decision in the 1857 U.S. **Supreme Court** case *Dred Scott v. Sanford* endorsed it.

The tenet that slavery was advantageous accompanied the birth of the nation. Before 1830, the Old South defended slavery, albeit in a contrite way, as a necessary evil, but still legal. Opposition to slavery in the South was limited to bluestocking pundits such as **Thomas Jefferson**, who rarely practiced what they preached, or more practical men like **George Washington**, **James Madison**, and **James Monroe**, who were benevolent enough to free their chattels upon their deaths.

In the 1830s, after the slave revolts of Denmark Vesey in Charleston, South Carolina, and Nat Turner in Southampton County, Virginia, the South's support of slavery was threatened in two incidents. In Virginia, the politicians of the Tidewater and the mountains debated the issue, which betokened the state's schism during the Civil War. Historians cite this **Great Debate** as evidence of slavery's many opponents in the South.

But the few abolition advocates in either section of the state believed the owner should be compensated and the freed slaves transported out of Virginia or back overseas. At the concurrent Tennessee constitutional convention, a debate on the issue failed when the committee reported that slavery was the only way whites and blacks could live together without fear of a holocaust as previously took place in **Haiti**.

But the most significant augury manifested in South Carolina, just as secession did 30 years later. This was the tenet of slavery as a positive good, for North and South, white and black. The Positive Good Doctrine preceded the abolitionist attack by several years, contrary to the popular belief that followed. The Slavery as a Positive Good argument was based on several principles: The South's definition of slavery was not the North's. Under the slaveholders' belief that their power was limited to property rights, Southerners argued that slaves merely lost their right in self-ownership. They still enjoyed the rights to life, marriage, happiness, and so on, provided they continued to serve master and mistress in return for their daily sustenance.

The historical argument for slavery was also a strong point of contention. In nearly every society, especially Jewish, Greek, and Roman, endurance and tolerance of slavery justified its righteousness. The South was notably cognizant that slaves were taken captive by the victors in wars, and their own slaves were losers in African intertribal wars. For centuries, international law thinkers espoused the condition to prevent wholesale slaughter of prisoners of war.

One argument posited that slavery or barbarism was inborn in the African. Their natural habitat in Africa sustained their condition as savages incapable of modern invention. In Haiti, they returned to the same status after gaining their freedom. In the British West Indies, abolition thwarted the local economies. At home, unable and unwilling to improve themselves, the free blacks' standard of living was barely above savagery. The North harbored its own racist beliefs, which ignored the legal and informal discriminations that perpetuated this condition.

The South wielded the theories of contemporary science to prove their points, emphasizing ethnicity—blacks were widely classified as inferior. Many Southerners admitted that slavery would be an abomination if blacks were biologically equal to whites. Craniology, as popular as spiritualism in the 19th century, played a strategic part. Dr. Samuel G. Morton pointed out that Caucasian skulls had a forehead slope of 80°, whereas blacks were about 70°, closer to the apes' 68°. In this pre-Darwinian age, scientists also believed in the distinct origins of the races; not one, but several creations.

Dr. Josiah Nott of Mobile was well versed in this field of study. His laboratory was filled with the skulls of whites, blacks, and apes on which he conducted comparisons. Nott and George Glidden wrote the 1854 classic, *Types of Mankind*. Nott's follow-up, *Indigenous Races of the Earth,* was published in 1857. Another "negro doctor" (a title that encompassed a multitude of sins), Dr. Samuel A. Cartwright theorized that an orangutan, not the serpent, had tempted Eve in the Garden of Eden. He based his theory on the hypothesis of the British Dr. Adam Clark that Eve's bait to iniquity walked erect, spoke, and reasoned. "If he had lived in Louisiana, instead of Britain," said Cartwright, "he would have recognized the NEGRO GARDENER." John L. Cabell of Virginia censured much of Cartwright's and Nott's claims out of hand.

The Bible was a powerful influence in Victorian America, and was cited many times to validate slavery. Documented sources ranged from the fourth and tenth commandments to the usual curse on the descendants of Ham from Genesis. John Fletcher of Natchez, Mississippi, wrote an 1852 tome, *Studies in Slavery in Easy Lessons*, which illustrated in biblical verses from Genesis, Leviticus, and Joshua in the Old Testament, Luke and several of Paul's Letters in the New Testament that black slavery was divinely inspired.

The social justifications of slavery were just as numerous. The South maintained that the hierarchy of classes and races confirmed the superiority of slave society over free society. By definition, slavery made all whites more equal to one another. The distinct class structure in the North distinguished the haves from the have-nots. Those without property indulged in various "isms" (Fourierism, anarchism, socialism, free rentism, free love-ism, perfectionism, Seventh-Day Adventism, Mormonism, and especially abolitionism) that forced government to place restrictions upon the lower classes. The 'Mudsill Theory' of South Carolina's **James Hammond** claimed that slavery was necessary for blacks to perform the drudgery of society to free the whites for higher purposes of intellect and governance. Also of South Carolina, **John C. Calhoun**'s position on this class struggle aspect of Northern society gave him the title the "Marx of the Master Class" one hundred years later.

According to this logic, if slavery were so good for society, certain reforms would benefit everyone. In the 1850s, the **Black Codes** of the South were amended to emphasize their "humane" features, to make slavery appear more attractive, and protect slaves from inhumane owners. The South then demanded the reopening of the **international slave trade** that the **Constitution** had closed in 1808. They believed such a Positive Good institution encompassing the benefits of civilization and Christianization must be extended and sustained. In May 1859, a Southern Commercial Convention at Vicksburg, Mississippi, proposed just that. But the Civil War ensued, invalidating the suggestion.

SLAVERY IN THE CITIES. Although the South was noted as a rural area when compared to the North, before the Civil War, it did have many important cities that exercised an influence disproportionate to their numbers. By 1860, there were 30 places of over

8,000 inhabitants, although most were located around the periphery of the region. These included New Orleans (the largest city in the South), Charleston, Mobile, Richmond, Baltimore, Washington and the District of Columbia, Louisville, St. Louis, Nashville, and Memphis.

The premier historian of slavery in Southern cities is Richard Wade. His principle argument is that by the time of the Civil War **slavery** was slowly disintegrating as an institution in the urban South. The decline was not economic. It involved slavery as a social institution of racial separation and control. The big problem was that the slave got lost track of in the city environment's great push toward individual anonymity, regardless of color.

In the eyes of the slaveholding South, according to Wade, the city was "corrupting" the slave system. The black slaves were losing track of their "proper," subordinate places in white society because of the complex nature of city life and the contact and interchange of attitudes and ideas. The result was that slaves began to act free. They became insolent, intractable, and totally worthless as slaves.

Social life included attending mixed-race balls, having casual acquaintances, attending the same churches, patronizing the same stores. There was also the chance for increased sexual contact, usually between white males and black females. Plantation isolation and discipline was missing.

But no matter what their stations in life, finally, blacks in the city were not under as much white supervision. It was a great place for **runaway slaves** to hide, to separate from whites in all aspects of life and enjoy being black without white interference. Essentially, the city demanded fluidity in life while the plantation enforced rigidity in life.

Given the breakdown in the rigidity of slave institutions, Wade says, white Southern authorities tried to compensate by developing new social constructs for the cities. The first was to get rid of blacks living in the city by selling slaves to the countryside where white control was more absolute. Since fieldhands were in great demand in the 1850s, city slaveowners could make a fine profit selling their slaves to plantations.

By the time of the Civil War, the major owners of slaves in the cities were those who practiced **industrial slavery**. The cities were becoming more white and the countryside more black. The city environment was destroying slavery as an institution between 1845 and 1860.

Finally, barring any decline in slaves in the city, Wade sees the Southern city as the place that segregation laws first appear in the South. This was a device to keep blacks and whites from getting too close and crossing "natural" racial "differences." Everything was to be sorted out conveniently by race.

Meanwhile, several other historians challenged Wade's notions by examining slavery in smaller towns and more extensively than Wade had in New Orleans. They painted a completely opposite picture of slavery in the cities. First, Wade's critics discovered that in New Orleans and the smaller Louisiana towns, few slaves were sold to the countryside. Second, the absolute numbers of slaves in the Louisiana towns and cities did not decrease but grew steadily between 1845 and 1860. An increasing white population was bringing more slaves into town for their own use and profit. Third, while segregation was ingrained in law, it was not present in practice. Indeed, all laws, including white patrols to curb slave infractions at night, curfew, liquor sale regulations, the sale and purchase of stolen property, and unsupervised assemblage, were ignored by whites and blacks alike. Finally, there was less competition between whites and blacks at various trades than Wade supposed. The tradesmen divided jobs up by race and some were allotted to blacks only.

The conclusion of Wade's critics was that slavery was far from a disintegrating institution in Southern urban areas. Rather it was a vigorous, growing institution that actually offered an entrance into slave ownership on a small scale that allowed white entrepreneurs to expand into other endeavors almost at will.

SLAVERY IN THE NORTH, ABOLITION OF. *See* ABOLITION OF SLAVERY IN THE NORTH.

SLAVERY IN WASHINGTON, D.C. *See* WASHINGTON, D.C., SLAVERY IN.

SLAVES, CARE AND MAINTENANCE OF. The master's expenditures for food, clothing, shelter, medical care, and old-age care were in a sense wages, but slaveowners referred to them as maintenance costs. How good these living standards were depended on the master's education, information, and disposition, where the plantation was located (those on the frontier had less), and the status of the slave (fieldhands got less attention, house servants received more). But all masters knew that the slaves were a notch above livestock in their needs.

Southerners were generally proud of the care the slaves received. Planters liked to compare slave living standards with free workers in the North, but they overlooked one big difference between slave and free labor. No matter how bad the living standards of free workers, free laborers always could improve their condition in life. The slave rarely got this chance.

The diet of the adult slave was something like a peck of cornmeal and three or four pounds of bacon or salt meat each week. Molasses was thrown in for sweetness. The meat, meal, and molasses combination has come to be known as the three Ms. The better plantations served coffee, but the others served coffee substitutes, like boiled acorns. A child counted as one-third of an adult for the purpose of rations. Few slaves starved, there was plenty of bulk, but the diet was not balanced. The other side of the story was that most masters rarely ate better, although they might get more. It was common for the slaves to eat their seven-day ration in five, and starve over the weekend. Hence all storerooms, smokehouses, and corncribs were under lock and key, generally kept in the hands of the **plantation mistress**.

There were lots of quack medical articles on nutrition before the Civil War in Southern agricultural journals. The health problems of white and black alike were not mitigated any by the poor medical treatment available. Medical science was practically non-existent in the 19th century. Bloodletting, castor oil, calomel, jalap, and salts were popular. The hygienic value of soap was poorly understood. There also existed a belief that blacks and whites were so different as to require different medical procedures. This led to the specialty of Negro medicine, often practiced by a veterinarian. It did have one advantage. Blacks relied more on folk remedies that usually kept them out of the hands of incompetent doctors. In general, when one sent for a doctor in the Old South, death was not far behind. *See also* SLAVERY.

SLAVES, RUNAWAY. *See* RUNAWAY SLAVES.

SLIDELL, JOHN (1793–1871). Originally from New York, John Slidell studied law at Columbia and entered the mercantile business only to be ruined by the **Embargo Act** and the **War of 1812**. He removed to New Orleans in 1819 to avoid arrest for **dueling** and practiced law. Slidell married into a prominent Creole family and became a Southerner in all but birth. He was a state **Democrat** legislator, U.S. District Attorney, a member of Congress, and U.S. Minister to Mexico. But as the **War with Mexico** was brewing, Mexico refused to receive him and he returned home. He was one of Louisiana's U.S. Senators in the 1850s and opposed **Stephen A. Douglas** and his Popular Sovereignty. He left the senate with Louisiana's **secession**.

At home, Slidell was allied with **Judah P. Benjamin** against **Pierre Soulé**, all of them by then being Democrats. When Soulé threatened to lead Louisiana in secession, Slidell and Benjamin returned home to take over the new movement and maintain their hold on Louisiana government. Benjamin was rewarded with a cabinet position in the Confederate government while Slidell received the appointment of roving ambassador to Europe.

Along with a co-appointee, James Y. Mason of Virginia, Slidell slipped through the Union blockade to Havana and took the British ship *Trent* to England. While at sea, the *Trent* was stopped by a Union warship and Slidell and Mason were arrested and kidnapped.

After a two-week confinement, Union President Abraham Lincoln released the two Confederate emissaries with an apology and they continued to Europe. While Mason went to Great Britain, Slidell concentrated on getting the French to recognize the Confederacy. He also helped negotiate the Erlanger loan for the South by marrying one of his daughters into the Erlanger family. Although the French-speaking Slidell was popular with the French government and people, Mason failed to get the British to act, and France would not recognize Southern independence without the prior backing of the British navy.

Slidell remained in France throughout the Civil War and neither sought nor was offered a pardon. He supported the French invasion of Mexico and, when that failed, he removed to London where he joined his old political ally, Benjamin.

SMITH, THOMAS. *See* RICE.

SOCIAL HIERARCHY. As with all societies, that of the Old South had a definite pecking order to it. The first and most obvious division was by race. The whites determined all that the blacks could do, legally. Although blacks were primarily the property of the white element, some few blacks were free by birth, or by action of themselves, purchasing their freedom by hiring out their time, or by their former masters through manumission papers.

The white part of society was patriarchal in authority. The father had absolute authority over his family, by law and tradition. Under his care were his wife and children, and possibly some extended family. At the top of white society were the slaveholders. Although modern readers automatically think of massive white plantation houses framed by towering pillars and approached by oak-tree-lined alleys, most **plantation masters** owned less than a half dozen slaves. They lived in double log houses with a covered breezeway between. Servants lived on one side and the family on the other. The white family worked alongside its slaves in the kitchen, supervised by the **plantation mistress**, or in the fields under the master's eye. On larger plantations, the slave force was usually divided into manageable groups of 50 or less, each led by a white **overseer**. If a planter were very wealthy, he might own several plantations in more than one state. Each group of plantations would be supervised by a **plantation steward** with the overseers reporting to him.

Most of the whites in the Old South were **non-slaveholders**. These people supported the slave system, however, seeing it as their way to future riches. The non-slaveholders included professional men (although many planters were doctors or lawyers on the side), skilled tradesmen (usually referred to as mechanics), industrialists (employing slave or free black labor or white mechanics, or a combination of both), storekeepers, and itinerant drummers (many of whom were Yankees). At the bottom were those condescendingly called poor whites, poor white trash, or "po' buckra" by the slaves of more important planters. But their prevalence is exaggerated in most stereotypes of the Old South; they belong more properly to the flotsam of the post–Civil War era.

While most white slaveholders owned fewer than a half dozen slaves, most black chattels were raised and worked on the larger plantations. At the top of the black society were the free people of color, some of whom had been free for generations. A few select freemen owned slaves, as many a hundred slaves in certain coastal sections of Louisiana. But almost all black slaveholders owned the members of their own family, who were free in actuality, if not by law.

Another oddity of slavery in the Old South was that not all slaves were coal black. Many of their ancestors came from African tribes that ranged in color from black to many shades of brown. In addition, **miscegenation** was common in America from the arrival of the first blacks. The result was that some slaves were virtually white in appearance. Very often the whiter slaves were used as domestic workers. In such capacities, they learned much about the white world and with the proper habits and clothing, could even pass for white and escape to freedom in a Southern city, the North, or Canada. The general rule was that if one looked white, was one-eighth or less black by blood, and acted white, one could probably pass for white, especially in the free states or British Canada. Thousands did it, although males seemed to be the most successful, as they were not burdened by children like women were.

Among the black slaves there were social classes, too. At the top were slave foremen, referred to as **drivers**. They set the pace in the fields, judiciously, so that the weaker would not be singled out as slow workers. Drivers were used when the plantation workforce was divided into gangs in which several slaves would labor at the same job. There were plow gangs (generally men), hoe gangs (both men and stronger women), and trash gangs (comprised of the old, weaker adults and children) that cleaned up after the others. On rice plantations in particular, the labor was assigned as a task. Here, each slave would handle an individual job with a daily quota. Often, if a slave completed the assigned quota ahead of time, the rest of the day was free time.

At a par with the foremen were a group of skilled slave artisans capable of working at a specific trade. These were blacksmiths, leather crafters, woodworkers, bricklayers, and the like, who made the plantation a self-sufficient place. Often such slaves were hired out by the master to nearby planters or non-slaveholding whites who needed a particular skilled tradesman for a specific job. Such slaves often made up the estate of a widow or spinster, who hired out her slaves and lived off their income. Owners never hired out an expensive slave if the job was considered dangerous—free white laborers like the Irish handled these onerous tasks. Particularly lucky skilled workers, usually in a town situation, would be allowed to hire themselves out and sometimes a percentage of their income would be placed against earning their eventual freedom.

Another step above the fieldhand was working in the Big House as a domestic. Maids, butlers, cooks, and nurses worked as body servants to the white family. They often slept on a pallet at the foot of their master and mistress' bed and were on beck and call 24 hours a day. These house servants are sometimes seen as spies in the black community for the white man, but the infiltration worked the other way around, too. House slaves picked up loads of information as they worked to serve meals, greeted plantation guests, and drove the master and mistress to town and other plantations.

Perhaps no house slave had a more important position than the black mammy. She was often a power unto herself. She supervised other servants, raised the white children even more than their own mothers right down to breastfeeding them as infants, and kept white and black in line with an iron hand. Few dared to contradict mammy; even smart planters generally let her have her way. She could be a white informer, but many a warning about bad things to come got to the quarters because of mammy's outward closeness to the white world and inward loyalty to the black.

It was standard practice in the Old South to rate every slave as a full or partial hand. There were quarter hands, half hands, three-quarter hands, and full hands. A hand could do a full day's work with a hoe in the field. The elderly, infirm, female, or young were usually given the partial ratings. Unlike the patriarchal white family, the black family was matriarchal, by law and by custom. Although the black father was not recognized by law as a part of the slave family, he did act in that manner by custom in the slave quarters. But his authority was always that which the white master allowed him. All in all, equality between genders was closer in the black, slave society than in the free, white society because of the uncertainties of the peculiar institution. *See also* SOCIALIZATION, WOMEN IN THE OLD SOUTH.

SOCIALIZATION. One of the common threads that can be woven between all classes and both races in the Old South was the enjoyment of leisure time. While many activities crossed class and racial lines, each major group in the Old South, the **plantation masters**, the poorer whites, and the blacks, slave and free, enjoyed different ways of recreating.

The planter class liked nothing better than a good horse race. Many plantations raised blooded stock and racing was quite competitive. Jockeys were often slave boys, lithe and weightless to the big thoroughbreds that pounded around the course. Nearer county seats and larger towns, the rich set up formal racecourses with grandstands and an exclusive country-club environment. Horseback riding was a perennial Southern skill for men and **women** alike, as the North would find out during the Civil War, when expert Confederate cavalry rode roughshod over many a Union war plan.

The wealthy did other things for recreation. They sat for portraits, utilizing the services of traveling artists. They held lavish receptions, parties, dances, and formal balls, and barbeques in the style described by Margaret Mitchell for the Twelve Oaks Plantation in *Gone with the Wind*. Such gatherings also included the slaves from many plantations, who not only served the guests, but partied on their own behind the scenes.

The white middle classes had their own more simple dances, horse races, and parties. Concerts offered by local fiddlers, pianists, and folk singers were popular. One activity that all classes and races especially liked was the circus. At first these were offered at taverns and the audience restricted to white males. But soon traveling shows featured acrobats, clowns, and various animal acts and drew men, women and children, slave and free alike. The circus could be a relatively expensive affair. Shows frequently charged as much as 75 cents for adults and two bits for children and slaves.

The white small farmers, who worked in the field with their few slaves, often made work part of their entertainment. The results were certain group activities that promoted community wealth. There were quiltings, hog killings, barn raisings, corn shuckings, and other harvest activities, all followed by a barbeque. Such activities also included sports competitions, including wrestling, boxing, and various tests of strength for men and their horse or mule teams. Marksmanship was prized, and contests involving such things as shooting the head off a turkey, driving nails into a log, or plinking other targets were popular. Sometimes everyone would gather after the dinner and engage in a mass hunt through the corn fields, shooting varmints that might damage future crops.

The slaves also enjoyed their own leisure enjoyments, generally under the supervision of their owners, but sometimes not. Because no one wanted to sit up all night and monitor slave activities, as soon as the planter and his family and minions were asleep, the quarters often hummed with secret meetings, visits to nearby plantations, and feasts on stolen food or poached game. Stories, songs, and folktales lasted into the night. Youngsters were carefully warned to keep mum about all of this so that the planter did not find out and punish the offenders. Nighttime visitation off the plantation had to be done with great stealth lest the violators be caught and whipped by the slave patrol, whites who patrolled the roads and trails to interdict such activities.

Particularly popular were holidays like Sundays, Christmas, New Years, and the Fourth of July. Each involved free time off from work and, for those who had been hard workers in the fields, passes to town or to nearby plantations to visit friends, lovers, relatives, and acquaintances. The slaves liked to show off their physical abilities and held sporting contests like ballplaying, wrestling, jumping, foot races, and boxing. Afterward there would be a barbeque, followed by a dance.

One of the favorite holidays for both races in the Old South was Christmas. The slaves often got several days off. There was caroling, gift giving, the burning of Yule logs, and, in some areas, Christmas tree decorating. Another favorite, July Fourth, would feature a reading of the Declaration of Independence, political speeches, a dinner or barbeque, and an endless round of toasts.

Perhaps the one leisure activity that caused many to look askance was interracial gambling at so-called "Negro Bars." While the planters would bet on anything without notice, authorities feared that this lower-class mixing of whites and blacks, slave and free promoted too many vices, like drunkenness and fights. The stakes for the bets often involved stolen goods. And it just looked untidy to the powers that be that the dregs of both races should be congregating in an unsupervised manner. *See also* SOCIAL HIERARCHY.

SOIL DEPLETION. *See* TOBACCO.

"SOOTHING SYRUP" PARTY. *See* CONSTITUTIONAL UNION PARTY.

SOULÉ, PIERRE (1802–1870). Pierre Soulé was born in Castillon, France, and educated in Jesuit schools in Toulouse and Bordeaux. Following his involvement in a plot to overthrow Louis XVIII, he fled to the Pyrenees, where he worked as a shepherd. After the regime change, he returned to France and, as a journalist, wrote a caustic treatise of the ministers of Charles X. Once again, he fled ahead of the police to Britain and then to **Haiti** and the United States. While working as a gardener and learning English, he lived in Maryland, Kentucky, and Tennessee before finally arriving in New Orleans. There he read law and was admitted to the bar.

Soulé fit in perfectly with French-speaking Louisiana. In 1845, he served one year in the Louisiana state senate and, in 1847, served one term in the U.S. Senate as a **Democrat**. Under the **Franklin Pierce** administration, Soulé was appointed minister to Spain and co-authored the controversial **Ostend Manifesto**, calling for the annexation of Cuba to the U.S. He was soon recalled to New Orleans and resumed his law practice. He backed **Stephen A. Douglas** for president in the **election of 1860** and, although a Unionist, he supported the **secession** of his state.

During the Civil War, Soulé made several diplomatic trips to Europe on behalf of the **Confederacy**. Back in occupied New Orleans, he was arrested and faced a firing squad, but a last-minute change in Union commanding generals saved his life. He then served as a staff officer for Gen. P. G. T. Beauregard at the Siege of Charleston, and made an unsuccessful bid to recruit a foreign legion to serve the Confederacy. After the war, he fled to Cuba and financed a program to settle Confederate veterans in Maximilian's Mexico. He later returned to New Orleans and practiced law until his death in 1870. *See also* SLIDEL, JOHN.

SOUTH CAROLINA EXPOSITION AND PROTEST. *See* CONCURRENT VOICE AND NULLIFICATION.

SOUTHAMPTON REVOLT (1831). Although many of the alleged 250 slave rebellions in the United States were unsubstantiated plots, the one in Southampton, Virginia, in 1831 definitely was not. Indeed, it was the bloodiest in American history. Southampton was a county in economic decline located on the south side of the James River. It was, like the rest of the South, noticing the rise of the **abolitionists** in the North for the first time. Virginia also was about to mull over the efficacy of slavery in the Great Debates as it drew up a new constitution.

Worse, from just across the North Carolina line came a free man of color, **David Walker**, who had moved to Boston, Massachusetts, and in 1829 published his *Appeal*, which declared the American slaves to be the most degraded persons in the world, held in such bondage and ignorance as not to realize how bad off they truly were. Walker called for revolt of the slaves and execution of the slaveholders. The *Appeal* spread all across the South despite attempts to cull it from the mails. Southampton was especially edgy because it had a large population of slaves shipped in from St. Domingue in years past, before it became the free black nation of **Haiti**. Walker's message was not muted any, even though he was found dead under suspicious circumstances shortly after issuing his *Appeal*.

All of these happenings were believed to have had an influence on Nat Turner, a slave preacher of great intelligence in his early thirties and an advocate of Old Testament teachings. Turner was prematurely balding and wore his facial hair in a sort of abbreviated Van Dyk style. His body was marked from countless scars. Yankees claimed it came from poor treatment and constant whippings. Southern whites asserted he obtained them in numerous knife fights. But Turner said he had them from birth—the mark of God, making him an unusual man. Fellow slaves seemed to agree with Turner and called him the "Prophet."

Turner had a vision of black revolution. He saw and communed with the spirits, divinely sent messengers from God who told him scientific truths about the elements, the sun, and the stars. He saw black and white angels fighting against each other, harbingers of what was to come on earth. Then God told Turner by way of an eclipse to get ready, for the day was at hand— 4 July 1831. But Turner was sick that day. God understood. He sent another sign. The sun appeared green in August for several days from atmospheric disturbances. Turner would move on Sunday, 21 August 1831.

Turner and six cohorts gathered on the fateful Sunday. They ate, drank, and planned. That evening they struck at Turner's own master, Joseph Travis, and the Travis family. Even though the Travises were kind owners, Turner and his men showed no mercy. By prior agreement, every white was to be killed regardless of gender or age. Within 48 hours, Turner's original six had expanded into a small company of 70 and laid waste to a 20-mile swath across the county, killing 55.

There was no opposition until the group approached the county seat at Jerusalem (Courtland today). Turner's men had paused for a rest and to recruit on surrounding plantations. The Virginia militia surprised them with their guard down and scattered the rebels. Then, with the aid of North Carolina militia and regular U.S. troops, the area was scoured and all suspects arrested or shot down. The contingent with Nat Turner at its head was defeated at a nearby plantation and all taken but Turner. In the end, 53 blacks were arrested and tried, of whom 20 were hanged, 12 transported to the West Indies, and 21 acquitted. Over 100 black suspects never made it to trial, dying at the hands of a vengeful militia in the wild.

Hiding for two and a half months in haystacks, a cave, and a fallen log, Turner was accidentally stumbled over by a local white and taken to Jerusalem. At his trial in November, Turner pled not guilty— or at least he said that he did not feel guilty. It did not matter. He was hanged on 11 November. Before he was hanged he "confessed" to his white attorney, Thomas R. Gray, who wrote the statement up and published it as *The Confessions of Nat Turner*. Later, modern novelist William Styron would cause much controversy by turning it into a look at Turner's whole life, only to be challenged as a white man who could not hope to comprehend a black man's true inner thoughts. *See also* SLAVE RESISTANCE AND REBELLION.

SOUTHERN MOVEMENT. *See* **COMPROMISE OF 1850.**

SOUTHWEST ORDINANCE. The South refused to ratify the U.S. **Constitution** unless provision was made for the expansion of slavery into the West, prohibited in the **Northwest Ordinance**. The North yielded. In exchange for repassage of the Articles of Confederation's Land Law of 1787 or Northwest Ordinance, Congress passed the Southwest Ordinance in 1790. It was for all practical purposes an extension of the Northwest Ordinance on territorial government and the Land Ordinance of 1784 on the rectangular survey.

But, as part of the agreement by which North Carolina ceded control of its Western land claims in what was to become Tennessee, no prohibition on slavery was inserted. The creation of the Mississippi Territory in 1798 opened the district of the present-day states of Alabama and Mississippi to slavery by making no prohibition of the institution, although some Northern congressmen wanted it, and made possible a final solution to the **Yazoo Land Frauds,** again with no exclusion or, rather, no mention of slavery being prohibited.

SPECIE CIRCULAR. *See* BANK WAR; PANIC OF 1837.

SPOILS SYSTEM. *See* JACKSON'S FIRST ADMINISTRATION.

SPOT RESOLUTION. *See* WAR WITH MEXICO.

SPREAD EAGLE FOREIGN POLICY. Under the **Franklin Pierce** and **James Buchanan** administrations, the United States undertook "Spread Eagle" foreign policy, embracing support for the Monroe Doctrine (Europe to stay out of the Americas, America to stay out of European questions) and expansion into the American West and Latin America. **Manifest Destiny**, the conviction that expansion was America's God-given right, was the term generally in use at the time.

Among Spread Eagle foreign policy's aspects was the precept of **"Young America,"** the view of the United States as a youthful, burgeoning republic, unlike the "effete monarchies" of Europe, which Americans considered on the decline. It was incumbent upon the United States to back the European revolutionaries of 1848: to give them military and political aid while fighting in the streets and grant them U.S. asylum after the revolutions failed. In their fervent single-mindedness, Americans ignored this blatant violation of the Monroe Doctrine.

Spread Eagle foreign policy also encompassed American interest in trade with the Orient. In accord with the old bromide, the United

States was to follow the setting sun to riches and glory. Hawaii was an integral leg of the voyage from the Isthmus of Panama to San Francisco. Because of tides and winds, Hawaii was the first port of call for California-bound ships en route to their continental destinations. The U.S. Senate rejected Franklin Pierce's attempts to annex Hawaii.

China also had great magnetism for the United States. British concessions won in the Opium Wars induced the United States to demand and receive trading rights in five Chinese ports in the 1844 Treaty of Wanghia, an example of "jackal diplomacy." It guaranteed America equal rights with any other power through any other treaty. In 1858, when Great Britain and France forced the Treaty of Tientsin on China, the earlier Treaty of Wanghia gave the United States the same expanded rights of trade.

Interest in Japan, an important stopover for coal and provisions, naturally followed. After extremist Christian missionary zeal resulted in dissatisfaction in Japan, she closed her ports to all Westerners. Com. Matthew C. Perry visited Tokyo Bay in 1852 with a great fleet that included the first steam warship the Japanese had ever seen. Claiming he was carrying letters from the American president to the Japanese emperor, Perry shunned all but the highest authorities. He threatened war if rebuffed, but departed after a 10-day stalemate.

He returned the following year with an even more imposing fleet. Under pressure from Japanese merchants, the government agreed to the Perry Pact, requiring fair treatment to shipwrecked sailors, fuel and water for ships in need, and some trade. The United States pledged not to request extraterritorial rights as other Western powers had in China. Townsend Harris arrived as the first American consul, persuading the wary Japanese to sign the Harris Treaty of 1858. The treaty, which lasted until 1911, opened more ports, secured trade and residence rights for Americans with extraterritorial judicial privileges, and expedited the exchange of ministers, or ambassadors.

Latin America was another region ripe for American expansion. But irregular military expeditions called **filibustering,** rather than formal diplomacy, was the norm there, popular among the sons of the slave South, especially Louisiana's.

SQUATTER SOVEREIGNTY. This arose out of the idea that a territory's residents could vote to abolish **slavery** any time prior to achieving statehood. As its strongest and most outspoken advocate, **Lewis Cass** of Michigan backed it as the **Democrat** candidate in the **election of 1848**. The inverse of the Southern-favored concept of **Popular Sovereignty**, it was a misleading formula excluding Southerners. It lacked the hostility instigated by the **Wilmot Proviso** as understood by its staunchest adversary **John C. Calhoun**, the most important Southern senator of the era and a key spokesman for the South. Yankees outnumbered Southerners in the territories and, with the support of anti-slave Mexicans, the Old South feared that they would wield control over territorial governments and vote for free soil before late-arriving Southern settlers could make their influence felt.

STAPLE CROPS. In British mercantilism, staple crops are the raw materials grown in colonies and sent to the mother country to be processed in home industry. It was this that gave value to the British North American colonies south of the **Mason–Dixon Line**. While the colonies to the north of the line tended to compete with home industries, or rely on subsistence agriculture, those to the south of the line grew products that could be made into something or emphasized commercial agriculture for the British home islands. Southern staples included **rice, indigo,** naval stores, and **tobacco** in the colonial era, with the addition of **cotton, sugar,** and **hemp** after the American Revolution. The South also produced much **corn** and **livestock** that tended to replace New England cod as the main food for slaves as the new nation expanded westward in the **Great Migration**.

STEPHENS, ALEXANDER H. (1812–1883). Born in Georgia, Alexander Stephens attended private institutions to prepare him for the ministry. But upon graduation from Franklin College, now the University of Georgia, he pursued law and then politics as a **Whig Party** legislator opposed to **Nullification**. After attending the Charleston Commercial Convention, he was elected to Congress in 1843. He backed the annexation of the Republic of Texas, but in his disagreement with President **John Tyler**'s course of action, he devised his own, which was the basis for Texas' admission to the Union. He backed his friend, Congressman **Abraham Lincoln** of Illinois, in protesting the **War with Mexico**. Nevertheless, he agreed that the result benefited the South and opposed the **Wilmot Proviso**'s limitation of **slavery** expansion.

In 1850, Stephens favored compromise over the Southern movement. In his Georgia Platform, he stated that the South would acknowledge the **Compromise of 1850** and continued Union, however reluctantly, but zealously continue to defend its rights. Stephens refused to back Whig presidential candidate, Bvt. Lt. Gen. **Winfield Scott** when Scott refused to support the Compromise of 1850 or offer his backing to the extension of slavery into the territories. When Stephens led the **Kansas–Nebraska Bill** to fruition in the House in 1854, the Southern Whigs broke off from their Northern counterparts for good. Stephens supported President **James Buchanan** on the **Popular Sovereignty** issue, but when Buchanan violated its principles in the **Kansas Settlement,** Stephens resigned his House seat.

Stephens supported **Stephen A. Douglas** in the **election of 1860**. In 1861, he favored cooperation with the Lincoln administration until it committed an overt act against the South. Nonetheless, Stephens backed the **secession** of Georgia, which won him the vice presidency of the provisional government of the Confederacy at Montgomery in 1860 and again in the **Confederate election of 1861**. In his famous "Cornerstone Speech" delivered at Savannah, he proclaimed slavery was the essence of the Confederacy. But Stephens' theories of state rights were at odds with the realities of war. The States Rights Faction in the **Confederate government** supported him, but instead of leading, he spent most of the war at home in Georgia. He blamed the **Jefferson Davis** administration for avoiding peace. In retaliation, Davis sent him to the Hampton Roads Peace Conference in 1865, where Stephens renewed his acquaintance with his old friend Lincoln but admitted Southern surrender was his only option.

In 1865, Stephens was arrested for treason at his home and lodged in Ft. Warren at Boston Harbor for six months. Upon his release, he was elected to the U.S. Senate but was not seated. During Reconstruction he authored *A Constitutional View of the Late War between the States*. In 1872, he lost another bid for the U.S. Senate, but served in the U.S. House from 1874 until 1882. He was elected governor of Georgia the following year but died while in office. Regardless of party or office, Stephens' political principles remained fixed: state sovereignty, local government, and the greatest liberty to the individual.

STEWARDS, PLANTATION. *See* PLANTATION STEWARDS.

SUGAR. In spite of numerous experiments in Louisiana during the French regime before 1803, there was no widespread sugar industry. Louisiana was actually on the northern fringes of the optimal sugar-growing climate, and competition from the Caribbean islands, particularly St. Domingue in the case of the French, undercut the price and the need.

But in 1795, Etienne Boré brought in a skilled sugar maker and developed a successful crop. This, the Hatian Revolution, skilled sugar émigrés coming to Louisiana, and the eventual American accession by way of the **Louisiana Purchase**, changed everything. Now there was a vast American market to access and Louisiana was well on its way to becoming one of the richest plantation areas in the United States.

Louisiana's climate was at a distinct disadvantage when compared to the West Indies. This meant more replanting and lower crop yields per acre—up to 50 percent less than the Caribbean islands. This was somewhat mitigated in 1817 when Jean Jacques Coiron introduced ribbon cane, a hardier variety than that found in the islands. Louisiana sugar was replanted from seed every third year. The rest of the crop was ratoons, the replanting of stalks from previous harvests, that had been pulled up and covered with leaves and trash to keep them from freezing in the winter. The result was a four-field system of crop rotation: one in peas, two in ratoons, and one in seed cane.

The sugar was harvested in October with a cane knife. The task was about five acres per hand, although the slaves generally worked in gangs. As it was cut, each stalk was topped for its seeds and stripped of its leaves. The stalks were then sent to the grinding house, where they were crushed. The leaves and stalk remnants were then sent to the trash or bagasse house and dried to be used as fuel for the kettles, where the juice was boiled down. The first kettle was the grande, where the sugar maker added lime to the juice. The amount of lime added was a matter of individual judgment—sugar making was an art, not a science. As impurities boiled to the top, they were ladled off.

Then the juice passed on to successive kettles called the flambeau, sirop, and batterie (which was also variously known as the tache or concentrator). The by-then crystallized sugar was stored in hogsheads and the molasses drained off on a regular basis. This was distilled into rum. About 70 percent of the crop was marketed as sugar, and the rest was sold as either molasses or rum. The slaves, sheds, boiling houses, cooling houses, distillery, and kettles were a large investment, but the **tariff**-protected high returns made it all worthwhile.

One of the most unique characteristics of Louisiana's sugar country was its political adherence to the **Whig Party**, and **Henry Clay** and his **American System** with its high tariff provisions, including protection for Louisiana sugar. The constant demand and the tariff kept prices inordinately high for the whole pre–Civil War period. Louisiana justified this state of affairs by pointing out that it purchased food, slaves, and manufactured goods that more than offset any disadvantage the rest of the South suffered from the 30-percent sugar tariff. *See also* ECONOMY.

SUMNER, CHARLES. *See* BROOKS, PRESTON S.

SUPREME COURT. The Supreme Court was central to both solving and creating many of the problems of the antebellum years of 19th-century America. Much of its influence came from its chief justices, **John Marshall** and **Roger B. Taney**. Marshall acted as a Federalist, lasting so long on the bench as to be the last Federalist officeholder many years after the party had died out and been replaced by the **Whigs**. He spent his years creating the concept of judicial review of the acts of Congress and the state legislatures, and carving out a place for a strong federal presence in the governance of the United States.

Taney replaced Marshall as chief justice and spent an almost equal amount of time modifying Marshall's strong federal presence, reserving a secure place for the states under the U.S. Constitution. But in one matter he paralleled Marshall's powerful federal government. That was in the field of slavery, where Taney ruled federal law in interference of the **extraterritoriality** of slavery unconstitutional, and disallowed states to interfere with the law of slavery in or out of the South.

SWAMP LANDS ACT (1848, 1854). *See* JACKSON AND THE PUBLIC LANDS.

– T –

TALLMADGE AMENDMENT. *See* MISSOURI COMPROMISE.

TANEY, ROGER BROOKE (1777–1864). When **Supreme Court** Justice **John Marshall** died in 1835, President **Andrew Jackson** needed a replacement who would overturn Marshall's decisions. For this reason and for his political loyalty, he nominated **Democrat** Roger B. Taney (pronounced Taw-ney), a former **Federalist**. Born, raised, and educated in Calvert County, Maryland, Taney bravely supported unpopular issues, such as defending Gen. James Wilkinson against treason charges under the **Thomas Jefferson** administration, and providing sustenance for Taney's own freed slaves.

As treasury secretary, he gained national recognition by helping President Jackson withdraw federal deposits to destroy the **Second Bank of the United States**, but the **Whig**-dominated U.S. Senate rejected him when Jackson initially nominated him to the federal bench for disassembling the banking system, so essential to their economic policy. Jackson renominated Taney to the bench after a Democratic victory in the **election of 1836**, and the newly elected Senate confirmed him. Over the next 28 years, Taney modified John Marshall's proto-Whig economic decisions, which had taken 34 years and roughly paralleled the Whig's **American System**.

As chief justice, Taney was a strict constructionist (a literal reader of the U.S. Constitution) rather than a states righter. He reinforced the federal government's jurisdiction over **slavery**. He did not favor states rights like **secession**. Important cases decided under Taney's regime included *Charles River Bridge v. Warren Bridge* (1836), on behalf of free enterprise over monopolies; *Briscoe v. the Bank of Kentucky* (1837), on the right of states to charter banks; *William & James Brown & Company v. Thomas McGran* **(1840)**, on the law of factorage; *Prigg v. Pennsylvania* **(1842)**, in support of the Fugitive Slave Law of 1793; the License cases (1847), defining the right of a state to legislate on interstate commerce; *Dred Scott v. Sanford* **(1857)**, ruling that slavery could not be excluded in the territories; *Ableman v. Booth* **(1859)**, reaffirming and reinforcing the Prigg case, in reference to the **Fugitive Slave Law of 1850**; *ex parte* **Merryman (1861)**, protesting President **Abraham Lincoln**'s use of executive orders to institute arbitrary arrests in Taney's home state of Maryland by deciding that only Congress has the power to suspend *habeas corpus*.

TARIFF. Between the **War of 1812** and the **War with Mexico**, no single issue came closer to breaking up the North and Old South than the tariff. The first tax to protect infant American industries, the Tariff of 1816 was something even **Alexander Hamilton** had been unable to pass in the 1790s. The early tariffs before 1816 were solely for revenue purposes—just enough money to finance the federal government. The only sections of the nation in favor of the protective tariff were the Middle States (Pennsylvania, New Jersey, New York), which had most of America's industry. The Northwest and Southwest voted for the measure because they hoped to gain industry in the future; the Southeast was opposed to the tariff, but passed it as a defensive measure in case of future wars. Only New England was against the measure because it was still primarily a shipping area and feared retaliation from abroad.

Although the Tariff of 1816 had established a mildly protective tariff, that is, a low rate to help finance the operations of the federal government and protect some infant American manufacturers, in 1824 things began to change. In the intervening years, New England's economic base shifted from shipping to manufacture. From opposing the revenue Tariff of 1816, New England now wanted a high protective tariff to protect its infant industries. In this they were seconded by the Middle Atlantic states (especially New York and Pennsylvania), which also had manufactures to guard.

The result was a raising of the rates to 33 percent on all imported finished goods. This allowed American firms to raise their prices to just under the cost of foreign goods and turn a better profit. The South was against this rise, but easily outvoted in Congress.

After the raising of the tariff in 1824, manufacturers in the states north of Virginia desired to raise the rates on manufactured goods once again, this time to 50 percent. This vote was rigged to allow Vice President **John C. Calhoun** to break the tie in the Senate by voting "no." This was the opposite of his votes for the **New Nationalism** and indicated to the South he was "right" on this more and more heated sectional, as well as economic, issue. But Calhoun was actually being set up by **Martin Van Buren** and his cronies for the following year's debate and vote.

Also known as the Tariff of Abominations, the Tariff of 1828 was crucial to Martin Van Buren's building of the coalition that would become the **Democratic** Party. Joining with the Old Northwest, New England and New York and Pennsylvania wrote the highest tariff bill passed before the Civil War. The rates averaged 47 percent. They included a tariff on imported manufactured goods and, for the first time, raw materials. This protected the products of both Northeast industry and Northwest agricultural and mining concerns.

It used to be thought that the Southeast and Old Southwest put in the high rates on raw materials to get New England to vote against the bill. But New England decided that the tariff principle was more important than cheap raw materials and fooled everyone by voting for the bill. More recently, the Tariff of 1828 has been seen as a measure put forth by Van Buren to build party coalitions. He intended to get a strong tariff passed to extend the support of **Andrew Jackson** for president from the South to the North.

Van Buren knew that the South would never vote for **John Quincy Adams**—he was too hated. But now, with the Tariff of 1828, Jackson would carry states that were the bailiwick of Adams or **Henry Clay** and his **American System**. Jackson was safe on the tariff, especially in New York and Pennsylvania. It worked. Jackson swept the South and Middle Atlantic states in the **election of 1828**, took the West, and confined his opponents to New England, Delaware, Maryland, and New Jersey.

But Jackson and Van Buren proved a bit too clever for South Carolina, which nullified the Tariff of Abominations, as the Tariff of 1828 was viewed there. To take the sting out of the tariff and meet South Carolina's objections, the Tariff of 1832 was a carefully worked-out set of schedules designed to please. The new tariff cut many rates, particularly the ones affecting finished goods imported by the slave South, to 25 percent. Other items competitive with Northern manufactures were increased to 50 percent. The overall effect was to lower the tariff rates and provide more fair protection.

Even the congressmen from South Carolina favored it. President **Andrew Jackson** signed it immediately. But the Nullifiers attacked it and pledged that no customs would be collected in South Carolina after 1 February 1833. Henry Clay and **John C. Calhoun** modified the Tariff of 1832 with the Compromise Tariff of 1833. This measure would reduce all tariff rates gradually until an average rate of 20 percent was reached in 1842. The Tariff of 1833 would go into effect as a part of the Compromise of 1833, stealing credit from Jackson for solving the crisis.

After winning the **election of 1840**, the Whigs wanted guaranteed distribution of public lands, a pet project of Henry Clay's American System, to the states as a part of the tariff. But when **William Henry Harrison** died, **John Tyler** took his place. Tyler was definitely against high tariffs. The Congress passed a Little Tariff, which was at the average rate of 30 percent from the Tariff of 1832, with a distribution provision, but designed to last only 30 days, until it could iron out all the problems with President John Tyler.

But he vetoed it, objecting to the idea of any distribution. Congress then passed the Tariff of 1842. This put the average rates at 30 percent, but allowed distribution to end if the rates ever went above 20 percent. Tyler vetoed this, too. The Whigs in the House tried to impeach Tyler but lacked the votes. Finally they passed the Tariff of 1842 and specifically ended distribution with rates averaging at 30 percent as they had in 1832. This time the president signed it.

When the Democrats regained the presidency and control of Congress in 1844, James K. Polk moved to reduce the tariff once again. Known as the Walker Tariff, after its author Robert J. Walker of Mississippi, the Tariff of 1846 lowered rates and changed the methods of calculation from specific to ad valorem. After a brief respite devoted to the Compromise of 1850 and the Kansas–Nebraska Act, the Democrats in 1857 lowered the tariff to its lowest rate since 1816 of 20 percent. It would last only a short period until the South seceded from the Union. Then the Republicans would raise the rates close to 50 percent by 1864, and ever higher after the war.

TARIFF OF ABOMINATIONS. *See* TARIFF.

TAYLOR, JOHN, OF CAROLINE. *See* RUFFIN, EDMUND.

TAYLOR, ZACHARY (1784–1850). Born in Virginia, but privately tutored in Kentucky, Zachary Taylor enlisted in the army in 1808 through the Kentucky militia. In the **War of 1812** he held Ft. Harrison, Indiana, against attack and also fought in the Black Hawk War, the Seminole War (victory at Lake Okeechobee), and commanded the District of Florida. As commander of the army of occupation, he reinforced the American claim to the Río Grande as the international border between Texas and Mexico. Soon after, Mexican troops fired upon his troops in an incident which began the **War with Mexico.** Taylor then led a string of victories that culminated in the Battle of Buena Vista and the presidency as the **Whig Party** candidate in the **election of 1848**.

His term as president exposed the slaveholding Taylor's opposition to Southern legal ideals, such as **Squatter Sovereignty** and **Popular Sovereignty** as regarded **slavery** in the territories. He called for immediate admission of all territories, avoiding the slavery question, and until his plan was passed through Congress, he refused to consider the **Compromise of 1850**. With the country on the brink of Civil War, Taylor vociferously defended the issue, but died suddenly of gastroenteritis after a July 4 picnic. Upon assuming the presidency, Millard Fillmore and compromise forces in Congress, led by Senator **Stephen A. Douglas** of Illinois and Representative **Alexander H. Stephens** of Georgia, passed the Compromise of 1850, delaying war for another decade.

TECUMSEH. *See* WAR OF 1812.

TERTIUM QUIDS. *See* RANDOLPH, JOHN; YAZOO LAND FRAUDS.

TEXAS ANNEXATION. When **James K. Polk** won the **election of 1844** by vowing the "Re-annexation of Texas and the Re-occupation of Oregon," sitting President **John Tyler** decided to extend the **Three-Fifths Compromise** westward once more. The more giddy, like Missouri's Senator **Thomas Hart Benton**, thought that from five to nine states might be created from the Texas Republic once it was admitted to the union. The people had spoken. Why wait for Polk to accede to power? Tyler took the Treaty of Annexation and presented it to the Senate.

But there was a problem with the treaty. It would require a two-thirds vote. That was unachievable. Northerners were aghast at what

His Accidency, as many called Tyler for having come to office upon **William Henry Harrison**'s death, was trying to do. Massachusetts threatened to secede from the Union. But Tyler was not to be stopped. Prodded on by **Alexander Stephens** of Georgia, Tyler decided he could get Texas admitted by a joint resolution of both houses of Congress. That would require a simple majority vote. But it would involve the House as well as the Senate. Tyler was not worried. The House had 19 members elected under the **Three-Fifths Compromise**.

Tyler reasoned that in the Texas situation, unlike the **Louisiana Purchase**, there were only two parties (Texas and the United States), both in favor of annexation. In the case of Louisiana there had been three (Louisiana, France, and the United States). After Tyler and the South exerted great patronage pressure in the Senate, the joint resolution of annexation passed by one vote. The House gave it a majority of 22, all 19 of the three-fifths members voting "aye." Slavery was on the move west once again. But next time, in the Mexican Cession in 1848, the North would respond ahead of annexation with the **Wilmot Proviso** to limit the extension of slavery in the newly obtained territories.

TEXAS REVOLUTION. *See* LONE STAR REBELLIONS.

THOMAS AMENDMENT. *See* MISSOURI COMPROMISE.

THREE-FIFTHS COMPROMISE. Also known as the Federal Ratio, the Three-Fifths Compromise was a part (art. I, sect. 2) of the U.S. **Constitution** that allowed three-fifths of the slaves in the nation to be counted for the purposes of representation in Congress and for direct taxation. Under the defunct **Articles of Confederation**, each state had only one vote in Congress, regardless of population. But the new Constitution was going to apportion the House of Representatives by population. All of a sudden, the South was caught short of white males. Since the North had freed or soon would free its few slaves, and the protective **tariff** provided most government income before the Civil War, eliminating the need for direct taxes, the slaveholding South benefited greatly from extra so-called "Negro representatives" (even though only whites could vote for or serve in public office), which numbered at least 18 by the 1850s.

Why three-fifths, one might reasonably ask. Under the old Articles of Confederation, where each state had one vote in Congress, it had been proposed that national taxes be levied on everyone but Native Americans. The South was not about to be taxed for its black slaves without getting something in return. Black slaves, chattels as opposed to indentures who might be white, were property, just like horses and cattle, the South maintained. Southern men offered to allow taxation of each slave as half a person, but the North countered with three-fourths. After the debates stagnated, the Articles' convention settled on land as the basis for taxation. But since no state had to pay unless it desired, and none did unless under attack from the British Army, few national taxes were ever paid.

The same debate over taxes came up again in the Constitutional Convention. This time **James Madison** of Virginia proposed that black slaves be counted as three-fifths for purposes of taxation. This was a compromise between the South's old one-half and the North's old three-fourths. But now the Congress would be divided up on the basis of population, not one vote per state. So the South demanded three-fifths for both taxation and representation. The North said no. The South said that there would be no Constitution without it. The North yielded within a day. The Northern delegates believed that the main job was to get the Constitution functioning—quarrels could come later.

Although the South was outnumbered in the first congresses, with the **Great Migration**, these three-fifths representatives were at the core of what the North came to call the **Slave Power Conspiracy,** which allowed the South to at least get a head start on all important national policies in the antebellum years. In the years from George Washington's first election to 1850, the South controlled the presidency for 50 years, the Speaker of the House's position for 41 years, and the chair of the House Ways and Means Committee for 42 years. In addition, 19 out of 31 **Supreme Court** justices were Southerners. Close to 60 percent of all civil service jobs were also in Southern hands.

Some of the measures that owed much of their efficacy to the Federal Ratio were the election of the **Virginia Dynasty** series of early presidents, the **Louisiana Purchase**, American expansion into West Florida and Texas through **Lone Star Rebellions**, the purchase of

East Florida in the **Adams–Onís Treaty**, the declarations of war in 1812 and 1848, and the repeal of the **Missouri Compromise** in the **Kansas–Nebraska Act**.

TIDEWATER. The land between the Atlantic Coast and the first waterfall (the **fall line**) on any navigable river in the South influenced by the rise and fall of the tides is called the Tidewater.

TIENTSIN, TREATY OF. *See* SPREAD EAGLE FOREIGN POLICY.

TIGHT PACKERS. *See* SLAVE TRADE, INTERNATIONAL.

TOBACCO. The mainstay crop of the upper South from Delaware to North Carolina was tobacco. Originating as a cash crop with the first settlements in Virginia, colonial tobacco had its position thanks to the experiments that John Rolfe did with several Native American varieties of the weed. The profits in London were fantastic. Prices were so high that the Virginia Company had to restrict production and force colonists to grow domestic food crops lest they starve while growing tobacco.

But tobacco won out in the end. The Virginia Company permitted settlers to organize their lands into large plantations called hundreds. Originally both black and white indentured servants worked the crop. Many of the indentures, again both black and white, became planters after their terms expired. In 1628, Virginia exported a half million pounds of tobacco; by 1700, the amount had increased 70-fold. This did not count the amounts smuggled out to foreign nations and their colonies.

Tobacco culture involved a long, painstaking routine. The plant was quite delicate and good leaf was hard to produce. It was sown in late winter, the field dressed with ashes or forest mold, and the seedlings transplanted, once they sprouted, into hills about three feet apart. The slave would pack dirt up around his foot and lower leg, withdraw his limb from the hill, and tamp it down around the seedlings.

A hand could work about 1,000 seedlings. The weeds had to be chopped out continuously. There were numerous pests and worms that had to be removed from the leaves by hand. When the leaf turned yellow in the fall, it was picked and hung out to cure in open-sided sheds. It would be shipped a year later in hogsheads, which were packed with a careful eye to the humidity. It had to be damp enough to make the leaves pliable, but not damp enough to encourage the growth of mold in the barrels.

Tobacco culture was hard on man and earth alike. Tobacco wore out the soil like nothing else grown in the Americas. Early planters used to run cattle in their fallow fields, hoping the manure would keep them fertile another season. It was believed that a worn-out soil yielded a rank-tasting leaf. So did late planting. So the colonies that grew tobacco, especially Virginia and Maryland, passed laws regulating planting time and quality of the shipped leaf. Since most of the crop was shipped from ports in the Chesapeake, the laws in effect regulated everyone who grew the crop.

Because tobacco led to ruinous soil depletion, it was a great impetus to the continual westward movement into the Piedmont beyond the Appalachians that was to be epitomized in the **Great Migration**. But it was not tobacco that crossed the mountains as much as it was the planters, who precipitated the shift to **upland cotton**.

The tobacco industry never fully recovered from the effects of the American Revolution, even though it spread into Kentucky and Tennessee. The Napoleonic Wars in Europe, fought in North America as the **War of 1812**, the **Panic of 1819**, and the **Panic of 1837** harmed the international trade. Most of the crop was used in domestic consumption. But in the 1850s, Eli and Elisha Slade of North Carolina accidentally discovered a new variety called bright leaf. It was great for smoking (as opposed to chewing) and led to a revival of the crop in Virginia and North Carolina by the time of the Civil War.

Tobacco cultivation changed little from colonial days. The major difference was the introduction of a four-field crop rotation system (**corn**, wheat, clover, tobacco) and the introduction of marl, lime, gypsum, marsh mud, ashes, sea ore, fish by-products, and guano as fertilizers. Some even used common salt. All sorts of vegetable matter was experimented with, from tree leaves to pine cones. The use of an iron moldboard plow allowed for a deeper cut to turn more soil.

It became customary to strip leaves from each plant until the strongest six or seven remained to grow to maturity. The stalk would be split longitudinally at harvest by one fieldhand and cut off at the bottom by a following slave. Then the stalk and leaves would be hung on poles in tobacco barns, with semi-open sides missing every other board and batten, to dry. Each acre produced about 1,000 pounds of tobacco and, by the time of the Civil War, a slave was expected to work three acres alone. *See also* ECONOMY.

TOMPKINS, DANIEL. *See* ELECTION OF 1816, ELECTION OF 1820.

TOPEKA CONSTITUTION. *See* KANSAS SETTLEMENT.

TRAIL OF DEATH. *See* INDIAN REMOVAL.

TRAIL OF TEARS. *See* INDIAN REMOVAL COMPLETED.

TRANSCONTINENTAL LINE. *See* ADAMS–ONÍS TREATY.

TRIST, NICHOLAS. *See* WAR WITH MEXICO.

TRUE AMERICAN. *See* CLAY, CASSIUS M.

TUBMAN, HARRIET (ca. 1821–1913). Illiterate but deeply religious, Harriet Tubman was born and raised on the eastern shore of Maryland in the 1820s. When she was but 13, she accidentally got hit in the head with a heavy lead weight thrown at another slave, whom she was trying to protect from punishment. She healed in time, but suffered from split vision and various physical and mental problems on and off for the rest of her life. As she recovered, she began to analyze and examine her life as a slave and found it wanting.

Harriet married a free man of color, John Tubman, and moved in with him, even though she was still a slave. Then she heard a rumor that she and her brothers were to be sold. She ran away to Philadelphia, worked as a domestic, and became involved the Philadelphia Vigilance Committee, set up by black **abolitionist** William Still and other abolitionists to protect **runaway slaves** from being returned to slavery. Somewhat later, Tubman heard that her sister and her children were going to be sold. She learned of probable trails and hiding places from the Vigilance Committee and went South to save her family members.

She soon began making regular trips into Maryland, armed with a rifle, to guide an estimated 300 others to freedom in a dozen raids over the years before the Civil War. She was the first and only **woman**, the only black, and one of the few fugitive slaves to work as a conductor on the **underground railroad**. Her efforts were so brazen and so successful that $40,000 in reward money was offered as a bounty on her head, and earned her the nickname, "Moses," among the slaves. When the Civil War broke out, she became the only woman to officially lead men into battle, acting as a scout and a spy while serving with the Union Army in South Carolina. When the war ended, her husband, John Tubman, died, and she married Nelson Davis, a black Union veteran, but kept Tubman as her last name. She engaged in philanthropic activities on behalf of blacks, operating out of her farm in Auburn, New York.

TUCKER, ST. GEORGE. *See* JEFFERSON, THOMAS, AND SLAVERY IN VIRGINIA; PRO-SLAVE THEORISTS AND THE OLD SOUTH.

TURNER, NAT. *See* SOUTHAMPTON REVOLT (1831).

TWELFTH AMENDMENT. Nothing condemned the United States to a long line of mediocre hack politicians as vice presidents after the **election of 1800** more than the Twelfth Amendment. Its purpose was to prevent the **Thomas Jefferson–Aaron Burr** imbroglio from being repeated at a later date with different participants.

Under the original Constitution, the Electoral College was to choose two men to be president. The one with the most votes became president, the other vice president. The president had to have a majority vote in the Electoral College. The vice president need only to have the next highest number. If no one received a majority vote or two men received an equal number of votes for president, the election was thrown into the House of Representatives, each state having one vote for its entire delegation. If two men tied for second place, the Senate would choose a vice president.

The Twelfth Amendment compelled the Constitution to recognize the political parties for the first time. The electors had to cast two ballots, one for president and one for vice president. If no majority or a tie occurred in the Electoral College, the president would be chosen by the House and the vice president by the Senate. The result was that the party's candidate for president has been coupled to a reliable party hack who could bring in a number of electoral votes from elsewhere.

There would never again be a **George Washington–John Adams** ticket or an Adams–**Thomas Jefferson** ballot. Now the vice presidents were men like George Clinton or Elbridge Gerry, both of whom expired before their terms did, and Daniel Tompkins, who was drunk as much as sober. The only really capable vice president elected before the Civil War was **John C. Calhoun** in 1824—and he ran on everyone's ticket. In a sense the Twelfth Amendment has done nothing to solve the problem. The House had to choose the president again in 1825 and 1877.

TYLER, JOHN (1790–1862). Born and raised on the Virginia peninsula east of Richmond, John Tyler was educated at William and Mary College and practiced law before serving in the state's House of Burgesses. He was congressman after the **War of 1812**, state governor, and U.S. Senator. He broke with **Andrew Jackson** and the **Democrats** over the **Concurrent Voice and Nullification** and the **Bank War**.

Because he was a friend of **Henry Clay** and a Jackson hater, Tyler seemed a good man to put on the **Whig** ticket with **William Henry Harrison** in the **election of 1840**. When Harrison died a month after the inauguration, Tyler became the first vice president in American history to accede to the presidency after the death of the president. There was some doubt, particularly in the mind of party leader Clay, whether Tyler should have full power. Tyler solved that by vetoing more measures than **Andrew Jackson**, the record holder, in one term than Old Hickory had in two.

What Tyler found as president was that he was a Whig only because he hated Jackson and **Martin Van Buren**. With these two out of politics, Tyler went back to the Democrats, using the **annexation of Texas** as an excuse. Tyler retired to his Virginia home until he chaired the **Washington Peace Conference** to slow **secession** in 1861. After the South left the Union, he served in the provisional Confederate Congress and was elected to the Confederate Congress, but died before assuming office.

– U –

UNDERGROUND RAILROAD. Before the Civil War, at least 20,000 slaves fled their plantation homes for freedom in the North and Canada. The trip to freedom was very risky and complicated, and the **runaway slaves** were at the mercy of unscrupulous whites everywhere who might betray them to Southern **slave catchers** for a price, especially after the **Compromise of 1850** made slave catching a national pastime. So **abolitionists**, many of whom were Quakers and others free blacks, began to organize a network of safe houses to assist these freedom seekers, centered in Ohio, New York, and Pennsylvania, for obvious geographical reasons. Many other nonabolitionist Northerners became involved, spreading the influence of the antislavery movement before the Civil War.

Taking its name from a disgusted Southern planter who had lost so many of his runaway slaves to what he said must be an "underground railroad," the network decided to use railroad terms to describe its activities. The people who conducted the fleeing slaves were called "conductors" and included people such as **Harriett Tubman**, Thomas Garrett, Dr. Alexander Ross, John Brown, and William Still. The safe houses became "depots." And the runaway slaves were "passengers." The depots were usually cellars, attics, barns, or even specially built hidden rooms in houses or underground. Some hideaways were connected by sophisticated tunnels to avoid detection. In addition to shelter, the underground railroad provided disguises, fake freedom papers, transportation, money, and guides to help spirit the runaways along the way.

At least that is what the legend of the underground railroad says. Some historians are not convinced that it was that well organized and believed that the runaways had to do most of the work on their own, often trusting to luck to effect a complete escape. After the Civil War, abolitionists elaborated the actual activities, aided by radical Southern secessionists who, before the war, had used the underground railroad to rally the South against the alleged Yankee menace it posed and to secure the strict **Fugitive Slave Act** as a part of the Compromise of 1850.

After the passage of the Compromise of 1850, which prevented local authorities from hindering slave catchers, the North was no longer a safe haven for escaped blacks. The underground railroad helped many blacks keep their freedom by sending them across the Canadian border, particularly to towns and farmlands in Ontario, many of which still exist today.

Among the Northern businessmen and philanthropists who helped finance the underground railroad were abolitionists William Lloyd Garrison, Wendell Phillips, Josiah Grinnell, Gerrit Smith, Levi Coffin, and Thomas Wentworth Higginson, the latter of whom led one of the first black regiments raised by the Union from escaped slaves in South Carolina.

UPSHUR, ABEL. *See* ELECTION OF 1844.

U.S. CONSTITUTION. *See* CONSTITUTION, U.S., AND SLAVERY.

– V –

VAN BUREN, MARTIN (1782–1862). His reputation in American history can be seen in his nicknames: "The Red Fox of Kinderhook," the "Master Spirit," and the "Little Magician." Martin Van Buren was seen as an artful, cunning, selfish lawyer who lived off public office all his life. Born in Kinderhook, New York, Van Buren grew up in his father's tavern, read law, and was admitted to the bar by 1803. He learned politics in one of the most conniving, back-stabbing, politically-minded states in the Union. He was good at it.

He served in the state legislature, was state attorney general, and came to head the Albany Regency, a political club that was the forerunner of the **Democrat** Party. Members wore the tails of deer in their hat bands and waved them during political gatherings, gaining the nickname Bucktails. Van Buren was an Old Republican. That is, he was a **Democratic Republican** like **Thomas Jefferson** and **James Madison** before they became presidents. He believed in a strong state government and a weak national government. There was a reason. New York had a strong state government and it had done some wonderful things, like building the Erie Canal. Van Buren was not about to permit the federal government to compete with New York or assist some other state to do it.

What Van Buren wanted to do was set up a national political coalition that would believe the same as he. The best place to find such people was in the South, where they opposed a strong federal government on principle. So, in the **election of 1824**, he supported William H. Crawford of Georgia. In the **election of 1828**, he was for **Andrew Jackson**. Van Buren used Jackson's popularity to front for his coalition. He was secretary of state and assisted in **Jackson's break with John C. Calhoun**, Old Hickory's vice president. Van Buren became vice president in 1832 because of his loyalty to **Jackson's first administration** and president in the **election of 1836** because of his loyalty to **Jackson's second administration**. Van Buren helped Jackson orchestrate the destruction of Philadelphia as the main economic engine of the nation in favor of New York City in the **Bank War**. It has remained that way ever since.

But as president, Van Buren was checked by the **Panic of 1837**. Against the worst depression before the Civil War, the Little Magician lost his charm and was crushed by **William Henry Harrison** in the **election of 1840**. Back home in New York, Van Buren opposed the **annexation of Texas**, which cost him re-nomination for the presidency in the **election of 1844**. He got involved with tumultuous state politics and emerged as a **Free-Soil** Party presidential hopeful in the **election of 1848**, opposing the extension of slavery into the West. He returned to the Democrat fold only to oppose **secession** and died in the midst of the Civil War. Van Buren's political flexibility was admired and criticized, then and now. As **John Randolph of Roanoke** once put it: "He always rowed to his objective with muffled oars."

VELASCO, TREATY OF. *See* LONE STAR REBELLIONS.

VESEY, DENMARK. *See* THE CHARLESTON REVOLT (1822).

VIOLENCE AND WHITE MILITANCY. Southern social mores did not change very fast from the 18th century. But those in the North did. By the 1830s, the North was where the South would be in the 1930s, a 100-year gap in social perceptions. In the 19th century, the South still believed in a closeness to the God of the Old Testament—the one who spoke of an eye for an eye. The South held that honor was the most important social value from which all the rest sprung:

government, law and order, family, and societal values. Important to one's self-worth was what the community at large thought. It was important to build this community sanction by displaying a ferocity of will as a sign of one's inner merit. Honor gave structure to life, gender, family, and community.

Hospitality, gambling, and personal combat were the three things that made an honorable man and determined in what part of society he belonged. Southern hospitality was a way to differentiate the South from the North. Sociability and manners were more important than intellect or book learning. Family name was a history of who one was. For this reason so many Southern men, and some **women**, had no common English first name. Rather a family name from the matrilineal branch or perhaps of a close family friend or relative was used. The Southern woman was stereotyped in the sanctity of virginity, glorification of motherhood, and the noble self-sacrifice as a matron. But she was subordinate to male concepts of what was proper.

Gambling, the willingness to take a chance, to risk all for victory was typically Southern. Wrestling, like what **Abraham Lincoln** indulged in on the Illinois frontier, was present in the South, but usually it took the form of "rough and tumble," meaning no holds barred. Men tried to bite off an opponent's ear or nose or rip a lip off to the chin. In lower classes on the frontier, men grew and trimmed and polished select fingernails so that they might assist in the plucking out of an opponent's eye. Men with missing fingers, eye patches, and maimed limbs were common enough to be noted in journals of Yankee and foreign visitors.

But as weapons became more sophisticated, men graduated from teeth and bare hands to Bowie knives and pistols. Street fights, like **Andrew Jackson**'s shootout with the Benton Brothers, were common and considered manly, especially if one's own side were outnumbered and won. James and Resin Bowie made their reputations on a sandbar fight in the middle of the Mississippi with the knife of their own design.

Formal duels were engaged in by, but not limited to, the upper-class gentry. The rules were well known in cosmopolitan places like New Orleans and Charleston. Just how well known the dueling rules were in backcountry locales is debatable. There were probably as few duelists as there were slaveholders, but dueling and other forms of violence were acceptable because of deficient political institutions and a highly refined sense of personal honor and integrity. Even hangings and tar and feathering forced the malefactor to suffer and served as a community offering to the values of the common man. But it had to be public to be virtuous. All of the various forms of combat were cheered and created adventure amidst rural monotony.

The rural nature of the South meant knives and guns for defense and horsemanship were essential. The Southern forests were almost primeval. The proximity to Indians and **runaways slaves** and white brigands like the Harpe gang on the Wilderness Road and the Murrell gang on the Natchez Trace made for a tense, sensitive fighting man in the average Southerner. There was a great reliance on self-defense, not on the authorities and the law. This was especially true with newspaper editors. **Cassius M. Clay**, one of the few outspoken **abolitionists** in Kentucky, had had his press and his life threatened so often that he stationed loaded cannons behind his front door to keep mobs at bay.

A Southerner seeking military service did not have to await foreign war; there was plenty to do defending his home against slave insurrection. The connection between slavery and martial spirit was universally recognized. Slaveowners found it desirable to build up a military force to keep their chattels under control. In this sense slavery was not just an economic and social good, but a military good as well. Private military schools inculcated Southerners with the value of serving and protecting the South from outsiders like Northern anti-slavery advocates.

Unlike in the North, the militia tradition in the South was kept intact throughout the period preceding the Civil War, and units tended to be well trained. Members included all white males between 18 and 45. Each potential soldier had to provide his own weapons, musket, bayonet, knapsack, and two spare flints. The distances between settlements in the South made a militia muster a good social get-together as well as a place to learn techniques of modern warfare.

There was always a strong feeling among Southerners that **slavery** ought to be extended into new lands. It would help relieve the numbers in older communities and bring more **Three-Fifths Compromise** states into the Union. Southern youth, especially the second and third sons, who might not inherit the plantation, volunteered quickly for **filibustering**. Such enthusiasm caused President **James Madison** to issue a proclamation against American citizens attacking the crumbling Spanish empire's province of Texas on 1 September 1815. But the problem was continual during the years before the American Civil War. After the **War with Mexico**, the Knights of the Golden Circle, a filibustering group, established "castles" to provide new recruits to soldier into Cuba and northern Mexico to gain more land for slave states.

Mark Twain once asserted that Sir Walter Scott caused the Civil War. Indeed, after the Bible, Scott's novels glorifying the medieval knight and chivalry were most read in the South. It was heroic fiction, which struck to the heart of the Southern male. After all, the leading characteristic of the Southerner was reckless bravery in battle, just like his Celtic forebears. The South generally fought against other outside influences and not against the North until after the **Compromise of 1850**. From then on, the South believed it was intentionally being mistreated in the Union. As the 1850s progressed, the South dared the North to fight. When a society is at stake, all classes band together and seek someone to blame—in this case, Yankees. It was but a short step to **secession** and Civil War. *See also* SLAVE RESISTENCE AND REBELLION; SOCIALIZATION.

VIRGINIA AND KENTUCKY RESOLVES (1798). *See* THE KENTUCKY AND VIRGINIA RESOLVES.

VIRGINIA DYNASTY. The series of U.S. presidents from **Thomas Jefferson** through **James Madison** to **James Monroe** is called the Virginia Dynasty. Some include **John Tyler** and **George Washington** in this group. But Tyler was never elected as president, being the first vice president to succeed a deceased president (Virginia-born William Henry Harrison), although he blocked the enactment of **Henry Clay's American System** and admitted Texas to the Union, making him a quintessential practitioner of what the North called the **Slave Power Conspiracy**.

Unlike Tyler, Washington is such an exception to all rules that he could be left out, except that Washington did do one thing that endeared him to more fervent Southerners. He approved Jefferson's suggestion, made as secretary of state, that the original apportionment of the House of Representatives called for in the Constitution, of one congressman for each 30,000 persons, be apportioned among the states and rounded off. The one per 30,000 should not be not among the nation as a whole.

This bit of chicanery would allow the total number of representatives for the North to increase by two instead of six. The South would still gain two, but the overall figures, which favored the North, would be lessened by two-thirds. **Alexander Hamilton** protested, but Washington yielded to the combined efforts of Jefferson and Attorney General Edmund Randolph of Virginia in the cabinet and Madison in Congress to issue the first presidential veto in American history. The Jefferson formula then became law, assisted by people's identification of their citizenship by state rather than by the nation as a whole.

Essentially, the Virginia Dynasty was the early apotheosis of the **Slave Power Conspiracy**, the national political advantage Southerners held in Washington before the Civil War because of the **Three-Fifths Compromise** in the Constitution.

VIRGINIA SLAVERY DEBATES (1832). Following the **Missouri Compromise**, and the fear that its debate had inspired Denmark Vesey's proposed slave uprising known as the **Charleston Plot** and Nat Turner's actual Virginia rebellion in the **Southampton Revolt**, the Virginia state legislature debated **slavery** and its eventual eradication by state action.

Slavery was a hot topic in Virginia even before the Nat Turner revolt in 1831. Two years earlier, Virginians had written a new state constitution that still contained the **Three-Fifths Compromise** of the U.S. Constitution, known as the Federal Ratio. This allowed three-fifths of Virginia's slaves to be counted for representation and direct taxation. Western counties had been desirous of getting rid of this ratio, which allowed the slaveholding eastern part of the state to dominate the state legislative agendas. Many in the western part of the state wanted to divide the state in half, generally on a line down the Appalachians.

On 11 January 1832, Representative William O. Goode proposed that the House agree that it was inexpedient to legislate on the topic of emancipation. A counterproposal, presented by Thomas Jefferson Randolph, reintoduced his grandfather's suggestion that slavery be got rid of by freeing all slaves born after 4 July 1840, males at age 21 and females at 18. Such freed persons would then be apprenticed out until they had earned the money for their deportation from the United States.

Randolph was part of a group of young politicians who still embodied the ideals of the Revolutionary generation and saw slavery as an evil and a denial of the Declaration of Independence. But they also agreed with pro-slave advocates that whites and blacks could not exist side-by-side in the same society. **Colonization** elsewhere would solve that one major objection to emancipation.

This view was widely held west of the mountains. But those east of the mountains also questioned the continued viability of slavery. Lands were worn out, slave populations were becoming increasingly large and, as Nat Turner had demonstrated, more dangerous. Slavery also kept the state from turning to other crops and industry and undercut fair wages for free white labor. Slavery also worked against public schools, internal improvements, and promoted race-mixing that white non-slaveholding Virginians found abominable. All of this led to a desire of western, white-dominated Virginia to separate from eastern, black-dominated Tidewater and Piedmont regions.

The debate centered on pro-slave advocates insisting that the reformers propose an acceptable plan for emancipation. The crux was in the details. There was also some trepidation about denying property rights, and the economic and social necessities for emancipation. Others believed that they ought to consult their constituents before acting on so grave a matter. The who, when, how, and why led to a defeat of the proposal by a decisive majority, made possible in part by the three-fifths delegate opposition to it. The legislature satisfied itself by passing a more comprehensive and stricter **Black Code**, tightening the bonds of slavery and discriminating against free persons of color.

The impetus for reforming slavery in Virginia died as quickly as it had been born. The **Nullification Crisis** diverted everyone's attention to more pressing problems. The panic from the Southampton Revolt ebbed, not to arise again until John Brown's **Harper's Ferry Raid** in 1859. The demand for more and more slaves in the growing Southwest siphoned off the slave surplus, bringing the white-black numbers into a more acceptable ratio. The notion of dividing the state in halved along the Blue Ridge Mountains died out until the Civil War reintroduced it and caused it to happen. And **Edmund Ruffin** published his work on calcareous manures, which offered hope in rejuvenating Virginia's worn-out **tobacco** lands.

The public mind-set changed so rapidly that the young politicians who had backed the reform of slavery in Virginia were turned out of office—at least those who did not change their public stances in short order. After 1832, the conditions that had given rise to the possibility of ending slavery ceased to exist. It had become impossible to devise a practicable plan of freedom for slaves and their colonization abroad.

Nothing revealed the shifting political climate of the South in favor of slavery better than the Tennessee constitutional convention of 1834. This time the convention refused to consider the eradication of slavery in any form. The committee in charge gave three reasons: slavery was the only way the races could live together; emancipation would lead to the creation of a black revolt as it had in **Haiti**; and the slaves were better treated than free factory laborers of the North. The goal now became not to apologize for the peculiar institution but to justify **slavery as a positive good**.

– W –

WAKARUSA WAR. *See* KANSAS–MISSOURI BORDER WARS.

WALKER, DAVID (1785–1830). Born in Wilmington, North Carolina, the son of a slave father and a free woman of color, David Walker was free by birth. Little is known of his youth, but Walker evidently was unable to live in a slave state without being goaded into open rebellion that would cost him his life. So he moved to Boston sometime around 1827.

In the North, Walker became an anti-slave agent of an abolitionist newspaper run by the first black graduate of Bowdoin College, John B. Russworm. After making numerous speeches against slavery, Walker published *David Walker's Appeal to the Colored Citizens of the World* (1829). Divided into four chapters, the *Appeal* portrayed the wretchedness of the slave in the South, the ignorance the institution bred, the propaganda of Christian ministers, and the colonization movement.

Walker concluded that the black person in American was treated akin to a talking ape, a condition that he blamed upon the writings of **Thomas Jefferson**. Black persons had to shed their servile attitudes and prove Jefferson's claim of innate black inferiority wrong, Walker said. He invoked the Declaration of Independence's statement that all men were created equal and stated that one who would not fight to be free deserved enslavement.

Walker's appeal was sent, unwanted but free, anonymously all over the South. Governors and state legislatures banned the book or its possession. The **Southampton Revolt** of Nat Turner in Virginia in 1831 was blamed on the incendiary nature of Walker's appeal. It was little wonder that Walker was found dead in the street in front of his Boston blacksmith shop, a death ruled to be of suspicious circumstances but never cleared up.

WALKER, ROBERT. See KANSAS–MISSOURI BORDER WARS.

WALKER, WILLIAM. See FILIBUSTERING.

WALKER TARIFF. See TARIFF.

WANGHIA, TREATY OF. See SPREAD EAGLE FOREIGN POLICY.

WAR HAWKS. The pro-war feeling that swept the United States in 1810 and 1811, marked by the **Lone Star Rebellion** in West Florida and the Battle of Tippecanoe in Indiana Territory, brought a new type of **Democratic-Republican** politician to the fore. These were the War Hawks (the first time the term was used in American history). These men were not interested in constitutional issues left over in the quarrels between **Thomas Jefferson, James Madison,** and **Alexander Hamilton.** They were American nationalists and territorial expansionists.

They wanted a tough, boisterous America that would conquer the Native Americans blocking the settlement of the Old Northwest and the Old Southwest, secure West Florida by a Lone Star Rebellion, and take control of British Canada. This was the prized 14th colony left over from the days of the American Revolution. The Americans had tried to conquer Canada in 1776 to "save" it from British tyranny, but had failed. Now they would finish the job of liberating North America.

Most of the War Hawks were from the South or the West. They included men like Kentuckians **Henry Clay** and **Richard Mentor Johnson**; South Carolinians **John C. Calhoun**, William Lowndes, and Langdon Cheves (pron. Ché-vis); Tennessean Felix Grundy; and western New Yorker Peter B. Porter. Although they were not numerically dominant, these men obtained influential committee chairmanships (congressional rules were different then). Clay was speaker, Cheves was chairman of the Naval Committee, and the others were in control of the Foreign Relations Committee. Clay and Calhoun would be big names in national politics in various capacities until 1850. It was these men who voted for the **War of 1812**.

WAR OF 1812. Also known as the Second War for American Independence, the War of 1812 was fought ostensibly to secure America's neutral shipping rights on the high seas. In the eyes of the Congressmen who declared war, known as the **War Hawks**, it was also a war to conquer Canada while Britain was busy with Napoleon in Europe, a failed objective from 1776. But for the purposes of the settlers of the Old Southwest and the Old Northwest, the War of 1812 can best be seen as an Indian War from which emerged two important political personages for the future: **William Henry Harrison** and **Andrew Jackson**. Their opponents were the allied tribes of the Shawnee in northern Indiana and the Creeks of the Alabama region. What made the Native Americans more dangerous than usual to the advancing white settlers was good leadership. For the Shawnee, Tecumseh and his half brother the Prophet provided better than usual political, military, and religious direction.

Indeed, one could make a good argument that the War of 1812 began as an Indian War in 1811, a year before Congress declared the conflict. In that year, the Shawnee war chief Tecumseh, seething from decades of white exploitation, brought to fruition his plan to unite all of the tribes between the Appalachians and the Mississippi River in one last campaign against the seizure of their lands by the westward movement of white farmers. In his ability to ally the disparate tribes, usually hostile to each other, Tecumseh was one of the great diplomats of his age. The Prophet did his part by giving the alliance a religious flavor, based on a return to the values of the Indian past.

The governor of Indiana Territory, Harrison, knew exactly what he faced and determined to attack before Tecumseh could complete his alliance. In 1811, Tecumseh announced that he was traveling south to join the Southern tribes to his budding alliance. He had no sooner gotten out of sight than Harrison advanced on the Shawnee Confederation's principle town, located on the banks of Tippecanoe Creek in northern Indiana. The alliance, led by the Prophet, attacked Harrison's force and nearly destroyed the white army.

But Harrison's men valiantly hung on, the Indians withdrew after their women and children got a head start, and Harrison declared a victory that would propel him to the presidency in 1840. After inept bungling by other so-called generals, Harrison took over the effort against the Indians and now the British, invaded Canada near Detroit, and crushed the Indian alliance at the Battle of the Thames in Ontario. Tecumseh died in the fighting, the credit for his death going to Colonel **Richard Mentor Johnson** of the First Kentucky Mounted Rifles, who would eventually rise to the vice presidency.

As Harrison was subduing the British–Native American alliance in the Old Northwest, the war spread to the Old Southwest in 1813. Encouraged by British and Spanish agents operating out of Pensacola with supplied guns and ammunition, the Creek nation attacked white settlers at Ft. Mimms. The settlers had grown sloppy after numerous false alarms, and when the attack came could not shut the fort's gates fast enough to contain the onslaught. Around 400 men, women, and children were cut down. The Ft. Mimms Massacre, as it was called, was the worst loss of white life in any single engagement in an Indian War in all of American history.

The American response was to call out the Tennessee state militia under its commander, Andrew Jackson. After some meaningless skirmishes, the militiamen went home to harvest crops over Jackson's vehement protests. But they returned the following spring after their corn was planted. Led by Jackson, the whites tore through the Creek homeland in Alabama. The Indians were cornered at Horseshoe Bend on the Alabama River, and vengeance for Ft. Mimms was exacted with no mercy shown. Up to 900 Native Americans died, including

Tecumseh's half-brother the Prophet, there on a diplomatic mission. The militia followed up the victory, burning everything in sight. Pursuing the Creeks without let-up, Jackson forced them to sign the Treaty of Ft. Jackson, in which they gave up all claims to Alabama's fertile belt of black soil, the future center of the **Cotton Kingdom**. Then Jackson turned to the British operating out of Pensacola with Spanish connivance. Seizing the town, Jackson burned it to the ground to deny it to the enemy as a base.

Meanwhile, Jackson heard of a large British invasion army and fleet coming through the Gulf. He rushed to Mobile and drove off a British probing attack. Then Jackson realized that the real prize on the Gulf was New Orleans. Using forced marches, he got there ahead of the British. In New Orleans, Jackson declared martial law and rounded up everyone he could find to defend the city. His force included civilians, white militia, free black militia, friendly Indians, and pirates under Jean Lafitte from their stronghold in the swamps at Barataria.

Establishing his force behind the Rodriguez Canal on Chalmette Plantation below the city, Jackson received the British attack. His position was strong with the Mississippi River on one flank and the swamps on the other. In a matter of hours Jackson won one of the most lop-sided victories in American military history, taking 14 casualties and inflicting 2,000 on the enemy.

This Battle of Chalmette, or the First Battle of New Orleans (the second would occur during the Civil War and a third during Reconstruction that followed), was fought on 15 January 1815. That is, it occurred one month after the signing of the Treaty of Ghent, which had ended the conflict with the formula *status quo ante bellum*. This meant that the British and Americans would withdraw to the border existing before the war. America's drive for Canada, the lost 14th colony of the Revolution, was over. But there was one exception to the peace formula. The United States kept West Florida (the area from Baton Rouge to Mobile), because it was originally seized by a **Lone Star Rebellion** in 1810 and Spain was not at the peace conference. Andrew Jackson had secured the South and become a hero for all time.

WAR WITH MEXICO. Although Northerners, particularly **abolitionists**, would claim that President **James K. Polk** was willing to settle for half of Oregon for the North in the **Oregon Treaty** of 1846, but insisted on obtaining all of Texas to the Río Grande for the South, this was untrue. Polk was willing to negotiate for the North, too. Part of the problem was that Mexico just did not trust the motives of the ministers the U.S. sent down to negotiate. The Americans wanted to reach some sort of compromise, but no matter what the compromise, the Americans wanted more than Mexico wanted to give. The first American Minister to Mexico was **Joel R. Poinsette** of South Carolina. The Mexicans doubted his motives so much as to ask his recall several times. The **Lone Star Rebellion** in Texas did nothing but confirm Mexico's worst feelings about the colossus to the North.

After the Texas revolution, it took some years until Mexico would even receive a new American Minister. But with the **election of 1844**, President James K. Polk sent **John Slidell**, a Louisiana **Democrat** who spoke fluent Spanish. Most histories boil down the problem between Mexico and the United States to where the boundary between the two nations ought to have been after the **Texas annexation**—the Nueces at Corpus Christi (Mexico's assertion from colonial days) or the Río Grande at Matamoros (agreed to in the repudiated 1836 Treaty of Velasco). But there was a persistent problem of claims owed by Mexico to Americans and Mexico's unwillingness to accept the loss of Texas at all.

Slidell was to offer Mexico $2 million to absorb the claims issue and accept the Nueces border. If not, Slidell was to ask for the Río Grande. Slidell was also to offer Mexico another $5 million for New Mexico (Santa Fé), and $5 million more for San Francisco. Or Mexico could receive $25 million for all of Alta California (the present-day U.S. state). Sadly, it did not matter what the U.S. wanted or offered. Any Mexican government that even talked to Slidell, much less took the cash, would be out of office overnight. To put on pressure and defend Texas from Mexican attack, Polk sent Maj. Gen. **Zachary Taylor** and the U.S. army to the Río Grande from New Orleans on 4 July 1845. But logistical problems dictated he stop at Corpus Christi.

Meanwhile, Slidell cooled his heels in Vera Cruz, as Mexico's minister to the U.S., Juan N. Almonte, meddled in American politics. He was a Centralist and a front man for the then-exiled Gen. Antonio

López de Santa Anna. Almonte got acquainted with many New England politicians and **abolitionists**, who convinced him that the United States was out to steal Texas for slavery, as its admission to statehood in December 1845 demonstrated. This was true enough, but Almonte thought these opponents to expansion were stronger politically than they were. He thought they would destroy America's war effort, something that was not so.

So the Federalists, those who realized that Texas was gone, could not negotiate with Slidell until the U.S. gave back Texas to Mexico all the way to the Sabine River. But there were enough doubts as to the democratic Federalists' patriotism that the Centralists staged a coup and put their own strongman, Antonio Paredes in power. He told Slidell to get out. Then he ordered the Mexican army to advance to Matamoros. Polk had already ordered Taylor to do the same. The two armies stared across the river at each other as the generals verbally argued fine points of possession.

On 23 April 1846, Paredes issued a declaration of defensive war. His orders were to defend Mexico and Texas by marching on New Orleans or even Mobile. On 24 April, Mexican dragoons crossed the Río Grande into no-man's land and captured an American cavalry patrol. Polk had drafted a weak message of double-talk asking Congress to declare war, but when the information of the hostilities arrived, he tore it up. The new message asked Congress to declare war because "American blood had been shed on American soil."

On 13 May, Congress obliged. **Whigs** protested vehemently. **Abraham Lincoln**, congressman from Illinois, introduced the Spot Resolution, asking Polk to point out the exact spot of American soil upon which American blood had been shed. Lincoln knew that the spot was on disputed ground. Democrats voted it down. Volunteers from the Northwest and Southwest hurried south, hoping the war would not end before they saw action. They need not have worried.

Polk's war strategy was based on two attacks. Taylor was to march across northern Mexico to protect the flank of the second column, under Brig. Gen. Stephen Watts Kearny, coming down the Santa Fé Trail, which would march all the way to California by way of the Gila River. Initial American victories under Taylor caused the Mexicans to turn to Santa Anna, who was in exile in Cuba for past political failures. Polk wanted Santa Anna back in Mexico, too. The general had agreed to talk the Centralist government into acceding to American territorial demands.

But no sooner had he landed at Vera Cruz than Santa Anna announced that he had come to lead Mexico to victory. He advanced northward to meet Taylor's forces at Buena Vista. The battle was touch and go for both sides, but in the end, aided by Col. **Jefferson Davis** and his Mississippi Rifle Regiment and Capt. Braxton Bragg and his light artillery, Taylor won the battle and assured his elevation to the presidency in the upcoming **election of 1848**.

Kearney, meanwhile, marched to Santa Fé and on to California. There he found that an exploration column, under Lt. **John Charles Frémont**, in the area from the year before, had stirred up a pro-American Bear Flag Revolt and, in cooperation with the U.S. Navy, had already secured the Mexican province for the United States. Frémont was the son-in-law of Senator **Thomas Hart Benton**, and when Gen. Kearney asked Lt. Frémont to turn everything over to him as military governor, Frémont claimed to be a civilian officer of the Bear Flag government and not under the general's command. Frémont's court-martial was short and final, despite his father-in-law's efforts to save him.

Although Polk had accomplished the extension of the United States to the Pacific, Mexico refused to yield. This caused Polk to send Maj. Gen. **Winfield Scott** on a wildly successful attack of Mexico City from Vera Cruz. Polk kept switching generals because they were all so effective—and as Whigs, potential **Democrat** political opponents. He believed in divide and rule. It did not work. Both Taylor and Scott would run for president on the Whig ticket, Taylor successfully in the **election of 1848**, Scott not so successfully in the **election of 1852**.

With the fall of Mexico City, Gen. Santa Anna had lost every battle he participated in. He was on the road to another exile overseas. Anxious for an end to the war before the election of 1848, Polk had sent Nicholas Trist of the State Department to negotiate a treaty any time he could get a Mexican delegation to talk. Opportunity came at Guadalupe Hidalgo north of Mexico City. Here Trist got Mexico to agree to make what was called the Mexican Cession. It gave the Desert Southwest to the United States for $15 million, with the international boundary the Gila River. (Trist was supposed to pay $20 million, but he deducted the difference for Mexico's "prolonging" the war). Mexico also gave up Alta California and recognized the Texas annexation, with the international border the Río Grande. The United States assumed all claims of its citizens against the Mexican government.

Although Polk and Congress accepted the provisions of the Treaty of Guadalupe Hidalgo, the South was not satisfied. Many had wanted all of Mexico, but **John C. Calhoun** had blocked that. The North was already angry enough at being short-changed in the Oregon Treaty to propose that slavery be excluded from the Mexican Cession by way of the **Wilmot Proviso**. It would take the massive **Compromise of 1850** to cool everyone off.

By 1853, the big issue with Mexico was a railroad route to California. Led by Secretary of War Jefferson Davis, the **Franklin Pierce** administration sent James Gadsden of Alabama to negotiate a Southern railroad route. Who should Gadsden meet as head of Mexico's government but General Santa Anna, back from exile once again. In desperate need of money to maintain himself in power, Santa Anna sold the Gadsden Purchase to the United States for $10 million. This extended the international boundary south from the Gila to its present location, roughly at the 31st parallel. Disgusted at this piece of chicanery, the Mexicans threw Santa Anna out for the last time.

The Mexican Cession was opposed by the North as a slave state grab for political power in Washington. It was the **Slave Power Conspiracy** at its worst. The South already had nearly 20 representatives in Congress, thanks to counting slaves in the **Three-Fifths Compromise** in the **Constitution**. The line was soon to be drawn violently in the **Kansas–Missouri Border Wars**. The Civil War and Southern **secession** were on the horizon.

WASHINGTON, D.C., SLAVERY IN. As the U.S. Constitution granted Congress the exclusive governance over the future District of Columbia (art. I, sect. 8), the South was particularly interested in where the District would be located. When the capital was in a Northern city, like New York or Philadelphia, there had been incidents where slaves had successfully fled their masters, congressmen from the South. It was difficult to enforce the fugitive slave laws in the North.

The usual story is that Secretary of State **Thomas Jefferson** held a dinner party at which Secretary of the Treasury **Alexander Hamilton** agreed to find Northern support for a location for the national capitol in the slave South if congressional **Democratic Republican** Party leader and Hamilton opponent **James Madison** would find Southern support to pass his **Funding and Assumption** measures, particularly the latter. This has been called the Compromise of 1790. In reality, President **George Washington**, Jefferson, and Madison thought a Southern location for the capital so critical that there was no deal necessary. Indeed, some slave states had already expressed great trepidation in ratifying the Constitution if that were not to be the case.

Ordinarily Washington was very careful of using his enormous prestige to influence political decisions. He knew he had an unfair advantage as victor of the Revolution. But Washington, backed by Jefferson and Madison, was willing to use his powerful influence to locate the capitol on a 10-mile square plot of land (two-thirds of which was in Maryland, the rest in Virginia) on the Potomac north of his home of Mount Vernon. The District's main town was at first Alexandria, Virginia. But in 1846 the federal government returned the Virginia part of the District as unneeded.

When the government moved to Washington in 1800, a fifth of the District's resident were slaves of government officials. There would be no need to worry about interference with the slaveowners' right to chattel property. No slave would be able to escape the **peculiar institution** by fleeing down the street to friendly **abolitionists'** hands. Slavery was as normal in the nation's capital as in the Mississippi Delta.

But it galled Northern congressional representatives to see slaves up close and in person. It especially bothered them to see the excellent slave jails, as Washington, D.C., became the center of the **domestic slave trade**. So after the **War with Mexico**, when slavery was the hottest topic in town and 76 slaves had been spirited out of town in the *Pearl* **incident**, Northerners insisted that the slave trade at least be abolished in the District as part of the **Compromise of 1850**. At least they would not have to see their fellow beings sold anymore. Slavery is why the capital of the United States, unlike the capitals of most nations, was located in a remote swamp on the Potomac instead of a premier city like Philadelphia or New York.

WASHINGTON, GEORGE (1732–1799). Born to wealth in Westmoreland County, George Washington lived most of his life at his brother's estate, Mount Vernon. The early death of his father left Washington relatively poor, so he had to settle for a colonial education rather than one in Britain. He was good at mathematics and became a surveyor for Lord Thomas Fairfax. He was at home in the woods. He traveled with his brother to Barbadoes and inherited Mount Vernon upon his brother's death.

His familiarity with the woods and the fact he had inherited his brother's commission as a lieutenant colonel of the Virginia militia made him a perfect candidate to go west in 1753 for Lt. Gov. Robert Dinwiddie and order the French out of Virginia's land claims around present-day Pittsburgh. A year later he took a military expedition back and was surrounded in an improvised Ft. Necessity and forced to surrender. These expeditions began the French and Indian Wars.

Washington returned again in 1755 leading the Virginia militia accompanying British Gen. Edward Braddock and was present at the column's massacre. He later participated in the British capture of Ft. Duquesne, which became Ft. Pitt and then Pittsburgh. These expeditions were the sum of military experience that Washington had to draw on for his command of the Continental Army during the Revolution.

At the end of his military service, Washington married Martha Dandridge Custis, a wealthy widow. They would have no children, which did much to make him look neutral among contending political factions, especially later. Washington served in the House of Burgesses before attending the First and Second Continental Congresses. He actively campaigned for the command of the army, wearing his militia uniform. Appointed as general in chief, Washington took over the militia forces besieging the British at Boston. Securing cannon from inland Ft. Ticonderoga, he planted them on Dorchester Heights, causing the British to withdraw without firing a shot.

Leading his army to the one place that the British had to have, New York harbor, Washington was defeated in successive battles at Brooklyn Heights, Harlem Heights, White Plains, and Ft. Lee, and driven across New Jersey. He kept the British off his back by arranging several sham conferences of surrender until he had crossed the Delaware River near Trenton. The British and their Hessian allies had weakened their forces in occupation duties. This allowed Washington to re-cross the Delaware and hit the outpost at Trenton on Christmas day 1776. He followed up this victory by striking a British relief force at Princeton, causing the British to withdraw to New York City for the winter.

The following year Washington discovered that the British had ferried their army to the head of Chesapeake Bay. He rushed his army south and was beaten at Chad's Ford in the Battle of Brandywine Creek. The colonial capital of Philadelphia soon fell and, after striking the British pursuit at Germantown, Washington retreated to Valley Forge where his army spent the worst winter of the war. He exposed and confronted the so-called Conway Cabal, securing his command of the army against all contenders.

The next year, with the entrance of France into the war on the American side, the British withdrew from Philadelphia by land, fearing an attack at sea by the French Navy. Washington hit the column at Monmouth but failed to mount a successful coordinated attack. The British then holed up in New York City and concentrated on fighting in the Southern colonies.

After several years of jockeying back and forth with the British around New York City, during which time his best subordinate Benedict Arnold switched sides, Washington stealthily sneaked his army away for a forced march to the Virginia peninsula. There, in conjunction with the French, he pinned the British Army of Lord Charles Cornwallis down at Yorktown and forced its surrender in October 1781.

Until the Treaty of Paris in 1783, Washington had to check attempts by his officers to march on Congress and install a military dictatorship with him as king. This he squelched in the so-called Newburgh Address, where he skillfully donned glasses no one knew he wore, because he had lost much of his sight in the service of the country, and promised he would personally negotiate for their back salary and better conditions. This may be the most important service he performed because it kept the United States from following the path of the later French and Latin American Revolutions to dictatorship.

Washington spent the 1780s farming. But he, like many Revolutionary veterans, thought the government of the **Articles of Confederation** was too weak. He acted as presiding officer at the Constitutional Convention and was unanimously elected as first president under the Constitution of 1787. During his administration, he backed a **Federalist** Party line, supporting the nationalistic programs and centralizing power in the hands of the federal government put forward by Secretary of State **Alexander Hamilton**. He retired from office after serving two terms, once again setting a precedent for moderation in the holding of power that others subsequently chose to ignore, forcing a constitutional amendment to secure.

Nowadays, Washington has been trashed for many things, including that he was a slaveholder. This overlooks the fact that he really was the "Father of His Country." He was a big man, one of the tallest presidents, with a volatile temper. He was very aloof, not because he was unfriendly, but because it allowed him to hold his temper in check and appear neutral among a group of political prima donnas like **Thomas Jefferson** and Hamilton. The reason that Hamilton won out was that Washington believed that his policies worked. But he never said that to either man.

WASHINGTON PEACE CONFERENCE (1861). Many of the compromise ideas in varied forms were presented in the House of Representatives' **Corwin Committee of Thirty-Three** and the Senate's **Crittenden Committee of Thirteen** and had already failed there. Most came up again in the Washington Peace Conference of 1861, a belated effort sponsored by the Border South to head off **secession** and war (after all, these states knew very well that any North-South war would be fought on their lands).

After much talk, the "Old Gentlemen's Convention," many of the sponsors and delegates elderly ex-**Whigs**, proposed a Thirteenth Amendment to the Constitution and a reunification of the nation under the old Constitution. This amendment would draw the 1820 **Missouri Compromise** line of 36°30' across the Western territories to the eastern border of California. Above the line slavery was not to be allowed. Below the line slavery was to be guaranteed. Territories would become states in the traditional manner. No new territories could be added to the United States without a majority of senators from both sections concurring.

The proposed amendment also guaranteed slavery in the states where it existed and in the District of Columbia so long as it existed in Maryland. Slavery could not be abolished in any state without concurrence of the slaveholders. All fugitive slaves were to be rendered back to their states of origin. If this could not be done because of mob action or the inaction of state or federal officials, the federal government would compensate the slaveholder, which action would end all claims on the fugitive. The slave trade was to be prohibited in the District of Columbia (already done in the **Compromise of 1850** by law) and between the United States and foreign countries (done by law in 1808). The amendment could not itself be amended without the agreement of all the states. But many in the North and South were fed up with compromise by this time, and **Abraham Lincoln**'s tough inaugural speech put an end to the effort. *See also* WASHINGTON D.C., SLAVERY IN.

WEBSTER, DANIEL (1782–1852). Considered one of three great statesmen (along with Southerners **Henry Clay** and **John C. Calhoun**) of the first half of the 19th century, Daniel Webster was originally from New Hampshire. With a swarthy complexion and dark hair and eyes, Webster was called "Black Dan" all his life. A graduate of Dartmouth, he early on showed that he was a master orator and politician who had a hard time keeping track of money and the amount of liquor he consumed. These problems would haunt his career all his life. But recognizing his political acumen, businessmen from New England would continue to bail him out of trouble to preserve his voice in the House and Senate in Washington.

Originally a **Federalist** and a quiet supporter of the **Hartford Convention**, Webster moved to Massachusetts after the **War of 1812**. Sent to Washington again, Webster opposed Henry Clay and the **American System**, especially the **tariff**. But as New England became more nationalistic during the 1820s, Webster followed along. By the time of **Andrew Jackson's first administration**, he was firmly on the side of the **National Republicans** and then the **Whigs**.

During the **Nullification** Crisis, Webster made a national reputation when he debated the nature of the Union with Robert Y. Hayne and John C. Calhoun, winning over Hayne but falling short with the more brilliant Calhoun. He ran for the presidency several times but was nominated only once in the **election of 1836**, which he lost to

Martin Van Buren. Webster served his party well as secretary of state during the **Canadian Boundary Dispute** during the 1840s and returned to the Senate.

It was here on 7 March 1850 that Webster spoke in favor of the **Compromise of 1850** and received the condemnation of his home state. He was castigated in John Greenleaf Whittier's poem, "Ichabod," a Hebrew name meaning without honor. He tried for the presidency in 1852, but lost out to Winfield Scott. Webster returned home and died before the **election of 1852**, heartbroken over the future of the Union he had fought so long to preserve.

WEBSTER–ASHBURTON TREATY (1842). See CANADIAN BOUNDARY DISPUTE.

WEBSTER–HAYNE DEBATES. See JACKSON'S BREAK WITH CALHOUN; NON-EXCLUSION DOCTRINE; NULLIFICATION CRISIS; WEBSTER, DANIEL.

WEED, THURLOW. See CHICAGO CONVENTION (1860); ELECTION OF 1840, FILLMORE, MILLARD.

WESTERN LANDS CESSION. Through the Peace of Paris (1783), which ended the Revolutionary War, Britain yielded all of the land from the Appalachian Mountains to the Mississippi River to the new, independent nation, the United States of America. But the lands were not the domain of the nation, but of merely some of the 13 states. This was a sticking point with the landless states, and caused one of them, Maryland, to hold up the creation of the new central government under the **Articles of Confederation** for four years until the lands were ceded to the nation as a whole.

There were several reasons the landless states demanded the cession. The lands had been fought for by all the states and all should share equally in them. Ceding the lands to the central government would strengthen the bond of the Union among all of the states. The central government had potentially greater resources to defend the lands from foreign incursion or Native American attacks. States with no lands would be at a disadvantage to those with lands when it came to taxing its population. Finally, land sales (no one envisioned them being for free) would help pay off the tremendous national debt from the Revolutionary War.

The most important claim held by any one state was that of Virginia, which ran to the Pacific west and northwest from Old Point Comfort. When Virginia ceded its claims at landless Maryland's insistence, the other states followed suit. Maryland then ratified the Articles of Confederation. Georgia was the last to yield its Western lands in 1802, just as the **Yazoo Land Frauds** were made public. Not all of the Western claims were totally ceded to the United States. Many states kept small tracts to pay off their Revolutionary War soldiers, like the Virginia Reserve around Cincinnati and the Connecticut Western Reserve at Cleveland. The **Land Ordinance** of 1785, the **Northwest Ordinance** of 1787, and the **Southwest Ordinance** of 1790 all provided for the survey, government, and settlement of these territories.

WHIG PARTY. Formed in 1832 by those in opposition to Andrew Jackson's presidential reelection, the Whig Party has faded into historical obscurity. Named after the colonial patriots and British politicians who protested King George III's tyranny during the American Revolution, the 19th century Whigs were so-called because they opposed "King Andrew I of veto memory." **Andrew Jackson** was the first president to use veto power to turn down actions that were not overtly unconstitutional.

At its onset, the Whig federation comprised three distinct groups who shared their opposition to Andrew Jackson. The first group, **Henry Clay** and the **National Republican**s, embraced a sophisticated economic policy that Clay's **American System** incorporated, mandating a strong central government. The second group contained **John C. Calhoun** and the South Carolina Nullifiers, who joined the new party out of hatred for Jackson and Van Buren, yet they advocated laisser-faire economics and a weak federal government. **John Tyler** and the Virginia Nullifiers formed the third group, Calhoun's sole supporters outside of South Carolina in 1833.

Two major weaknesses hindered the party: **Daniel Webster**, whose native New England provided the largest bloc of party votes in national elections, questioned Clay's leadership that drove the party. Second, Calhoun and Tyler were perpetually against the party's economic dogma, regardless of its leader. They saw the American System and its belief in a high **tariff** unconstitutional and discriminatory toward the South. But their disdain for Jackson, and especially **Martin Van Buren**'s presence as Jackson's successor, prevailed, keeping them party adherents until their foes lost national elections. Clay moderated his economic programs until the Whigs won the presidency in 1840 with **William Henry Harrison**.

After the 1830s, the party attracted upper-class Yankee businessmen and Southern planters who advocated similar economic policies. The party then split into the Conscience Whigs and the Cotton Whigs. The former were old-money New England shipping magnates who preferred principle over victory and opposed the extension of **slavery** into the West. The Cotton Whigs were the nouveau riche **cotton**-milling manufacturing class in New England. As the 1840s approached and the slavery quarrel intensified, some Cotton Whigs altered their view on slavery. But generally they ignored slavery and backed the Southern cotton planters who provided raw materials for their cotton mills, and the **sugar** planters, who supported a high tariff to eliminate cheap foreign sugar competition.

The Whigs brought several policies to the fore. They spearheaded a viable economic development program, the American System, which remained strong during its 25-year existence. They were the pioneers of progressive campaign methods such as sloganeering and high-profile advertising. However, they were unable to win enough votes to ensure the presidency on the basis of their platform. To that end, they put forth military heroes such as **William Henry Harrison**, **Zachary Taylor**, and **Winfield Scott**. Their only alternative was their recurrent candidate, party leader **Henry Clay**, who seemed perpetually tainted with political corruption.

As the **War with Mexico** ended, the Whigs, encumbered by their diversity, splintered into factions over the slavery issue. The **Democrats** tended to share Southern opinions on the role of slavery in the **Constitution** and the day-to-day settlement of the West, but the Cotton Whigs, at least the Southern elements, began to defect to the Democratic party. Few traces remained in the **election of 1856** as the **American Party**, but the Whig Party was formally dissolved by the **election of 1860**.

WHITE, HUGH LAWSON (1773–1840). Originally from North Carolina, Hugh Lawson White crossed the mountains into Tennessee with his family in 1787. He was secretary to Governor William Blount and was prominent in the Cherokee wars, where he was credited with killing Chief Kingfisher in hand-to-hand combat.

Going to Philadelphia, White studied law and was admitted to the bar in Tennessee. He served in various judgeships and as a state senator. He ran the state Bank of Tennessee at Knoxville, managing it so well that it was the only Western bank to survive the **Panic of 1819** intact. After serving on a claims commission, White was elected to succeed **Andrew Jackson** as U.S. Senator in 1825.

When Jackson became president, White supported him throughout his administration. But White believed that Jackson's concept of active rotation in office led to lousy appointments. By 1836, White led the opposition to **Martin Van Buren** succeeding Jackson and shifted over to the **Whig** Party. When the state legislature instructed him to vote for Van Buren's independent sub-treasury system, White refused and resigned from the Senate. He died shortly afterward. His integrity caused many to eulogize him as the "Cato of the Senate."

WHITNEY, ELI (1765–1825). Born in Massachusetts, Eli Whitney attended Yale College, paying his tuition through teaching and day labor jobs. He went to Georgia as a tutor and soon came under the patronage of the widow of Gen. Nathaniel Greene. This allowed Whitney time to pursue the study of law while he resided on her estate.

The demand for **cotton** had expanded greatly worldwide after the American Revolution, and Whitney learned that the American South had the perfect answer in an ideal climate to grow green seed or **upland cotton**. There was one great problem with upland cotton—the seeds were very difficult to remove from the fibers by hand. This severely limited the marketing of the crop in volume. Whether Whitney did the work himself, or stole the idea from a neighborhood slave artisan as some assert, he developed a small box with a hopper that could be filled with raw cotton. The fibers would be run through two crank-operated spiked rollers working in opposition to each other to strip the seeds from the cotton and throw them aside. This meant that American upland cotton could now meet the demands of world trade, especially after the cotton engine (hence the term **cotton gin**) was married to the steam engine.

Somewhere along the line, the plans to Whitney's device were stolen and made available to the public. The inventor tried desperately to protect the proceeds from his device, but he had no patent. He soon exhausted all monies including a $5,000 gift from the South Carolina legislature. Returning north, Whitney became involved in the production of firearms using interchangeable parts, which allowed the parts of one gunlock and barrel to be switched with those of another at will. He made a fortune on this invention and on January 8, 1825, died in Connecticut a rich man.

WIGFALL, LOUIS T. (1816–1873). South Carolina–born and educated, Louis T. Wigfall enlisted for the Second Seminole War in which he served as a lieutenant of infantry. He then studied law at the University of Virginia before he removed to Texas in 1846. Wigfall established a law business at Marshall and was elected to the state legislature as a Democrat. By 1860 he was elected a member of the state senate.

Soon after joining the Texas state senate, Wigfall was elected to the U.S. Senate, where he became a leading figure in the **first secession** movement. He remained in the Senate until he was expelled in July 1860 for treasonous activity on behalf of the secession cause. He represented Texas at Montgomery in 1861 and was a signer of the **Confederate Constitution**.

As soon as the crisis developed at Ft. Sumter in Charleston, South Carolina, Wigfall returned to his home state and effected the fort's surrender through his personal negotiation. He immediately went to Richmond and secured a commission as colonel of the Second Texas Volunteer Infantry. He never served with the regiment, but instead parlayed his political connections into a brigadier generalship in the fall of 1861.

Wigfall received the command of the Texas Brigade in Virginia, later famous as Brig. Gen. John B. Hood's Brigade. But opportunity beckoned from the Confederate Senate, to which he had been elected by a grateful Texas legislature. While in the Confederate Senate, Wigfall rallied anti-**Jefferson Davis** politicians, angry at Confederate war policy. Upon Confederate defeat he fled to England. He lived there three years before returning to live in Baltimore, Maryland. He died on a trip to his Texas home shortly afterward on February 18, 1874.

WILDCAT. *See* INDIAN REMOVAL COMPLETED.

WILKINSON, JAMES. *See* BURR, AARON.

WILLIAM & JAMES BROWN & COMPANY *v.* THOMAS McGRAN (1840). Because Southern agriculture operated to sell its **staple crops** through cotton **factors**, who operated for their own interest as well as the planters', there was much litigation to establish legal boundaries in their business relationship. U.S. **Supreme Court** Associate Justice Joseph Story wrote the law of factorage in the McGran case in 1840, which was publicized all over the South and very well-known.

The rules codified the customs that had been in use since colonial days. The planter had to set the conditions to control the sale of his crop. The factor was obliged to obey any instructions given to him. If the planter gave no instructions, the factor had the right to sell according to his own best judgment, using sound discretion and the customs of the area in which he operated. Should a factor disobey orders, he had to absorb all losses incurred by his actions. But a factor could sell at a lower price than the planter desired if he correctly believed that the price would not rise.

If a factor informed a planter by letter that he would not follow his instructions, and the planter did not advise him otherwise, the factor could act on his own and suffer no loss. A factor could sell earlier than instructed, providing he had a lien on the crop. A lien existed only if the factor had bought supplies for the planter whose crop he was selling. But a planter did not have to sell his crop through any factor, even if the factor had bought supplies for him on credit.

The Court emphasized that all transactions had to be written out to be legal. But here the Court ran up against Southern social proprieties. The word of a gentleman was enough on all matters in the South. Indeed, for a factor to insist on a written contract might be deemed insulting enough to be settled on the **dueling** ground.

Planters often dealt openly through several factors at the same time. They might begin with one factor at the beginning of the season and then switch to another half-way through the growing season.

It was expected that a new factor would pay off all the debts the planter owed to his former factor.

Because of the planters' constant shifting from factor to factor, some factors, especially at New Orleans, kept a black list of planters they would not represent. But in any case, a factor was obliged by law, custom, and tradition to seek the highest price available for crop sales and the lowest price available when buying supplies. No factor could speculate with a crop he was representing. But he could speculate with any crop that he bought outright from another factor.

WILMOT PROVISO (1846, 1848). The Wilmot Proviso represented the radical **anti-slavery** view of the North, stating that **slavery** should be forbidden in any Western territories acquired as the result of victory in the **War with Mexico**. David Wilmot, a Democratic Pennsylvania congressman, presented it as a rider on the Army Appropriations Bill of 1846. Wilmot and many Northeastern **Democrats** believed that President **James K. Polk** had stolen the presidential nomination from their candidate, **Martin Van Buren**.

Their agenda consisted of introducing an anti-slavery measure to set off Polk and Southern Democrats by forcing them to oppose the measure in Congress. This would prove that the purpose of the War with Mexico was blatant conquest, provoked under the intent of spreading slavery into the West and adding slave states. It was correctly seen as flagrant Democratic politics when Wilmot introduced it in 1846, so it faced no opposition. The so-called Federal Ratio, the **Three-Fifths Compromise** in the **Constitution** that gave the South extra representation in Congress by counting that proportion of its slaves, caused its defeat. In effect, the Proviso isolated the **Slave Power Conspiracy** as Wilmot wished to do.

It was reintroduced in 1848 undisguised as a measure to prohibit slavery in the Western territories, which immediately raised a hue and cry. Northerners saw it as a practical means of limiting the spread of slavery. It had precedents: under the **Articles of Confederation** through the **Northwest Land Ordinance** of 1787, which prohibited slavery north of the Ohio River; and under the Constitution by way of the **Missouri Compromise**, which prohibited slavery in the West (the 36°30' line). Southerners believed it prevented them from enjoying the fruits of the war which they had fought with greater conviction than the anti-slave Northeast. They felt the earlier compromises denied their rights in the West and were unconstitutional.

The North feared slavery expansion into the West would bring in more potential slave states under the Federal Ratio. This issue prevailed in the **election of 1848,** ultimately provoking **secession** and the Civil War.

WIRT, WILLIAM. *See* ELECTION OF 1832.

WITHLACOOCHIE, BATTLE OF (1836). *See* INDIAN REMOVAL COMPLETED.

WOMEN IN THE OLD SOUTH. Before the Civil War, the Old South was a patriarchal society right out of the Middle Ages in the sense that it was pre-capitalistic and almost feudal in nature. It tended to compartmentalize men and women into different spheres. Men operated in a public capacity where they provided for their families and property, operated businesses, and conducted local, sectional, and national politics. Women worked their magic behind the scenes, as it were. They were to embrace femininity, beauty, simplicity, and submissiveness. They were to be nurturing mothers, dutiful wives, and social moral pillars. The women in the Old South stood high on the public pedestal and men protected them there.

This meant that the Southern woman was subordinate to the men in her life, be they her father, husband, brothers, or sons. The only property a woman could legally own was that inherited from the men in her life. By yielding to the male dominance in society, at least publicly, the Southern women legitimatized male gallantry, benevolence, and masculinity through their own outward moral purity.

Many historians consider the Southern woman to have been a victim of the slave society. But females worked to empower themselves, particularly after 1840 and especially after the Confederate loss of the Civil War, through their own **education** as reflected in their activities in religious and secular organizations. These promoted aid to the ill and downtrodden, promotion of temperance, control of sexual promiscuity, and even women's rights.

As a daughter, the girl's every act reflected upon her family name and her father's social status. As a wife the same held true of her husband's name and social position. One of the places that Southern women learned to promote themselves and their own abilities was through education. Girls between the ages of 12 and 14 were sent away to young ladies' academies and boarding schools. Not only did they learn the etiquette necessary for proper conduct in public affairs, they acquired knowledge in various formal school topics such as moral philosophy, Christianity, natural history, foreign languages (especially French), music, literature, math, and science. This was the opportunity of their lives. But their fathers expected less of them in education than they demanded from their sons.

After attending the academy, the young lady became eligible for marriage. But there was often no hurry. Young ladies often gloried in this period of dances, balls, and what was deemed appropriate interaction between young men and women. Often the **church and religion** took the lead in bringing young people together in Christian activities like picnics and Bible studies. One might dance and flirt with a beau, but only at a safe distance. Touching was limited in contact and duration.

Engagement came next. This was not to be entered into lightly. A broken engagement was tantamount to a divorce in its adverse social implications. It meant that the family and father were insulted, not only the girl's but her betrothed's, too. An engagement was a marriage without legal documentation. When the actual marriage took place, the Southern lady went from being the coy center of attention in the eyes of her man to becoming a submissive wife. A proper wife did not try to control or oppose her husband in any manner. Her one chore was to run the household. This could be relatively simple for a middle-class woman or more complex for a **plantation mistress**. But her husband was not financially responsible for anything but the bare necessities of housekeeping. Her main personal responsibility was to bear a male heir to carry on the family name.

But deep within the expected role of the Southern women was a fault. While at the academies, the young ladies no longer had to submit to men. They learned to be feminine, dainty, and loyal; but they also found out how to be tough and commanding in real life. Many women tried to expand their interests from the household to a wider world. This was possible so long as one did not cross the line between being a lady and "unsexing" herself in a man's occupation.

Where that line actually was, no one really knew. She could teach, care for children, and write poetry and light literature, but running a business was supposed to be beyond her ken, and politics was completely forbidden. Working in the cotton fields or the cotton, millinery, and iron mills or taking in laundry was definitely borderline, except for middle-class non-slaveholding families. Indeed, much of the labor handled by slaves in a planter's family was carried out by white women in less rich circumstances. Those few female slaves that the middle-class family might have worked side by side with white women.

Women in the Old South acquired an "inner stamina" to handle household and even business demands on their own—attributes that were reinforced when they took over the home front as their men went off to fight for Southern political independence in the Civil War. Women managed slaves and made daily decisions regarding planting, harvesting, food supply, nursing, and survival skills. They, particularly those who owned no slaves, worked in jobs requiring tedious labor, like gunpowder mills, iron works, and warehouses and groceries.

The **Confederate government** called on women to support the war in addition to everyday tasks. This involved writing letters to the troops away at war, knitting socks, sewing uniforms, making shirts and pants, saving urine for niter production, and organizing ladies' aid societies to coordinate such work. The result was that the Southern women came off the pedestal, hit the ground running, and never looked back.

Through it all, they managed the task with a consummate grace that concealed the grief and hardship the war brought. Yet in the end, it was the exhaustion of the Southern women that may have caused the collapse of the Confederacy. The toll of being woman, protector, and provider for her family, her slaves, and those less fortunate was too much. Feminism, submissiveness, and piety were ultimately lost along with the war. But before the War for Southern Independence changed everything, a woman's status in the Old South was dependent upon her character and that of her husband.

If white women learned strength because of the vicissitudes of war, black women learned it through the travail of **slavery** itself. The day of a female slave was usually longer than that of the male. For, in addition to her tasks in the field or cooking and caring for the white family, she had to look after her own. The tasks of the female fieldhand could be so exhausting that there was little energy to devote to familial responsibilities.

Larger plantations recognized this by providing nurseries for the black children and meal preparation for all slaves. On smaller farms, the white and black women shared the familial tasks with little regard to race. It was those slave women in units that were too big to see the white planter and his wife working alongside the slaves and not big enough to devote one or two hands to child care and cooking who frequently returned from her day's work too tired to do anything but collapse in bed.

It was not that slave women cared little for their children, as some pro-slave theorists callously asserted. The problem was that the system allowed so little time for a mother to see her children, except just before the morning bell summoned them to work or the evening bell sent them home after dark, and on weekends with their free time. Pregnancy was often quite difficult. Better slaveowners allowed a pregnant slaves a month or so off before the birth of her child and recuperation and nursing time afterward. But illness and "women's problems," both real and as a way to avoid work, were constant on the plantation.

Because of the contradictory position of the male slave as master of his family but not of his destiny or their existence, the black woman often stepped into the breech and provided family leadership. Above all, she had to see that the constant emasculation of the male slave under the demands of the white **overseer** did not make him less of a man at home in the quarters. This made black men and women much more equal within the family structure than whites were. A slave family was seen under law and custom to be the mother and her children, quite matriarchal as opposed to the male-dominated white society. This could protect the child from being sent or sold away from his mother, but usually only until about age 10 or so. After that, all bets were off. When it came to the realities of slavery, the father would be sold without a second thought, and the children at any age if the settlement of an estate made it monetarily necessary. *See also* SOCIAL HIERARCHY, SOCIALIZATION.

WORCESTER v. GEORGIA (1832). See INDIAN REMOVAL.

WORTH, COL. WILLIAM. See INDIAN REMOVAL COMPLETED.

– X –

X, Y, Z AFFAIR. See QUASI-WAR.

– Y –

YANCEY, WILLIAM L. (1814–1863). Born in Georgia, William L. Yancey lost his father at an early age. His mother married a New York man who took the family North, where young Yancey finished his education at several private academies. He briefly attended Williams College but never graduated because of lack of money. Yancey returned to the South and read law and was admitted to the South Carolina bar. He also met and married Sarah Earle, from a wealthy Greenville family, and thereby became an immediate slaveowner.

As a newspaper editor in Greenville, Yancey opposed **Nullification and the Concurrent Voice** as put forward by John C. Calhoun and his allies in the 1830s. Yancey decided to move his wife and her slaves to Alabama, but his plantation failed when in a dispute with a neighbor all of his wells were poisoned, killing most of his slaves.

Yancey entered law with John A. Elmore at Cahaba and became quite wealthy. Moving to Montgomery, Yancey entered state politics and served in both houses of the state legislature and the U.S. Congress. At this time Yancey began to change his political views to embody the **Non-Exclusion Doctrine** and **extraterritoriality** of slavery, which he put forward in the **Democratic** convention of 1848 as the Alabama Platform.

With the Compromise of 1850, Yancey became a full-fledged **fire-eater** in favor of immediate **secession**, a position that he pushed until it became a reality in 1861. He was instrumental in breaking up the Democratic convention during the **election of 1860**, advocating the Alabama Platform, until the party sundered. Yancey supported **John

C. Breckinridge** and the Southern wing of the party in the **election of 1860**.

After the secession of the South, the conservative Confederate government got rid of Yancey by making him a roving ambassador to Europe, trying to obtain recognition for the Confederacy. He failed in his efforts, being anything but diplomatic. Returning to the Old South, Yancey was elected to the Confederate Congress, where he opposed the government of **Jefferson Davis** on nearly every issue, He died suddenly in July 1863.

YAZOO LAND FRAUDS. By the time of the presidential **election of 1804**, President **Thomas Jefferson** had alienated a small group of ideologically pure **Democratic Republicans** enough for them to bolt the party. Led by **John Randolph** of Roanoke, these men called themselves the Tertium Quids. They opposed Jefferson's willingness to play fast and loose with the Constitution just as Alexander Hamilton had in the 1790s with **Funding and Assumption** and the **Bank of United States**. The Quids protested the **Louisiana Purchase** and Jefferson's willingness to continue most **Federalist** programs. But the thing they hated most was Jefferson's acceptance of the Yazoo Land Frauds.

The Yazoo district was essentially present-day Alabama and Mississippi above the 31st parallel. It was claimed by Georgia from its colonial charter and was the reason that Georgia would not make its **Western Lands Cession** until 1802. With the signing of **Pinckney's Treaty** in 1795, the Yazoo district was confirmed as belonging to Georgia and the United Sates. The state decided to sell the lands to a group of land speculators. Legend has it that a Yazoo lobbyist threatened legislators with a loaded whip handle, but he did not have to. Only one member's vote in the legislature was not bought.

The act was so crooked that the governor vetoed it. The legislature repassed it over his veto. The governor then went into a huddle with the lobbyists, and his price was met. A united front was presented to the people, and the Yazoo district went to the land company for $500,000. Georgians did not fall for this larceny. They booted the governor and the legislature out at the next election. The sale law was repealed and burned in a public ceremony to wipe the stain from the books. Then Georgia relinquished control over the Yazoo district to the United States government in 1802.

The Yazoo land men, who turned out to be mostly **Federalists** from the North, immediately asked the **Democratic Republican** federal government of **Thomas Jefferson** for compensation. They claimed that the Georgia repeal law had illegally seized their property and implied that the state legislature could declare its own laws unconstitutional, all of which was patent nonsense. Besides, there was no provision in the U.S. Constitution to pay off shady land deals. But the Yazoo men were correct about one thing. They had resold some of the land to purchasers who bought in good faith.

Jefferson assembled a commission under Secretary of State **James Madison** to review the case. Then he asked Congress to set aside $5 million to pay off any legal claimants. Led by John Randolph of Roanoke, a small group of Jefferson's own party, called the Tertium Quids, exploded in protest. They maintained that the government was endorsing a fraud through an act that was unconstitutional on its face. Randolph was chairman of the Ways and Means Committee in the House. He blocked any compensation.

Angered, Jefferson got the party to kick Randolph off the committee. Still Randolph ranted against the Yazoo settlement. He also blocked the pending annexation of West Florida. But most immediately he broke with Jefferson's seeking a second term. Eventually the Yazoo company would sue Georgia in a case that reached the U.S. **Supreme Court** as *Fletcher v. Peck* (1810). Here Chief Justice **John Marshall** wrote a decision that said that the original Yazoo law was a contract that could not be broken without the consent of both parties. The Yazoo men were paid off at last. And Georgia managed to retrieve the Yazoo district, after the payoffs, and resell it to the United States for $1.2 million. The only losers were Randolph and principle.

YOUNG, BRIGHAM. *See* MORMON WAR.

YOUNG AMERICA. This was a component of the American movement called **Manifest Destiny.** In 1848, the citizens of the United States widely supported the revolutions in Europe for constitutional government, with or without monarchy, so reminiscent of the American Revolution of 1776. The European revolutionaries formed societies named after their nations, or hoped-for nations, such as Young Italy, Young Hungary, Young Germany, Young Ireland, and such.

Following suit, in 1850, Edwin De Leon of South Carolina inspired Americans to form Young America, who sent armed mercenaries to assist the European revolutionaries. The federal government appointed A. Dudley Mann, a professional diplomat who later served in the Confederate diplomatic corps, as its minister to the Hungarian Revolution which, prior to his arrival, suffered great oppression at the hands of the Russians. The Austrian government forcefully protested this American interference but was rebuffed and challenged by Secretary of State **Daniel Webster**. In another incident, Martin Koszta, a Hungarian revolutionary who had visited the United States and tried to become an American citizen, was arrested upon his return to Europe by an Austrian officer in the Ottoman Empire. The United States deployed a warship to secure his release.

Americans welcomed the exiled heroes of the European revolution who had escaped violent suppression. Hungarian revolutionary leader Lajos Kossuth was greeted with enthusiasm on his visit to the United States in 1851. Over 100,000 cheering, waving supporters lined the railroad tracks as he passed. He made an eloquent speech before the Ohio state legislature, declaring 1803 a great year because both he and the state of Ohio were born. In Washington, D.C., Webster demanded Hungarian independence, self-government, and control of that nation's destinies. The dour old **James Buchanan**, U.S. Minister to the Court at St. James, entertained Kossuth and all the European states in London, although his subordinate, George N. Sanders, later implicated in the Lincoln kidnap and assassination conspiracies, did the legwork. It was an American ideal to support the world's revolutionaries in the 19th century, an integral part of America's **"Spread Eagle" foreign policy** of the 1850s.

Select Bibliography

CONTENTS

I.	General	384
II.	The Old South in Early America, 1783–1828	385
	1. The Confederation and the Constitution	385
	2. The Cotton Gin and the New Slave Economy	386
	3. George Washington and Alexander Hamilton	387
	4. The Federalist Era	388
	5. The Age of Thomas Jefferson and the Louisiana Purchase	390
	6. James Madison, the War of 1812, and the First Seminole War	392
	7. The Era of Good Feelings and the Missouri Compromise	393
	8. The Great Migration	394
III.	The Old South in the Jacksonian Era, 1829–1848	396
	1. The Age of Andrew Jackson	396
	2. The Native Americans and Indian Removal	397
	3. Slavery, the Nullification Crisis, and the Tariff	399
	4. Jacksonian Economics and the Bank War	400
	5. Texas Independence and the War with Mexico	400
	6. After Jackson	401
IV.	Slavery in the Old South, 1783–1865	403
	1. General	403
	2. State and Local Studies	404
	3. Profitability, Slave Management, and the Economics of Slavery	406
	4. Life and Society on the Plantation	408
	5. International and Domestic Slave Trade	410
	6. Industrial and Urban Slavery	412

	7. Abolition, Colonization, Passive Resistance, and Slave Rebellion	413
	8. Slavery, Abolitionists, and Abolition in the North and Haiti	415
	9. Slave Hiring-Out and Free People of Color	417
V.	The Law of Slavery and the Constitution	419
VI.	Class and Society in the Old South, 1783–1865	420
	1. General	420
	2. The Planter Class and Its Cohorts	421
	3. Non-Slaveholding Whites	423
	4. Southern Women	424
	5. Religion and Education	425
	6. Family Life and Leisure Pursuits, Benign and Deadly	426
	7. The Mind of the Old South	428
	8. Agriculture and the Southern Economy	429
VII	The Old South and the Era of Sectional Controversy, 1849–1861	430
	1. The Wilmot Proviso and the Compromise of 1850	430
	2. The Kansas Imbroglio, Popular Sovereignty, and Dred Scott	432
	3. The Expansion of Slavery at Home and Abroad	433
	4. Politics and Slavery	434
	5. Biographies	437
	6. The Road to Secession	439
VIII.	The Confederacy, 1861–1865	441
	1. Confederate Government and Ideology	441
	2. Confederate Political Leaders	442
	3. Confederate Military Leaders	443
	4. The Armies in the Field	443
	5. The South and the Northern Enemy	444

I. GENERAL

Boles, John B. and Evelyn Thomas Nolen (eds.). *Interpreting Southern History; Historiographical Essays in Honor of Sanford W. Higgnbotham*. Baton Rouge: Louisiana State University Press, 1987.

Current, Richard N. *et al*. (eds.). *Encyclopedia of the Confederacy*. 4 vols. New York: Simon & Schuster, 1993.

Dodd, Donald B. and Wynelle S. Dodd (comps.). *Historical Statistics of the South, 1790–1970*. University: University of Alabama Press, 1973.

Ericson, David F. *The Shaping of American Liberalism: The Debates over Ratification, Nullification, and Slavery*. Chicago; University of Chicago Press, 1993.

Fehrenbacher, Don E. *The South and Three Sectional Crises*. Baton Rouge: Louisiana State University Press, 1980.

Finkelman, Paul (ed.). *Slavery, Race, and the American Legal System, 1700–1872*. 16 vols. New York: Garland, 1988.

Foster, Gaines M. "Guilt over Slavery: A Historiographical Analysis," *Journal of Southern History*, 56 (1990), 665–94.

Gordon, David (ed.). *Secession, State, & Liberty*. New Brunswick, N.J.: Transaction Publishers, 1998.

Green, Fletcher M. and J. Isaac Copeland. *The Old South*. Arlington Heights, Ill.: AHM Publishing, 1980.

Klein, Martin A. *Historical Dictionary of Slavery and Abolition*. Lanham, Md.: Scarecrow Press, 2002.

Link, Arthur S. and Rembert W. Patrick (eds.). *Writing Southern History: Essays in Honor of Fletcher M. Green*. Baton Rouge: Louisiana State University Press, 1967.

McPherson, James M. and William J. Cooper (eds.). *Writing the Civil War: The Quest to Understand*. Columbia: University of South Carolina Press, 1998.

Miller, Randall M. and John David Smith (eds.). *The Dictionary of Afro-American Slavery*. Westport, Conn.: Praeger, 1997.

Phillips, Ulrich B. "The Central Theme of Southern History," *American Historical Review*, 34 (1928), 30–43.

Richter, William L. *Historical Dictionary of the Civil War and Reconstruction*. Lanham, Md.: Scarecrow Press, 2004.

Roller, David C. and Robert W. Twyman (eds.). *Encyclopedia of Southern History*. Baton Rouge: Louisiana State University Press, 1979.

Vandiver, Frank E. (ed.). *The Idea of the South: The Pursuit of a Central Theme*. Chicago: University of Chicago Press, 1964.

Waldstreicher, David. *In the Midst of Perpetual Fêtes: The Making of American Nationalism, 1776–1920*. Chapel Hill: University of North Carolina Press, 1997.

Wilson, Charles R. and William Ferris (eds.). *Encyclopedia of Southern Culture*. Chapel Hill: University of North Carolina Press, 1989.

Woodward, C. Vann. *American Counterpoint: Slavery and Racism in the North-South Dialogue*. Boston: Little, Brown, 1971.

———. *The Burden of Southern History*. New York: Mentor Books, 1968 (rev. ed).

II. THE OLD SOUTH IN EARLY AMERICA, 1783–1828

1. The Confederation and the Constitution

Ambler, Charles Henry. *Sectionalism in Virginia, from 1776 to 1861*. New York: Russell & Russell, 1910.

Bailyn, Bernard. *Ideological Origins of the American Revolution*. Cambridge, Mass.: Harvard University Press, 1967.
Banning, Lance. *The Sacred Fire of Liberty: James Madison and the Founding of the Federal Republic*. Ithaca, N.Y.: Cornell University Press, 1995.
Beeman, Ruchard, et al. (eds.). *Beyond Confederation: Origins of the Constitution and American National Identity*. Chapel Hill: University of North Carolina Press, 1987.
Brady, Patrick S. "The Slave Trade and Sectionalism in South Carolina, 1787–1808," *Journal of Southern History*, 38 (1972), 601–20.
Brookhiser, Richard. *Gentleman Revolutionary: Gouverneur Morris—The Rake Who Wrote the Constitution*. New York: Free Press, 2003.
Freehling, William W. "The Founding Fathers and Slavery," *American Historical Review*, 77 (1972), 81–93.
Lynd, Stoughton (ed.). *Class Conflict, Slavery, and the United States Constitution: Ten Essays*. Indianapolis: Bobbs-Merrill. 1967.
MacLeod, Duncan J. *Slavery, Race, and the American Revolution*. Cambridge, Mass.: Harvard University Press, 1974.
Nagel, Paul C. *One Nation Indivisible: The Union in American Thought, 1776–1861*. New York: Oxford University Press, 1964.
Ohline, Howard A. "Republicanism and Slavery: Origins of the Three-fifths Clause in the United States Constitution," *William and Mary Quarterly*, 3rd Ser., 28 (1971), 563–94.
Onuf, Peter. "From Constitution to Higher Law: The Reinterpretation of the Northwest Ordinance," *Ohio History*, 94 (1985), 5–33.
Rakove, Jack N. *Original Meanings: Politics and Ideas in the Making of the Constitution*. New York: Knopf, 1996.
Richards, Leonard L. *The Slave Power: The Free North and Southern Domination, 1780–1860*. Baton Rouge: Louisiana State University Press, 2000.
Rodell, Fred. *Fifty-Five Men: The Story of the Constitution Based on the Day-by-Day Notes of James Madison*. Harrisburg, Penn.: Stackpole, 1986.
St. George, Judith. *Mason and Dixon's Line of Fire*. New York: Putnam, 1991.
Wallace, David Duncan. *The Life of Henry Laurens*. New York: Russell & Russell, 1967 [orig. 1915].
Zahniser, Marvin R. *Charles Cotesworth Pinckney: Founding Father.* Chapel Hill: University of North Carolina Press, 1967.

2. The Cotton Gin and the New Slave Economy

Abernethy, Thomas P. *The South in the New Nation, 1789–1819*. Baton Rouge: Louisiana State University Press, 1961.
Breen, T. H. *Tobacco Culture: The Mentality of the Great Tidewater Planters on the Eve of the American Revolution*. Princeton: University of Princeton, N.J. Press, 1985.

Britton, Karen G. *Bale o' Cotton: The Mechanical Art of Cotton Ginning.* College Station: Texas A&M Press, 1992.
Carney, Judith A. *Black Rice: The African Origins of Rice.* Cambridge, Mass.: Harvard University Press, 2001.
Clark, John G. *New Orleans, 1718–1812: An Economic History.* Baton Rouge: Louisiana State University Press, 1970.
Green, Constance. *Eli Whitney and the Birth of American Technology.* Boston; Little, Brown, 1956.
Ohline, Howard A. "Slavery, Economics, and Congressional Politics," *Journal of Southern History*, 46 (1980), 335–60.
Palmer, Paul C. "Servant into Slave: The Evolution of the Legal Status of the Negro Laborer in Colonial Virginia," *South Atlantic Quarterly*, 65 (1966), 355–70.
Ragsdale, Bruce A. *A Planter's Republic: The Search for Economic Independence in Revolutionary Virginia.* Madison: University of Wisconsin Press, 1994.
Robinson, Donald L. *Slavery in the Structure of American Politics, 1765–1820.* New York: Norton, 1971.
St. George, Judith. *Mason and Dixon's Line of Fire.* New York: Putnam, 1991.
Unser, Daniel. *Indians, Settlers, and Slaves in a Frontier Exchange Economy: The Lower Mississippi Valley before 1803.* Chapel Hill: University of North Carolina Press, 1992.

3. George Washington and Alexander Hamilton

Alden, John R. *George Washington: A Biography.* Baton Rouge: Louisiana State University Press, 1984.
Brookhiser, Richard. *Alexander Hamilton, American.* New York: Free Press, 1999.
———. *Founding Father: Rediscovering George Washington.* New York: Free Press, 1996.
Chernow, Ron. *Alexander Hamilton.* New York: Penguin Press, 2004.
Flexner, James Thomas. *George Washington: A Biography.* Boston: Little, Brown, 1965–1972.
Freeman, Douglas S. *George Washington: A Biography.* 7 vols. New York: Charles Scribner's Sons, 1948–1957.
Hirschfeld, Fritz. *George Washington and Slavery: A Documentary Portrayal.* Columbia: University of Missouri Press, 1997.
Longmore, Paul. *The Invention of George Washington.* Berkeley: University of California Press, 1988.
McDonald, Forrest. *Alexander Hamilton: A Biography.* New York: Norton, 1979.
Mitchell, Broadus. *Alexander Hamilton.* 2 vols. New York: Macmillan, 1957–1962.
Spalding, Matthew and Patrick J. Garrity. *A Sacred Union of Citizens: George Washington's Farewell Address and the American Character.* Lanham, Md.: Rowman & Littlefield, 1996.
Wills, Garry. *Cincinnatus: George Washington and the Enlightenment.* Garden City, N.Y.: Doubleday, 1984.

4. The Federalist Era

Abernethy, Thomas P. *The South in the New Nation, 1789–1819.* Baton Rouge: Louisiana State University Press, 1961.

Anderson, William G. *Price of Liberty: The Public Debt of the American Revolution.* Charlottesville: University Press of Virginia, 1983.

Appleby, Joyce. *Capitalism and a New Social Order: The Republican Vision of the 1790s.* New York: New York University Press, 1984.

Arnbeck, Bob. *Through a Fiery Trial: Building Washington, 1790–1800.* Lanham, Md., Madison Books, 1991.

Bemis, Samuel Flagg. *Jay's Treaty: A Study in Commerce and Diplomacy.* New Haven, Conn.: Yale University Press, 1962.

Borden, Morton. *Parties and Politics in the Early Republic, 1789–1815.* New York: Crowell, 1967.

Bowling, Kenneth. "Dinner at Jefferson's: A Note on Jacob E. Cooke's 'The Compromise of 1790'," *William and Mary Quarterly*, 3rd Ser., 28 (1971), 629–48.

———. *The Creation of Washington, D.C.: The Idea and Location of the American Capital.* Fairfax, Va.: George Mason University Press, 1991.

Brookhiser, Richard. *America's First Dynasty: The Adamses, 1735–1918.* New York: Free Press, 2002.

———. *Gentleman Revolutionary: Gouverneur Morris—The Rake Who Wrote the Constitution.* New York: Free Press, 2003.

Broussard, James H. *The Southern Federalists, 1800–1816.* Baton Rouge: Louisiana State University Press, 1978.

Brown, Ralph A. *The Presidency of John Adams.* Lawrence: University of Kansas Press, 1993.

Buel, Richard, Jr. *Securing the Revolution: Ideology in American Politics, 1789–1815.* Ithaca, N.Y.: Cornell University Press, 1972.

Carpenter, Jesse T. *The South as a Conscious Minority, 1789–1861: A Study in Political Thought.* New York: New York University Press, 1930.

Chambers, William N. *Political Parties in a New Nation.* New York: Oxford University Press, 1963.

Charles, Joseph. *The Origins of the American Party System.* Williamsburg: Institute of Early American History and Culture, 1956.

Colbourn, Trevor (ed.). *Fame and the Founding Fathers: Essays by Douglass Adair.* New York: Norton, 1974.

Combs, Jerald A. *The Jay Treaty: Political Background of the Founding Fathers.* Berkeley: University of California Press, 1970.

Cooke, Jacob E. "The Compromise of 1790," *William and Mary Quarterly*, 3rd Ser., 27 (1970), 523–45.

Dauer, Manning. *The Adams Federalists.* Baltimore, Md.: The Johns Hopkins University Press, 1953.

Elkins, Stanley M. and Eric McKitrick. *The Age of Federalism: The Early Republic, 1787–1800.* New York: Oxford University Press, 1993.

Ellis, Joseph J. *Founding Brothers: The Revolutionary Generation*. New York: Vintage Books, 2002.
Ferguson, E. James. *The Power of the Purse: A History of American Public Finance*. Chapel Hill: University of North Carolina Press, 1961.
Finkelman, Paul. "The Kidnapping of John Davis and the Adoption of the Fugitive Slave Law of 1793," *Journal of Southern History*, 56 (1990), 397–422.
Hammond, Bray. *Banks and Politics in America from the Revolution to the Civil War*. Princeton: University of Princeton, N.J. Press, 1957.
Harris, C. M. "Washington's Gamble, L'Enfant's Dream: Politics, Design, and the Founding of the National Capital," *William and Mary Quarterly*, 3rd Ser., 56 (July 1999), 527–64.
Hobson, Charles F. *The Great Chief Justice: John Marshall and the Rule of Law*. Lawrence: University of Kansas Press, 1996.
Hofstadter, Richard. *The Idea of a Party System: The Rise of Legitimate Opposition in the United States, 1780–1840*. Berkeley: University of California Press, 1969.
Howe, John R., Jr. "Republican Thought and the Political Violence of the 1790s," *American Quarterly*, 19 (Summer 1967), 147–65.
Koch, Adreinne. *Jefferson and Madison: The Great Collaboration*. New York: Knopf. 1950.
Koch, Adrienne and Henry Ammon, "The Virginia and Kentucky Resolves: An Episode in Jefferson's and Madison's Defense of Civil Liberties," *William and Mary Quarterly*, 3rd Ser., 5 (1945), 170–89.
Kurtz, Stephen G. *The Presidency of John Adams: The Collapse of Federalism, 1795–1800*. Philadelphia: University of Pennsylvania Press, 1957.
Morgan, Edmund S. "John Adams and the Puritan Tradition," *New England Quarterly*, 34 (1961), 518–29.
Morton, Louis. *Robert Carter of Nomini Hall*. Charlottesville: University Press of Virginia, 1941.
Newman, Richard S. "Prelude to the Gag Rule: Southern Reaction to Antislavery Petitions in the First Federal Congress," *Journal of the Early Republic*, 46 (1996), 571–99.
Richards, Leonard L. *The Slave Power: The Free North and Southern Domination, 1780–1860*. Baton Rouge: Louisiana State University Press, 2000.
Risjord, Norman K. "The Compromise of 1790: New Evidence on the Dinner Table Bargain," *William and Mary Quarterly*, 3rd Ser., 33 (1976), 309–14.
———. *Chesapeake Politics, 1781–1800*. New York: Columbia University Press, 1978.
———. *The Early American Party System*. New York: Columbia University Press, 1969.
Robinson, Donald L. *Slavery in the Structure of American Politics, 1765–1820*. New York: Norton, 1971.
Rose, Lisle A. *Prologue to Democracy: The Federalists in the South, 1789–1800*. Lexington: University of Kentucky Press, 1968.

Sharp, Roger. *American Politics in the Early Republic: The New Nation in Crisis.* New Haven, Conn.: Yale University Press, 1993.

Sloan, Herbert E. *Thomas Jefferson and the Problem of Debt.* New York: Oxford University Press, 1995.

Smelser, Martin. "The Federalist Period as an Age of Passion," *American Quarterly,* 10 (Winter 1958), 391–419.

Smith, James Morton. *The Alien and Sedition Acts and American Civil Liberties.* Ithaca, N.Y.: Cornell University Press, 1956.

Smith, Page. *John Adams.* 2 vols. Garden City, N.Y.: Doubleday, 1962.

Thompson, C. Bradley. *John Adams and the Spirit of Liberty.* Lawrence: University of Kansas Press, 1998.

Zahniser, Marvin R. *Charles Cotesworth Pinckney: Founding Father.* Chapel Hill: University of North Carolina Press, 1967.

5. The Age of Thomas Jefferson and the Louisiana Purchase

Abernethy, Thomas P. *The South in the New Nation, 1789–1819.* Baton Rouge: Louisiana State University Press, 1961.

Adams, Henry. *History of the United States during the Administrations of Jefferson and Madison.* 9 vols. New York: Charles Scribner's Sons, 1889–1891.

Banning, Lance. *The Jeffersonian Persuasion: Evolution of a Party Ideology.* Ithaca, N.Y.: Cornell University Press, 1978.

Borden, Morton. *Parties and Politics in the Early Republic, 1789–1815.* New York: Crowell, 1967.

Brookhiser, Richard. *Gentleman Revolutionary: Gouverneur Morris—The Rake Who Wrote the Constitution.* New York: Free Press, 2003.

Buel, Richard, Jr. *Securing the Revolution: Ideology in American Politics, 1789–1815.* Ithaca, N.Y.: Cornell University Press, 1972.

Carpenter, Jesse T. *The South as a Conscious Minority, 1789–1861: A Study in Political Thought.* New York: New York University Press, 1930.

Cunningham, Noble E. *In Pursuit of Reason: The Life of Thomas Jefferson.* Baton Rouge: Louisiana State University Press, 1987.

———. *The Jeffersonian Republicans: The Formation of Party Organization, 1789–1801.* Chapel Hill: University of North Carolina Press, 1957.

———. *The Jeffersonian Republicans in Power: Party Operations, 1801–1809.* Chapel Hill: University of North Carolina Press, 1963.

Davis, David Brion. *Was Jefferson an Authentic Enemy of Slavery?* Oxford: Clarendon, 1970.

De Conde, Alexander. *This Affair of Louisiana.* New York: Charles Scribner's Sons, 1976.

Ellis, Joseph J. *American Sphinx: The Character of Thomas Jefferson.* New York: Knopf, 1997.

Finkelman, Paul. *Slavery and the Founders: Race and Liberty in the Age of Jefferson.* London: M. E. Sharp, 1996.

Freeman, Joanne. "Dueling as Politics: A Reinterpretation of the Burr-Hamilton Duel," *William and Mary Quarterly*, 3rd Ser., 53 (April 1996), 289–318.

Hofstadter, Richard. *The Idea of a Party System: The Rise of Legitimate Opposition in the United States, 1780–1840.* Berkeley: University of California Press, 1969.

Hosmer, James K. *The History of the Louisiana Purchase.* New York: D. Appleton, 1992.

Kaplan, Lawrence. *Entangling Alliances with None: American Foreign Policy in the Age of Jefferson.* Kent, Ohio: Kent State University Press, 1987.

Kerber, Linda. *Federalists in Dissent: Image and Ideology in Jeffersonian America.* Ithaca, N.Y.: Cornell University Press, 1970.

Lewis, Jan and Peter S. Onuf. *Sally Hemmings and Thomas Jefferson.* Charlottesville, University Press of Virginia, 1999.

Lomask, Milton. *Aaron Burr.* 2 vols. New York: Farrar, Strauss, and Giroux, 1979–1982.

Malone, Dumas. *Jefferson and His Time.* 6 vols. Boston: Little, Brown, 1948–1981.

McColley, Robert. *Slavery in Jeffersonian Virginia.* Urbana: University of Illinois Press, 1964.

McCoy, Drew R. *Elusive Republic: Political Economy in Jeffersonian America.* Chapel Hill: University of North Carolina Press, 1980.

Miller, John Chester. *The Wolf by the Ears: Thomas Jefferson and Slavery.* New York: Meridian, 1977.

Nagel, Paul C. *One Nation Indivisible: The Union in American Thought, 1776–1861.* New York: Oxford University Press, 1964.

Newmyer, R. Kent. *John Marshall and the Heroic Age of the Supreme Court.* Baton Rouge: Louisiana State University Press, 2001.

Richards, Leonard L. *The Life and Times of Congressman John Quincy Adams.* New York: Oxford University Press, 1986.

———. *The Slave Power: The Free North and Southern Domination, 1780–1860.* Baton Rouge: Louisiana State University Press, 2000.

Risjord, Norman K. *The Old Republicans: Southern Conservatism in the Age of Jefferson.* New York: Columbia University Press, 1965.

Robinson, Donald L. *Slavery in the Structure of American Politics, 1765–1820.* New York: Norton, 1971.

Shalhope, Robert E. "Thomas Jefferson's Republicanism and Antebellum Thought," *Journal of Southern History*, 72 (1976), 529–56.

———. "Toward a Republican Synthesis: The Emergence of an Understanding of Republicanism in American Historiography," *William and Mary Quarterly*, 3rd Ser., 29 (1972), 49–80.

Sharp, Roger. *American Politics in the Early Republic: The New Nation in Crisis.* New Haven, Conn.: Yale University Press, 1993.

Sloan, Herbert E. *Thomas Jefferson and the Problem of Debt.* New York: Oxford University Press, 1995.

Siegel, Adrienne. *The Marshall Court, 1801–1835.* Millwood, N.Y.: Associated Faculty Press, 1995.

Smith, Jean Edward. *John Marshall: Definer of a Nation*. New York: Henry Holt & Co., 1996.
Wallace, Anthony F. C. *Jefferson and the Indians: The Tragic Fate of the First Americans*. Cambridge, Mass.: Belknap Press, 1999.
Whitaker, Arthur P. *The Mississippi Question, 1795–1803*. New York: American Historical Association, 1934.
Young, James Sterling. *The Washington Community, 1800–1828*. New York: Columbia University Press, 1966.
Zahniser, Marvin R. *Charles Cotesworth Pinckney: Founding Father.* Chapel Hill: University of North Carolina Press, 1967.

6. James Madison, the War of 1812, and the First Seminole War

Abernethy, Thomas P. *The South in the New Nation, 1789–1819*. Baton Rouge: Louisiana State University Press, 1961.
Adams, Henry. *History of the United States during the Administrations of Jefferson and Madison*. 9 vols. New York: Charles Scribner's Sons, 1889–1891.
Brant, Irving. *James Madison*. 6 vols. Indianapolis: Bobbs-Merrill, 1941–1961.
Buel, Richard, Jr. *Securing the Revolution: Ideology in American Politics, 1789–1815*. Ithaca, N.Y.: Cornell University Press, 1972.
Carpenter, Jesse T. *The South as a Conscious Minority, 1789–1861: A Study in Political Thought*. New York: New York University Press, 1930.
Covington, James W. "The Negro Fort," *Gulf Coast Historical Review*, 4 (1996), 78–91.
Heidler, Davis S. and Jeanne T. Heidler. *Encyclopedia of the War of 1812*. Mechanicsburg, Penn.: Stackpole, 1997.
———. *Old Hickory's War: Andrew Jackson and the Quest for Empire*. Mechanicsburg, Penn.: Stackpole, 1996.
Hofstadter, Richard. *The Idea of a Party System: The Rise of Legitimate Opposition in the United States, 1780–1840*. Berkeley: University of California Press, 1969.
Horsman, Reginald. *The War of 1812*. New York: Knopf, 1969.
Ketcham, Ralph L. *James Madison: A Biography*. New York: Macmillan, 1971.
Koch, Adreinne. *Jefferson and Madison: The Great Collaboration*. New York: Knopf. 1950.
McCoy, Drew R. *The Last of the Fathers: James Madison and the Republican Legacy*. Cambridge, Mass.: Harvard University Press, 1989.
Newmyer, R. Kent. *John Marshall and the Heroic Age of the Supreme Court*. Baton Rouge: Louisiana State University Press, 2001.
Owsley, Frank Lawrence, Jr. *Struggle for the Gulf Borderlands: The Creek War and the Battle of New Orleans, 1812–1815*. Gainesville: University of Florida Press, 1981.
Rakove, Jack N. *James Madison and the Creation of the Federal Republic*. Glenview, Ill.: Scott Foresman/Little, Brown, 1990.

Richards, Leonard L. *The Slave Power: The Free North and Southern Domination, 1780–1860.* Baton Rouge: Louisiana State University Press, 2000.
Robinson, Donald L. *Slavery in the Structure of American Politics, 1765–1820.* New York: Norton, 1971.
Stagg, J. C. A. *Mr. Madison's War: Politics, Diplomacy and Warfare in the Early American Republic, 1783–1830.* Princeton, N.J.: Princeton, N.J. University Press, 1983.

7. The Era of Good Feelings and the Missouri Compromise

Abernethy, Thomas P. *The South in the New Nation, 1789–1819.* Baton Rouge: Louisiana State University Press, 1961.
Ambler, Charles Henry. *Thomas Ritchie: A Study in Virginia Politics.* Richmond, Va.: N. pub., 1913.
Ammon, Harry. *James Monroe and the Quest for National Identity.* New York: McGraw-Hill, 1971.
Bemis, Samuel Flagg. *John Quincy Adams and the Union.* New York: Knopf, 1956.
Brown, Richard. "The Missouri Crisis, Slavery, and the Politics of Jacksonianism," *South Atlantic Quarterly,* 65 (1966), 55–72.
Bruce, W. C. *John Randolph of Roanoke, 1773–1833.* New York: Octagon, 1970 [orig. 1922].
Brugger, Robert J. *Beverly Tucker: Heart over Mind in the Old South.* Baltimore, Md.: The Johns Hopkins University Press, 1978.
Carpenter, Jesse T. *The South as a Conscious Minority, 1789–1861: A Study in Political Thought.* New York: New York University Press, 1930.
Cunningham, Noble E. *The Presidency of James Monroe.* Lawrence: University of Kansas Press, 1996.
Dangerfield, George. *Era of Good Feelings.* New York: Harcourt, Brace & World, 1952.
Dawidoff, Robert. *The Education of John Randolph.* New York: Norton, 1979.
Eslinger, Ellen. "The Shape of Slavery on the Kentucky Frontier, 1775–1800," *Register of the Kentucky Historical Society,* 92 (1994), 1–23.
Fehrenbacher, Don E. "The Missouri Controversy and the Sources of Southern Separatism," *Southern Review,* 14 (1978), 653–67.
Hammond, Bray. *Banks and Politics in America from the Revolution to the Civil War.* Princeton, N.J.: University of Princeton, N.J. Press, 1957.
Hargreaves, Mary W. M. *The Presidency of John Quincy Adams.* Lawrence: University of Kansas Press, 1985.
Hofstadter, Richard. *The Idea of a Party System: The Rise of Legitimate Opposition in the United States, 1780–1840.* Berkeley: University of California Press, 1969.
Kirk, Russell B. *John Randolph of Roanoke.* Indianapolis: Liberty Press, 1978.
Miller, John Chester. *The Wolf by the Ears: Thomas Jefferson and Slavery.* New York: Meridian, 1977.

Mooney, Chase C. *William H. Crawford, 1772–1834*. Lexington: University of Kentucky Press, 1974.
Moore, Glover. *The Missouri Controversy, 1819–1821*. Lexington: University of Kentucky Press, 1966.
Newmyer, R. Kent. *John Marshall and the Heroic Age of the Supreme Court*. Baton Rouge: Louisiana State University Press, 2001.
Remini, Robert V. *Martin Van Buren and the Making of the Democratic Party*. New York: Columbia University Press, 1959.
——. *The Election of Andrew Jackson*. Philadelphia: Lippincott, 1963.
Richards, Leonard L. *The Slave Power: The Free North and Southern Domination, 1780–1860*. Baton Rouge: Louisiana State University Press, 2000.
Robinson, Donald L. *Slavery in the Structure of American Politics, 1765–1820*. New York: Norton, 1971.
Shalhope, Robert E. *John Taylor of Caroline: Pastoral Republican*. Columbia: University of South Carolina Press, 1980.
Siegel, Adrienne. *The Marshall Court, 1801–1835*. Millwood, N.Y.: Associated Faculty Press, 1995.
Smith, Jean Edward. *John Marshall: Definer of a Nation*. New York: Henry Holt & Co., 1996.
Stafford, Francis J. "Illegal Importations: Enforcement of the Slave Trade Laws along the Florida Coast, 1810–1828," *Florida Historical Quarterly*, 46 (1967), 124–33.
Staudenraus, P. J. *The African Colonization Movement, 1816–1865*. New York: Columbia University Press, 1961.
Sydnor, Charles S. *The Development of Southern Sectionalism, 1819–1848*. Baton Rouge: Louisiana State University Press, 1948.
Vipperman, Carl J. *William Lowndes and the Transition of Southern Politics, 1782–1822*. Chapel Hill: University of North Carolina Press, 1989.
Walters, Ronald G. and Eric Foner. *American Reformers, 1815–1860*. New York: Hill and Wang, 1997.
Wetzel, Charles. *James Monroe*. New York: Chelsea, 1989.
Young, James Sterling. *The Washington Community, 1800–1828*. New York: Columbia University Press, 1966.

8. The Great Migration

Abernethy, Thomas P. *The South in the New Nation, 1789–1819*. Baton Rouge: Louisiana State University Press, 1961.
——. *The Formative Period in Alabama, 1815–1828*. University: University of Alabama Press, 1965.
Bailey, Hugh C. "John Williams Walker and the 'Georgia Machine' in Early Alabama Politics," *Alabama Review*, 48 (1995), 96–113.

Barker, Eugene C. *The Life of Stephen F. Austin, Founder of Texas, 1793–1836: A Chapter in the Westward Movement of the Anglo-American People*. Austin: University of Texas Press, 1949.

Barnett, Todd H. "Virginians Moving West: The Early Evolution of Slavery in the Bluegrass," *Filson Club Historical Quarterly*, 73 (1999), 221–23, 239–43.

Censer, Jane Turner. "Southwestern Migration among North Carolina Planter Families: The 'Disposition to Emigrate'," *Journal of Southern History*, 57 (1991), 407–26.

Chipman, Donald E. *Spanish Texas, 1519–1821*. Austin: University of Texas Press, 1992.

Clark, Thomas D. and John W. Guice. *Frontiers in Conflict: The Old Southwest, 1795–1830*. Albuquerque: University of New Mexico Press, 1989.

Combs, H. Jason. "The South's Slave Culture Transplanted to the Western Frontier," *The Professional Geographer*, 56 (2004), 361–71.

Daniels, Jonathan. *The Devil's Backbone: The Story of the Natchez Trace*. New York: McGraw-Hill, 1998.

Dick, Everett. *The Dixie Frontier: A Social History of the Southern Frontier from the First Transmontane Beginnings to the Civil War*. New York: Knopf, 1948.

Fisher, David Hackett and James C. Kelly. *Away, I'm Bound Away: Virginia and the Westward Movement*. Richmond, Va.: Virginia Historical Society, 1993.

Foust, James D. *The Yeoman Farmer and Westward Expansion of U.S. Cotton Production*. New York: Arno Press, 1975.

Horsman, Reginald. *The Frontier in the Formative Years, 1783–1815*. New York: Holt, Rinehart and Winston, 1970.

Hudson, John. "North American Origins of Middlewestern Frontier Populations," *Annals of the Association of American Geographers*, 78 (1988), 395–413.

Lewis, James E. *The American Union and the Problem of Neighborhood: The United States and the Collapse of the Spanish Empire, 1783–1829*. Chapel Hill: University of North Carolina Press, 1998.

Lynch, William O. "The Westward Flow of Southern Colonists before 1861," *Journal of Southern History*, 9 (1943), 303–27.

McIlwraith, Thomas, and Edward Muller (eds.). *North America: The Historical Geography of a Changing Continent*. Lanham, Md.: Rowman and Littlefield, 2001.

Parker, William N. *Commerce, Cotton, and Westward Expansion, 1820–1860*. Chicago: Scott, Foresman, 1964.

Porter, Kenneth Wiggins. *The Negro on the American Frontier*. New York: Arno, 1971.

Roberts, Frances. "Politics and Public Land Disposal in Alabama's Formative Period," *Alabama Review*, 22 (1969), 163–74.

Unser, Daniel. *Indians, Settlers, and Slaves in a Frontier Exchange Economy: The Lower Mississippi Valley before 1803*. Chapel Hill: University of North Carolina Press, 1992.

Wallace, Anthony F. C. *Jefferson and the Indians: The Tragic Fate of the First Americans*. Cambridge, Mass.: Belknap Press, 1999.
Weber, David. *The Spanish Frontier in North America*. New Haven, Conn.: Yale University Press, 1992.
Wexler, Alan. *Atlas of Westward Expansion*. New York: Facts on File, 1995.
Whitaker, Arthur P. *The Mississippi Question, 1795–1803*. New York: American Historical Association, 1934.

III. THE OLD SOUTH IN THE JACKSONIAN ERA, 1829–1848

1. The Age of Andrew Jackson

Baxter, Maurice G. *Henry Clay and the American System*. Lexington: University of Kentucky Press, 1995.
———. *One and Inseparable: Daniel Webster and the Union*. Cambridge, Mass.: Harvard University Press, 1984.
Cain, Marvin R. "William Wirt against Andrew Jackson: Reflection of an Era," *Mid-America*, 47 (1965), 113–38.
Carroll, E. M. *Origins of the Whig Party*. Durham: Duke University Press, 1970.
Cole, Donald B. *The Presidency of Andrew Jackson*. Lawrence: University of Kansas Press: 1993.
Curtis, James C. *Andrew Jackson and the Search for Vindication*. Boston: Little, Brown, 1976.
Eaton, Clement. *Henry Clay and the Art of American Politics*. Boston: Little, Brown, 1957.
Hofstadter, Richard. *The Idea of a Party System: The Rise of Legitimate Opposition in the United States, 1780–1840*. Berkeley: University of California Press, 1969.
Gresham, L. Paul. "The Public Career of Hugh Lawson White," *Tennessee Historical Quarterly*, 3 (1944), 291–318.
Haites, Erik F., et al. *Western River Transportation: The Era of Internal Improvement, 1810–1860*. Baltimore, Md.: The Johns Hopkins University Press, 1975.
Johnson, Gerald W. *America's Silver Age: The Statecraft of Clay—Webster—Calhoun*. New York: Harper Bros., 1939.
Latner, Richard B. *The Presidency of Andrew Jackson: White House Politics, 1829–1837*. Athens: University of Georgia Press, 1979.
Marszalek, John F. *The Petticoat Affair: Manners, Mutiny, and Sex in Andrew Jackson's White House*. New York: Free Press, 1997.
McCormick, Richard P. *The Second American Party System: Party Formation in the Jacksonian Era*. Chapel Hill: University of North Carolina Press, 1966.
Mead, Walter Russell. "The Jacksonian Tradition and American Foreign Policy," *The National Interest*, 58 (Winter 1999–2000), 5–29.
Meyers, Marvin. *The Jacksonian Persuasion: Politics and Belief*. Palo Alto: Stanford University Press, 1960.

Newmyer, R. Kent. *John Marshall and the Heroic Age of the Supreme Court*. Baton Rouge: Louisiana State University Press, 2001.
Pessen, Edward (ed.). *The Many-Faceted Jacksonian Era: New Interpretations*. Westport, Conn.: Greenwood, 1977.
Peterson, Merrill D. *The Great Triumvirate: Webster, Clay, and Calhoun*. New York: Oxford University Press, 1987.
Poague, George R. *Henry Clay and the Whig Party*. Chapel Hill: University of North Carolina Press, 1936.
Remini, Robert V. *Andrew Jackson*. 3 vols. New York; Harper & Row, 1984.
———. *Daniel Webster: The Man and His Time*. New York: Norton, 1997.
———. *Henry Clay: Statesman for the Union*. New York: Norton, 1991.
———. *The Legacy of Andrew Jackson: Essays on Democracy, Indian Removal, and Slavery*. Baton Rouge: Louisiana State University Press, 1988.
Remini, Robert V. (ed.). *The Age of Jackson*. Columbia: University of South Carolina, 1972.
Rippy, J. Fred. *Joel R. Poinsett, Versatile American*. New York: Greenwood, 1968 [orig. 1935].
Sellers, Charles Grier, Jr. *Jacksonian Democracy*. Washington, D.C.: Service Center for Teachers of History, 1958.
Siegel, Adrienne. *The Marshall Court, 1801–1835*. Millwood, N.Y.: Associated Faculty Press, 1995.
Smith, Jean Edward. *John Marshall: Definer of a Nation*. New York: Henry Holt & Co., 1996.
Sydnor, Charles S. *The Development of Southern Sectionalism, 1819–1848*. Baton Rouge: Louisiana State University Press, 1948.
Vaughn, William P. *The Anti-Masonic Party in the United States, 1826–1843*. Lexington: University of Kentucky Press, 1983.
Walters, Ronald G. and Eric Foner. *American Reformers, 1815–1860*. New York: Hill and Wang, 1997.
Ward, John William. *Andrew Jackson: Symbol for an Age*. New York: Oxford University Press, 1955.
Watson, Harry L. *Andrew Jackson vs. Henry Clay: Democracy and Development in Antebellum America*. Boston: Bedford/St. Martin's, 1998.
———. *Jacksonian Politics and Community Conflict*. Baton Rouge: Louisiana State University Press, 1981.
———. *Liberty and Power: The Politics of Jacksonian America*. New York: Hill and Wang, 1990.
Wyatt-Brown, Bertram. "Andrew Jackson's Honor," *Journal of the Early Republic*, 17 (1997), 1–36.

2. The Native Americans and Indian Removal

Braund, Kathleen E. Holland. "The Creek Indians, Blacks, and Slavery," *Journal of Southern History*, 57 (1991), 607–18.

SELECT BIBLIOGRAPHY

Cotterill, R. S. *The Southern Tribes: The Story of the Civilized Tribes before Removal.* Norman: University of Oklahoma Press, 1954.

De Rosier, Arthur H. *The Removal of the Choctaw Indians.* Knoxville: University of Tennessee Press, 1970.

Drinnon, Richard. *Facing West: The Metaphysics of Indian-Hating and Empire Building.* Minneapolis: University of Minnesota Press, 1980.

Gibson, Arrell M. *The Chickasaws.* Norman: University of Oklahoma Press, 1971.

Halliburton, R., Jr. *Red over Black: Black Slavery among the Cherokee.* Westport, Conn.: Greenwood Press, 1977.

Jacobs, Wilbur R. *Dispossessing the American Indian.* New York: Charles Scribner's Sons, 1972.

James, Marquis. *The Raven: A Biography of Sam Houston.* Indianapolis: Bobbs-Merrill, 1929.

Littlefield, Daniel F., Jr. *Africans and Creeks: From the Colonial Period to the Civil War.* Westport, Conn.: Greenwood Press, 1979.

———. *Africans and Seminoles: From Removal to Emancipation.* Westport, Conn.: Greenwood Press, 1977.

Mahon, John K. *History of the Second Seminole War, 1835–1842.* Gainesville: University of Florida Press, 1967.

———. (ed.). *Indians of the Southwest.* Gainesville: University of Florida Press, 1975.

Miles, Edwin A. "After John Marshall's Decision: *Worcester v. Georgia* and the Nullification Crisis," *Journal of Southern History*, 39 (1973), 519–44.

Moulton, Gary E. *John Ross, Cherokee Chief.* Athens: University of Georgia Press, 1975.

Perdu, Theda. *Slavery and the Evolution of Cherokee Society, 1540–1866.* Knoxville: University of Tennessee Press, 1979.

Porter, Kenneth Wiggins. "Florida Slaves and Free Negroes in the Seminole War, 1835–1842," *Journal of Negro History*, 28 (1943), 390–421.

Prucha, Francis Paul. "Andrew Jackson's Indian Policy: A Reassessment," *Journal of American History*, 56 (1969), 527–39.

———, (ed.). *The Indian in American History.* New York: Holt, Rinehart and Winston, 1971.

Remini, Robert V. *The Legacy of Andrew Jackson: Essays on Democracy, Indian Removal, and Slavery.* Baton Rouge: Louisiana State University Press, 1988.

Rogin, Michael Paul. *Fathers and Children: Andrew Jackson and the Subjugation of the American Indian.* New Brunswick, N.J.: Transaction Publishers, 1991.

Royce, Charles C. *Indian Land Cessions in the United States.* Washington, D.C.: Smithsonian Institution, 1900.

Satz, Ronald N. *American Indian Policy in the Jacksonian Era.* Lincoln: University of Nebraska Press, 1975.

Wallace, Anthony F. C. *Jefferson and the Indians: The Tragic Fate of the First Americans.* Cambridge, Mass.: Belknap Press, 1999.

———. *The Long, Bitter Trail: Andrew Jackson and the Indians*. New York; Hill and Wang. 1993.
Williams, David. *The Georgia Gold Rush: Twenty-Niners, Cherokee, and Gold Fever*. Columbia: University of South Carolina Press, 1993.
Woodward, Grace S. *The Cherokees*. Norman: University of Oklahoma Press, 1954.

3. Slavery, the Nullification Crisis, and the Tariff

Bartlett, Irving H. *Calhoun: A Biography*. New York: Norton, 1993.
Bergeron, Paul. "The Nullification Controversy Revisited," *Tennessee Historical Quarterly*, 35 (1976), 263–75.
———. "Tennessee's Response to the Nullification Crisis," *Journal of Southern History*, 39 (1973), 23–44.
Bruce, Dickson D., Jr. *Rhetoric of Conservatism: The Virginia Convention of 1829–1830 and the Conservative Tradition in the South*. San Marino: Huntington Library, 1982.
Carpenter, Jesse T. *The South as a Conscious Minority, 1789–1861: A Study in Political Thought*. New York: New York University Press, 1930.
Cooper, William J., Jr. *Liberty and Slavery: Southern Politics to 1860*. New York: Knopf, 1983.
Coulter, E. Merton. "The Nullification Movement in Georgia," *Georgia Historical Quarterly*, 5 (1921), 3–39.
Ellis, Richard E. *The Union at Risk: Jacksonian Democracy, States' Rights, and the Nullification Crisis*. New York: Oxford University Press, 1987.
Freehling, Alison Goodyear. *Drift toward Dissolution: The Virginia Slavery Debate of 1831–1832*. Baton Rouge: Louisiana State University Press, 1982.
———. *Prelude to Civil War: The Nullification Crisis in South Carolina, 1816–1836*. New York: Harper & Row, 1965.
Green, Edwin. *George McDuffie*. Columbia: The State Company, 1936.
Harris, J. William. "Last of the Classical Republicans: An Interpretation of John C. Calhoun," *Civil War History*, 30 (1984), 255–67.
Hofstadter, Richard. *The American Political Tradition and the Men Who Made It*. New York: Knopf, 1948.
Jervey, Theodore D. *Robert Y. Hayne and His Times*. New York: Da Capo, 1970.
Malone, Dumas. *The Public Life of Thomas Cooper*. New Haven, Conn.: Yale University Press, 1926.
Nagel, Paul C. *One Nation Indivisible: The Union in American Thought, 1776–1861*. New York: Oxford University Press, 1964.
Niven, John. *John C. Calhoun and the Price of Union: A Biography*. Baton Rouge: Louisiana State University Press, 1988.
Parker, William N. *Commerce, Cotton, and Westward Expansion, 1820–1860*. Chicago: Scott, Foresman, 1964.

Pessen, Edward (ed.). *The Many-Faceted Jacksonian Era: New Interpretations.* Westport, Conn.: Greenwood, 1977.

Peterson, Merrill D. *The Great Triumvirate: Webster, Clay, and Calhoun.* New York: Oxford University Press, 1987.

———. *Olive Branch and Sword—The Compromise of 1833.* Baton Rouge: Louisiana State University Press, 1982.

Remini, Robert V. *The Legacy of Andrew Jackson: Essays on Democracy, Indian Removal, and Slavery.* Baton Rouge: Louisiana State University Press, 1988.

———. "Martin Van Buren and the Tariff of Abominations," *American Historical Review*, 63 (1958), 903–17.

Robert, Joseph Clarke. *The Road from Monticello: A Study of the Virginia Slavery Debate of 1832.* Durham: Duke University Press, 1941.

Rippy, J. Fred. *Joel R. Poinsett, Versatile American.* New York: Greenwood, 1968 [orig. 1935].

Wiltse, Charles W. *John C. Calhoun.* 3 vols. Indianapolis: Bobbs-Merrill, 1944–1951.

4. Jacksonian Economics and the Bank War

Haites, Erik F. et al. *Western River Transportation: The Era of Internal Improvement, 1810–1860.* Baltimore, Md.: The Johns Hopkins University Press, 1975.

Hammond, Bray. *Banks and Politics in America from the Revolution to the Civil War.* Princeton, N.J.: University of Princeton, N.J. Press, 1957.

Parker, William N. *Commerce, Cotton, and Westward Expansion, 1820–1860.* Chicago: Scott, Foresman, 1964.

Remini, Robert V. *Andrew Jackson and the Bank War: A Study in the Growth of Presidential Power.* New York: Norton, 1967.

Schweikart, Larry. *Banking in the American South from the Age of Jackson to Reconstruction.* Baton Rouge: Louisiana State University Press, 1987.

Sellers, Charles Grier, Jr. *The Market Revolution: Jacksonian America, 1815–1846.* New York: Oxford University Press, 1991.

Sharp, James Roger. *The Jacksonians versus the Banks: Politics in the States after the Panic of 1837.* New York: Columbia University Press, 1970.

Wilburn, Jean Alexander. *Biddle's Bank: The Crucial Years.* New York: Columbia University Press, 1967.

5. Texas Independence and the War with Mexico

Bauer, K. Jack. *The Mexican War, 1846–1848.* New York: Macmillan, 1974.

———. *Zachary Taylor: Soldier, Planter, Statesman of the Old Southwest.* Baton Rouge: Louisiana State University Press, 1985.

Campbell, Randolph B. *An Empire for Slavery: The Peculiar Institution in Texas, 1821–1865.* Baton Rouge: Louisiana State University Press, 1989.

Connor, Seymour V. and Odie B. Faulk. *North America Divided: The Mexican War, 1846–1848.* New York: Oxford University Press, 1971.

Davis, William C. *Three Roads to the Alamo: The Lives of Davis Crockett, James Bowie, and William Barrett Travis.* New York: HarperCollins, 1998.

Franklin, John Hope, "The Southern Expansionists of 1846," *Journal of Southern History,* 25 (1959), 323–38.

Faulk, Odie. *Too Far North, Too Far South* [the Gadsden Purchase]. Los Angeles: Westernlore Press, 1967.

James, Marquis. *The Raven: A Biography of Sam Houston.* Indianapolis: Bobbs-Merrill, 1929.

Johnson, Timothy D. *Winfield Scott: The Quest for Military Glory.* Lawrence: University Press of Kansas, 1998.

Lack, Paul D. *The Texas Revolutionary Experience: A Political and Social History, 1835–1836.* College Station: Texas A&M University Press, 1992.

McKinley, Silas Bent. *Old Rough and Ready: The Life and Times of Zachary Taylor.* New York: Vanguard Press, 1946.

Merk, Frederick. *Slavery and the Annexation of Texas.* New York; Knopf, 1972.

Smith, Arthur D. H. *Old Fuss and Feathers: The Life and Exploits of Lt.-General Winfield Scott . . . .* New York: Greystone, 1937.

Williams, John Hoyt. *Sam Houston: A Biography of the Father of Texas.* New York: Simon & Schuster, 1992.

6. After Jackson

Ashworth, John. *"Agrarians" and "Aristocrats": Party Political Ideology in the United States, 1837–1846.* Cambridge, Eng.: Cambridge University Press, 1987.

Brauer, Kinley. *Cotton versus Conscience: Massachusetts Whig Politics and Southwestern Expansion, 1843–1848.* Lexington: University of Kentucky Press, 1967.

Brock, William R. *Parties and Political Conscience: American Dilemmas, 1840–1850.* New York: KTO Press, 1979.

Brown, Thomas. *Politics and Statesmanship: Essays on the American Whig Party.* New York: Columbia University Press, 1985.

Cleaves, Freeman. *Old Tippecanoe: William Henry Harrison and His Time.* New York: Charles Scribner's Sons, 1939.

Cole, Arthur C. *The Whig Party in the South.* Gloucester, Mass.: Peter Smith, 1962.

Cole, Donald B. *Martin Van Buren and the American Political System.* Princeton: University of Princeton, N.J. Press, 1984.

Cooper, William J., Jr. *Liberty and Slavery: Southern Politics to 1860.* New York: Knopf, 1983.

Falkof, Lucille. *John Tyler, Tenth President of the United* States. Ada, Okla.: Garrett, 1990.

Holt, Michael F. *To Rescue Public Liberty: A History of the American Whig Party.* New York: Oxford University Press, 1999.

Howe, Daniel W. *The Political Culture of American Whigs.* Chicago: University of Chicago Press, 1979.

Johnson, Gerald W. *America's Silver Age: The Statecraft of Clay—Webster—Calhoun.* New York: Harper Bros., 1939.

McCormick, Richard P. *The Second American Party System: Party Formation in the Jacksonian Era.* Chapel Hill: University of North Carolina Press, 1966.

McCoy, Charles Allan. *Polk and the Presidency.* Austin: University of Texas Press, 1960.

Meyer, Leland W. *The Life and Times of Colonel Richard Mentor Johnson of Kentucky.* New York: AMS Press, 1932.

Niven, John. *Martin Van Buren: The Romantic Age of American Politics.* New York: 1983.

Pessen, Edward (ed.). *The Many-Faceted Jacksonian Era: New Interpretations.* Westport, Conn.: Greenwood, 1977.

Peterson, Merrill D. *The Great Triumvirate: Webster, Clay, and Calhoun.* New York: Oxford University Press, 1987.

Poague, George R. *Henry Clay and the Whig Party.* Chapel Hill: University of North Carolina Press, 1936.

Porter, Kirk Harold and Donald Bruce Johnson. *National Party Platforms, 1840–1964.* Urbana: University of Illinois Press, 1966.

Quaife, Milo M. *The Diary of James K. Polk during His Presidency, 1845–1849.* 4 vols. Chicago: A. C. McClurg, 1910.

Richards, Leonard L. *The Life and Times of Congressman John Quincy Adams.* New York: Oxford University Press, 1986.

Richards, Leonard L. *The Slave Power: The Free North and Southern Domination, 1780–1860.* Baton Rouge: Louisiana State University Press, 2000.

Seager, Robert, II. *And Tyler Too: A Biography of John and Julia Gardiner Tyler.* Norwalk, Conn.: Easton Press, 1989 [orig. 1963].

Sellers, Charles Grier, Jr. *James K. Polk, Jacksonian.* 2 vols. Princeton: Princeton, N.J. University Press, 1957–1966.

Sewell, Richard H. *Ballots for Freedom: Antislavery Politics in the United States, 1837–1860.* New York: Oxford University Press, 1976.

Shade, William G. *Democratizing the Old Dominion: Virginia and the Second Party System, 1824–1861.* Charlottesville: The University Press of Virginia, 1996.

Silbey, Joel. *The Shrine of Party: Congressional Voting Behavior, 1841–1852.* Pittsburgh: University of Pittsburgh Press, 1967.

Sydnor, Charles S. *The Development of Southern Sectionalism, 1819–1848.* Baton Rouge: Louisiana State University Press, 1948.

Vaughn, William P. *The Anti-Masonic Party in the United States, 1826–1843.* Lexington: University of Kentucky Press, 1983.

Volpe, Vernon. *Forlorn Hope of Freedom: The Liberty Party in the Old Northwest.* Kent: Kent State University Press, 1990.

Walters, Ronald G. and Eric Foner. *American Reformers, 1815–1860*. New York: Hill and Wang, 1997.
Watson, Harry L. *Jacksonian Politics and Community Conflict*. Baton Rouge: Louisiana State University Press, 1981.
Watson, Harry L. *Liberty and Power: The Politics of Jacksonian America*. New York: Hill and Wang, 1990.

IV. SLAVERY IN THE OLD SOUTH, 1783–1865

1. General

Abzug, Robert H. and Stephen E. Maizlish (eds.). *New Perspectives on Race and Slavery in America: Essays in Honor of Kenneth M. Stampp*. Lexington: University of Kentucky Press, 1986.
Boles, John B. *Black Southerners, 1619–1869*. Lexington: University of Kentucky Press, 1983.
Elkins, Stanley M. *Slavery: A Problem in American Institutional and Intellectual Life*. Chicago: University of Chicago Press, 1959.
Fogel, Robert W. et al (eds.). *Without Consent or Contract: The Rise and Fall of American Slavery*. New York: Norton, 1989.
Foner, Laura and Eugene D. Genovese (eds.). *Slavery in the New World: A Reader in Comparative History*. Englewood Cliffs, N.J.: Prentice-Hall, 1969.
Genovese, Eugene D. *In Red and Black: Marxian Explorations in Southern and Afro-American History*. New York: Vintage, 1971.
Hudson, Larry E., Jr. *Working toward Freedom: Slave Society and Domestic Economy in the American South*. Rochester, N.Y.: University of Rochester Press, 1994.
Jones, Bobby Frank. "A Cultural Middle Passage." Unpublished Ph.D. Dissertation, University of North Carolina, Chapel Hill, 1965.
Kolchin, Peter. "More Time on the Cross? An Evaluation of Robert William Fogel's *Without Consent or Contract*," *Journal of Southern History*, 58 (1992), 491–502.
———. "Toward a Reinterpretation of Slavery," *Journal of Social History*, 9 (1975), 99–113.
———. *American Slavery, 1619–1877*. New York: Hill & Wang, 1993.
Lane, Ann J. *The Debate over Slavery: Stanley Elkins and his Critics*. Urbana: University of Illinois Press, 1971.
Menn, J. K. "The Large Slaveholders of the Deep South, 1860." Unpublished Ph.D. Dissertation, University of Texas, Austin, 1964.
Nash, Gary B. *Race and Revolution*. Madison: University of Wisconsin Press. 1990.
Nelson, B. H. "Some Aspects of Negro Life in North Carolina during the Civil War," *North Carolina Historical Review*, 25 (1848), 166.
Parish, Peter J. *Slavery: History and the Historians*. New York: Harper & Row, 1989.

Phillips, Ulrich B. *American Negro Slavery*. Baton Rouge: Louisiana State University Press, 1966 (rev. ed.).

———. *Life and Labor in the Old South*. Boston: Little Brown & Co., 1929.

———. "Plantations with Slave Labor and Free," *American Historical Review*, 30 (1925), 738–53.

Prichard, Walter. "Routine on a Louisiana Sugar Plantation under the Slavery Regime," *Mississippi Valley Historical Review*, 14 (1927), 168–78.

Proctor, William G. "Slavery in Southwest Georgia," *Georgia Historical Quarterly*, 49 (1965), 1–22.

Rawick, George P. *The American Slave: A Composite Autobiography*. Westport, Conn.: 41 vols. Greenwood Press, 1972–1979.

Reuter, Edward Byron. *The Mulatto in the United States*. New York: Negro Universities Press, 1969 [orig. 1918].

Shore, Laurence. "The Poverty of Tragedy in Historical Writing on Southern Slavery," *South Atlantic Quarterly*, 85 (1986), 147–64.

Sio, Arnold A. "Interpretations of Slavery: The Slave Status in the Americas," *Comparative Studies in History and Society*, 7 (1965), 289–308.

Smith, Mark M. *Mastered by the Clock: Time, Slavery, and Freedom in the American South*. Chapel Hill: University of North Carolina Press, 1997.

Stampp, Kenneth M. *The Peculiar Institution: Slavery in the Antebellum South*. New York: Knopf, 1956.

Tannenbaum, Frank. *Slave and Citizen: The Negro in the Americas*. New York: Knopf, 1956.

Walker, Clarence E. *Deromanticizing Black History: Critical Essays and Reappraisals*. Nashville: University of Tennessee Press, 1991.

Walsh, Lorena S. "Rural African Americans in the Constitutional Era in Maryland," *Maryland Historical Magazine*, 84 (1989), 327–41.

Weld, Theodore Dwight. *American Slavery as It Is: Testimony of a Thousand Witnesses*. New York: American Antislavery Society, 1839.

Wood, Betty. *The Origins of American Slavery: Freedom and Bondage in the English Colonies*. New York: Hill & Wang, 1997.

Wiley, Bell Irvin. "The Movement to Humanize the Institution of Slavery during the Confederacy," *Emory University Quarterly*, 5 (1949), 207–20.

———. *Southern Negroes, 1861–1865*. New Haven, Conn.: Yale University Press, 1938.

2. State and Local Studies

Arroyo, Elizabeth Fortson. "Poor Whites, Slaves, and Free Blacks in Tennessee, 1796–1861," *Tennessee Historical Quarterly*, 55 (1996), 57–64.

Bassett, John Spencer. *Slavery in the State of North Carolina*. Baltimore, Md.: The Johns Hopkins University Press, 1899.

Bolton, Charles S. *Arkansas, 1800–1860: Remote and Restless*. Fayetteville: University of Arkansas Press, 1998.

Boyd, Minnie C. *Alabama in the Fifties: A Social Study.* New York: AMS Press, 1931.
Brackett, Jeffrey R. *The Negro in Maryland.* Baltimore, Md.: The Johns Hopkins University Press, 1889.
Campbell, Randolph B. *An Empire for Slavery: The Peculiar Institution in Texas, 1821–1865.* Baton Rouge: Louisiana State University Press, 1989.
Chaplin, Joyce E. "Tidal Rice Cultivation and the Problem of Slavery in South Carolina and Georgia, 1760–1815, *William and Mary Quarterly,* 3rd Ser., 49 (1992), 29–61, 583–84.
Chatham, Katherine. "Plantation Slavery in Middle Florida." Unpublished M.A. Thesis, University of North Carolina, Chapel Hill, 1938.
Coleman, J. Winston. *Slavery Times in Kentucky.* Chapel Hill: University of North Carolina Press, 1940.
Corlew, Robert E. "Some Aspects of Slavery in Dickson County," *Tennessee Historical Quarterly,* 10 (1951), 224–48.
Coulter, E. Merton. "Slavery and Freedom: Athens, Georgia, 1860–1866," *Georgia Historical Quarterly,* 49 (1965), 264–93.
Davis, Charles S. *Cotton Kingdom in Alabama.* Montgomery: University of Alabama Press, 1939.
Din, Gilbert C. *Spaniards, Planters, and Slaves: The Spanish Regulation of Slavery in Louisiana, 1763–1803.* College Station: Texas A&M University Press, 1999.
Dormon, James H. (ed,). *Creoles of Color in the Gulf South.* Knoxville: University of Tennessee Press, 1996.
Dorsett, Lyle Wesley. "Slaveholding in Jackson County, Missouri," *Missouri Historical Society Bulletin,* 20 (October 1963), 25–37.
Dunbar-Nelson, Alice. "The People of Color in Louisiana," *Journal of Negro History,* 2 (1917), 51–78.
England, E. Merton. "The Free Negro in Antebellum Tennessee," *Journal of Southern History,* 21 (1955), 37–58.
Fields, Barbara Jeanne. *Slavery and Freedom on the Middle Ground: Maryland during the Nineteenth Century.* New Haven, Conn.: Yale University Press, 1985.
Flanders, Ralph B. *Plantation Slavery in Georgia.* Chapel Hill: University of North Carolina Press, 1933.
Foner, Laura. "The Free People of Color in Louisiana and St. Domingue: A Cooperative Portrait of Two Three-Caste Societies," *Journal of Social History,* 3 (1970), 406–30.
Hall, Gwendolyn Midlo. *Africans in Colonial Louisiana: The Development of Afro-Creole Culture in the Eighteenth Century.* Baton Rouge: Louisiana State University Press, 1992.
Hering, Julia. "Plantation Economy in Leon County, 1830–1840," *Florida Historical Quarterly,* 23 (1954), 45.
Hurt, R. Douglas. *Agriculture and Slavery in Missouri's Little Dixie.* Columbia: University of Missouri Press, 1992.

Jewett, Clayton E. and John O. Allen. *Slavery in the South: A State-by-State History*. Westport, Conn.: Greenwood Press, 2004.
Johnston, James Higo. *Race Relations in Virginia and Miscegenation in the South, 1776–1860*. Amherst: University of Massachusetts Press, 1960.
Jordan, Weymouth T. *Antebellum Alabama: Town and Country*. Tallahassee: Florida State University Press, 1957.
Kulikoff, Alan. "A 'Proflick' People: Black Population Growth in the Chesapeake Colonies, 1700–1790," *Southern Studies*, 16 (1977), 391–428.
——. "The Origins of Afro-American Society in Tidewater Maryland and Virginia, 1700 to 1790," *William and Mary Quarterly*, 3rd Series, 35 (1978), 229–31.
——. *Tobacco and Slaves: The Development of Southern Cultures in the Chesapeake, 1680–1800*. Chapel Hill: University of North Carolina Press, 1986.
Marten, James. "Slaves and Rebels: The Peculiar Institution in Texas, 1861–1865," *East Texas Historical Journal*, 28 (Spring 1990), 29–36.
Mooney, Chase C. *Slavery in Tennessee*. Bloomington: Indiana University Press, 1957.
Patterson, Caleb Perry. *The Negro in Tennessee, 1790–1865*. New York: Negro Universities Press, 1968.
Rivers, Larry Eugene. *Slavery in Florida: Territorial Days to Emancipation*. Gainesville: University of Florida Press, 2000.
Rogers, Jane Harris. "The Model Farm of Missouri and Its Owner," *Missouri Historical Review*, 18 (1924), 146–57.
Sellers, James B. *Slavery in Alabama*. 2nd ed., University: University of Alabama Press, 1950.
Sitterson, J. Carlyle. "Hired Labor on Sugar Plantations of the Antebellum South," *Journal of Southern History*, 14 (1948), 192–205.
Smith, Julia Floyd. *Slavery and Plantation Growth in Antebellum Florida, 1821–1860*. Gainesville: University of Florida Press, 1973.
Sydnor, Charles S. *Slavery in Mississippi*. New York: D. Appleton, 1933.
Taylor, Joe Gray. *Negro Slavery in Louisiana*. Westport, Conn.: Greenwood Press, 1963.
Trexler, Harrison Anthony. *Slavery in Missouri, 1804–1865*. Baltimore, Md.: The Johns Hopkins University Press, 1914.
Turner, Wallace B. "Kentucky Slavery in the Last Antebellum Decade," *Kentucky Historical Society Review*, 58 (1960), 298.
Williamson, Joel. *The New People: Miscegenation and Mulattoes in the United States*. New York: Free Press, 1980.

3. Profitability, Slave Management, and the Economics of Slavery

Aitken, Hugh G. J. (ed.). *Did Slavery Pay? Readings in the Economics of Black Slavery in the United States*. Boston: Houghton Mifflin, 1971.
Breeden, James O. (ed.). *Advice among Masters: The Ideal in Slave Management in the Old South*. Westport, Conn.: Greenwood Press, 1980.

Clifton, James M. "The Rice Driver: His Role in Slave Management," *South Carolina Historical Magazine*, 92 (1981), 331–53.

Coles, Harry L., Jr. "Some Notes on Slaveownership and Landownership in Louisiana, 1850–1860," *Journal of Southern History*, 9 (1943), 381–94.

Conrad, Alfred H. and John R. Meyer. "The Economics of Slavery in the Antebellum South," *Journal of Political Economy*, 66 (1958), 95–130.

———. *The Economics of Slavery and Other Studies in Econometric History*. Chicago: University of Chicago Press, 1964.

David, Paul A. et al (eds.). *Reckoning with Slavery: A Critical Study in the Quantitative History of American Negro Slavery*. New York: Oxford University Press, 1976.

Davis, David Brion. "Slavery and the Post-World War II Historians," *Daedalus*, 103 (Spring 1974), 1–16.

———. *The Problem of Slavery in the Age of Revolution*. Ithaca, N.Y.: Cornell University Press, 1975.

Doyle, Bertram Wilbur. *The Etiquette of Race Relations in the South: A Study in Social Control*. Chicago: University of Chicago Press, 1937.

Fogel, Robert W. and Stanley L. Engerman. *Time on the Cross: The Economics of American Negro Slavery*. 2 vols. Boston: Little, Brown, 1974.

Genovese, Eugene D. "Medical and Insurance Costs of Slaveholding in the Cotton Belt," *Journal of Negro History*, 45 (2960), 141–55.

———. *The Political Economy of Slavery: Studies in the Economy and Society of the Slave South*. New York: Pantheon, 1965.

Gutman, Herbert G. *Slavery and the Numbers Game: A Critique of* Time on the Cross. Urbana: University of Illinois Press, 1975.

Owsley, Frank L and Harriet C. "The Economic Basis of Society in the late Antebellum South," *Journal of Southern History*, 6 (1940), 20–45.

Parker, William N. "Slavery and Southern Economic Development: An Hypothesis and Some Evidence," *Agricultural History*, 44 (1970), 115–25.

Pessen, Edward. "How Different Were the Antebellum North and South?" *American Historical Review*, 85 (1980), 1119–49.

Phillips, Ulrich B. *The Slave Economy of the Old South: Selected Essays in Economic and Social History*. Ed. by Eugene D. Genovese. Baton Rouge: Louisiana State University Press, 1968.

Smith, Robert Worthington. "Was Slavery Profitable in the Antebellum South?" *Agricultural History*, 20 (1946), 62–64.

Stone, James Herbert. "Black Leadership in the Old South: The Slave Drivers of the Rice Kingdom." Unpublished Ph.D. Dissertation, Florida State University, Tallahassee, 1976.

Van Deburg, William L. *The Slave Drivers: Black Agricultural Labor in the Antebellum South*. Westport, Conn.: Greenwood Press, 1979.

Woodman, Harold D. "Economic History and Economic Theory: The New Economic History in America," *Journal of Interdisciplinary History*, 3 (1972), 323–50.

———. "The Profitability of Slavery: A Historical Perennial," *Journal of Southern History*, 29 (1963), 303–25.

4. Life and Society on the Plantation

Alford, Terry. *Prince among Slaves*. New York: Harcourt Brace Jovanovich, 1977.

Berlin, Ira and Philip D. Morgan (eds.). *Cultivation and Culture: Labor and the Shaping of Slave Life in the Americas*. Charlottesville: University of Virginia Press, 1993.

Berlin, Ira and Richard Hoffman (eds.). *Slavery and Freedom in the Age of the American Revolution*. Charlottesville: University Press of Virginia, 1983.

Berlin, Ira. *Many Thousands Gone: The First Two Centuries of Slavery in North America*. Cambridge, Mass.: Harvard University Press, 1998.

Blassingame, John W. *The Slave Community: Plantation Life in the Antebellum South*. New York: Oxford University Press, 1972.

Bruce, Dickson D., Jr. "The 'John and Old Master' Stories and the World of Slavery: A Study in Folktales and History," *Phylon*, 35 (1974), 418–29.

Campbell, Edward D. C., Jr. and Kym S. Rice. *Before Freedom Came: African-American Life in the Antebellum South*. Richmond, Va.: Museum of the Confederacy, 1991.

Campbell, John. "Work, Pregnancy, and Infant Mortality of American Slaves from Childhood to Maturity," *Journal of Economic History*, 46 (1986), 721–41.

Cody, Cheryll Ann. "Naming, Kinship, and Estate Dispersal: Notes on Slave Family Life on a South Carolina Plantation, 1786 to 1833," *William and Mary Quarterly*, 3rd Ser., 39 (1982), 192–211.

Epstein, Dena S. *Sinful Tunes and Spirituals: Black Folk Music to the Civil War*. Urbana: University of Illinois Press, 1977.

Fett, Sharon M. *Working Cure: Healing, Health, and Power on Southern Slave Plantations*. Chapel Hill: University of North Carolina Press, 2002.

Fisher, Miles Mark. *Negro Slave Songs in the United States*. Ithaca, N.Y.: Cornell University Press, 1953.

Flusche, Michaelk. "Joel Chandler Harris and the Folklore of Slavery," *Journal of American Studies*, 9 1975), 347–63.

Fox-Genovese, Elizabeth. *Within the Plantation Household: Black and White Women of the Old South*. Chapel Hill: University of North Carolina Press, 1988.

Frazier, E. Franklin. "The Negro Slave Family," *Journal of Negro History*, 15 (1930), 198–259.

Genovese, Eugene D. *Roll Jordan Roll: The World the Slaves Made*. New York: Pantheon, 1974.

Gorn, Elliott J. "Black Spirits: The Ghost Folklore of Afro-American Slaves," *American Quarterly*, 36 (1984), 549–65.

Gutman, Herbert G. *The Black Family in Slavery and Freedom*. New York: Pantheon, 1976.

Johnson, Michael P. "Work, Culture, and the Slave Community: Slave Occupations in the Cotton Belt in 1860," *Labor History*, 27 (1986), 325–55.

Jones, Jacqueline. *Labor of Love, Labor of Sorrow: Black Women, Work, and the Family from Slavery to the Present*. New York: Basic Books, 1985.

Joyner, Charles. *Down by the Riverside: A South Carolina Slave Community*. Urbana: University of Illinois, 1984.
Katz, Bernard (ed.). *Social Implications of Early Negro Music in the United States*. New York: Arno Press, 1969.
Kiple, Kenneth F. and Virginia Himmelsteib King. *Another Dimension to the Black Diaspora: Diet, Disease, and Racism*. Cambridge, Mass.: Cambridge, Mass. University Press, 1981.
Kolchin, Peter. "Reevaluating the Antebellum Slave Community: A Comparative Perspective," *Journal of American History*, 70 (1983), 579–601.
Levine, Lawrence W. *Black Culture and Black Consciousness: Afro-American Folk Thought from Slavery to Freedom*. New York: Oxford University Press, 1977.
Malone, Ann Patton. *Sweet Chariot: Slave Family and Household Structure in Nineteenth Century Louisiana*. Chapel Hill: University of North Carolina Press, 1992.
Margo, Robert A. and Richard H. Steckel. "The Heights of American Slaves: New Evidence on Slave Nutrition and Health," *Social Science History*, 14 (1984), 516–38.
Marks, Bayly E. "Skilled Blacks in Antebellum St. Mary's County, Maryland," *Journal of Southern History*, 53 (1987), 537–64.
Miller, Elinor and Eugene D. Genovese. *Plantation, Town, and Country: Essays on the Local History of American Slave Society*. Urbana: University of Illinois Press, 1974.
Morgan, Philip D. "The Ownership of Property by Slaves in the Mid-Nineteenth-Century Low Country," *Journal of Southern History*, 49 (1983), 399–420.
———. "Work and Culture: The Task System and the World of Lowcounry Blacks," *William and Mary Quarterly*, 3rd Ser., 39 (1982), 563–99.
Morris, Richard B. "The Measure of Bondage in the Slave States," *Mississippi Valley Historical Review*, 41 (1954), 219–40.
Mullin, Gerald W. *Africa in America: Slave Acculturation and Resistance in the American South and the British Caribbean, 1736–1831*. Urbana: University of Illinois Press, 1992.
Olsen, John F. "The Occupational Structure of Plantation Slave Labor in the late Antebellum South." Unpublished Ph.D. Dissertation, University of Rochester, 1983.
Owens, Harry P. (ed.), *Perspectives and Irony in American Slavery*. Jackson: University Of Mississippi Press, 1976.
Owens, Leslie Howard. *This Species of Property: Slave Life and Custom in the Old South*. New York: Oxford, 1976.
Parkhurst. Jessie W. "The Role of the Black Mammy in the Plantation Household," *Journal of Negro History*, 23 (1938), 349–69.
Postell, William Dosite. *The Health of Slaves on the Southern Plantations*. Baton Rouge: Louisiana State University Press, 1951.
Raboteau, Albert J. *Slave Religion: The 'Invisible Institution' in the Antebellum South*. New York: Oxford University Press, 1978.

Roediger, David R. "And Die in Dixie: Funerals, Death & Heaven in the Slave Community, 1700–1965," *Massachusetts Review*, 22 (1981), 163–88.
Savitt, Todd L. *Medicine and Slavery: The Diseases and Health Care of Blacks in Antebellum Virginia*. Urbana: University of Illinois Press, 1978.
Schwartz, Marie Jenkins. "Family Life in the Slave Quarters: Survival Strategies," *Magazine of History*, 15 (2001), 36–41.
Southern, Eileen. *The Music of Black Americans: A History*. New York: Norton, 1971.
Stampp, Kenneth M. "Rebels and Sambos: The Search for the Negro's Personality in Slavery," *Journal of Southern History*, 37 (1971), 367–92.
Starobin, Robert S. (ed.). *Blacks in Bondage: Letters of American Slaves*. New York: New Viewpoints, 1974.
———. "Privileged Bondsmen and the Process of Accommodation: The Role of Houseservants and Drivers as Seen in Their Own Letters," *Journal of Social History*, 5 (1971), 46–70.
Steckel, Richard H. "A Dreadful Childhood: The Excess Mortality of American Slaves," *Social Science History*, 10 (1986), 427–65.
Steckel, Richard H. "Slave Marriage and the Family," *Journal of Family History*, 5 (1980), 406–21.
Stevenson, Brenda E. *Life in Black and White: Family and Community in the Slave South*. New York: Oxford University Press, 1996.
Stuckey, Sterling. "Through the Prism of Folklore: The Black Ethos in Slavery," *Massachusetts Review*, 9 (1968), 417–37.
Wetherell, Charles. "Slave Kinship: A Case Study of the South Carolina Good Hope Plantation, 1835–1856," *Journal of Family History*, 6 (1981), 294–308.
White, Deborah Gray. *Ar'n't I a Woman? Female Slaves in the Plantation South*. New York: Norton, 1985.
Wiggins, David K. "The Play of Slave Children in the Plantation Communities of the Old South, 1920–1860," *Journal of Sport History*, 7 (1980), 21–39.
Wyatt-Brown, Bertram. The Mask of Obedience: Male Slave Psychology in the Old South," *American Historical Review*, 93 (1988), 1228–52.

5. International and Domestic Slave Trade

Bancroft, Frederick. *Slave Trading in the Old South*. Baltimore, Md.: The Johns Hopkins University Press, 1931.
Calderhead, William. "How Extensive Was the Border State Slave Trade: A New Look," *Civil War History*, 18 (1972), 42–55.
Cody, Cheryll Ann. "Naming, Kinship, and Estate Dispersal: Notes on Slave Family Life on a South Carolina Plantation, 1786 to 1833," *William and Mary Quarterly*, 3rd Ser., 39 (1982), 192–211.

SELECT BIBLIOGRAPHY • 411

Coleman, J. Winston. "Lexington's Slave Dealers and Their Southern Trade," *Filson Club Historical Quarterly*, 12 (1938), 1–23.

Collins, Winfield. *The Domestic Slave Trade of the Southern States*. New York: Broadway Publishing, 1904.

Curtin, Philip D. *The Atlantic Slave Trade: A Census*. Madison: University of Wisconsin, 1969.

Davidson, Basil. *The African Slave Trade: Precolonial History, 1450–1850*. Boston: Little, Brown, 1961.

Eltis, David. "Free and Coerced Transatlantic Migrations: Some Comparisons," *American Historical Review*, 88 (1983), 251–80.

Ewald, Janet J. "Slavery in Africa and the Slave Trades from Africa," *American Historical Review*, 97 (1992), 465–85.

Fornell, Earl W. "The Abduction of Free Negroes and Slaves in Texas," *Southwestern Historical Quarterly*, 60 (1956–1957), 369–80.

Freudenberger, Herman and Jonathan B. Prichett. "The Domestic United States Slave Trade: New Evidence," *Journal of Interdisciplinary History*, 21 (1991), 447–78.

Inikori, Joseph E. and Stanley L. Engerman (eds.). *The Atlantic Slave Trade: Effects on Economies, Societies, and Peoples in Africa, the Americas, and Europe*. Durham: Duke University Press, 1992.

Johnson, Walter. *Soul by Soul: Life inside the Antebellum Slave Market*. Cambridge, Mass.: Harvard University Press, 1999.

Klein, Herbert S. *The Middle Passage: Comparative Studies in the Atlantic Slave Trade*. Princeton: University of Princeton, N.J. Press, 1978.

Lightner, David L. "The Interstate Slave Trade in Anti-slavery Politics," *Civil War History*, 36 (1990), 119–36.

Lovejoy, Paul E. "The Impact of the Atlantic Slave Trade on Africa: A Review of the Literature," *Journal of African History*, 30 (1989), 365–94.

Mannix, Daniel P. and Malcolm Cowley. *Black Cargoes: A History of the Atlantic Slave Trade, 1518–1865*. New York: 1962.

McGettington, James. "Boone County Slaves: Sales, Estate Divisions, and Families, 1820–1865," *Missouri Historical Review*, 72 (1978), 176–97.

Rawley, James A. *The Transatlantic Slave Trade: A History*. New York: Norton, 1981.

Stafford, Francis J. "Illegal Importations: Enforcement of the Slave Trade Laws along the Florida Coast, 1810–1828," *Florida Historical Quarterly*, 46 (1967), 124–33.

Stephenson, Wendell Holmes. *Isaac Franklin: Slave Trader and Planter of the Old South, with Plantation Records*. Baton Rouge: Louisiana State University Press, 1938.

Sweig, Donald M. "Reassessing the Human Dimension of the Interstate Slave Trade," *Prologue*, 12 (1980), 5–21.

Tadman, Michael. *Speculators and Slaves: Masters, Traders, and Slaves in the Old South*. Madison: University of Wisconsin Press, 1989.

Takaki, Ronald T. *A Pro-Slavery Crusade: The Agitation to Reopen the African Slave Trade.* New York: Free Press, 1971.

Thomas, Hugh. *The Slave Trade: The Story of the Atlantic Slave Trade.* London: Picador, 1997.

6. Industrial and Urban Slavery

Bateman, Fred and Thomas Weiss. *A Deplorable Scarcity: The Failure of Industrialism in the Slave Economy.* Chapel Hill: University of North Carolina Press, 1981.

Blassingame, John W. *Black New Orleans.* Chicago: University of Chicago Press, 1973.

Dew, Charles B. "Disciplining Slave Ironworkers in the Antebellum South: Coercion, Conciliation, and Accommodation," *American Historical Review*, 79 (1974), 393–418.

———. *Bond of Iron: Master and Slave at Buffalo Forge.* New York: Norton, 1994.

Fleisig, Heywood. "Slavery, the Supply of Agricultural Labor, and the Industrialization of the South," *Journal of Economic History*, 36 (1976), 572–97.

Goldin, Claudia Dale. *Urban Slavery in the American South, 1820–1860.* Chicago: University of Chicago Press, 1976.

Goodstein, Anita S. "Black History on the Nashville Frontier, 1780–1810," *Tennessee Historical Quarterly*, 38 (1979), 401–20.

Hanger, Kimberly. *Bounded Lives, Bounded Places: Free Black Society in Colonial New Orleans, 1769–1803.* Durham: Duke University Press, 1997.

Ingersoll, Thomas N. *Mammon and Manon in Early New Orleans: The First Slave Society in the Deep South, 1718–1819.* Knoxville: University of Tennessee Press, 1999.

Jernegan, Marcus W. "Slavery and the Beginnings of Industrialism in America," *American Historical Review*, 25 (1920), 220–40.

Jordan, Weymouth T. *Antebellum Alabama: Town and Country.* Tallahassee: Florida State University Press, 1957.

Lander, Ernest M., Jr. "Manufacturing in South Carolina, 1815–1860," *Business History Review*, 28 (1954), 60–66.

Lewis, Ronald L. *Coal, Iron, and Slaves: Industrial Slavery in Maryland and Virginia, 1715–1865.* Westport, Conn.: Greenwood Press, 1979.

Miller, Elinor and Eugene D. Genovese. *Plantation, Town, and Country: Essays on the Local History of American Slave Society.* Urbana: University of Illinois Press, 1974.

Phillips, Christopher. *Freedom's Port: The African American Community in Baltimore, Md., 1790–1860.* Urbana: University of Illinois Press, 1997.

Reinders, Robert C. "Slavery in New Orleans in the Decade before the Civil War," *Mid-America*, 44 (1962), 211–21.

Richter, William L. "Slavery in Antebellum Baton Rouge, 1820–1860," *Louisiana History*, 10 (1969), 125–46.
Seip, Terry L. "Slaves and Free Negroes in Alexandria," *Louisiana History*, 10 (1969), 147–65.
Sheldon, Marianne B. "Black-White Relations in Richmond, Virginia, 1782–1820," *Journal of Southern History*, 45 (1979), 26–44.
Starobin, Robert S. *Industrial Slavery in the Old South*. New York: Oxford University Press, 1970.
Tregle, Joseph G., Jr. "Early New Orleans Society: A Reappraisal," *Journal of Southern History*, 18 (1952), 20–36.
Tyler-McGraw, Marie. *In Bondage and Freedom: Antebellum Black Life in Richmond, Virginia*. Richmond, Va.: Valentine Museum, 1988.
Wade, Richard C. *Slavery in the Cities: The South, 1820–1860*. New York: Oxford University Press, 1964.

7. Abolition, Colonization, Passive Resistance, and Slave Rebellion

Aptheker, Herbert. "Maroons within the Present Limits of the United States," *Journal of Negro History*, 24 (1939), 167–84.
——. *American Negro Slave Revolts*. New York: Columbia University Press, 1943.
——. *Nat Turner's Slave Revolt*. New York: Columbia University Press, 1944.
Bauer, Raymond and Alice. "Day to Day Resistance to Slavery," *Journal of Negro History*, 27 (1942), 399–419.
Bracey, John H. et al. (eds.). *American Slavery: The Question of Resistance*. Belmont, Calif.: Wadsworth Publishing Co., 1971.
Carroll, Joseph Cephas. *Insurrections in the United States 1800–1865*. New York: Negro Universities Press, 1968.
Davis, David Brion. "Abolitionists and the Freedmen: An Essay Review," *Journal of Southern History*, 31 (1965), 164–70.
Dew, Charles B. "Black Ironworkers and the Slave Insurrection Panic of 1856," *Journal of Southern History*, 41 (1975), 321–38.
Dillon, Merton L. "The Failure of American Abolitionists," *Journal of Southern History*, 25 (1959), 159–77.
Duberman, Martin (ed.). *The Antislavery Vanguard: New Essays on the Abolitionists*. Princeton: Princeton, N.J. University Press, 1965.
DuBois, W. E. Burghardt. *John Brown*. New York: International Publishers, 1962.
——. *The Suppression of the African Slave Trade to the United States of America, 1638–1870*. Baton Rouge: Louisiana State University Press, 1969.
Egerton, Douglas R. "Gabriel's Conspiracy and the Election of 1800," *Journal of Southern History*, 56 (1990), 191–214.

———. *Gabriel's Rebellion: The Virginia Slave Conspiracies of 1800 and 1802*. Chapel Hill: University of North Carolina Press, 1993.

———. *He Shall Go Out Free: The Lives of Denmark Vesey*. Madison: University of Wisconsin Press, 1999.

Flanigan, Daniel J. "Criminal Procedure in Slave Trials in the Antebellum South," *Journal of Southern History*, 40 (1974), 537–64.

Franklin, John Hope and Loren Schweninger. *Runaway Slaves: Rebels on the Plantation*. New York: Oxford University Press, 1999.

Frederickson, George M. and Christopher Lasch. "Resistance to Slavery," *Civil War History*, 13 (1967), 315–29.

Frey, Sylvia R. *Water from the Rock: Black Resistance in a Revolutionary Age*. Princeton: University of Princeton, N.J. Press, 1991.

Genovese, Eugene D. *From Rebellion to Revolution: Afro-American Slave Revolts in the Making of the New World*. Baton Rouge: Louisiana State University Press, 1979.

———. "Rebelliousness and Docility in the Negro Slave: A Critique of the Elkins Thesis," *Civil War History*, 13 (1967), 293–314.

Halasz, Nicholas. *The Rattling Chains: Slave Unrest and Revolt in the Antebellum South*. New York: D. McKay, 1966.

Jervey, Edward D. and C. Harold Huber. "The *Creole* Affair," *Journal of Negro History*, 65 (1980), 196–212.

Johnson, Michael P. "Runaway Slaves and the Slave Communities in South Carolina, 1799–1830," *William and Mary* Quarterly, 3rd Ser., 38 (1981), 418–41.

Jones, Howard. *Mutiny on the Amistad: The Saga of a Slave Revolt and Its Impact on American Abolition, Law, and Diplomacy*. New York: Norton, 1987.

———. "The Peculiar Institution and National Honor: The Case of the *Creole* Slave Revolt," *Civil War History*, 21 (1975), 28–50.

Kilson, Marion D. de B. "Towards Freedom: An Analysis of Slave Revolts in the United States," *Phylon*, 25 (1964), 175–87.

Kolchin, Peter. "The Process of Confrontation: Patterns of Resistance to Bondage in Nineteenth-Century Russia and the United States," *Journal of Social History*, 9 (1978), 457–90.

Lofton, John. *Denmark Vesey's Revolt: The Slave Plot That Lit the Fuse to Fort Sumter*. Kent, Ohio: Kent State University Press, 1983.

Miles, Edwin A. "The Mississippi Slave Insurrection Scare of 1835," *Journal of Negro History*, 42 (1957), 46–60.

Mullin, Gerald W. *Africa in America: Slave Acculturation and Resistance in the American South and the British Caribbean, 1736–1831*. Urbana: University of Illinois Press, 1992.

———. *Flight and Rebellion: Slave Resistance in Eighteenth-Century Virginia*. New York: Oxford University Press, 1972.

Nash, A. E. Kier. "Fairness and Formalism in the Trials of Blacks in the State Supreme Courts of the Old South," *Virginia Law Review*, 56 (1970), 64–100.

Oates, Stephen B. *The Fires of Jubilee: Nat Turner's Fierce Rebellion*. New York: Harper & Row, 1975.

Robertson, David. *Denmark Vesey*. New York: Knopf, 1999.

Starobin, Robert S. *Denmark Vesey: The Slave Conspiracy of 1822*. Englewood Cliffs, N.J.: Doubleday, 1979.

Tragle, Henry Irving (ed.). *The Southampton Slave Revolt of 1831: A Compilation of Source Material*. Amherst: University of Massachusetts Press, 1971.

Wade, Richard C. "The Vesey Plot: A Reconsideration," *Journal of Southern History*, 30 (1964), 143–61.

White, William W. "The Texas Slave Insurrection of 1860," *Southwestern Historical Quarterly*, 52 (1949), 259–85.

Wish, Harvey. "The Slave Insurrection Panic of 1856," *Journal of Southern History*, 5 (1939), 206–22.

8. Slavery, Abolitionists, and Abolition in the North and Haiti

Adams, Alice Dana. *The Neglected Period of Anti-Slavery in America, 1800–1831*. Gloucester, Mass.: P. Smith, 1964 [c1908].

Baur, John. "International Repercussions of the Haitian Revolution," *Americas*, 26 (1970), 394–418.

Breyfogle, William. *Make Free: The Story of the Underground Railroad*. Philadelphia: Lippincott, 1958.

Buckmaster, Henrietta. *Let My People Go: The Story of the Underground Railroad and the Growth of the Abolitionist Movement*. New York: Harper & Brothers, 1941.

Campbell, Penelope. *Maryland in Africa: The Maryland State Colonization Society, 1831–1857*. Urbana: University of Illinois Press, 1971.

Campbell, Stanley. *The Slave Catchers: Enforcement of the Fugitive Slave Law, 1850–1860*. Chapel Hill: University of North Carolina Press, 1970.

Cover, Robert M. *Justice Accused: Antislavery and Judicial Process*. New Haven, Conn.: Yale University Press, 1975.

Gara, Larry. *The Liberty Line: The Legend of the Underground Railroad*. Lexington: University of Kentucky Press, 1961.

Henry, H. M. *Police Control of the Slave in South Carolina*. New York: Negro Universities Press, 1968 [orig., 1914].

Hodges, Graham Russell. *Slavery and Freedom in the Rural North: African Americans in Monmouth County, New Jersey, 1665–1865*. Madison: University of Wisconsin Press, 1996.

Hunt, Alfred N. *Haiti's Influence on Antebellum America: Slumbering Volcano in the Caribbean*. Baton Rouge: Louisiana State University Press, 1988.

James, C. L. R. *The Black Jacobins: Toussaint L'Ouverture and the San Domingo Revolution*. New York: Vintage, 1963.

Magdol, Edward. *The Antislavery Rank and File: A Social Profile of the Abolitionists' Constituency*. Westport, Conn.: Greenwood Press, 1986.

Malin, James C. *John Brown and the Legend of Fifty-Six*. Philadelphia: American Philosophical Society, 1942.
Martin, Asa Earl. *The Antislavery Movement in Kentucky Prior to 1850*. Louisville: Standard Printing Co., 1918.
Martin, Waldo E., Jr. *The Mind of Frederick Douglass*. Chapel Hill: University of North Carolina Press, 1984.
Mayer, Henry. *All on Fire: William Lloyd Garrison and the Abolition of Slavery*. New York: St. Martin's, 1998.
McFeely, William S. *Frederick Douglass*. New York: Norton, 1990.
McManus, Edgar J. *Black Bondage in the North*. Syracuse: Syracuse University Press, 1973.
Melish, Joanne Pope. *Disowning Slavery: Gradual Emancipation and "Race" In New England, 1780–1860*. Ithaca, N.Y.: Cornell University Press, 1998.
Nash, Gary B. and Jean R. Soderlund. *Freedom by Degrees: Emancipation in Pennsylvania and Its Aftermath*. New York: Oxford University Press, 1991.
Oates, Stephen B. *"To Purge This Land with Blood": A Biography of John Brown*. New York: Harper & Row, 1970.
Paulson, Timothy J. *Days of Sorrow, Years of Glory, 1831–1850: From the Nat Turner Revolt to the Fugitive Act*. New York: Chelsea, 1994.
Pease, William H. and Jane H. *The Fugitive Law and Anthony Burns: A Problem in Law Enforcement*. Philadelphia: J. B. Lippincott, 1975.
Preston, Dickson J. *Young Frederick Douglass: The Maryland Years*. Baltimore, Md.: The Johns Hopkins University Press, 1980.
Quarles, Benjamin. *Black Abolitionists*. New York: Oxford University Press, 1969.
Renehan, Edward J., Jr. *The Secret Six: How a Circle of Northern Aristocrats Helped Light the Fuse of the Civil War*. New York: Crown, 1995.
Schwartz, Philip J. *Twice Condemned: Slaves and the Criminal Laws of Virginia, 1705–1865*. Baton Rouge: Louisiana State University Press, 1988.
Still, William. *The Underground Railroad*. New York: Arno Press, 1970 [orig. 1872].
Stoddard, Lothrop. *The French Revolution in Santo Domingo*. Westport, Conn.: Negro Universities Press,1970 [orig. 1914].
Venet, Wendy Hamand. *Neither Ballots nor Bullets: Women Abolitionists and the Civil War*. Charlottesville: University of Virginia Press, 1991.
Walters, Ronald G. and Eric Foner. *American Reformers, 1815–1860*. New York: Hill and Wang, 1997.
White, Shane. *Somewhat More Independent: The End of Slavery in New York City*. Athens: University of Georgia Press, 1991.
Whitman, T. Stephen. *The Price of Freedom: Slavery and Manumission in Baltimore and Early National Maryland*. Lexington: University of Kentucky Press, 1997.
Wilson, Hill Peebles. *John Brown, Soldier of Fortune: A Critique*. Lawrence, Kan.: H. P. Wilson, 1913.

Zilversmit, Alfred. *The First Emancipation: The Abolition of Slavery in the North.* Chicago: University of Chicago Press, 1967.

9. Slave Hiring-Out and Free People of Color

Arroyo, Elizabeth Fortson. "Poor Whites, Slaves, and Free Blacks in Tennessee, 1796–1861," *Tennessee Historical Quarterly,* 55 (1996), 57–64.
Berkeley, Edmund. "Prophet without Honor: Christopher, Free Person of Color," *Virginia Magazine of History and Biography,* 77 (1969), 180–90.
Berlin, Ira. *Slaves without Masters.* New York: Pantheon, 1974.
Bolster, W. Jeffrey. *Black Jacks: African American Seamen in the Age of Sail.* Cambridge, Mass.: Harvard University Press, 1997.
Brown, Letitia. *Free Negroes in the District of Columbia, 1790–1846.* New York: Oxford University Press, 1972.
Coulter, E. Merton. "Slavery and Freedom: Athens, Georgia, 1860–1866," *Georgia Historical Quarterly,* 49 (1965), 264–93.
Curry, Leonard P. *The Free Black in Urban America, 1800–1850: The Shadow of a Dream.* Chicago: University of Chicago Press, 1981.
Davis, Edwin Adams and William Ransom Hogan. *The Barber of Natchez.* Baton Rouge: Louisiana State University Press, 1973.
Eaton, Clement. "Slave Hiring: A Step toward Freedom in the Upper South," *Mississippi Valley Historical Review,* 46 (1960), 663–78.
Evans, W. A. "Free Negroes in Monroe County During Slavery," *Journal of Mississippi History,* 3 (1941), 37–43.
Everett, Donald Edward. "Free Persons of Color in New Orleans, 1803–1865." Unpublished Ph.D. Dissertation, Tulane University, New Orleans, 1952.
Fitchett, Horace. "The Traditions of the Free Negro in Charleston, South Carolina," *Journal of Negro History,* 25 (1940), 139–52.
Flanders, Ralph B. "The Free Negro in Antebellum Georgia," *North Carolina Historical Review,* 9 (1932), 250–72.
Foner, Philip S. *Frederick Douglass: A Biography.* New York: Citadel, 1964.
Franklin, John Hope. "James Boon, Free Negro Artisan," *Journal of Negro History,* 30 (1945), 150–80.
———. *The Free Negro in North Carolina, 1790–1860.* Chapel Hill: University of North Carolina Press, 1943.
Garvin, Russell. "The Free Negro in Florida before the Civil War," *Florida Historical Quarterly,* 46 (1967), 1–18.
Gutman, Herbert G. *The Black Family in Slavery and Freedom.* New York: Pantheon, 1976.
Hudson, Larry E., Jr. *Working toward Freedom: Slave Society and Domestic Economy in the American South.* Rochester, N.Y.: University of Rochester Press, 1994.
Hughes, Sarah S. "Slaves for Hire: The Allocation of Black Labor in Elizabeth County, Virginia, 1782 to 1810," *William and Mary Quarterly,* 3rd Ser., 35 (1978), 260–86.

Jackson, Luther P. "The Virginia Free Negro Farmer and Property Owner, 1830–1860," *Journal of Negro History*, 24 (1939), 390–421.

Johnson, Michael P. and James L. Roark. *Black Masters: A Free Family of Color in the Old South*. New York: Norton, 1984.

Koger, Larry. *Black Slaveowners: Free Black Slave Masters in South Carolina, 1790–1860*. Jefferson, N.C.: McFarland & Company, Inc., 1985.

Landers, Jane G. "Acquisition and Loss on a Spanish Frontier: The Free Black Homesteaders of Florida, 1784–1821," *Slavery and Abolition*, 17 (1996), 85–101.

Lebstock, Suzanne. *The Free Women of Petersburg: Status and Culture in a Southern Town, 1784–1860*. New York: Norton, 1984.

McConnell, Roland C. *Negro Troops of Antebellum Louisiana: A History of the Battalion of the Free Men of Color*. Baton Rouge: Louisiana State University Press, 1968.

Muir, Andrew Forrest. "The Free Negro in Jefferson and Orange Counties, Texas," *Journal of Negro History*, 35 (1950), 183–206.

Reinders, Robert C. "The Decline of the New Orleans Free Negro in the Decade before the Civil War," *Journal of Mississippi History*, 24 (1962), 88–98.

Roark, James L. *Black Masters: A Free Family of Color in the Old South*. New York: Norton, 1984.

Russell, John H. *The Free Negro in Virginia, 1619–1865*. Baltimore, Md.: The Johns Hopkins University Press, 1913.

Schoen, Harold. "The Free Negro in the Republic of Texas," *Southwestern Historical Quarterly*, 39 (1935–1936), 292–308; 40 (1936–1937), 85–113.

Schwartz, Philip J. "Emancipators, Protectors, and Anomalies: Free Black Slaveowners in Virginia," *Virginia Magazine of History and Biography*, 95 (1987), 317–38.

Schweninger, Loren. "Slave Independence and Enterprise in South Carolina, 1780–1865," *South Carolina Historical Magazine*, 93 (1992), 101–25.

———. "The Underside of Slavery: The Internal Economy, Self-Hire, and Quasi-Freedom, 1780–1865," *Slavery and Abolition*, 12 (1991), 10–21.

———. *Black Property Owners in the South, 1790–1915*. Urbana: University of Illinois Press, 1990.

Seip, Terry L. "Slaves and Free Negroes in Alexandria," *Louisiana History*, 10 (1969), 147–65.

Senese, Donald J. "The Free Negro and the South Carolina Courts, 1790–1860," *South Carolina Historical Magazine*, 68 (1967), 140–53.

Shugg, Roger W. "Negro Voting in the Antebellum South," *Journal of Negro History*, 21 (1936), 357–64.

Sterkx, Herbert E. *The Free Negro in Antebellum Louisiana*. Rutherford, N.J.: Fairleigh Dickinson University Press, 1972.

Sydnor, Charles S. "The Free Negro in Mississippi Before the Civil War," *American Historical Review*, 32 (1927), 769–88.

Wikramanayake, Marina. *A World in Shadow: The Free Black in Antebellum South Carolina*. Columbia: University of South Carolina Press, 1973.

Woodson, Carter G. *Free Negro Owners of Slaves in the United States in 1830*. Washington, D.C.: The Association for the Study of Negro Life and History, Inc., 1924.

V. THE LAW OF SLAVERY AND THE CONSTITUTION

Bestor, Arthur. "State Sovereignty and Slavery: A Reinterpretation of Pro-Slavery Constitutional Doctrine, 1846–1860," Illinois State Historical Society, *Journal*, 53 (1960), 117–80.

Catterall, Helen Tunnicliff (ed.). *Judicial Cases Concerning American Slavery and the Negro*. 5 vols. Washington, D.C.: Carnegie Institution, 1926–1937.

Cobb, Thomas R. R. *An Inquiry into the Law of Negro Slavery*. Intro. by Paul Finkelman, Athens: University of Georgia Press, 1999.

Finkelman, Paul. *An Imperfect Union: Slavery, Federalism, and Comity*. Chapel Hill: University of North Carolina Press, 1981.

Goodell, William. *The American Slave Code in Theory and Practice*. London: Clarke, Beeton, 1853.

Hall, Kermit L. (ed.). *The Law of American Slavery: Major Interpretations*. New York: Gartland, 1987.

Howard, W. S. *American Slaves and the Federal Law, 1837–1862*. Berkeley: University of California Press, 1963.

Hurd, John Codman. *The Law of Freedom and Bondage in the United States*. Boston: Little, Brown & Co., 1858–1862.

Ingersoll, Thomas N. "Slave Codes and Judicial Practice in New Orleans, 1718–1807," *Louisiana Historical Review*, 13 (1995), 28–39.

McGeachy, Katherine Ann. "The North Carolina Slave Code." Unpublished M.A. Thesis, University of North Carolina, 1948.

Morris, Thomas D. *Southern Slavery and the Law, 1619–1860*. Chapel Hill: University of North Carolina Press, 1996.

Nieman, Donald G. *Promises to Keep: African Americans and the Constitutional Order, 1776–1989*. New York: Oxford University Press, 1990.

Nye, Russell B. *Fettered Freedom: Civil Liberties and the Slavery Controversy, 1830–1860*. East Lansing: Michigan State College Press, 1949.

O'Neall, John B. *The Negro Law of South Carolina*. Columbia: J. G. Bowman, 1848.

Paludan, Phillip S. *A Covenant with Death: The Constitution, Law, and Equality in the Civil War Era*. Urbana: University of Illinois University Press, 1975.

Tushnet, Mark V. *The American Law of Slavery, 1810–1860: Considerations of Humanity and Interest*. Princeton: University of Princeton, N.J. Press, 1981.

Wahl, Jenny B. *The Bondsman's Burden: An Economic Analysis of the Common Law of Southern Slavery*. New York: Cambridge, Mass. University Press, 1998.
Watson, Alan. *Slave Law in the Americas*. Athens: University of Georgia Press, 1989.
Wiecek, William. "Slavery and Abolition before the United States Supreme Court," *Journal of American History*, 65 (1978), 34–59.
———. *The Sources of Antislavery Constitutionalism in America, 1760–1848*. Ithaca, N.Y.: Cornell University Press, 1877.

VI. CLASS AND SOCIETY IN THE OLD SOUTH, 1783–1865

1. General

Ayers, Edward L. *Vengeance and Justice: Crime and Punishment in the 19th Century American South*. New York: Oxford University Press, 1984.
Boman, Martha. "A City in the Old South: Jackson, Mississippi," *Journal of Mississippi History*, 15 (1953), 1–32.
Brownell, Blair A. and David R. Goldfield (eds.). *The City in Southern History: The Growth of Urban Civilization in the South*. Port Washington, N.Y.; Kennikat Press, 1977.
Burton, Orville Vernon and Robert C. McMath, Jr. (eds.). *Class, Conflict, and Consensus: Antebellum Southern Community Studies*. Westport, Conn.: Greenwood Press, 1982.
Eaton, Clement. *The Growth of Southern Civilization, 1790–1860*. New York: Harper & Row, 1961.
Freehling, William W. (ed.). *Slavery and Freedom*. New York: Oxford University Press, 1982.
Goldfield, David R. *Urban Growth in the Age of Sectionalism: Virginia, 1847–1861*. Baton Rouge: Louisiana State University Press, 1977.
Green, Fletcher M. *Constitutional Development in the South Atlantic States, 1776–1860*. Chapel Hill: University of North Carolina Press, 1930.
Hindus, Michael Stephen. *Prison and Plantation: Crime, Justice, and Authority in Massachusetts and South Carolina, 1767–1878*. Chapel Hill: University of North Carolina Press, 1980.
Oakes, James. *Slavery and Freedom: An Interpretation of the Old South*. New York: Norton, 1990.
Sydnor, Charles S. "The Southerner and the Laws," *Journal of Southern History*, 6 (1940), 3–24.
Taylor, William R. *Cavalier and Yankee: The Old South and the American National Character*. Garden City, N.Y.: George Brazillier, 1961.
Tobias, J. J. *Crime and Industrial Society in the Nineteenth Century*. New York: Schocken, 1968.

Wooster, Ralph A. *Politicians, Planters and Plain Folks: Courthouse and Statehouse in the Upper South, 1850–1860*. Knoxville: University of Tennessee Press, 1975.

———. *The People in Power: Courthouse and Statehouse in the Lower South*. Knoxville: University of Tennessee Press, 1969.

Wyatt-Brown, Bertram. *Yankee Saints and Southern Sinners*. Baton Rouge: Louisiana State University Press, 1985.

2. The Planter Class and Its Cohorts

Bell, Malcolm, Jr. *Major Butler's Legacy: Five Generations of a Slaveholding Family*. Athens: University of Georgia Press, 1987.

Campbell, Randolph B. and Richard G. Lowe. *Wealth and Power in Antebellum Texas*. College Station: Texas A&M University Press, 1977.

Cash, W. J. *The Mind of the South*. New York: Knopf, 1941.

Censer, Jane Turner. *North Carolina Planters and Their Children, 1800–1860*. Baton Rouge: Louisiana State University Press, 1984.

Clement, William Edwards. *Plantation Life on the Mississippi*. New Orleans: Pelican, 1952.

Clifton, James M. "Jehossee Island: The Antebellum South's Largest Rice Plantation," *Agricultural History*, 59 (1985), 56–65.

Coclanis, Peter A. *The Shadow of a Dream: Economic Life and Death in the South Carolina Low Country, 1670–1920*. New York: Oxford University Press, 1989.

Collins, Bruce. *White Society in the Antebellum South*. New York: Longmans, 1985.

Craven, Avery O. *Edmund Ruffin: Southerner*. Baton Rouge: Louisiana State University Press, 1966.

Faust, Drew Gilpin. *James Henry Hammond and the Old South: A Design for Mastery*. Baton Rouge: Louisiana State University Press, 1982.

Gaines, Francis Pendleton. *The Southern Plantation: A Study in the Development and Accuracy of a Tradition*. Gloucester, Mass.: Peter Smith, 1962.

Genovese, Eugene D. *The World the Slaveholders Made: Two Essays in Interpretation*. New York: Pantheon Books, 1969

Greenberg, Kenneth S. *Masters and Statesmen: The Political Culture of American Slavery*. Baltimore, Md.: The Johns Hopkins University Press, 1985.

Harris, J. William. *Plain Folk and Gentry in a Slave Society: White Liberty and Black Slavery in Augusta's Hinterlands*. Middletown, Conn.: Wesleyan University Press, 1985.

———. *Society and Culture in the Slave South*. New York: Routledge, 1992.

Hermann, Janet S. *Joseph E. Davis: Pioneer Patriarch*. Jackson: University Press of Mississippi, 1990.

Hofstadter, Richard. "U. B. Phillips and the Plantation Legend," *Journal of Negro History*, 29 (1944), 109–24.

Johnson, Guion Griffis. *A Social History of the Sea Islands, with Special Reference to St. Helena Island, South Carolina*. Chapel Hill: University of North Carolina Press, 1930.

Johnson, Michael P. "Planters and Patriarchy: Charleston, 1800–1860," *Journal of Southern History*, 46 (1980), 45–72.

Jordan, Weymouth T. *Hugh Davis and His Alabama Plantation*. University, Ala.: University of Alabama Press, 1948.

Klein, Rachel N. *Unification of a Slave State: The Rise of the Planter Class in the South Carolina Backcountry, 1760–1808*. Chapel Hill: University of North Carolina Press, 1990.

Luraghi, Raimondo. *The Rise and Fall of the Plantation South*. New York: New Viewpoints, 1978.

McNeilly, Donald P. *The Old South Frontier: Cotton Plantations and the Formation of Arkansas Society, 1819–1861*. Fayetteville: University of Arkansas Press, 2000.

Miller, James David. *South by Southwest: Planter Emigration and Identity in the Slave South*. Charlottesville: University Press of Virginia, 2002.

Moffat, Charles H. "Charles Tait, Planter, Politician, and Scientist of the Old South," *Journal of Southern History*, 14 (1948), 206–33.

Moore, John Hebron. *The Emergence of the Cotton Kingdom in the Old Southwest: Mississippi, 1770–1860*. Baton Rouge: Louisiana State University Press, 1989.

Morris, Christopher. *Becoming Southern: The Evolution of a Way of Life, Warren County and Vicksburg, Mississippi, 1770–1860*. New York: Oxford University Press, 1995.

Oakes, James. *The Ruling Race: A History of American Slaveholders*. New York: Knopf, 1982.

Osterweis, Rollin G. *Romanticism and Nationalism in the Old South*. New Haven, Conn.: Yale University Press, 1949.

Peterson, Thomas Virgil. *Ham and Japhet: The Mythic World of Whites in the Antebellum South*. Metchuen: Scarecrow, 1978.

Phifer, Edward W. "Slavery in Microcosm: Burke County, North Carolina," *Journal of Southern History*, 29 (1962), 137–65.

Rosengarten, Theodore. *Tombee: The Portrait of a Cotton Planter*. New York: Quill/William Morrow, 1986.

Scarborough, William K. *The Overseer: Plantation Management in the Old South*. Baton Rouge: Louisiana State University Press, 1966.

———. "Southern Plantation Overseer: A Reevaluation," *Agricultural History*, 38 (1964), 13–20.

Shore, Laurence. *Southern Capitalists: The Ideological Leadership of an Elite, 1832–1885*. Chapel Hill: University of North Carolina Press, 1986.

Stowe, Steven M. *Intimacy and Power in the Old South: Rituals in the Lives of the Planters*. Baltimore, Md.: The Johns Hopkins University Press, 1987.

Taylor, Rosser H. "The Gentry of Antebellum South Carolina," *North Carolina Historical Review*, 17 (1940), 114–33.

Tracey, Susan Jean. *In the Master's Eye: Representations of Women, Blacks, and Poor Whites in Antebellum Southern Literature*. Amherst: University of Massachusetts Press, 1996.

Troutman, Richard L. "The Physical Setting of the Bluegrass Planter," *Kentucky Historical Society Register*, 66 (1968), 367–77.

Vlach, John Michael. *Back of the Big House: The Architecture of Plantation Slavery*. Chapel Hill; University of North Carolina Press, 1993.

Woodman, Harold D. *King Cotton and His Retainers: Financing and Marketing the Cotton Crop of the South, 1800–1925*. Lexington: University of Kentucky Press, 1968.

Young, Jeffrey Robert. *Domesticating Slavery; The Master Class in Georgia and South Carolina, 1670–1837*. Chapel Hill: University of North Carolina Press, 1999.

3. Non-Slaveholding Whites

Arroyo, Elizabeth Fortson. "Poor Whites, Slaves, and Free Blacks in Tennessee, 1796–1861," *Tennessee Historical Quarterly*, 55 (1996), 57–64.

Bolton, Charles C. *Poor Whites of the Antebellum South: Tenants and Laborers in Central North Carolina and Northeast Mississippi*. Durham: Duke University Press, 1994.

Bonner, James C. *Georgia's Last Frontier: The Development of Carroll County*. Athens: University of Georgia Press, 1971.

Buck, Paul. "The Poor Whites in the Antebellum South," *American Historical Review*, 31 (1925), 41–54.

Cash, W. J. *The Mind of the South*. New York: Knopf, 1941.

Cecil-Fransman, Bill. *Common Whites: Class and Culture in Antebellum North Carolina*. Lexington: University of Kentucky Press, 1992.

Clark, Blanche Henry. *Tennessee Yeomen, 1840–1860*. Nashville: Vanderbilt University Press, 1945.

Collins, Bruce. *White Society in the Antebellum South*. New York: Longmans, 1985.

Craven, Avery O. "Poor Whites and Negroes of the Antebellum South," *Journal of Negro History*, 15 (1930), 14–25.

Hahn, Steve. *The Roots of Southern Populism: Yeoman Farmers and the Transformation of the Georgia Upcountry, 1850–1890*. New York: Oxford University Press, 1983.

Harris, J. William. *Plain Folk and Gentry in a Slave Society: White Liberty and Black Slavery in Augusta's Hinterlands*. Middletown, Conn.: Wesleyan University Press, 1985.

———. *Society and Culture in the Slave South*. New York: Routledge, 1992.

Hyde, Samuel C., Jr. (ed.). *Plain Folk of the Old South Revisited*. Baton Rouge: Louisiana State University Press, 1997.

Inscoe, John C. *Mountain Masters, Slavery, and the Sectional Crisis in Western North Carolina*. Knoxville: University of Tennessee Press, 1989.

Linden, Fabian. "Economic Democracy in the Slave South: An Appraisal of Some Recent Views," *Journal of Negro History*, 31 (1946), 140–89.
Magdol, Edward and Jon Wakelyn (eds.). *The Southern Common People: Studies in Nineteenth-Century Social History*. Westport, Conn.: Greenwood Press, 1980.
McCurry, Stephanie. *Masters of Small Worlds: Yeoman Households, Gender Relations, and the Political Culture of the Antebellum South Carolina Lowland*. New York: Oxford University Press, 1995.
McDonald, Forrest and Grady McWhiney. "The Antebellum Southern Herdsman: A Reinterpretation, *"Journal of Southern History*, 41 (1975), 147–66.
———. "The South from Self-Sufficiency to Peonage: An Interpretation," *American Historical Review*, 85 (1980), 1095–1118.
McWhiney, Grady. *Cracker Culture: Celtic Ways in the Old South*. Tuscaloosa: University of Alabama Press, 1988.
Owsley, Frank L. and Harriet C. "The Economic Basis of Society in the Late Antebellum South," *Journal of Southern History*, 6 (1940), 20–45.
Owsley, Frank Lawrence. *Plain Folk of the Old South*. Baton Rouge: Louisiana State University Press, 1949.
Russel, Robert R. "The Effects of Slavery upon Nonslaveholders in the Antebellum South," *Agricultural History*, 15 (1941), 112–26.
Tracey, Susan Jean. *In the Master's Eye: Representations of Women, Blacks, and Poor Whites in Antebellum Southern Literature*. Amherst: University of Massachusetts Press, 1996.
Weaver, Herbert. *Mississippi Farmers, 1850–1860*. Nashville: Vanderbilt University Press, 1968.
Winters, Donald L. "'Plain Folk' of the Old South Reexamined: Economic Democracy in Tennessee," *Journal of Southern History*, 53 (1987), 565–86.
Wright, Gavin. "'Economic Democracy' and the Concentration of Agricultural Wealth in the Cotton South, 1850–1860," *Agricultural History*, 44 (1970), 63–93.

4. Southern Women

Brown, Alexis Girardin. "The Women Left Behind: Transformation of the Southern Belle, 1840–1880," *The Historian*, 62 (No. 4, 2000), 759–78.
Bynum, Victoria E. *Unruly Women: The Politics of Social and Sexual Control in the Old South*. Chapel Hill: University of North Carolina Press, 1992.
Clinton, Catherine. *The Plantation Mistress: Woman's World in the Old South*. New York: Pantheon, 1982.
Fox-Genovese, Elizabeth. *Within the Plantation Household: Black and White Women of the Old South*. Chapel Hill: University of North Carolina Press, 1988.
Jones, Jacqueline. *Labor of Love, Labor of Sorrow: Black Women, Work, and the Family from Slavery to the Present*. New York: Basic Books, 1985.
Lebstock, Suzanne. *The Free Women of Petersburg: Status and Culture in a Southern Town, 1784–1860*. New York: Norton, 1984.

McCurry, Stephanie. *Masters of Small Worlds: Yeoman Households, Gender Relations, and the Political Culture of the Antebellum South Carolina Lowland*. New York: Oxford University Press, 1995.
McMillan, Sally G. *Motherhood in the Old South: Pregnancy, Childbirth, and Infant Rearing*. Baton Rouge: Louisiana State University Press, 1990.
McMillan, Sally G. *Southern Women: Black and White in the Old South*. Arlington Heights, Il: Harlan Davidson, 1992.
Parkhurst. Jessie W. "The Role of the Black Mammy in the Plantation Household," *Journal of Negro History*, 23 (1938), 349–69.
Scott, Anne Firor. *The Southern Lady: From Pedestal to Politics, 1830–1930*. Chicago: University of Chicago Press, 1970.
Tracey, Susan Jean. *In the Master's Eye: Representations of Women, Blacks, and Poor Whites in Antebellum Southern Literature*. Amherst: University of Massachusetts Press, 1996.
White, Deborah Gray. *Ar'n't I a Woman? Female Slaves in the Plantation South*. New York: Norton, 1985.

5. Religion and Education

Bailey, David. *Shadow on the Church: Southwestern Evangelical Religion and the Issue of Slavery, 1783–1860*. Ithaca, N.Y.: Cornell University Press, 1985.
Boles, John B. *The Great Revival, 1787–1805: The Origins of the Southern Evangelical Mind*. Lexington: University of Kentucky Press, 1972.
———. (ed.). *Masters & Slaves in the House of the Lord: Race and Religion in the American South, 1740–1870*. Lexington: University of Kentucky Press, 1988.
Brigham, R. I. "Negro Education in Antebellum Missouri," *Journal of Negro History*, 30 (1945), 405–20.
Brooks, Walter H. "Evolution of the Negro Baptist Church," *Journal of Negro History*, 7 (1922), 11–22.
Calhoon, Tobert M. *Evangelicals and Conservatives in the Early South, 1740–1861*. Columbia: University of South Carolina Press, 1988.
Carwardine, Richard J. *Evangelicals and Politics in Antebellum America*. New Haven, Conn.: Yale University Press, 1993.
Cornelius, Janet Duitsman. *"When Can I Read My Title Clear": Literacy, Slavery, and Religion in the Antebellum South*. Columbia: University of South Carolina Press, 1991.
Frazier, E. Franklin. *The Negro Church in America*. New York: Schocken, 1963.
Heyrman, Christine Leigh. *Southern Cross: The Beginnings of the Bible Belt*. New York: Knopf, 1997.
Hill, Samuel S. *The South and North in American Religion*. Athens: University of Georgia Press, 1980.
Hudson, Winthrop S. *Nationalism and Religion in America: Concepts of American Identity and Mission*. Gloucester, Mass.: Peter Smith, 1970.

Jackson, Luther P. "Religious Instruction of Negroes, 1830–1860, with Special Reference to South Carolina," *Journal of Negro History*, 15 (1930), 72–114.

Jernegan, Marcus W. "Slavery and Conversion in the American Colonies," *American Historical Review*, 21 (1916), 504–27.

Johnson, Guion Griffis. "The Camp Meeting in Antebellum North Carolina," *North Carolina Historical Review*, 10 (1933), 95–110.

Korn, Bertram W. *Jews and Negro Slavery in the Old South, 1789–1865*. Elkins Park, Penn.: Reform Congregation Keneseth Israel, 1961.

Loveland, Anne C. *Southern Evangelicals and the Social Order, 1800–1860*. Baton Rouge: Louisiana State University Press, 1980.

Mathews, Donald G. *Religion in the Old South*. Chicago: University of Chicago Press, 1977.

Parkinson, Ralph Thomas. The Religious Instruction of Slaves, 1820–1860." Unpublished Ph.D. Dissertation, University of North Carolina, 1948.

Raboteau, Albert J. *Slave Religion: The 'Invisible Institution' in the Antebellum South*. New York: Oxford University Press, 1978.

Sernett, Milton C. *Black Religion and Evangelicalism: White Protestants, Plantation Missions, and the Flowering of Negro Christianity, 1787–1865*. Metuchen: Scarecrow, 1975.

Snay, Mitchell. *Gospel of Disunion: Religion and Separatism in the Antebellum South*. Cambridge: Cambridge, Mass. University Press, 1993.

Sobel, Mechal. *Trabelin' On: The Slave Journey to an Afro-Baptist Faith*. Westport, Conn.: Greenwood Press, 1979.

Startup, Kenneth Moore. *The Root of All Evil: The Protestant Clergy and the Economic Mind of the Old South*. Athens: University of Georgia Press, 1997.

Tracey, Susan Jean. *In the Master's Eye: Representations of Women, Blacks, and Poor Whites in Antebellum Southern Literature*. Amherst: University of Massachusetts Press, 1996.

Wakelyn, Jon L. and Randall M. Miller. *Catholics in the Old South: Essays on Church and Culture*. Macon: Mercer University Press, 1983.

Wamble, Gaston Hugh. "Negroes and Missouri Protestant Churches Before and After the Civil War," *Missouri Historical Review*, 61 (1967), 321–47.

Woodson, Carter G. *The Education of the Negro Prior to 1861*. Washington, D.C.: Associated Publishers, 1919.

Wyatt-Brown, Bertram. *Southern Honor: Ethics and Behavior in the Old South*. New York: Oxford University Press, 1982.

6. Family Life and Leisure Pursuits, Benign and Deadly

Bardaglio, Peter W. *Reconstructing the Household: Family, Sex, and the Law in the Nineteenth-Century South*. Chapel Hill: University of North Carolina Press, 1995.

Bruce, Dickson D., Jr. *Violence and Culture in the Antebellum South.* Austin: University of Texas Press, 1979.

Burton, Orville Vernon. *In My Father's House Are Many Mansions: Family and Community in Edgefield, South Carolina.* Chapel Hill: University of North Carolina Press, 1985.

Cashin, Joan E. *A Family Venture: Men and Women on the Southern Frontier.* New York: Oxford University Press, 1991.

Cochrane, Hamilton. *Noted American Duels and Hostile Encounters.* Philadelphia: Chilton, 1962.

Duffy, John. "Medical Practice in the Antebellum South," *Journal of Southern History*, 25 (1959), 53–72.

Franklin, John Hope. *The Militant South.* Cambridge, Mass.: Beacon Press, 1956.

Gorn, Elliott J. "'Gouge and Bite, Pull Hair and Scratch': The Social Significance of Fighting in the Southern Backcountry," *American Historical Review*, 90 (1985), 18–43.

Greenberg, Kenneth S. "The Nose, the Lie, and the Duel in the Antebellum South," *American Historical Review*, 95 (1990), 57–74.

Gutman, Herbert G. *The Black Family in Slavery and Freedom.* New York: Pantheon, 1976.

Johnson, Guion Griffis. "Courtship and Marriage Customs in Antebellum North Carolina," *North Carolina Historical Review*, 8 (1931), 384–402.

LeClercq, Anne Sinker Whaley. *An Antebellum Plantation Household.* Columbia: University of South Carolina Press, 1966.

Malone, Ann Patton. *Sweet Chariot: Slave Family and Household Structure in Nineteenth-Century Louisiana.* Chapel Hill: University of North Carolina Press, 1992.

McMillan, Sally G. *Motherhood in the Old South: Pregnancy, Childbirth, and Infant Rearing.* Baton Rouge: Louisiana State University Press, 1990.

Mitchell, M. C. "Health and the Medical Profession in the Lower South," *Journal of Southern History*, 19 (1944), 424–46.

Rorabaugh, W. J. "The Political Duel in Early America," *Journal of the Early Republic*, 15 (Spring 1995), 1–23.

Seitz, Don C. *Famous American Duels.* New York: Thomas Y. Crowell, 1919.

Shryock, Richard H. "Medical Practice in the Old South," *South Atlantic Quarterly*, 29 (1930), 172–82.

Stowe, Steven M. *Intimacy and Power in the Old South: Rituals in the Lives of the Planters.* Baltimore, Md.: The Johns Hopkins University Press, 1987.

Williams, Jack Kenny. *Dueling in the Old South.* College Station: Texas A&M Press, 1980.

Wyatt-Brown, Bertram. "Andrew Jackson's Honor," *Journal of the Early Republic*, 17 (1997), 1–36.

―――. *Southern Honor: Ethics and Behavior in the Old South.* New York: Oxford University Press, 1982.

7. The Mind of the Old South

Cash, W. J. *The Mind of the South*. New York: Knopf, 1941.
Eaton, Clement. *The Freedom-of-Thought Struggle in the Old South*. New York: Harper & Row, 1964 [rev. ed].
———. *The Mind of the Old South*. Baton Rouge: Louisiana State University Press, 1967 [rev. ed].
Faust, Drew Gilpin. *The Ideology of Slavery: Proslavery Thought in the Antebellum South, 1830–1869*. Baton Rouge: Louisiana State University Press, 1981.
———. *A Sacred Circle: The Dilemma of the Intellectual in the Old South, 1840–1860*. Baltimore, Md.: The Johns Hopkins University Press, 1977.
Fehrenbacher, Don E. *Constitutions and Constitutionalism in the Slaveholding South*. Athens: University of Georgia Press, 1989.
Fields, Barbara J. "Slavery, Race, and Ideology in the United States of America," *New Left Review*, 181 (1990), 95–118.
Ford, Lacy K., Jr. *Origins of Southern Radicalism: The South Carolina Upcountry, 1800–1860*. New York: Oxford University Press, 1980.
Frederickson, George M. *The Black Image in the White Mind: The Debate on Afro-American Character and Destiny, 1817–1914*. New York: Harper & Row, 1971.
Genovese, Eugene D. *The Slaveholder's Dilemma: Freedom and Progress in Southern Conservative Thought, 1820–1860*. Columbia: University of South Carolina Press, 1992.
Horsman, Reginald. *Josiah Nott of Mobile: Southerner, Physician, and Racial Theorist*. Baton Rouge: Louisiana State University Press, 1987.
Jenkins, William Sumner. *Pro-Slavery Thought in the Old South*. Chapel Hill: University of North Carolina Press, 1935.
Jordan, Winthrop. *White over Black: American Attitudes toward the Negro, 1550–1812*. Chapel Hill: University of North Carolina Press, 1968.
McCardell, John. *The Idea of a Southern Nation: Southern Nationalists and Nationalism, 1830–1860*. New York: Norton, 1979.
Osterweis, Rollin G. *Romanticism and Nationalism in the Old South*. New Haven, Conn.: Yale University Press, 1949.
Shalhope, Robert E. "Race, Class, Slavery and the Antebellum Southern Mind," *Journal of Southern History*, 37 (1971), 557–74.
Shore, Laurence. *Southern Capitalists: The Ideological Leadership of an Elite, 1832–1885*. Chapel Hill: University of North Carolina Press, 1986.
Stanton, William. *The Leopard's Spots: Scientific Attitudes Toward Race in America, 1815–1859*. Chicago: University of Chicago Press, 1960.
Startup, Kenneth Moore. *The Root of All Evil: The Protestant Clergy and the Economic Mind of the Old South*. Athens: University of Georgia Press, 1997.
Tise, Larry. *Proslavery: A History of the Defense of Slavery in America, 1701–1840*. Athens: University of Georgia Press, 1987.
Wish, Harvey. *George Fitzhugh: Propagandist of the Old South*. Baton Rouge: Louisiana State University Press, 1943.

8. Agriculture and the Southern Economy

Bonner, James C. *A History of Georgia Agriculture, 1732–1860*. Athens: University of Georgia Press, 1964.

Britton, Karen G. *Bale o' Cotton: The Mechanical Art of Cotton Ginning*. College Station: Texas A&M Press, 1992.

Carney, Judith A. *Black Rice: The African Origins of Rice*. Cambridge, Mass.: Harvard University Press, 2001.

Chaplin, Joyce E. *An Anxious Pursuit: Agricultural Innovation and Modernity in the Lower South, 1730–1815*. Chapel Hill: University of North Carolina Press, 1993.

Coclanis, Peter A. *The Shadow of a Dream: Economic Life and Death in the South Carolina Low Country, 1670–1920*. New York: Oxford University Press, 1989.

Craven, Avery O. *Soil Exhaustion as a Factor in the Agricultural History of Virginia and Maryland, 1606–1860*. Urbana: University of Illinois Press, 1926.

Dethloff, Henry C. *A History of the American Rice Industry, 1685–1985*. College Station: Texas A&M University Press, 1988.

Eaton, Miles. "The Development and Later Decline of the Hemp Industry in Missouri," *Missouri Historical Review*, 43 (1949), 344–59.

Gray, Lewis C. *History of Agriculture in the Southern States to 1850*. 2 vols. Washington, D.C.: Carnegie Institution, 1933.

Heyward, Duncan Clinch. *Seed from Madagascar*. Chapel Hill: University of North Carolina Press, 1937.

Hilliard, Sam Bowers. *Atlas of Antebellum Southern Agriculture*. Baton Rouge: Louisiana State University Press, 1984.

———. *Hog Meat and Hoecake: Food Supply in the Old South, 1840–1860*. Carbondale, Ill.: Southern Illinois University Press, 1972.

Hutchinson, W. K. and S. H. Williamson. "The Self-Sufficiency of the Antebellum South: Estimates of the Food Supply," *Journal of Economic History*, 31 (1971), 491–612.

Jordan, Terry C. *Trail to Texas: Southern Roots of Western Cattle Ranching*. Lincoln: University of Nebraska Press, 1981.

Kellar, Herbert Anthony (ed.). *Solon Robinson: Pioneer and Agriculturalist*. 2 vols. Indianapolis: Bobbs-Merrill, 1936.

Murray, Chalmers S. *This Is Our Land: The Story of the Agricultural Society of South Carolina*. Charleston: Carolina Art Association, 1949.

Otto, John S. *The Southern Frontiers, 1607–1860: The Agricultural Evolution of the Colonial and Antebellum South*. New York: Greenwood, 1989.

Robert, Joseph Clarke. *The Tobacco Kingdom: Plantation, Market, and Facotry in Virginia and North Carolina, 1800–1860*. Durham: Duke University Press, 1938.

Russel, Robert R. *Economic Aspects of Southern Nationalism, 1840–1861*. Urbana: University of Illinois Press, 1923.

Sheehan, Bernard. *Seeds of Extinction*. Chapel Hill: University of North Carolina Press, 1973.

Siegel, Frederick F. *The Roots of Southern Distinctiveness: Tobacco and Society in Danville, Virginia, 1780–1865*. Chapel Hill: University of North Carolina Press, 1987.
Sitterson, J. Carlyle. *Sugar Country: The Sugar Industry in the South, 1753–1950*. Lexington: University of Kentucky Press, 1953.
Wright, Gavin. "Slavery and the Cotton Boom," *Explorations in Economic History*, 12 (1975), 439–51.
———. *The Political Economy of the Cotton South: Households, Markets, and Wealth in the Nineteenth Century*. New York: Norton, 1978.

VII. THE OLD SOUTH AND THE ERA OF SECTIONAL CONTROVERSY, 1849–1861

1. The Wilmot Proviso and the Compromise of 1850

Bauer, K. Jack. *Zachary Taylor: Soldier, Planter, Statesman of the Old Southwest*. Baton Rouge: Louisiana State University Press, 1985.
Brauer, Kinley. *Cotton versus Conscience: Massachusetts Whig Politics and Southwestern Expansion, 1843–1848*. Lexington: University of Kentucky Press, 1967.
Brock, William R. *Parties and Political Conscience: American Dilemmas, 1840–1850*. New York: KTO Press, 1979.
Brown, Thomas. *Politics and Statesmanship: Essays on the American Whig Party*. New York: Columbia University Press, 1985.
Carpenter, Jesse T. *The South as a Conscious Minority, 1789–1861: A Study in Political Thought*. New York: New York University Press, 1930.
Cole, Arthur C. *The Irrepressible Conflict, 1850–1865*. New York: Macmillan, 1938.
Cooper, William J., Jr. *Liberty and Slavery: Southern Politics to 1860*. New York: Knopf, 1983.
Craven, Avery O. *The Growth of Southern Nationalism, 1848–1861*. Baton Rouge: Louisiana State University Press, 1953.
Eaton, Clement. *Henry Clay and the Art of American Politics*. Boston: Little, Brown, 1957.
Elliott, Charles Winslow. *Winfield Scott: The Soldier and the Man*. New York: Macmillan, 1937.
Escott, Paul D. "Jefferson Davis and Slavery in the Territories," *Journal of Mississippi History*, 39 (1977), 97–116.
Fadeland, Betty L. *James Gillespie Birney: Slaveholder to Abolitionist*. New York: Greenwood, 1969.
Faulk, Odie. *Too Far North, Too Far South* [the Gadsden Purchase]. Los Angeles: Westernlore Press, 1967.
Foner, Eric. "The Wilmot Proviso Revisited," *Journal of American History*, 56 (1969), 262–79.

Foster, Herbert D. "Webster's Seventh of March Speech and the Secession Movement, 1850," *American Historical Review*, 27 (1922), 245–70.
Gara, Larry. "Antislavery Congressmen, 1848–1856: Their Contribution to the Debate between the Sections," *Civil War History*, 15 (1969), 197–207.
Going, Charles B. *David Wilmot, Free-Soiler: A Biography of the Great Advocate of the Wilmot Proviso*. New York: D. Appleton & Co., 1924.
Grayson, Benson Lee. *The Unknown President: The Administration of President Millard Fillmore*. Washington, D.C.: University Press of America, 1981.
Hamilton, Holman. *Prelude to Conflict: The Crisis and Compromise of 1850*. Lexington: University of Kentucky Press, 1964.
———. *Zachary Taylor: Soldier in the White House*. Indianapolis: Bobbs-Merrill, 1951.
Harmon, George D. "Douglas and the Compromise of 1850," Illinois State Historical Society, *Journal*, 21 (1929), 477–79.
Hodder, Frank H. "The Authorship of the Compromise of 1850," *Mississippi Valley Historical Review*, 22 (1936), 525–36.
Holt, Michael F. *The Political Crisis of the 1850s*. New York: John Wiley and Sons, 1978.
Jennings, Thelma N. *The Nashville Convention: Southern Movement for Unity, 1848–1851*. Memphis: Memphis, Tenn. State University Press, 1980.
Johnson, Gerald W. *America's Silver Age: The Statecraft of Clay—Webster—Calhoun*. New York: Harper Bros., 1939.
Johnson, Vicki Vaughn. *The Men and Vision of the Southern Commercial Conventions. 1845–1871*. Columbia: University of Missouri Press, 1992.
McKinley, Silas Bent. *Old Rough and Ready: The Life and Times of Zachary Taylor*. New York: Vanguard Press, 1946.
McLaughlin, Andrew Cunningham. *Lewis Cass*. New York: AMS Press, 1972.
Morris, Thomas D. *Free Men All: The Personal Liberty Laws of the North, 1780–1861*. Baltimore, Md.: The Johns Hopkins University Press, 1974.
Morrison, Chaplain. *Democratic Politics and Sectionalism: The Wilmot Proviso Controversy*. Chapel Hill: University of North Carolina Press, 1967.
Peterson, Merrill D. *The Great Triumvirate: Webster, Clay, and Calhoun*. New York: Oxford University Press, 1987.
Quaife, Milo M. *The Doctrine of Non-Intervention with Slavery in the Territories*. Chicago: M. C. Chamberlain, 1910.
Ramsdell, Charles W. "The Natural Limits of Slavery Expansion," *Mississippi Valley Historical Review*, 16 (1929), 151–71.
Rayback, Joseph G. *Free Soil: The Election of 1848*. Lexington: University of Kentucky Press, 1970.
Russel, Robert R. "Constitutional Doctrines with Regard to Slavery in the Territories," *Journal of Southern History*, 32 (1966), 466–85.
Scarry, Robert J. *Millard Fillmore*. Jefferson, N.C.: McFarland, 2001.
Silbey, Joel. *The Shrine of Party: Congressional Voting Behavior, 1841–1852*. Pittsburgh: University of Pittsburgh Press, 1967.

Smith, Elbert B. *The Presidencies of Zachary Taylor and Millard Fillmore.* Lawrence: University Press of Kansas, 1988.
Stegmaier, Mark J. *Texas, New Mexico, and the Compromise of 1850: Boundary Dispute and Sectional Crisis.* Kent, Ohio: Kent State University Press, 1996.
Wofford, Frank B. *Lewis Cass: The Last Jeffersonian.* New York: Octagon Books, 1973, rev. ed.

2. The Kansas Imbroglio, Popular Sovereignty, and Dred Scott

Cole, Arthur C. *The Irrepressible Conflict, 1850–1865.* New York: Macmillan, 1938.
Cooper, William J., Jr. *Liberty and Slavery: Southern Politics to 1860.* New York: Knopf, 1983.
———. *The South and the Politics of Slavery, 1852–1856.* Baton Rouge: Louisiana State University Press, 1978.
Craven, Avery O. *The Growth of Southern Nationalism, 1848–1861.* Baton Rouge: Louisiana State University Press, 1953.
Fehrenbacher, Don E. *The Dred Scott Case: Its Significance in American Law and Politics.* New York: Oxford University Press, 1978.
Fleming, Walter Lynwood. "The Buford Expedition to Kansas," *American Historical Review*, 6 (1900), 39–43.
Gara, Larry. "Antislavery Congressmen, 1848–1856: Their Contribution to the Debate between the Sections," *Civil War History*, 15 (1969), 197–207.
———. *The Presidency of Franklin Pierce.* Lawrence: University Press of Kansas, 1991.
———. "Results of the Fugitive Slave Law," *Civil War Times Illustrated*, 2 (October 1963), 30–37.
Goodrich, Thomas. *War to the Knife: Bleeding Kansas.* Lincoln: University of Nebraska Press, 2004.
Herklotz, Hildegarde R. "Jayhawkers in Missouri, 1858–1863," *Missouri Historical Review*, 17 (1923), 266–84.
Hodder, Frank H. "The Railroad Background of the Kansas–Nebraska Act," *Mississippi Valley Historical Review*, 12 (1925), 3–22.
———. "Some Aspects of the English Bill for the Admission of Kansas." American Historical Association, *Annual Report* (1906), I, 202–10.
Hoffert, Sylvia. "The Brooks-Sumner Affair." *Civil War Times Illustrated*, 11 (October 1972), 35–40.
Holt, Michael F. *The Political Crisis of the 1850s.* New York: John Wiley and Sons, 1978.
Hopkins, Vincent C. *Dred Scott's Case.* New York: Fordham University Press, 1951.
Johannsen, Robert W. "Lecompton Constitutional Convention," *Kansas Historical Quarterly*, 23 (1957), 226–34.

———. "Stephen A. Douglas, *Harper's Magazine*, and Popular Sovereignty," *Mississippi Valley Historical Review*, 45 (1959), 606–31.
Johnson, Samuel A. *Battle Cry of Freedom: The New England Emigrant Aid Company in the Kansas Crusade*. Lawrence: University Press of Kansas, 1954.
Kutler, Stanley I. (ed.). *The Dred Scott Decision: Law or Politics?* Boston: Houghton Mifflin Co., 1967.
Lynch, William. "The Influence of Population Movements on Missouri before 1861," *Missouri Historical Review*, 15 (1922), 506–16.
Malin, James C. "The Pro-Slavery Background of the Kansas Struggle," *Mississippi Valley Historical Review*, 10 (1923), 287–97.
———. *The Nebraska Question, 1852–1854*. Lawrence: University Press of Kansas, 1953.
McCormick, E. I. "Justice Campbell and the Dred Scott Decision," *Mississippi Valley Historical Review*, 19 (1933), 565–71.
Milton, George Fort. *Eve of Conflict: Stephen A. Douglas and the Needless War* (Boston: Houghton Mifflin, 1934.
Nevins, Allan, *The Constitution, Slavery, and the Territories*. Boston: Boston University Press, 1953.
Rawley, James A. *Race and Politics: "Bleeding Kansas" and the Coming of the Civil War*. Philadelphia: Lippincott, 1969.
Ray, P. Orman. *The Repeal of the Missouri Compromise, Its Origin and Authorship*. Cleveland: Arthur H. Clark, 1909.
Rosenberg, M. "The Kansas–Nebraska Act: A Case Study," *Annals of Iowa*, 26 (1964), 436–57.
Russel, Robert R. "The Issues in the Congressional Struggle over the Kansas–Nebraska Bill, 1854," *Journal of Southern History*, 29 (1963), 187–210.
Siegel, Martin. *The Taney Court, 1836–1864*. Millwood, N.Y.: Associated Faculty Press, 1995.
Wolff, Gerald. "The Slaveocracy and the Homestead Problem of 1854," *Agricultural History*, 40 (1966), 101–11.

3. The Expansion of Slavery at Home and Abroad

Berwanger, Eugene H. *The Frontier against Slavery: Western Anti-Negro Prejudice and the Slavery Extension Controversy*. Urbana: University of Illinois Press, 1967.
Binder, Frederick Moore. *James Buchanan and the American Empire*. Selinsgrove, Penn.: Susquehanna University Press, 1994.
Bridges, C. A. "The Knights of the Golden Circle: A Filibustering Fantasy," *Southwestern Historical Quarterly*, 44 (1940–1941), 287–302
Brown, Charles A. *Agents of Manifest Destiny: The Lives and Times of the Filibusters*. Chapel Hill: University of North Carolina Press, 1980.
Cole, Arthur C. *The Irrepressible Conflict, 1850–1865*. New York: Macmillan, 1938.

Craven, Avery O. *The Growth of Southern Nationalism, 1848–1861*. Baton Rouge: Louisiana State University Press, 1953.

Crenshaw, Ollinger. "The Knights of the Golden Circle," *American Historical Review*, 47 (1941), 23–50.

Curti, Merle E. "'Young America,'" *American Historical Review*, 32 (October 1926), 34–55.

De Forest, Tim. "Southern Attempts to Annex Cuba," *America's Civil War*, 10 (May 1997), 38–44.

Hall, James O. "A Magnificent Charlatan: George Washington Lafayette Bickley Made a Career of Deceit," *Civil War Times Illustrated.*, 18 (February 1980), 40–42.

Jordan, Terry. "The Imprint of the Upper and Lower South on Mid-Nineteenth-Century Texas," *Annals of the Association of American Geographers*, 57 (1967), 667–90.

May, Robert E. *The Southern Dream of a Caribbean Empire, 1854–1861*. Baton Rouge: Louisiana State University Press, 1973.

Morrison, Michael A. *Slavery and the American West: The Eclipse of Manifest Destiny and the Coming of the Civil War*. Chapel Hill: University of North Carolina Press, 1997.

Nevins, Allan, *The Constitution, Slavery, and the Territories*. Boston: Boston University Press, 1953.

Parker, William N. *Commerce, Cotton, and Westward Expansion, 1820–1860*. Chicago: Scott, Foresman, 1964.

Riepma, Siert F. "Young America: A Study in American Nationalism before the Civil War," Ph.D. Dissertation, Western Reserve University, Cleveland, OH, 1939.

Rogers, Tommy. "The Great Population Exodus from South Carolina, 1850–1860," *South Carolina Historical Magazine*, 68 (1967), 14–21.

Rogers, Tommy. "Migration Patterns of Alabama's Population, 1850 and 1860," *Alabama Historical Quarterly*, 28 (1966), 45–48.

Schaefer, Donald F. "A Statistical Profile of Frontier and New South Migration, 1850–1860," *Agricultural History*, 59 (1985), 563–78.

Stout, Joe A., Jr., *The Liberators: Filibustering Expeditions into Mexico, 1848–1862, and the Last Gasp of Manifest Destiny*. Los Angeles: Westernlore Press, 1973.

4. Politics and Slavery

Alexander, Thomas B. *Sectional Stress and Party Strength: A Computer Analysis of Roll-Call Voting Patterns in the United States House of Representatives, 1836–1860*. Nashville: Vanderbilt University Press, 1967.

Anbinde, Tyler. *Nativism and Slavery: The Northern Know Nothings and the Politics of the 1850s*. New York: Oxford University Press, 1992.

Baker, Jean H. *Affairs of Party: The Political Culture of Northern Democrats in the Mid-Nineteenth Century*. Ithaca, N.Y.: Cornell University Press, 1983.

———. *The Politics of Continuity: Maryland and Political Parties from 1858 to 1870*. Baltimore, Md.: The Johns Hopkins University Press, 1973.

Billington, Ray A. *The Origins of Nativism in the United States*. New York: Arno, 1974.

Blue, Frederick J. *The Free Soilers: Third Party Politics, 1848–1854*. Urbana: University of Illinois Press, 1973.

Boykin, James H. *North Carolina in 1861*. New York: Pageant Press, 1958.

Carey, Anthony Gene. *Parties, Slavery, and Union in Antebellum Georgia*. Athens: University of Georgia Press, 1997.

Cole, Arthur C. *The Irrepressible Conflict, 1850–1865*. New York: Macmillan, 1938.

Cooper, William J., Jr. *Liberty and Slavery: Southern Politics to 1860*. New York: Knopf, 1983.

Craven, Avery O. *The Growth of Southern Nationalism, 1848–1861*. Baton Rouge: Louisiana State University Press, 1953.

Eaton, Clement. *The Freedom-of-Thought Struggle in the Old South*. New York: Harper & Row, 1964 [rev. ed].

Davis, David Brion. *The Slave Power Conspiracy and the Paranoid Style*. Baton Rouge: Louisiana State University Press, 1969.

Durden, Robert F. *The Self-Inflicted Wound: Southern Politics in the Nineteenth Century*. Lexington: University of Kentucky Press, 1985.

Fehrenbacher, Don E. *The Dred Scott Case: Its Significance in American Law and Politics*. New York: Oxford University Press, 1978.

Fields, Barbara J. "Slavery, Race, and Ideology in the United States of America," *New Left Review*, 181 (1990), 95–118.

Finkelman, Paul. "The Nationalization of Slavery: A Counter-Factual Approach to the 1860s," *Louisiana Studies*, 14 (1975), 213–40.

Foner, Eric. *Free Soil, Free Labor, Free Men: The Ideology of the Republican Party before the Civil War*. New York: Oxford University Press, 1970.

Gara, Larry. "Antislavery Congressmen, 1848–1856: Their Contribution to the Debate between the Sections," *Civil War History*, 15 (1969), 197–207.

———. "Slavery and the Slave Power: A Crucial Distinction," *Civil War History*, 15 (1969), 5–18.

Gienapp, William E. *The Origins of the Republican Party, 1852–1860*. New York: Oxford University Press, 1987.

Greeley, Andrew M. *An Ugly Little Secret: Anti-Catholicism in North America*. Kansas City: Sheed, Andrews, and McMeel, 1977.

Holt, Michael F. "The Politics of Impatience: The Origins of Know Nothingism," *Journal of American History*, 60 (1973), 309–31.

———. *Political Parties and American Political Development from the Age of Jackson to the Age of Lincoln*. Baton Rouge: Louisiana State University Press, 1992.

———. *Rise and Fall of the Whig Party: Jacksonian Politics and the Onset of the Civil War*. New York: Oxford University Press, 1999.

———. *To Rescue Public Liberty: A History of the American Whig Party*. New York: Oxford University Press, 1999.

———. *The Political Crisis of the 1850s*. New York: John Wiley and Sons, 1978.

Howe, Daniel W. *The Political Culture of American Whigs*. Chicago: University of Chicago Press, 1979.

Hyman, Harold M., and William Wiecek. *Equal Justice under Law: Constitutional Development, 1835–1875*. New York: Harper & Row, 1982.

Jeffrey, Thomas. *State Parties and National Politics: North Carolina, 1815–1861*. Athens: University of Georgia Press, 1989

Kruman, Marc W. *Parties and Politics in North Carolina, 1836–1865*. Baton Rouge: Louisiana State University Press, 1983.

Levin, Daniel Lessard. *Representing Popular Sovereignty: The Constitution in American Political Culture*. Albany: State University of New York Press, 1999.

Mazlisch, Stephen E. and John J. Kushma (eds.). *Essays on American Antebellum Politics, 1840–1860*. College Station: Texas A&M University Press, 1982.

Miller, William Lee. *Arguing about Slavery: The Great Battle in the United States Congress*. New York: Knopf, 1996.

Milton, George Fort. *Eve of Conflict: Stephen A. Douglas and the Needless War* (Boston: Houghton Mifflin, 1934.

Mulkern, John R. *The Know-Nothing Party in Massachusetts: The Rise and Fall of a People's Movement*. Boston: Northeastern University Press, 1990.

Nagel, Paul C. *One Nation Indivisible: The Union in American Thought, 1776–1861*. New York: Oxford University Press, 1964.

Nevins, Allan. *The Emergence of Lincoln*. 2 vols. New York: Charles Scribner's Sons, 1950.

———. *The Ordeal of the Union*. 2 vols. New York: Charles Scribner's Sons, 1947.

Nichols, Roy F. *The Democratic Machine, 1850–1854*. New York: Columbia University Press, 1923.

Nichols, Roy F. *The Disruption of the American Democracy*. New York: Macmillan, 1948.

———. *The Invention of the American Party System*. New York: Macmillan, 1967.

Overdyke, W. Darrell. *The Know-Nothing Party in the South*. Baton Rouge: Louisiana State University Press, 1950.

Phillips, Ulrich B. *Georgia and State Rights*. Yellow Springs, Ohio: Antioch Press 1968 [orig. 1902].

Porter, Kirk Harold, and Donald Bruce Johnson. *National Party Platforms, 1840–1964*. Urbana: University of Illinois Press, 1966.

Potter, David M. *The Impending Crisis, 1848–1861*. New York: Harper & Row, 1976.

Richards, Leonard L. *The Slave Power: The Free North and Southern Domination, 1780–1860*. Baton Rouge: Louisiana State University Press, 2000.

Sewell, Richard H. *Ballots for Freedom: Antislavery Politics in the United States, 1837–1860*. New York: Oxford University Press, 1976.

———. *A House Divided: Sectionalism and the Coming of the Civil War, 1848–1865*. Baltimore, Md.: The Johns Hopkins University Press, 1988.
Stampp, Kenneth M. *America in 1857: A Nation on the Brink*. New York: Oxford University Press, 1990.
Thornton, J. Mills, III. *Politics and Power in a Slave Society: Alabama, 1800–1860*. Baton Rouge: Louisiana State University Press, 1978.
Walters, Ronald G. and Eric Foner. *American Reformers, 1815–1860*. New York: Hill and Wang, 1997.

5. Biographies

Allmendinger, David F. *Ruffin: Family and Reform in the Old South*. New York: Oxford University Press, 1990.
Ambler, Charles Henry. *The Life and Diary of John Floyd, Governor of Virginia, an Apostle of Secession, and the Father of the Oregon Country*. Richmond: Richmond, Va. Press, 1918.
Bailey, Hugh C. *Hinton Rowan Helper: Abolitionist-Racist*. University, Ala.: University of Alabama Press, 1965.
Crist, Lynda Lasswell. "A 'Duty Man': Jefferson Davis as Senator," *Journal of Mississippi History*, 51 (1989), 281–96.
Curtis [sic], Merle E. "George Sanders—American Patriot of the Fifties," *South Atlantic Quarterly*, 27 (January 1928), 79–87.
Davis, William C. *Robert Barnwell Rhett: The Life and Times of a Fire-Eater*. Columbia: University of South Carolina Press, 2001.
Dubay, Robert W. *John Jones Pettus, Mississippi Fire-Eater: His Life and Times, 1813–1867*. Jackson: University Press of Mississippi, 1975.
DuBose, J. W. *The Life and Times of William Lowndes Yancey*. 2 vols. Birmingham: Roberts & Sons, 1892.
Edmunds, John B. *Francis W. Pickens and the Politics of Destruction*. Chapel Hill: University of North Carolina Press, 1977.
Hentig, Gerald S. *Henry Winter Davis: Antebellum and Civil War Congressman from Maryland*. New York: Twayne, 1973.
Johannsen, Robert W. *Stephen A. Douglas*. New York: Oxford University Press, 1973.
Johnson, Allen. *Stephen A. Douglas: A Study in American Politics*. New York: Macmillan, 1908.
Johnson, Z. T. *The Political Policies of Howell Cobb*. Nashville: George Peabody, 1929.
King, Alvy L. *Louis Wigfall: Southern Fire-Eater*. Baton Rouge: Louisiana State University Press, 1970.
Kirwan, Albert D. *John J. Crittenden: The Struggle for the Union*. Lexington: University of Kentucky Press, 1962.
Klein, Philip S. *James Buchanan: A Biography*. University Park: Pennsylvania State University Press, 1995.

Klunder, Willard Carl. *Lewis Cass and the Politics of Moderation*. Kent: Kent State University Press, 1996.

Langheim, Eric. *Jefferson Davis, Patriot: A Biography*. New York: Vantage Press, 1962.

Leemhuis, Roger P. *James L. Orr and the Sectional Conflict*. Washington, D.C.: University Press of America, 1979.

May, Robert E. *John A. Quitman: Old South Crusader*. Baton Rouge: Louisiana State University Press, 1985.

McNash, William. *Thomas R. R. Cobb (1823–1862): The Making of a Southern Nationalist*. Macon: Mercer University Press, 1983.

Mitchell, Broadus. *Frederick Law Olmsted, a Critic of the Old South*. Baltimore, Md.: The Johns Hopkins University Press, 1924.

Montgomery, Horace. *Howell Cobb: A Confederate Career*. Tuscaloosa: Confederate Publishing Co., 1959.

Nichols, Roy F. *Franklin Pierce: Young Hickory of the Granite Hills*. Philadelphia: University of Pennsylvania Press, 1931.

Nuremburger, Ruth Ketring. *The Clays of Alabama: A Planter-Lawyer-Politician Family*. Lexington: University of Kentucky Press, 1958.

Parks, Joseph H. *John Bell of Tennessee*. Baton Rouge: Louisiana State University Press, 1950.

Parrish, William E. *David Rice Atchison of Missouri: Border Politician*. Columbia: University of Missouri Press, 1961.

Phillips, Ulrich B. *The Life of Robert Toombs*. New York: B. Franklin, 1968 [orig. 1913].

Richardson, Edward H. *Cassius Marcellus Clay: Firebrand of Freedom*. Lexington: University of Kentucky Press, 1996.

Robbins, Peggy. "The Greatest Scoundrel [Jacob Thompson]," *Civil War Times Illustrated*, 31 (November/December 1992), 54–59, 89–90.

Sansing, David. "A Happy Interlude: Jefferson Davis and the War Department," *Journal of Mississippi History*, 51 (1989), 297–312.

Shenton, James P. *Robert John Walker: A Politician from Jackson to Lincoln*. New York: Columbia University Press, 1961.

Simpson, John Eddins. *Howell Cobb: The Politics of Ambition*. Chicago: Adams Press, 1973.

Smiley, David L. *Lion of Whitehall: The Life of Cassius M. Clay*. Madison: University of Wisconsin Press, 1962.

Swisher, Carl B. *Roger B. Taney*. New York: MacMillan, 1935.

Thompson, William Y. *Robert Toombs of Georgia*. Baton Rouge: Louisiana State University Press, 1966.

Todd, John Emerson. *Frederick Law Olmsted*. Boston: Twayne, 1982.

Wakelyn, Jon L. *The Politics of a Literary Man: William Gilmore Simms*. Westport, Conn.: Greenwood Press, 1973.

White, Laura Amanda. *Robert Barnwell Rhett: Father of Secession*. Gloucester, Mass: P. Smith, 1965.

6. The Road to Secession

Auer, J. Jeffry (ed.). *Antislavery and Disunion, 1857–1861: Studies in Rhetoric of Compromise and Conflict*. New York: Harper & Row, 1963.

Barney, William L. *The Road to Secession: A New Perspective on the Old South*. New York: Praeger, 1972.

———. *The Secessionist Impulse: Alabama and Mississippi in 1860*. Princeton, N.J.: Princeton University Press, 1974.

Bestor, Arthur, "The American Civil War as a Constitutional Crisis," *American Historical Review*, 69 (1964), 327–54.

Buenger, Walter L. *Secession and Union in Texas*. Austin: University of Texas Press, 1984.

Carey, Anthony Gene. *Parties, Slavery, and Union in Antebellum Georgia*. Athens: University of Georgia Press, 1997.

Channing, Steven A. *Crisis of Fear: Secession in South Carolina*. New York: Norton, 1970.

Cobb, James C. "The Making of a Secessionist: Henry L. Benning and the Coming of the Civil War," *Georgia Historical Quarterly*, 60 (1976), 313–23.

Cole, Arthur C. *The Irrepressible Conflict, 1850–1865*. New York: Macmillan, 1938.

Cooper, William J., Jr. *Liberty and Slavery: Southern Politics to 1860*. New York: Knopf, 1983.

Craven, Avery O. *The Growth of Southern Nationalism, 1848–1861*. Baton Rouge: Louisiana State University Press, 1953.

Crenshaw, Ollinger. "The Speakership Contest of 1859–1860," *Mississippi Valley Historical Review*, 29 (1942), 323–38.

Denman, Clarence P. *The Secession Movement in Alabama*. Freeport, N.Y.: Books for Libraries Press, 1971.

Donnelly, William J. "Conspiracy or Popular Movement: The Historiography of Southern Support for Secession," *North Carolina Historical Review*, 42 (1965), 70–84.

Freehling, William W. *The Reintegration of American History: Slavery and the Civil War*. New York: Oxford University Press, 1994.

———. *The Road to Disunion: Secessionists at Bay*. New York: Oxford University Press, 1990.

Freehling, William W. and Craig M. Simpson (eds.). *Secession Debated: Georgia's Showdown in 1860*. New York: Oxford University Press, 1992.

Graebner, Norman A. (ed.). *Politics and the Crisis of 1860*. Urbana: University of Illinois Press, 1961.

Gunderson, Robert Gray. *The Old Gentlemen's Convention: The Washington Peace Conference of 1861*. Madison: University of Wisconsin Press, 1961.

Heidler, Davis S. *Pulling the Temple Down; The Fire-Eaters and the Destruction of the Union*. Mechanicsburg, Penn.: Stackpole, 1994.

Hicken, Victor. "John A. McClernand and the House Speakership Struggle of 1859," Illinois State Historical Society, *Journal*, 53 (1960), 163–78.

Huston, James L. *Calculating the Value of the Union: Slavery, Property Rights, and the Economic Origins of the Civil War.* Chapel Hill: University of North Carolina Press, 2003.

———. *The Panic of 1857 and the Coming of the Civil War.* Baton Rouge: Louisiana State University Press, 1987.

———. "Southerners against Secession: The Arguments of the Constitutional Unionists in 1850–1851," *Civil War History*, 46 (2000), 291–99.

Johnson, Michael P. *Toward a Patriarchal Republic: The Secession of Georgia.* Baton Rouge: Louisiana State University Press, 1977.

Klein, Maury. *Days of Defiance: Sumter, Secession, and the Coming of the Civil War.* New York: Knopf, 1997.

Knupfer, Peter B. *The Union as It Was: Constitutional Unionism and Sectional Compromise, 1787–1861.* Chapel Hill: University of North Carolina Press, 1991.

Levine, Bruce. *Half Slave and Half Free: The Roots of the Civil War.* New York: Hill and Wang, 1992.

Long, Durwood. "Alabama's Secession Commissioners," *Civil War History*, 9 (1963), 55–66.

May, John A. and Joan R. Faunt. *South Carolina Secedes.* Columbia: University of South Carolina Press, 1960.

McCrary, Peyton, et al. "Class and Party in the Secession Crisis: Voting Behavior in the Deep South," *Journal of Interdisciplinary History*, 8 (1978), 429–57.

Milton, George Fort. *Eve of Conflict: Stephen A. Douglas and the Needless War* (Boston: Houghton Mifflin, 1934.

Oates, Stephen B. *"To Purge This Land with Blood": A Biography of John Brown.* New York: Harper & Row, 1970.

Pease, William H. and Jane H. *James Louis Petigru: Southern Conservative, Southern Dissenter.* Athens: University of Georgia Press, 1995.

Phillips, Ulrich B. *The Course of the South to Secession: An Interpretation.* New York: Appleton-Century, 1939.

Potter, David M. *Lincoln and His Party in the Secession Crisis.* New Haven, Conn.: Yale University Press, 1962, 2nd rev. ed.

———. *The South and Sectional Conflict.* Baton Rouge: Louisiana State University Press, 1968.

Rainwater, Percy Lee. *Mississippi: Storm Center of Secession, 1856–1861.* New York: Da Capo Press, 1969.

Randall, James G. "The Blundering Generation," *Mississippi Valley Historical Review*, 47 (1940), 3–28.

Ransom, Roger L. *Conflict and Compromise: The Political Economy of Slavery, Emancipation and the Civil War.* Cambridge: Cambridge, Mass. University Press, 1989.

Renehan, Edward J., Jr. *The Secret Six: How a Circle of Northern Aristocrats Helped Light the Fuse of the Civil War.* New York: Crown, 1995.

Shanks, Henry Thomas. *The Secession Movement in Virginia, 1847–1861.* Richmond, Va.: Garrett and Massie, 1934.

Sitterson, J. Carlyle. *The Secession Movement in North Carolina*. Chapel Hill: University of North Carolina Press, 1939.

Stampp, Kenneth M. *And the War Came: The North and the Secession Crisis, 1860–1861*. Baton Rouge: Louisiana State University Press, 1950.

———. *The Imperiled Union: Essays on the Background of the Civil War*. New York: Oxford University Press, 1980.

Walther, Eric H. *The Fire-Eaters*. Baton Rouge: Louisiana State University Press, 1992.

Wood, James M. *Rebellion and Realignment: Arkansas' Road to Secession*. Fayetteville: University of Arkansas Press, 1987.

Wooster, Ralph A. "The Secession of the Lower South: An Amalgamation of Changing Interpretations," *Civil War History*, 7 (1961), 117–27.

Wooster, Ralph A. *The Secession Conventions of the South*. Princeton: Princeton, N.J. University Press, 1962.

Wright, William C. *The Secession Movement in the Middle Atlantic States*. Rutherford: Fairleigh Dickinson University Press, 1973.

VIII. THE CONFEDERACY, 1861–1865

1. Confederate Government and Ideology

Alexander, Thomas B. and Richard E. Beringer. *Anatomy of the Confederate Congress: A Study of the Influence of Member Characteristics on Legislative Voting Behavior, 1861–1865*. Nashville: Vanderbilt University Press, 1972.

Coulter, E. Merton. *Confederate States of America, 1861–1865*. Baton Rouge: Louisiana State University Press, 1950.

Creason, Joe. "Kentucky's Efforts to Remain Neutral," *Civil War Times*, 2 (January 1961), 8–9.

Crofts, Daniel W. *Reluctant Confederates: Upper South Unionists in the Secession Crisis*. Chapel Hill: University of North Carolina Press, 1989.

Davis, William C. *A Government of Our Own: The Making of the Confederacy*. New York: Free Press, 1974.

DeRosa, Marshall L. *The Confederate Constitution of 1861*. Columbia: University of Missouri Press, 1991.

Dew, Charles B. *Apostles of Disunion: Southern Secession Commissioners and the Causes of the Civil War*. Charlottesville: University Press of Virginia, 2001.

Genovese, Eugene D. *A Consuming Fire: The Fall of the Confederacy in the Mind of the White Christian South*. Athens: University of Georgia Press, 1998.

Grimsley, Mark. "Conciliation and Failure, 1861–1862," *Civil War History*, 39 (1993), 317–35.

Lee, Charles R. Jr. *The Confederate Constitutions*. Chapel Hill: University of North Carolina Press, 1963.

Martis, Kenneth C. *Historical Atlas of the Congresses of the Confederate States of America, 1861–1865*. New York: Free Press, 1994.
Nevins, Allan. *The War for the Union*. 4 vols. New York: Charles Scribner's Sons, 1959–1971.
Owsley, Frank Lawrence. *State Rights in the Confederacy*. Chicago: University of Chicago Press, 1925.
Phillips, Kevin. *The Cousins' Wars: Religion, Politics, and the Triumph of Anglo-America*. New York: Basic Books, 1999.
Rabel, George C. *Confederate Republic: A Revolution against Politics*. Chapel Hill: University of North Carolina Press, 1994.
Rafuse, Ethan S. "Why the Confederate Insurgency Failed: Another Take on the Essential Question," *North & South*, VII (November 2004), 24–33.
Ringold, May S. *The Role of State Legislatures in the Confederacy*. Athens: University of Georgia Press, 1966.
Thomas, Emory M. *The Confederacy as a Revolutionary Experience*. Englewood Cliffs, N.J.: Prentice Hall, 1991.
———. *The Confederate Nation, 1861–1865*. New York: Harper & Row, 1979.

2. Confederate Political Leaders

Canfield, Cass. *The Iron Will of Jefferson Davis*. New York: Harcourt Brace Jovanovich, 1978.
Cooper, William J., Jr. *Jefferson Davis, American*. New York; Knopf, 2000.
Davis, William C. *Breckinridge: Statesman, Soldier, Symbol*. Baton Rouge: Louisiana State University Press, 1992.
———. "The Conduct of 'Mr. Thompson'," *Civil War Times Illustrated*, 9 (May 1970), 4–7, 43–47.
———. *Jefferson Davis: The Man and His Hour*. New York: HarperCollins, 1991.
Eaton, Clement. *Jefferson Davis*. New York: Free Press, 1977.
Escott, Paul D. *After Secession: Jefferson Davis and the Failure of Confederate Nationalism*. Baton Rouge: Louisiana State University Press, 1878.
Evans, Eli N. *Judah P. Benjamin: The Jewish Confederate*. New York: Free Press, 1988.
Faust, Drew Gilpin. *The Creation of Confederate Nationalism: Ideology and Identity in the Civil War South*. Baton Rouge: Louisiana State University Press, 1988.
Grimsley, Mark. "'We Will Vindicate the Right': An Account of the Life of Jefferson Davis," *Civil War Times Illustrated*, 30 (July/August 1996), [Special Issue].
Heck, Frank H. *Proud Kentuckian: John C. Breckinridge, 1821–1875*. Lexington: University of Kentucky, 1976.
Meade, Robert Douthat. *Judah P. Benjamin: Confederate Statesman*. New York: Oxford University Press, 1943.
———. "The Relations between Judah P. Benjamin and Jefferson Davis," *Journal of Southern History*, 5 (1939), 468–78.

Nevins, Allan. *The War for the Union.* 4 vols. New York: Charles Scribner's Sons, 1959–1971.
Schott, Thomas E. *Alexander H. Stephens of Georgia.* Baton Rouge: Louisiana State University Press, 1988.
Von Abele, Rudolph R. *Alexander H. Stephens: A Biography.* Westport, Conn.: Negro Universities Press, 1971 [orig. 1946].
Wiley, Bell I. "Jefferson Davis: An Appraisal," *Civil War Times Illustrated,* 6 (April 1967), 4–11, 44–49.

3. Confederate Military Leaders

Bandow, Doug. "The Marble man," *National Review,* 43 (October 21, 1991), 48–49.
Castle, Albert. *General Sterling Price and the Civil War in the West.* Baton Rouge: Louisiana State University Press, 1968.
Connelly, Thomas L. *The Marble Man: Robert E. Lee and His Image in American Society.* New York: Knopf, 1977.
Dew, Charles B. *Ironmaker to the Confederacy: Joseph R. Anderson and the Tredegar Iron Works.* New Haven, Conn. Yale University Press, 1966.
Freeman, Douglas S. *R. E. Lee.* 4 vols. New York: Charles Scribner's Sons, 1934–1935.
Holladay, Florence Elizabeth. "The Extraordinary Powers and Functions of the General Commanding the Trans-Mississippi Department of the Southern Confederacy." M.A. thesis, University of Texas, 1914.
Nevins, Allan. *The War for the Union.* 4 vols. New York: Charles Scribner's Sons, 1959–1971.
Nolan, Alan T. *Lee Considered: General Robert E. Lee and Civil War History.* Chapel Hill: University of North Carolina Press, 1991.
Robertson, James I., Jr. *Stonewall Jackson: The Man, the Soldier, the Legend.* New York: Macmillan, 1997.
Shalhope, Robert E. *Sterling Price: Portrait of a Southerner.* Columbia: University of Missouri, 1971.
Thomas, Emory M. *Robert E. Lee: A Biography.* New York: Norton, 1995.
Woodworth, Steven E. *Jefferson Davis and His Generals: The Failure of Confederate Command in the West.* Lawrence: University of Kansas Press, 1990.

4. The Armies in the Field

Ash, Stephen V. *When the Yankees Came: Conflict and Chaos in the Occupied South, 1861–1865.* Chapel Hill: University of North Carolina Press, 1995.
Connelly, Thomas L. *Army of the Heartland; The Army of Tennessee, 1861–1862.* Baton Rouge: Louisiana State University Press, 1967.
——. *Autumn of Glory: The Army of Tennessee, 1862–1865.* Baton Rouge: Louisiana State University Press, 1971.

Freeman, Douglas S. *Lee's Lieutenants: A Study in Command*. 3 vols. New York: Charles Scribner's Sons, 1942–1944.
Josephy, Alvin M., Jr. *The Civil War in the American West*. New York: Knopf, 1991.
Kerby, Robert L. *Kirby Smith's Confederacy: The Trans-Mississippi South, 1863–1865*. New York: Columbia University Press, 1972.
Linderman, Gerald F. *Embattled Courage: The Experience of Combat in the American Civil War*. New York: Free Press, 1987.
Manning, Chandra Miller. "'Our Liberties and Institutions': What the Union and Confederate Soldiers Thought the Civil War Was About," *North & South*, 7 (October 2004), 12–25.
Monaghan, Jay. *Civil War on the Western Border, 1854–1865*. Boston: Little, Brown & Co., 1955.
Massey, Mary E. *Refugee Life in the Confederacy*. Baton Rouge: Louisiana State University Press, 1964.
Nevins, Allan. *The War for the Union*. 4 vols. New York: Charles Scribner's Sons, 1959–1971.
Rabel, George C. *Civil Wars: Women in the Crisis of Southern Nationalism*. Urbana: University of Illinois Press, 1989.

5. The South and the Northern Enemy

Bennett, Lerone, Jr., *Forced into Glory: Abraham Lincoln's White Dream*. Chicago: Johnson Publishing, 2000.
Bradford, M. E. "The Lincoln Legacy: A Long View." In *Remembering Who We Are: Observations of a Southern Conservative*, edited by M. E. Bradford, 143–56. Athens: University of Georgia Press, 1985.
Current, Richard N. *The Lincoln Nobody Knows*. New York: McGraw Hill Book Co., 1958.
———. *Lincoln's Loyalists: Union Soldiers from the Confederacy*. Boston: Northeastern University Press, 1992.
DiLorenzo, Thomas. *The Real Lincoln: A New Look at Abraham Lincoln, His Agenda, and an Unnecessary War*. New York: Forum, 2002.
Donald, David H. *Lincoln*. New York: Simon & Schuster, 1995.
Fleming, Thomas. "Lincoln's Tragic Heroism," *National Review*, 41 (December 8, 1989), 38–40.
Jaffa, Harry V. "Lincoln's Character Assassins," *National Review*, 42 (January 22, 1990), 34–38.
May, J. Thomas. "The Medical Care of Blacks in Louisiana During Occupation and Reconstruction, 1862–1868." Unpublished Ph.D. Dissertation, Tulane University, New Orleans, 1970.
Nevins, Allan. *The War for the Union*. 4 vols. New York: Charles Scribner's Sons, 1959–1971.

Pratt, Fletcher. *Stanton: Lincoln's Secretary of War.* Westport, Conn.: Greenwood Press, 1953, reprint 1970.

Rose, Willie Lee. *Rehearsal for Reconstruction: The Port Royal Experiment.* New York: Oxford University Press, 1976.

Thomas, Benjamin. *Abraham Lincoln: A Biography.* New York: Alfred A. Knopf, 1953.

Appendix A
U.S. Governments during the Antebellum Era, 1790–1861

Party	President	V. Pres.	State	War	Treasury	Post. Gen.	Atty. Gen.	Navy	Interior
Federalist, 1790–1793	George Washington	John Adams	Thomas Jefferson	Henry Knox, Timothy Pickering	Alexander Hamilton		Edmund Randolph		
Federalist, 1793–1797	George Washington	John Adams	Edmund Randolph, Timothy Pickering	Timothy Pickering, James McHenry	Oliver Wolcott, Jr.		William Bradford, Charles Lee		
Federalist, 1797–1801	John Adams	Thomas Jefferson	Timothy Pickering, John Marshall	James McHenry, Samuel Dexter	Oliver Wolcott, Jr., Samuel Dexter		Charles Lee	Benjamin Stoddart	
Dem/Rep, 1801–1805	Thomas Jefferson	Aaron Burr	James Madison	Henry Dearborn	Samuel Dexter, Albert Gallatin		Levi Lincoln	Benjamin Stoddart, Robert Smith	
Dem/Rep, 1805–1809	Thomas Jefferson	George Clinton	James Madison	Henry Dearborn	Albert Gallatin		Jno. Breckinridge, Caesar A. Rodney	Robert Smith	
Dem/Rep, 1809–1813	James Madison	George Clinton	Robert Smith, James Monroe	William Eustis, James Monroe, John Armstrong	Albert Gallatin, George W. Campbell, Alexander J. Dallas		Ceasar A. Rodney, William Pinckney	Robert Smith, Paul Hamilton, William Jones	
Dem/Rep, 1813–1817	James Madison	Elbridge Gerry	James Monroe	James Monroe, William H. Crawford, George Graham	William H. Crawford		Richard Rush	Benjamin Crowninshield	

Party, Years	President	Vice President	Secretary of State	Secretary of Treasury	Secretary of War	Attorney General	Postmaster General	Secretary of Navy
Dem/Rep, 1817–1821	James Monroe	Daniel D. Tompkins	John Quincy Adams	William H. Crawford	John C. Calhoun	Richard Rush, William Wirt		Benjamin Crowninshield, Smith Thompson
Dem/Rep, 1821–1825	James Monroe	Daniel D. Tompkins	John Quincy Adams	William H. Crawford	John C. Calhoun	William Wirt		Samuel L. Southard
Nat'l/Rep, 1825–1829	John Quincy Adams	John C. Calhoun	Henry Clay	Richard Rush	James Barbour, Peter B. Porter	William Wirt		Samuel L. Southard
Democrat, 1829–1833	Andrew Jackson	John C. Calhoun	Martin Van Buren, Edward Livingston	Samuel D. Ingham, Louis McLane	John Eaton, Lewis Cass	John M. Berrien, Roger B. Taney		John Branch, Levi Woodbury
Democrat, 1833–1837	Andrew Jackson	Martin Van Buren	Louis McLane, John Forsyth	William J. Duane, Roger B. Taney, Levi Woodbury	Lewis Cass	Benjamin F. Butler	William T. Barry, Amos Kendall	Levi Woodbury, Mahlon P. Dickerson
Democrat, 1837–1841	**Martin Van Buren**	Richard M. Johnson	John Forsyth	Levi Woodbury	Joel R. Poinsett	Benjamin F. Butler, Felix Grundy, Henry D. Gilpin	John M. Niles	Mahlon P. Dickerson, James K. Paulding
Whig, 1841	**William Henry Harrison**	John Tyler	Daniel Webster	Thomas Ewing	John Bell	John J. Crittenden	Francis Granger	George E. Badger

(continued)

Party	President	V. Pres.	State	War	Treasury	Post. Gen.	Atty. Gen.	Navy	Interior
Whig, 1841–1845	John Tyler		*Abel P. Upshur, John C. Calhoun*	John C. Spencer, William Wilkins	*Walter Forward, John C. Spencer, George M. Bibb*	*Charles A. Wickliffe*	*Hugh S. Legaré, John Nelson*	*Abel P. Upshur, David Henshaw, Thomas W. Gilmer, John Y. Mason*	
Democrat, 1845–1849	*James K. Polk*	George M. Dallas	James Buchanan	William L. Marcy	*Robert J. Walker*	*Cave Johnson*	*John Y. Mason, Nathan Clifford, Isaac Toucey*	*George Bancroft, John Y. Mason*	
Whig, 1849–1851	Zachary Taylor	Millard Fillmore	John M. Clayton	*George W. Crawford*	William M. Meredith	Jacob Collamer	Reverdy Johnson	*William B. Preston*	Thomas Ewing
Whig, 1851–1853	**Millard Fillmore**		Daniel Webster, Edward Everett	*Charles M. Conrad*	Thomas Corwin	Nathan K. Hall, Samuel D. Hubbard	*John J. Crittenden*	*William A. Graham, John P. Kennedy*	Thos. M.T. McKennan, Alexander H. H. Stuart
Democrat, 1853–1857	**Franklin Pierce**	*William R. King*	*William L. Marcy*	*Charles M. Conrad, Jefferson Davis*	James Guthrie	James Campbell	Caleb Cushing	*James C. Dobbin*	Robert McClelland
Democrat, 1857–1861	**James Buchanan**	*John C. Breckinridge*	Lewis Cass, Jeremiah S. Black	*John B. Floyd,* Joseph Holt	*Howell Cobb, Philip F. Thomas,* John A. Dix	*Aaron V. Brown,* Joseph Holt, *Horatio King*	Jeremiah S. Black, Edwin M. Stanton	Isaac Toucey	*Jacob Thompson*

(Southerners italicized, Northern doughface presidents in bold)

Appendix B
U.S. and Confederate Governments during the Civil War, 1861–1865

Party	President	V. Pres.	State	War	Treasury	Post. Gen.	Atty. Gen.	Navy	Interior
U.S.A., Republican, 1861–1865	Abraham Lincoln	Hannibal Hamlin	William F. Seward, Edwin M. Stanton	Simon Cameron, William P. Fessenden	Salmon P. Chase, William Dennison	Montgomery Blair, James Speed	Edward Bates	Gideon Welles, John P. Usher	Caleb B. Smith
U.S.A., Republican, 1865–1869	Abraham Lincoln	Andrew Johnson	William F. Seward	Edwin M. Stanton	Hugh McCullough	Alexander W. Randall	Henry Stanberry	Gideon Welles	James Harlan
C.S.A., No Party, 1861–1865	Jefferson Davis	Alexander H. Stevens, R. M. T. Hunter, Judah P. Benjamin	Robert Toombs, Judah P. Benjamin, George W. Randolph, James Seddon, John P. Breckinridge	Leroy P. Walker, George A. Trenholm	Christopher G. Memminger	John H. Reagan, Thomas Bragg, Thomas H. Watts, George Davis	Judah P. Benjamin	Stephen A. Mallory	NONE

Appendix C
The Articles of Confederation and Perpetual Union, 1781

To all to whom these presents shall come, we the undersigned delegates of the states affixed to our names, send greeting:

Whereas the delegates of the United States of America in Congress assembled, did, on the fifteenth day of November in the year of our Lord seventeen seventy-seven, and in the second year of the Independence of America, agree to Certain Articles of Confederation and perpetual union between the states of New Hampshire, Massachusetts Bay, Rhode Island and Providence Plantations, Connecticut, New York, New Jersey, Pennsylvania, Delaware, Maryland, Virginia, North Carolina, South Carolina and Georgia in the words following, viz:

Articles of Confederation and Perpetual Union Between the States of New Hampshire, Massachusetts Bay, Rhode Island and Providence Plantations, Connecticut, New York, New Jersey, Pennsylvania, Delaware, Maryland, Virginia, North Carolina, South Carolina and Georgia.

ARTICLE I

The style of this Confederacy shall be "The United States of America."

ARTICLE II

Each state retains its sovereignty, freedom and independence, and every power, jurisdiction and right which is not by this Confederation expressly delegated to the United States in Congress assembled.

ARTICLE III

The said states hereby severally enter into a firm league of friendship with each other for their common defence, the security of their liberties, and their mutual and general welfare, binding themselves to assist each other against all force offered to, or attacks made upon them, or any of them, on account of religion, sovereignty, trade, or any other pretence whatever.

ARTICLE IV

The better to secure and perpetuate mutual friendship and intercourse among the people of the different States in this Union, the free inhabitants of each of these states, paupers, vagabonds and fugitives from justice excepted, shall be entitled to all privileges and immunities of free citizens in the several states; and the people of each state shall have free ingress and regress to and from any other state, and shall enjoy therein all the privileges of trade and commerce, subject to the same duties, impositions and restrictions as the inhabitants thereof respectively; provided, that such restrictions shall not extend so far as to prevent the removal of property imported into any state, to any other state of which the owner is an inhabitant; provided also, that no imposition, duties or restriction shall be laid by any state on the property of the United States, or either of them.

If any person guilty of or charged with treason, felony, or other high misdemeanor in any state, shall flee from justice, and be found in any of the United States, he shall upon demand of the governor or executive power of the state from which he fled, be delivered up and removed to the state having jurisdiction of his offense.

Full faith and credit shall be given in each of these states to the records, acts and judicial proceedings of the courts and magistrates of every other state.

ARTICLE V

For the more convenient management of the general interests of the United States, delegates shall be annually appointed in such manner as the legislature of each state shall direct, to meet in Congress on the first Monday in November, in every year, with a power, reserved to each state, to recall its delegates, or any of them, at any time within the year, and to send others in their stead, for the remainder of the year.

No state shall be represented in Congress by less than two, nor by more than seven members; and no person shall be capable of being a delegate for more than three years in any term of six years; nor shall any person, being a delegate, be capable of holding any office under the United States, for which he, or another for his benefit receives any salary, fees or emolument of any kind.

Each state shall maintain its own delegates in a meeting of the states, and while they act as members of the committee of the states.

In determining questions in the United States, in Congress assembled, each state shall have one vote.

Freedom of speech and debate in Congress shall not be impeached or questioned in any court, or place out of Congress, and the members of Congress shall be protected in their persons from arrests and imprisonments, during the time of their going to and from, and attendance on Congress, except for treason, felony, or breach of the peace.

ARTICLE VI

No state without the consent of the United States in Congress assembled, shall send any embassy to, or receive any embassy from, or enter into any conference, agreement, alliance or treaty with any king, prince or state; nor shall any person holding any office of profit or trust under the United States, or any of them, accept of any, present, emolument, office or title of any kind whatever from any king, prince or foreign state; nor shall the United States in Congress assembled, or any of them, grant any title of nobility.

No two or more states shall enter into any treaty, confederation or alliance whatever between them, without the consent of the United States in Congress assembled, specifying accurately the purposes for which the same is to be entered into, and how long it shall continue.

No state shall lay any impost or duties, which may interfere with any stipulations in treaties, entered into by the United States in Congress assembled, with any king, prince or state, in pursuance of any treaties already proposed by Congress to the courts of France and Spain.

No vessels of war shall be kept up in time of peace by any state, except such number only as shall be deemed necessary by the United States in Congress assembled, for the defence of such state, or its trade; nor shall any body of forces be kept up by any state, in time of peace except such number only, as in the judgment of the United States, Congress assembled, shall be deemed requisite to garrison the forts necessary for the defence of such state; but every state shall always keep up a well regulated and disciplined militia, sufficiently armed and accoutered, and shall provide and constantly have ready for use, in public stores, a due number of field pieces and tents, and a proper quantity of arms, ammunition and camp equipage.

No state shall engage in any war without the consent of the United States in Congress assembled, unless such state be actually invaded by enemies, or shall have received certain advice of a resolution being formed by some nation of Indians to invade such state, and the danger is so imminent as not to admit of a delay, till the United States in Congress assembled can be consulted: nor shall any state grant commissions to any ships or vessels of war, nor letters of marque or reprisal, except it be after a declaration of war by the United States in Congress assembled, and then only against the kingdom or state and the subjects thereof, against which war has been so declared, and under such regulations as shall be established by the United States in Congress assembled, unless such state be infested by pirates, in which case vessels of war be fitted out for that occasion, and kept so long as the danger shall continue, or until the United States in Congress assembled shall determine otherwise.

ARTICLE VII

When land forces are raised by any state for the common defence, all officers of or under the rank of colonel, shall be appointed by the Legislature of each state respectively by whom such forces shall be raised, or in such manner as such state shall direct, all vacancies shall be filled up by the state which first made the appointment.

ARTICLE VIII

All charges of war, and all other expenses that shall be incurred for the common defence or general welfare, and allowed by the United States in Congress assembled, shall be defrayed out of a common treasury, which shall be supplied by the several states, in proportion to the value of all land within each state, granted to or surveyed for any person, as such land and the buildings and improvements thereon shall be estimated according to such mode as the United States in Congress assembled, shall from time to time direct and appoint.

The taxes for paying that proportion shall be laid and levied by the authority and direction of the legislatures of the several states within the time agreed upon by the United States in Congress assembled.

ARTICLE IX

The United States in Congress assembled, shall have the sole and exclusive right and power of determining on peace and war except in the cases mentioned in the sixth article; of sending and receiving ambassadors; entering into treaties and alliances; provided that no treaty of commerce shall be made whereby the legislative power of the respective states shall be restrained from imposing such imposts and duties on foreigners, as their own people are subjected to, or from prohibiting the exportation or importation of any species of goods or commodities whatsoever; of establishing rules for deciding in all cases, what captures on land or water shall be legal, and in what manner prizes taken by land or naval forces in the service of the United States shall be divided or appropriated; of granting letters of marque and reprisal in times of peace; appointing courts for the trial of piracies and felonies committed on the high seas and establishing courts for receiving and determining finally appeals in all cases of captures, provided that no member of Congress shall be appointed a judge of any of said courts.

The United States in Congress assembled shall also be the last resort on appeal in all disputes and differences now subsisting or that hereafter may arise between two or more states concerning boundary, jurisdiction or any other cause whatever; which authority shall always be exercised in the manner following. Whenever the legislative or executive authority or lawful agent of any state in controversy with another shall present a petition to Congress, stating the matter in question and praying for a hearing, notice thereof shall be given by order of Congress to the legislative or executive authority of the other state in controversy, and a day assigned for the appearance of the parties by their lawful agents, who shall then be directed to appoint by joint consent commissioners or judges to constitute a court for hearing and determining the matter in question: but if they can not agree, Congress shall name three persons out of each of the United States, and from the list of such persons each party shall alternately strike out one, the petitioners beginning, until the number shall be reduced to thirteen; and from that number not less than seven, nor more than nine names, as Congress shall direct, shall in the presence of Congress be drawn out by lot, and the persons whose names shall be so drawn or any five of them, shall be commissioners or judges, to hear and finally determine the controversy, so always as a major part of the judges who shall hear the cause shall agree in the determination: and if either party shall neglect to attend at the day appointed, without showing reasons, which Congress judge sufficient, or being present shall refuse to strike, the Congress shall proceed to nominate three persons out of each state, and the Secretary of Congress shall strike in behalf of such party absent or refusing; and the judgment and sentence of the court to be appointed, in the manner before prescribed, shall be final and conclusive; and if any of the parties shall refuse to submit to the authority of such court, or to appear or defend their claim or cause, the court shall, nevertheless proceed to pronounce sentence, or judgment, which shall in like manner be final and decisive, the judgment or sentence and other proceeds being in either case transmitted to Congress, and lodged among the acts of Congress for the security of the parties concerned: provided that every commissioner, before he sits in judgment, shall take an oath to be administered by one of the judges of the supreme or superior court of the state where the cause shall be tried, "well and truly to hear and determine the matter in question, according to the best of his judgment without favor, affection, or hope of reward":

provided also that no state shall be deprived of territory for the benefit of the United States.

All controversies concerning the private right of soil claimed under different grants of two or more states, whose jurisdiction as they may respect such lands, and the states which passed such grants are adjusted, the said grants or either of them being at the same time claimed to have originated antecedent to such settlement of jurisdiction, shall on the petition of either party to the Congress of the United States, be finally determined as near as may be in the same manner as is before prescribed for deciding disputes respecting territorial jurisdiction between the different states.

The United States in Congress assembled shall also have the sole and exclusive right and power of regulating the alloy and value of coin struck by their own authority, or by that of respective state fixing the standard of weights and measures throughout the United States regulating the trade, and managing all affairs with the Indians, not members of any of the states, provided that the legislative right of state within its own limits be not infringed or violated; establishing and regulating post offices from one state to another, throughout all the United States, and exacting such postage on the papers passing through the same as may be requisite to defray the expenses of the said office; appointing all officers of the land forces, in the service of the United States, excepting regimental officers; appointing all the officers of the naval forces, and commissioning all officers whatever in the service of the United States; making rules for the government and regulation of said land and naval forces, and directing their operations.

The United States in Congress assembled shall have authority to appoint a committee, to sit in the recess of Congress, to be denominated "a Committee of the States," and to consist of one delegate from each state; and to appoint such other committees and civil officers as may be necessary for managing the general affairs of the United States under their direction; to appoint one of their number to preside, provided that no person be allowed to serve in the office of president more than one year in any term of three years; to ascertain the necessary sums of money to be raised for the service of the United States, and to appropriate and apply the same for defraying the public expenses; to borrow money, or emit bills on the credit of the United States, transmitting every half year to the respective states an account of the sums of money so borrowed or emitted; to build and equip a navy; to agree upon the number of land forces, and to make requisitions from each state for its quota, in proportion to the number of white inhabitants in such state; which requisition shall be binding, and therepon the legislature of each state shall appoint the regimental officers, raise the men and clothe, arm and equip them in a soldierlike manner, at the expense of the United States; and the officers and men so clothed, armed and equipped shall march to the place appointed, and within the time agreed on by the United States in Congress assembled: but if the United States in Congress assembled shall, on consideration of circumstances judge proper that any state should not raise men, or should raise a smaller number than its quota, and that any other state should raise a greater number of men than the quota thereof, such extra number shall be raised, officered, clothed, armed and equipped in the same manner as the quota of such state, unless the legislature of such state shall judge that such extra number can not be safely spared out of the same, in which case they shall raise, officer, clothe, arm and equip as many of such extra number as they judge can be safely spared. And the officers and men so clothed, armed and equipped, shall march to the place appointed, and within the time agreed on by the United States in Congress assembled.

The United States in Congress assembled shall never engage in war, nor grant letters of marque and reprisal in time of peace, nor enter into any treaties or alliances, nor coin money, nor regulate the value thereof, nor ascertain the sums and expenses necessary for the defense and welfare of the United States, or any of them, nor emit bills, nor borrow money on the credit of the United States, nor appropriate money, nor agree upon the number of vessels of war, to be built or purchased, or the number of land or sea forces to be raised, nor appoint a commander-in-chief of the army or navy, unless nine states assent to the same: nor shall a question on any other point, except for adjourning from day to day be determined, unless by the votes of a majority of the United States in Congress assembled.

The Congress of the United States shall have power to adjourn to any time within the year, and to any place within the United States, so that no period of adjournment be for a longer duration than the space of six months; and shall publish the journal of their proceedings monthly, except such parts thereof relating to treaties, alliances or military operations, as in their judgment require secrecy; and the yeas and nays of the delegates of each state on any question shall be entered on the journal, when it is desired by any delegate; and the delegates of a state, or any of them, at his or their request, shall be furnished with transcript of the said journal, except such parts as are above excepted to lay before the legislatures of the several states.

ARTICLE X

The Committee of the States, or any nine of them shall be authorized to execute, in the recess of Congress, such of the powers of Congress as the United States in Congress assembled, by the consent of nine states, shall from time to time think expedient to vest them with; provided that no power be delegated to the said committee for the exercise of which, by the Articles of Confederation, the voice of nine states in the Congress of the United States assembled is requisite.

ARTICLE XI

Canada acceding to this Confederation, and joining in the measures of the United States, shall be admitted into, and entitled to all the advantages of this Union: but no other colony shall be admitted into the same, unless such admission be agreed to by nine states.

ARTICLE XII

All bills of credit emitted, moneys borrowed and debts contracted by, or under the authority of Congress, before the assembling of the United States, in pursuance of the present Confederation, shall be deemed and considered as a charge against the United States, for payment and satisfaction whereof the said United States and the public faith are hereby solemnly pledged.

ARTICLE XIII

Every state shall abide by the determinations of the United States in Congress assembled, on all quesions which by this Confederation are submitted to them. And the Articles of this Confederation shall be inviolably observed by every state, and the Union shall be perpetual; nor shall any alteration at any time hereafter be made in any of them, unless such alteration be agreed to in a Congress of the United States, and be afterwards confirmed by the legislatures of every state.

AND WHEREAS it hath pleased the Great Governor of the world to incline the hearts of the legislatures we respectively represent in Congress, to approve of, and to authorize us to ratify the said Articles of Confederation and perpetual Union. Know ye that we the undersigned delegates, by virtue of the power and authority to us given for that purpose, do by these presents, in the name and in behalf of our respective constituents, fully and entirely ratify and confirm each and every of the said Articles of Confederation and perpetual Union, and all and singular the matters and things therein contained: and we do further solemnly plight and engage the faith of our respective constituents, that they shall abide by the determinations of the United States Congress assembled, on all questions, which by the said Confederation are submitted to them. And that the articles thereof shall be inviolably observed by the states we respectively represent, and that the Union shall be perpetual.

IN WITNESS WHEREOF we have hereunto set our hands in Congress. Done at Philadelphia in the State of Pennsylvania the ninth day of July in the year of our Lord one thousand seven hundred and seventy-eight, and in the third year of the independence of America.

On the part and behalf of the State of New Hampshire.
Josiah Bartlett   John Wentworth, Junr.   August 8th, 1778

On the part and behalf of the State of Massachusetts Bay.
John Hancock   Francis Dana   Samuel Adams
James Lovell   Elbridge Gerry   Samuel Holton

On the part and behalf of the State of Rhode Island and Providence Plantations.

William Ellery   John Collins   Henry Marchant

On the part and behalf of the State of Connecticut.
Roger Sherman   Titus Hosmer   Samuel Huntington
Andrew Adams   Oliver Wolcott

On the part and behalf of the State of New York.
Jas. Duane   Wm. Duer   Fra. Lewis
Gouv. Morris

On the part and behalf of the State of New Jersey (Novr. 26, 1778.)
Jno. Witherspoon   Nathl. Scudder

On the part and behalf of the State of Pennsylvania.
Robt. Morris   William Clingan   Daniel Roberdeau
Joseph Reed   Jona. Bayard Smith 22d July 1778

On the part and behalf of the State of Delaware.
Tho. M'Kean   John Dickinson   Nicholas Van Dyke
Feby. 12, 1779   May 5th, 1779

On the part and behalf of the State of Maryland.
John Hanson   Daniel Carroll   March 1, 1781

On the part and behalf of the State of Virginia.
Richard Henry Lee   Jno. Harvie   John Banister
Francis Lightfoot Lee Thomas Adams

On the part and behalf of the State of North Carolina.
John Penn   Corns. Harnett
July 21st, 1778   Jno. Williams

On the part and behalf of the State of South Carolina.
Henry Laurens   Richd. Hutson   William Henry Drayton
Thos. Heyward Junr. Jno. Mathews

On the part and behalf of the State of Georgia.

Jno. Walton Edwd. Telfair 24th July, 1778
Edwd. Langworthy

Appendix D
Constitution of the
Confederate States of America, 1861

PREAMBLE

We, the people of the Confederate States, each State acting in its sovereign and independent character, in order to form a permanent, Federal Government, establish justice, insure domestic tranquillity, and secure the blessings of Liberty to ourselves and our posterity—invoking the favor and guidance of Almighty God—do ordain and establish this Constitution for the Confederate States of America:

ARTICLE I

Section I

All legislative powers herein delegated shall be vested in a Congress of the Confederate States which shall consist of a Senate and House of Representatives.

Section II

1. The House of Representatives shall be composed of members chosen every second year by the people of the several States—and the electors in each State shall be citizens of the Confederate States, and have the qualifications requisite for electors of the most numerous branch of the State Legislature; but no person of foreign birth, not a citizen of the Confederate States, shall be allowed to vote for any officer, civil or political, State or Federal.

2. No person shall be a Representative, who shall not have attained the age of twenty-five years and be a citizen of the Confederate States, and

who shall not, when elected, be an inhabitant of that State in which he shall be chosen.

3. Representatives and direct taxes shall be apportioned among the several States which may be included within this Confederacy according to their respective numbers, which shall be determined by adding to the whole number of free persons, including those bound to service for a term of years, and excluding Indians not taxed, three-fifths of all slaves. The actual enumeration shall be made within three years after the first meeting of the Congress of the Confederate States, and within every subsequent term of ten years, in such manner as they shall, by law, direct. The number of Representatives shall not exceed one for every fifty thousand, but each State shall have, at least, one Representative; and until such enumeration shall be made, the State of South Carolina shall be entitled to choose six—the State of Georgia ten—the State of Alabama nine—the State of Florida two—the State of Mississippi seven—the State of Louisiana six, and the State of Texas six.

4. When vacancies happen in the representation from any State, the Executive authority thereof shall issue writs of election to fill such vacancies.

5. The House of Representatives shall choose their Speaker and other officers; and shall have the sole power of impeachment; except that any judicial or other federal officer resident and acting solely within the limits of any State, may be impeached by a vote of two-thirds of both branches of the Legislature thereof.

Section III

1. The Senate of the Confederate States shall be composed of two Senators from each State, chosen for six years, by the Legislature thereof, at the regular session next immediately preceding the commencement of the term of service; and each Senator shall have one vote.

2. Immediately after they shall be assembled in consequence of the first election, they shall be divided, as equally as may be, into three classes. The seats of the Senators of the first class shall be vacated at the expi-

ration of the second year, of the second class at the expiration of the fourth, and of the third class at the expiration of the sixth year, so that one-third may be chosen every second year; and if vacancies happen, by resignation or otherwise, during the recess of the Legislature of any State, the Executive thereof may make temporary appointments until the next meeting of the Legislature, which shall then fill such vacancies.

3. No person shall be a Senator who shall not have attained the age of thirty years, and be a citizen of the Confederate States, and who shall not, when elected, be an inhabitant of the State for which be shall be chosen.

4. The Vice President of the Confederate States shall be President of the Senate, but shall have no vote, unless they be equally divided.

5. The Senate shall choose their other officers, and also a President pro tempore, in the absence of the Vice President, or when he shall exercise the office of President of the Confederate States.

6. The Senate shall have the sole power to try all impeachments. When sitting for that purpose, they shall be on oath or affirmation. When the President of the Confederate States is tried, the Chief Justice shall preside; and no person shall be convicted without the concurrence of two-thirds of the members present.

7. Judgment, in cases of impeachment, shall not extend further than to removal from office, and disqualification to hold and enjoy any office of honor, trust or profit under the Confederate States; but the party convicted shall nevertheless be liable and subject to indictment, trial, judgment and punishment, according to law.

Section IV

1. The times, places and manner of holding elections for Senators and Representatives shall be prescribed in each State by the Legislature thereof, subject to the provisions of this Constitution; but the Congress may, at any time by law, make or alter such regulations, except as to the times and places of choosing Senators.

2. The Congress shall assemble at least once in every year, and such meeting shall be on the first Monday in December, unless they shall by law appoint a different day.

Section V

1. Each House shall be the judge of the elections, returns and qualifications of its own members, and a majority of each shall constitute a quorum to do business; but a smaller number may adjourn from day to day, and may be authorized to compel the attendance of absent members, in such manner and under such penalties as each House may provide.

2. Each House may determine the rules of its proceedings, punish its members for disorderly behavior, and, with the concurrence of two-thirds of the whole number, expel a member.

3. Each House shall keep a journal of its proceedings, and from time to time publish the same, excepting such parts as may, in their judgment, require secrecy; and the yeas and nays of the members of either House on any question shall, at the desire of one-fifth of those present, be entered on the journal.

4. Neither House, during the Session of Congress, shall, without the consent of the other, adjourn for more than three days, nor to any other place than that in which the two Houses shall be sitting.

Section VI

1. The Senators and Representatives shall receive a compensation for their services, to be ascertained by law, and paid out of the Treasury of the Confederate States. They shall in all cases, except treason, felony, and breach of the peace, be privileged from arrest during their attendance at the session of their respective Houses, and in going to and returning from the same; and for any speech or debate in either House, they shall not be questioned in any other place.

2. No Senator or Representative shall, during the time for which he was elected, be appointed to any civil office under the authority of the Con-

federate States, which shall have been created, or the emoluments whereof shall have been increased, during such time; and no person holding any office under the Confederate States shall be a member of either House during his continuance in office; but Congress may by law grant to the principal officer in each of the Executive Departments a seat upon the floor of either House, with the privilege of discussing any measures appertaining to his department.

Section VII

1. All bills for raising revenue shall originate in the House of Representatives; but the Senate may propose or concur with amendments, as on other bills.

2. Every bill which shall have passed both Houses, shall, before it becomes a law, be presented to the President of the Confederate States; if he approve, he shall sign it; but if not, he shall return it, with his objections, to that House in which it shall have originated, who shall enter the objections at large on their journal, and proceed to reconsider it. If, after such reconsideration, two-thirds of that House shall agree to pass the bill, it shall be sent, together with the objections, to the other House, by which it shall likewise be reconsidered, and if approved by two-thirds of that House, it shall become a law. But in all such cases the votes of both Houses shall be determined by yeas and nays, and the names of the persons voting for and against the bill shall be entered on the journal of each House respectively. If any bill shall not be returned by the President within ten days (Sundays excepted) after it shall have been presented to him, the same shall be a law in like manner as if he had signed it, unless the Congress by their adjournment prevent its return, in which case it shall not be a law. The President may approve any appropriation and disapprove any other appropriation in the same bill. In such case he shall, in signing the bill, designate the appropriations disapproved; and shall return a copy of such appropriations, with his objections, to the House in which the bill shall have originated; and the same proceedings shall then be had as in case of other bills disapproved by the President.

3. Every order, resolution, or vote, to which the concurrence of both Houses may be necessary, (except on a question of adjournment,) shall

be presented to the President of the Confederate States; and before the same shall take effect, shall be approved by him, or, being disapproved by him, shall be re-passed by two-thirds of both Houses, according to the rules and limitations prescribed in the case of a bill.

Section VIII

The Congress shall have power—

1. To lay and collect taxes, duties, imposts, and excises, for revenue necessary to pay the debts, provide for the common defense and carry on the Government of the Confederate States; but no bounties shall be granted from the Treasury, nor shall any duties or taxes on importations from foreign nations be laid to promote or foster any branch of industry; and all duties, imposts and excises shall be uniform throughout the Confederate States.

2. To borrow money on the credit of the Confederate States.

3. To regulate commerce with foreign nations, and among the several States, and with the Indian tribes; but neither this nor any other clause contained in the Constitution shall ever be construed to delegate the power to Congress to appropriate money for any internal improvement, intended to facilitate commerce, except for the purpose of furnishing lights, beacons and buoys, and other aids to navigation upon the coasts, and the improvement of harbors and the removing of obstructions in river navigation; in all which cases such duties shall be laid on the navigation facilitated thereby, as may be necessary to pay the costs and expenses thereof.

4. To establish uniform laws of naturalization, and uniform laws on the subject of bankruptcies, throughout the Confederate States; but no law of Congress shall discharge any debt contracted before the passage of the same.

5. To coin money, regulate the value thereof, and of foreign coin, and fix the standard of weights and measures.

6. To provide for the punishment of counterfeiting the securities and current coin of the Confederate States.

7. To establish post-offices and post-roads: but the expenses of the Post-office Department, after the first day of March, in the year of our Lord eighteen hundred and sixty-three, shall be paid out of its own revenues.

8. To promote the progress of science and useful arts by securing for limited times to authors and inventors the exclusive right to their respective writings and discoveries.

9. To constitute tribunals inferior to the Supreme Court.

10. To define and punish piracies and felonies committed on the high seas and offences against the law of nations.

11. To declare war, grant letters of marque and reprisal, and make rules concerning captures on land and water.

12. To raise and support armies; but no appropriation of money to that use shall be for a longer term than two years.

13. To provide and maintain a navy.

14. To make rules for the government and regulation of the land and naval forces.

15. To provide for calling forth the militia to execute the laws of the Confederate States, suppress insurrections, and repel invasions.

16. To provide for organizing, arming, and disciplining the militia, and for governing such part of them as may be employed in the service of the Confederate States, reserving to the States respectively the appointment of the officers and the authority of training the militia according to the discipline prescribed by Congress.

17. To exercise exclusive legislation, in all cases whatsoever, over such districts (not exceeding ten miles square) as may, by cession of one or more States and the acceptance of Congress, become the seat of Government of the Confederate States; and to exercise like authority over all places purchased, by the consent of the Legislature of the State in

which the same shall be, for the erection of forts, magazines, arsenals, dockyards, and other needful buildings: and,

18. To make all laws which shall be necessary and proper for carrying into execution the foregoing powers, and all other powers vested by this Constitution in the Government of the Confederate States, or in any department or officer thereof.

Section IX

1. The importation of negroes of the African race from any foreign country other than the slaveholding States or Territories of the United States of America, is hereby forbidden, and Congress is required to pass such laws as shall effectually prevent the same.

2. Congress shall also have power to prohibit the introduction of slaves from any State not a member of, or Territory not belonging to, this Confederacy.

3. The privilege of the writ of habeas corpus shall not be suspended, unless, when in cases of rebellion or invasion, the public safety may require it.

4. No bill of attainder, ex post facto law, or law denying or impairing the right of property in negro slaves, shall be passed.

5. No capitation or other direct tax shall be laid, unless in proportion to the census or enumeration herein before directed to be taken.

6. No tax or duty shall be laid on articles exported from any State except by a vote of two-thirds of both Houses.

7. No preference shall be given by any regulation of commerce, or revenue to the ports of one State over those of another.

8. No money shall be drawn from the treasury, but in consequence of appropriations made by law; and a regular statement and account of the

receipts and expenditures of all public money, shall be published from time to time.

9. Congress shall appropriate no money from the Treasury except by a vote of two-thirds of both Houses, taken by yeas and nays, unless it be asked and estimated for by some one of the Heads of Department and submitted to Congress by the President; or for the purpose of paying its own expenses and contingencies; or for the payment of claims against the Confederate States, the justice of which shall have been judicially declared by a tribunal for the investigation of claims against the Government, which it is hereby made the duty of Congress to establish.

10. All bills appropriating money, shall specify, in Federal currency, the exact amount of each appropriation, and the purposes for which it is made, and Congress shall grant no extra compensation to any public contractor, officer, agent or servant, after such contract shall have been made, or such service rendered.

11. No title of nobility shall be granted by the Confederate States and no person holding any office of profit or trust under them, shall, without the consent of the Congress, accept of any present, emolument, office, or title of any kind whatever, from any king, prince or foreign State.

12. Congress shall make no law respecting an establishment of religion, or prohibiting the free exercise thereof; or abridging the freedom of speech, or of the press; or the right of the people peaceably to assemble and petition the Government for a redress of grievances.

13. A well regulated militia being necessary to the security of a free State, the right of the People to keep and bear arms, shall not be infringed.

14. No soldier shall, in time of peace, be quartered in any house, without the consent of the owner; nor in time of war, but in a manner to be prescribed by law.

15. The right of the people to be secure in their persons, houses, papers and effects, against unreasonable searches and seizures, shall not be violated; and no warrant shall issue, but upon probable cause, supported by oath or affirmation, and particularly describing the place to be searched, and the persons or things to be seized.

16. No person shall be held to answer for a capital or otherwise infamous crime, unless on a presentment or indictment of a grand jury, except in cases arising in the land or naval forces, or in the militia, when in actual service in time of war or public danger; nor shall any person be subject for the same offence to be twice put in jeopardy of life or limb; nor be compelled in any criminal case to be a witness against himself, nor be deprived of life, liberty or property, without due process of law; nor shall private property be taken for public use, without just compensation.

17. In all criminal prosecutions, the accused shall enjoy the right to a speedy and public trial, by an impartial jury of the State and district wherein the crime shall have been committed, which district shall have been previously ascertained by law, and to be informed of the nature and cause of the accusation; to be confronted with the witnesses against him; to have compulsory process for obtaining witnesses in his favor, and to have the assistance of counsel for his defense.

18. In suits at common law, where the value in controversy shall exceed twenty dollars, the right of trial by jury shall be preserved, and no fact so tried by a jury shall be otherwise re-examined in any court of the Confederacy than according to the rules of the common law.

19. Excessive bail shall not be required, nor excessive fines imposed, nor cruel and unusual punishments inflicted.

20. Every law, or resolution having the force of law, shall relate to but one subject, and that shall be expressed in the title.

Section X

1. No State shall enter into any treaty, alliance or confederation; grant letters of marque and reprisal; coin money; make anything but gold and

silver coin a tender in payment of debts; pass any bill of attainder, ex post facto law, or law impairing the obligation of contracts; or grant any title of nobility.

2. No State shall, without the consent of the Congress, lay any imposts or duties on imports or exports, except what may be absolutely necessary for executing its inspection laws; and the net produce of all duties and imposts, laid by any State on imports or exports, shall be for the use of the Treasury of the Confederate States; and all such laws shall be subject to the revision and control of Congress.

3. No State shall, without the consent of Congress, lay any duty on tonnage, except on sea-going vessels, for the improvement of its rivers and harbors, navigated by the said vessels; but such duties shall not conflict with any treaties of the Confederate States with foreign nations; and any surplus revenue thus derived shall, after making such improvement, be paid into the common treasury; nor shall any State keep troops or ships of war in time of peace, enter into any agreement or compact with another State or with a foreign power, or engage in war unless actually invaded, or in such imminent danger as will not admit of delay; but when any river divides or flows through two or more States, they may enter into compacts with each other to improve the navigation thereof.

ARTICLE II

Section I

1. The Executive power shall be vested in a President of the Confederate States of America. He and the Vice-President shall hold their offices for the term of six years; but the President shall not be re-eligible. The President and Vice-President shall be elected as follows:

2. Each State shall appoint, in such manner as the Legislature thereof may direct, a number of electors, equal to the whole number of Senators and Representatives to which the State may be entitled in the Congress; but no Senator or Representative, or person holding an

office of trust or profit under the Confederate States, shall be appointed an Elector.

3. The electors shall meet in their respective States and vote by ballot for President and Vice-President, one of whom at least shall not be an inhabitant of the same State with themselves.—They shall name in their ballots the person voted for as President, and in distinct ballots the person voted for as Vice-President, and they shall make distinct lists of all persons voted for as President and of all persons voted for as Vice-President, and of the number of votes for each, which lists they shall sign and certify and transmit, sealed, to the seat of Government of the Confederate States, directed to the President of the Senate. The President of the Senate shall, in the presence of the Senate and House of Representatives, open all the certificates, and the votes shall then be counted; the person having the greatest number of votes for President shall be the President, if such number be a majority of the whole number of electors appointed, and if no person have such majority, then from the persons having the highest numbers not exceeding three on the list of those voted for as President, the House of Representatives shall choose immediately by ballot the President. But in choosing the President the votes shall be taken by States, the Representation from each State having one vote. A quorum for this purpose shall consist of a member or members from two-thirds of the States and a majority of all the States shall be necessary to a choice; and if the House of Representatives shall not choose a President, whenever the right of choice shall devolve upon them, before the fourth day of March next following, then the Vice President shall act as President as in case of the death or other constitutional disability of the President.

4. The person having the greatest number of votes as Vice-President shall be the Vice-President, if such number be a majority of the whole number of electors appointed; and if no person have a majority, then from the two highest numbers on the list the Senate shall choose the Vice-President. A quorum for the purpose shall consist of two-thirds of the whole number of Senators, and a majority of the whole number shall be necessary to a choice.

5. But no person constitutionally ineligible to the office of President shall be eligible to that of Vice-President of the Confederate States.

6. The Congress may determine the time of choosing the electors, and the day on which they shall give their votes, which day shall be the same throughout the Confederate States.

7. No person, except a natural-born citizen of the Confederate States, or a citizen, thereof at the time of the adoption of this Constitution, or citizen thereof born in the United States prior to the twentieth of December, 1860, shall be eligible to the office of President; neither shall any person be eligible to that office who shall not have attained the age of thirty-five years, and been fourteen years a resident within the limits of the Confederate States as they may exist at the time of his election.

8. In case of the removal of the President from office, or of his death, resignation, or inability to discharge the powers and duties of said office, the same shall devolve on the Vice-President and the Congress may by law provide for the case of removal, death, resignation, or inability, both of the President and Vice-President, declaring what officer shall then act as President; and such officer shall act accordingly until the disability be removed or a President shall be elected.

9. The President shall, at stated times, receive for his services a compensation, which shall neither be increased nor diminished during the period for which he shall have been elected, and he shall not receive within that period any other emolument from the Confederate States, or any of them.

10. Before he enters on the execution of his office, he shall take the following oath or affirmation:

"I do solemnly swear (or affirm) that I will faithfully execute the office of President of the Confederate States, and will, to the best of my ability, preserve, protect and defend the Constitution thereof."

Section II

1. The President shall be Commander-in-Chief of the army and navy of the Confederate States, and of the militia of the several States, when called into the actual service of the Confederate States; he may require

the opinion, in writing, of the principal officer in each of the Executive Departments, upon any subject relating to the duties of their respective offices; and he shall have power to grant reprieves and pardons for offences against the Confederate States, except in cases of impeachment.

2. He shall have power, by and with the advice and consent of the Senate, to make treaties, provided two-thirds of the Senators present concur; and he shall nominate, and by and with the advice and consent of the Senate, shall appoint Ambassadors, other public Ministers and Consuls, Judges of the Supreme Court and all other officers of the Confederate States, whose appointments are not herein otherwise provided for, and which shall be established by law; but the Congress may by law vest the appointment of such inferior officers, as they think proper, in the President alone, in the courts of law, or in the Heads of Departments.

3. The principal officer in each of the Executive Departments, and all persons connected with the diplomatic service, may be removed from office at the pleasure of the President.— All other civil officers, of the Executive Department, may be removed at any time by the President, or other appointing power, when their services are unnecessary, or for dishonesty, incapacity, inefficiency, misconduct or neglect of duty; and when so removed the removal shall be reported to the Senate, together with the reasons therefore.

4. The President shall have power to fill all vacancies that may happen during the recess of the Senate, by granting commissions which shall expire at the end of their next session; but no person rejected by the Senate shall be reappointed to the same office during their ensuing recess.

Section III

1. The President shall from time to time, give to the Congress information, of the state of the Confederacy, and recommend to their consideration such measures as he shall judge necessary and expedient; he may, on extraordinary occasions, convene both Houses, or either of them; and in case of disagreement between them, with respect to the time of adjournment, he may adjourn them to such time as he shall think proper;

he shall receive Ambassadors and other Public Ministers; he shall take care that the laws be faithfully executed, and shall commission all the officers of the Confederate States.

Section IV

The President, Vice-President, and all civil officers of the Confederate States, shall be removed from office on impeachment for, and conviction of treason, bribery or other high crimes and misdemeanors.

ARTICLE III

Section I

1. The judicial power of the Confederate States shall be vested in one Supreme Court, and in such inferior courts as the Congress may from time to time ordain and establish. The Judges, both of the supreme and inferior courts, shall hold their offices during good behavior; and shall, at stated times, receive for their services a compensation, which shall not be diminished during their continuance in office.

Section II

1. The Judicial power shall extend to all cases arising under this Constitution, the laws of the Confederate States, and treaties made, or which shall be made, under their authority; to all cases affecting Ambassadors, other public ministers and consuls; to all cases of admiralty and maritime jurisdiction; to controversies to which the Confederate States shall be a party; to controversies between two or more States; between a State and citizen of another State, where the State is plaintiff; between citizens claiming lands under grants of different States; and between a State, or the citizens thereof, and foreign States, citizens, or subjects; but no State shall be sued by a citizen or subject of any foreign State.

2. In all cases affecting Ambassadors, other public Ministers and Consuls, and those in which a State shall be a party, the Supreme Court shall

have original jurisdiction. In all the other cases before mentioned, the Supreme Court shall have appellate jurisdiction, both as to law and fact, with such exceptions and under such regulations as the Congress shall make.

3. The trial of all crimes, except in cases of impeachment, shall be by jury; and such trial shall be held in the State where the said crimes shall have been committed; but when not committed within any State, the trial shall be at such place or places as the Congress may by law have directed.

Section III

1. Treason against the Confederate States shall consist only in levying war against them, or in adhering to their enemies, giving them aid and comfort. No person shall be convicted of treason unless on the testimony of two witnesses to the same overt act, or on confession in open court.

2. The Congress shall have power to declare the punishment of treason, but no attainder of treason shall work corruption of blood, or forfeiture, except during the life of the person attainted.

ARTICLE IV

Section I

1. Full faith and credit shall be given in each State to the public acts. records and judicial proceedings of every other State. And the Congress may by general laws prescribe the manner in which such acts, records and proceedings shall be proved, and the effect thereof.

Section II

1. The citizens of each State shall be entitled to all the privileges and immunities of citizens in the several States, and shall have the right of transit and sojourn in any State of this Confederacy, with their slaves

and other property; and the right of property in said slaves shall not be thereby impaired.

2. A person charged in any State with treason, felony or other crime, against the laws of such State, who shall flee from justice, and be found in another State, shall, on demand of the Executive authority of the State from which he fled, be delivered up, to be removed to the State having jurisdiction of the crime.

3. No slave or other person held to service or labor in any State or Territory of the Confederate States, under the laws thereof, escaping, or lawfully carried into another, shall, in consequence of any law or regulation therein, be discharged from such service or labor; but shall be delivered up on claim of the party to whom such slave belongs, or to whom such service or labor may be due.

Section III

1. Other States may be admitted into this Confederacy by a vote of two-thirds of the whole House of Representatives, and two-thirds of the Senate—the Senate voting, by States; but no new State shall be formed or erected within the jurisdiction of any other State; nor any State be formed by the junction of two or more States or parts of States, without the consent of the Legislatures of the States concerned, as well as of the Congress.

2. The Congress shall have power to dispose of and make all needful rules and regulations concerning the property of the Confederate States, including the lands thereof.

3. The Confederate States may acquire new territory, and Congress shall have power to legislate and provide governments for the inhabitants of all territory belonging to the Confederate States lying without the limits of the several States, and may permit them, at such times and in such manner as it may by law provide, to form States to be admitted into the Confederacy. In all such territory, the institution of negro slavery, as it now exists in the Confederate States, shall be recognized and protected by Congress, and by the Territorial Government; and the inhabitants of

the several Confederate States and Territories shall have the right to take to such territory any slaves lawfully held by them, in any of the States or Territories of the Confederate States.

4. The Confederate States shall guarantee to every State that now is, or hereafter may become, a member of this Confederacy, a republican form of government, and shall protect each of them against invasion; and on application of the Legislature, or of the Executive when the Legislature is not in session, against domestic violence.

ARTICLE V

Section I

1. Upon the demand of any three States, legally assembled in their several Conventions, the Congress shall summon a Convention of all the States to take into consideration such amendments to the Constitution as the said States shall concur in suggesting at the time when the said demand is made; and should any of the proposed amendments to the Constitution be agreed on by the said Convention, voting by States, and the same be ratified by the Legislatures of two-thirds of the several States, or by Conventions in two-thirds thereof, as the one or the other mode of ratification may be proposed by the General Convention, they shall thenceforward form a part of this Constitution. But no State shall, without its consent, be deprived of its equal representation in the Senate.

ARTICLE VI

Section I

The Government established by this Constitution is the successor of the Provisional Government of the Confederate States of America, and all the laws passed by the latter shall continue in force until the same shall be repealed or modified; and all the officers appointed by the same shall remain in office until their successors are appointed and qualified, or the offices abolished.

Section II

All debts contracted and engagements entered into before the adoption of this Constitution, shall be as valid against the Confederate States, under this Constitution, as under the Provisional Government.

Section III

This Constitution and the laws of the Confederate States, made in pursuance thereof, and all treaties made, or which shall be made under the authority of the Confederate States, shall be the supreme law of the land; and the Judges in every State shall be bound thereby, anything in the Constitution or laws of any State to the contrary notwithstanding.

Section IV

The Senators and Representatives before mentioned, and the members of the several State Legislatures, and all executive and judicial officers, both of the Confederate States and of the several States, shall be bound by oath or affirmation to support this Constitution; but no religious test shall ever be required as a qualification to any office or public trust under the Confederate States.

Section V

The enumeration in the Constitution of certain rights shall not be construed to deny or disparage others retained by the people of the several States.

Section VI

The powers not delegated to the Confederate States by the Constitution, nor prohibited by it to the States, are reserved to the States respectively, or to the people thereof.

ARTICLE VII

1. The ratification of the Conventions of five States shall be sufficient for the establishment of this Constitution between the States so ratifying the same.

2. When five States shall have ratified this Constitution, in the manner before specified, the Congress, under the Provisional Constitution, shall prescribe the time for holding the election of President and Vice-President, and for the meeting of the electoral college, and for counting the votes, and inaugurating the President. They shall also prescribe the time for holding the first election of members of Congress under this Constitution, and the time for assembling the same. Until the assembling of such Congress, the Congress under the Provisional Constitution shall continue to exercise the legislative powers granted them, not extending beyond the time limited by the Constitution of the Provisional Government.

EXTRACT FROM THE JOURNAL OF THE CONGRESS

Congress, March 11, 1861

On the question of the adoption of the Constitution of the Confederate States of America, the vote was taken by yeas and nays; and the Constitution was unanimously adopted, as follows:

Those who voted in the affirmative being Messrs. Walker, Smith, Curry, Hale, McRae, Shorter and Fern, of Alabama, (Messrs. Chilton and Lewis being absent); Messrs. Morton, Anderson and Owens, of Florida; Messrs. Toombs, Howell Cobb, Bartow, Nisbet, Hill, Wright, Thomas, R. R. Cobb and Stephens, of Georgia, (Messrs. Crawford and Kenan being absent); Messrs. Perkins, DeClonet, Conrad, Kenner, Sparrow and Marshall, of Louisiana; Messrs. Harris, Brooke, Wilson, Clayton, Barry and Harrison, of Mississippi; (Mr. Campbell being absent), Messrs. Rhett, Barnwell, Keitt, Chesnut, Memminger, Miles, Withers and Boyce, of South Carolina; Messrs. Reagan, Hemphill, Waul, Gregg, Oldham and Ochiltree, of Texas (Mr. Wigfall being absent.)

A true copy:

J. J. Hooper,
Secretary of the Congress.

Congress, March 11, 1861

I do hereby certify that the, foregoing are, respectively, true and correct copies of "The Constitution of the Confederate States of America," unanimously adopted this day, and of the yeas and nays, on the question of the adoption thereof.

Howell Cobb,
President of the Congress.

Appendix E
Constitution of the
United States of America as of 1860

PREAMBLE

We the People of the United States, in order to form a more perfect union, establish justice, insure domestic tranquility, provide for the common defence, promote the general welfare, and secure the blessings of liberty to ourselves and our posterity, do ordain and establish this Constitution for the United States of America.

ARTICLE I

Section 1

All legislative powers herein granted shall be vested in a Congress of the United States, which shall consist of a Senate and House of Representatives.

Section 2

The House of Representatives shall be composed of members chosen every second year by the people of the several states, and the electors in each state shall have the qualifications requisite for electors of the most numerous branch of the state legislature.

No person shall be a representative who shall not have attained to the age of twenty-five years, and been seven years a citizen of the United States, and who shall not, when elected, be an inhabitant of that state in which he shall be chosen.

Representatives and direct taxes shall be apportioned among the several states which may be included within this Union, according to their respective numbers, which shall be determined by adding to the whole number of free persons, including those bound to service for a term of years, and excluding Indians not taxed, three-fifths of all other persons. The actual enumeration shall be made within three years after the first meeting of the Congress of the United States, and within every subsequent term of ten years, in such manner as they shall by law direct. The number of representatives shall not exceed one for every thirty thousand, but each state shall have at least one representative; and until such enumeration shall be made, the state of New Hampshire shall be entitled to chuse three, Massachusetts eight, Rhode-Island and Providence Plantations one, Connecticut five, New-York six, New-Jersey four, Pennsylvania eight, Delaware one, Maryland six, Virginia ten, North-Carolina five, South-Carolina five, and Georgia three.

When vacancies happen in the representation from any state, the Executive authority thereof shall issue writs of election to fill such vacancies.

The House of Representatives shall choose their Speaker and other officers; and shall have the sole power of impeachment.

Section 3

The Senate of the United States shall be composed of two senators from each state, chosen by the legislature thereof, for six years; and each senator shall have one vote.

Immediately after they shall be assembled in consequence of the first election, they shall be divided as equally as may be into three classes. The seats of the senators of the first class shall be vacated at the expiration of the second year, of the second class at the expiration of the fourth year, and of the third class at the expiration of the sixth year, so that one-third may be chosen every second year; and if vacancies happen by resignation, or otherwise, during the recess of the Legislature of any state, the Executive thereof may make temporary appointments until the next meeting of the Legislature, which shall then fill such vacancies.

No person shall be a Senator who shall not have attained to the age of thirty years, and been nine years a citizen of the United States and who shall not, when elected, be an inhabitant of that state for which he shall be chosen.

The Vice President of the United States shall be President of the Senate, but shall have no vote, unless they be equally divided.

The Senate shall choose their other officers, and also a President pro tempore, in the absence of the Vice President, or when he shall exercise the office of President of the United States.

The Senate shall have the sole power to try all impeachments. When sitting for that purpose, they shall be on oath or affirmation. When the President of the United States is tried, the Chief Justice shall preside: And no person shall be convicted without the concurrence of two-thirds of the members present.

Judgment in cases of impeachment shall not extend further than to removal from office, and disqualification to hold and enjoy any office of honor, trust or profit under the United States: but the party convicted shall nevertheless be liable and subject to indictment, trial, judgment and punishment, according to law.

Section 4

The times, places and manner of holding elections for Senators and Representatives, shall be prescribed in each state by the legislature thereof; but the Congress may at any time by law make or alter such regulations, except as to the places of choosing Senators.

The Congress shall assemble at least once in every year, and such meeting shall be on the first Monday in December, unless they shall by law appoint a different day.

Section 5

Each House shall be the judge of the elections, returns and qualifications of its own members, and a majority of each shall constitute a quorum to do business; but a smaller number may adjourn from day to day, and may be authorized to compel the attendance of absent members, in such manner, and under such penalties as each House may provide.

Each House may determine the rules of its proceedings, punish its members for disorderly behavior, and, with the concurrence of two-thirds, expel a member.

Each House shall keep a journal of its proceedings, and from time to time publish the same, excepting such parts as may in their judgment require secrecy; and the yeas and nays of the members of either House on any question shall, at the desire of one-fifth of those present, be entered on the journal.

Neither House, during the session of Congress, shall, without the consent of the other, adjourn for more than three days, nor to any other place than that in which the two Houses shall be sitting.

Section 6

The Senators and Representatives shall receive a compensation for their services, to be ascertained by law, and paid out of the treasury of the United States. They shall in all cases, except treason, felony and breach of the peace, be privileged from arrest during their attendance at the session of their respective Houses, and in going to and returning from the same; and for any speech or debate in either House, they shall not be questioned in any other place.

No Senator or Representative shall, during the time for which he was elected, be appointed to any civil office under the authority of the United States, which shall have been created, or the emoluments whereof shall have been increased during such time: and no person holding any office under the United States, shall be a member of either House during his continuance in office.

Section 7

All bills for raising revenue shall originate in the House of Representatives; but the Senate may propose or concur with amendments as on other Bills.

Every bill which shall have passed the House of Representatives and the Senate, shall, before it become a law, be presented to the President of the United States; if he approve he shall sign it, but if not he shall return it, with his objections to that House in which it shall have originated, who shall enter the objections at large on their journal, and proceed to reconsider it. If after such reconsideration two-thirds of that House shall agree to pass the bill, it shall be sent, together with the objections, to the other House, by which it shall likewise be reconsidered, and if approved by two-thirds of that House, it shall become a law. But in all such cases the votes of both Houses shall be determined by yeas and nays, and the names of the persons voting for and against the bill shall be entered on the journal of each House respectively. If any bill shall not be returned by the President within ten days (Sundays excepted) after it shall have been presented to him, the same shall be a law, in like manner as if he had signed it, unless the Congress by their adjournment prevent its return, in which case it shall not be a law.

Every order, resolution, or vote to which the concurrence of the Senate and House of Representatives may be necessary (except on a question of adjournment) shall be presented to the President of the United States; and before the same shall take effect, shall be approved by him, or being disapproved by him, shall be repassed by two-thirds of the Senate and House of Representatives, according to the rules and limitations prescribed in the case of a bill.

Section 8

The Congress shall have power to lay and collect taxes, duties, imposts and excises, to pay the debts and provide for the common defense and general welfare of the United States; but all duties, imposts and excises shall be uniform throughout the United States;

To borrow money on the credit of the United States;

To regulate commerce with foreign nations, and among the several states, and with the Indian tribes;

To establish a uniform rule of naturalization, and uniform laws on the subject of bankruptcies throughout the United States;

To coin money, regulate the value thereof, and of foreign coin, and fix the standard of weights and measures;

To provide for the punishment of counterfeiting the securities and current coin of the United States;

To establish post offices and post roads;

To promote the progress of science and useful arts, by securing for limited times to authors and inventors the exclusive right to their respective writings and discoveries;

To constitute tribunals inferior to the Supreme Court;

To define and punish piracies and felonies committed on the high seas, and offenses against the law of nations;

To declare war, grant letters of marque and reprisal, and make rules concerning captures on land and water;

To raise and support armies, but no appropriation of money to that use shall be for a longer term than two years;

To provide and maintain a navy;

To make rules for the government and regulation of the land and naval forces;

To provide for calling forth the militia to execute the laws of the union, suppress insurrections and repel invasions;

To provide for organizing, arming, and disciplining the militia, and for governing such part of them as may be employed in the service of the United States, reserving to the states respectively, the appointment of the officers, and the authority of training the militia according to the discipline prescribed by Congress;

To exercise exclusive legislation in all cases whatsoever, over such District (not exceeding ten miles square) as may, by cession of particular states, and the acceptance of Congress, become the seat of the government of the United States, and to exercise like authority over all places purchased by the consent of the legislature of the state in which the same shall be, for the erection of forts, magazines, arsenals, dockyards, and other needful buildings;—And

To make all laws which shall be necessary and proper for carrying into execution the foregoing powers, and all other powers vested by this Constitution in the government of the United States, or in any department or officer thereof.

Section 9

The migration or importation of such persons as any of the states now existing shall think proper to admit, shall not be prohibited by the Congress prior to the year one thousand eight hundred and eight, but a tax or duty may be imposed on such importation, not exceeding ten dollars for each person.

The privilege of the writ of habeas corpus shall not be suspended, unless when in cases of rebellion or invasion the public safety may require it.

No bill of attainder or ex post facto Law shall be passed.

No capitation, or other direct, tax shall be laid, unless in proportion to the census or enumeration herein before directed to be taken.

No tax or duty shall be laid on articles exported from any state.

No preference shall be given by any regulation of commerce or revenue to the ports of one state over those of another: nor shall vessels bound to, or from, one state, be obliged to enter, clear or pay duties in another.

No money shall be drawn from the treasury, but in consequence of appropriations made by law; and a regular statement and account of receipts and expenditures of all public money shall be published from time to time.

No title of nobility shall be granted by the United States: and no person holding any office of profit or trust under them, shall, without the consent of the Congress, accept of any present, emolument, office, or title, of any kind whatever, from any king, prince, or foreign state.

Section 10

No state shall enter into any treaty, alliance, or confederation; grant letters of marque and reprisal; coin money; emit bills of credit; make anything but gold and silver coin a tender in payment of debts; pass any bill of attainder, ex post facto law, or law impairing the obligation of contracts, or grant any title of nobility.

No state shall, without the consent of the Congress, lay any imposts or duties on imports or exports, except what may be absolutely necessary for executing its inspection laws: and the net produce of all duties and imposts, laid by any state on imports or exports, shall be for the use of the treasury of the United States; and all such laws shall be subject to the revision and control of the Congress.

No state shall, without the consent of Congress, lay any duty of tonnage, keep troops, or ships of war in time of peace, enter into any agreement or compact with another state, or with a foreign power, or engage in war, unless actually invaded, or in such imminent danger as will not admit of delay.

ARTICLE II

Section 1

The executive power shall be vested in a President of the United States of America. He shall hold his office during the term of four years, and, together with the Vice President, chosen for the same term, be elected, as follows:

Each state shall appoint, in such manner as the Legislature thereof may direct, a number of electors, equal to the whole number of Senators and Representatives to which the State may be entitled in the Congress: but no Senator or Representative, or person holding an office of trust or profit under the United States, shall be appointed an elector.

The electors shall meet in their respective states, and vote by ballot for two persons, of whom one at least shall not be an inhabitant of the same state with themselves. And they shall make a list of all the persons voted for, and of the number of votes for each; which list they shall sign and certify, and transmit sealed to the seat of the government of the United States, directed to the President of the Senate. The President of the Senate shall, in the presence of the Senate and House of Representatives, open all the certificates, and the votes shall then be counted. The person having the greatest number of votes shall be the President, if such number be a majority of the whole number of electors appointed; and if there be more than one who have such majority, and have an equal number of votes, then the House of Representatives shall immediately choose by ballot one of them for President; and if no person have a majority, then from the five highest on the list the said House shall in like manner choose the President. But in choosing the President, the votes shall be taken by States, the representation from each state having one vote; a quorum for this purpose shall consist of a member or members from two-thirds of the states, and a majority of all the states shall be necessary to a choice. In every case, after the choice of the President, the person having the greatest number of votes of the electors shall be the Vice President. But if there should remain two or more who have equal votes, the Senate shall choose from them by ballot the Vice President.

The Congress may determine the time of choosing the electors, and the day on which they shall give their votes; which day shall be the same throughout the United States.

No person except a natural-born citizen, or a citizen of the United States, at the time of the adoption of this Constitution, shall be eligible to the office of President; neither shall any person be eligible to that office who shall not have attained to the age of thirty-five years, and been fourteen Years a resident within the United States.

In case of the removal of the President from office, or of his death, resignation, or inability to discharge the powers and duties of the said office, the same shall devolve on the Vice President, and the Congress may by law provide for the case of removal, death, resignation or inability, both of the President and Vice President, declaring what officer shall then act as President, and such officer shall act accordingly, until the disability be removed, or a President shall be elected.

The President shall, at stated times, receive for his services, a compensation, which shall neither be increased nor diminished during the period for which he shall have been elected, and he shall not receive within that period any other emolument from the United States, or any of them.

Before he enter on the execution of his office, he shall take the following oath or affirmation:—"I do solemnly swear (or affirm) that I will faithfully execute the office of President of the United States, and will to the best of my ability, preserve, protect and defend the Constitution of the United States."

Section 2

The President shall be commander in chief of the Army and Navy of the United States, and of the militia of the several states, when called into the actual service of the United States; he may require the opinion, in writing, of the principal officer in each of the executive departments, upon any subject relating to the duties of their respective offices, and he shall have power to grant reprieves and pardons for offenses against the United States, except in cases of impeachment.

He shall have power, by and with the advice and consent of the Senate, to make treaties, provided two thirds of the Senators present concur; and he shall nominate, and by and with the advice and consent of the Senate, shall appoint ambassadors, other public ministers and consuls, judges of the Supreme Court, and all other officers of the United States, whose appointments are not herein otherwise provided for, and which shall be established by law: but the Congress may by law vest the appointment of such inferior officers, as they think proper, in the President alone, in the courts of law, or in the heads of departments.

The President shall have power to fill up all vacancies that may happen during the recess of the Senate, by granting commissions which shall expire at the end of their next session.

Section 3

He shall from time to time give to the Congress information of the state of the union, and recommend to their consideration such measures as he shall judge necessary and expedient; he may, on extraordinary occasions, convene both Houses, or either of them, and in case of disagreement between them, with respect to the time of adjournment, he may adjourn them to such time as he shall think proper; he shall receive ambassadors and other public ministers; he shall take care that the laws be faithfully executed, and shall commission all the officers of the United States.

Section 4

The President, Vice President and all civil officers of the United States, shall be removed from office on impeachment for, and conviction of, treason, bribery, or other high crimes and misdemeanors.

ARTICLE III

Section 1

The judicial power of the United States, shall be vested in one Supreme Court, and in such inferior courts as the Congress may from time to time ordain and establish. The judges, both of the supreme and inferior courts, shall hold their offices during good behaviour, and shall, at stated times, receive for their services, a compensation, which shall not be diminished during their continuance in office.

Section 2

The judicial power shall extend to all cases, in law and equity, arising under this Constitution, the laws of the United States, and treaties made, or which shall be made, under their authority;—to all cases affecting ambassadors, other public ministers and consuls;—to all cases of admiralty and maritime jurisdiction;—to controversies to which the United States shall be a party;—to controversies between two or more states;—between a state and citizens of another state;— between citizens of different states;—between citizens of the same state claiming lands under grants of different states, and between a state, or the citizens thereof, and foreign states, citizens or subjects.

In all cases affecting ambassadors, other public ministers and consuls, and those in which a state shall be party, the Supreme Court shall have original jurisdiction. In all the other cases before mentioned, the Supreme Court shall have appellate jurisdiction, both as to law and fact, with such exceptions, and under such regulations as the Congress shall make.

The trial of all crimes, except in cases of impeachment, shall be by jury; and such trial shall be held in the state where the said crimes shall have been committed; but when not committed within any state, the trial shall be at such place or places as the Congress may by law have directed.

Section 3

Treason against the United States, shall consist only in levying war against them, or in adhering to their enemies, giving them aid and comfort. No person shall be convicted of treason unless on the testimony of two witnesses to the same overt act, or on confession in open court.

The Congress shall have power to declare the punishment of treason, but no attainder of treason shall work corruption of blood, or forfeiture except during the life of the person attainted.

ARTICLE IV

Section 1

Full faith and credit shall be given in each state to the public acts, records, and judicial proceedings of every other state. And the Congress may by general laws prescribe the manner in which such acts, records, and proceedings shall be proved, and the effect thereof.

Section 2

The citizens of each state shall be entitled to all privileges and immunities of citizens in the several states.

A person charged in any state with treason, felony, or other crime, who shall flee from justice, and be found in another state, shall on demand of the executive authority of the state from which he fled, be delivered up, to be removed to the state having jurisdiction of the crime.

No person held to service or labor in one state, under the laws thereof, escaping into another, shall, in consequence of any law or regulation therein, be discharged from such service or labor, but shall be delivered up on claim of the party to whom such service or labor may be due.

Section 3

New states may be admitted by the Congress into this union; but no new states shall be formed or erected within the jurisdiction of any other state; nor any state be formed by the junction of two or more states, or parts of states, without the consent of the legislatures of the states concerned as well as of the Congress.

The Congress shall have power to dispose of and make all needful rules and regulations respecting the territory or other property belonging to the United States; and nothing in this Constitution shall be so construed as to prejudice any claims of the United States, or of any particular state.

Section 4

The United States shall guarantee to every state in this union a republican form of government, and shall protect each of them against invasion; and on application of the legislature, or of the executive (when the legislature cannot be convened) against domestic violence.

ARTICLE V

The Congress, whenever two thirds of both houses shall deem it necessary, shall propose amendments to this Constitution, or, on the application of the legislatures of two-thirds of the several states, shall call a convention for proposing amendments, which, in either case, shall be valid to all intents and purposes, as part of this Constitution, when ratified by the legislatures of three-fourths of the several states, or by conventions in three-fourths thereof, as the one or the other mode of ratification may be proposed by the Congress; provided that no amendment which may be made prior to the year one thousand eight hundred and eight shall in any manner affect the first and fourth clauses in the ninth section of the first article; and that no state, without its consent, shall be deprived of its equal suffrage in the Senate.

ARTICLE VI

All debts contracted and engagements entered into, before the adoption of this Constitution, shall be as valid against the United States under this Constitution, as under the Confederation.

This Constitution, and the laws of the United States which shall be made in pursuance thereof; and all treaties made, or which shall be made, under the authority of the United States, shall be the supreme law of the land; and the judges in every state shall be bound thereby, anything in the Constitution or laws of any State to the contrary notwithstanding.

The Senators and Representatives before mentioned, and the members of the several state legislatures, and all executive and judicial officers, both of the United States and of the several states, shall be bound by oath or affirmation, to support this Constitution; but no religious test shall ever be required as a qualification to any office or public trust under the United States.

ARTICLE VII

The ratification of the conventions of nine states, shall be sufficient for the establishment of this Constitution between the states so ratifying the same.

Done in convention by the unanimous consent of the states present the seventeenth day of September in the year of our Lord one thousand seven hundred and eighty seven and of the independence of the United States of America the twelfth. In witness whereof We have hereunto subscribed our Names,

G. Washington
—Presidt. and deputy from Virginia

New Hampshire:
John Langdon, Nicholas Gilman

Massachusetts:
Nathaniel Gorham, Rufus King

Connecticut:
Wm. Saml. Johnson, Roger Sherman

New York:
Alexander Hamilton

New Jersey:
Wil. Livingston, David Brearley, Wm. Paterson, Jona. Dayton

Pennsylvania:
B. Franklin, Thomas Mifflin, Robt. Morris, Geo. Clymer, Thos. FitzSimons, Jared Ingersoll, James Wilson, Gouv. Morris

Delaware:
Geo. Read, Gunning Bedford Jr., John Dickinson, Richard Bassett, Jaco. Broom

Maryland:
James M'Henry, Daniel of St. Thos. Jenifer, Danl. Carrol

Virginia:
John Blair, James Madison Jr.

North Carolina:
Wm. Blount, Richd. Dobbs Spaight, Hugh Williamson

South Carolina:
J. Rutledge, Charles Cotesworth Pinckney, Charles Pinckney, Pierce Butler

Georgia:
William Few, Abr. Baldwin

AMENDMENTS TO THE CONSTITUTION OF THE UNITED STATES BEFORE 1860

The Bill of Rights

Amendment I (1791)

Congress shall make no law respecting an establishment of religion, or prohibiting the free exercise thereof; or abridging the freedom of speech, or of the press; or the right of the people peaceably to assemble, and to petition the government for a redress of grievances.

Amendment II (1791)

A well regulated militia, being necessary to the security of a free state, the right of the people to keep and bear arms, shall not be infringed.

Amendment III (1791)

No soldier shall, in time of peace be quartered in any house, without the consent of the owner, nor in time of war, but in a manner to be prescribed by law.

Amendment IV (1791)

The right of the people to be secure in their persons, houses, papers, and effects, against unreasonable searches and seizures, shall not be violated, and no warrants shall issue, but upon probable cause, supported by oath or affirmation, and particularly describing the place to be searched, and the persons or things to be seized.

Amendment V (1791)

No person shall be held to answer for a capital, or otherwise infamous crime, unless on a presentment or indictment of a grand jury, except in cases arising in the land or naval forces, or in the militia, when in actual service in time of war or public danger; nor shall any person be subject for the same offense to be twice put in jeopardy of life or limb; nor shall be compelled in any criminal case to be a witness against himself, nor be deprived of life, liberty, or property, without due process of law; nor shall private property be taken for public use, without just compensation.

Amendment VI (1791)

In all criminal prosecutions, the accused shall enjoy the right to a speedy and public trial, by an impartial jury of the state and district wherein the crime shall have been committed, which district shall have been previously ascertained by law, and to be informed of the nature and cause of the accusation; to be confronted with the witnesses against him; to have compulsory process for obtaining witnesses in his favor, and to have the assistance of counsel for his defense.

Amendment VII (1791)

In suits at common law, where the value in controversy shall exceed twenty dollars, the right of trial by jury shall be preserved, and no fact tried by a jury, shall be otherwise reexamined in any court of the United States, than according to the rules of the common law.

Amendment VIII (1791)

Excessive bail shall not be required, nor excessive fines imposed, nor cruel and unusual punishments inflicted.

Amendment IX (1791)

The enumeration in the Constitution, of certain rights, shall not be construed to deny or disparage others retained by the people.

Amendment X (1791)

The powers not delegated to the United States by the Constitution, nor prohibited by it to the states, are reserved to the states respectively, or to the people.

Other Pre–Civil War Amendments

Amendment XI (1798)

The judicial power of the United States shall not be construed to extend to any suit in law or equity, commenced or prosecuted against one of the United States by citizens of another state, or by citizens or subjects of any foreign state.

Amendment XII (1804)

The electors shall meet in their respective states and vote by ballot for President and Vice-President, one of whom, at least, shall not be an inhabitant of the same state with themselves; they shall name in their ballots the person voted for as President, and in distinct ballots the person voted for as Vice-President, and they shall make distinct lists of all persons voted for as President, and of all persons voted for as Vice-President, and of the number of votes for each, which lists they shall sign and certify, and transmit sealed to the seat of the government of the United States, directed to the President of the Senate;—The President of the Senate shall, in the presence of the Senate and House of Representatives, open all the certificates and the votes shall then be counted;—the person having the greatest number of votes for President, shall be the President, if such number be a majority of the whole number of electors appointed; and if no person have such majority, then from the persons having the highest numbers not exceeding three on the list of those voted for as President, the House of Representatives shall choose immediately, by ballot, the President. But in choosing the President, the votes shall be taken by states, the representation from each state having one vote; a quorum for this purpose shall consist of a member or members from two-thirds of the states, and a majority of all the states shall be necessary to a choice. And if the House of Representatives shall not choose a President whenever the right of choice shall devolve upon them, before the fourth day of March next following, then the Vice-President shall act as President, as in the case of the death or other constitutional disability of the President. The person having the greatest number of votes as Vice-President, shall be the Vice-President, if such number be a majority of the whole number of electors appointed, and if no person have a majority, then from the two highest numbers on the list, the Senate shall choose the Vice-President; a quorum for the purpose shall consist of two-thirds of the whole number of Senators, and a majority of the whole number shall be necessary to a choice. But no person constitutionally ineligible to the office of President shall be eligible to that of Vice-President of the United States.

About the Author

William L. Richter (B.A. M.A. Arizona State University, M.L.S. University of Arizona, Ph.D. Louisiana State University) is an academically trained historian-turned-cowboy, retired from operating his own horseshoeing business out of Tucson, Arizona. He has researched and written extensively in the areas of the Antebellum South, the Civil War, and Reconstruction. He has two dozen articles and book reviews to his credit and is the author of several books: *The Army in Texas during Reconstruction, 1865–1870* (1987); *Overreached on All Sides: The Freedmen's Bureau Administrators in Texas, 1865–1868* (1991); *The ABC-Clio Companion to Transportation* (1995); and *The ABC-Clio Companion to American Reconstruction, 1862–1877* (1996). He is also co-author with Ronald D. Smith of *Fascinating People and Astounding Events in American History* (1993), a volume of American history anecdotes. Finally, he has written a historical novel, *The Last Confederate Heroes* (2002), about the people who assassinated Abraham Lincoln. His most recent work is *A Historical Dictionary of the Civil War and Reconstruction* (2004). He can be reached at www.williamrichter.com.